Web Applications of Consumer Behavior

Strategic Applications of Consumer Behavior

Consumer Behavior

About the Author

Dr. Henry Assael is a professor of marketing at New York University's Stern School of Business. He joined NYU in 1966 and served as chairman of Stern's Marketing Department from 1979 to 1991.

Dr. Assael received a BA from Harvard, graduating *cum laude,* an MBA from the Wharton School, and a Ph.D from the Columbia Graduate School of Business. His research interests and publications are primarily in the areas of consumer research; namely, market segmentation, product positioning, advertising evaluation, media selection, and survey research methods. He has written over thirty articles for scholarly journals; edited a thirty-three-volume series on the history of marketing; and is the author of *Consumer Behavior and Marketing Action* (six editions), *Marketing: Principles and Strategy* (two editions), and *Marketing Management: Strategy and Action.*

Dr. Assael has consulted for AT&T, Avon, CBS, Nestlé, Pepsi Cola, the New York Stock Exchange, the Kennedy Center, and the National Academy of Sciences. In addition, he is listed in *Who's Who in America.*

Consumer Behavior

A Strategic Approach

Henry Assael

New York University

HOUGHTON MIFFLIN COMPANY

Boston   New York

For Alyce Assael

Publisher: Charles Hartford

Editor in Chief: George T. Hoffman

Associate Sponsoring Editor: Joanne Dauksewicz

Project Editor: Paula Kmetz

Senior Production/Design Coordinator: Jill Haber

Manufacturing Manager: Florence Cadran

Senior Marketing Manager: Steven W. Mikels

Marketing Associate: Lisa E. Boden

Cover illustration © Dennis Harms/The Stock Illustration Source

Printed in the U.S.A.

Library of Congress Control Number: 2002109350

ISBN: 0-618-22215-4

23456789–QV– 07 06 05 04

Brief Contents

Contents

CHAPTER 3   Consumer Learning, Habit, and Brand Loyalty 56

CHAPTER 4   Low-Involvment Consumer Decision Making 88

CHAPTER 5   Situational Influences in Decision Making   120

PART FIVE

Marketing Action   499

CHAPTER 17   The Marketing Communications Process   500

Preface

As the name implies, *Consumer Behavior: A Strategic Approach* is designed to link the conceptual foundations of consumer behavior with strategic marketing applications. Such a linkage is essential in any business curriculum if conceptually based courses such as Consumer Behavior are to be considered in a managerial and planning framework. To paraphrase Peter Drucker, the central purpose of the business firm is to satisfy customer needs. Therefore, business managers must understand the nature of these needs as a foundation for strategy development.

A former version of this book had a successful history of being one of the first consumer behavior texts to establish such a key linkage through six editions. Given the changes in the field—the increasing importance of the Web as a source of information, the increasingly macro orientation of consumer behavior in both a societal and global context, the basic fragmentation of the American marketplace—it was decided that it is time to break new ground. This book takes a fresh new look at the field of consumer behavior while retaining the strength and orientation of the former version.

TEXTBOOK FEATURES

This book initially establishes a basic model of consumer decision making as an organizational framework and then relates it to strategic applications in key areas, particularly segmentation, positioning, and communications. A central focus throughout is web-based applications of consumer behavior concepts.

▮ Conceptual Framework

The starting point is a simple model of consumer behavior. The model makes consumer decision making the central focus. We consider consumer decisions under various conditions—high versus low involvement and complex versus routinized decisions—examining the different strategic implications under each of these conditions.

We then consider the micro and macro forces that influence consumer behavior; namely, the consumer's psychological processes in arriving at a decision and the environmental influences on the consumer. The psychological processes—need recognition, motivation, perception, and attitude formation—represent a more traditional cognitive perspective in approaching consumer behavior. The environmental forces reflect a more experiential view, focusing on group and societal influences.

The basic model defines the three key sections of the book. After the introductory chapter, we consider consumer decision making in Part Two, individual influences in Part Three, and environmental forces in Part Four.

▮ Strategic Framework

Each chapter has a section on strategic applications. For example, in Part Two, Consumer Decision Making, we consider the advertising, pricing, and distribution implications of low versus high levels of consumer product involvement. We deal with the ways situational influences might affect market segmentation and product development with new uses in mind. We explore the communications implications when consumers buy repeatedly out of commitment or as a result of inertia.

Part Three, The Individual Consumer, focuses on the psychological influences on consumer decisions. In this part, we consider how marketers can utilize concepts of perceptual generalization and discrimination to influence consumer perceptions and how they can attempt to reduce perceived risk. We also describe how attitudinal concepts and theories can be used to develop strategies to reinforce and change consumer attitudes. In Part Four, Group and Cultural Influences, we describe how marketers can encourage word-of-mouth communications within groups by appealing to opinion leaders and by using spokespersons in advertising. We also describe how marketers can encourage a process of diffusion of positive communications about the product across groups.

Part Five of the text, Marketing Action, considers the consumer behavior implications for marketing strategy on an integrated basis. This last section describes advertising strategies within the framework of a communications model, approaches to market segmentation, and the ability to implement micromarketing strategies through mass customization and relationship marketing. The final chapter deals with consumer rights in the marketplace and the social responsibility of business firms to ensure these rights.

In addition to the integration of applications with concepts, many chapters have boxed items that provide mini-cases representing strategic applications of the chapter materials. The chapter on decision making, for instance, evaluates Mercedes Benz's approach in conveying information in both a utilitarian and hedonic context. The chapter on attitudes considers Kmart's attempts to change consumer attitudes in its repositioning strategy. The chapter on reference groups evaluates the conditions under which spokespersons should be used as experts or referents.

▌A Web-Based Orientation

The focus throughout this book is on the importance of information to the consumer. Information empowers consumers with the ability to make informed decisions. Chapters on perceptions, information processing, and attitude formation emphasize the information base for consumer decision making.

The text emphasizes Internet applications in almost every chapter. We deal with the Internet as a key source of information and make the distinction between active and passive processing on the Web. We describe utilitarian and hedonic motivations for surfing on the Web. We consider the Web as a vehicle for group influence by describing the role of chatrooms and communities of interest as well as the potential for marketers to stimulate communications through viral marketing strategies. And we focus on the interactivity, personalization, and customization that the Web provides as a basis for micromarketing and mass customization.

Further, boxed items deal with web-based applications in most chapters. Specific topics include:

- ▌Cognitive learning on the Web
- ▌The role of the Web in promoting low-involvement products
- ▌Gift giving on the Web

- The sacred and secular dimensions of consumption on the Web
- Different patterns of Internet usage in Japan and the United States
- The role of Web communities of interest, relationships, and transactions
- The socialization of children on the Web
- The effects of negative word of mouth on the Web

A Global Perspective

Global communications have produced similar needs and tastes among consumers worldwide, yet regional differences in tastes and customs still dominate in many product categories. The text devotes a chapter (Chapter 13) to these orientations by focusing on the global versus cross-cultural influences on consumer behavior that result in world-brand and localized strategies. A key perspective is the attempt to take advantage of both a global and a localized view of consumer behavior through a strategy of flexible globalization reflected in the statement, "Think global, act local." Other chapters also extend the focus to global issues. For example, Chapter 9, "Demographics and Social Class," compares trends in the United States and globally.

Many chapters have boxed items applying a global perspective to chapter content. Specific topics include:

- Procter & Gamble's failure to export its U.S. strategies abroad
- How product involvement differs across cultures
- The nature of social class in China
- Differences in the perspectives and values of Gen X'ers in Japan versus the United States
- Micromarketing in Russia
- Consumerism and consumer rights in Europe and Asia

A Perspective on Consumer Rights and Social Responsibility

As noted, the final chapter considers consumer rights in the marketplace. It deals with basic issues such as advertising to children, the legitimacy of health claims, environmental protection, privacy on the Web, and ensuring truth in advertising and packaging. The chapter serves two purposes. First, it provides a balance between the strategic focus throughout the book and a focus on consumer rights. Second, it conforms to the current emphasis on ethical issues in the business curriculum.

Further, the chapter focuses on the consumer movement—that is, the attempt by consumer advocates and government to protect consumer rights, both in the United States and abroad. In this respect, it traces the development of a consumerist perspective domestically and globally.

Beyond the coverage in this chapter, ethical issues are woven into discussions of strategic applications in many chapters in the book. For example, the chapter on consumer involvement (Chapter 4) considers the desirability of increasing involvement with social issues such as AIDs prevention and teenage drinking. The chapter on information processing (Chapter 7) considers the less-efficient processing capabilities of younger and older consumers and raises the question of business's responsibilities to these two groups. The chapter on subcultures (Chapter 12) deals with targeting cigarettes and alcohol to minority groups. The chapter on marketing communications (Chapter 17) considers the potential for consumers to misperceive advertising claims and the responsibilities of marketers to ensure that claims are not deceptive and irresponsible.

PEDAGOGICAL FEATURES

The text has a number of pedagogical features, meant to enhance the value of the text for students. These features include:

Opening Vignettes. A case history is presented at the beginning of each chapter, which sets the stage for the conceptual and strategic content of the chapter. The example is often carried through in the chapter providing an integrated focus. Examples of opening vignette topics are:

- The use of infomediaries such as autobytel.com in helping consumers make informed decisions (Chapter 2)
- How Timex positions its watches by how they are used (Chapter 5)
- How Nike facilitates online information search (Chapter 7)
- BMW's attempt to target professional women (Chapter 9)
- Nestle's localized strategy compared to Levi Strauss's attempt to become a world brand (Chapter 13)
- The use of viral marketing strategies to stimulate word of mouth and diffusion on the Web (Chapter 16)
- Volvo's attempt to expand its customer base beyond appeals to safety (Chapter 18)
- The Body Shop's strategy of advocating social causes (Chapter 19)

Research Assignments. Each chapter has a set of research assignments, which can serve as bases for course projects. About half of these have a web component. The research assignments are of several types, as follows:

- Conducting focus groups to investigate issues such as consumer motivations, attitudes, brand images, and decision processes
- Conducting experiments to test the effects of sensory and marketing stimuli on consumers
- Undertaking short surveys to test hypotheses related to issues such as differences in characteristics between high- and low-involvement consumers for a product category
- Conducting online searches utilizing search engines and BOTS to help evaluate product categories, or going online to determine the nature of chatrooms and communities of interest and relationships

Additional Features.

- Each chapter has a *Questions for Discussion* section at the end. These questions are meant to provide a basis for applying chapter concepts to specific situations and examples, rather than just asking students to feed back information.
- As noted, each chapter has *feature boxes* that serve as mini-cases. They are of three types: (1) web-based applications of consumer behavior, (2) strategic

applications of consumer behavior, and (3) global applications of consumer behavior.

▌ A comprehensive *glossary* at the end of the book defines items in bold letters in the text.

ANCILLARIES

A variety of ancillary material provides instructors and students with support in using the text in an integrated manner. The instructor package includes:

Instructor's Manual. Contrary to the usual practice, the Instructor's Manual was prepared by the author. It provides additional materials not found in the text, for use in the classroom. There is also a detailed guide to the end-of-chapter questions and research assignments. Each chapter in the manual is organized as follows:

▌ *Chapter objectives*

▌ *Teaching suggestions,* which provide a full set of materials to enhance classroom presentation beyond the scope of the text. This section provides additional conceptual material as well as additional examples of strategic applications, to expand on material in the text.

▌ *Answers and guides to end-of-chapter questions.* Guidelines are presented for each question in the form of answers or directions for classroom discussion.

▌ *Guidelines for research assignments,* to assist students in implementing these assignments.

Test Bank and Computerized Test Bank. The test bank contains multiple choice and true/false questions, as well as short essay questions. In addition, *HM Testing,* an electronic, Windows version of the Test Bank allows instructors to generate and change tests easily on the computer. The program will also print an answer key for each version of the text. A call-in test service (800-733-1717), which allows instructors to select items from the Test Bank and order printed tests, is also available.

Videos. The video package highlights global companies and corresponds with the concepts and topics highlighted in the text. The video guide provides complete teaching notes to help instructors prepare for each video and includes in-class discussion ideas.

PowerPoint. This classroom presentation package (downloadable from the Web) provides clear, concise text and art to create a total presentation package. Instructors who have access to PowerPoint can edit slides to customize them for their presentations. Slides can also be printed as lecture notes for class distribution.

Instructor web site. This password-protected site provides lecture notes and PowerPoint slides for downloading, as well as additional classroom resources.

The student package includes:

Student web site. This resource includes chapter study aids, ACE practice test questions, and special web links that allow students to further explore consumer behavior issues and resources.

Wall Street Journal *subscription offer.* Students whose instructors have adopted the *WSJ* with this text will receive, shrink-wrapped with their book, a registration card for the ten-week print and online subscription to the *WSJ*. Students must fill out and return the registration card found in text to initiate the subscription privileges. The text package will also include a copy of the Wall Street Journal Student Subscriber Handbook, which explains how to use both print and online versions of the newspaper. The cost of the *WSJ* is $13.50 in addition to the net cost of the core text. This is sold as a package with new textbooks only. *WSJ* subscriptions cannot be sold as a standalone item.

ACKNOWLEDGEMENTS

I am indebted to a number of people at Houghton Mifflin who made this book possible. My editor, now editor-in-chief, George Hoffman, supported the key idea that there have been sufficient changes in the field to warrant a new consumer behavior book, one that builds on strategic applications and takes a more web-based view of the field. His vision made this book possible. I am also deeply indebted to Joanne Dauksewicz, associate sponsoring editor, for her constant support in overseeing every facet of the book and being an active participant in the revision process. Joanne was a rare combination of production and developmental editor rolled into one.

I am very grateful to Paula Kmetz, project editor, for her constant help and support in managing every stage of the book, from organizing exhibits to consulting on permissions to insuring the consistency of the final version. Her organizational skills were sorely needed and very much appreciated. I am also indebted to two excellent photo researchers, Julie Low and Connie Gardner, for their support in providing meaningful exhibits for the book. And I would like to thank Jill Haber, production and design coordinator, for organizing a book that students can relate to.

Finally, I would like to thank an excellent group of reviewers for providing suggestions that were truly consumer-oriented. These suggestions helped make the book more student-friendly while maintaining its basic precepts of being conceptually sound and strategically oriented. In particular, I would like to thank: Roshan D. Ahuja, Xavier University; Myra Jo Bates, Ft. Hayes State University; Marjorie Bonavia, University of Maryland; James Cagley, University of Tulsa; Paul Chao, University of Northern Iowa; Amanda Diekman, Purdue University; Richard W. Easley, Baylor University; Paul Herbig, Tri-State University; Fahri Karakaya, University of Massachusetts; Dr. Cherie Keen, Fairfield University; Barry E. Langford, Florida Gulf Coast University; Mark Mitchell, University of South Carolina, Spartanburg; James O'Donnell, Huntington College; Cliff Olson, Southern Adventist University; Melodie Philhours, Akansas State University; Michelle Reiss, Spaulding University; Paul A. Scipione, Montclaire State University; Michael Shapiro, Dowling College; Jane Z. Sojka, Ohio University; and Dr. Jane B. Thomas, Winthrop University.

H.A.

Introduction to Consumer Behavior

CHAPTER 1

Consumer Behavior: A Managerial Perspective

Consumer behavior determines a firm's profitability. Further, profitability is established in the long term by developing a *loyal* consumer base, that is, a group of consumers who are satisfied with the marketer's brand and continue to buy it over time. At the heart of all marketing strategies is the need to satisfy consumers so as to establish such a loyal consumer base.

Marketers have come to realize that their effectiveness in meeting consumer needs directly influences their profitability. The better they understand the factors underlying consumer behavior, the better able they are to develop effective marketing strategies to meet consumer needs.

This introductory chapter establishes a managerial orientation to the study of consumer behavior. It considers the reasons why the study of consumer behavior is important. In so doing, the chapter

- defines the strategic applications of consumer behavior,
- describes the information required to understand consumer behavior,
- considers differing approaches in studying consumer behavior,
- considers the importance of the Web in providing consumers with information and empowering them to make better choices, and
- reviews the organization of the text.

The next chapter begins to describe consumers in more detail by considering how they go about making decisions for brands and products.

Levi Strauss & Co. Begins to Focus on the Consumer

In the past, many business firms were not concerned with understanding consumer behavior. They were more focused on tracking sales results with little concern for why consumers did what they did. Consider Levi Strauss & Co. Until the mid-1980s, the company sold jeans to a mass market. It did not have to understand the dynamics behind the sales of jeans or be concerned with segmenting its markets as long as the sales of jeans kept rising. But by 1985 the jeans market began to take a slide, and it showed anemic growth in the booming 1990s.[1] Why? Basic demographic and lifestyle trends started affecting sales. The most significant of these demographic trends was the aging of the baby-boom generation (those born between 1946 and 1964). Baby boomers were getting out of jeans into more comfortable fitting slacks. Further, teens—the most loyal of jeans purchasers—represented a shrinking proportion of the market because of lower birthrates.

Levi Strauss quickly came to recognize that it was facing different demographic and lifestyle segments with different needs regarding casual wear. It realized it would have to appeal to baby boomers, Generation Xers (those born between 1965 and 1976), and teens differently. It also became sensitive to the different needs of women regarding fit and design. The days of mass marketing were over. Levi Strauss began to embark wholeheartedly on a strategy of market segmentation.

As a result, the company broadened its line to include slacks and then targeted different lines to different consumer segments. It first introduced baggy cotton slacks (the Dockers® line) for the baby boomers' expanding waistlines, then comfortable Action Slacks for the over-50 group. Then, Levi Strauss further segmented the market by introducing Loose jeans, a line of fashion-oriented denim slacks targeted to Generation Xers, 501® buttonfly jeans targeted to teens, and in 1994, a new line of jeans positioned for kids ages 8 to 14.

In another illustration of the company's savvy in targeting consumers, Levi Strauss foresaw the trend to casual wear in the office, a trend that saw the percentage of companies allowing casual wear at least once a week to grow from 36 percent in 1992 to 75 percent in 1996.[2] To keep pace with this trend, Levi Strauss introduced Slates® pants in 1996 and refined the brand in 1999 to offer savvy styles that fill the niche between khakis and traditional business dress for the 25- to 34-year-old market (see Exhibit 1.1).[3]

In 1998 and 1999, Levi Strauss again had to revise its marketing strategy as it saw worldwide sales decline, particularly among its core market of teens and young adults aged 15 to 24.[4] This time the decline was due to a change in the tastes and lifestyles of the new teen market, Generation Y (those born between 1977 and 1994). This group

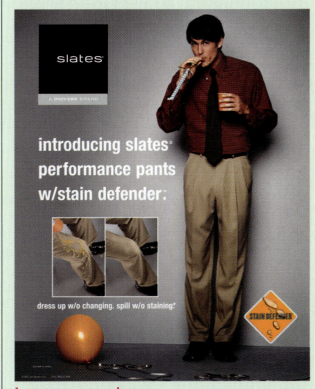

| EXHIBIT 1.1 |

With Slates clothing, Levi Strauss targets men and women looking for casual wear at the office.

Photographer, Jennifer Livingston; ad agency, FCB; client, Slates.

began buying urban street styles rather than the traditional brands like Levi's and needed fashion styles that appealed to their changing tastes. Levi Strauss introduced new urban brands like Wide Legs and Hard Jeans, Original Spin custom fit jeans, and Dockers K-1 khakis. In 2000, Levi Strauss introduced Engineered Jeans, a radical-looking style with an odd silhouette, ergonomically designed to accommodate the body's contours.[5] Levi Strauss has also attempted to improve its image among teens with a line of hip e-outerwear jackets that feature a built-in mobile phone and MP3 player connected by wires in the garment.[6]

In a further effort to change the perception among teens that its jeans were traditional, Levi Strauss launched a worldwide advertising campaign in the late 1990s using music sponsorships and events to develop more positive attitudes toward its new product lines. It is also using less traditional forms of advertising, like its worldwide sponsorship of Christina Aguilera, the Goo Goo Dolls, Third Eye Blind, and other music groups and an interactive web site featuring games, music, chatrooms, and fashion.[7]

Levi Strauss is not resting on its capacity to better target the market. It is also moving from a market segmentation strategy to a *micromarketing* strategy; that is, a strategy that targets individual consumers by allowing them to customize the Levi Strauss product. For example, in 2000 Levi Strauss began targeting women through a personal pair program, which allows them to create custom fit jeans at original Levi's stores. Personal pair jeans allow customers to have jeans personally cut and sewn to fit the exact measurements of their bodies.

As part of its micromarketing strategy, Levi Strauss is also customizing the information it provides on its web site to better meet the needs of individual consumers. As part of its global strategy, Levi Strauss's web site includes separate sites for the United States, Europe, Asia Pacific, and Latin America; and the Dockers.com and Slates.com web sites include a site for the United States and Europe offering unique content for each country. Levi Strauss will continue using its web sites as a marketing and information tool to target consumers around the world.[8]

Rapid changes in the marketing environment such as those experienced by Levi Strauss & Co. have led marketing managers to analyze more closely the factors that influence consumer choice. Managers are now concerned with delivering benefits to consumers, learning about and changing consumers' attitudes, and influencing consumer perceptions. They realize that marketing plans must be based on the psychological and social forces that are likely to condition consumer behavior—forces such as the aging of baby boomers, increasing concern with health and nutrition, greater information access through the Internet, greater emphasis on value, and greater focus on a clean environment.

The result of this realization is a new emphasis on consumer information. The most successful companies will be those that get their hands on information that identifies and explains the needs and behavior of consumers. Companies that develop a fuller understanding of consumers will be better able to develop marketing strategies to meet their needs. This book fosters such an understanding of consumer behavior.

Consumer Behavior and Marketing Action

Much of this text is devoted to a better understanding of terms such as "consumer benefits," "perceptions," and "attitudes" and how they influence development of successful marketing strategies. Because global teens began viewing Levi Strauss as a more traditional brand, the company changed its line to a more up-to-date, "hipper" look. Levi Strauss wanted its jeans to regain "badge value" among teens from Bangkok to Berlin. Levi Strauss also had to change perceptions of jeans as a male-oriented product if it was to target females successfully. In changing consumer perceptions, Levi Strauss was trying to develop more positive attitudes toward its new product lines, thus increasing the chances that the targeted demographic groups would buy.

Companies that fail to recognize consumer needs are more likely to make costly mistakes. Consider Sears, the number one retailer in the United States until 1990, when it fell to third place. Before its slide, Sears had a clear focus on how to satisfy its customers—offer a wide variety of low-priced merchandise to middle America. However, Sears failed to see the implications of the increase in the number of working women and the greater affluence of dual-earning households in the United States. These demographic shifts meant that consumers wanted a greater variety of name brands at reasonable prices.

While other mass merchandisers were moving to specialty, name-brand goods, Sears continued to offer what consumers perceived as lower-priced merchandise and price-oriented displays in older stores. By 1993, the company recognized it needed a drastic repositioning. It put more emphasis on fashion by emphasizing name-brand apparel in a boutique-like setting and introduced a cosmetic line. Part of the focus on fashion was a new advertising campaign, "The Softer Side of Sears," introduced in 1993. The campaign helped increase sales of its lines and attracted female shoppers, but by 1999 growth had tapered off and Sears needed to modify its strategy again.[9] Sears launched a revised campaign in 1999 and early 2000 that focused more on the value of its merchandise than on a change in image (see Exhibit 1.2). With its heavy spending on advertising and continuous refinement of its message, Sears may again increase sales and profitability.

As the Levi Strauss and Sears examples demonstrate, the basic philosophy required for

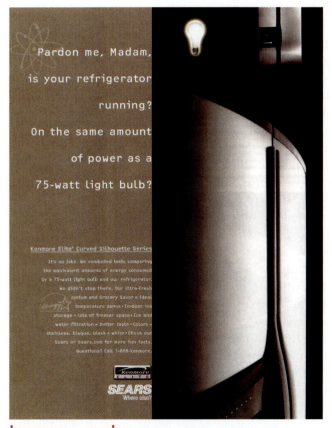

| **EXHIBIT 1.2** |

Sears changed its advertising focus from fashion to functionality.

Reprinted by arrangement with Sears, Roebuck and Co. and protected under copyright. No duplication is permitted.

successful marketing—the importance of satisfying customers—may be simple; but its implementation is complex. It requires that the company do the following:

▌ Define consumer needs

▌ Identify consumer segments that have these needs

▌ Position new products or reposition existing products to meet these needs

▌ Where possible, try to satisfy consumer needs at the individual level through interactive technologies

▌ Develop marketing strategies to communicate and deliver product benefits

▌ Evaluate these strategies for their effectiveness

▌ Ensure that such strategies do not deceive or mislead consumers and are implemented in a socially responsible manner

Underlying these strategic requirements is the importance of obtaining information on consumer needs, consumer perceptions of new and existing brands, attitudes toward these brands, intentions to buy, and past purchasing behavior.

Developing a Consumer-Oriented View of Marketing Strategy: The Marketing Concept

The philosophy that marketing strategies rely on a better knowledge of the consumer is known as the **marketing concept.*** The marketing concept states that marketers must first define the benefits consumers seek in the marketplace and gear marketing strategies accordingly. Acceptance of this concept has provided the impetus for studying consumer behavior in a marketing context.

First formulated in the 1950s, the marketing concept seems so logical today that we may wonder why marketers did not turn to it sooner. There are two reasons. First, marketing institutions were not sufficiently developed before 1950 to accept the marketing concept. Consumer behavior research was in its infancy. Moreover, advertising and distributive facilities were more suited to the mass-production and mass-marketing strategies of that time. The implementation of the marketing concept requires a diversity of facilities for promoting and distributing products that meet the needs of smaller and more diverse market segments. This diversity in marketing institutions did not exist before 1950. Instead, the emphasis was on economies of scale in production and marketing. Before the 1950s, for example, Coca-Cola was a one-product company, worldwide.

The second reason the marketing concept was not accepted until the 1950s is that this was the decade that many economies began emerging from the ravages of World War II and, prior to that, the global depression. Consumer goods began assuming more importance, and purchasing power began growing. For the first time in many decades, demand began exceeding supply *and* purchasing power existed to take up the slack. Growth was exponential, particularly in Germany and Japan. For a time, global marketers could ignore targeting specific consumer needs with better products because of pent-up demand. But as supply caught up with

---

* All terms in bold type are defined in the Glossary at the back of the text.

demand, a more marketing-oriented view was required to stay competitive. No longer could marketers take a sales-oriented approach by saying "We will sell what we make" without concern for researching the marketplace. They now had to identify consumer needs and develop products to meet these needs.

Just as marketers in domestic markets had to be more attuned to the needs of their consumers, global marketers had to become more aware of differences in needs and usage patterns as a function of different cultures and values. This meant that marketers exporting abroad could no longer rely on homegrown strategies and assume they would be successful. They had to adapt to the differing needs of the global marketplace.

The result of these changes was that marketers began thinking in behavioral terms. In this more consumer-driven context, a product must be developed and positioned to deliver a set of benefits to a defined segment of consumers. The goals of advertising are to communicate symbols and images that show how the brand delivers these benefits, to create a favorable attitude toward the brand, and to induce trial. Advertising is also intended to reinforce the consumers' choices to influence them to repurchase. Distribution is designed to ensure that consumers get the right product at the right time and place, and to provide the services to facilitate this task.

Micromarketing, that is, directing marketing strategies to meet the needs of individual consumers, is the natural culmination of the marketing concept. New technologies have made it possible to more effectively develop products and provide information to enable consumers to better meet their needs. Firms are increasingly customizing both products and information to consumer specifications, as Levi Strauss has done. Consumers can gather more extensive information from the Web to enable them to better meet their needs. The term **mass customization** has come to mean the ability of marketers to offer customized products to large segments of the population. As we will see, micromarketing and mass customization have empowered consumers in the marketplace through wider choices and more information. Such strategies have increased the need for more information and an even better understanding of consumers to allow marketers to direct strategies to individual consumers.

Implications for Consumer Behavior

The shift to a more consumer-driven orientation is still going on today. Avon Products reflects this shift. Before 1980, the company's sales-oriented management failed to see the potential impact of an increasing proportion of working women on its primary means of distribution—door-to-door sales of cosmetics. The simple fact was that fewer women were at home to open the door for the Avon salesperson. More affluent and aware female consumers were beginning to look down on Avon's low-price, bargain basement image.[10] Further, in its expansion abroad, the company had to face the problem that door-to-door selling ran against cultural values and mores in many countries.

The shift to a consumer orientation required a new management team, which promptly commissioned a large-scale study of women's cosmetic needs and attitudes toward Avon products. On the basis of the study, the company repositioned

| **EXHIBIT 1.3** |

Avon attempts to develop a unified global image.

Courtesy Avon.

itself to appeal to affluent working women with new products, such as higher-priced prestige perfumes, and began distributing them through department stores, such as J.C. Penney and Sears.[11] To reinforce a more savvy and up-to-date image, Avon became an official sponsor of the 1996 U.S. Olympic team. In 1998, Avon spent nearly $10 million on its "Women of the Earth" campaign to promote its high-end perfume in more than fifty-four countries.[12] Additionally, in the spring of 2000, Avon began a ten-week mall kiosk tour that took place each weekend at a different mall, to further modernize its image with the female marketplace.[13]

Avon's 2000 marketing campaign, "Let's Talk," was its first global marketing campaign (see Exhibit 1.3). The goal of the campaign, according to the then-new CEO, Andrea Jung, was to build on Avon's brand image and to update its door-to-door sales strategy to make it more contemporary for modern women. This $100 million global branding campaign focused on more television ads and Internet marketing geared toward teenagers.[14] Avon has also extended its brand through its web site, which offers convenient online shopping and product information. As an extension of this strategy, Avon plans to launch a new global operation aimed at teenage girls in 2003. The plan is to use teens on a worldwide basis to sell beauty products to other teens through the Web, direct selling, and catalogs.[15]

The shift to a consumer orientation by companies such as Avon and Levi Strauss & Co. has changed the nature of marketing operations in several ways:

■ *By providing a spur to consumer behavior research.* Both Levi Strauss & Co. and Avon conducted studies of consumer needs, attitudes, and purchasing behavior as a basis for their shift in strategy.

■ *By creating a more customer-oriented framework for marketing strategies.* Levi Strauss & Co. could no longer rely on a mass-market approach. It recognized it had to broaden its line beyond jeans to satisfy teens globally. It also realized it would have to differentiate its appeals based on the needs of different segments—an appeal to baby boomers based primarily on fit, and to teens based on a more "hip" image.

■ *By encouraging measurement of the factors that influence consumers to purchase.* Levi Strauss & Co. had to determine what factors influence choice of slacks among its various age segments.

GLOBAL APPLICATIONS

Procter & Gamble Fails to Export Its Consumer Savvy to Japan

Lack of adequate knowledge of foreign consumers' needs and customs often results in American companies mismarketing abroad. Consider Procter & Gamble (P&G), a company renowned for its ability to meet the needs of American consumers with leading packaged goods such as Tide detergent, Crest toothpaste, Folgers coffee, and Pampers disposable diapers. Until recently, when it came to marketing in Japan, P&G appeared to be a novice. It made the basic mistake of assuming the marketing strategies that worked at home would also work abroad.

Its experience in disposable diapers was instructive. In the words of its current CEO, when P&G introduced Pampers in Japan in 1977, it used "American products, American advertising, and American sales methods and promotional strategies." The product was relatively thick and bulky, designed for American mothers who intended to leave diapers on their babies for longer periods. P&G did not realize that Japanese women are among the most compulsive cleaners in the world and change their babies' diapers twice as often as the average American mother. Japanese companies saw an opening and introduced a thinner, leak-resistant diaper better suited to the needs of Japanese mothers. As a result, Pampers' market share in Japan plummeted from 90 percent in 1977 to 7 percent in 1985.

At that point, a new head of international operations, Edward Artzt, recognized the fallacy of ignoring cross-cultural differences and encouraged development of an improved diaper with one-third the thickness of the original model. By 1990, the new diaper captured almost one-third of the Japanese market and became the prototype for Ultra Pampers in the United States.

P&G is now a company attuned to cross-cultural differences. Former CEO Durk Jager, known for his unconventional solutions and targeted marketing, restructured the company along product lines, rather than the four geographical business units. This effort globalized its brands while still adapting each product to meet local customer needs. Operating in 140 countries and reaching 5 billion people, the company will continue to aggressively expand its 300-brand portfolio worldwide, including Asia, Eastern Europe, and Latin America.

In each case, it is not doing so hesitantly, given its newfound confidence in defining and meeting the needs of foreign consumers. In 2000, under new president and CEO A.G. Lafley, the company looked for new competitive advantages through the development of the corporate web site, *www.pg.com,* and higher pricing strategies on key global brands. To uniquely promote the branding of their premier products, individual web sites have also been created such as Tide.com, where you can put your clothing stains up against the "stain detective," which will recommend the best methods for getting clothes clean. Plus, P&G has utilized the Web to gauge consumer demand and promote new products.

Sources: "Procter & Gamble Is Following Its Nose," *Business Week* (April 22, 1991), p. 28; "At Procter & Gamble, Change Under Artzt Isn't Just Cosmetic," *Wall Street Journal* (March 5, 1991), pp. A1, A8; "Japan Rises to P&G's No. 3 Market," *Advertising Age* (December 10, 1990), p. 42; Edward Artzt, "Winning in Japan: Keys to Global Success," *Business Quarterly* (Winter 1989), pp. 12–16; "P&G Will Make Jager CEO Ahead of Schedule," *Wall Street Journal* (September 10, 1998), p. B1; "Bulky P&G Looks for Speed," *Money*, No. 1999, p. 30; "P&G Weds Data, Sales," *Advertising Age* (October 23, 2000), pp. 76–77; and "Piling on Procter & Gamble," *Advertising Age* (December 11, 2000) p. 51.

■ *By emphasizing market segmentation.* As we saw, Levi Strauss & Co. grouped its customers primarily into age segments. Avon also had to identify segments such as affluent working women (targets for more expensive perfumes and in-store displays), less affluent working women (targets for sales calls at the workplace), as well as women working at home, often on a part-time basis, and the more traditional stay-at-home consumers (both targets for sales calls at home).

■ *By emphasizing product positioning to meet consumer needs.* Products are developed and advertised to establish qualities that set them apart from competition and to relate these qualities to the needs of a defined market segment. Based on the theme "We're going to make you feel beautiful," Avon developed a campaign for its products positioned to less affluent working women. How did it arrive at this positioning strategy? Avon conducted research, showing that less affluent working women wanted to improve their feelings about themselves and to accept themselves more.

■ *By focusing more on the individual consumer.* Both Levi Strauss and Avon have implemented micromarketing strategies directed to individual consumers. Levi Strauss offers customized products and information on its web site. Avon targets its catalogs to individual consumers through direct mail. It is also broadening its base beyond door-to-door selling by relying on more direct customer orders online.

In summary, in accepting the marketing concept, marketing management has recognized that the determinants of consumer behavior have a direct bearing on the formulation of marketing strategies.

Current Trends in Consumer Behavior

The preceding historical perspective shows that successful companies adapt to changing consumer needs and environmental trends—the needs of aging baby boomers in the case of Levi Strauss, and the needs of an increasing proportion of working women in the case of Avon.

The late 1990s and early 2000s have seen equally important consumer behavior trends that will influence marketing strategies. A few in particular are a greater value orientation on the part of consumers, a desire for and access to more information, a more fragmented marketplace, an increase in time poverty, and a desire for more customized products to fit consumer needs. The culmination of many of these trends is greater consumer empowerment.

A GREATER VALUE ORIENTATION

Steep recessions in the early 1980s and 1990s and the economic downturn that started in 2000 have made consumers more price sensitive. Today, with the realization that growth is not unbridled and that there are limits to future purchasing power, consumers are viewing price more in the context of value, that is, getting one's money's worth. The emphasis on value has led to a preponderance of "cross-shoppers"; that is, people who buy suits at Brooks Brothers, but go to Kmart to buy socks, or consumers who buy premium ice cream and generic paper towels.[16] This dichotomy makes sense to consumers seeing value at both high price ends and low price ends in certain product categories.

Greater sensitivity to value has led companies to keep prices down without sacrificing quality. Companies have introduced product offerings at both the high and low ends of the price spectrum—for example, The Gap Inc. positions Banana Republic on the high end and Old Navy on the low end. Retailers such as Nordstrom and Saks Fifth Avenue, both prestige department stores, have opened discount clearinghouses, and Mercedes has developed less expensive models that advertise performance and safety over snob appeal.[17] The emphasis on EDLP (everyday low prices) by leading marketers such as Procter & Gamble and Wal-Mart is also an indication of a greater value orientation. Another is the resurgence of emphasis on building brand equity—that is, communicating the value of a brand in the context of quality and price.

GREATER INTEREST IN AND ACCESS TO INFORMATION VIA THE WEB

The American consumer is becoming a more aware and self-assured shopper. One reason for this is the greater accessibility of information and shopping options. More consumers than ever before have access to virtually unlimited information through the use of the Internet (see boxed insert entitled "Bertelsmann Appeals to Individual Consumers through Online Book Sales," on page 18). The greater incidences of home computers and advances in interactive technologies have expanded the availability of product information in cyberspace. With the increasing educational levels of American consumers, these additional information sources are likely to be used.

The strategic consequences of these changes on consumer behavior are yet to be felt. It is likely that marketers will expand the range of product options available to consumers and ensure that fuller product information is provided than is now typically the case. Marketers will also consider a broader range of media options in communicating to consumers as well as a broader range of delivery options (home shopping channels, telephone buying, electronic kiosks, buying on the Internet).

One indication of future change is Procter & Gamble's introduction of web sites for more than forty of its brands, most of which have customized sites for several countries. The web site for Hugo Boss men's fragrances comes with cutting-edge color graphics, free screensavers and e-cards, and even an interactive "movie maker" on the Hugo Dark Blue site, all targeted to Generation Xers. Forrester Research predicts ad spending on the Web to reach $15 billion by 2005, quite a startling increase if it comes to pass, when one considers ad spending on the Web was only $74 million in 1996.

FRAGMENTATION OF THE MARKETPLACE

The American marketplace has seen increased fragmentation along demographic and social lines, accelerated by a decrease in the traditional family and increase in nontraditional households. For example, in 1972 an estimated 5 percent of children were living in single-parent homes; today that figure is estimated at 18 percent. Couples with no children are also a growing segment, from 16 percent in 1972 to 33 percent today.[18] Fragmentation has also occurred within segments defined by ethnic and national origin. The Hispanic market is no longer thought of as homogeneous. Marketers now typically divide this group into Cuban-American, Mexican-American, and Puerto Rican subsegments. Companies have tried to appeal to more narrowly defined segments by adopting selective marketing messages to reach these audiences. For example, Anheuser Busch has developed advertising with separate themes for each subsegment of the Hispanic audience.

Marketers are also viewing age groupings through a more fragmented lens. What was once referred to as the mature market (those over 50) is now defined as young mature (50s), transitionals (60s), older (70s), and aged (80s). Technology has facilitated companies' ability to customize their messages and build greater customer relationships through product personalization.

INCREASING TIME POVERTY

Consumers are busier than ever and now must face an ever-decreasing amount of free time. Time is divided not just between work and recreation, but also increasingly among family and community commitments. This means that consumers have less and less time to spend searching for information, shopping, and making purchase decisions. The strategic implication is that marketers must emphasize service as well as price, using technology to reduce transaction time, building environments conducive to one-stop shopping, and adding value by providing fast and easy access to information.

A DESIRE FOR MORE CUSTOMIZED PRODUCTS

The greater sophistication of consumers, their access to more information, and their emphasis on value have led them to desire products more closely fitted to their needs. Consumers today are looking for more options at lower prices. They want sneakers for different activities, snacks for different times of day, clothing that is custom-fitted, and cars with a specific set of options and accessories. Consider the following examples of customization:

- Ford builds its Thunderbirds with 69,120 combinations, meaning consumers can come close to designing their own cars.

- Nike launched the "Nike iD" section of its web site *(www.nike.com)* to allow consumers to select the color and size of a particular style of running shoe, and then to customize it even further by selecting a message of up to eight characters that would be sewn onto the back (see Exhibit 1.4).[19]

| EXHIBIT 1.4 |
Nike customizes its running shoes online.

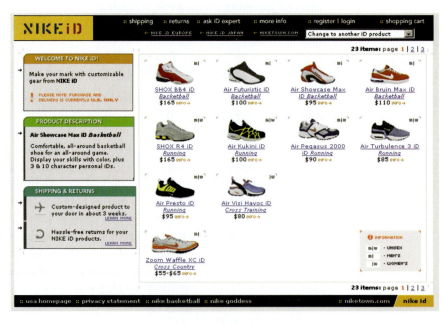

- ■ Motorola offers 29 million different combinations of pager features designed to customer orders.[20]

- ■ Nikon's sunglasses division markets five lens types and more than thirty frames for activities ranging from skiing to driving to water sports.[21]

Because of this trend, some marketers believe that a totally new set of marketing strategies will arise in the future. Instead of product managers selling one product at a time to as many customers as possible (a one-manufacturer-to-many-consumers strategy), *customer managers* will sell more customized products to one consumer at a time (a one-manufacturer-to-one-customer strategy).[22] As the trend to customization accelerates, such strategies will become more feasible and likely.

Consumer Empowerment through the Web

Consumer empowerment stems from the flood of information now available to consumers, the potential for forming discussion and/or buying groups, the ability of consumers to rate and issue warnings on the Web about products and services, and the proliferation of mass-customized products.[23] With close to 150 million American consumers having access to the Internet as of 2001, companies are beginning to recognize the power of consumers to fully exploit the new technological revolution.[24]

Consumer empowerment on the Web has changed every stage of brand building, affecting each of the "4 Ps" of marketing—promotion, place, price, and the product itself.

PROMOTION

In the past, marketers have controlled advertising and promotions directed to consumers by (1) identifying the target market, (2) developing ads to address their needs, and (3) selecting the appropriate media to reach the target (a one-to-many strategy). This process still exists today, but with one large change: the increasing recognition by marketers of the importance of **permission marketing.** This term, coined by the former vice president of direct marketing at Yahoo!, applies to marketing on the Web and implies that in the age of electronic communication, consumers are able to choose which web sites they want to visit and what messages they want to receive.[25] What this means is that marketers on the Web must now ask consumers directly for permission to market to them (a one-to-one strategy). Permission marketing has given consumers the power to decide when they want to be exposed to advertisements. This affects the types of promotion in which marketers engage.

The result of this shift of power means that marketers must develop new ways to build *relationships* with their consumers, making it more likely that those consumers will continue to grant such permission. Lasting bonds such as the ones many packaged goods marketers are seeking do not come easily because products such as paper towels, detergents, or disposable diapers are often not important enough to consumers to form strong loyalties. But companies are becoming more and more creative with regard to establishing relationships with consumers.[26] Sites like *www.pampers.com* offer a parenting email newsletter that provides information on baby care to new parents. In so doing, the site tries to link important issues to the brand and thus establish recognition and loyalty for Pampers.

Kraft has attempted to increase involvement with its brands by offering an entire interactive kitchen on its web site *(www.Kraft.com),* which contains easy recipes and dinner solutions referencing multiple Kraft products. The site is set up in such a way as to encourage consumers (particularly busy moms) to come back to the site repeatedly, looking for the next big recipe of the day.

PRODUCT

The Web has moved marketing of packaged goods from the traditional one-to-many format *(i.e.,* one manufacturer selling to many consumers via television or print media advertisements) to a revolutionary one-to-one format. Marketers now have an unprecedented opportunity to offer consumers a truly engaging experience, one that provides for complete interactivity and enough choices to allow customers to develop not only their own customized information search, but in some cases, their own customized product.

To offer personalized information, many companies now allow consumers to design their own personal web sites. Ivillage *(www.ivillage.com)* and Yahoo! *(www.yahoo.com)* both contain very popular personalization features that allow consumers to develop their own searches and customized information content.

Companies are increasingly offering consumers the opportunity to customize the products as well. The previous section cited customization implemented by companies such as Ford, Motorola, Nikon, and Nike. Customizing cars, pagers, sunglasses, and running shoes is feasible because these products offer many different features that can be bundled into the product that consumers desire. Customization is beginning to be introduced into more frequently purchased everyday products. For example, in November 1999, Procter & Gamble launched a website, *www.Reflect.com,* that employs a mass customization model to allow buyers to customize their own beauty products.[27] The site allows customers to create a skin care, hair care, or cosmetics product that is suited to their individual needs. P&G, a company that had grown to mammoth size based on its skills at mass marketing, determined the necessity to market on an individual level, granting consumers the power to decide what characteristics the product would have.

PLACE

Perhaps even more compelling is the ability of consumers to determine where they want to make a purchase. Thanks to the Web, consumers now have available to them more information than they ever had before, allowing them to choose between many more manufacturers and between many more retailers selling identical items. In particular, search-and-comparison tools called **BOTS** (or **shopping agents**) have made it much easier for consumers to locate a greater variety of items on line. According to Jupiter Research, 83 percent of online shoppers say they comparison-shop before making a purchase.[28] Of course, consumers have always had the power to comparison-shop, but the widespread use of the Web has significantly cut down on the cost of such an information search. Furthermore, the Web gives consumers the ability to have access to the right product at the right time and place, with global reach from home even for items previously unavailable.

PRICE

Price is directly affected by the advent of consumer marketing on the Web. Consumers now have an almost unlimited ability to search for price alternatives and obtain previously unavailable price information. For example, sites such as *www.edwards.com* allow consumers to obtain the dealer's and list prices of vehicles prior to entering the dealership. This empowers the consumer in negotiating a lower price. With this new power comes a logical shift from shopping on the basis of convenience to shopping on the basis of price. Marketers must now consider the pricing strategies of their competitors much more closely.

The Information Base for Understanding Consumer Behavior

Most marketing firms have a marketing information system designed to provide data on what consumers do and why. Such a system is obviously important in understanding consumer behavior and developing marketing strategies. A marketing information system should have the capability of collecting two types of data, secondary and primary. **Secondary data** are existing data from published sources or from company records. **Primary data** are data collected by the company for the specific purpose of answering its research questions.

SECONDARY DATA

Generally, companies first analyze secondary data before collecting primary data. Three important sources of secondary data in understanding consumers are census data from the U.S. government, syndicated services that track consumer trends, and databases that provide information on the characteristics of purchasers of certain products and services.

▌ **Census Data**   Census data provide a storehouse of demographic information that is constantly used by marketers. We have seen that important demographic trends such as the aging of baby boomers and the increasing proportion of working women have influenced Levi Strauss and Avon to change their long-term marketing strategies. The 2000 census has been important in tracking demographic trends such as the increasing proportion of nontraditional families and the sharp rise in the Hispanic-American population, surpassing African Americans as the largest group in the United States based on ethnicity or national origin.

▌ **Syndicated Services**   Syndicated services are offered by firms that collect data periodically and sell it to subscribing companies. Syndicated services serve two important functions in the context of consumer behavior. First, they track behavior in the form of sales data. Second, they provide a basis for understanding such behavior by periodically collecting information on consumer attitudes, perceptions, and lifestyles.

Two companies, A. C. Nielsen and Information Resources Inc., provide information on consumer behavior by reporting scanner data from retail stores. Such data break out sales by type of product, retail store, price, and region. These firms also maintain panels of consumers who use special coded cards when purchasing that identify their demographic and lifestyle characteristics. This permits marketers to tie in what people buy to who they are.

Syndicated services also track consumer attitudes, opinions, and lifestyles and divide consumers into segments that might better explain their purchasing behavior. For example, one service, the Value and Lifestyle Survey (VALS), interviews 2,500 respondents yearly and divides them into segments such as achievers (affluent people who get satisfaction from their jobs and families) and experiencers (younger people who strive for wealth and power and spend heavily on new products). Marketers can determine what products these segments are buying and can thereby get a better understanding of their purchasing behavior.

Companies also provide services based on **geodemographic analysis,** that is, the identification of consumer characteristics and purchasing habits based on where they live. The basic assumption in this type of analysis is that people with similar values, backgrounds, and needs live in the same neighborhoods. Therefore, these neighborhoods can be grouped into clusters that exhibit similar demographic and lifestyle characteristics. One syndicated service, PRIZM, has identified sixty-two such clusters based on census data. These clusters are formed by grouping zip codes areas with similar demographic and social characteristics.[29] Currently, similar systems are being formed on a global basis to group consumers with similar characteristics in neighborhoods in, say, Milan, Paris, and New York. Marketers use this information to more accurately target their brands to individuals in various geographic areas.

▌ **Database Marketing** **Database marketing** utilizes information about individual consumers and allows companies to customize their offerings accordingly. Database marketing represents the informational underpinnings of micromarketing and has been made possible by interactive technologies that allow companies to track individual consumer responses to company offers and inquiries.

An example is the facility Levi Strauss established in allowing customers to provide alterations data directly in their stores through in-store computers and on the Web. In so doing, Levi Strauss gained a valuable database on individual consumers. By maintaining files of these consumers in a database, Levi Strauss can now reach them with direct mail promotions.

Such a database raises issues of invasion of privacy. There is a thin line between using consumer data collected in the course of doing business and invading consumers' privacy regarding personal information. One logical solution is to inform consumers that data are available regarding their characteristics and purchasing patterns and ask their permission to use it.

PRIMARY DATA

In most cases, secondary data is not sufficient to develop marketing strategies to meet consumer needs; therefore, companies collect primary data to meet their informational needs. They conduct surveys to determine consumers' attitudes toward their products as well as their intentions to buy. They determine consumer reactions to advertisements, price promotions, and new product concepts. And they test new products on select consumer groups. Consumer researchers collect primary data by utilizing qualitative research, survey research, experimentation, and observation.

▌ Qualitative Research **Qualitative research** is designed to learn more about consumers' underlying motives by asking them questions in an unstructured manner. It allows researchers to form hypotheses regarding consumer actions and to better define research areas so as to know the kinds of questions to ask in more structured surveys or experiments. The two most frequently used qualitative approaches are focus group interviews and projective techniques.

Focus group interviews are informal, open-ended group discussions that are guided by a trained moderator who keeps the discussion focused on a series of topics of interest to the marketing firm. One airline used focus groups to research fear of flying among businesspeople. Group discussions allowed consumers to be open about their fears. These focus groups showed that it was not so much fear of flying that deterred businesspeople as guilt that if they died they would leave behind their loved ones. As a result, the airline developed an ad campaign that focused on the joy of coming back to the family from a business trip rather than the more rational appeals of direct flights and on-time arrivals.

Projective techniques involve presenting ambiguous materials to consumers designed to induce them to project subconscious feelings and attitudes. If the desired information is very personal or deep-seated, consumers can be given a cartoon and asked to fill in the bubble, given an unfinished sentence and asked to complete it, or given a situation and asked to project the people they would associate with it. In each case, consumers are likely to project their true feelings because the questions are not asked directly.

Panasonic used projective techniques to determine whether its positive image in consumer electronics could carry over to office automation. Researchers asked consumers to select photos of people they associated with IBM, Xerox, Canon, and Panasonic products. Respondents associated photos of older, distinguished, and affluent people with IBM and Xerox. They selected photos of younger, upstart professionals with Panasonic.[30] The company used these findings to develop an ad campaign for its office automation products, "The Panasonic boom, the next generation," showing the independent baby boomers of the 1960s and 1970s now in management positions.

▌ Survey Research Survey research is designed to collect structured data through a questionnaire from a sample of respondents that is representative of a population. If General Motors wanted to determine attitudes toward GM cars among foreign car owners, it might develop a questionnaire to elicit attitudes toward domestic and foreign cars, and ask these questions among a representative sample of foreign car owners (the population). GM could then determine the reasons for resistance toward its particular divisions among foreign car owners, the characteristics of car owners holding these negative views, and whether it can develop strategies to change these attitudes.

The GM survey is known as a *cross-sectional design;* that is, it conducts research at a particular point in time. If GM were to track changes in attitudes and behavior among the same sample of foreign car owners over time, this would be a *longitudinal design.* Companies frequently conduct longitudinal studies by forming panels of consumers to track changes in attitudes and behavior. One of the first such longitudinal panels was formed by General Electric in the late 1960s to track the acquisition of major appliances among new households.

Experimental Research   Experimental research attempts to test for cause-and-effect relationships under controlled conditions. Researchers try to determine the effects of marketing stimuli such as alternative product characteristics, advertising themes, or price levels (the cause) on consumer responses (the effect). In trying to establish such cause-and-effect relationships, the researcher must try to control all factors except the marketing stimulus being tested so that consumer responses can be attributed to that stimulus.

Frito-Lay ran experiments under controlled conditions and found it could reduce the oil in its light chip line (the stimulus or cause) by one-third without a

WEB APPLICATIONS OF CONSUMER BEHAVIOR

Bertelsmann Appeals to Individual Consumers through Online Book Sales

The largest media company in Europe, Bertelsmann, has invested heavily to develop an online presence worldwide. With businesses in book publishing, music, television, radio, magazines, newspapers, and print and media services, Bertelsmann has leveraged its position as the world's largest book publisher into partnerships with strong Internet booksellers like Barnesandnoble.com in the United States and building its own online media superstore, Bertelsmann Online, or BOL, to focus on selling books in Europe.

The German-based company was late to the U.S. online book game, buying a 50 percent share of Barnesandnoble.com in 1998. However, the 1998 launch of its BOL sites was still relatively early to the European market. The German Retail Association predicted electronic commerce sales would reach 17.9 million euros by 2003 (approximately $19.2 billion at the current exchange rate), and BOL wants a piece of the e-commerce revenue pie.

BOL.com has a 5-million-title database and has sites customized by language and content for Germany, the United Kingdom, France, Spain, Switzerland, and the Netherlands. The BOL.com sites were built to offer personalization by designing the sites with the needs of local consumers in mind. "The issue for us as the architects of this site and as the builders of it was really to come up with a design that was global with initial designs . . . and had flexibility to localize," said site creator Kit Cody.

Each BOL site has the same clean blue and white design, with standard search, browse, and shopping functions, as well as sections on bestsellers, gift ideas, and recommendations. However, each site promotes different books on the home page, based on local bestsellers and interests, and carries a different inventory of books in each language. The sites can be further customized by completing the "My BOL" profile, which asks customers to select their favorite book categories (such as business management or science fiction) and authors and asks for a name, email address, and password to create the account. After a "My BOL" account has been created, customers returning to the home page type in their email address and password and are greeted by name and shown a personalized home page. The home page includes several targeted book selections to match the interests specified in the profile. BOL will also send a customized newsletter each month via email containing suggested book titles. As one of the leading book club companies in the world, Bertelsmann is using its offline experience in customized marketing to create a personalized online experience for customers around the world.

Sources: "German Publisher to Join Web Booksellers," *Computerworld* (June 1, 1998), p. 37; "Euro E-comm: Giant Bertelsmann Tests Site," *Adweek*, Print Media Edition: Eastern edition (November 30, 1998), p. 33; www.BOL.com web site, as of November 2000; www.bertelsmann.com web site, as of November 2000; "World Watch," *Wall Street Journal* (January 23, 2002), p. A17.

decrease in consumer taste ratings (the response or effect). Beyond that level, taste ratings plummeted. Frito-Lay gave groups formulations with one-sixth less oil, one-third less, one-half less, and so on. When it ran tests on these various formulations, the company matched each group on key consumer characteristics to make sure that the results were due to the oil level in the chip rather than to some extraneous factor like frequency of snacking or age of the respondent.

■ **Observational Research**   Researchers also observe consumers to determine what they do in the process of buying a product, using it, or being exposed to a marketing communication. For example, how long do consumers examine products in a supermarket before putting it in the shopping cart, or how accurately do consumers follow directions on a label in food preparation?

In 2000, Best Western paid a number of 55+ consumers to tape themselves on cross-country trips. The effort convinced the company it did not have to boost its 10 percent discounts to seniors because the tapes showed that seniors were more interested in the thrill of talking the hotel clerk into a discount than the actual size of the discount.[31] Curad Battle Ribbon adhesives were also developed as a result of direct observation of children decorating bandages with crayons and felt-tip pens. These studies are *obtrusive* in that respondents are aware of the presence of researchers, and such awareness can influence results. In an example of *unobtrusive observation,* researchers determined they could not get reliable estimates of alcohol consumption through direct questioning, so they measured the number of empty bottles in the garbage.[32]

Another form of observation is *participant observation,* in which a researcher observes or sometimes lives with a group or family in a particular culture and observes their behavior. Such in-depth observation is derived from cultural anthropology and is called **ethnographic research.** Ethnographic studies are occasionally used by marketers. 3Com spent four months videotaping 645 households in three cities to see exactly how they used various devices to organize their day. A crucial discovery was that it took over an hour for consumers to log on to a computer after deciding to use it, whereas it took only ten seconds to log onto a Palm handheld after making the decision to use it. As a result, 3Com designed their new Audrey handheld device more as a tool rather than a planned activity, with an extremely compact size and simple design.[33]

Approaches to Studying Consumer Behavior: A Managerial versus a Holistic Approach

There are two broad approaches to the study of consumer behavior. A *managerial approach* views consumer behavior as an applied social science. It is studied as an adjunct to and a basis for developing marketing strategies. A *holistic approach* views consumer behavior as a pure rather than applied social science. In this view, consumer behavior is a legitimate focus of inquiry in and of itself without necessarily being applied to marketing. Although it may appear that the first view has more credence for marketers, in reality, a holistic approach also provides a useful perspective for marketing strategy in many cases.

A MANAGERIAL APPROACH

A managerial approach to consumer behavior tends to be more micro and cognitive in nature. It is *micro* in emphasizing the individual consumer, his or her attitudes, perceptions, lifestyle, and demographic characteristics. More macro environmental effects—reference groups, the family, culture—are studied in the context of how they influence the individual consumer. In being more micro, a managerial orientation is also more *cognitive;* that is, it emphasizes the thought processes of individual consumers and the factors that go into influencing their decisions.

Marketing managers find such a focus on the individual only natural. The goal of all marketing strategy should be to satisfy the needs of individual consumers in a socially responsible manner. Information is collected on the consumer's needs (desired product benefits), thought processes (attitudes and perceptions), and characteristics (lifestyle and demographics). This information is then aggregated to define segments of consumers that can be targeted with the company's offerings. Thus, a more affluent, older baby-boom segment might be identified that likes casual wear and emphasizes performance over status. Identification of such a segment would have implications for marketers for everything from clothes to home computers and from yogurt to cars.

But there are risks in taking too rigid a managerial perspective. First, it might overemphasize the rationality of consumers. The cognitive view is that consumers search for and process information in some systematic manner in an attempt to meet their needs. But in many cases, such systematic processing may not occur, as when consumers buy products for their symbolic value, on impulse, or on an addictive basis. Using a strictly cognitive approach may not reveal the underlying nature of the consumer's decision in these cases.

Second, a micro view might overlook the dynamics of environmental factors independent of the individual. For example, a perspective on gift giving in the context of ritual behavior would be culturally derived and might be insightful for many marketers. Yet such a perspective might be overlooked if the focus is primarily on individual consumers.

Third, a managerial perspective tends to focus more on purchase than on consumption. This is only natural because marketing managers emphasize sales results as represented by purchasing behavior. But recently, the focus has increasingly shifted to what happens after the purchase. Satisfaction is generally defined by the consumption, not the purchase experience. A whole new area in marketing, called **relationship marketing,** recognizes that marketers must connect with consumers before the purchase *and* maintain an ongoing relationship after the purchase. And to a large degree, this relationship is dependent on the consumption experience. The Web has enabled marketers to enhance relationship marketing efforts through interactive communication with customers, by email, chatrooms, and message boards.

A HOLISTIC APPROACH

A holistic approach is more macro in its orientation. It is *macro* in that it tends to focus more on the nature of the consumption experience than on the purchasing process, stressing the broader, culturally derived context of consumption.

Consumption is seen as being symbolic as well as functional, antisocial as well as social, and idiosyncratic as well as normative. Purchase behavior is of little inherent interest outside of its impact on the consumption experience. When it is studied, it is in the context of shopping rather than decision making because shopping is frequently culturally derived.

Whereas a managerial orientation is more interested in predicting what the consumer might do in the future, the holistic approach is more interested in understanding the environmental context of the consumer's actions at present.

A holistic approach also has its drawbacks. The most important is that findings regarding culturally derived meaning of consumer actions and consumption experiences may not be actionable from a marketer's perspective. This need not bother those who study consumer behavior for its own sake, but findings from consumer behavior should be actionable for marketing strategies in a business context—thus the reference in the title of this book to a *strategic approach* for consumer behavior.

Second, a holistic approach does not put sufficient emphasis on purchase decisions. Marketers must understand how consumers reach decisions if they are to influence them. Third, although many consumer decisions are not made through a process of systematic processing, many are. Some understanding of such cognitive processes is necessary if marketers are to attempt to meet consumer needs.

A BALANCED VIEW

This book clearly takes a managerial perspective in viewing the study of consumer behavior as a basis for developing marketing strategies to meet consumer needs. But it also recognizes the value of a broader, holistic perspective in moderating a strictly cognitive and micro view. For example, the discussion of consumer decision making considers both information processing and the symbolic role of products. The discussion of the consumer environment considers its effects on both consumer purchases and the consumption experience.

A Model of Consumer Behavior

As noted, the premise of this text is that marketing strategies must be based on the factors that influence consumer behavior. Figure 1.1, a simple model of consumer behavior, emphasizes the interaction between the marketer and the consumer. Consumer decision making—that is, the process of perceiving and evaluating brand information, considering how brand alternatives meet the consumer's needs, and deciding on a brand—is the central component of the model.

Two broad influences determine the consumer's choice. The first is the individual consumer whose needs, perceptions of brand characteristics, and attitudes toward alternatives influence brand choice. In addition, the consumer's demographics, lifestyle, and personality characteristics influence brand choice.

The second influence on consumer decision making is the environment. The consumer's purchasing environment is represented by culture (the norms and values of society), subcultures (a part of society with distinct norms and values in

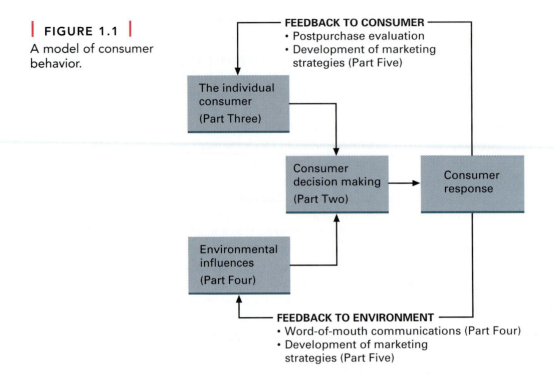

certain respects), and face-to-face groups (friends, family members, and reference groups). Marketing organizations are also part of the consumer's environment, because these organizations provide the offerings that can satisfy consumer needs.

Once the consumer has made a decision, postpurchase evaluation, represented as feedback to the individual consumer, takes place. During evaluation, the consumer will learn from the experience and may change his or her pattern of acquiring information, evaluating brands, and selecting a brand. Consumption experience will directly influence whether the consumer will buy the same brand again. A feedback loop also leads back to the environment. Consumers use word of mouth to communicate their purchase and consumption experiences to friends and families.

Figure 1.1 also shows that consumer feedback is the basis for marketing strategies. Marketers seek information from consumers (top loop). They track consumer responses in the form of market share and sales data. However, such information neither tells the marketer why the consumer purchased nor provides information on the strengths and weaknesses of the marketer's brand relative to those of the competition. Therefore, marketing research is also required at this step to determine consumer reactions to the brand and future purchase intent. This information permits management to reformulate marketing strategy to better meet consumer needs.

Marketers also seek information from the environment (bottom loop). They want to determine the nature of word-of-mouth communications regarding their brands. They also want to determine how cultural and social norms might impact the purchases of their products. On a broader dimension, marketers seek consumer opinions regarding their corporate image in the context of social responsibility.

Organization of This Text

This text considers the components of the model in Figure 1.1 in detail, and, in so doing, emphasizes consumer behavior applications to marketing strategy. Figure 1.1 shows that we will consider a portion of the model in each of the sections of this text.

In Part Two, we review consumer decision making. The process by which consumers make purchasing decisions must be understood to develop strategic applications. As we will see, consumer decision making is not a uniform process. It varies by the importance of the purchase to the consumer, the degree to which the consumer is satisfied with the purchase, and the willingness of the consumer to search for information and brand alternatives.

Part Three discusses the individual consumer. The way in which the individual consumer influences the decision process is central to understanding consumer behavior. In this section, we consider consumers' *thought processes;* that is, the cognitive factors that influence decision making. We also consider consumers' *experiential processes;* that is, decisions that are governed more by the emotions of consumers in seeking pleasure rather than purely utility from products. This distinction between *hedonic* and *utilitarian* products will be a common theme in this section. Part Two also considers the individual consumer's *characteristics,* namely demographic, lifestyle, and personality characteristics that influence consumers' decisions. Demographic and lifestyle trends are considered for the United States and abroad.

In Part Four, we cover the environmental factors influencing behavior. We start with the broadest set of environmental influences, **culture;** that is, the widely shared norms and patterns of behavior of the society in which the consumer lives. We also consider **subcultures,** groups with norms and values that distinguish them from the culture as a whole, and **cross-cultural influences** that identify differences in cultural values between nations. We then consider face-to-face groups and how they influence consumer behavior. One chapter describes **reference groups,** so-called because they provide consumers with a means of comparing and evaluating their attitudes and behavior with the group's. Another describes the most important group of all, the family. A chapter is also devoted to describing word-of-mouth influences within groups and a broader process of the diffusion of information and influence across groups.

In Part Five, we summarize many of the strategic applications discussed throughout the book in two chapters, one dealing with targeting consumers and the other with influencing them. Targeting consumers requires identifying market segments and positioning products accordingly. The Web has allowed such targeting to become a one-to-one process through micromarketing; that is, manufacturers targeting individual consumers with customized information and products. Influencing consumers requires developing marketing communications geared to consumer needs, and transmitting information and influence through various media vehicles including the Web.

In the concluding chapter of Part Five, we consider consumer rights, such as the right to safe products and accurate information. We focus on the role of government and consumer advocates in furthering and protecting these rights. We also consider the social responsibility of business in protecting the consumer and the environment.

SUMMARY

This introductory chapter has established the text's orientation by linking consumer behavior to marketing strategy. The need for consumer information to establish marketing strategies is recognized. Such consumer information permits marketing managers to

- define consumer needs,
- identify consumer segments that have these needs,
- develop marketing strategies targeted to these segments,
- evaluate marketing strategies, and
- ensure that marketing strategies are implemented in a socially responsible manner.

A historical perspective shows that a consumer orientation developed out of economic necessity as the economic environment became more competitive. As a result, marketing managers had to begin to identify consumer needs to remain competitive, and to gear marketing strategies accordingly. A better understanding of consumer needs, perceptions, attitudes, and intentions became necessary.

The culmination of the marketing environment is micromarketing; that is, an attempt to meet the needs of individual consumers by empowering them to determine the information they want and the characteristics of the products they need.

Current trends suggest that marketers must continue to be sensitive to changes in consumer needs, demographic characteristics, and lifestyles to develop effective marketing strategies. Changes that are most likely to have an impact on marketers include the following:

1. A greater value orientation on the part of consumers
2. Greater interest in and access to information on products and services
3. Fragmentation of the marketplace
4. Increased time poverty
5. The desire for more customized products

Perhaps the most important trend is the empowerment of consumers through new technologies. Consumer empowerment has influenced every facet of marketing strategy because of the greater access to information on the part of the consumer.

Marketing firms need some systematic basis for collecting information. Most have a marketing information system designed to provide data on what consumers do and why. Such information systems are designed to collect both secondary data (existing data from published sources or company records) and primary data (data collected by the company to answer its research questions).

The common sources of secondary data are the U.S. government, syndicated services, and databases on individual consumer characteristics that allow companies to customize their offerings. The usual means of collecting primary data are qualitative research, surveys, experimentation, and observation.

Although this text takes a managerial approach to the study of consumer behavior, it also recognizes the usefulness of an alternative view—a holistic approach. A managerial approach tends to emphasize individual consumers, their thought processes, and the impact of the environment on their needs and attitudes. A holistic approach tends to stress consumer experiences—primarily consumption—rather than purchase behavior, and the general context of the consumer's environment. One following a holistic approach tends to view consumer behavior as a field of study in and of itself without necessarily deriving managerial and strategic implications.

The text is organized after the model in Figure 1.1, which has four components: consumer decision making, the two key elements that influence consumer decision making—the individual consumer and the consumer's environment, and marketing strategies geared to meeting consumer needs based on an understanding of these influences.

QUESTIONS FOR DISCUSSION

1. Explain the ways in which the study of consumer behavior is linked to the development of marketing strategies.

2. Why did Levi Strauss & Co. switch from a mass-market strategy to a strategy of market segmentation? How did it adjust its product line to reflect changes in consumer demographics and lifestyles?

3. Have Levi Strauss and Avon implemented a micromarketing strategy?

4. A vice president of marketing for a large soft drink company often states that sales are the ultimate criterion for judging marketing effectiveness, and therefore one must look primarily at the relationship between marketing stimuli (price, advertising, deals, coupons) and sales. What arguments could you, as director of marketing research, present in support of the role of consumer research in demonstrating that sales figures alone are not sufficient to evaluate marketing strategies?

5. What were the conditions leading to the development of the marketing concept?

6. Why are micromarketing and mass customization logical culminations of the marketing concept?

7. What caused Avon to shift from a sales to a marketing orientation in the 1980s? What Avon strategies reflected this shift?

8. What is the relation between a greater value orientation on the part of consumers and the "cross-shopper" effect? What are the strategic implications of a greater value orientation?

9. In what ways did P&G fail to meet consumers' needs in marketing their products in Japan? How have they changed their strategy to market internationally? What role has the Internet played?

10. In what ways does the consumer have more access to information today? Are consumers likely to use these new information sources? How are marketers responding to their availability?

11. What is meant by the prediction that instead of product managers selling one product to many consumers, we will begin to see customer managers selling many products to one customer? Why did analysts make this prediction?

12. In what ways have consumers become more empowered because of new technologies? What are the strategic implications for marketers of this empowerment?

13. In what ways has Bertelsmann customized its online web site? What benefits are to be gained from customization?

14. What are the roles of primary and secondary data in conducting consumer research? What are the roles of qualitative and survey research in collecting primary data?

15. What is the distinction between a managerial and a holistic approach to the study of consumer behavior? What are the advantages and disadvantages of both?

RESEARCH ASSIGNMENTS

1 Log onto Levi Strauss's worldwide web site. Browse the seven sections and answer the following questions:

- Levi Strauss is assuming there is a global youth market. Is there any support for this assumption from Levi Strauss's approach?

- In what ways is Levi Strauss trying to appeal to the global youth market?

- What type of product information is Levi Strauss supplying?

- What are the distinctions between the seven sections of Levi Strauss's site? What purpose does each section serve?

2 Do a content analysis of two issues of *Advertising Age,* one from about 1960 and one current issue, by determining the frequency of the appearance of certain basic marketing references.

- How frequently mentioned in the 1960 and the current issues are (a) marketing research, (b) test marketing, (c) new product development, (d) market segmentation, (e) product positioning (f) lifestyles, (g) advertising regulation, (h) environmental concerns, and (i) advertising to ethnic segments such as Hispanic Americans?

3 Visit the *Ivillage.com* web site and customize the delivery of your content by creating a personalized content page. Participate in chatrooms and message boards about select consumer products. Discuss the various ways the site establishes a relationship with consumers and suggest methods that Ivillage could use to improve its relationship efforts.

4 Attempt to trace the development of the marketing concept and evolutions of a behavioral orientation for a large manufacturer of consumer packaged goods. Do so by tracing references to the company in business periodicals, the evolution of the company's annual reports, and, when possible, by interviewing company executives who have been with the company in marketing for ten years or more.

- What has been the change in marketing research procedures, particularly in regard to (a) product testing, (b) advertising evaluation, (c) in-store testing, and (d) utilization of concepts of market segmentation and product positioning?

- What changes have occurred in the organization of the research function?

NOTES

1. "Can Levi's Be Cool Again?," *Business Week* (March 13, 2000), p. 144.
2. "Levi's vs. the Dress Code," *Business Week* (April 1, 1996), pp. 57–58.
3. "Slates Backgrounder," Press release from www.levistrauss.com (January 2001).
4. "Red, White and Blue: An American Icon Fades Away," *Ad Week* (April 26, 1999), pp. 28–35.
5. "Assessing Levi's Patch Job," *Brandweek* (November 6, 2000), p. 34.
6. "Wired Set Looks to Haberdasher-e," *Europe* (October 2000), p. 6.
7. "Levi's Uses Music to Woo Youth Market/ Hefty Sums Spent to Sponsor Concerts," *San Francisco Chronicle* (March 8, 1999), p. A1; "Can Levi's Ever Be Cool Again?" *Marketing* (April 15, 1999), pp. 28–29; and *www.levistrauss.com*, as of July 2000.
8. "Levi's Sta-Prest Makes an Impression on Youth Culture," *Marketing* (March 25, 1999), p. 24; and "More Lost Than Ever," *Business 2.com* (February 6, 2001), p. 70.
9. "Sears Drops 'Soft Side' Image in Face of Discount Challenge," *Discount Store News* (March 8, 1999), p. 1.
10. "Direct Selling Is Alive and Well," *Sales & Marketing Management* (August 1988), p. 76; and "Fresher Face at Avon," *Management Today* (December 1984), p. S-4.
11. "Avon Confirms Negotiations with J.C. Penney and Sears," *PR Newswire* (September 18, 2000).
12. "Avon's $10M Says, 'We Are Women'," *Brandweek* (September 21, 1998), p. 12.
13. "Tour de Face," *Brandweek* (May 29, 2000), p. 34.
14. "Avon's Calling Beyond In-house," *Advertising Age* (June 19, 2000), p. 1.
15. "Avon to Target Teens," *Direct Marketing* (November 2001), p. 22.
16. "Consumer Schizophrenia: Extremism in the Marketplace," *Planning Review* (July/August 1992), pp. 18–22.
17. *John Naisbitt's Trendletter* (September 1995/February 1996), p. 5.
18. "Advertisers Are Cautious as Household Makeup Shifts," *Wall Street Journal* (May 15, 2001), pp. B1 and B4.
19. "Custom Manufacturing—Nike Model Shows Web Limtations," *Internetweek* (December 6, 1999), pp. 1, 12.
20. "Mass Customization Sparks Sea Change," *Business Marketing* (November 1993), p. 43.
21. *John Naisbitt's Trendletter* (September 1995/February 1996), p. 9.
22. Don Peppers and Martha Rogers, *The One-to-One Future: Building Relationships One Customer at a Time* (New York: Currency Doubleday, 1993).
23. "Regarding Customers as Business Collaborator," *New York Times* (February 9, 2000), p. C10.
24. "Exploration of World Wide Web Tilts from Eclectic to Mundane," *New York Times* (August 26, 2001), pp. 1, 22; www.nua.ie/surveys, "U.S. Department of Commerce: U.S. Digital Divide Narrows" (October 18, 2000).
25. "Have You Got Permission?" *Marketing* (June 22, 2000), pp. 28–29.
26. "E-Goods," *Advertising Age* Vol. 70, No. 39(1999), pp. 66 and 75.
27. "The New Brand Management," *Advertising Age* (November 8, 1999), pp. S2, S19.
28. "Revenge of the BOTS," *The Industry Standard* (November 22–29), 1999, pp. 263–271.
29. PRIZM Cluster Narratives, Claritas Inc., 1999.
30. "Matching Face with Image," *Business Marketing* (March 1989), p. 58.
31. "Consumers in the Mist," *Business Week* (February 26, 2001), p. 92.
32. David A. Aaker and George S. Day, *Marketing Research* (New York: John Wiley & Sons, 1980), p. 102.
33. "Consumers in the Mist," *Business Week* (February 26, 2001), pp. 92, 94.

Consumer Decision Making

Complex Decision Making: Purchase and Consumption

This chapter presents a model of complex decision making. A detailed example of a couple deciding on the purchase of a new car is used to describe this process.

Complex decision making includes many of the important behavioral concepts used throughout the text. For example, it requires a consumer who is involved with the product and, as a result, actively searches for information. Therefore, concepts of involvement and consumer information processing are introduced. Complex decision making also involves the evaluation of alternative brands. Therefore, the process consumers use to assess products in light of their needs is also considered. Finally, complex decision making involves the consumers' evaluation of the brand after purchasing it. Therefore, concepts of consumer satisfaction and post-purchase evaluation are formulated.

Since the basis for evaluating the product after the purchase is consumption, this chapter considers not only the purchasing process but also the consumption experience. It highlights the fact that products can be purchased and consumed for both utilitarian and emotional reasons.

Autobytel.com Helps Empower the Car Purchaser

The purchase of a car is a good example of complex decision making since it is a large purchase (next to the purchase of a home, the purchase of a new car is the second-largest purchase most consumers will ever make), and it usually involves all of the steps described in this chapter.

One relatively recent and major change in car purchasing is that consumers can now obtain information on prices and features of alternative cars from the Web. In the vast majority of cases, consumers obtain this information and then go to dealerships to purchase. Few actually buy online, although the option is available.

Certain web sites, known as **infomediaries,** serve to bring together information from various sources. When used for auto purchases, infomediaries allow consumers to make side-by-side comparisons of cars, to determine the dealer's invoice price in advance, to buy the car on a "no price haggling" basis online, and to obtain information about financing, insurance, and service.

One such web site is *www.Autobytel.com* (see Exhibit 2.1). Autobytel was the first company to recognize the need for a car infomediary on the Web. The site aggregates various auto information service providers, such as Edmund's, Kelley Blue Book, Pace Publication's CarPrice.com, and Intellichoice, to assist consumers in gathering information.

Once consumers have gathered information from these sources, Autobytel then allows them to customize their car by selecting the make, model, and exact series and then adding whatever option packages they want. Most important, consumers can determine the dealer's invoice price and manufacturer's suggested list price for the specified car. Such information was not ordinarily available to the consumer before the advent of the Web. Consumers can buy online from Autobytel by submitting a free, no-obligation purchase request for the vehicle they designed. A dealer assigned by Autobytel will then call the consumer with a fair, no-haggle price and, if

EXHIBIT 2.1

Autobytel was the first company to recognize the need for a car infomediary on the Web.

Reprinted with permission of Autobytel.com.

requested, will deliver the car to the consumer's door.[1]

Alternatively, consumers can visit a dealership, using the price knowledge gleaned from the Autobytel site to improve their negotiating position with the dealer. In either case, Autobytel provides substantial value to consumers that was never before available.

Most recently, Autobytel expanded its services to several European countries, Japan, and Australia, competing against such online sites as Auto Trade Interactive, Virgincars.com, and OneSwoop. These sites serve to walk consumers through nearly every step of the complex decision-making process. As soon as the consumer recognizes the need for a new car, Autobytel and other sites can aid in the search for information, evaluation of alternatives, and final choice, and then follow up with postpurchase services such as financing, insurance, and even car maintenance.[2]

As noted, most consumers use infomediaries for free information and then make their purchases from traditional car dealerships. Recent research has shown that, due to the perceived risk of making such a large purchase sight unseen (*i.e.,* the "tire-kicking" factor), although over 60 percent of consumers research their cars online before buying them offline, only 5 to 8 percent of new cars are bought online.[3] If this trend continues, online services such as Autobytel will have difficulty maintaining a revenue stream, because they do not charge for information.

Consumer use of Autobytel reflects a general trend—using the Web primarily for information with purchasing being a distant second. It is the information rather than the purchasing capabilities that have truly empowered consumers. As a result, it is likely that infomediaries such as Autobytel will evolve by charging consumers a fee for information access, with limited revenue from online purchases.

The Nature of Complex Decision Making

The process by which consumers make purchasing decisions must be understood to develop strategic applications. Consumer decision making is not a single process. Deciding to buy a car is a more important and complex decision than deciding to buy toothpaste. In **complex decision making,** consumers evaluate brands in a detailed and comprehensive manner. More information is sought and more brands are evaluated than in other types of buying decisions. In this chapter, we consider complex decision making. In Chapters 3 and 4, we consider consumer decisions that require less information and deliberation.

CONDITIONS FOR COMPLEX DECISION MAKING

Complex decision making is most likely when consumers are **involved** with the product; that is, when the product is important to consumers. This means that complex decision making is most likely for

- high-priced products.
- products associated with performance risks (medical products, automobiles).
- complex products (compact disc players, personal computers).
- products associated with one's ego (clothing, cosmetics).

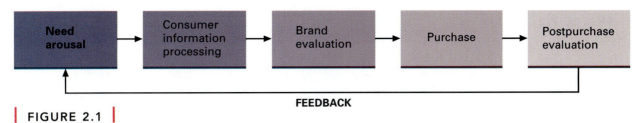

| FIGURE 2.1 |

A basic model of complex decision making.

The nature of the product is not the only condition for complex decision making. Certain *facilitating* conditions also need to exist. The most important is adequate *time* for extensive information search and processing.[4] Complex decision making will not occur if a decision must be made quickly. For example, if a washing machine breaks down in a family with eight children, it is unlikely the parents will spend several weeks establishing purchasing criteria and evaluating alternative brands. Also, consumers may not have the time to devote to extensive information processing because business or social obligations may have a higher priority. A recent law school graduate working fourteen-hour days is unlikely to spend a great deal of time replacing a broken-down stereo system.

A second condition for complex decision making is the availability of *adequate information* to evaluate alternative brands. A study by Greenleaf and Lehmann found that consumers sometimes delay a decision because of insufficient or inaccurate information. The same study also found that decision making is delayed when there are too many product characteristics and features to consider. Such confusion means that complex decision making also requires a consumer's *ability to process information.*[5]

A MODEL OF COMPLEX DECISION MAKING

Research on decision making has identified five phases in the decision process: (1) problem recognition, (2) search for information, (3) evaluation of alternatives, (4) choice, and (5) outcome of the choice.[6] For a consumer engaging in complex decision making, these steps can be translated into (1) need arousal, (2) consumer information processing, (3) brand evaluation, (4) purchase, and (5) postpurchase evaluation. A model of complex decision making representing these five steps is presented in Figure 2.1.

Each of these five processes is considered in more detail to introduce some of the important behavioral concepts that will appear in later chapters. The model of complex decision making is illustrated by an example, that of a couple purchasing an automobile.

Need Arousal

Need arousal, or recognition of a need, represents a disparity between a consumer's current situation and some desired goal (*e.g.,* need for a more economical means of transportation, desire for more stylish clothing). Such a disparity produces a motivation to act. Need recognition shapes the benefits consumers seek in a brand and

FIGURE 2.2

Need arousal.

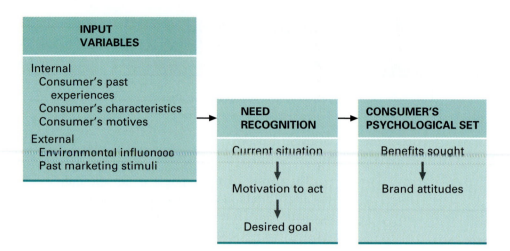

FIGURE 2.2

Need arousal.

brand attitudes. Desired benefits and brand attitudes determine the consumer's **psychological set;** that is, the mindset of the consumer toward various brands prior to seeking and processing information. Need arousal, as outlined in Figure 2.2, is a function of various internal and external input variables.

INPUT VARIABLES

The various input variables that affect need arousal are (1) the consumer's past experiences, (2) consumer characteristics, (3) consumer motives, (4) environmental influences (face-to-face groups, culture, social class, and the buying situation), and (5) marketing stimuli (seeing advertising, noticing the product on the shelf, hearing about the product from salespeople).

Consider the following example. Rob and Linda Greene are a couple in their late 20s with a 3-year-old daughter, and they live in a middle-class suburban neighborhood of a large metropolitan area. They both work and use public transportation to get to their jobs. Their daughter is in a daycare center during the week. They are a one-car family. The Greenes are also users of the Internet and in the past have used the Internet to purchase furniture and home electronics.

■ **Consumers' Past Experiences** Rob inherited his parents' Oldsmobile when he married Linda five years ago. The Greenes use their Olds primarily on weekends and for shopping needs, and it has served them well according to these needs. As a result, their past experiences with the car have been positive. Rob and Linda have also developed a set of expectations regarding a car. They have come to expect good service and a car that performs consistently over time. Any deviations from these expectations might cause them to consider alternative models.

■ **Consumer Characteristics** The benefits consumers seek and their brand attitudes are partially conditioned by their characteristics—their demographics, lifestyles, and personalities. Income may affect the type of car purchased—compact, standard, or luxury. Age, marital status, and number of children may affect the class of car—sports car, sedan, or station wagon. Lifestyle may affect the choice of make. A socially oriented, outer-directed couple may want a car that impresses others and may stress styling and size of car. A family that travels a lot may emphasize the benefits of comfort at the expense of styling. Even personality has an influence. The power-oriented, aggressive individual may want a car with a great deal of acceleration. The compulsive individual may stress regular service benefits and the alleviation of anxieties with better warranty terms.

Rob and Linda are both starting out in careers—Rob as a financial analyst, Linda as a product manager for a food company. Their dual incomes will define the price range they can afford. Rob and Linda like to take long car trips with their daughter on their vacations. They are more interested in the functional aspects of a car than the status communicated by a car. They place more importance on economy, service dependability, performance, and comfort, in that order. Given the importance of the purchase, they see substantial financial and performance risks in buying. As a result, they are highly involved in the purchase decision.

▌ **Consumer Motives** **Motives** are general drives that direct a consumer's behavior toward attaining his or her needs. The greater the disparity between a consumer's current situation and desired goals, the greater the motivational drive to act to satisfy consumer needs.

The motivational drive directly affects the specific benefit criteria consumers use to evaluate brands. If Rob and Linda are motivated by a drive to meet the need for status, two important benefit criteria will be the size and styling of the car. If the need for economy drives the motivation to act, then benefit criteria may be gas mileage, service costs, and sticker price.

▌ **Environmental Influences** Consumers purchase and use many products in a social setting. The purchase of a car is frequently a family decision, and each member of the family influences the decision. Neighbors and business associates may also be important sources of information and influence. Rob and Linda began their search by seeking general information about cars online. Having been referred to the Kelley Blue Book web site *(www.kbb.com)* by a neighbor who had purchased a new car the previous year, the Greenes were pleased to find the link to Autobytel.com, a site that allowed them to select the specific criteria that mattered to them most. They used the site to search for various models based on their emphasis on economy, service, and comfort.

A car is a symbol as well as a means of transport. As a result, social and cultural norms may also influence the purchase of a car and the way it is used. Teenagers are more likely to use a car as a means of socialization, adults as a symbol of socioeconomic status.

▌ **Past Marketing Stimuli** Past information about brand characteristics and prices will also affect consumers' needs. Consumers obtain such information from advertising, in-store stimuli, sales representatives, and the Web.

NEED RECOGNITION

The various input variables in Figure 2.2 determine a consumer's current state of mind. Consumers recognize a need when there is a disparity between their current state and some desired end state. This disparity creates tension and arouses a *motivation to act.*

Rob and Linda were motivated to act because of their current state of affairs. They learned that the Oldsmobile needed a transmission overhaul. This fact, in addition to poor gas mileage, caused them to begin considering alternative makes. One additional factor prompted them to act. Both Rob and Linda believed the Olds had a stodgy image, and they agreed they should consider getting a sportier, more up-to-date-looking car. Rob remembered an ad campaign meant to counteract the Olds' image based on the theme "This is not your father's Oldsmobile." Rob had found that campaign amusing since the Olds used to be his father's car. The ad had done little to counter Rob and Linda's perception of the Olds.

■ A Hierarchy of Needs

Abraham Maslow developed a motivational theory based on a *hierarchy of needs.*[7] According to Maslow, consumers are motivated to act by first satisfying the lowest level of needs before the next higher level of needs becomes activated. Once these needs have been satisfied, the individual then attempts to satisfy the next higher level, and so on. Thus, the unfulfilled needs lead to action. Maslow defined five levels of needs, from lowest to highest:

1. Physiological (food, water, shelter, sex)
2. Safety (protection, security, stability)
3. Social (affection, friendship, acceptance)
4. Ego (prestige, success, self-esteem)
5. Self-actualization (self-fulfillment)

Marketers can appeal to a range of needs within Maslow's five levels. For example, they can appeal to the following:

- Physiological needs through sexual appeals, as in ads for personal grooming products

- Safety needs, as emphasized in messages advertising safer cars or promoting a safer environment

- Social needs, by showing group acceptance as a result of wearing certain types of clothing or using a brand of soap or deodorant

- Ego needs, by linking a product to success in business (credit cards) or in sports activities (athletic shoes)

- Self-actualization needs, by showing self-fulfillment through travel, education, or cultural pursuits

According to Maslow, few people satisfy their social and ego needs and move to the fifth level. In fact, most advertising appeals focus on satisfying social and ego needs, whether it is an appeal for the status of a luxury car or the more mundane appeal for the social protection a deodorant affords.

One researcher equates Maslow's theory to three stages in a family's life cycle.[8] In the first stage, young adults acquire material possessions primarily to gain acceptance and to emulate their peers (Maslow's Level 3). Having established themselves in their middle years, consumers view possessions as a means of demonstrating success and gaining self-esteem (Maslow's Level 4). As adults reach older age, possessions are no longer important. They now seek experiences that provide emotional satisfaction and self-realization (Maslow's Level 5).

▎ Utilitarian versus Hedonic Needs   In addition to Maslow's classification, needs can be classified even more basically as utilitarian or hedonic. Rob and Linda's purchase of a car assumes that they make decisions objectively by collecting information on utilitarian product attributes such as service costs, gas mileage, repairs, and performance. This is not always the case. As we all know, we sometimes make decisions based on emotional factors that are the result of our more innate desires and fantasies.

Utilitarian needs seek to achieve some practical benefit such as a durable car, an economical computer, or warm clothing. Such needs are identified with functional product attributes (durability, economy, warmth) that define product performance. Hence, the utilitarian purchase maintains an informational focus and emphasizes the purchase process itself. **Hedonic needs** seek to achieve pleasure from a product. They are more likely to be associated with emotions or fantasies derived from consuming a product. In being more closely identified with the consumption process, hedonic needs are more experiential. A hedonic need might be the desire to appear more masculine or feminine, to be associated with a winning sports team, or to feel at one with nature.

In satisfying hedonic needs, consumers frequently use emotional, rather than utilitarian, criteria in evaluating alternative brands. (We use the term "emotional" rather than "irrational" and the term "utilitarian" rather than "rational" because emotional criteria such as "feel behind the wheel" could be as rational as utilitarian criteria such as "service costs.") Buying a Gucci scarf for twice as much as the same scarf with a store label cannot be justified based on the functional benefits of a scarf, but it can certainly be justified based on its hedonic benefits.

Marketing strategies used in appealing to utilitarian and hedonic needs are very different. Advertising that appeals to utilitarian needs tends to be more informative to reduce the financial and performance risks typically associated with utilitarian purchases. Print ads offer an ideal medium for utilitarian advertising, because they allow for detailed messages to convey information. The Web may also be a highly effective medium for utilitarian advertising due to its interactive nature and ability to convey concrete, detailed product information. An ad for a bicycle might advertise durability, a comfortable ride, and ease in shifting gears. Advertising that appeals to hedonic needs tends to be more symbolic and emotional to address the social and psychological risks often related to hedonic purchases. Given the emphasis on imagery, television is perhaps the most effective medium for hedonic ads.

The ad for the Jaguar XJR in Exhibit 2.2 is symbolic and emotional in that it appeals to the thrill of speed and power embodied in the Jaguar. Given

370 horsepower leaves people no choice but to talk behind your back.

XJ | www.jaguar.com

JAGUAR
THE ART *of* PERFORMANCE

▎ EXHIBIT 2.2 ▎

This Jaguar ad appeals to hedonic needs.

Jaguar Cars North America, 2001. Ad created by Young & Rubicam Advertising.

the experiential and emotional tone of the ad, functional benefits do not have to be cited.

THE CONSUMER'S PSYCHOLOGICAL SET

The consumer's psychological set is his or her state of mind at the time needs are recognized and motives are aroused. In the context of consumer decision making, the consumer's psychological set is directed to brand, product, or store evaluations. The psychological set is made up of two components: benefits sought and brand attitudes.

❚ **Benefits Sought**   **Benefit criteria** are the factors consumers consider important in deciding on one brand or another. Rob and Linda's most important criteria were economy and service dependability; but other criteria such as road performance, comfort, styling, and safety were also relevant. Marketers identify **benefit segments** by grouping consumers that emphasize the same benefit criteria. In identifying consumer segments that emphasize benefits such as economy, performance, and style, marketers try to develop product characteristics that satisfy these benefits. The car manufacturer that appeals to a performance segment might advertise product characteristics such as quick acceleration and a smooth ride.

Consumers regard product characteristics as goal objects that may or may not satisfy desired benefits. Thus, the goal object consumers use to evaluate economy may include gas mileage and service costs.

The distinction between hedonic and utilitarian needs also applies to benefits and goal objects. Hedonic needs will lead to defining pleasure-oriented benefits and goal objects in satisfying these needs. The relationships between needs, motives, benefits, and goal objects for both utilitarian and hedonic needs are provided in the following chart:

Needs	Motivation	Benefits sought	Goal objects
Utilitarian:			
Adequate transportation	Drive to act to meet needs	Economy	Gas mileage Service costs Sticker price
Hedonic:			
Pleasure in driving	Drive to act to meet needs	Good feeling behind wheel	Purring engine Smell of the car Smooth ride

❚ **Brand Attitudes**   Brand attitudes are consumers' predispositions to evaluate a brand favorably or unfavorably. They are represented by three factors: beliefs about brands, evaluation of brands, and tendency to act.[9] The assumption is that these components operate in sequence as follows:

1. Beliefs are formed about the brand that influence . . .

2. attitudes toward the brand, which then influence . . .

3. an intention to buy (or not to buy).

That is, if brand beliefs result in positive attitudes, there is a greater chance the consumer will buy the brand.

STRATEGIC APPLICATIONS

Mercedes-Benz Appeals to Hedonic and Utilitarian Motives

Mercedes-Benz's introduction of the A-class car series illustrates the importance of complex decision making for marketers. Mercedes introduced the unique A-class cars in Europe in mid-1998 to compete in the small-car segment against makers like Fiat and Volkswagen. The move from its traditionally upscale market into the low-priced, small-car segment met with resistance in the industry from marketing analysts who criticized Mercedes for diluting its brand and likened it to "Rolex putting Bugs Bunny on a watch." Despite the resistance, Juergen Schrempp, chairman of Daimler-Benz, Mercedes-Benz's parent company, supported the launch of the compact A-class car as part of a strategy to become a player in the growing lower-end market.

The A-class car caught the attention of many Europeans with its unusual design and creative advertising. Termed the "little giant" by the company, the cars were designed to be compact in length for easy driving and parking, yet the height and redesigned body made the interior surprisingly roomy (see Exhibit 2.3). The cars can be customized by three model lines, ten exterior and twenty-three interior colors, various engine options, and additional luxury features like a sunroof and remote central locking. With all of its features and functionality, the A-class

Mercedes still sells in the lower-end $14,000 range.

Through its advertising of the A-class, Mercedes-Benz has focused on the functionality and utility as well as the uniqueness and style of the car. In addition to advertising its utilitarian features—lower price and great design, Mercedes-Benz also emphasized the hedonic features of the car—the full quality and luxury experience with a sporty feel. Advertising was targeted to up-and-coming professionals, especially women, with statements like "the Elegance is a car to be seen in" and "Translate vision into reality." Starting in 2003, Mercedes offered the A-class to the American automobile market.

The strong attachment of many buyers to the car shows that car buying goes beyond strictly utilitarian criteria. Mercedes-Benz highlights the emotional nature of the car-buying experience online, where it showcases the stories of seven A-class owners, like Maxine Wright, a senior underwriter in Kent, United Kingdom, who bought her red Avant-Garde from her local dealer. It is her first Mercedes and she says she "love(s) it when other A-class owners wave, and can't wait for the warmer weather so (she) can let the sunshine in." Mercedes is attempting to personalize its relationship with its consumers by offering trips to their customer center in Rastatt, Germany, for buyers picking up a new A-class car. Mercedes will provide a full tour through the plant and information on staying at nearby hotels, and it will even help plan excursions to the nearby Black Forest.

Clearly, Mercedes-Benz is successfully expanding its well-respected brand into the small car segment with the A-class series. Through utilitarian and hedonic messages, it has succeeded in convincing buyers that the A-class is a viable alternative to the numerous other brands in the small car market.

Sources: "Test-Driving the A-Car," *Fortune* (November 10, 1997), p. 150; "A-Class Damage Control at Daimler-Benz," *Business Week* (November 24, 1997), p. 62; Mercedes-Benz United Kingdom home page at www.mercedes-benz.co.uk, as of March 2000; "Quirky Ads Boost Mercedes," *Marketing* (October 8, 1998), p. 23.

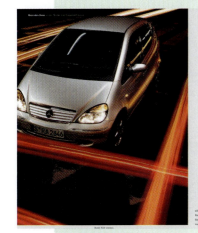

| **EXHIBIT 2.3** |

The Mercedes A-Class series.

Courtesy DaimlerChrysler AG.

This sequence has been referred to as a **hierarchy of effects** model of consumer decision making. It stipulates the sequence of stages consumers go through in purchasing, a sequence involving thinking (beliefs), feelings (evaluations), and actions (the intention to buy the brand).[10]

Returning to the Greenes, Rob and Linda's *beliefs* about an Olds were that it provides performance and comfort, but they questioned its economy because of the increasing costs of maintenance. Because of web searches, advertising, and comments from friends, Linda eventually suggested to Rob that they consider a Toyota Corolla and a Saturn because both are nicely styled, provide comfort, and are not expensive to maintain.

An important link exists between beliefs and desired benefits. When beliefs about a brand conform to the benefits consumers desire, consumers will evaluate the brand favorably. Favorable brand evaluation is more likely to lead to an intention to buy the brand. Given that Rob and Linda's primary benefit criteria were economy and service dependability, they preferred a car (brand evaluation) that had those characteristics (their beliefs) and would probably plan to buy such a car (their tendency to act).

Consumer Information Search and Processing

Consumer information search and processing involves the exposure to and perception of information, and its retention in memory. These processes are represented in Figure 2.3 and are summarized next. They are considered in detail in Chapters 6 and 7.

STIMULUS EXPOSURE

Once a need is recognized, consumers are more likely to search for and process information relevant to that need. Rob and Linda were more likely to notice stimuli related to cars such as advertisements on television and in web banners, comments friends made about their cars, and cars in showrooms and on the street. They

| FIGURE 2.3 |
Consumer information search and processing.

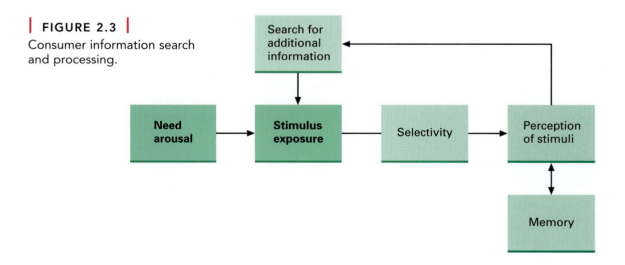

were also more likely to be aware of information that affects the cost of owning and operating a car, such as sticker prices, trade-in allowances, gasoline mileage, and cost for service and parts.

Consumers' exposure to stimuli is often *selective.* People tend to choose friends who support their views, reinforce their egos, and parallel their lifestyles. They often seek commercials that support recent purchases in an attempt to justify them. They also frequently tune out information that conflicts with their needs or beliefs. The recent car buyer may ignore the negative experiences of a friend with the same make or may rationalize poor performance by thinking the car is not yet broken in. Therefore, stimulus exposure is a selective process that is directed by the need to reinforce existing brand attitudes and perceptions and to seek additional information.

PERCEPTION OF STIMULI

Perception is the process by which consumers select, organize, and interpret stimuli to make sense of them. Stimuli are more likely to be perceived when they

▌ conform to consumers' past experiences.

▌ conform to consumers' current beliefs about a brand.

▌ are not too complex.

▌ are believable.

▌ relate to a set of current needs.

▌ do not produce excessive fears and anxieties.

It is clear that consumers' perceptions of stimuli, as well as their exposure to stimuli, are selective. Ads that reinforce consumers' beliefs and experiences are more likely to be noticed and retained. Also, consumers are more likely to dismiss or reinterpret those ads that contradict past experiences and current beliefs about a brand. By perceiving stimuli selectively, consumers attempt to achieve a state of psychological equilibrium; namely, a state that lacks conflict and avoids contradictory information.

MEMORY

Retained information is stored in consumers' **memory,** which is composed of past information and experiences. Once stored in memory, information can be recalled for future use, as shown by the double arrow in Figure 2.3 between memory and perception of stimuli. (Memory processes are described in Chapter 7 as part of a detailed discussion of consumer information processing.)

SEARCH FOR ADDITIONAL INFORMATION

Sometimes consumers may not have enough information to make adequate decisions. In such cases, they search for additional information. Such a search is most likely when consumers

▌ are highly involved with the product.

▌ believe that alternative brands being considered are inadequate.

▌ have insufficient information about the brands under consideration.

- receive information from friends or media sources that conflicts with past experiences and current information.

- are close to deciding on a particular brand and would like to confirm expectations regarding its performance.

Involvement and Information Processing

As noted, greater involvement tends to encourage more information search. This link is confirmed in several studies. In a study of involvement with tennis and tennis equipment, Celsi and Olson found that people who are more involved devote more attention to ads for tennis products and process the product information in the ads more extensively.[11] Similarly, Gensch and Javalgi found that farmers who were more involved with learning about farming methods were likely to use more attributes in evaluating alternative suppliers. Among involved farmers, 47 percent used three or more attributes in evaluating alternative retail stores. Among uninvolved farmers, only 15 percent used three or more attributes.[12]

About two weeks after deciding to purchase a new car, Linda checked out several copies of *Consumer Reports* from the library to determine ratings of various makes from an impartial source. On occasion, Rob and Linda asked friends who owned one of the makes under consideration about their experiences. At that point, Linda decided to spend some time searching on the Web for automobile information. There were three stages in her search. First, she went to general search engines such as google.com, yahoo.com, and hotbot.com for general information. Consumers may seek information on all these sites by entering keywords or phrases, which are used by the search engines to identify the most relevant web sources. Because these search engines frequently overlap in the information provided, consumers tend to select one or two preferred search engines to perform their information gathering.

Second, Linda turned to several sites to help her select the best car makes to satisfy her needs and Rob's. She first went to a site recommended by a friend, *www.womansmotorist.com*. The site provides reviews of various car makes and information on maintenance. She then went to *www.consumerreports.org* to get expert ratings on the various features of the makes she and Rob were considering. Linda went to these sites because at that point, she knew the makes and models she was interested in. For less savvy consumers, there are sites known as "shopping BOTS" that make recommendations regarding the best products to fill a consumer's needs based on specific input as to the nature and priority of those needs.

On the basis of the results from these two Web sites and their prior information search, Rob and Linda narrowed their choice to three cars—Toyota Corolla, Honda Accord, and Saturn—and dropped the Olds from consideration. Having arrived at this decision set, Linda went into the third stage of her web search by going to specific car information and buying sites such as Autobytel. She obtained information on invoice price, model specifications, and ratings for each of the three models.

Figure 2.3 shows that the search for additional information feeds back to stimulus exposure, as additional information may stimulate further search. Linda's search on the Web stimulated further search. This process illustrates the dynamic nature of consumers' decision-making processes. The components of information processing and brand evaluation are not discrete; they occur on an ongoing basis until consumers reach a final decision.

▌The Limits of Information Search   Complex decision making does not always lead to greater information search. Extensive information search occurs only when consumers consider the additional information collected worth the cost of obtaining it. One study found that when consumers were presented with information on sixteen alternative brands, they used only 2 percent of the information available in making a decision.[13] Another study found that one-half of all consumers studied visited only one store or showroom when buying cars and major appliances.[14] A limited search does not necessarily reflect consumers' lack of concern about the purchase. It may mean that many consumers rely on past experience in deciding on a brand or believe they have enough information at the time of purchase.

Similarly, consumers typically develop a short list of preferred web sites for their online information gathering needs. One reason is that consumers still face transaction costs in terms of additional time required to identify useful sites, to conduct the actual search, and to download information, which can be particularly cumbersome without high-speed Internet access lines.

Brand Evaluation

Brand evaluation is illustrated in Figure 2.4. As a result of information processing, consumers use past and current information to associate brands they are aware of with their desired benefits. Consumers prefer the brand they expect will give the most satisfaction based on the benefits they seek.

BENEFIT ASSOCIATION

In benefit association, one must develop a priority of desired benefits and relate a brand's characteristics to these benefits. Rob and Linda's priorities were, by order of importance, economy, safety, service dependability, performance, comfort, and styling. Rob and Linda used these benefit criteria to evaluate the characteristics of the three makes they were considering. They gathered objective ratings with regard

▌ FIGURE 2.4 ▐
Brand evaluation.

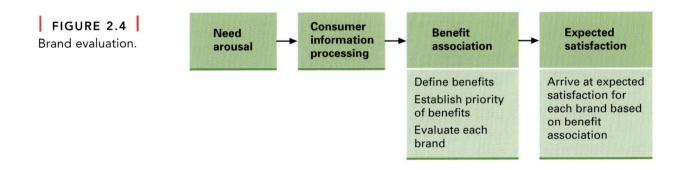

to these criteria from Autobytel, J.D. Power and Associates, and Edmunds.com. Although they gave greater weight to benefits they regarded as most important, they also included other benefits in assessing the relative merits of each car. On this basis, Rob and Linda determined that the Saturn and Corolla do best on economy, the Saturn and Accord scored best on service dependability, and all three makes were rated close to equal on safety and performance. However, the Saturn scored worst on styling. Rob and Linda selected the Saturn, despite the negative rating on styling, because it scored highest on the most important benefits.

Rob and Linda used utilitarian criteria in selecting a car, but as mentioned previously, consumers can also use more *hedonic* criteria, such as the feeling of freedom in driving or the pleasurable feeling of being behind the wheel. Saturn's advertising appealed more to emotional than utilitarian benefits by portraying Saturn owners as free spirits with pride in ownership. The evaluative procedure Rob and Linda used to evaluate alternative cars is known as a *compensatory* method of evaluation because a negative rating on one criterion can be made up by a positive rating on another. Thus, even though the Saturn scored lowest on styling, its high ratings on economy and service dependability resulted in Rob and Linda choosing the car.

In the compensatory method, consumers evaluate each brand across all benefit criteria. The alternative is a *noncompensatory* method of evaluation in which consumers evaluate brands one criterion at a time across all brands. For example, Rob and Linda might first evaluate the three cars by economy and might eliminate the Accord on this basis. They would then evaluate the two remaining cars by the next most important criterion, safety, and find the Saturn and Toyota equal on this criterion. They would then go to service dependability and eliminate the Corolla, leaving the Saturn as the choice. Thus, consumers may use different decision rules in evaluating brands.[15]

Two factors are likely to determine which method of evaluation is used—the nature of consumer needs and the level of involvement. When consumers are driven by functional needs, they are more likely to use a compensatory system. Consumers are likely to use multiple criteria in evaluating a car's economy, dependability, or comfort. In evaluating economy, reasonable service costs and good gas mileage could counterbalance a higher sticker price. When consumers are driven by hedonic needs, a "one strike and you're out" decision rule is more likely. If a car does not give the consumer a pleasurable feeling behind the wheel and a sense of driving enjoyment, it would be immediately out of the running.

Consumers are also more likely to use noncompensatory decision rules for less involving decisions such as those for detergents and toothpaste. In such cases, it may not be worth the time and effort to choose a brand by the more extensive processing requirements of a compensatory method.

EXPECTED SATISFACTION

Both the compensatory and noncompensatory models agree that consumers develop a set of expectations based on the degree to which a brand or product satisfies the benefits consumers desire. The brand that comes closest to satisfying the most important benefits is expected to provide the most satisfaction. For Rob and Linda, the Saturn had the highest expected satisfaction because it did best on their most important benefit criterion, economy.

Purchase and Postpurchase Evaluation

The outcome of brand evaluation is an intention to buy (or not to buy). The final sequence in complex decision making involves purchasing the intended brand, evaluating the brand during consumption, and storing this information for future use (*i.e.,* feedback). These steps are outlined in Figure 2.5.

INTENTION TO BUY

Once consumers evaluate brands, they intend to purchase those achieving the highest level of expected satisfaction. Purchasing in complex decision making is not likely to be immediate. Rob and Linda may still have some shopping to do to obtain the best trade-in value on their present car, and they may have to obtain financing. Therefore, a period of time will ensue before Rob and Linda purchase the Saturn. To purchase the car, they might do several things called *instrumental actions:* select a dealer; determine when to purchase; go to the place of purchase; and, as is often the case with an automobile purchase, arrange for financing. Moreover, they may have to decide on options such as air conditioning or a CD player.

Having chosen a Saturn, Rob and Linda decided to visit several dealerships. They knew the invoice and manufacturer's list price from Autobytel and were therefore armed with information that would give them some advantage in price negotiations. They also decided to place a purchase request for the specific Saturn through Autobytel to compare the Autobytel price to the prices from various dealers. They also investigated alternative financing options.

NO PURCHASE

The consumer decision-making model shows that a decision might be made to delay purchase or not to buy. Rob and Linda might have decided not to buy a new car because they estimated that, in the long run, it would be cheaper to fix the Olds. Or, having evaluated the various brands, they may have decided to wait and see if some additional options may be introduced in next year's models.

| FIGURE 2.5 |

Purchase and postpurchase evaluation.

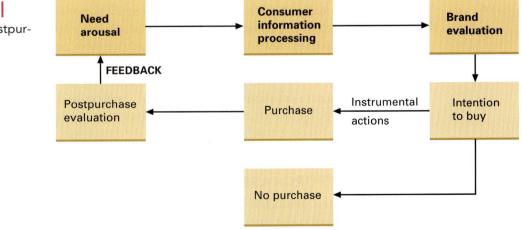

The study by Greenleaf and Lehmann cited earlier found a number of reasons why consumers might delay a decision, namely that they[16]

- are too busy to devote time to the decision.
- do not like shopping for the item.
- are concerned that the purchase may make other people think less well of them (social risk).
- are concerned that they might have made the wrong decision or that the product might not work (ego and performance risk).
- need more information about the item.
- believe that the product's price may soon decrease or that a better item may soon become available.

A study by Luce found that another reason consumers might delay a purchase is the simple desire to avoid a decision.[17] For example, some consumers might find the financial or performance risk in buying a car so great that they might decide the status quo is the best option. Or they might find two models so closely based on their needs that they avoid the decision for fear of making the wrong decision.

The decision-making process may also be terminated or delayed at any stage because of outside constraints. For example, the Saturn may not be available when expected, or the price of the Saturn may increase unexpectedly due to cost overruns in production.

PURCHASE

Figure 2.5 demonstrates that the link between intention to buy and actual purchase requires instrumental action. The time lag between intention and purchase is likely to be greater in complex decision making because of the greater number of actions required for a purchase to take place.

Of the instrumental actions required for a purchase, store selection is most important. In fact, store selection may require a decision-making process of its own. Where to purchase a suit or dress may be more critical than what brand to buy. The act of purchasing may also require Rob and Linda to negotiate to get the best terms regarding price, used-car allowance, and financing. Rob and Linda will select the dealer that gives them the best terms, or they will choose to buy through Autobytel, in which case they know they will be given a low, no-haggle price and related services such as financing, insurance, extended warranty option, assistance with selling their used car, and a host of other tips and pertinent car ownership information.

In this case, Rob and Linda made their decision to buy a certain car prior to visiting dealerships. For many goods, decision and purchase are almost simultaneous because consumers make the brand decision in the store. For example, by a glance at the supermarket shelf, a consumer may be reminded of a need for canned peas. With no strong brand loyalties, the consumer may just select the lowest-priced brand.

POSTPURCHASE EVALUATION

Once the product is purchased, the consumer evaluates its performance in the process of consumption.

▌ Purchasing versus Consuming   It is important to distinguish between purchase and consumption for three reasons. First, the product may be purchased by one person and consumed by another. The consumer, not the purchaser, determines product satisfaction. Second, the purchase depends on consumer expectations of the degree to which brands are likely to satisfy needs. Consumption determines whether these expectations are confirmed. Third, a consumer's postpurchase evaluation determines whether the brand is likely to be repurchased. It is unlikely that any brand can survive over time without some degree of loyalty. The consumer's dissatisfaction will lead to no further purchases, negative word-of-mouth communication about the brand, and lost sales.

A study by Cooke, Meyvis, and Schwartz confirms the importance of the consumption experience.[18] They found that information learned after the purchase has greater impact on determining satisfaction with a brand than information learned before. In other words, what is learned in the process of consumption is more important in determining satisfaction than what is learned during the purchasing process.

▌ Satisfaction versus Dissatisfaction   Satisfaction occurs when consumer expectations are met or exceeded and the purchase decision is reinforced. Such reinforcement is represented in Figure 2.5 as feedback from postpurchase evaluation. Satisfaction reinforces positive attitudes toward the brand, leading to a greater likelihood that the consumer will repurchase the same brand. Dissatisfaction results when consumer expectations are not met. Such *disconfirmation of expectations* is likely to lead to negative brand attitudes and lessens the likelihood that the consumer will buy the same brand again.

POSTPURCHASE DISSONANCE

In many cases, a decision involves two or more close alternatives and could go either way. Having made their decisions, consumers may feel insecure, particularly if substantial financial or social risks are involved. Any negative information about the chosen product causes postpurchase dissonance; that is, conflict resulting from two contradictory beliefs.

Assume in Rob and Linda's decision-making process that the Toyota Corolla was a close second to the Saturn. The likelihood of postpurchase dissonance increases. The financial risks of purchasing the car make dissonance even more likely. There are also the social risks of buying a car that may not conform to the norms of friends and neighbors, and there is the psychological risk that the wrong decision may have been made.

Suppose that shortly after the purchase, Linda meets a friend who also purchased a Saturn and who relates some negative experiences, such as lower-than-expected gas mileage and mechanical failures. At about the same time, Rob learns that Toyota will be introducing a more economical model next year. This information produces postpurchase doubt, as Rob and Linda believe they should have perhaps delayed the purchase. Such doubt is psychologically uncomfortable. The tendency is to reduce doubt by confirming the purchase. Consumers do this by

▌ ignoring the dissonant information.

▌ selectively interpreting the information, saying, for example, that any brand will have an occasional lemon.

■ lowering the level of expectations, saying that even if there are a few problems with the car, it still is an acceptable choice.

■ seeking positive information about the brand.

■ convincing others you made a good choice, and in doing so convincing yourself.

In each case, dissonance is reduced.[19]

Now assume that after six months, Rob finds the Saturn's gas mileage is about 10 percent lower than dealer and advertising claims. Linda determines that service costs are somewhat higher than expected. In other respects (styling, comfort, performance), the car meets expectations. The theory of postpurchase dissonance says that Rob and Linda will focus on the positive performance and tend to dismiss or rationalize the negative performance. If, as is true with Rob and Linda, the disparity between prior expectations and subsequent product performance is not great, an **assimilation effect** occurs. That is, consumers ignore the product's defects and their evaluation of the product remains positive.

If there is a great disparity between prior expectations and performance, however, a **contrast effect** is likely to take place in which consumers recognize and magnify poor performance.[20] Thus, if the Saturn's gas mileage is half of that claimed in the advertising, it is unlikely that Rob and Linda would focus solely on the positive aspects of performance. They would probably be extremely dissatisfied, have negative attitudes toward the selected brand, and be unlikely to consider that brand next time.

To minimize or eliminate postpurchase dissonance, marketers can employ several tactics after the purchase. These tactics include providing additional information about product care, offering warranties, developing ad campaigns to reconfirm customers' decisions ("Aren't you really glad you bought a Buick?"), and following up with direct contact.

Reducing postpurchase dissonance is particularly important for products purchased on the Web because consumers tend to view such purchases as risky, particularly for higher-priced products and those where prior examination of the product is important (*e.g.,* clothing). In these cases, the Web is used to reassure customers on at least four dimensions: security, ease of use, quality of the relationship between the web site and the customer, and postpurchase follow-through (*e.g.,* on-time delivery, undamaged goods, accurate orders, etc.). Follow-through is particularly important in reducing dissonance on the Web. Web-based strategies for addressing adequate follow-through include making returns easier, providing two-way communication for companies to obtain feedback and for customers to voice problems, and facilitating refunds.

The Consumption Experience: Hedonic Consumption and Product Symbolism

So far, we have focused on the consumer's purchasing process. But as discussed, consumption determines the level of satisfaction and repeat purchasing behavior. Therefore, the consumption experience is at the center of future purchase decisions. Two distinctions are important in better understanding the consumption experience: (1) the difference between consuming products versus services and (2) the difference between consumption that satisfies hedonic versus utilitarian needs.

PRODUCT VERSUS SERVICE CONSUMPTION

Products are tangible entities that are produced by manufacturers, purchased, and then consumed. *Services* are intangible offerings that are produced and consumed simultaneously; an airplane flight, a college course, or a financial service is being consumed as the marketer is offering them. The consumption experience involves direct interaction with a service provider—the airline attendant, the college professor, or the financial consultant.

The intervention of a service provider means that the consumption experience is likely to be much more variable for services than products. A student might find a professor challenging and engaging in one lecture and dull in another; a traveler may have a flawless flight on one occasion but have her baggage lost on the next. Such variability makes it more difficult for consumers to assess services than products, and the level of dissatisfaction is likely to be higher because prior expectations are not as likely to be met.

How can marketers try to reduce the potential for dissatisfaction with the consumption experience? They can minimize service variability and establish a longer-term customer relationship. Companies attempt to minimize service variability by trying to instill a customer-oriented focus in service providers and ensuring constancy in service. McDonald's attempts to control the operations of its franchises by insisting on uniform training and facilities; FedEx ensures on-time delivery through a rigid adherence to routine.

Service marketers have also relied on establishing a one-to-one relationship with consumers over time. American Express, for example, has been able to target specific promotional offerings to card users based on their expenditure patterns. To illustrate, a frequenter of Italian restaurants could be offered a reduced-price coupon to several neighborhood Italian restaurants.

UTILITARIAN VERSUS HEDONIC CONSUMPTION

The same distinction between hedonic and utilitarian needs in the purchasing processes applies to the consumption experience. Utilitarian consumption involves using a product for some functional purpose—detergents to wash dishes or clothes, cereals for a nutritious breakfast, a car as transportation to work. The cognitive processes of postpurchase evaluation cited previously work fairly well in assessing satisfaction in these cases. Satisfaction is determined by the degree to which the product meets prior expectations on functional attributes such as softness and whiteness for a detergent, or gas mileage and comfort for a car.

Hedonic consumption involves use of a product to fulfill fantasies and satisfy emotions. Level of satisfaction cannot be determined in the same orderly manner for hedonic consumption as for utilitarian consumption. It is more likely to be based on the pleasurable experiences and emotions that result from using the brand rather than on the brand's utilitarian performance and economic value. As a result, the consumer is likely to arrive at some overall judgment of satisfaction based on the totality of the consumption experience. Satisfaction is assessed on a simple like/dislike (or in a more emotional context, love/hate) dimension.

The same product can be consumed in both a hedonic and utilitarian manner. Rob and Linda purchased the Saturn based on utilitarian criteria. But after buying it, they got caught up in the mystique of the car among owners, tooting at other

---

STRATEGIC APPLICATIONS

OF CONSUMER BEHAVIOR

From Heavy Metal to Cologne: Harley Davidson Changes Its Symbols

Harley-Davidson has long recognized that bikers choose motorcycles for their symbolism as much as their performance. Until the 1980s, Harley's symbols were the heavy metal and black leather associated with big bikes—a throwback to the days of James Dean and Marlon Brando. Harley had a virtual monopoly of the big bike market. However, by the 1980s, the black leather crowd was dwindling; and Harley knew it would have to look to a new customer base.

The new customer base Harley went after—baby boomers—was a complete reversal of form. By the mid-1980s, many baby boomers were heading toward midlife crises and were looking for some escape from everyday cares. The stock market crash of 1987 further fueled the search for fantasy. Harley felt big bikes might provide it.

But the symbolism needed to change, and with it, Harley's image. Harley changed its image to appeal to a more affluent, white-collar market in several ways. Out went the heavy metal look in its advertising; in came a softer approach. One ad featured a baby in a Harley T-shirt with the tag line, "When did it start for you?" Harley also began to use celebrities such as Kurt Russell and Elizabeth Taylor in its advertising. In addition, the company began to sell items such as cologne and wine coolers with the Harley name in its dealerships. Since 1997 Harley customers have even been able to grab a cup of coffee at The Dirty Cup coffee shops in the Harley-Davidson superstores, which also boast a wide selection of Harley clothing, dishes, jewelry, and other products.

Harley's success in attracting baby boomers is reflected in the fact that most of its buyers are 40-something, attended college, and have a median household income of $70,000, and the company boasts of a threefold rise in revenues and earnings. As *Business Week* reported in its May 28, 2001 issue, "Baby boomers are dedicated to the sport. They are perhaps the youngest 50 through 60 year olds that the country has ever seen—in better shape and with more of an appetite for adventure. Once the kids leave for college . . . they are riding motorcycles, not lumbering along in Winnebagos." As a result of catching this trend, by 1998 Harley owned 56 percent of the U.S. market for large motorcycles, and its U.S. sales increased by 20 percent in both 1999 and 2000.

Its sales were also growing worldwide, where the Harley mystique extended to Europe, Japan, Australia, and other countries. More than 50,000 bikes were sold in Japan, and demand is still rising. And of the nearly 400,000 Harley Owners Group members (HOGs), a Harley-Davidson enthusiast group, nearly 30,000 members are in Europe. Success can also be seen in Harley-Davidson's continued growth, with a current market cap of more than $9 billion.

Buying a Harley may still be a good example of symbolic purchasing behavior, but the symbolism has certainly changed.

Sources: "Trouble Ahead on Thunder Road?" *Business Week* (May 28, 2001), p. 94E2; "Cult Followings," *Advertising Age* (March 28, 1994), p. S-12; "The Power of Cult Brands," *Adweek's Marketing Week* (February 24, 1992), pp. 18–21; "After Nearly Stalling, Harley-Davidson Finds New Crowd of Riders," *Wall Street Journal* (August 31, 1990), pp. A1, A6; "Bikers Ride into Middle Age," *American Demographics* (December 1991), p. 15; "Ea$y Rider$ Harley Revs Up Boomer Marketing," *Denver Post* (July 7, 1997), p. B2; "Japan's Bikers: The Tame Ones," *Business Week* (October 6, 1997), p. 30D; www.bigcharts.com for HDI as of November 29, 1999.

Saturn owners and being tooted at in turn; they even took the company up on its offer to host a weekend for Saturn owners in Spring Hill, Tennessee. They used the car for shopping trips, but they also found themselves taking more outings with their daughter partly because of the sheer pleasure of driving the car.

Advertisers attempt to appeal to the hedonic motives of consumers through emotional themes and the utilitarian motives through product information. The ad for WalkerInformation data collection services, shown in Exhibit 2.4, appeals to both. The bottom portion of the ad is clearly informational; the top portion and insert relies on a direct appeal to the buyer's emotions with the tag line "Trust."

In summary, complex decision making should incorporate consumer evaluations of brands as both objective entities and subjective symbols. Because consumers frequently employ products as symbols in a social setting, the role of product symbolism in consumer behavior will become more evident when we cover group influences later in the text.

| **EXHIBIT 2.4** |

This WalkerInformation ad appeals to both hedonic and utilitarian needs.

© 2002 Walker Information. Designed by Scofield Design and Communications.

Complex Decision Making and Store Choice

Until now, we have focused on decision making for brands. However, consumers also make decisions regarding the stores in which they shop. In buying a car, consumers determine the make of car first and then choose the dealer to buy from. But frequently, consumers' choice of store comes first and influences their choice of brand. For example, we generally make a decision regarding the store first and then the brand when we shop for clothes. Similarly, we often make a brand decision in the store when we shop for appliances or electronics. In these cases, store choice conditions brand choice.

A MODEL OF STORE CHOICE

Consumers' decision-making process for a store is similar to that for a brand. The model of store choice in Figure 2.6 is an adaptation of the basic model of complex decision making in Figure 2.1. Consider the business school student who is purchasing a notebook computer. One of the first decisions she has to make is what stores to visit to gather information about alternative brands. The model in Figure 2.6 shows that there are two components to need arousal in store choice: first, a purchasing need (recognition of a need to buy a computer) and second, a shopping need (need to search for alternatives in various stores). Shopping needs can be complex. Some consumers consider the process of shopping time-consuming and not particularly enjoyable. Others like to search for bargains and enjoy interacting with salespeople.

Need arousal establishes certain priorities as to the store or stores that consumers select. Assume our student is time-oriented and does not enjoy shopping. Based on her purchase and shopping needs, she is looking for conveniently located stores with knowledgeable salespeople and competitive prices. Information search involves asking friends which stores are reliable and searching for store ads with information on prices and models.

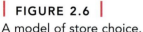

| FIGURE 2.6 |
A model of store choice.

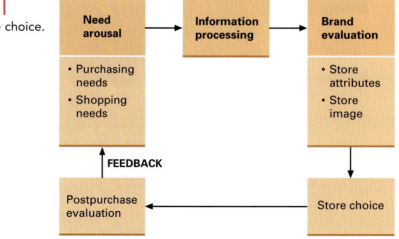

On this basis, our consumer will evaluate stores and choose several to visit. In the process, she will develop an image of each store. The more closely the store fulfills her needs (knowledgeable and helpful salespeople, good service, competitive prices), the more likely it is she will buy the computer from that store. Therefore, store choice depends on the degree to which the consumer's image of the store relates to his or her purchasing and shopping needs.

Say our consumer decides to purchase a Toshiba. Once having made the brand decision, she selects the store based on price, service, and convenience. In postpurchase evaluation, she evaluates both the brand and the store. The two are closely related; satisfaction with the brand leads to satisfaction with the store. However, some components of postpurchase evaluation are specific to the store; for example, a car buyer who is satisfied with the purchase may be dissatisfied with the service the dealer offers.

STORE CHOICE AND BRAND CHOICE

In the preceding example, our consumer selected the brand first and then the store. It is possible that a consumer might make a computer decision in the store (*i.e.,* put store choice before brand choice).

Under what circumstances is store choice most likely to influence brand choice?

- *When store loyalty is high.* Consumers loyal to a particular department store are more likely to shop there first for desired items.

- *When brand loyalty is low.* Consumers with no strong loyalties to a particular brand are more likely to select the store first and make a brand decision within the store.

- *When brand information is inadequate.* Consumers who have little brand experience or information are more likely to rely on sales personnel for assistance. Brand choice is, therefore, more likely to be made in the store.

HEDONIC VERSUS UTILITARIAN SHOPPING BEHAVIOR

The distinction between hedonic and utilitarian consumption applies to shopping behavior. Typically, consumers view shopping as a necessary task to acquire goods. For the utilitarian shopper, shopping is not inherently pleasurable. It is simply a means to an end.

But for many the shopping task is a pleasurable event. The thrill in finding a bargain or the satisfaction in beating out someone else to the last item in stock can be highly rewarding. Shopping expeditions with friends are regarded as a social experience for the hedonic shopper. Shopping also offers an opportunity to communicate with salespeople. Stores and shopping malls are viewed as gathering places for such social interaction. In France, local shops traditionally serve as a center to gather and gossip with neighbors and tradespeople. In these cases, shopping serves a purpose beyond the selection of goods.

SUMMARY

This chapter presented a comprehensive model of complex decision making. Complex decision making occurs when consumers are involved with the product and go through an extensive decision process to arrive at a choice. The chapter used the example of a couple buying a new automobile to illustrate this model.

Complex decision making assumes that adequate information is available for a decision and that the consumer has the time and ability to process information extensively.

A model of complex decision making has several phases:

1. *Need arousal* initiates a decision process. Consumers are prompted to act by a disparity between their current situation and a desired goal. Such a disparity results in tension and a motivation to act. Several factors influence the consumer's current situation and desired goals; namely, the consumer's lifestyles, demographics, and personality characteristics, as well as environmental influences such as group norms and family needs.

2. *Consumer information processing* involves exposure to and perception of information from various sources. Information processing is selective; consumers choose information that is (a) most relevant to the benefits they seek and (b) likely to conform to their beliefs and attitudes. Processing of information involves a series of steps—exposure, attention, comprehension, retention in memory, and search for additional information. The Web plays a key role in information search and subsequent brand evaluation by offering greater efficiency and access to information. The result is to empower consumers in transactions with marketers for products such as cars, electronic goods, and other big-ticket items.

3. In the process of *brand evaluation,* consumers evaluate the characteristics of various brands and determine their expected satisfaction for each brand.

4. Consumers *purchase* the brand most likely to satisfy their desired benefits. In so doing, various instrumental actions are required, such as selecting a store, determining when to purchase, and possibly obtaining financing.

5. Once consumers have made purchases, *postpurchase evaluation* occurs. If performance has met the consumers' expectations, consumers are likely to be satisfied with the product. If not, dissatisfaction will occur, reducing the probability that consumers will repurchase the same brand. In cases in which consumers had difficulty making up their minds, dissonance is likely. Dissonance or postpurchase conflict results from doubts about the decision. As dissonance is not a desirable state, consumers may seek to reduce it by ignoring negative information or by seeking positive information about the brand. From the marketer's perspective, the Internet offers additional tools to reduce and control for postpurchase dissonance.

Central to the decision-making process is the consumption experience. Consumption determines the level of satisfaction with the product or service and influences future decision making. Two distinctions were drawn in understanding consumption: the difference between consuming products and services and the difference between consuming products for utilitarian and hedonic purposes. Since services are intangible and more variable, they are more difficult to evaluate, and consumers are more likely to be dissatisfied. As a result, marketers try to follow strategies to decrease variability and increase the tangibility of services.

Hedonic consumption is driven by emotional and pleasure-seeking criteria. Consumers consume products for what they mean rather than for what they can do. Examples of hedonic consumer products are motorcycles, perfume, and clothing. Marketing strategies attempt to associate products with symbols that generate positive feelings for such products.

Although most of the chapter was devoted to brand decision making, we noted that consumers also make store decisions. At times, the store decision may determine brand choice. A model of store decision making is essentially the same as that for brands, except that consumers are evaluating store attributes and selecting stores according to shopping as well as purchasing needs.

The next chapter shifts the focus from complex decision making to habit.

QUESTIONS FOR DISCUSSION

1. What advantages does Autobytel offer consumers? What are the limitations of the site?

2. Use the model of complex decision making in this chapter to describe the steps in the decision-making process for the following cases:
   - A businessperson considers adopting a new video conferencing system for communication between branches of the firm.
   - A college student considers purchasing a laptop computer.
   - A consumer considers purchasing a headache remedy that is advertised as stronger and more effective.

3. What are the implications for marketing strategy based on your description of the decision-making process for each of the three cases in Question 2, particularly implications for (a) market segmentation, (b) advertising, (c) pricing, (d) distribution, and (e) development of new products?

4. Of what use might the model of complex decision making be to a marketing manager in the following situations?
   - Kellogg's introduces a new line of adult cereals.
   - General Motors introduces its new line of Saturn cars.
   - Procter & Gamble introduces an improved version of Pampers disposable diapers with better absorbency.

5. What differences in the decision-making process might exist for Rob and Linda Greene in the following situations?
   - They have never purchased a car before.
   - They are in a lower-income group.
   - They are buying a car for business purposes.

6. Linda Greene went through three stages of information search on the Web in evaluating car purchases. What was the purpose of each stage of her web search?

7. What are the distinctions between utilitarian and hedonic needs? What are the implications for marketing strategy of targeting consumers who purchase a car to fulfill hedonic versus utilitarian needs?

8. In some cases, consumers buy almost immediately after reaching a decision. In other cases, there might be a gap between intention and purchase. What are the possible reasons for such a delay? What are implications for advertising and selling strategies?

9. What is the distinction between purchasing versus consuming? What causes postpurchase dissonance, and how do consumers typically react?

10. Why is postpurchase dissonance more likely for web purchases? What strategies are available to web marketers to reduce such dissonance?

11. What types of products are consumers most likely to purchase because of their symbolism? Why?

12. Select a product category that consumers are more likely to purchase on a utilitarian basis and a product category that consumers are more likely to purchase on a hedonic basis.
   - What types of attributes are consumers likely to use in evaluating alternative brands for the utilitarian product? for the hedonic product?
   - What are the implications for advertising the utilitarian product? the hedonic product?

13. The Internet is generally associated with utilitarian purchases. Can it be used to purchase hedonic products? Cite an example.

14. A large retailer of sports equipment in an urban area finds sales slipping. As a result, the retailer wishes to conduct a study to determine (a) how consumers decide on a store for sports equipment and (b) the image of the store relative to that of the competition. Specify how the model of store choice in Figure 2.6 might help in determining the required information.

RESEARCH ASSIGNMENTS

1 Select a product that is more utilitarian in nature (*e.g.,* washing machine, refrigerator, vacuum cleaner). Conduct a focus group interview* with six to ten consumers who bought the item in the last year and focus the discussion on how they decided on what brand to buy. Now select a product that is more hedonic in nature (*e.g.,* perfume, designer clothes); conduct a focus group with consumers who bought the item in the last year (or less, depending on the product) and ask them how they decided on the brand.

- What are the differences in the nature of information search, the attributes used for evaluation, and the way the brands were evaluated?

- What are the implications of these differences for advertising strategy?

2 Log onto the Internet site *www.mysimon.com.* Select a product category of your choice. Enter your preferences based on the questions asked in the "product search" section.

- How well do the results fit your selection criteria?

- Did the site ask appropriate questions for the product category selected?

- What other information should be collected from you for improved results?

3 Select an electronics product that is likely to cost several hundred dollars or more (*e.g.,* a videocassette recorder, compact disc player, or personal computer). Conduct focus group interviews with consumers who have purchased the item within the past year or who are currently considering purchasing.

- Describe the decision-making process for both the decision to buy the product and the particular brand to be purchased.

- Does the decision-making process conform to the model in this chapter?

- What are the implications of the decision-making process for (a) market segmentation, (b) product positioning, and (c) advertising strategy?

4 Now select an electronics product that is likely to cost under $100 (*e.g.,* portable headphones, telephone answering machine, calculator). Conduct depth interviews with consumers who have purchased the item within the past year or who are currently considering purchasing.

- How does the decision-making process differ from that described in the first assignment?

- What are the implications of the decision-making process for (a) market segmentation, (b) product positioning, and (c) advertising strategy?

5 Select a product category in which the choice of a store is particularly important (*e.g.,* clothing, furniture, rugs and carpets). Identify consumers who have bought an item in the category within the past six months. Conduct seven or eight depth interviews with the consumers to identify the process of store choice.

- Describe the decision process.

- Does the process of store choice conform to the model described in Figure 2.6?

- What are the strategic implications of the decision process for the retailer?

---

* Many of the research assignments proposed in this text will involve conducting focus group interviews among a group of six to ten consumers. The researcher does not ask specific questions; rather, he or she acts as a moderator or passive listener. The researcher may develop a list of areas to be covered in the discussion and may steer the conversation to these topics. (See Chapter 1 for a further description of focus group interviews.)

NOTES

1. See *Autobytel.Com* (Cambridge, Mass.: Harvard Business School Publishing, 1999), pp. 1–21.
2. "Autobytel to Expand Services," *Automotive News* (February 4, 2002), p. 36.
3. National Automobile Dealers Association, "State of Dealership Internet Operations: The Changing Landscape," 2000.
4. See Sharon E. Beatty and Scott M. Smith, "External Search Effort: An Investigation Across Several Product Categories," *Journal of Consumer Research* 14 (June 1987), pp. 83–95.
5. Eric A. Greenleaf and Donald R. Lehmann, "Reasons for Substantial Delay in Consumer Decision Making," *Journal of Consumer Research* 22 (September 1995), pp. 186–199.
6. See John Dewey, *How We Think* (New York: Heath, 1910), and Orville G. Brim Jr., David C. Glass, David E. Lavin, and Norman Goodman, *Personality and Decision Processes* (Stanford, Calif.: Stanford University Press, 1962).
7. Abraham H. Maslow, *Motivation and Personality* (New York: Harper & Row, 1954).
8. "Marketing to Mature Adults Requires a State of Being," *Marketing News* (December 9, 1991), p. 10.
9. Michael L. Ray, "Attitudes in Consumer Behavior," in Leon G. Schiffman and Leslie L. Kanuk, eds., *Consumer Behavior* (Englewood Cliffs, N.J.: Prentice-Hall, 1978), pp. 150–154.
10. Robert J. Lavidge and Gary A. Steiner, "A Model for Predictive Measurements of Advertising Effectiveness," *Journal of Marketing* 25 (October 1961), pp. 59–62; and Michael L. Ray, "Marketing Communication and the Hierarchy of Effects," in Peter Clarke, ed., *New Models for Mass Communication Research* (Beverly Hills, Calif.: Sage, 1973), pp. 147–175.
11. Richard L. Celsi and Jerry C. Olson, "The Role of Involvement in Attention and Comprehension Processes," *Journal of Consumer Research* 15 (September 1988), pp. 210–224.
12. Dennis H. Gensch and Rajshekhar G. Javalgi, "The Influence of Involvement on Disaggregate Attribute Choice Models," *Journal of Consumer Research* 14 (June 1987), pp. 71–82.
13. Jacob Jacoby, Robert W. Chestnut, K. C. Weigl, and W. Fisher, "Pre-Purchase Information Acquisition," in Beverlee B. Anderson, ed., *Advances in Consumer Research,* Vol. 3 (Atlanta: Association for Consumer Research, 1975), pp. 306–314.
14. Joseph W. Newman and Richard Staelin, "Prepurchase Information Seeking for New Cars and Major Household Appliances," *Journal of Marketing Research* 9 (August 1972), pp. 249–257.
15. For a good review of compensatory and noncompensatory models, see William L. Wilkie and Edgar A. Pessemier, "Issues in Marketing's Use of Multi-Attribute Attitude Models," *Journal of Marketing Research* 10 (November 1973), pp. 435–438.
16. Greenleaf and Lehmann, "Reasons for Substantial Delay," p. 192.
17. Mary Frances Luce, "Choosing to Avoid: Coping with Negatively Emotion-Laden Consumer Decisions," *Journal of Consumer Research* 24 (March 1998), pp. 409–433.
18. Alan J. Cooke, Tom Meyvis, and Alan Shwartz, "Avoiding Future Regret in Purchase-Timing Decisions," *Journal of Consumer Research* 27 (March 2001), pp. 447–459.
19. For a review of the literature on postpurchase dissonance, see William H. Cummings and M. Venkatesan, "Cognitive Dissonance and Consumer Behavior: A Review of the Evidence," in Mary Jane Schlinger, ed., *Advances in Consumer Research,* Vol. 2 (Ann Arbor, Mich.: Association for Consumer Research, 1975), pp. 21–31.
20. For a description of assimilation versus contrast theories, see Rolph E. Anderson, "Consumer Dissatisfaction: The Effect of Disconfirmed Expectancy on Perceived Product Performance," *Journal of Marketing Research* 10 (February 1973), pp. 38–44.

CHAPTER 3

Consumer Learning, Habit, and Brand Loyalty

This chapter describes the opposite of complex decision making—habit. A consumer's prior satisfaction with a brand results in purchasing it on a routinized basis. For such purchases, the consumer finds little need to evaluate brand alternatives. Recognizing a need leads directly to a purchase. Therefore, habit is a way of ensuring satisfaction based on past experience and of simplifying decision making by reducing information search and brand evaluation.

Understanding habit requires understanding the principles of consumer learning, as learning theory can help explain whether consumers will develop consistent behavior over time. Such consistent behavior can be the result of brand loyalty or inertia. **Brand loyalty** is repeat buying because of commitment to a brand, whereas **inertia** is repeat buying without commitment. For unimportant purchases, if a brand is reasonably satisfactory, a consumer may buy again because it is not worth the time and trouble to go through a decision process.

The Rebirth of Brand Loyalty:
Coke Is It, and So Is McDonald's, Tide, and Intel

The strategic importance of brand loyalty is demonstrated by one of the leading brands in the world—Coke. Coca-Cola executives estimate that the name of their flagship brand is worth close to $100 billion, independent of all the manufacturing, bottling, and distribution facilities.[1] This figure represents the value of the brand in the consumer's mind—known as **brand equity.** How did Coke achieve this equity? First, it accomplished brand equity by being available on a widespread basis from the turn of the century, giving satisfied consumers a constant opportunity to buy again. Second, Coke used symbols such as the hourglass-shaped bottle and the red-and-white can that resulted in consumers *learning* to associate these symbols with past brand satisfaction. Third, Coke used constant advertising *reinforcing* these positive associations. And fourth, it established learning, reinforcement, and brand loyalty on a global basis so that today Coke is considered a worldwide icon.[2]

The hue and cry that arose when Coca-Cola announced a change in the formula of its flagship brand in 1985 attests to the depth of commitment for a brand, even when it is typically purchased on a routine basis. Taste tests showed that a majority of consumers preferred New Coke to the regular brand. But loyal consumers were committed to more than the physical ingredients of the brand. They had an emotional association with the brand based on past experiences that transcended the physical product. Once Coca-Cola realized the depth of feeling of many of its consumers for the brand, it brought back the original formula. Had the company insisted on the introduction of New Coke, satisfaction, for many, would have turned to dissatisfaction, and reinforcement to extinction; that is, the elimination of the positive association between past experience and the brand.

Brand loyalty is not a constant in marketing. In the 1980s and early 1990s many marketers thought

brand loyalty was in permanent decline (see the Marlboro experience in the Strategic Applications box on page 65). Lower-priced private brands were making substantial inroads into the sales of national brands because many national brands were overpriced, and because consumers were more price sensitive as a result of steep recessions in the early 1980s and again in the early 1990s.

But national brands began experiencing something of a renaissance because marketers recognized the consumer's desire for quality at reasonable prices. Many national brands lowered their prices to become more competitive with private brands and to better satisfy the consumer's need for value. Led by Procter & Gamble and Wal-Mart in the early

| **EXHIBIT 3.1** |
Establishing brand equity for a high-technology product.
Courtesy Intel Corporation.

1990s, many packaged goods marketers and mass merchandisers began instituting a policy of everyday low prices (EDLP) for national brands to assure consumers that lower prices were permanent rather than just a temporary promotion. Leading brands in diverse categories such as McDonald's, Tide, and Levi lowered prices, maintained quality, and saw their market shares rise. As a result, growth of private brands plateaued in the mid-1990s and began to decrease. In 1996, private brands represented 19.6 percent of supermarket sales. By 2000, they were 15.4 percent.[3]

Even high-technology brands began developing substantial brand equity. Although consumers do not directly buy an Intel computer chip, Intel is still able to command loyalty through product quality and advertising awareness. Witness the positive association in consumers' minds between the brand and its advertising tag line, "Intel Inside" (see Exhibit 3.1).

By the mid-1990s, it appeared that brand loyalty was back overall, as a result of price and advertising appeals to a value-driven consumer.

In this chapter, we elaborate on many of the terms used in the preceding section: "learning," "habit," "reinforcement," "extinction," and ultimately, "brand loyalty." We first describe learning as a process that can sometimes lead to repetitive behavior. Then, we describe habit and consider two possible outcomes of habitual purchase behavior: brand loyalty and inertia.

Consumer Learning

Consumers learn from past experience, and their future behavior is conditioned by such learning. In fact, **learning** can be defined as a change in behavior occurring as a result of past experience. As consumers gain experience in purchasing and consuming products, they learn not only what brands they like and do not like, but also the features they like most in particular brands. They then adjust their future behavior based on past experience. After wearing the brand repeatedly, a consumer might determine that a pair of Reebok running shoes is the most comfortable and provides the best support. Continued satisfaction with the brand leads this consumer to buy Reeboks every time he needs new athletic shoes. Thus, continued satisfaction reinforces past experience and increases the probability that the consumer will buy the same brand the next time.

There are two schools of thought in understanding the process of consumer learning: the behaviorist and the cognitive. The **behaviorist school** is concerned with observing changes in an individual's responses as a result of exposure to stimuli. Behaviorist psychologists have developed two types of learning theories: classical conditioning and instrumental conditioning. **Classical conditioning** views behavior as the result of a close association (contiguity) between a primary stimulus (social success) and a secondary stimulus (a brand of toothpaste, deodorant, or soap). **Instrumental conditioning** views behavior as a function of the consumer's assessment of the degree to which purchase behavior leads to satisfac-

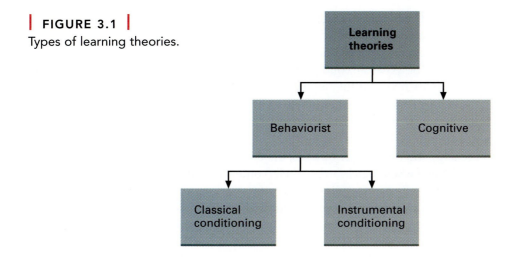

tion. Satisfaction leads to reinforcement and to an increase in the probability of repurchasing.

The **cognitive school** views learning as problem solving and focuses on changes in the consumer's psychological set (the consumer's attitudes and desired benefits) as a result of learning. In this respect, the cognitive school more closely describes learning within a framework of complex decision making. However, the concepts are relevant to habit, because complex decision making may lead to routinized purchases when the consumer is satisfied with the brand and repurchases it over a period of time.

Figure 3.1 illustrates the cognitive and the behaviorist schools of learning and, within the behaviorist school, classical and instrumental conditioning. These three theories of learning—classical conditioning, instrumental conditioning, and cognitive learning—will be considered next.[4]

CLASSICAL CONDITIONING

In *classical conditioning,* a secondary stimulus is paired with a primary stimulus that already elicits a particular response. As a result of this pairing, an association is formed. Eventually, the secondary stimulus will elicit the same reaction as the primary stimulus. An effective advertising campaign may link a product to a stimulus that evokes a positive feeling. A good example is one of the most successful and longest-running advertising campaigns in history, the Marlboro Cowboy campaign. Although some might rightfully object to cigarette advertising, there is no denying that the campaign is highly effective. The basis for the Marlboro Cowboy campaign was the fact that many people viewed a cowboy as conveying strength, masculinity, and quiet security. The cowboy is the **primary** or **unconditioned stimulus.** The positive feeling that the cowboy evokes (strength, masculinity) is the **unconditioned response.**

Consumers associate Marlboro cigarettes with the cowboy through (1) repetitive advertising and (2) contiguity between the unconditioned and conditioned stimulus (cowboy always linked to Marlboro). The product then becomes a **secondary** or **conditioned stimulus** because it evokes the same positive feeling as does the cowboy. The Marlboro campaign was successful because of this positive link. As a result, the cowboy influenced smokers to buy Marlboro and reminded Marlboro smokers to repurchase. The brand purchase is the **conditioned response.**

Theories of classical conditioning[5] are reflected in Pavlov's famous experiments.[6] Pavlov reasoned that because his dogs salivated (unconditioned response) at the sight of food (unconditioned stimulus), a neutral stimulus such as a bell could also cause the dogs to salivate if it was closely associated with the unconditioned stimulus (food). To test his theory, Pavlov rang a bell when presenting food to the dogs. After a number of trials, the dogs learned the connection between bell and food; and when they heard the bell (conditioned stimulus) even in the absence of food, they salivated (conditioned response).

These associations are represented at the top of Figure 3.2. The association between the conditioned stimulus and unconditioned stimulus is represented as

| **FIGURE 3.2** |

Summary of three learning theories.

Source: Adapted from Kenneth E. Runyon and David W. Stewart, *Consumer Behavior and the Practice of Marketing,* 3/e, Macmillan College Publishing Company, Inc., 1987.

CLASSICAL CONDITIONING

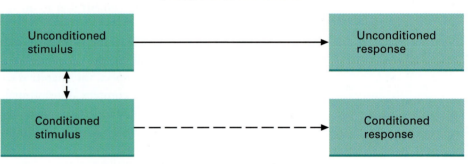

Emphasis: Association through repetition and contiguity

INSTRUMENTAL CONDITIONING

Emphasis: Reinforcement; dependence of outcome on learner's actions

COGNITIVE LEARNING THEORY

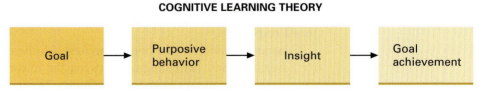

Emphasis: Problem solving; understanding relationships

a dotted arrow because it is a learned association. The association between conditioned stimulus and conditioned response is also learned. The two key concepts are repetition and contiguity. To establish a conditioned response, the conditioned stimulus must be frequently repeated in close contiguity to the unconditioned stimulus.

Classical conditioning can be applied to marketing in an effort to associate a product with a positive stimulus. For example, Miller Lite Beer is frequently advertised during exciting sports events. Because of the repetitive pairing of the product with sports events, the excitement the sports event produces may eventually carry over to Miller Lite. This association may influence people to buy the brand. Similarly, companies frequently use celebrities who have some legitimate link with the product as spokespersons to establish positive associations—for example, Marion Jones for the National Fluid Milk Processor Promotion Board (see Exhibit 3.2).

▌ Associative Learning: Beyond Pavlov's Dogs   When consumers establish a link between an unconditioned and a conditioned stimulus, they are

▌ EXHIBIT 3.2 ▌

Using celebrity spokespersons to establish a positive link with the product.

© America's Dairy Farmers and Milk Processors.

engaging in learning through association. If we take Pavlov's experiments as our frame of reference, such *associative learning* is based on contiguity between the unconditioned and the conditioned stimulus requiring no thought. But consumers rarely act on such a mindless basis. They go through a thought process in linking a cowboy to Marlboro, or a doughboy to Pillsbury. This link is stronger if consumers recognize that it is associated with their needs. Therefore, contiguity must be coupled with relevance or need recognition if consumers are to establish a strong connection between an unconditioned and conditioned stimulus.

A study by Janiszewski and Warlop found that consumers considered the link between an unconditioned and a conditioned stimulus informative and that such a link often leads to the search for additional information.[7] Sports enthusiasts might value Miller Lite more highly compared with other beers because of its association with sports events in advertising, and they might pay more attention to ads for Miller Lite as a result. Such associative learning is not mindless; it is consciously developed.

As a result, it is not enough for marketers to rely on repetitive advertising showing the association between the unconditioned and the conditioned stimulus. They must do so in some meaningful way that relates to consumer needs, whether it is the need for masculinity associated with the cowboy, or the need for a vicarious identification with a winning team associated with Miller Lite.

WEB APPLICATIONS

Has the Internet Lessened Brand Loyalty?

By 1996, many marketing analysts believed that there might be another turn of the brand loyalty wheel with a reduction in loyalty as Internet usage proliferated. The Web gave consumers an unparalleled opportunity to search out the lowest-priced brands and purchase products on the Web at steep discounts. As we saw in the last chapter, car buyers could now enter dealerships knowing the dealer's invoice price. Similarly, airline travelers, computer buyers, and purchasers of an array of electronic products could seek out the lowest prices on the Web. Price seemed to matter more and brand names less.

But as Web usage expanded, it became increasingly apparent that the Web was not a threat to national brands and could actually reinforce brand loyalty in certain instances. By 2000, it was clear that consumers tended to use the Web more for informational purposes rather than to seek low-price bargains (airline tickets being one important exception). When consumers found the lowest prices for computers, cars, or electronics, they compared price to value in terms of brand reputation as they always did. The Web did not change the nature of brand loyalty; it merely gave consumers a wider range of information on which to make decisions.

Further, web sites often promote brand equity by reinforcing the image of the brand established by advertising and by providing more information about the brand. Key brands such as Nike, Levi Strauss, and McDonald's, and even packaged goods such as Tide and Pampers, link their sites to the established brand image while providing useful information.

In short, brand loyalty is as strong today as it was prior to the advent of the Web.

▌ Strategic Applications of Classical Conditioning Advertisers accepted classical conditioning concepts of repetition and contiguity on a more widespread basis before 1950 than they did after that time. Before 1950, advertisers used jingles and themes frequently in radio commercials. But then the advent of television lent a new dimension to advertising by providing more variability through the video component. In addition, a more consumer-oriented approach to advertising resulted in greater variation as advertisements were directed to particular consumer segments. A mass advertising approach based on a single repeated theme was not as viable a strategy. As a result, advertisers now only rarely attempt to establish associations solely through repetition.

The shift in advertising emphasis away from classical conditioning also implied a shift toward principles of cognitive learning. Measures of recall are still used in evaluating ads to determine whether basic brand associations have been established. However, measures of attitude change (changes in brand beliefs, preferences, and intention as a result of advertising) are also used as criteria for advertising effectiveness. This change means that criteria of effectiveness have shifted from measures of association (such as recall) to measures of change in the consumer's psychological set (*e.g.,* brand perceptions and attitude change).

Today, advertisers still recognize the importance of principles of classical conditioning and attempt to associate products with positive symbols and images. One successful advertising symbol, which has been around since 1925, is the Jolly Green Giant. Another application is the recent swing back to using past advertising themes and symbols that were so successfully bonded to the product that consumers still associate the brand with the theme. Examples of past campaigns that have been brought back are Timex (It takes a lickin' and keeps on tickin'), Memorex tapes (Is It Live or Is It Memorex?), Campbell's Soup (M'm, M'm, Good!), and Wonder Bread (Helps build strong bodies twelve ways).[8]

INSTRUMENTAL CONDITIONING

Instrumental conditioning also requires the development of a link between a stimulus and response. However, the individual determines the response that provides the greatest satisfaction. That is, no previous stimulus-response connection is required; response is within the conscious control of the individual. In classical conditioning, the unconditioned stimulus is already linked to a response, and response is more reflexive. Instrumental conditioning can best be illustrated by a hypothetical experiment. Suppose Pavlov had provided his dogs with two levers instead of one. When pushed, one lever would produce food; the other, a shock. The dogs would have quickly learned to press the lever that produced food and to avoid the lever that produced a shock. Learning occurs because the same act is repeatedly rewarded or reinforced.

The foremost proponent of instrumental conditioning was B. F. Skinner. In Skinner's experiments, the subject was free to act in a variety of ways.[9] The consequences of the act (degree of satisfaction or dissatisfaction) influence future behavior. These associations are summarized in the middle of Figure 3.2. Behavior results in an evaluation of degree of reward or punishment obtained from past behavior. Reward will increase the probability of repeating the behavior; punishment will decrease that probability.

Antismoking commercials rely on principles of instrumental conditioning by linking smoking to a shortened life span. This link, which is meant to create avoidance, would be analogous to the lever producing an electric shock. In contrast, Philip Morris was relying on principles of classical conditioning by trying to condition smokers' responses based on the positive association of the cowboy with the product.

▌ Reinforcement Instrumental conditioning comes closer than classical conditioning to describing the formation of habit in consumer purchasing. The consumer has control over his or her purchasing behavior. Continuous **reinforcement** (repeated satisfaction) resulting from product usage increases the probability that the consumer will repurchase. Initially, the consumer undergoes a decision process; but with continuous reinforcement, the probability of buying the same brand increases until the consumer establishes a habit and buying is routinized.

A study by Bennett and Mandel illustrates the role of reinforcement in producing habit.[10] They asked a sample of recent car purchasers to recall the cars they had purchased in the past and to determine the amount of information seeking in their most recent purchase. Although Bennett and Mandel found that information seeking did not decrease with the number of car purchases made in the past, it did decrease if the consumer purchased the same car repeatedly. In other words, past experience alone will not reduce information seeking. Rather, it is reduced only by past experience that leads to satisfaction and repeat purchase of the same brand. Therefore, a necessary condition for the formation of habit is reinforcement of past purchase behavior.

The purchase of a car or other high-priced item by habit may seem questionable. We might assume that consumers would want to maximize value and reduce risk through extensive information search and brand evaluation. But in a study of French car buyers, Lapersonne, Laurent, and Le Goff found that 17 percent of consumers engaged in little or no search behavior and considered only their current make for purchase. The researchers concluded that these buyers were so satisfied with their current model and dealer that the value of collecting additional information and considering other brands was small.[11]

Stimuli other than the product can also be positive reinforcers. In the Lapersonne et al. study, French consumers strongly identified the dealer as well as the car as a basis for satisfaction. French consumers tend to have stronger personal relationships with local retailers. But as we saw in Chapter 2, Saturn owners experienced the same positive reinforcement from dealers. Other reinforcers may be a special sale on the consumer's regular brand; a new, improved version of it; or positive word-of-mouth communication about the brand from friends and relatives.

▌ Extinction and Forgetting Theories of instrumental conditioning also help us understand the events that may lead a consumer to cease buying by habit. If a consumer is no longer satisfied with the product, a process of **extinction**—that is, the elimination of the link between stimulus and expected reward—takes place. Extinction leads to a rapid decrease in the probability that the consumer will repurchase the same brand. Successful antismoking commercials create extinction by eliminating the link between a cigarette and the pleasure of smoking (see Exhibit 3.3).

The Marlboro Cowboy: Still Riding Tall in the Saddle?

It was Friday, April 2, 1993, and Philip Morris had just announced a 20 percent price cut for its flagship brand, Marlboro. The reaction on Wall Street was immediate, an almost fifteen-point drop in Philip Morris's stock price, representing a loss of $13 billion in market value. In the coming week, other producers of packaged goods—PepsiCo, Coca-Cola, P&G, Gillette—would experience a similar drop in their stock prices.

What happened? Investors were reacting to changes in consumer buying habits that were building for a decade. The 1991–1992 recession hit the bastion of brand loyalty—the middle class—hardest. In moving from the free-spending 1980s into the 1990s, this group became more price- and value-conscious. Higher-priced national brands, such as Marlboro, were out. Lower-priced private brands (*i.e.,* brands sponsored by retailers or wholesalers) and lower-priced manufacturers' brands, such as Doral, Viceroy, and Bucks, were in because they were often of equal quality to the national brands. Marlboro was particularly hard hit by the shift. The brand's market share went from 26.2 percent in 1989 to 22.1 percent in 1993, representing a loss of close to $2 billion a year in sales.

Once Philip Morris decided to satisfy the consumer's greater price sensitivity, the Marlboro Cowboy began to be downplayed. The company began relying more on coupons, price promotions, and special offers to sell Marlboro than on advertising. As one analyst said, "Today a campaign [such as the Marlboro Cowboy] won't have much impact on puffers who want to snag a bargain" (*Wall Street Journal* [June 23, 1992], p. B1).

The result of the price reductions was to recapture many of the customers Marlboro lost to private and lower-priced brands. By the first quarter of 1995, Marlboro's share had increased to 30.6 percent, well above what it was in 1989. And the brand's share continued to increase so that by 2001 it was up to a whopping 38 percent.

Why did customers switch back to Marlboro? Consumers recognized the value of national brands once their prices decreased. They viewed the price of Marlboro relative to its value as in line with the prices of private and discount brands. Once price was in line with value perceptions, brand equity was reestablished and strengthened.

But what happened to the Marlboro Cowboy? He is still the dominant component in Marlboro's advertising strategy with one major change—today Philip Morris's price promotions are more central in keeping consumer loyalty than was true in the past.

The Marlboro story shows that brand loyalty is not a constant. If consumers view price as being out of line with value, brand loyalty will suffer, regardless of the strength of images like the Marlboro Cowboy. But once Philip Morris got price back into line with value perceptions, the Marlboro Cowboy was back in the saddle.

Sources: "Whoa Horse," *New York Times* (March 21, 1995), p. D5; "Up in Smoke," *Adweek* (June 21, 1993), pp. 24–32; "Brands on the Run," *Business Week* (April 19, 1993), pp. 26–28; "Marlboro's 2-Fisted Pitch," *New York Times* (April 6, 1993), pp. D1, D22; and "More Shoppers Bypass Big-Name Brands and Steer Carts to Private-Label Products," *Wall Street Journal* (October 20, 1992), pp. B1, B5; "Billboards into the Ashcan; Outdoor Ads for Cigarettes Coming Down as Part of Pact," *Los Angeles Times* (April 22, 1999), p. 1; www.philipmorris.com web site as of November 30, 1999; "'Marlboro Man' Suit Against Tobacco Goes to Court of Appeals," *Wall Street Journal* (August 30, 1999); www.whitehouse.gov web site as of November 30, 1999 in publications archives "Statement on Filing Suit Against Tobacco Companies" September 22, 1999; "The Century's Masters," *Marketing* (November 25, 1999), p. 22; "The Marlboro Man Lives!" *U.S. News & World Report* (September 21, 1998), p. 58; "Marlboro Man Winning War for Hearts and Lungs of Turks," *Houston Chronicle* (September 20, 1998), p. 3; "US Tobacco Firms Push Eagerly into Asian Market," *Marketing News,* (January 21, 1991), p. 2.

Tobacco kills over 400,000 Americans a year. That's more than AIDS, murder, suicide, alcohol, illicit drugs and traffic accidents combined.

| EXHIBIT 3.3 |

An attempt to extinguish the link between cigarettes and pleasure.

Courtesy American Legacy Foundation.

Forgetting differs from extinction. **Forgetting** occurs when the stimulus is no longer repeated or perceived. If a product is not used or if its advertising is discontinued, consumers may forget that product. At the turn of the century, Sapolio soap was on a par with Ivory as a leading brand. When the company decided that Sapolio was so well known that a reduction in advertising was warranted, both the company and the product began their demise. In this case, extinction did not occur since the brand still satisfied consumers. Rather, the company's action resulted in forgetting and a long-term decline in sales. Another cause of forgetting is competitive advertising, which causes interference with receipt of the message. The consumer may become confused by advertising clutter, and the link between stimulus and reward weakens.

Marketers can combat forgetting by repetition. By simply maintaining the level of advertising expenditures relative to competition, a company can generally avoid any serious forgetting on the consumer's part. However, repetition, in itself, is of limited use because showing the same ad again and again may merely irritate the consumer. It is more important to avoid extinction, because lack of sufficient reward can mean the quick end of any brand. The most important vehicle for avoiding extinction is delivering sufficient benefits to a defined target segment.

Figure 3.3 presents learning curves that reflect the processes of reinforcement, extinction, and forgetting as related to advertising exposure. Reinforcement occurs if repetitive exposures to an ad campaign increase the probability of repurchase. Extinction quickly decreases that probability because of a negative stimulus, even if

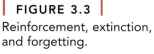

FIGURE 3.3

Reinforcement, extinction, and forgetting.

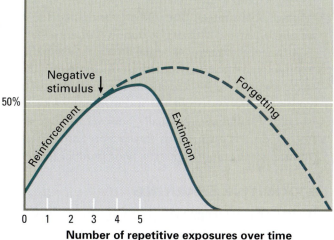

the consumer continues to see the ad campaign for the product. Forgetting results in a longer-term decline in the probability of repurchase due to a decrease in advertising frequency.

An unforeseen potential for extinction occurred in 1999 when schoolchildren in Belgium became ill after drinking from what were believed to be contaminated Coke bottles. The company was slow to respond to the crisis during the time Coke products were being recalled in Belgium and France. Instead of remembering that customer perceptions are what count, Coke attempted to dispute the claims and generally ignored the issue. As a result of Coke's initial reaction, consumers' perception of Coke became even worse, and the company eventually had to issue a public apology concerning its slow reaction to the situation. The Coke brand was strong enough to survive, but because of the company's slow reaction, it took longer for Europeans to again be completely comfortable with Coke products.[12]

The importance of the effects of forgetting is illustrated by an antitrust action against Kraft Foods, owners of Post cereals, for its acquisition of Nabisco Shredded Wheat in 1994. The government argued that the acquisition would extinguish the link between Nabisco and shredded wheat, thus destroying the brand's equity and lessening competition in the cereal market. Kraft (which was allowed to use the Nabisco and Post names on shredded wheat until 1997 when it became Post only) successfully argued that consumers would be on the forgetting rather than the extinction portion of the learning curve (see Figure 3.3). Kraft won its case because it convinced the court that it would be many years before consumers stopped associating shredded wheat with Nabisco. To this day, most consumers tend to associate the term "shredded wheat" with Nabisco rather than Post.

■ Applications of Instrumental Conditioning to Marketing   Instrumental conditioning is important in marketing because the theory focuses on reinforcement. Quite simply, consumers repurchase when they are satisfied. Therefore, the objective of all marketing strategy should be to reinforce the consumer's purchase through product satisfaction. This thesis is the very basis of the marketing concept: Develop marketing strategies that deliver known consumer benefits. Only in this manner can a brand achieve repeat purchases and a core of loyal users.

Principles of instrumental conditioning can be applied to advertising and sales promotional strategy. The role of advertising is to increase consumers' expectation of reinforcement. This can be done by communicating product benefits to convince consumers that they will be satisfied if they buy the product. The role of sales promotion is to create an initial inducement to try the product by offering free samples, coupons, or price deals. If the product is satisfactory, many consumers will continue to buy, even if the incentives are withdrawn. Coupons and price deals should be withdrawn gradually, however.[13] These strategies can be successful only if the product is a source of satisfaction and reinforcement. Advertising and price inducements cannot support a poor product for very long.

COGNITIVE LEARNING

Cognitive psychology views learning as a problem-solving process rather than the development of connections between stimulus and response. Cognitive learning for consumers is a process of perceiving stimuli, associating stimuli to needs, evaluating alternative brands, and assessing whether products meet expectations. Learning is equated to a process of complex decision making because of the emphasis on problem solving.

▌ **Cognitive Learning Theory**   Markin compares the cognitive orientation to learning with the behaviorist orientation:

> The behaviorist is inclined to ask, "What has the subject learned to do?" The cognitivist, on the other hand, would be inclined to ask, "How has the subject learned to perceive the situation?" The cognitivist is interested in examining a learning situation in terms of such factors as motivation, the perceived goals, the overall nature of the situation, and the beliefs, values, and personality of the subject—in short, the entire range of the subject's psychological field. The cognitivist, as opposed to the behaviorist, contends that consumers do not respond simply to stimuli but instead act on beliefs, express attitudes, and strive toward goals.[14]

This statement reflects the fact that **cognitive learning theory** emphasizes the thought process involved in consumer learning, whereas classical and instrumental conditioning emphasize results based on the stimulus associations.

Cognitive learning theory is an outgrowth of Kohler's experiments on apes conducted in the early 1920s.[15] In one experiment, Kohler placed a chimpanzee in a cage with several boxes, and bananas were hung from the roof. After trying to reach the food and failing, the chimp solved the problem by placing a box under the bananas and then stepping onto it to reach the fruit. Learning was not a result of contiguity between stimulus and response or reinforcement; it was the result of insight. The cognitive approach to learning is presented at the bottom of Figure 3.2 as recognition of a goal, purposive behavior to achieve the goal, insight as to a solution, and goal achievement. Reinforcement is a recognized part of cognitive learning, as there must be an awareness of goal achievement for learning to take place. However, the nature of the goal is understood from the beginning, and the reward (such as eating the bananas) is anticipated. In instrumental conditioning, the reward is not apparent until after behavior takes place.

▌ **Vicarious Learning**   A type of cognitive learning that has important marketing applications is **vicarious,** or **observational, learning.** Through vicarious

WEB APPLICATIONS

Cognitive Learning on the Internet

Cognitive learning is particularly important in understanding the nature of Internet usage. Adoption of the Internet has grown exponentially, and with it the nature of the learning process on the Web. Internet usage was estimated at more than 150 million Internet users in late 2000, up from 100 million users in 1999. According to Jupiter Communications, a market research firm, that number is expected to grow to 194 million in the United States by the end of 2005. Internet use is also rapidly expanding outside the United States. By late 2000, more than 60 percent of the online population resided outside the United States.

Learning on the Internet takes place in two ways. Browsing—discovering web sites at random—is one mode of learning. But such learning is largely *incidental,* and discovery is often serendipitous. Another mode of learning on the Internet is *purposeful learning;* that is, going directly to web sites of interest.

Recent evidence suggests that the mode of Internet learning is rapidly shifting from browsing to purposeful learning. One analyst suggests that the Web is no longer driven by a browser's "eclectic imagination" in terms of the desire to find interesting sites as a means of stimulation and entertainment. Rather, today the Web has become more routine. Web users typically use a half-dozen sites to get news, financial information, travel tips, and other information they need on a regular basis. Many users develop "personalized portals" to display information they are interested in when they log on.

Further demonstrating the shift from browsing to purposeful learning is the number of sites visited in a typical month. In 2000, 60 percent of

Internet users visited more than twenty web sites a month according to Jupiter Media Metrix, a research firm that measures traffic on the Web. As of August 2001, only about 30 percent of users visited more than twenty sites a month. Further, the number of people using search engines as a starting point also dropped because most users know what sites they want to visit.

Another indication of the purposeful nature of learning on the Web, according to Jupiter Media Metrix, is that most users said they were spending more time online, but on fewer sites, and the reason most often cited for spending more time online was for school or work. This again suggests that Web users are utilizing the medium more for information gathering than as a purchasing facility.

The early days of the Web as a novelty that warranted learning through browsing seem to be waning. Although there is still a learning curve associated with Internet use, learning is becoming increasingly directed to Web usage in a purposeful and directed manner.

Sources: "Exploration of World Wide Web Tilts from Eclectic to Mundane," *New York Times* (August 26, 2001), pp. 1, 22; "Follow-Up Survey Reports Growth in Internet Users," *New York Times* (August 14, 1996), p. D2; "Internet Population Rises 36 percent in North America: Study," *Computer Dealer News* (September 14, 1998), p. 20; "Internet Commerce Will Rocket to More Than $1 Trillion by 2003, According to IDC," press release from IDC web site (www.idc.com) as of June 28, 1999; "Non-U.S. Internet Commerce to Account for Almost Half of Worldwide Spending by 2003, IDC Reports," press release from IDC web site (www.idc.com) as of August 25, 1999; "The Net: Europeans Aren't Buying," *Business Week* (September 6, 1999), p. 8; "Internet Users Now Exceed 100 Million," *New York Times* (November 12, 1999), p. 8; Nua Internet Surveys, www.nua.ie/surveys/how_many_online/index.html.

learning, people imitate the behavior of others as a result of observing them. To be effective, the consumer should have the ability to perform the behavior, and it should appear useful to the consumer. Starter jackets are officially licensed by the National Football and Hockey Leagues. Starter advertises its jackets by showing sports stars wearing them. A sports enthusiast can emulate the behavior of a Mike Piazza, for example, by wearing a New York Mets jacket made by Starter.

Marketers frequently show the positive results of using their products—attractive models using cosmetics or perfumes that result in social success or wearing clothes that result in business success. Sometimes typical consumers are portrayed providing testimonials for the product, as in Saturn car ads. In each case, the consumer learns by associating the actions of others with some positive consequence and emulating those actions.

In these examples, the consumer sees the positive consequences of imitating the behavior of others. The other side of the coin is seeing the negative consequences of another's actions and avoiding them. The social embarrassment of not using a deodorant or a denture adhesive stimulates negative vicarious learning.

▌ Marketing Applications of Cognitive Learning
Cognitive learning is relevant in understanding the process of consumer decision making. The model of complex decision making in Chapter 2 described a process of cognitive learning. Consumers recognize a need, evaluate alternatives to meet that need (purposive behavior in Figure 3.2), select the product they believe will most likely satisfy them (insight), and then evaluate the degree to which the product meets the need (goal achievement).

A study of the purchasing patterns of recent residents of a community reflects a process of cognitive learning. Andreasen and Durkson studied the purchasing patterns of three groups of households, selected according to the time they had been living in the Philadelphia area: less than three months, one and a half to two years, and three years or more.[16] The researchers believed there would be little difference among the three groups for national brands. However, for local brands, they predicted that the longer a family lived in the area, the closer brand awareness and purchasing would be to those of established residents. Results confirmed their hypothesis. The families living in the area one and a half to two years were closer to the purchase patterns of the established residents than were families living in the area three months or less.[17]

Andreasen and Durkson identified three learning tasks in a new market environment: (1) brand identification, (2) brand evaluation, and (3) establishment of regular behavioral patterns with respect to the evaluated brands. This perspective clearly reflects a cognitive orientation to learning.

RELEVANCE OF THE COGNITIVE VERSUS BEHAVIORIST PERSPECTIVE

It is apparent that the cognitive and behaviorist approaches to learning are very different. Therefore, it is reasonable to ask in what marketing situations one is more likely to be relevant than another.

As the behaviorist approach places little emphasis on thought processes and consumer attitudes, it might be most relevant when the consumer's cognitive activity is minimal. As we will see in Chapter 4, this is most likely to occur when the consumer is not involved with the product. Taking an instrumental conditioning perspective, consumers in a passive, uninvolved state may be more receptive to buying what they purchased before as long as it is reasonably satisfactory. Perhaps if they spent more time searching for information on soap, toothpaste, or paper towels, they might find a better brand. However, for many products, it is simply not worth the effort. Positive reinforcement produces a satisfactory but by no means optimal choice.

Principles of classical conditioning can also be applied to low-involvement purchasing behavior. According to Allen and Madden, when the consumer is in a passive state, it is easier to establish a link between a product and a positive stimulus.[18] For example, a brand of toothpaste might be linked to a nice smile or a brand of disposable diapers to a contented baby, with little thought on the part of the consumer. If the link is repeated frequently enough, the consumer may see the brand in the store and buy it based on these positive associations.

Cognitive learning theory is more relevant for important and involving products. In these cases, a consumer's problem solving takes place through a process of information search and brand evaluation. Goal achievement through purposive behavior is more descriptive of decisions for buying cars, clothing, or furniture than those for toothpaste, paper towels, or detergents.

Habit

Habit can be defined as repetitive behavior; that is, a routinized response resulting in a limitation or absence of (1) information seeking and (2) evaluation of alternative choices. Learning leads to habitual purchasing behavior if the consumer is satisfied with the brand over time. After repetitive purchases, the consumer will buy the brand again with little information seeking or brand evaluation. Such an absence of cognitive activity can also be described as *routinized decision making* to distinguish it from the more extensive information processing in complex decision making.

In this section, we consider the nature of habit, or routinized decision making. We then consider brand loyalty as a likely result of habitual purchasing behavior.

A MODEL OF HABITUAL PURCHASING BEHAVIOR

A model showing the process of habitual purchasing behavior is presented in Figure 3.4. The consumer has settled on a regular brand, for example, Coca-Cola Classic

| FIGURE 3.4 |
A model of habitual purchasing behavior.

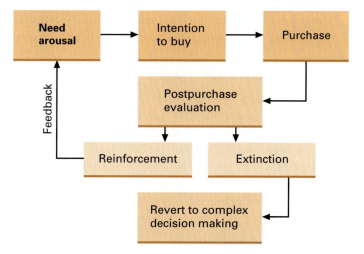

(hereafter, Coke), based on past experience and has become a loyal purchaser. Need arousal may occur simply because the consumer is out of stock or may be due to a simple stimulus such as thirst.

Information processing is limited or nonexistent. That is, recognition of a need is likely to lead directly to an intention to buy. Being out of the brand may be sufficient reason to add Coke to the shopping list, or perhaps the loyal consumer will be reminded by seeing Coke on the store shelf. The consumer evaluates the brand after purchase and expects to receive the same satisfaction from the brand as experienced previously. This is very likely, because prepackaged products generally ensure standardization. Continued satisfaction results in a high probability that the consumer will repurchase the brand.

However, the possibility exists that the product will not meet the consumer's expectations, resulting in extinction of the link between brand usage and positive rewards. For example, the consumer may find a box of cereal is half-empty when purchased or may not like the taste of a reformulation of a brand of toothpaste. As a result, the consumer considers alternative brands, initiating a process of decision making.

Other factors besides dissatisfaction may cause extinction and a change from habit to complex decision making. For instance, a new product comes on the market; the consumer becomes aware of it and considers purchasing. Information search and brand evaluation result. In another case, additional information may cause a change in needs and may result in decision making. Information on the negative effects of smoking might cause a smoker to reassess the favored brand of cigarettes.

Also, boredom with a brand may prompt the consumer to look for something new. Howard and Sheth state that at times consumers get tired of buying by habit: "The buyer, after attaining routinization of his decision process [habit], may find himself in too simple a situation. He is likely to feel monotony or boredom associated with such repetitive decision making. . . . He feels a need to complicate his buying situation by considering new brands."[19] The result, once again, is a move away from habit to more complex decision making.

Finally, extinction may result because of constraints on purchasing the same brand. For example, if the store was out of the preferred brand, the consumer then considers other brands and finds a preferred alternative. There may also be a change in price. If the price of a less-preferred brand is reduced or that of the regular brand increased, the consumer may consider other alternatives.

FUNCTIONS OF HABIT

Purchasing by habit provides two important benefits to the consumer. First, it reduces risk; second, it facilitates decision making. When consumers are highly involved with the product, habit is a means of reducing purchase risk. Buying the same brand again and again reduces the risk of product failure and financial loss for important purchases. Frequently, when information is limited, consumers buy the most popular brand as the safest choice. Several studies cite such brand loyalty as a means of reducing risk. Roselius questioned consumers on ways of reducing purchase risk and found that brand loyalty and buying a well-known brand were mentioned most frequently.[20]

Habit also simplifies decision making by minimizing the need for information search, resulting in routinized decision making. When consumers are not involved with a product, they try to minimize search because it is not worth the time and energy involved. A typical shopping list may easily include twenty items or more, many of which are relatively unimportant. Consider the amount of time the consumer would spend in prepurchase deliberation or in-store selection if each item required an examination of brand alternatives.

A study by Kass examined the role of habit in new mothers' purchases of baby products.[21] As mothers became more experienced and knowledgeable, the number of information sources they used in evaluating alternative baby products and the amount of information they sought decreased. Clearly, habit formation was taking place. The findings also showed that as purchases become more routinized, not only is information seeking reduced, but the type of information also changes. For example, purchasing by habit resulted in the following:

1. A shift in the type of information sought from general product information to specific brand information

2. More reliance on information on price or availability, with less reliance on product-specific information such as freshness and vitamin content

Consumers were learning to be more efficient purchasers by selecting a favorite brand. However, they were also watching for price specials on competitive brands and for the appearance of new brands.

HABIT VERSUS COMPLEX DECISION MAKING

Complex decision making and habit (routinized decision making) are two extremes of a continuum. In between is what might be called *limited decision making*. The left-hand graph of Figure 3.5 presents complex decision making, limited decision

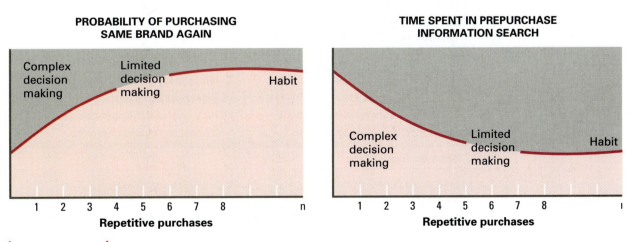

| FIGURE 3.5 |

As the probability of purchasing the same brand increases, the amount of information search and prepurchase deliberation decreases.

making, and habit on a continuum based on the probability of repurchase. Consumers purchase more frequently those products bought by habit. With each successive purchase of the same brand, the chances of buying again increase until there is a high probability consumers will continue to repurchase. As the probability of repurchasing increases, the time consumers spend on information search and prepurchase deliberation decreases, as shown in the right-hand graph of Figure 3.5.

The curve in the left-hand graph of Figure 3.5 is a learning curve because it shows that over time consumers learn which brand satisfies them. The result is an increase in the probability that consumers will continue to purchase the brand.

Table 3.1 further distinguishes between complex decision making and habit. Consumers are more likely to use complex decision making for more expensive products and products they are more likely to be involved with on an emotional level. Low-cost products purchased frequently with little commitment are more likely to be subject to routinized behavior. Consumers are more likely to use compensatory decision rules in purchasing by complex decision making; that is, evaluating brands by many product attributes simultaneously, so as to reduce risk. Simpler, noncompensatory decision rules involving one criterion at a time are more likely to be used for routinized purchases because it is not worth the time and effort to engage in more extensive brand evaluations.

STRATEGIC IMPLICATIONS OF HABIT VERSUS COMPLEX DECISION MAKING

It is important for marketing managers to identify the position of a brand on the continuum from habit to complex decision making. The strategic implications of this position apply to every facet of marketing strategy and are summarized on the bottom of Table 3.1.

TABLE 3.1
Characteristics of complex decision making versus habit

Habit (routinized decision making)	Complex decision making
Little or no information processing	Extensive information processing
Frequently purchased products	Infrequently purchased products
Lower-priced products	Higher-priced products
Low level of consumer involvement	High level of consumer involvement
Noncompensatory decision rules	Compensatory decision rules
Strategic implications	
Extensive distribution	Selective distribution
Few service requirements	Service often required
Personal selling unimportant	Personal selling important
Sales promotions important	Sales promotions unimportant
Advertising used for reminder effect	Advertising used to provide information
Greater price sensitivity	Less price sensitivity

■ **Distribution** Because brands consumers purchase by habit are likely to be high-turnover, low-margin items, they should be distributed extensively. Widespread distribution is important for those consumers who purchase by habit because seeing the item reminds them to buy. The classic example is Hershey's sole reliance, until the early 1970s, on intensive distribution rather than on advertising to promote its chocolate bar. Manufacturers are more likely to distribute products purchased by complex decision making selectively or exclusively.

■ **Product** Products consumers purchase by complex decision making, primarily appliances and durables, tend to be technically more complex. Personal selling is more important for these products, and service is more likely to be required. Products consumers purchase by habit are generally packaged goods involving few service requirements and little direct selling.

■ **Advertising and In-Store Promotions** The nature of advertising and promotions differs according to the product's position on the decision-making continuum. Products consumers purchase by habit are more likely to use advertising as a reminder. Repetitive advertising is more important. A Czech ad for Coke uses the symbol of a yo-yo to repeatedly remind consumers that they should return the bottle, and in so doing, reminds them to buy. In-store promotions are also more effective for low-involvement products because consumers often make the purchase decision once they are in the store.

In contrast, products consumers purchase by complex decision making are more likely to use advertising selectively to convey information to specific audiences. The ad for the Chevy Tahoe Z71 in Exhibit 3.4 is a good example in explicitly listing the advantages of the car.

| EXHIBIT 3.4 |
Advertising used to inform customers.
Courtesy Chevrolet Motor Division.

■ **Pricing** Pricing policies are also likely to differ. When consumers purchase brands by habit, frequently the only way a competitor can get a brand-loyal consumer to try an alternative brand is to introduce a price deal or special sale. Another method of inducing trial among brand loyalists is to provide free samples in the hope the loyal consumer will consider buying the alternative brand. Price deals or free samples are less effective in influencing consumers purchasing by complex decision making because the risks of buying just to save money may be too great. In addition, the marketer's costs for free samples or price deals for specialty items may be prohibitive.

INDUCING A SWITCH FROM HABIT TO DECISION MAKING

Generally, consumers are more likely to purchase the market leader in a product category by habit. This is because many consumers buy the leading brand to avoid risk and the need to search for information. Buying the market leader is a safe way to routinize purchase behavior.

Marketers who want their brands to challenge the leading brand must induce consumers to switch from habit to decision making. Various marketing strategies can induce consumers who buy by habit to consider other brands:[22]

- Create awareness of an alternative to the leading brand. Net2phone, a secondary company to the market leaders, compares its rates with Sprint, MCI, and AT&T.

- Advertise a new feature in an existing brand. Plaque-fighting properties in toothpaste or hexachlorophene in soap may induce consumers to switch brands.

- Try to change consumer priorities by introducing a feature consumers had not previously considered. Toothpaste in pump dispensers was a feature that appealed to many consumers, for instance.

- Encourage consumers to use the product as a substitute for another category. Trying to convince consumers to drink Pepsi instead of coffee in the morning or to eat Special K cereals instead of cookies in the afternoon are examples.

- Use free product samples, coupons, or price specials to get consumers to switch from their favored brand.

- Introduce a line extension of an existing brand that offers a new benefit. Colgate in gel form provides better taste.

Conversely, marketers of the market leader try to retain habitual purchasers by repetitive advertising that reinforces satisfaction and attempts to simplify the choice process. Coke's former advertising slogan "Coke Is It" implied that once consumers choose Coke, they are satisfied and further information search is not necessary. One reason the introduction of a new Coke formula was a mistake is that it prompted many habitual Coke users to reassess their choice (*i.e.,* to switch from habit to decision making).

Brand Loyalty

A close link exists among learning, habit, and brand loyalty. **Brand loyalty** represents a favorable attitude toward a brand resulting in consistent purchase of the brand over time. It is the result of consumers learning that one brand can satisfy their needs.

Two approaches to the study of brand loyalty have dominated the marketing literature. The first, an instrumental conditioning approach, views consistent purchasing of one brand over time as an indication of brand loyalty. Consumers' repeat purchasing behavior is assumed to reflect reinforcement and a strong stimulus-to-response link. The second approach to the study of brand loyalty is based on cognitive theories. Some researchers believe that behavior alone does not reflect brand loyalty. Loyalty implies a commitment to a brand that may not be reflected by just measuring continuous behavior. A family may buy a particular brand because it is the lowest-priced brand on the market. A slight increase in price may cause the family to shift to another brand. In this case, continuous purchasing does not reflect reinforcement or loyalty. The stimulus (product) and reward links are not strong. An attitudinal measure combined with a behavioral measure is required to identify true loyalty.

The differences between a behavioral and a cognitive orientation in defining brand loyalty and habit are best illustrated by the statements of two researchers. Tucker takes a strong behavioral position: "No consideration should be given to what the subject thinks or what goes on in his central nervous system; his behavior is the full statement of what brand loyalty is."[23] Jacoby takes a clear cognitive position: "To exhibit brand loyalty implies repeat purchasing behavior based on cognitive, affective, evaluative and predispositional factors—the classical primary components of an attitude."[24] He also states: "Brand loyalty is a function of psychological (decision-making, evaluative) processes."[25] In this discussion, behavioral (instrumental conditioning) and attitudinal (cognitive) approaches to understanding brand loyalty will be considered.

BEHAVIORAL APPROACH TO BRAND LOYALTY

Recent developments in data collection have given more impetus to the behavioral as opposed to the cognitive school in measuring brand loyalty. The availability of electronically recorded purchases through in-store scanners has made it possible to provide managers with quick information on what people do. As a result, marketers are relying more on behavioral data generated through scanners and less on attitudinal and perceptual data generated through surveys.

The problem with relying primarily on behavioral data in developing and assessing marketing strategies is, in the words of one marketing expert, that "what people do does not say anything about why they do it. There is no surrogate available for talking to the consumer."[26]

COGNITIVE APPROACH TO BRAND LOYALTY

The limitations of a strictly behavioral approach in measuring brand loyalty are overcome when loyalty includes both attitudes and behavior. Day states that to be truly loyal, the consumer must hold a favorable attitude toward the brand in addition to purchasing it repeatedly.[27] Day recognizes that consumers might continue to buy the same brand because other brands are not readily available, a brand offers a long series of price deals, or consumers want to minimize decision making. Day defines these conditions as "spurious loyalty" because they do not reflect commitment.

Evidence suggests that utilizing both the attitudinal and behavioral components provides a more powerful definition of brand loyalty. In his study, Day found that when he attempted to predict brand loyalty, the predictive power of the model using both attitude and behavior measures was almost twice as good as the model using behavior alone. Furthermore, when the behavior measure alone was used, over 70 percent of the sample was defined as brand loyal. Adding the attitudinal component reduced the proportion of brand-loyal consumers to under 50 percent. In other words, defining loyalty based only on repeat purchasing overstates the degree of loyalty.[28]

THE BRAND-LOYAL CONSUMER

Several researchers have attempted to define the characteristics of a brand-loyal consumer. Their studies have uniformly shown that there is no general, brand-loyal consumer; that is, a consumer who tends to be loyal regardless of product category.[29] Brand loyalty is product-specific. Consumers will be loyal to brands in one category and will have little loyalty to brands in other categories.

Despite the product-specific nature of brand loyalty, some generalizations can be made about those who tend to be brand loyal:

1. The brand-loyal consumer tends to be more self-confident in his or her choice. Both Day[30] and Carman[31] found this relationship to be true in separate studies of consumer packaged goods.

2. Brand-loyal consumers are more likely to perceive a higher level of risk in the purchase and to use repeat purchasing of a single brand as a means of reducing risk.[32]

3. The brand-loyal consumer is more likely to be store loyal. Carman states that the consumer who restricts the number of stores visited thereby restricts the opportunity to be disloyal to the brands the store sells. Therefore, "store loyalty is a regulator of brand loyalty."[33]

4. Minority group consumers tend to be more brand loyal. Some studies have found that African-American and Hispanic-American consumers tend to be more brand loyal.[34] Loyalty may be the result of concern about financial risk in purchases and a desire to "play it safe."

BRAND LOYALTY AND PRODUCT INVOLVEMENT

The cognitive definition of brand loyalty means that loyalty represents commitment and, therefore, involvement with the purchase. (See Exhibit 3.5 for the ultimate example of commitment resulting in brand loyalty.) A study by J. Walter

| **EXHIBIT 3.5** |
A humorous example of commitment and brand loyalty.

Reprinted with permission of Bill Whitehead.

"Brand loyalty isn't just an empty phrase to Arthur!"

Thompson, a large advertising agency, found that brand loyalty is highest when consumers are personally involved with the brand and find the purchase risky.[35] In these cases, the brand is a source of self-identification (cosmetics, automobiles, cigarettes).

Inertia—that is, repeat purchasing of a brand without commitment—represents habitual purchasing with a low level of involvement. In this case, the consumer has no strong opinions or feelings about the brand. The consumer bases purchasing on what is most familiar. Repeat purchase of a brand does not represent commitment; it merely represents acceptance.

Consumer Loyalty, Consumer Equity, and Micromarketing

Traditionally, marketers have viewed brand loyalty in aggregate terms. For example, Coca-Cola might say that based on repetitive purchases and positive attitudes toward the brand, 60 percent of purchasers can be defined as brand loyal. An oft-quoted figure in the cigarette industry, citing it as one of the most brand-loyal categories, is that between 90 and 95 percent of smokers are committed to a usual brand.[36]

This perspective reflects the "one-to-many" marketing focus cited in Chapter 1; namely, one brand being marketed to many consumers representing a particular target for the brand. But as Chapter 1 also noted, the increasing fragmentation of the marketplace coupled with new technology has enabled marketers to increasingly focus on individual consumers, what was referred to as a "one-to-one" approach, or *micromarketing*. The capability to micromarket to individual consumers has led to a shift in the concept of brand loyalty. Increasingly, marketers are talking about *consumer loyalty;* that is, implementing strategies designed to maintain the loyalty of individual customers to the brand and the company over time.

Micromarketing requires developing consumer loyalty through strategies both before and after the purchase. Prior to the purchase, marketers can offer consumers the opportunity to customize information on the Web to suit their needs and, for some product categories, the opportunity to customize the design of the product. After the purchase, marketers seek to maintain the relationship with the customer through a variety of strategies that maintain their interest in the product and the company. As we saw in the previous chapter, these postpurchase strategies have come to be known as **relationship marketing.** The success of relationship marketing programs means that consumer loyalty is translated into **consumer equity**— that is, a long-term commitment to the brand and the company based on interactive relationships.

The primary objective of micromarketing is to establish consumer equity at the individual level by delivering the best product to meet the consumer's needs and by establishing a unique relationship with the consumer after the purchase. The development of the Internet and other interactive devices makes it more efficient and cheaper to communicate with consumers after the purchase. For example, the cost of sending a customized email is much less expensive than a broadly based direct-mail campaign. Communications between buyer and seller can lead to an ongoing relationship that makes it easier to target each individual consumer.[37]

As a result of these changes, marketers are beginning to shift their focus from marketing brands on a national scale in the mass media to developing more customized strategies to target individual consumers. If one were to extend micromarketing to its logical conclusion, the goal of a company like Procter & Gamble would be to find a variety of products for each consumer instead of trying to find a variety of consumers for one product. This does not necessarily mean selling P&G products on the Web, but rather viewing the constellation of products needed by individual consumers and developing customized messages and information for these products. Some marketing analysts even feel that companies like Procter & Gamble or Kellogg will someday have the capacity to customize their products to individual consumers much like Dell Computers does today—for example, putting raisins in Cheerios based on individual customer tastes.[38]

To build consumer equity, marketers need information on individual consumers—what web sites consumers visit most often, what their preferences are, what products they purchase most frequently, and what brands they prefer. Such information should be made available in the context of *permission marketing;* that is, with the consumer's knowledge and concurrence. The benefit of such targeted marketing is not only increased customer equity but also increased referrals through word-of-mouth communications. Such referrals further expand the marketer's database for micromarketing.

Micromarketing is still in its early stages. As technology becomes more advanced and large corporations embrace mass customization both in an informational and product context, there will be an increasing shift in strategic focus from brand equity to consumer equity.

Store Loyalty

Consumers are loyal to stores just as they are to brands. At times, store loyalty may be stronger than brand loyalty. A young lawyer may religiously shop at one particular department store because it conforms to his self-image as being upwardly mobile and achievement oriented. Given this link between his self-image and his image of the store, our shopper's loyalties to this department store are likely to be stronger than his loyalty to any of the items of merchandise it carries.

As with brand loyalty, store loyalty may also reflect inertia. Our young lawyer may shop at a particular department store not because of any strong commitment to the store, but because his time is limited and it is simply easier to shop in one place for clothing and accessories.

STORE-LOYAL CONSUMERS

In the previous section, we noted that brand-loyal consumers also tend to be store loyal. It is possible that consumers who wish to reduce the time and effort in brand selection also seek to minimize time and effort in store selection. Another possibility is that shopping in the same store fosters loyalty for brands carried by that store, particularly private (retailer-controlled) brands.

Reynolds, Darden, and Martin related lifestyle characteristics to store loyalty.[39] They identified store loyalty by the willingness of a sample of women to shop in the same stores and to avoid the risk of shopping in new stores. They found that the store-loyal woman tends to be older and more downscale (lower income, less educated) than one who is not loyal.

Goldman supported these findings in his study.[40] He found that store-loyal consumers engaged in less prepurchase search, knew about fewer stores, and were less likely to shop even in other stores known to them. Goldman concluded that store-loyal behavior appears to be "part of a low search, low knowledge and low utilization level shopping style" and that this shopping style is more likely to exist among low-income consumers because they are constrained by their inability to shop much.[41] The clear implication is that store loyalty is an inefficient mode of shopping and is more likely to exist among low-income consumers because of limited information and less discretionary income.

The two studies just cited also found that store-loyal consumers see more risk in shopping.[42] The lower income and educational level of the store-loyal consumer may heighten the sense of risk in shopping behavior. The careful and conservative nature of these customers suggests that store loyalty may be a means of reducing the risk of shopping in unknown stores. One obvious strategy in reducing risk in store choice is to shop in one or a select number of stores.

LEVEL OF STORE LOYALTY

Consumers' greater price sensitivity as a result of the two recessions in the 1980s and 1990s has led to an erosion of store loyalty. A study by Yankelovich, Skelly, and White, a marketing research firm, found that almost 50 percent of all shoppers said they switched from their favorite supermarket to one with lower prices during the 1980–1982 recession.[43] The 1991–1992 recession promoted comparison shopping and further discouraged store loyalty. The recession of 2001–2002 has further increased price sensitivity and the role of price promotions in the marketing mix. This has been reflected by a significant shift in promotional dollars from advertising to price promotions.

But there is a countervailing trend to greater price sensitivity. The increase in the number of dual-earning households has increased the premium on convenience and reduced the time for comparison-shopping. The greater number of single-parent households has also limited the amount of time available for shopping. For these consumers, the additional cost of being store or brand loyal is worth the time saved.

As a result, store loyalty is likely to be pulled by two opposing trends. Consumers' greater value orientation is likely to cause them to comparison-shop, eroding store loyalty. But demographic trends such as the increased numbers of working women and single-parent households are likely to put a premium on time, encouraging store loyalty.

WEB SITE LOYALTY

With the emergence of the Internet, a new dimension of loyal consumer behavior is browser and web site loyalty. The greater incidence of purposeful learning on the

Web, as cited in the Web Applications box on page 62, means that consumers are visiting fewer sites more often. One study found that 90 percent of consumers visited only one site for books, and 80 percent only one site for CDs.[44] As a result, loyalty to specific web sites is increasing.

Purposeful learning on the Web means that the sites consumers are most likely to visit are for specific informational purposes. Sites visited most frequently relate to health, weather, general news, and travel destination information. The sites most frequently visited for purchases on the Web are to buy books, records, flowers, gifts, and airline tickets.[45]

Several factors encourage web site loyalty:

▪ Consumers who are loyal to an offline retailer are more likely to be *loyal to its online representative.* For example, consumers who shop at The Gap or Barnes & Noble regularly may be more loyal to their respective web sites, as long as the companies have done a good job in transferring their brand image and equity to the site.

▪ Consumers tend to face limits in the *time utility* of their information search. Over time, they learn how to best navigate certain sites and are likely to "settle into" these sites rather than spend the time to learn the protocols for other sites.

▪ There may be substantial *switching costs* in using another site if the consumer had made an investment of time and contributed information to a certain site. For example, if a consumer has designed a personalized news or financial page on AOL.com, switching to another portal would require repersonalizing the page. Or if a consumer has provided demographic and behavioral information to Amazon to allow it to make recommendations regarding books or music, she may be reluctant to go to another site. She feels secure with Amazon and does not want to unnecessarily divulge personal information.

The implications of web site loyalty are hard to gauge since it is still relatively early to define habitual behavior emerging on the Web. Web site loyalty has the potential to reinforce brand loyalty if marketers are successful in establishing relationships with customers who visit their sites regularly. On the other hand, loyalty to sites that compare prices and brands could also have the potential for expanding the range of options consumers are considering, thus diminishing the potential for brand loyalty.

Societal Implications of Brand and Store Loyalty

The preceding description of brand and store loyalty suggests that it may not be the most efficient mode of decision making for consumers. On the positive side, brand and store loyalty save consumers time and effort in evaluating alternatives. However, such loyalty may lead consumers to repurchase the same brand even if it is higher priced or of inferior quality.

IMPLICATIONS FOR BRAND LOYALTY

Name brands often trade on their national reputation and frequent advertising to charge higher prices. Many consumers are swayed by the name appeal alone and establish strong brand loyalties based on image. Blind taste tests have shown that many consumers cannot tell the difference between Pepsi and Coke or Miller and Budweiser. However, when the name is revealed, the consumers exhibit strong preferences. Clearly, loyalty is a function of brand name and image rather than any functional brand attributes. Similarly, bleach is a fairly standardized product; however, Clorox can charge more than other brands because it is a known commodity.

Consumers have a right to develop brand loyalties based on image alone. However, the fact that brand and store loyalties tend to be stronger for minority consumers and older, downscale consumers is disturbing. These consumers are often the ones who can least afford the higher prices of national brands.

In this respect, the recent move to everyday low prices for national brands may be beneficial from a societal standpoint. Increasingly, consumers are showing more willingness to shop around for value. Shopping for value could mean trying a lower-priced brand of toothpaste or a private brand of disposable diapers. As a result, we are witnessing the development of more efficient and economical consumers.

Unfortunately, this move to more effective modes of brand choice is more characteristic of middle-income consumers, not lower-income consumers. Because lower-income consumers are less likely to be aware of brand and price alternatives, a key question is whether there should be a governmental role in increasing price and brand awareness for these consumers.

IMPLICATIONS FOR STORE LOYALTY

The same considerations apply to store loyalty. Store loyalty may be a convenient mode of shopping and does save time and effort, but it inhibits comparisons of brand alternatives by restricting choice to one store.

Any erosion of store loyalty may be beneficial from a societal viewpoint in encouraging consumers to shop for alternatives. As a result, consumers are more likely to be aware of lower-priced alternatives. Here again, the problem is that older, downscale consumers and disadvantaged minorities continue to be the most store loyal. Low-income consumers often lack the mobility to engage in comparison-shopping. Goldman's description of store-loyal consumers as exhibiting a low-knowledge and low-utilization style of shopping applies most to downscale consumers.[46] However, these are the consumers who can most benefit by increasing their range of alternatives.

In this regard, government could have a role in increasing the mobility of lower-income, disadvantaged consumers through improved modes of transportation to facilitate comparison-shopping.

SUMMARY

Consumer learning, habit, and brand loyalty are closely linked concepts. Habitual purchasing behavior is the result of consumer learning from reinforcement. Consumers will repeatedly buy what satisfies them best. This behavior leads to brand loyalty.

Concepts of learning are necessary to understand habit. The distinction is made between behavioral and cognitive approaches to learning. Behavioral learning focuses on the stimuli that affect behavior and on behavior itself. Cognitive learning focuses on problem solving and emphasizes the consumer thought variables that influence learning. Learning on the Web is a form of problem solving, with the form of learning shifting from random to purposeful search behavior as consumers become more accustomed to the sites that are most helpful.

Within the behavioral school, a key distinction is made between classical and instrumental conditioning. Classical conditioning explains behavior based on the establishment of a close association between a primary and a secondary stimulus. Instrumental conditioning views behavior as a function of the consumer's actions. Satisfaction leads to reinforcement and to an increase in the probability of repurchasing a brand.

Learning leads to repetitive buying and habit. In a model representing habitual purchasing behavior, a consumer's need arousal leads directly to an intention to buy, a subsequent purchase, and postpurchase evaluation. Information search and brand evaluation are minimal.

Habit serves two important functions. It reduces risk for high-involvement purchases and saves time and energy for low-involvement products.

Habit frequently leads to brand loyalty; that is, repetitive buying based on a commitment to the brand. The different learning theories describe two views of brand loyalty. An instrumental conditioning approach suggests that a consumer's consistent purchase of a brand is a reflection of brand loyalty. But such loyalty may lack commitment to the brand and reflect repeat buying based on inertia. The cognitive school believes that behavior is an insufficient measure of loyalty. Attitudinal commitment to the brand is also required.

Brand-loyal consumers also tend to be store loyal. But store loyalty may be an inefficient mode of shopping because it is likely to result in the consumer paying more because of a lack of search for alternatives.

A shift of emphasis is beginning to occur from brand loyalty to consumer loyalty as marketers begin to implement micromarketing strategies. Marketers are customizing information and products to suit consumer needs and establishing relationships with consumers after the purchase based on interactive communications. As a result, the focus is increasingly on individual consumers rather than brand marketing through the mass media to larger groups.

Chapter 4 focuses on the low-involvement conditions that encourage inertia, often in the form of brand and store loyalty.

QUESTIONS FOR DISCUSSION

1. How can principles of classical conditioning be applied to advertising? What are the shortcomings of such applications?

2. What conditions are necessary for classical conditioning to work in advertising? Provide some examples.

3. This chapter implies that the emphasis in advertising strategy has shifted from an adherence to classical learning theory before 1950 to an adherence to cognitive theories of learning after 1950.
   - How would such a shift be reflected in advertising strategy?
   - Do you agree that such a shift has taken place in advertising in the past fifty years?

4. Why was the Marlboro campaign less effective in the early 1990s compared with its success in previous years? How can learning theory explain this development?

5. Why did Marlboro recapture market share after 1993?

6. How can principles of instrumental conditioning be applied to advertising? In what ways do applications of instrumental conditioning differ from those of classical conditioning?

7. What are the implications of extinction and forgetting in the antitrust case brought against Kraft for its acquisition of Nabisco Shredded Wheat?

8. As a member of the Federal Trade Commission, what principles of conditioning would you use in deciding whether a company engaging in misleading advertising should either correct its advertising or simply stop it? If corrective advertising were ordered, what principles of conditioning would you use to determine if this action had the desired effects?

9. The chapter cites a shift in learning on the Web from nonpurposeful to purposeful. What does this mean? What are the implications of such a shift?

10. A good example of the operation of cognitive learning is to determine how new residents in a community learn about new products not available in their previous community. What evidence might demonstrate that a process of learning is taking place among new residents of a community?

11. What are the marketing strategy implications of positive and negative vicarious learning?

12. If habit is based on reinforcement and an increased likelihood of consumers buying the same product, why have certain dominant brands, once purchased by habit, become extinct or experienced a substantial loss in market share (*e.g.*, Sapolio soap)?

13. How can a crisis affect a consumer's reaction to a loyal brand? What actions should a company take to protect its brand in a time of crisis?

14. This chapter suggests that consumers' boredom and desire for variety may result in a change from habit to decision making.
    - Is this more likely for certain product categories than for others?
    - Is this more likely for certain consumers than for others? That is, is there a "stick-with-it" type as opposed to a "novelty-seeker" type?

15. Habit serves two different purposes for high- and low-involvement situations.
    - What are they?
    - Can you cite examples of habit in a high-involvement situation? in a low-involvement situation?

16. What are the strategic implications of the erosion of brand loyalty in the 1990s?

17. What is meant by a shift in emphasis from brand loyalty to consumer loyalty? What are the reasons behind this shift? What are the strategic implications?

18. Under what circumstances are brand and store loyalty inefficient models of consumer choice? What are the societal implications?

RESEARCH ASSIGNMENTS

1 Develop an experiment in which you ask consumers to evaluate three brands in a product category. Each brand should be placed in a separate room with background music. Make sure the brands are in the same price range and of the same quality. Play rock music in one room, classical in the second, and country and western in the third. Ask consumers to state their preference for one of the three brands. Ask consumers their musical preferences, as well.

- Are brand preferences related to preferences for the background music played?
- What learning theories could you use to explain your results?
- What are the implications of your results for marketing strategy?

Sources for this assignment: M. Elizabeth Blair and Terence Shimp, "Consequences of an Unpleasant Experience with Music: A Second-Order Negative Conditioning Perspective," *Journal of Advertising* 21 (March 1992), pp. 35–43; and Gerald Gorn, "The Effects of Music in Advertising on Choice Behavior: A Classical Conditioning Approach," *Journal of Marketing* 46 (Winter 1982), pp. 94–101.

2 Identify specific web sites that you believe reflect relationship marketing strategies. In what way do they do so? Do you believe these strategies are effective? Now identify one or two sites that do not reflect any attempt to establish long-lasting relationships with their customers. Do you believe they should do so? Why or why not?

3 Instruct two or three respondents to undertake a search for information on a certain product category without instructing them as to what web sites to visit. Then select two or three other respondents and provide them with specific guidance on the nature of the sites that can be provided for information. Instruct both sets of consumers to select a product in the category that best fits their needs. What strategies did the first set of consumers use to determine the best sites for information on the category? Were there any disadvantages in giving the second set of consumers specific instructions as to what sites to visit?

4 Develop a measure of brand loyalty using either a behavioral or a cognitive approach. Interview a sample of from thirty to fifty consumers of a frequently purchased packaged product (coffee, toothpaste, frozen orange juice). Identify those who are loyal to a brand versus those who are not.

- Are there any differences between the two groups in terms of (a) demographic characteristics, (b) importance placed on need criteria in selecting brands, (c) brand attitudes, (d) advertising recall, and (e) price paid?
- What are the implications of the differences between loyalists and nonloyalists for (a) attempts at increasing the number of loyal users, (b) product positioning, and (c) utilization of deals and coupons?

5 Develop a measure of loyalty incorporating both behavior and brand attitudes. Interview a sample of consumers of a frequently purchased packaged good. Distinguish between true loyalists and those who buy regularly out of inertia.

- What are the differences between the two groups according to the five criteria in Assignment 4?
- According to your findings, should marketers try to influence consumers who buy their brand out of inertia to become truly loyal? What are the advantages and disadvantages of such a strategy?
- What other marketing implications emerge from your findings?

NOTES

1. "The Brand's the Thing," *Fortune* (March 4, 1996), pp. 72–86
2. Ibid.
3. "Private Labels Bring Big Profits to Retailers," *St. Louis Post-Dispatch* (March 12, 2001), p. BP8; and "Private Label Goes Premium," *Discount Store News* (November 4, 1996), p. F38.
4. For a good summary of these three learning theories, see Michael L. Ray and Peter H. Webb, "Three Learning Theory Traditions and Their Application in Marketing," in Ronald C. Curhan, ed., *Combined Proceedings of the American Marketing Association,* Series No. 36 (Chicago: American Marketing Association, 1974), pp. 100–103.
5. Edward L. Thorndike, *The Psychology of Learning* (New York: Teacher's College, 1913); and John B. Watson and Rosalie Rayner, "Conditioned Emotional Reactions," *Journal of Experimental Psychology* 3 (1920), pp. 1–14.
6. Ivan Pavlov, *Conditioned Reflexes. An Investigation of the Physiological Activity of the Cerebral Cortex,* G. V. Anrep, ed. (London: Oxford University Press, 1927).
7. Chris Janiszewski and Luk Warlop, "The Influence of Classical Conditioning Procedures on Subsequent Attention to the Conditioned Brand," *Journal of Consumer Research* 20 (September 1993), pp. 171–189. For a further elaboration of

associative learning, see Stijn M. J. van Osselaer and Chris Janiszewski, "The Two Ways of Learning Brand Associations," *Journal of Consumer Research* 28 (September 2001), pp. 202–223.
8. "Hostess, Wonder Bread Target Kids Again," *Wall Street Journal* (November 17, 1995), p. B6.
9. B. F. Skinner, *The Behavior of Organisms: An Experimental Analysis* (New York: Appleton-Century-Crofts, 1938).
10. Peter D. Bennett and Robert M. Mandel, "Prepurchase Information Seeking Behavior of New Car Purchasers—The Learning Hypothesis," *Journal of Marketing Research* 6 (November 1969), pp. 430–433.
11. Eric Lapersonne, Gilles Laurent, and Jean-Jacques Le Goff, "Consideration Sets of Size One: An Empirical Investigation of Automobile Purchases," *International Journal of Research in Marketing* 12 (1995), pp. 55–66.
12. Constance Hays, with Alan Cowell and Craig R Whitney, NY Times News Service, "Execs Admit Stumbling in Coke Contamination," *New Orleans (La.) Times-Picayune* (June 30, 1999), p. C6.
13. Michael L. Rothschild and William C. Gadis, "Behavioral Learning Theory: Its Relevance to Marketing and Promotions," *Journal of Marketing* 45 (Spring 1981), pp. 70–78.

14. Rom J. Markin, Jr., *Consumer Behavior, A Cognitive Orientation* (New York: Macmillan, 1974), p. 239.

15. Wolfgang Kohler, *The Mentality of Apes* (New York: Harcourt Brace & World, 1925).

16. Alan R. Andreasen and Peter G. Durkson, "Market Learning of New Residents," *Journal of Marketing Research* 5 (May 1968), pp. 166–176.

17. Ibid.

18. Chris T. Allen and Thomas J. Madden, "A Closer Look at Classical Conditioning," *Journal of Consumer Research* 12 (December 1985), pp. 301–315.

19. John A. Howard and Jagdish Sheth, *The Theory of Buyer Behavior* (New York: John Wiley, 1969), pp. 27–28.

20. Ted Roselius, "Consumer Rankings of Risk Reduction Methods," *Journal of Marketing* 35 (January 1971), pp. 56–61.

21. Klaus Peter Kass, "Consumer Habit Forming, Information Acquisition, and Buying Behavior," *Journal of Business Research* 10 (March 1982), pp. 3–15.

22. See Brian Wasnick and Cynthia Huffman, "Perceiving, Choosing, and Using: A Framework for Revitalizing Mature Brands," working paper, The Wharton School of Business, May 1996.

23. W. T. Tucker, "The Development of Brand Loyalty," *Journal of Marketing Research* 1 (August 1964), p. 32.

24. Jacob Jacoby, "A Model of Multi-Brand Loyalty," *Journal of Advertising Research* 11 (June 1971), p. 26.

25. Jacob Jacoby and David B. Kyner, "Brand Loyalty vs. Repeat Purchasing Behavior," *Journal of Marketing Research* 10 (February 1973), p. 2.

26. "What Do People Want, Anyway?" *New York Times* (November 8, 1987), p. F4.

27. George S. Day, "A Two-Dimensional Concept of Brand Loyalty," *Journal of Advertising Research* 9 (September 1969), pp. 29–36.

28. Ibid.

29. See *Are There Consumer Types?* (New York: Advertising Research Foundation, 1964); and Ronald E. Frank, William F. Massy, and Thomas M. Lodahl, "Purchasing Behavior and Personal Attributes," *Journal of Advertising Research* 9 (December 1969), pp. 15–24.

30. Day, "A Two-Dimensional Concept," pp. 29–36.

31. James M. Carman, "Correlates of Brand Loyalty: Some Positive Results," *Journal of Marketing Research* 7 (February 1970), pp. 7–76.

32. Roselius, "Consumer Rankings," pp. 56–61; and Jagdish Sheth and M. Venkatesan, "Risk-Reduction Processes in Repetitive Consumer Behavior," *Journal of Marketing Research* 3 (August 1968), pp. 307–311.

33. Carman, "Correlates of Brand Loyalty," pp. 7–76.

34. "Traditional Brand Loyalty," *Advertising Age* (May 18, 1981), p. S2; and "Hispanics: All for One?" *Advertising Age* (September 13, 1984), p. 3.

35. "Brand Loyalty Beats Price in Some Product Categories," *Marketing News* (November 28, 1980), p. 1.

36. *Philip Morris: Marlboro Friday (A)* (Cambridge, Mass.: Harvard Business School Publishing, 1995), pp. 9–11; Philip Morris communication, August 2001.

37. Don Peppers and Martha Rogers, "The End of Mass Marketing," *Marketing Tools* (March/April 1995), pp. 42–52.

38. Ibid.

39. Fred D. Reynolds, William R. Darden, and Warren S. Martin, "Developing an Image of the Store-Loyal Customer," *Journal of Retailing* 50 (Winter 1974–1975), pp. 73–84.

40. Arieh Goldman, "The Shopping Style Explanation for Store Loyalty," *Journal of Retailing* 53 (Winter 1977–1978), pp. 33–46.

41. Ibid.

42. Robert D. Hisrich, Ronald J. Dornoff, and Jerome B. Kernan, "Perceived Risk in Store Selection," *Journal of Marketing Research* 9 (November 1972), pp. 435–439; and Joseph F. Dash, Leon G. Schiffman, and Conrad Berenson, "Risk and Personality Related Dimensions of Store Choice," *Journal of Marketing* 40 (January 1976), pp. 32–39.

43. *Supermarket Shoppers in a Period of Economic Uncertainty* (New York: Yankelovich, Skelly, and White, Inc. 1982), p. 16.

44. "Why Shoppers' Loyalty to Familiar Web Sites Isn't So Crazy After All," *Wall Street Journal* (August 13, 2001), p. B1.

45. "Exploration of World Wide Web Tilts from Eclectic to Mundane," *New York Times* (August 26, 2001), p. 22.

46. Goldman, "The Shopping Style Explanation for Store Loyalty," pp. 33–46.

4

Low-Involvement Consumer Decision Making

In describing complex decision making and brand loyalty in Chapters 2 and 3, we assumed that consumers were highly involved with the purchasing decision. However, when we consider the variety of more mundane products purchased on an everyday basis—toothpaste, detergents, cereals, deodorants—it is not surprising that most purchases are low in consumer involvement.[1] A **low-involvement purchase** is one in which consumers do not consider the product important and do not strongly identify with it.

Marketers like to think that consumers are involved with their products because involved consumers are more likely to pay attention to advertising, evaluate brands carefully, and become brand loyal. Where consumer involvement is lacking, marketers try to create it by introducing new product attributes that are important to consumers or by linking uninvolving products to involving situations and issues.

Can Procter & Gamble Increase the Level of Product Involvement through the Web?

In the late 1990s, Procter & Gamble (P&G), the packaged goods giant (and the world's largest advertiser), entered the information age when it went online to try to increase involvement with its basically uninvolving brands.[2] P&G's managers recognized several trends in Internet usage that could have tremendous implications for the company's marketing strategy:[3]

- In the United States, Internet usage was expected to increase from 150 million people in 2000 to close to 200 million by 2005.
- There were 407 million worldwide users of the Internet in 2000.
- The diffusion of Internet usage has increased to the point where lower-income consumers are increasingly likely to be web users. This is reflected in the fact that the average household income of Internet users has been dropping steadily in the last five years.
- By 2000, roughly 50 percent of Internet users were women.

This last trend, in particular, offered significant opportunities to P&G and other consumer goods manufacturers, as women usually make the purchase decisions for most of P&G's product categories.

P&G set out to use these trends to its advantage by leveraging the interactivity of the Web to strengthen its customer relationships. In the process, the company has attempted to increase consumer involvement with products like Pampers, Tide, and Crest. P&G has been engaged in a process of further increasing the equity of strongly established brands by building a relationship with the consumer on a one-to-one basis, rather than simply delivering an advertising message through the mass media.

Through the Internet, consumer packaged goods manufacturers can provide a new level of information to their consumers, creating value that was not previously available. The "stain detective" section on the Tide site (*www.Tide.com*), the "Pampers Parenting Institute free e-mail newsletter" on the Pampers site (*www.Pampers.com*), and the "Dental Appointment Reminder e-postcard" option on the Crest site (*www.Crest.com*) are just a few examples of the interactive potential of the Internet and of the ways in which the Internet can increase brand involvement through greater interactivity between consumer and marketer.[4] P&G has gone further and now allows web users to download the "Tide stain detective" to handheld devices and supports the information on parenting on Pampers' site in six separate languages (see Exhibit 4.1).

| **EXHIBIT 4.1** |

Tide's international presence on the Web: the Italian and Polish home pages.
Copyright © The Procter & Gamble Company. Used by permission.

The Internet has allowed P&G to move beyond traditional advertising and to build involvement by providing interactivity, community, and personalization opportunities for its brands. However, because marketers of low-involvement products like P&G still need to use price promotions or other incentives as well as advertising to attract consumers, P&G recognizes that efforts to build web-based relationships for low-involvement products bring limited results. On the other hand, that is not to say that a brand like Tide, Crest, or Pampers has no place on the Web. Even conveying product information on the Web and, perhaps, offering benefits to which consumers would not otherwise have access might be enough to make a web presence worthwhile.[5] But it is questionable whether such a presence is sufficient to increase consumer involvement with P&G's brands.

This chapter focuses on purchase decisions in which consumers are not highly involved. The importance of a low-involvement perspective is considered first. Next, consumer decisions are classified by level of product involvement. Several theoretical bases for low-involvement purchase behavior are described. Strategic implications of high- versus low-involvement situations are considered, with special emphasis on advertising strategy.

The Nature of Involvement

The level of involvement with a product varies by individual. Some individuals may be highly involved with the purchase of jeans because they associate the product with personal appearance and social acceptance. Others may not be as highly involved because they view jeans as just another piece of casual clothing with few personal associations. Thus, consumer involvement with a product can vary on a continuum from high to low. The position of the consumer on this continuum depends on several factors. Generally, a consumer is more likely to be involved with a product when it

- *is important to the consumer.* A product is most likely to be important when (a) the consumer's self-image is tied to the product (*e.g.,* the Toyota ad in Exhibit 4.2 portraying a link between the car and the owner's personality); (b) it has symbolic meaning tied to consumer values (*e.g.,* owning a BMW represents power and success to baby boomers; wearing Nike sneakers represents athletic prowess to teenagers); (c) it is expensive; or (d) it has some important functional role, such as the transportation provided by a car or the quick cooking facilities provided by a microwave oven.

- *has emotional appeal.* Consumers do not seek only functional benefits in products. They often seek benefits that trigger an emotional response. The very ownership of a Saturn car or Harley-Davidson motorcycle produces a kinship with other owners for many buyers. This kinship often results in a cultlike following frequently referred to for these two brands. Clearly, any such kinship goes beyond functional benefits and is a more emotional response to the product.

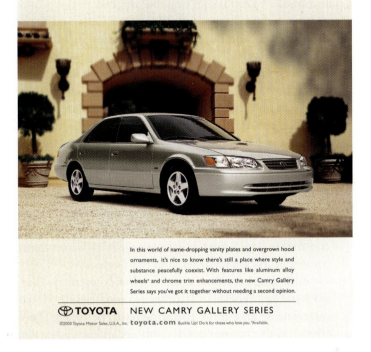

- *is continually of interest to the consumer.* The fashion-conscious consumer, for example, has an ongoing interest in clothing, and the car buff has an ongoing interest in cars.

- *entails significant risks.* Among these risks would be the financial risk of buying a house, the technological risk of buying a personal computer, the social risk of changing one's wardrobe, or the physical risk of buying an unsafe car or the wrong medication.

- *is identified with the norms of a group.* That is, the product has sign or "badge" value.[6]

These conditions are likely to result in complex decision making. As most brands lack significant self-identity, interest, risk, emotion, or badge value, it is not surprising that buying by inertia is more widespread than purchasing by complex decision making.

TYPES OF INVOLVEMENT

Behavioral researchers have identified two types of involvement with products: situational and enduring.[7] **Situational involvement** occurs only in specific situations and is temporary, whereas **enduring involvement** is continuous and more permanent. Situational involvement generally occurs when a purchase decision is required. For example, an MBA graduate may not be particularly fashion-conscious, but she must buy a suit for job interviewing. This graduate will be highly involved with clothes in that particular situation but not afterward. Another MBA graduate may be very fashion-conscious. She may also be looking for a suit for job interviews, but her interest in clothes is enduring, not situational. Such enduring involvement requires an ongoing interest in the product category, whether a purchase is required or not. According to Celsi and Olson, "The emphasis is on the product itself, and the inherent satisfaction its usage provides, rather than on some (situational) goal."[8]

For the situationally involved, the Web is a tremendous resource for accumulating information quickly; for example, product alternatives, specifications, and prices. Many **high-involvement purchases** are made on a situational basis. For example, one-third of car purchases are made by consumers who wake up in the morning not knowing they will purchase a car that day. In this context, the Web enables quick comparison and evaluation of purchasing alternatives.

For those consumers who have a continuous interest in a product (*e.g.,* Harley-Davidson devotees), the Web is a useful vehicle for staying connected to other enthusiasts in an interactive way. Additionally, the smart marketer may sponsor chatrooms or other forums to encourage the enduring involvement of interested consumers (*e.g.,* Saturn hosts message boards and chatrooms on its web site to keep owners of its cars involved with their vehicles).

Both situational and enduring involvement are likely to result in complex decision making. Whether the college graduate is interested in clothes because of a job interview or on a more enduring basis, he or she is aware of fashion information, considers alternative lines of clothing, and evaluates them carefully before making a decision.

Marketers take a very different approach in targeting those with enduring versus situational involvement. The deep-seated nature of enduring involvement means that symbols and images are more likely to be used to connect the consumer with the product. In targeting the situationally involved consumer, more specific appeals to the particular context of the purchase are made. The first ad for Godiva chocolates in Exhibit 4.3 targets those who believe that quality time can be spent in a museum enjoying a delicious chocolate. The second ad focuses on a particular situation, gift-giving for Valentine's Day, without the rich symbolism of the first. Whereas the former individual may be a chocoholic who buys chocolates all year, the latter consumer is involved only on gift-giving occasions and has been given additional incentive with the possibility of winning a valuable prize.

THE MULTIDIMENSIONAL NATURE OF INVOLVEMENT

The five conditions for involvement suggest that consumers can be involved with a product on several dimensions. In their study, Kapferer and Laurent[9] confirmed the multidimensional nature of involvement. They asked eight hundred women to agree or disagree with statements about twenty product categories. The statements were closely related to the five components of involvement: product importance, interest, risk, emotion, and badge value. Scales were developed for each component of involvement.

Depicting enduring versus situational involvement for a brand.

(left) Photo credit: Grace Huang. Courtesy Godiva Chocolatier, Inc.; (right) © 2000 Steve Hellerstein. Courtesy Godiva Chocolatier, Inc.

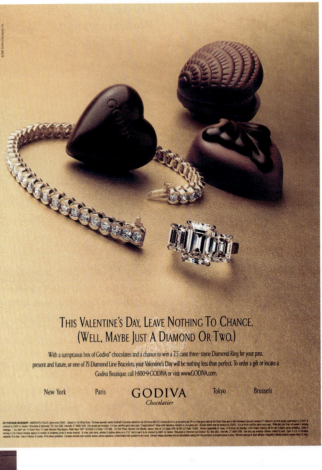

The scores for ten of the products are shown in Table 4.1 (with 100 as an average score). Clearly, for this sample of women, clothing and perfume were involving across all components, except for risk. This suggests that consumers are more likely to be involved with these items on an enduring, rather than a situational, basis. Champagne was involving for all components except continuous interest, suggesting that consumers are involved with champagne on a situational basis (*i.e.*, for special occasions). Chocolate was involving only in its emotional appeal, suggesting possible pleasurable childhood associations with the product. Detergents and facial soap were not involving in any respect. The value of the study is in showing that products can be involving in different ways. For example, washing machines and vacuum cleaners were high in product importance, possibly because they serve a support role in the household. However, neither product had pleasure (emotional) or badge value, because they were associated with housework.[10] If the promotional objective is to create consumer involvement, advertisements for both washing machines and vacuum cleaners might emphasize their time-liberating value to increase their emotional appeal.

TABLE 4.1

Product categories by components of involvement

Product	Components of Involvement				
	Continuous interest	Emotion	Budget value	Product importance	Risk
Clothing	123	147	166	129	99
Perfume	120	154	164	116	97
Champagne	75	128	123	123	119
Washing Machine	130	111	104	136	102
Vacuum Cleaner	108	94	78	130	111
Detergent	80	44	77	75	94
Facial Soap	88	91	99	78	85
Shampoo	99	78	93	94	102
Yogurt	95	105	73	72	73
Chocolate	94	130	86	76	91

Source: From Jean-Noel Kapferer and Giles Laurent, "Consumer Involvement Profiles: A New Practical Approach to Consumer Involvement," *Journal of Advertising Research* 25 (December 1985–January 1986), p. 51. Reprinted with permission.

INVOLVEMENT WITH THE MEDIUM

Although researchers have established that consumers have varying levels of involvement with the products they purchase, it is also important to note the different levels of involvement consumers have among the various media by which they receive advertising messages.

Television is a passive medium. Consumers often switch channels, perform other tasks, or simply ignore commercials when they appear. They generally do not process the information contained in these ad messages actively; rather, they often remember the ads later when in the presence of the product. As a result, TV is the medium of choice for low-involvement products, and it reaches the largest base of consumers.

The Internet, on the other hand, is extremely high in involvement. The interactive nature of the Web draws consumers in by requiring action on their part. Consumers can not only direct online search and determine the information they want, they can also express their opinions to their peers or contact marketers to communicate product specifications or reactions to products. This type of purposeful communication requires motivation and interaction. One might assume this forum is best suited for high-involvement products. However, less involving products have staked out their territory in the digital domain, as we saw with Pampers, Crest, and Tide, to increase the experiential value of these types of products.

Marketers also attempt to create synergies between advertising media and the Web to reinforce the brand. Nike created an ad campaign to integrate both television and the Web in order to increase involvement with its shoes. The TV ads featured story lines that resulted in cliffhanger endings. To find out the ending of the ad, consumers had to log on to "whatever.nike.com". Once online, consumers could

Kellogg Increases Involvement with Cereals

Kellogg followed a strategy of encouraging involvement in the 1980s with profound consequences for the cereal industry when it created the adult cereal market. Until then, cereals were primarily a children's product; by 1980, however, the market was stagnating because of a declining birthrate. Kellogg saw an opportunity to target cereals to nutritionally oriented baby boomers. To do so, it had to get these consumers more involved in cereal by convincing them it was not just kid stuff.

Kellogg did so in the most direct way. In 1984, it began touting the high-fiber content of its All-Bran cereal as helping to prevent cancer. It followed by targeting a new line of cereals— Common Sense, Just Right, Mueslix—to diet-conscious, health-oriented, and fitness segments. As a result, adults began seeing cereal as part of a healthier lifestyle, a highly involving issue. Kellogg's success in transforming cereal from a less to a more involving product doubled the growth rate for cereals.

As baby boomers age, they continue to be interested in maintaining their health. Research shows that 52 percent of the general public believes in the efficacy of food products to help reduce cancer and disease. As a result, Kellogg and other cereal manufacturers have an opportunity to expand their offerings of healthy cereals. As a part of this effort, Kellogg created the Functional Foods Division in 1997 to research

and develop disease-preventive foods. "The trend is really about marketers capitalizing on the wellness issue, where consumers increasingly dissatisfied with conventional medicine and disillusioned with the whole drug industry are realizing nutrition is something they can do on their own," said Clare Hasler, director of the Functional Foods for Health Program at the University of Illinois.[11] In 1999, Kellogg introduced Special K Plus, a calcium- and iron-fortified version of Special K, targeted to women. Kellogg also created a new program, K-sentials, which fortifies many of its existing cereals with essential vitamins and nutrients.

The messages are changing, too. Rather than telling consumers about the harmful ingredients absent in products (no fat, low salt, etc.), marketers are promoting the positive ingredients in products (natural ingredients, vitamins).

Kellogg's strategy is clear: Make cereals an important nutritional supplement for adults, and in so doing, increase the involvement with the product category.

Sources: "Kellogg Seeks FDA Approval for Health Claim by Asserting a Link Between Wheat Bran Intake and Reduced Risk of Colon Cancer," *Chicago Tribune* (June 4, 1997), p. 3; "Eyeing an Aging America, Food Giants Broaden Inroads into Nutraceuticals," *Brandweek* (January 6, 1997), p. 8; "The New Product Crunch," *Supermarket Business* (August 1999), p. 29; "Food Firms' Resolution: Focus on Health Bennies," *Brandweek* (January 4, 1999), p. 9; and "Special K Drops Thin Models for Health Theme," *Marketing News* (March 2, 1998), p. 8.

also access product information, styles, and so on, creating increased interest and involvement with the product.

Involvement with print media, such as newspapers and magazines, falls somewhere in between TV and the Web. Though the content is static, the consumer is in complete control in regard to the pacing and amount of time spent with a particular message.

THE CROSS-CULTURAL NATURE OF INVOLVEMENT

Differences in product involvement also occur on a cross-cultural basis. For example, bicycles are more important in China, where they are the primary means of transportation, than they are in the United States. A Chinese consumer might be as involved in buying a bicycle as an American consumer is in buying a car. Zaichowsky and Sood surveyed business students in fifteen countries to determine involvement levels for eight product categories.[12] Involvement in the purchase of beer among English and American students was significantly higher than that for students from South American countries. This difference probably reflects the cultural role of beer in these countries. English and American students associate beer with relaxation and social occasions, whereas no such association exists for students from South American countries. Students' involvement with soft drinks was uniformly low for all countries, except China. Apparently, soft drinks in China are a valued commodity, particularly with the introduction of Western brands in the last ten years. Involvement with blue jeans was fairly uniform across countries, probably as a result of similar perceptions of the product among students worldwide.

These findings suggest that international marketers must adjust their strategies on a country-by-country basis, depending on the cultural role and importance of certain products.

The Importance of a Low-Involvement Perspective

Most consumers' purchases are not involving. Kassarjian and Kassarjian support the view that most purchase decisions do not greatly involve consumers: "Subjects just do not care about products; they are unimportant to them. Although issues such as racial equality . . . may stir them up, products do not."[13]

INVOLVEMENT AND THE HIERARCHY OF EFFECTS

If low involvement characterizes much of purchasing, why have marketers focused on high-involvement decisions (*i.e.,* complex decision making and brand loyalty)? There are two reasons. First, because marketers are highly involved with their products, they easily assume consumers are also highly involved. [14] Tyebjee notes the reluctance of product and advertising managers to consider an uninvolved consumer:

> These individuals [product and advertising managers] spend a major part of their waking hours thinking about their brand. Therefore, when they evaluate the advertising strategy they do so as highly involved individuals, unlike the target consumer. Highly cluttered, complex advertising copy is often a result of agency and brand group decision makers who are unable to view the product from the perspective of the [uninvolved] consumer.[15]

Exhibit 4.4 is a good illustration of the marketer's assumption that consumers are involved with mundane products.

A second reason that marketers tend to focus on high-involvement decisions is that it is easier for them to understand and influence consumers if they assume consumers employ a cognitive process of brand evaluation. Complex decision making assumes a sequence in the consumers' choice process (referred to as a **hierarchy of effects**) that leads consumers to think before they act. That is, they first form brand beliefs (the cognitive component of attitudes), then evaluate brands (the affective component), and then make a purchase decision (the behavioral component). The

*"And now a message of importance to those of you who
have been giving serious thought to the purchase of a
new tube of toothpaste."*

beliefs/evaluation/behavior hierarchy assumes involved consumers. The assumption that such a high-involvement hierarchy of effects describes consumer choice has dominated marketing thought since consumer behavior became an integrated field of study.

LOW-INVOLVEMENT HIERARCHY

Consumer behavior researchers are directing more attention to a low-involvement hierarchy of effects. This hierarchy stipulates that consumers may act without thinking. For example, when purchasing table salt, it is unlikely that the consumer initiates a process of information search to determine brand characteristics. Nor is the consumer likely to evaluate alternative brands to identify the most favored one.

Rather than searching for information, the consumer receives information passively. The consumer sits in front of the television and sees an advertisement for Morton salt that describes it as "easy to pour." Stifling a yawn, the consumer is thinking about anything but salt. The consumer is not really evaluating the advertisement. Rather, in just seeing the ad, the consumer is storing information in a few bits and pieces without any active cognitive process. However, over time, the consumer establishes an association of Morton salt with ease in pouring. Lastovicka refers to this process as "information catching" rather than "information processing."[16]

A need arises simply because the amount of salt in the house is running low. The consumer buys Morton salt because of the familiarity that repetitive advertising produces. The consumer sees the brand on the store shelf, associates it with the advertising theme, and has sufficient stimulus to purchase Morton salt. Under these conditions, the consumer does not form an attitude toward the brand and has no favorable or unfavorable reaction. Instead, the consumer regards the brand as

TABLE 4.2
A comparison of low- and high-involvement hierarchies

Low-involvement hierarchy	High-involvement hierarchy
1. Brand beliefs are formed first by *passive* learning.	1. Brand beliefs are formed first by *active* learning.
2. A purchase decision is made.	2. Brands are evaluated.
3. The brand may or may not be evaluated afterward.	3. A purchase decision is made.

relatively neutral, since it is not associated with any important benefits tied to self or group identification.

Therefore, the hierarchy of effects for low-involvement products is quite different from that for high involvement, as indicated in Table 4.2. Consumers become aware of the product and form beliefs about it passively. They make a purchase decision with little brand information and then evaluate the brand after the purchase to determine the level of satisfaction. At this point, consumers may develop weak attitudes toward the brand—for example, if a new feature such as a convenient spout is introduced (favorable evaluation) or if the brand performs poorly (sticks to the container, producing an unfavorable reaction). If such attitudes develop, they occur after the purchase and are weakly held.[17]

Several studies have supported the distinction between a high- and a low-involvement hierarchy. Joseph E. Seagram & Sons and Time, Inc., jointly conducted a study of consumer choice of liquor brands and found that an increase in brand awareness was related to a subsequent purchase of the advertised brand. However, there was no change in attitudes toward the brand as a result of brand evaluation. The study concluded that the findings "tend to contradict the long-accepted belief that first you change people's attitudes, then you change their buying habits."[18] The findings supported a beliefs/behavior/attitude hierarchy.

In a later study, Beatty and Kahle distinguished between consumers who are and who are not involved with soft drinks. The more involved consumers tended to make choices based on favorable attitudes toward the preferred brands. Attitudes did not play an important role in the decision for less involved consumers.[19]

LOW INVOLVEMENT AND BRAND EVALUATION

The Morton salt example cited in the last subsection suggests that in low-involvement decision making, consumers do very little brand evaluation and information processing. This is because consumers are generally governed by a principle of *cognitive economy*—they search for only as much information as they feel is necessary to adequately evaluate brands.[20] In low-involvement conditions, consumers are not motivated to actively evaluate brands. The product being evaluated is not particularly risky, expensive, important, or personally relevant. This lack of motivation to process information is why brand beliefs are formed in a passive state.

Research supports the lower levels of brand evaluation and information processing for low-involvement conditions. Mulvey et al. examined consumers' evaluation of tennis rackets and found involved consumers used more complex means of evaluation. For example, less involved consumers thought of the quality of a tennis racket in the abstract, whereas more involved consumers could articulate what makes a high-quality tennis racket, using criteria such as head size, grip, and materials.[21]

LOW-INVOLVEMENT DECISION CRITERIA

If brand evaluation is minimal in low-involvement conditions, then how do consumers make decisions? They follow relatively simple decision rules that reflect principles of cognitive economy by minimizing the time and effort in shopping and decision making.

One rule cited in the Morton salt example is to pick the most familiar brand. A study by Hoyer and Brown supports this type of decision making in low-involvement purchases. They found that consumers who are aware of one brand in a product category repeatedly choose it, even if it is lower in quality compared with that of other brands.[22]

Another simple decision rule is to pick the brand used the last time if it was adequate. A study by Lynch, Marmorstein, and Weigold found that uninvolved

---

GLOBAL APPLICATIONS

OF CONSUMER BEHAVIOR

What Is Low Involvement at Home May Be High Involvement Abroad

Many products that are taken for granted by consumers in more advanced economies may be valuable items in other countries. For example, hair spray is a low-involvement product for most consumers in the United States, but in Poland it is likely to arouse intense consumer interest. The product was almost unknown during the Communist years. When Poland converted to a free-market system, the novelty and initial scarcity of the product aroused consumer interest. Polish consumers attached badge value to the product—a well-groomed look enhanced social status. They also became personally involved as a result. And they were willing to pay more for the product on a relative price basis than American consumers.

Many products that are regarded as commonplace in the United States are assigned more importance abroad because they are regarded as American icons. McDonald's is an example. Considering the history of poor service

in Eastern European countries and those of the former Soviet Union, McDonald's standards of uniformity, tasty food, and child-friendly tables created instant involvement with fast-food establishments. As one executive said, "The world is becoming a service society, but in many countries they don't get any except at McDonald's." But the novelty of good service is not the only reason Eastern European and Russian consumers are more involved with McDonald's. The price of a meal for a family of four often equals a week's pay.

Hair spray in Poland and McDonald's in Russia demonstrate that involvement is consumer, not product, related. Differences in a consumer's economic and cultural environment mean that a low-involvement product in one country can be totally absorbing in another.

Source: "That Golden Touch to the Arches: In Russia McDonald's Is Unsung Bearer of Western Civilization," *Christian Science Monitor* (March 4, 1997), p. 1.

consumers make decisions on this basis by recalling previously formed brand evaluations.[23] Finally, if uninvolved consumers have few prior associations with brands, the simplest expedient is to pick the least expensive alternative.

In each of these cases, consumers are making quick decisions (generally in the store) with little or no brand evaluation.

Four Types of Consumer Behavior

In Chapter 1, we described four types of consumer choice processes based on the level of involvement and decision making: complex decision making, brand loyalty, inertia, and limited decision making. Figure 4.1 shows that a different hierarchy of effects describes each of these processes.[24] The high- and low-involvement processes are also described by different learning theories based on these decision hierarchies.

COMPLEX DECISION MAKING AND BRAND LOYALTY

The upper left-hand box of Figure 4.1 represents the process of complex decision making described by the traditional "think-before-you-act" hierarchy. The learning theory that best describes this process is cognitive learning; that is, a process that requires the consumers' development of brand attitudes and a detailed evaluation of brand alternatives.

The lower left-hand box describes brand loyalty; that is, consumers make purchases with little deliberation because of past satisfaction and a strong commitment

| FIGURE 4.1 |

Four types of consumer behavior.

	HIGH INVOLVEMENT	**LOW INVOLVEMENT**
DECISION MAKING	**Decision process** Complex decision making **Hierarchy of effects** Beliefs Evaluation Behavior **Theory** Cognitive learning	**Decision process** Limited decision making **Hierarchy of effects** Beliefs Behavior Evaluation **Theory** Passive learning
HABIT	**Decision process** Brand loyalty **Hierarchy of effects** (Beliefs) (Evaluation) Behavior **Theory** Instrumental conditioning	**Decision process** Inertia **Hierarchy of effects** Beliefs Behavior (Evaluation) **Theory** Classical conditioning

to the brand as a result. The Web offers consumers the ability to save time by purchasing a known brand online. Additionally, consumers can develop customized specifications for purchasing a known brand, for example, Dell computers. The learning theory that best describes brand loyalty is instrumental conditioning (positive reinforcement based on satisfaction with the brand, leading to repetitive behavior). Both high-involvement processes are described by a beliefs/evaluation/behavior hierarchy, except that forming beliefs and evaluating brands are not a necessary part of the choice process in brand loyalty. Complex decision making was described in Chapter 2 and brand loyalty in Chapter 3. In this chapter, we focus on the two low-involvement processes shown in Figure 4.1—inertia and limited decision making.

INERTIA

The lower right-hand box of Figure 4.1 represents the Morton salt example—buying based on **inertia.** As we saw, when a low-involvement hierarchy operates, a consumer forms beliefs passively, makes a decision with little information processing, and then evaluates the brand after the purchase. Because inertia involves repetitive buying of the same brand to avoid making a decision, the consumer does not make a subsequent brand evaluation until after the first few purchases. If the brand achieves a certain minimum level of satisfaction, the consumer will repurchase it on a routinized basis. This process is sometimes referred to as **spurious loyalty** because repetitive purchases may make it appear that the consumer is loyal to the brand when actually no such loyalty exists. The Web enables consumers facing time poverty the convenience of ordering items online and having them delivered. VitaminShoppe.com offers a service online that allows its customers to receive email reminders when supplies of a previously purchased product are running low, thereby enabling consumers to purchase by inertia.

The learning theory that best describes inertia is classical conditioning. When the consumer is not involved with the product, contiguity between a stimulus and a response could be established more easily through repetitive advertising because the consumer is in a passive state. The consumer forms the association without thinking. When the consumer goes into a store, the association may be triggered by seeing the product; and the easiest thing to do is to buy the product with little deliberation. Thus, repetitive exposure to a theme like "the quicker, thicker picker upper" for Bounty paper towels might create an association between absorbency and the product for a low-involvement product category.

Various studies have demonstrated the effectiveness of repeating advertising themes in low-involvement conditions. Batra and Ray showed that repeating an advertising message results in more favorable brand attitudes for low-involvement purchases.[25] In the high-involvement case, repetition had an initial favorable impact; but after a while, repetition became counterproductive. Similarly, Hawkins and Hoch found that for low-involvement purchases, repetition resulted in greater acceptance of the truth of advertising claims.[26] In both cases, repetition created familiarity, allowing consumers to more easily associate known claims with a particular brand.

Because of the dominance of low-involvement products, inertia is probably much more common than most marketing managers would like to admit. Product managers and advertisers sometimes use marketing strategies that assume consumers care. Most consumers do not.

LIMITED DECISION MAKING

Occasionally, low-involvement purchases warrant some decision making (upper right-hand box in Figure 4.1), in contrast to the process of routinized decision making that characterizes inertia. The introduction of a new product, a change in the existing brand, or a desire for variety might cause a consumer to switch from routinized to limited decision making. For example, assume a new, thicker paper towel is introduced and is advertised as being so strong, it can be reused. A consumer who consistently buys Bounty notices the ad. Involvement with the category is low, but introduction of the new product is enough to arouse mild interest and curiosity. The decision process conforms to a low-involvement hierarchy, as there is little information seeking and brand evaluation. The consumer forms beliefs about the brand (thick, strong, can be reused), purchases the brand, and then evaluates it based on initial trial.

Although limited decision making involves cognitive processes, the relevant learning process is described as passive rather than cognitive learning, because no active information search and brand evaluation takes place. The consumer receives information about the new paper towel passively and puts it in the back of his or her mind. Seeing the brand in the store triggers recall; the consumer examines the package and purchases the product for trial.

Information search engines on the Web may encourage limited decision making by minimizing the time required to find the right product for a particular need. A consumer looking for advice on removing a paint stain might not be particularly involved with the subject and uses google.com to quickly determine the relevant site and information for the purpose. Such efficient information search is a prime advantage of the Web in low-involvement conditions.

An important form of limited decision making is *variety seeking*. Consumers often try a variety of brands out of boredom simply because many low-involvement products are ordinary and mundane. One study found that under these conditions, consumers often switch to a less preferred brand just to experience a variety of alternatives.[27] For example, it is unlikely that consumers develop strong preferences for a brand of salad dressing. A consumer may consciously buy various brands for the sake of variety, even less preferred ones; thus, purchases are made without brand evaluation or changes in brand attitude. The chosen brand is evaluated while being consumed.

R. H. Bruskin, a large marketing research firm, found evidence of variety-seeking behavior. Bruskin found that for certain low-involvement products such as toothpaste, potato chips, and salad dressing, most consumers who switched to other brands continued to have favorable attitudes toward their former brand. The study concluded that consumers do not switch to other brands because of dissatisfaction but "just to try something new."[28] Because the level of involvement is low, the consumer is not likely to be seriously dissatisfied. Rather, the motivation to switch brands is a desire for change and a search for novelty.

Browsing on the Web can lead to variety-seeking behavior. As a consumer is searching items on the Web, links may lead to a new product or item, which may result in a purchase on- or offline. It is very simple to shop virtually and browse the aisles of an online grocery store such as Peapod.com. Just as there is prime placement in real grocery stores to induce variety seeking, so is there strategic placement of products online. And in many respects it is easier to seek out unknown alternatives online than in a real store, because browsing is facilitated and encouraged.

Unplanned Purchasing Behavior

When consumers are not involved with a product, they often make a purchase decision inside the store, because there is insufficient motivation to preplan a purchase. Such unplanned decisions are generally made by inertia or by limited decision making. In contrast, complex decision making assumes a preplanning process. There are two basic reasons for an **unplanned purchase.** First, the time and effort involved in searching for alternatives outside the store may not be worth the trouble, and consumers buy largely on a reminder basis (*i.e.,* by inertia). Second, consumers may seek variety or novelty and thus buy on impulse (*i.e.,* by limited decision making).

The influence of in-store stimuli such as displays, shelf position, packaging, and price become more important for unplanned purchases than preplanned purchase decisions. This does not mean that advertising and in-store stimuli are separate. As we know, advertising can reinforce in-store stimuli by reminding consumers of the brand once they see it on the shelf. Conversely, displays and good shelf position are a necessity if advertising is to be effective. As a result, the role of advertising differs markedly, depending on the type of purchase. For preplanned purchases, advertising attempts to create demand beforehand. For unplanned purchases, advertising is meant to tie in with in-store stimuli that influence consumers at the point of sale.

As unplanned purchases are often instigated by the reminder effect, it is becoming easier for marketers to effectively prompt consumers via directed email messages. Amazon.com or barnesandnoble.com can prompt consumers to buy the newest book by a favorite author or the latest release by a preferred artist. Web sites are also becoming effective in suggesting products that a consumer will like, based on past purchases or on the purchases of consumers with similar tastes. Such targeting based on consumer preferences and behavior can encourage **impulse buying** on the Web.

Three Theories of Low-Involvement Consumer Behavior

A better understanding of low-involvement choice has evolved in marketing because of three theories: (1) the theory of passive learning developed by Krugman,[29] (2) the theory of social judgment developed by Sherif,[30] and (3) the elaboration likelihood model developed by Petty and Cacioppo.[31]

KRUGMAN'S THEORY OF PASSIVE LEARNING

Krugman's theory of passive learning provided one of the first perspectives on low-involvement consumer behavior. Studying the effects of television as a medium in the 1960s, Krugman sought an answer to why TV ads produced high levels of brand recall yet little change in consumers' brand attitudes. He hypothesized that television is a low-involvement medium that results in **passive learning.** The viewer is in a relaxed state and does not pay attention to the message. In this low-involvement environment, the viewer does not link the message to his or her needs, brand beliefs, and past experiences (as is assumed in the high-involvement case). The viewer retains information randomly because of repetition of the message. As a result, a respondent can show a high level of recall for a particular television advertisement, but the advertisement has little influence on brand attitudes.

Why is television a low-involvement medium? First, television advertising is animate, whereas the viewer is inanimate (passive). Second, the pace of viewing is out of the viewer's control, and the viewer has little opportunity for reflection or making connections.[32] In contrast, print media (magazines and newspapers) are high-involvement media because advertising is inanimate, whereas the reader is animate. The pace of exposure is within the reader's control, and the reader has more opportunity to reflect on the advertising.

Krugman predicted that television would be more effective for low-involvement cases and print advertising would be more effective for high-involvement cases. In their study, Grass and Wallace confirmed this view.[33] They found that for unmotivated consumers, television was more effective in conveying a message than print ads were. For motivated consumers, print ads were somewhat more effective. A study by Childers and Houston concluded that verbal messages (such as print ads) are best for high-involvement audiences and visual messages (such as TV ads) are best for low-involvement audiences.[34] Krugman summarized his view of television by saying, "The public lets down its guard to the repetitive commercial use of television. . . . It easily changes its ways of perceiving products and brands and its purchasing behavior without thinking very much about it at the time of TV exposure."[35] In other words, consumers can change beliefs about a brand, leading to a purchase decision with very little thought and deliberation involved.

Krugman's theory of passive learning also has implications for the nature of advertising. If consumers are passive and disinterested, brand evaluation is unlikely to occur. Therefore, conveying product benefits through an informational approach is unlikely to work. Advertising must use noninformational means such as symbols and imagery to convey the message.

▮ Consumer Behavior Implications of Passive Learning   Krugman's view of a **passive consumer** has stood many of the traditional behavioral concepts in marketing on their head. Table 4.3 lists the traditional behavioral concepts associated with an involved, active consumer and the parallel concepts of an uninvolved, passive consumer.

The newer low-involvement view holds the following principles:

1. *Consumers learn information at random.* Krugman views uninvolved consumers as those who learn from repetitive advertising, much as children learn nonsense syllables, by just picking up random stimuli and retaining them.

TABLE 4.3

The low-involvement, passive consumer versus the high-involvement, active consumer

Newer, low-involvement view of a passive consumer	Traditional, high-involvement view of an active consumer
1. Consumers learn information at random.	1. Consumers are information processors.
2. Consumers are information catchers.	2. Consumers are information seekers.
3. Consumers represent a passive audience for advertising. As a result, the effect of advertising on the consumers is strong.	3. Consumers represent an active audience for advertising. As a result, the effect of advertising on the consumer is weak.
4. Consumers buy first. If they do evaluate brands, it is done after the purchase.	4. Consumers evaluate brands before buying.
5. Consumers seek some acceptable level of satisfaction. As a result, consumers buy the brand least likely to give them problems and buy based on a few attributes. Familiarity is the key.	5. Consumers seek to maximize expected satisfaction. As a result, consumers compare brands to see which provide the most benefits related to needs and buy based on multi-attribute comparisons of brands.
6. Personality and lifestyle characteristics are not related to consumer behavior because the product is not closely tied to the consumer's identity and belief system.	6. Personality and lifestyle characteristics are related to consumer behavior because the product is closely tied to the consumer's identity and belief system.
7. Reference groups exert little influence on product choice because products are unlikely to be related to group norms and values.	7. Reference groups influence consumer behavior because of the importance of the product to group norms and values.

2. *Consumers are information catchers.* In the low-involvement case, consumers are information catchers; that is, passive receivers of information. High-involvement consumers are regarded as information seekers, actively searching for information from alternative sources and engaging in shopping behavior.

3. *Consumers represent a passive audience for advertising.* The low-involvement perspective views advertising as most effective when it deals with unimportant matters. Under these conditions, advertising is a much more effective medium for inducing purchasing behavior in low-involvement conditions. In Krugman's view, just being exposed to a commercial is persuasive and may lead consumers to purchase without the intervening step of comprehension.

The traditional active audience view is tied to the assumption that consumers are involved information seekers with strongly held brand attitudes. Under such conditions, consumers are likely to resist advertising that does not conform to prior beliefs (selective perception). This view logically leads to the conclusion that advertising is a weak vehicle for changing people's minds and is better suited to confirming strongly held beliefs. On balance, when consumers are passive and the message is relatively unimportant, the low-involvement view considers advertising a more powerful medium than does the traditional active audience view.

4. *Consumers evaluate brands after buying.* Krugman states that uninvolved consumers may buy simply due to a reminder effect since most such purchases are

unplanned. As a result, consumers often make the connection between a need and the brand in the store. Brand evaluation occurs after the purchase. For example, consumers select a lower-priced brand of paper towels in the store and then evaluate the brand after using it. The traditional view holds that consumers evaluate alternative brands before purchasing them.

5. *Consumers seek an acceptable rather than optimal level of satisfaction.* In the low-involvement case, consumers do not seek to maximize brand satisfaction. The energy required in search of the best product is not worth the expected benefits. A lower level of satisfaction is acceptable. Active consumers seek to maximize satisfaction by extensively evaluating brands. Comparing brand attributes, consumers select the brand that best meets their needs.

6. *Personality and lifestyle characteristics are not related to consumer behavior.* There is no reason to assume that personality variables such as compulsiveness and lifestyle variables such as sociability are related to behavior for uninvolved consumers. Most products consumers purchase are not central to their beliefs or self-identity. In contrast, the traditional view assumes that the consumer's personality and lifestyle are related to the purchase decision. Such relationships are assumed to exist because a high level of involvement assumes the product is important to the consumer's belief system and self-identity.

7. *Reference groups exert little influence on consumers in low-involvement conditions.* A study by Cocanougher and Bruce supports this view.[36] Since reference groups are not very important for low-involvement products, much of the advertising portraying social approval in the use of products such as floor wax or room deodorizers may be misplaced. The more relevant approach may be to portray the problems such products can eliminate. Involved consumers are more likely to be influenced by reference groups because a high-involvement product is likely to reflect the norms and values of the group. Products such as automobiles, homes, and stereo sets are visible and have important connotations as to status.

SHERIF'S THEORY OF SOCIAL JUDGMENT

A second theory that sheds additional light on uninvolved consumers is Sherif's **social judgment theory.** Sherif described an individual's position on an issue according to his or her involvement with the issue.[37] He identified a latitude of acceptance (the positions the individual accepts), a latitude of rejection (positions the individual rejects), and a latitude of noncommitment (positions toward which the individual is neutral). A highly involved individual who has a definite opinion about an issue would accept very few other positions and would reject a wide number of positions (narrow latitude of acceptance and wide latitude of rejection). An uninvolved individual would find more positions acceptable (wide latitude of acceptance) or would have no opinion about the issue (wide latitude of noncommitment).

A highly involved individual who agrees with a message (within his or her latitude of acceptance) interprets it as more positive than it actually is. This reaction represents an **assimilation effect.** A message that the individual disagrees with (within the latitude of rejection) is interpreted as more negative than it actually is. This reaction represents a **contrast effect.** For example, a car buff who just bought

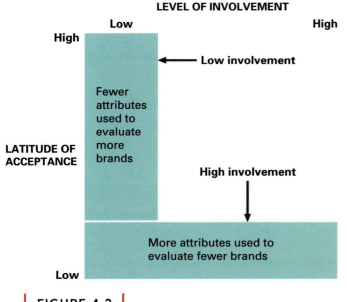

LEVEL OF INVOLVEMENT

Low — High

High

Low involvement ←

Fewer attributes used to evaluate more brands

LATITUDE OF ACCEPTANCE

High involvement ↓

More attributes used to evaluate fewer brands

Low

| **FIGURE 4.2** |

Social judgment theory applied to consumer behavior.

a Chevy Blazer and is very satisfied with the car might recall some comments a friend made about it as more positive than they were (assimilation). However, if very disappointed with the Blazer, the car buff may recall the same comments by the friend as more negative than they actually were (contrast). Therefore, the highly involved individual is more likely to perceive messages selectively based on his or her preconceptions and biases. The uninvolved individual is less likely to perceive the message selectively, and an assimilation or contrast effect is less likely to occur.

Sherif's theory as applied to consumer behavior is illustrated in Figure 4.2. Active, involved consumers would find fewer brands acceptable and would actively process information, whereas less involved consumers would find many brands acceptable and would engage in less information processing.

Sherif's theory conforms well to Krugman's concept of passive learning and provides more insight into passive consumers. Uninvolved consumers are willing to consider a wider number of brands because of a lack of commitment to one or several brands, but they do not search for alternatives. Given a lack of commitment, they are less willing to spend time interpreting advertising messages and evaluating brands. As a result, they perceive advertising with little cognitive activity and purchase brands in the easiest way possible—by purchasing the most familiar brand and buying the same brand repetitively. On this basis, social judgment theory and the theory of passive learning both agree that uninvolved consumers seek a satisfactory solution to problem solving, whereas involved consumers seek a more optimal solution.

Rothschild and Houston extend Sherif's theory to predict that highly involved consumers use more attributes to evaluate fewer brands (horizontal bar in Figure 4.2), while less involved consumers use fewer attributes to consider more brands (vertical bar in Figure 4.2).[38] This assumption makes sense, since more involved consumers' latitude of acceptance is narrower (fewer brands considered) and their level of information processing is greater (more attributes used in evaluation), whereas the reverse is true for less involved consumers.

ELABORATION LIKELIHOOD MODEL

Petty and Cacioppo's **elaboration likelihood model (ELM)** is a third theory that provides insight into uninvolved consumers. Illustrating how consumers process information in high- and low-involvement conditions,[39] the model presents a continuum from elaborate (central) processing to nonelaborate (peripheral) processing. The degree of elaboration depends on consumers' motivation to process information. If consumers are more involved, they are more motivated to process information, leading to more elaborate (central) processing. Less involved consumers are less motivated to process information, leading to nonelaborate (peripheral) processing.

Motivation to process the message is closely related to its relevance in meeting consumer needs.[40] The more relevant the message, the more likely consumers are to develop thoughts in support of or counter to its content (*i.e.,* the more consumers elaborate on the message). Thus, the arthritic consumer viewing a commercial for a pain reliever that claims to relieve the pain of arthritis is more likely to elaborate on the message by injecting his or her thoughts (such as, "This product might help me." or "This product could upset my stomach.") compared with the consumer who rarely encounters such pain. Uninvolved consumers are unlikely to develop such message-relevant thoughts. Elaboration is minimal because consumers are not motivated to process the information. They act as passive recipients of information.

Petty and Cacioppo's distinction between high and low elaboration is similar to Krugman's distinction between active and passive consumers, shown in Table 4.3. The difference is that the ELM focuses on the consumers' response to the message (in support of or against) and the nature of the stimuli that are most likely to persuade the active or passive information processor, whereas Krugman's model focuses on message exposure and comprehension.

In support of the ELM, Petty, Cacioppo, and Goldman found that involved consumers are more likely to be influenced by the quality and strength of the message (central cues). In contrast, less involved consumers are more likely to be influenced by stimuli that are peripheral to the message—for example, the use of color in the ad, the nature of the background, or the use of an expert spokesperson.[41] Such peripheral cues had little influence on involved consumers. Advertising to involved consumers should emphasize central message cues dealing with performance. Advertising to uninvolved consumers should use peripheral cues that might create a positive environment to stimulate the passive receipt of information.[42]

Strategic Implications of Low-Involvement Decision Making

The low-involvement perspective and the theories of Krugman, Sherif, and Petty and Cacioppo have implications for every facet of marketing strategy. This section reviews the strategic implications of low-involvement decision making and some strategic issues that arise from this perspective.

MARKETING STRATEGY

The most important implications of a low-involvement perspective are for advertising strategy. Important implications apply to other facets of marketing strategy as well.

▎ **Advertising**   Advertising strategy for a low-involvement product should be very different than for a high-involvement product. Differences in advertising approaches, as reflected in the theories cited, suggest the following strategies for low-involvement products:

1. *Advertising dollars should be spent in a campaign of high repetition and should use short-duration messages.*[43] As Krugman notes, repetition is necessary to gain exposure, even though processing the message may be minimal.[44] High repetition and short messages encourage passive learning and ensure brand familiarity.

An example is the constant repetition of Budweiser's "Whassup" ad campaign. The message was short, did not require the consumers' attention, and could, therefore, be processed passively. However, consumers remembered and easily linked it to the brand once they were in the store. In-store promotions and print ads with the same theme reinforced the television campaign.

2. *Advertising should focus on a few key points rather than on a broad-based information campaign.* Where there is little consumer interest or attention, there is limited ability to process and assimilate information. A proper campaign in the low-involvement case "utilizes short messages emphasizing a few key points."[45] Bic attempted this when it ran its campaign for a new product—Parfum Bic. It was short and to the point, having only two messages—disposability and a Parisian flavor. Interestingly, the product was a failure because many consumers viewed perfume as an involving product that did not require the disposability that Bic thought was a benefit. Bic fell into the trap of advertising an involving product with an uninvolving benefit.

3. *Visual and nonmessage components should be emphasized.*[46] Because uninvolved consumers learn passively and forget quickly, it is important to keep the product visually in front of them. In-store displays and packaging are important communication tools. Television advertising is more likely to be effective than print media because of the active visual component in television commercials. Where print is used, the product should be in the foreground and any peripheral cues in the background.

4. *Advertising should be the primary means of differentiating the product from that of the competition.* Because there are no substantial brand differences for many low-involvement products, advertising becomes a primary means of competitive differentiation. Advertisers use symbols and imagery as substitutes for actual product differences and to maintain interest in undifferentiated brands. In this respect, symbols that can be positively identified with the brand, such as the Pillsbury Doughboy, should be used. As Tyebjee states, "Communication differentiation rather than product differentiation is the strategic role of the sales proposition of low-involvement advertising."[47]

5. *Television rather than print media should be the primary vehicle for communication.* If less product information is required, a low-involvement medium such as television is more suitable. This is because television does not require consumers to evaluate the content of the communication as closely as they would for print. Print media are more suitable if the audience is active in seeking information and evaluating it.

▍ **Product Positioning**   Low-involvement products are more likely to be positioned to minimize problems, whereas high-involvement products are more likely to be positioned to maximize desired benefits. This is true because uninvolved consumers seek acceptable, not optimal, products.

Taking a high-involvement view, a product such as plastic wrap might be positioned to stress benefits such as extra strength and the protection it affords food. A low-involvement positioning might emphasize problem minimization such as a wrap that is less likely to shred or one that avoids freezer burn. Frequent reference to avoiding problems such as dirty floors, stained glasses, or "ring around the collar" suggests the prevalence of a problem minimization approach for low-involvement products.

▌ **Price**   Consumers buying low-involvement products are more likely to be price sensitive than consumers of high-involvement products. They frequently purchase on the basis of price alone, because brand comparisons are unimportant and there are few differences between brands. Therefore, a decrease in price or a coupon offer may be enough to influence the consumer to buy.

A study by Gotlieb, Schlacter, and St. Louis confirmed the greater price sensitivity of less involved consumers.[48] They found that it took less of a price difference to get uninvolved consumers to switch from their current brand compared to more involved consumers. In his study of margarine purchasers, Lastovicka also demonstrated the importance of price for uninvolved consumers. Among those who said the purchase was unimportant, 52 percent said price was the determining factor. Among those who thought the purchase important, only 22 percent said that price was the determinant.[49]

▌ **In-Store Stimuli**   Because most low-involvement purchases are unplanned, in-store stimuli such as coupons, displays, or price deals are more likely to be important when consumers are uninvolved. Consumers may purchase the brand at eye level or the one with the largest shelf space simply because of the reminder effect. The package may be more influential for low-involvement goods because it is encountered in the store.

▌ **Distribution**   Widespread distribution is particularly important for low-involvement products because consumers are not motivated to search for a brand. If a favored brand is not in the store, consumers are likely to make another choice. Marketing strategy must ensure in-store availability to discourage the likelihood of a brand switch.

▌ **Product Trial**   Attempts at inducing trial are particularly important for low-involvement products, because consumers may form a favorable attitude toward the brand after the purchase.[50] For instance, a consumer may try a free sample of toothpaste, like the taste, and purchase it. Not seeking to maximize satisfaction, the consumer may continue to purchase the toothpaste just because the brand is adequate.[51] Information search and further brand evaluation are not warranted. Due to inertia, trial may be sufficient to induce the consumer to continue purchasing the brand.

What strategies can the marketer use to encourage trial under low-involvement conditions? Free samples, deals and coupons, joint promotions with other products, in-store displays, and intensive distribution are all useful.

STRATEGIC ISSUES

Several strategic issues dealing with low-involvement decision making remain to be considered:

▌ Should marketers attempt to increase consumers' involvement for low-involvement products? If so, how?

▌ Given low involvement, should marketers attempt to shift consumers from a pattern of repetitive buying that reflects inertia to variety-seeking behavior?

■ Should marketers segment markets by degree of involvement so that different strategies are directed to high-involvement and low-involvement consumers for a particular product category?

■ **Shifting Consumers from Low to High Involvement** It would make sense for a marketer to try to get consumers more involved in a product. Because involvement means commitment, involved consumers are more likely to remain loyal to the marketer's brand in the face of competitive activity. What strategies can the marketer use to involve consumers with the product?

1. *Link the product to an involving issue.* Rothschild and Houston use Sherif's theory in citing one strategy as an attempt to widen the latitude of rejection of competitive brands. This can be done by linking the advertised brand to an involving issue.[52] Total initiated a campaign to link cereal (an uninvolving product) to the issue of individuals receiving the proper amount of calcium in their diets (a highly involving issue as a result of increased awareness of bone-mass loss as one ages). One Total ad suggested that its cereal was good for the bones because it provides 100 percent of the daily requirement of calcium.

    The Pampers and Crest web sites cited earlier were designed to link uninvolving products with involving issues—Pampers with advice for new parents, and Crest with cavity prevention.

2. *Create a problem and solve it.* Madison Avenue has tried to increase involvement in mundane products by trying to convince consumers they have problems they never knew about. In the 1940s and 1950s it was halitosis and body odor; in the 1960s and 1970s it was coffee nerves and dishpan hands; in the 1980s it was vaginal yeast infections. Pepsi-Cola tried a similar strategy in 1994 when it tried to convince consumers of the importance of dating cola cans. Stale cola never occurred to most consumers as a problem, and for good reason—most colas are consumed before they lose their fizz. As a result, Pepsi's attempt to create awareness of a problem fell flat.[53]

3. *Link the product to an involving personal situation.* Another strategy is to associate a low-involvement product with an involving situation. Tyebjee suggests relating the product to an activity in which the consumer is engaged.[54] He cites examples such as an early morning coffee commercial, advertisements of automobile products on radio during rush hours, and messages about sleep aids on nighttime television shows. In each case, involvement with the product increases because of the situation's relevance.

4. *Link the product to involving advertising.* A fourth strategy is to create involvement with the advertising in the hope that consumers will establish some link with the product. Lutz notes that just because "some products may be inherently low in involvement, their advertising need not be."[55] He cites two types of ads that may create involvement. An ego-defensive ad would help consumers defend themselves against inadequacy (*e.g.,* Marlboro smokers are masculine). A value-expressive advertisement expresses the consumers' values and beliefs. The ad for Dreft in Exhibit 4.5 links the laundry product to family values. It tries to create an emotional attachment for an uninvolving product.

    A third ad approach is to give an uninvolving product badge value through advertising. A Häagen-Dazs ad, for example, shows the product in the middle

Gentleness. Bottled. Dreft evokes a special kind of warmth. It's the first detergent made just for babies. It rinses out thoroughly, leaving towels soft. And it's the number one choice of pediatricians. Dreft embodies a clean you can trust.

of an elegant table setting with the statement, "It is now socially acceptable to eat Häagen-Dazs ice cream with your fingers." The ad tries to increase involvement with an uninvolving product category by a tongue-in-cheek attempt at creating snob appeal.

5. *Change the importance of product benefits.* A more difficult strategy is to try to change the importance consumers attach to product benefits. For example, Seven Up began advertising its flagship brand as having no caffeine, even though this was not a new attribute. With the greater health consciousness of American consumers, Seven Up felt it could increase the importance attached to caffeine content in soft drinks and thereby increase the involvement with its product.

6. *Introduce an important characteristic in the product.* Boyd, Ray, and Strong cite the possibility of introducing into a product an attribute that had not been considered important or that did not previously exist.[56] Examples include using additives in gasoline, adding bran to cereals, and introducing automatic rewinds in cameras.

These six strategies would assist the marketer in creating more product involvement—but involvement is relative. Creating greater involvement for toothpaste or ice cream does not mean that consumers are likely to engage in complex decision making when they evaluate brands. It means only that a moderate amount of cognitive activity may be stimulated through advertising and product policies.

Shifting Consumers from Inertia to Variety Seeking

Under a condition of low involvement, another question is whether marketers should encourage consumers to switch brands in a search for variety or to avoid product search and stay with the same brand (inertia) because of familiarity. (See Exhibit 4.6 for an example of switching from inertia to variety seeking.)

If a brand is a market leader, it would be in the brand's interest for the marketer to encourage inertia. If it is a lesser-known brand, the marketer should encourage variety seeking. In a low-involvement situation, consumers may purchase the market leader because of familiarity. In such conditions, the marketer should use advertising as a reminder. In-store conditions would also be important to maintain brand familiarity. To keep the brand in front of consumers, the market leader would place the brand in the dominant shelf space in the store. For less familiar brands, the marketer would attempt to encourage variety seeking by using deals, lower prices, coupons, and free samples to encourage trial. The objective is to induce consumers to switch brands and gain wider experience. Sherif's theory would support this view. In a low-involvement condition, the consumer has a wide latitude of acceptance, which suggests a greater willingness to try a diversity of brands.

"I've been faithful to this brand for 27 years. . . . Maybe it's time for a little fling!"

| EXHIBIT 4.6 |

Changing from inertia to variety seeking.

Reprinted with permission of Bill Whitehead.

Campbell's Soup is a good example of a market leader in a low-involvement category. Campbell's strategy has consistently been to advertise frequently to maintain familiarity and to dominate shelf space within the store. Other canned soups have occasionally been introduced. Competitors' strategies have reflected attempts to induce trial by lower prices, free samples, and appeals to variety in advertising. However, Campbell's high-frequency advertising campaigns and in-store dominance have made entry into the canned soup market difficult for other brands.

Segmenting Markets by Degree of Consumer Involvement

Because involvement can be measured on an individual level, markets can be segmented by consumer involvement. Purchasers of toothpaste can be categorized as high-, medium-, and low-involvement consumers. Therefore, should marketing strategies for a given product category be differentiated by the degree of consumer involvement? Is it feasible to direct different advertising strategies to a high- versus a low-involvement segment for the same product? Such an approach would be expensive and could confuse consumers. A more realistic approach would be to differentiate product rather than advertising strategy.

A good example is cereal. Ordinarily, cereal is regarded as a low-involvement product; however, to consumers concerned with nutritional and health benefits, it is more involving. A company would introduce a cereal brand to more involved consumers through print as well as TV advertising by communicating the benefits of the brand in an informationally oriented campaign. Deals and coupons would not be emphasized, but nutritional information would be prominently displayed in the ads and on the package.

To direct a brand to the low-involvement segment, marketers would use deals and coupons to induce trial and place less emphasis on nutritional information. The marketer would also seek in-store displays and eye-level shelf space for the brand to encourage impulse buying.

In short, where it is possible to identify high- and low-involvement segments, marketers should consider differentiating their strategies by offering different brands.

Societal Implications of Low-Involvement Decision Making

Consumers are involved with issues as well as with products. Some consumers are more highly involved than others with issues such as environmental protection, drug abuse, teenage drinking, and AIDS prevention. Whereas it would not necessarily benefit society to increase consumer involvement with bleach, toothpaste, or cars, it would be of benefit to increase involvement with the preceding societal issues.

The problem is that consumers who are not involved reflect the profile of Krugman's passive consumer—low awareness of the issues, little processing of information regarding these issues, and little or no consideration of alternative solutions. What kinds of consumers are least likely to be involved with societal issues? A few studies have been conducted to identify these consumers. For example, Webster's study of the ecologically conscious consumer found that those least likely to be involved with ecological issues were older, less educated, and less likely to be upwardly mobile.[57] Studies of political involvement indicate that those least involved have the exact same profile—older, less educated, lower income.[58]

A key question is how to increase involvement with societal issues among those least involved. Three groups—business, government, and consumer groups—have a role. At times, companies have played a constructive role. For example, American Airlines has attempted to increase awareness of cystic fibrosis for approximately the last two decades by raising money to help research the disease through its promotion of the Celebrity Ski weekend (see Exhibit 4.7). Consumer groups have played an active role in trying to increase awareness of and involvement in key issues. For example, the Environmental Defense Fund has mounted advertising campaigns to increase awareness of recycling; the Partnership for a Drug-Free America has run a nationwide campaign to increase awareness of drug abuse; and organizations such as Momentum have been instrumental in increasing awareness of AIDS prevention.

Government plays an indirect role in increasing involvement by trying to encourage participation in the political process and by publicizing legislation and activities at the federal, state, and local levels regarding issues such as pollution

EXHIBIT 4.7

Attempting to increase involvement with a societal issue.

American Airlines 2000 Celebrity Ski ad produced by Temerlin McClain.

control. A key question is whether the federal government should do more to provide information to those who might be most at risk—for example, providing more effective information on AIDS prevention to drug abusers or increasing awareness of the dangers of drinking and driving among teenagers.

SUMMARY

This chapter has focused on consumer choice in low-involvement situations. Four types of consumer behavior were identified using two dimensions: level of consumer involvement and level of decision making.

1. Complex decision making requires high consumer involvement and extensive information processing. Consumers form beliefs about brands, evaluate them, and then choose. This think-before-you-act model conforms to a traditional hierarchy of effects.

2. Brand loyalty requires high involvement but little information processing. Positive reinforcement results in the consumers' purchase of the same brand repetitively.

3. Inertia assumes a low level of involvement and little information processing. The consumer has found a reasonably satisfactory brand and will stick with it. There is little incentive to search for information and to evaluate alternative brands. Price deals and coupons may induce brand switching.

4. Limited decision making assumes a low level of involvement but a moderate amount of information processing. Consumers may switch from

inertia to limited decision making because of the introduction of a new product or changes in the existing product. Variety seeking because of boredom is an important example of limited decision making.

Although the Web tends to be associated with more involving products like cars, computers, and electronics, its growth as a means to reach and influence consumers has caused companies to evaluate this new medium as a way to market low-involvement products as well. The Web affords consumers more access to information, thus allowing them to become more involved with decision making for even low-involvement products.

Unplanned purchases are an important manifestation of low-involvement purchasing behavior, because consumers make most unplanned purchase decisions in the store. As a result, in-store stimuli such as displays, coupons, and price specials are more likely to be influential.

Three theories were presented as a basis for understanding low-involvement decision making. Krugman's theory of passive learning suggests that when consumers are not involved, they do not cognitively evaluate advertising messages. Exposure to advertising could occur without recall and comprehension. Sherif's theory of social judgment suggests that in conditions of low involvement, consumers are willing to consider many brands; they are likely to use only a few attributes to evaluate them, however. Petty and Cacioppo's elaboration likelihood model suggests that uninvolved consumers are more likely to react to nonmessage stimuli in communications than they are to the message itself.

The implications of low-involvement decision making for the development of marketing strategy were described. Several important strategic questions were raised:

- How can marketers get consumers more involved with low-involvement products?

- How can marketers of lesser-known brands get consumers to switch from inertia to variety-seeking behavior?

- Should marketers segment markets by consumers' degree of involvement?

The chapter closed by considering the societal implications of a lack of involvement in key issues such as environmental control, teenage drinking, and drug abuse and the role of business, consumer agencies, and government in increasing awareness and involvement.

Having focused on consumers' decision processes in Chapters 2 through 4, we next turn our attention to the individual consumer and how the consumer's psychological set and characteristics influence behavior.

QUESTIONS FOR DISCUSSION

1. Why did P&G establish web sites for Tide, Pampers, and Crest? Do you believe this is a wise investment of P&G's resources?

2. What is the strategic value of companies like Kellogg and Seven Up increasing consumer involvement with their products?

3. What are some of the ways a company can promote enduring involvement with its products in an online environment?

4. This chapter suggests that many consumers are not involved with the brand purchased and that they make decisions frequently based on inertia.
- If this is true, why do most marketing strategies assume an involved consumer?
- Why is it hard for a marketing manager to believe that most consumers might not be involved in the purchase of the company's brand?

5. Assume that a paper towel manufacturer has identified a segment of paper towel users who are more involved with the product because they recognize many usage situations that require a high-quality towel. The company decides to introduce a heavier-weight/high-quality towel to this involved segment. How would the marketing strategy used for this brand differ from that for most other paper towel brands?

6. Develop a profile of the involved consumer for paper towels versus the uninvolved consumer. Use Table 4.3 as a basis for profiling these two segments.

7. One group of consumers usually determines what cereal it will buy in advance and then goes to the store and buys it. Another usually makes its decision in the store. What differences might be employed in marketing to each group?

8. Why is variety seeking considered a form of low-involvement consumer behavior?

9. The elaboration likelihood model (ELM) suggests that nonmessage cues in advertising are more influential in low-involvement conditions.
   • Why is this true?
   • How can nonmessage cues be used in advertising strategies?

10. Discuss the two arguments that (a) advertising is a weak communications medium because of consumer involvement resulting in selective exposure (the active audience view) versus (b) advertising is a strong communications medium because of a lack of consumer involvement resulting in retention of the message with little cognitive activity (the passive audience view).
    • What is the predominant view in advertising today? Why?
    • Can you cite advertising examples that tend to support recognition on the part of advertisers of a passive audience?

11. Pick a low-involvement product category. Assume you are introducing a new brand in this category. Devise a strategy for creating higher involvement with the brand by utilizing the five strategies for shifting consumers from low to high involvement described in the chapter.

12. Consider the product you selected in Question 11.
    • Under what conditions would a marketer of a brand encourage variety seeking?
    • Under what conditions would the marketer encourage inertia?

13. Is it realistic to develop separate brand and marketing strategies for high- and low-involvement segments of a product category?

14. Should business, government, and consumer groups have a role in increasing consumer involvement with societal issues such as pollu-

tion control or teenage drinking? If so, what should that role be?

RESEARCH ASSIGNMENTS

1 Select a high-involvement and a low-involvement product being marketed or promoted on the Web.

• How do the web sites differ? Specifically, are there differences in (a) the amount of information offered, (b) the types of information, and (c) the number of links to other sites?

• How does the organization of each web site differ? Is one site more focused on brand equity than the other? Do the web sites differ in the amount of promotional materials offered?

• On this basis, why would you identify one web site as more involving than the other?

2 Select what you regard as a high-involvement and a low-involvement product category. Develop a means of measuring degree of consumer involvement for these two product categories using a consumer's rating of (a) the importance of the product, (b) the risk associated with the product, and (c) the emotional appeal of the product. Interview a small sample of consumers applying this measure.

• Was your assumption correct? That is, are significantly more consumers involved in what you identify as the high-involvement category compared with the low?

• Determine the following information for each consumer: (1) number of brands considered, (2) number of attributes cited as important in evaluating brands for each product, and (3) advertising recall for key brands.

Now categorize the sample into those above and below average on level of involvement for each product category. Are there differences in characteristics between those more and less involved according to the three preceding areas of information? Do your findings conform to the theories of (a) passive learning, (b) social judgment, and (c) elaboration likelihood?

NOTES

1. For a review of low-involvement consumer behavior, see Scott A. Hawkins and Stephen J. Hoch, "Low Involvement Learning: Memory Without Evaluation," *Journal of Consumer Research* 19 (September 1992), pp. 212–225; John C. Maloney and Bernard Silverman, eds., *Attitude Research Plays for High Stakes* (Chicago: American Marketing Association, 1979); and William L. Wilkie, ed., *Advances in Consumer Research*, Vol. 6 (Ann Arbor: Association for Consumer Research, 1979), pp. 174–199. See also the following sources: Judith L. Zaichowsky, "Measuring the Involvement Construct," *Journal of Consumer Research* 12 (December 1985), pp. 341–352; Marsha L. Richins and Peter H. Bloch, "After the New Wears Off: The Temporal Context of Product Involvement," *Journal of Consumer Research* 13 (September 1986), pp. 280–285; Banwari Mittal and Myung-Soo Lee, "Separating Brand-Choice Involvement from Product Involvement via Consumer Involvement Profiles," in Michael J. Houston, ed., *Advances in Consumer Research*, Vol. 15 (Provo, Utah: Association for Consumer Research, 1987), pp. 43–49; Sharon E. Beatty, Lynn R. Kahle, and Pamela Homer, "The Involvement-Commitment Model: Theory and Implications," *Journal of Business Research* 16 (March 1988), pp. 149–168; Carolyn L. Costley, "Meta Analysis of Involvement Research," in Houston, *Advances in Consumer Research*, Vol. 15, pp. 554–562; Richard L. Celsi and Jerry C. Olson, "The Role of Involvement in Attention and Comprehension Processes," *Journal of Consumer Research* 15 (September 1988), pp. 210–224; Dennis H. Gensch and Rajshekhar G. Javalgi, "The Influence of Involvement on Disaggregate Attribute Choice Models," *Journal of Consumer Research* 14 (June 1987), pp. 71–82; and Jean-Noel Kapferer and Gilles Laurent, "Consumer Involvement Profiles: A New Practical Approach to Consumer Involvement," *Journal of Advertising Research* 25 (December 1985–January 1986), pp. 48–56.

2. University of Michigan Business School, Case: *Procter & Gamble Online: Tide and Pampers Hit the Web* (1999).

3. "Exploration of World Wide Web Tilts From Eclectic to Mundane," *New York Times* (August 26, 2001), pp. 1, 22; "Internet Users Now Exceed 100 Million," *New York Times* (November 12, 1999), p. 8.

4. University of Michigan Business School, Case: *Procter & Gamble Online: Tide and Pampers Hit the Web* (1999).

5. David Kiley and Gerry Khermouch, "Going Internet for the Brand Makeover," www.brandweek.com, as of June 19, 2000.

6. See Giles Laurent and Jean-Noel Kapferer, "Measuring Consumer Involvement Profiles," *Journal of Marketing Research* 22 (February 1985), pp. 41–53.

7. Michael J. Houston and Michael L. Rothschild, "Conceptual and Methodological Perspectives on Involvement," in Subhash C. Jain, ed., *1978 Educators' Proceedings* (Chicago: American Marketing Association, 1978), pp. 184–187.

8. Celsi and Olson, "The Role of Involvement," pp. 210–224.

9. Kapferer and Laurent, "Consumer Involvement Profiles," pp. 48–56.

10. Laurent and Kapferer, "Measuring Consumer Involvement Profiles," pp. 41–53.

11. "How King Kellogg Beat the Blahs," *Fortune* (August 29, 1988), pp. 55–64.

12. Judith L. Zaichowsky and James H. Sood, "A Global Look at Consumer Involvement and Use of Products," *International Marketing Review* 6 (February 1988), pp. 20–34.

13. Harold H. Kassarjian and Waltraud M. Kassarjian, "Attitudes Under Low Commitment Conditions," in Maloney and Silverman, *Attitude Research Plays for High Stakes*, p. 8.

14. Nancy T. Hupfer and David M. Gardner, "Differential Involvement with Products and Issues: An Exploratory Study," in David M. Gardner, ed., *Proceedings of the 2nd Annual Conference of the Association for Consumer Research* (College Park, MD: Association for Consumer Research, 1971), pp. 262–269.

15. Tyzoon T. Tyebjee, "Refinement of the Involvement Concept: An Advertising Planning Point of View," in Maloney and Silverman, *Attitude Research Plays for High Stakes*, p. 106.

16. John L. Lastovicka, "Questioning the Concept of Involvement Defined Product Classes," in Wilkie, *Advances in Consumer Research*, pp. 174–179.

17. See Michael L. Rothschild, "Advertising Strategies for High and Low Involvement Situations," in Maloney and Silverman, *Attitude Research Plays for High Stakes*, pp. 74–93. Recent research has suggested that attitudes are formed in low-involvement conditions on a noncognitive basis. Yet these attitudes are likely to be weaker than those formed on a cognitive basis in high-involvement conditions. See Chris Janiszewski, "Preconscious Processing Effects: The Independence of Attitude Formation and Conscious Thought," *Journal of Consumer Research* 15 (September 1988), pp. 199–209.

18. "Major Study Details Ads' Effects on Sales," *Advertising Age* (June 21, 1982), pp. 1, 80.

19. Sharon E. Beatty and Lynn R. Kahle, "Alternative Hierarchies of the Attitude-Behavior Relationship: The Impact of Brand Commitment and Habit," *Journal of the Academy of Marketing Science* 16 (Summer 1988), pp. 1–10.

20. Robert S. Wyer and Thoas K. Srull, "Human Cognition in Its Social Context," *Psychological Review* 93 (July 1986), pp. 322–359.

21. Michael S. Mulvey, Jerry C. Olson, Richard L. Celsi, and Beth A. Walker, "Exploring the Relationships Between Means-End Knowledge and Involvement," *Advances in Consumer Research*, Vol. 21 (Provo, Utah: Association for Consumer Research, 1994), pp. 51–57.

22. Wayne D. Hoyer and Steven P. Brown, "Effects of Brand Awareness on Choice for a Common, Repeat-Purchase Product," *Journal of Consumer Research* 17 (September 1990), pp. 141–148.

23. John G. Lynch, Howard Marmorstein, and Michael F. Weigold, "Choices from Sets Including Remembered Brands: Use of Recalled Attributes and Prior Evaluations," *Journal of Consumer Research* 15 (September 1988), pp. 169–184.

24. For a similar four-part classification, see F. Steward DeBruicker, "An Appraisal of Low-Involvement Consumer Information Processing," in Maloney and Silverman, *Attitude Research Plays for High Stakes,* p. 124.

25. Rajeev Batra and Michael L. Ray, "Situational Effects of Advertising Repetition: The Moderating Influence of Motivation, Ability, and Opportunity to Respond," *Journal of Consumer Research* 12 (March 1986), pp. 432–445.

26. Hawkins and Hoch, "Low Involvement Learning," pp. 212–225.

27. Rebecca K. Rattner, Baarbara E. Kahn, and Daniel Kahneman, "Choosing Less-Preferred Experiences for the Sake of Variety," *Journal of Consumer Research* 26 (June 1999), pp. 1–15.

28. "Former Customers are Good Prospects," *Wall Street Journal* (April 22, 1982), p. 31.

29. Herbert E. Krugman, "The Impact of Television Advertising: Learning Without Involvement," *Public Opinion Quarterly* 29 (Fall 1965), pp. 349–356.

30. C. W. Sherif, M. Sherif, and R. W. Nebergall, *Attitude and Attitude Change* (Philadelphia: Saunders, 1965).

31. Richard E. Petty and John T. Cacioppo, *Attitudes and Persuasion: Classic and Contemporary Approaches* (Dubuque, IA: William C. Brown, 1981); and Richard E. Petty, John T. Cacioppo, and David Schumann, "Central and Peripheral Routes to Advertising Effectiveness: The Moderating Role of Involvement," *Journal of Consumer Research* 10 (September 1983), pp. 135–146.

32. Herbert E. Krugman, "The Measurement of Advertising Involvement," *Public Opinion Quarterly* 30 (Winter 1966), pp. 584–585.

33. Robert C. Grass and Wallace H. Wallace, "Advertising Communication: Print vs. TV," *Journal of Advertising Research* 14 (October 1974), pp. 19–23.

34. Terry L. Childers and Michael J. Houston, "Conditions for a Picture-Superiority Effect on Consumer Memory," *Journal of Consumer Research* 11 (September 1984), p. 652.

35. Krugman, "The Impact of Television Advertising . . . ," p. 354.

36. A. Benton Cocanougher and Grady Bruce, "Socially Distant Reference Groups and Consumer Aspirations," *Journal of Marketing Research* 8 (August 1971), pp. 378–381.

37. Sherif, Sherif, and Nebergall, *Attitude and Attitude Change*; and M. Sherif and C. E. Hovland, *Social Judgment* (New Haven, Conn.: Yale University Press, 1964).

38. Michael L. Rothschild and Michael J. Houston, "The Consumer Involvement Matrix: Some Preliminary Findings," in Barnett A. Greenberg and Danny N. Bellenger, *Proceedings of the American Marketing Association Educators' Conference,* Series. No. 41 (1977), pp. 95–98.

39. Petty, Cacioppo, and Schumann, "Central and Peripheral Routes to Advertising Effectiveness," pp. 135–146.

40. For a study showing that central processing is directed to consumer needs, see Jennifer L. Aaker and Angela Y. Lee, "'I' Seek Pleasures and 'We' Avoid Pains: The Role of Self-Regulatory Goals in Information Processing and Persuasion," *Journal of Consumer Research* 28 (June 2001), pp. 33–49.

41. Richard E. Petty, John T. Cacioppo, and Rachel Goldman, "Personal Involvement as a Determinant of Argument-Based Persuasion," *Journal of Personality and Social Psychology* 41 (November 1981), pp. 847–855; and Petty, Cacioppo, and Schumann, "Central and Peripheral Routes to Advertising Effectiveness," pp. 135–146.

42. For the conditions in which peripheral cues in advertising are most likely to be effective, see Jaideep Sengupta, Ronald C. Goodstein, and David S. Boniger, "All Cases Are Not Created Equal: Obtaining Attitude Persistence Under Low Involvement Conditions," *Journal of Consumer Research* 23 (March 1997), pp. 351–361; and Laura Peracchio and Joan Meyers-Levy, "Evaluating Persuasion-Enhancing Techniques From a Resource-matching Perspective," *Journal of Consumer Research* 24 (September 1997), pp. 178–191.

43. Rothschild, "Advertising Strategies for High and Low Involvement Situations," p. 84.

44. Krugman, "The Measurement of Advertising Involvement," pp. 584–585.

45. Rothschild, "Advertising Strategies for High and Low Involvement Situations," p. 84.

46. Krugman, "The Measurement of Advertising Involvement," pp. 584–585.

47. Tyebjee, "Refinement of the Involvement Concept," p. 97.

48. Jerry B. Gotlieb, John L. Schlacter, and Robert D. St. Louis, "Consumer Decision Making: A Model of the Effects of Involvement, Source Credibility, and Location on the Size of the Price Difference Required to Induce Consumers to Change Suppliers," *Psychology & Marketing* 9 (May/June 1992), pp. 191–206.

49. John L. Lastovicka, "The Low Involvement Point-of-Purchase: A Case Study of Margarine Buyers," paper presented at the first Consumer Involvement Conference, New York University, June 1982.

50. Thomas S. Robertson, "Low-Commitment Consumer Behavior," *Journal of Advertising Research* 16 (April 1976), p. 23; and Henry Assael, "The Conceptualization of a Construct of Variety-Seeking Behavior," Working Paper Series #79–43, Stern School of Business, New York University, May 1979, p. 5.

51. Peter L. Wright, "The Choice of a Choice Strategy: Simplifying vs. Optimizing," Faculty Working Paper No. 163, University of Illinois, Department of Business Administration, 1974.

52. Rothschild and Houston, "The Consumer Involvement Matrix," pp. 95–98.

53. "Pepsi-Cola to Stamp Dates for Freshness on Soda Cans," *New York Times* (March 31, 1994), pp. D1, D18.

54. Tyebjee, "Refinement of the Involvement Concept," p. 100.

55. Richard J. Lutz, "A Functional Theory Framework for Designing and Pretesting Advertising Themes," in Maloney and Silverman, *Attitude Research Plays for High Stakes,* p. 47.

56. Harper W. Boyd, Jr., Michael L. Ray, and Edward C. Strong, "An Attitudinal Framework for Advertising Strategy," *Journal of Marketing* 36 (April 1972), p. 31.

57. Frederick E. Webster, Jr., "Determining the Characteristics of the Socially Conscious Consumer," *Journal of Consumer Research* 2 (December 1975), pp. 188–196.

58. Lester W. Milbrath and M. L. Goel, *Political Participation,* 2nd ed. (New York: New York University Press, 1982).

Situational Influences in Decision Making

In Chapters 2 through 4, we saw how consumers go about making decisions and how at times their decisions become habitual. Because purchasing and consuming are the objectives of consumer decisions, the situation in which consumers purchase and consume products and services influences what they buy.

Regarding the purchase, the type of store (small boutique or department store), the purpose of the purchase (as a gift or for oneself), and the context of the purchase (shopping alone, with friends, assisted by a salesperson) are likely to influence the consumer. Regarding consumption, a consumer could easily say: "The brand I select depends on how, when, where, and why I'm going to use it." A consumer may prefer one brand of paper towels for heavy-duty cleaning and another for wiping, one brand of coffee to have alone and another to serve guests, and one make of automobile for long business trips and another for local shopping trips. These consumption situations directly affect purchasing behavior.

In this chapter, three types of situations—the purchase situation, the consumption situation, and the communication situation (the setting in which consumers are exposed to information)—are examined as influences on consumer decisions. The following topics are considered:

▌ The nature of these situational influences

▌ A model of consumer behavior based on situational effects

▌ Recent studies that account for consumption and purchase situations

▌ The use of situational variables in developing marketing strategies

Timex Positions Its Watches by How People Use Them

The consumption situation can be the basis for introducing and positioning a product. Timex has positioned its watches based on the consumption situation in appealing to the fitness segment. It switched from plain, low-priced watches to more stylish models positioned to younger, sports-oriented consumers and geared to specific situations. One watch, the Ironman, is designed for joggers and has features such as a stopwatch to count time and laps, storage for best times, and multiple alarms. Another, the Skiathlom, can fit over a parka and gloves and records temperature as well as time. The Expedition line of watches is designed for use during outdoor activities, like hiking, camping, or trailblazing. It features a digital compass, a countdown timer, and a stopwatch[1] (see Exhibit 5.1). As a result of Timex's repositioning to focus on particular sports situations, sales soared.

Leveraging this success, in 1994 Timex introduced a new line of watches, Timex Data Link watches, specifically geared to busy executives. These watches provided users with the ability to upload appointments and phone numbers from an electronic day-planner on a personal computer to the watch's memory. This upload occurred by simply pointing the watch at the computer screen. By 1996, the watch line had won numerous awards and was compatible with a popular electronic day-planner, Schedule1 for Windows 95. In 1998, Timex entered a joint arrangement with Motorola and introduced "Beepwear" functionality for its executive technology watches.[2] This is yet another example of Timex introducing a watch based on a consumption situation, scheduling and planning day-to-day activities.

By 2000, Timex was launching watches geared toward children. Rather than just changing the colors and presenting a generic Timex watch, Timex developed a unique watch for the consumption situation of children. Children use watches in a less serious way than adults and want something fun and cool to wear. The TMX watch is a brightly colored watch with a "mystery answer" function, so kids can ask a question and press a button to get one of fourteen random answers, and a screensaver function that displays neat, computer-like graphics.[3] Timex realized that even children may have unique consumption experiences, and it targeted watches to match those needs.

| EXHIBIT 5.1 |

Timex positions its watches by the usage situation.

© Chuck Swartzell/Visuals Unlimited.

The purchase situation as well as the consumption situation is central to marketing strategies. For example, the gift-giving situation is often the basis for advertising products such as watches, electronics, and toys. Manufacturers frequently advertise products for Father's or Mother's Day and for holidays, particularly Christmas. In many retail businesses, 50 percent of sales occur between Thanksgiving and Christmas, and most are for gift-giving occasions.

In this chapter, we consider the nature of situational influences on consumers, particularly the purchase and consumption situations, and their strategic importance in positioning products to consumers.

The Nature of Situational Influences

Situational influences are temporary conditions or settings that occur in the environment at a specific time and place. Examples are shopping for a gift, going skiing, and jogging. Because the usage situation is so important in affecting brand choice, it is surprising that most marketing studies do not account for the situation. Consumers are asked to rate brands on nutrition, taste, convenience, and other variables without reference to the usage situation. The assumption seems to be that brand attitudes, brand preferences, and consumer choice are the same regardless of the situation.

Clearly, if marketing strategy is to be geared to consumer needs and preferences, marketers must understand these needs and preferences for a particular usage situation. To gain such an understanding, we consider (1) the types of situations that influence consumers' decisions, (2) the characteristics of these situations, and (3) how they affect consumer behavior in the context of a model of situational influences.

Types of Situations

In this section, the three types of situations relevant to marketers are described—the purchase situation, the consumption situation, and the communication situation.[4]

PURCHASE SITUATION

The purchase situation affects many consumer decisions. Three factors are particularly important in affecting marketing strategy based on the purchasing situation: (1) the in-store purchase situation, (2) whether the purchase situation is for a gift-giving occasion, and (3) whether the purchase situation is unanticipated.

▌ In-Store Situations　　We saw the importance of store influences on shopping behavior when we discussed store choice in Chapters 2 and 3. In-store stimuli such as product availability, shelf position, pricing promotions, displays, and ease of shopping are important in influencing consumer purchasing decisions, especially for unplanned purchases.

The importance of the purchase situation is documented in many studies that have demonstrated the effects of price changes, displays, and salesperson influences on consumer behavior as a result of the in-store environment.[5] One such study of beauty aids found that the following situational factors were instrumental in influencing unplanned purchases:[6]

▮ *Price promotions.* Fifty-six percent of respondents bought more unplanned items because of these in-store stimuli.

▮ *Free samples.* Thirty-five percent of respondents bought more unplanned items because of free samples.

▮ *Displays.* Twenty-seven percent of respondents bought more unplanned items because of displays.

The importance of in-store stimuli is further demonstrated by the fact that expenditures on sales promotions have risen more rapidly than those on advertising. In 1988, total expenditures on sales promotions exceeded those for advertising for the first time; they have continued to increase at a more rapid rate since then, and the majority of such expenditures are for in-store stimuli such as price promotions, displays, and coupons.[7]

Because of these influences, it is important for marketers to identify various in-store situations and ask consumers how they would respond. For example, assume a manufacturer of a leading line of cereals conducts a survey and asks a sample of consumers how the following purchase-related situations may affect their brand choice:

▮ You are in the store and find your favorite brand of cereal is not in stock. (Do you go to another store, buy a substitute brand, or delay the purchase?)

▮ Your favorite brand of cereal costs five cents more than it did the last time you bought it. (Do you continue to buy it?)

▮ A brand of cereal that you have used occasionally has a price deal. (Do you consider buying?)

▮ You need cereal, but as you come into the store, you notice a long line at the checkout counter. (Do you go to another store?)

▮ You have some difficulty finding your favorite brand of cereal. (Do you ask a clerk for help or buy a competitive brand?)

Responses to these in-store situations may affect brand strategies. One essential indicator of brand loyalty, for example, is whether consumers stick with their favorite brand, regardless of in-store stimuli, or whether such stimuli influence them to try a competitive brand.

▮ **Gift-Giving Situations** A second purchase-related situation is whether consumers buy the product as a gift or for themselves. Marketers target a wide range of products from candy to clothing to electronics for holidays and other gift-giving occasions.

Purchasing a gift is likely to be more involving for consumers than purchasing a product for themselves. As Belk notes, when consumers give gifts, they are giving not only the physical product but also a symbolic message with it.[8] They want to ensure that they are sending the right message in terms of the type of gift, its price, and the brand name. As a result, they frequently spend more time selecting products for gifts than when selecting products for their own use. Consumers use different criteria in evaluating brands and are likely to select a different brand than if the purchase were for themselves.

Even if the products themselves are uninvolving, when placed in a gift-giving context, consumers are likely to be more involved. Clarke and Belk found that when buying uninvolving products such as bubble bath or blankets, consumers visited more stores and spent more time in information search when the purchase was for a gift.[9]

One result of this greater involvement in gift giving is that consumers are likely to see more risk in the selection. As a result, consumers are more likely to buy brand names and to shop in well-known stores. For example, a study by Ryan found that consumers are more likely to purchase small appliances for gifts from stores with a high-quality image.[10]

The gift-giving situation has been described as a *cultural ritual.* The consumer acquires a gift, removes the price tag, wraps the item, delivers it, awaits a reaction, receives a gift in return in some circumstances, and conveys a reaction. This process of exchanging gifts creates bonds of trust and dependence between the parties.

The nature of the gift-giving ritual is also culturally bound. One study found that in China, gift-giving rituals are more prescribed and related to social propriety and family values than they are in the United States.[11] Similarly, the Japanese view gifts as part of the bonding process in a highly group-oriented society, and they define more gift-giving occasions and give gifts to a much wider network of friends, acquaintances, and family.

Although gift giving has generally positive connotations, Wooten found that it often creates anxiety in the selection process, particularly if the gift giver is highly motivated and pessimistic about the chances that the gift will be a success.[12] Sherry, McGrath, and Levy go so far as to describe a darker side of gift giving in the context of rituals. Using depth interviews and ethnographic techniques (see Chapter 1), they found that many consumers saw gift giving and receiving as creating interpersonal conflicts. Consider the following narrative between husband and wife during a gift-giving occasion:[13]

JOHN: Mabel, why did your brother send me this plaid shirt?

MABEL: Billy called and asked if you liked the way he dressed. I couldn't hurt his feelings.

JOHN: Isn't it funny how your gift is so pretty and mine looks like a roving used car salesman's loungewear?

MABEL: John, just throw it away or give it to the Goodwill and let the whole matter drop.

JOHN: I don't want to let it drop, I paid good money to buy Bill and Nancy a gift that we thought was nice. We got them a set of very expensive wineglasses from Neiman Marcus.

MABEL: I told you what to do with the shirt once. Plus last year they got us both a really nice gift.

JOHN: Yeah, you can talk. Your gift is great. Mine is really garbage. Next year nothing, nothing. The damn cheapskates.

WEB APPLICATIONS

Gift Giving on the Web

Although the Web has not achieved its expectations as a source of purchasing, consumers seem to find the Web a useful source for gift ideas and purchases. Department stores such as Nordstrom and Neiman Marcus have sections for gift ideas and facilitate gift purchasing on the Web. They also maintain gift registries and wish lists that provide interested parties with suggestions from prospective recipients for occasions such as weddings or anniversaries. Sites such as Godiva.com, redenvelope.com, and calyxandcorolla.com specialize in particular types of gifts—from chocolates to flowers. Even though each of these sites can be used for purchasing items for oneself, the majority of users use them for purchasing gifts.

One of the advantages of these sites is that they make recommendations for consumers based on particular gift-giving situations—Mother's Day, birthdays, Christmas, and so on.

Additionally, they make it easy for consumers to have the gifts sent to one or more recipients, as opposed to having it sent to the purchaser; and there are generally multiple options for delivery—ranging from standard U.S. mail to overnight express delivery. Consumers are generally willing to pay more for a gift because the convenience and service are worth the additional cost; consequently, these sites are usually able to maintain slightly higher margins than a traditional shopping site.

Generally, consumers are most likely to buy gifts on the Web if (1) the items purchased are standardized and do not have to be examined (music, books); (2) the products are associated with a known brand name (Godiva, Tiffany's); (3) the item is unique to the site and cannot be purchased elsewhere; and (4) the consumer is pressed for time and is seeking delivery direct to the recipient.

OF CONSUMER BEHAVIOR

MABEL: Let me tell you something. That's my brother. I don't complain when your mother gives me a pair of KMart stockings which no one wears.

Most gift-giving occasions do not approach this degree of negativity, but in many cases there is underlying resentment at the obligatory nature of gift giving, the shopping task required, and the time deadlines involved. As Sherry et al. note, "Gift giving frequently becomes a contest, even an ordeal. Both giver and receiver may be caught in the snares of temporal deadlines and unattainable expectations."[14]

■ **Unanticipated Purchase Situations**   Purchase situations can sometimes be unanticipated. For example, if unexpected guests arrive, consumers may make a special shopping trip and pay higher prices to obtain needed items quickly. Cote, McCullough, and Reilly studied several unanticipated purchase situations, such as an unexpected price change, bumping into friends who might influence choice, and being short of time.[15] Among the products studied, unanticipated situations were particularly important in explaining the purchase of hamburgers, beer, and potato chips, items that typically can serve as last-minute fill-ins for unexpected situations. The study also found that consumer behavior for most of the food items studied was better predicted when unexpected situations were included as variables.

Two unanticipated situations—out-of-stock products and product failures—are particularly important because they precipitate the need for making a choice.

Consumers finding a food item out of stock may make a special purchase trip if the item is important enough. Product failures for durable goods like appliances and automobiles require consumers to make decisions to repair or replace the item. One study found that 60 percent of purchases of major home appliances resulted from breakdowns or the need for repairs.[16]

CONSUMPTION SITUATION

The consumption situation defines the context in which the consumer uses the brand. A consumer may use a particular brand of perfume or cologne for special occasions and another brand for everyday use. Another consumer may consider different brands of personal computers for home versus business use. A consumer might use regular coffee to serve to guests but instant when drinking coffee alone. Each of these consumption situations affects brand choice.

Marketers must identify consumption situations relevant to the product category. Bearden and Woodside identified the following consumption situations for beer:

▪ Entertaining close friends at home

▪ Going to a restaurant or lounge on Friday or Saturday night

▪ Watching a sports event or a favorite TV show

▪ Engaging in a sports activity or hobby

▪ Taking a weekend trip

▪ Working at home on the yard, house, or car

▪ Relaxing at home[17]

The consumption situation is also likely to affect consumers' choice of services. Gehrt and Pinto identified the following consumption situations for health-care services:[18]

▪ Whether the health problem is major or minor

▪ Whether the health problem affects the consumer or another member of the family

▪ Whether the health problem occurs at home or away from home

These situations directly affect the type of health care consumers choose. For example, going to a hospital's emergency room for a major health problem is more likely when consumers are away from home than it is when they are at home.

COMMUNICATION SITUATION

The communication situation is the setting in which consumers are exposed to information. It can be person to person (word-of-mouth communications between friends and neighbors or information from a salesperson) or impersonal (advertising, in-store displays). The communication situation could determine whether consumers notice, comprehend, and retain the information. Three types of situations may affect consumer response—the exposure situation, the context of the communication, and the consumer's mood state while receiving the communication.

Regarding the first factor, the following define various situations for advertising exposure:

■ Did the consumer hear a radio commercial while riding in the car or while sitting in the living room?

■ Did the consumer read a magazine inside or outside the home?

■ Did the consumer read the magazine as a pass-on issue?

■ Did the consumer see a TV commercial alone or with a group of people?

■ Did the consumer see the TV commercial in the context of watching an involving program?

■ Did the consumer see an ad or promotion online?

All these situations are likely to influence the effectiveness of the advertisement, independent of its content.

A second situational variable that is likely to affect reaction to the communication is the context in which it appears—for example, the type of programming in which a TV commercial appears. One study found that "happy" programming, in contrast to "sad" programming, led consumers to have more positive thoughts during exposure to the commercial and a higher level of recall.[19] Program content led some major advertisers to withdraw from reality shows because of their graphic content or sexual explicitness.

A third situational variable is the consumer's mood state when receiving the communication. Research has shown that whether consumers are happy or sad affects the processing and recall of brand information.[20] As a result, the consumer's mood state is also likely to affect comprehension and retention of the advertising message.[21]

The consumption and purchase situations are considered in the remainder of this chapter. Communication situations are explored further in Chapter 17.

Characteristics of Consumption and Purchase Situations

It is necessary not only to identify specific types of consumption or purchase situations, but also to consider the more general characteristics of such situations. Belk identified five characteristics:[22]

1. *Physical surroundings*—for example, a store's decor and shelf layout, being indoors or outside when using a product, being in a noisy room when watching TV.

2. *Social surroundings*—whether guests are present, the social occasion, the importance of friends and neighbors who are present when purchasing or consuming a product.

3. *Time*—whether it is breakfast, lunchtime, or between meals; seasonal factors such as winter versus summer relative to clothing; the time that has passed since the product was last consumed.

4. *Task definition*—shopping for oneself or for the family; shopping for a gift; cooking for oneself, for the family, or for guests.

5. *Antecedent states*—momentary conditions such as shopping when tired or anxious, buying a product on impulse, using a product when in an excited state. The consumer's mood when buying or using a product would be an antecedent state. Antecedent states are internal to consumers because they are determined by the consumer's state of mind. The four other situational characteristics are determined by the environment and are, therefore, external to consumers.

Situations are likely to be made up of several of these characteristics. For example, the purchase situation "shopping for a snack that the family can eat while watching television in the evening" is made up of the physical surroundings (at home), social surroundings (family), time (evening), and task definition (consumer is doing the shopping and family does the eating).

One study of attitudes toward do-it-yourself auto maintenance examined situations that might influence these attitudes such as physical surroundings (convenient area to work, tools available), time availability, and antecedent states (knowledge of maintenance procedures before starting work). These characteristics were found to affect willingness to engage in auto maintenance.[23]

THE EXPERIENTIAL NATURE OF SITUATIONAL INFLUENCES

Of the three types of situations cited—consumption, purchase, and communications—marketers have tended to concentrate on the purchase situation because they quite naturally focus on sales results. The purchase decision reflects consumer choice, but it is the consumption *experience* that ultimately determines whether the consumer is satisfied and repurchases the product. In determining the potential for a new interactive set-top box, for example, marketers could reasonably ask the following questions:

■ Under what circumstances is the new product most likely to be used (*physical surroundings*)?

■ Will it be used in a social context (*social surroundings*)?

■ When will it be used (*time*)?

■ What tasks are required for usage (*task definition*)?

■ What are the various attitudes and emotions that are likely to affect usage at various times (*antecedent states*)?

These questions reflect the nature of the consumption experience. Many marketers like Timex develop and position their products to reflect these experiences. In recent years, advertisers have begun to focus more on the emotional context of products with appeals to pleasure seeking, social status, and fantasy, for example. Such ads are designed to portray the experiential nature of the product as it is being consumed—the Harley-Davidson rider experiencing the freedom of the road, the young adult wearing Calvin Klein jeans enjoying their badge value, the wearer of Air Jordans experiencing the vicarious thrill of the Jordan name on the basketball court.

Why are advertisers relying more on the experiential nature of products? Because in an increasingly competitive environment, portraying a product such as jeans, motorcycles, or basketball shoes in an involving usage context can provide them with a competitive edge.

CHARACTERISTICS OF THE PURCHASE AND CONSUMPTION EXPERIENCE ON THE WEB

The Internet provides a particular focus on the purchase and consumption experience. In a broad sense, most Internet users are "consuming" information when using the Web to help them make purchase decisions. Therefore, their experiences in the consumption of information largely determine future usage. The same criteria used to evaluate purchase and consumption situations for products can be used to evaluate Internet usage, as follows:

- *Physical surroundings.* Internet usage can take place at home or at the office.

- *Social surroundings.* Using the Web as a solitary pursuit is different from using it in a social context.

- *Time.* Time poverty is one of the biggest motivators for Web usage. Consumers can now perform tasks ranging from banking and bill payment to gift purchasing on the Web. The main downside, however, is that with the proliferation of information on the Web, it can take a significant amount of time to surf and find the exact information a consumer is searching for.

- *Task definition.* There are multiple tasks for which consumers use the Web to find information or to make purchases. These include:
  - Hedonic search tasks—Consumers use the Web as a form of entertainment and often take pleasure in the search itself.
  - Utilitarian search tasks—Many consumers use the Web strictly as a utilitarian source of information. For example, if a consumer is looking for information to make a purchase, on- or offline, he or she may use the Web simply as a way to compare price or product alternatives before making a purchase.

- *Antecedent states.* Antecedent states can have both positive and negative effects on Web usage. Some web users enjoy the process of browsing and searching the Web and get involved to the point where they lose track of time and place. This has been described as a "flow state," meaning that Internet usage provides a "hedonic lift" to the user.[24] On the negative side, some users may approach the Web with a degree of trepidation because they are not comfortable with technology or do not trust that their privacy is protected.

A Model of Situational Influences

The simple model of consumer behavior in Chapter 1 described three possible influences on purchasing behavior: (1) the consumer, (2) environmental influences, and (3) marketing strategy. A model of situational determinants on consumer behavior describes behavior as a function of the same three basic forces, except that

| FIGURE 5.1 |

A model of situational
determinants of consumer
behavior.

Source: Figure adapted from
Russell W. Belk, "Situational
Variables and Consumer Behavior,"
Journal of Consumer Research 2
(December 1975), p. 158. Reprinted
with permission from The
University of Chicago Press.

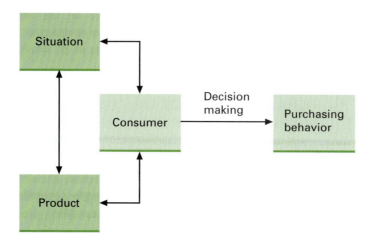

the consumers' environment is represented by the consumption, purchase, or communications situation and marketing strategy is represented by the product being consumed.

This model of situational influences is presented in Figure 5.1. The two outside forces acting on consumers are the product and the situation. The consumer reacts to the product and the situation and decides on the brand to be purchased. The interaction between the consumer's psychological set (needs, attitudes, and preferences), the situation, and the product results in a process of choice leading to behavior. The situation and the product can also be viewed in terms of the principle of **context,** which states that consumers organize stimuli into **figure** (foreground) and **ground** (background) by distinguishing stimuli that are prominent from those that are less prominent. This distinction is clear in viewing almost any print advertisement. The product generally appears in the foreground and the situation in the background. The ads in Exhibit 5.2 are examples. The ad for Benjamin Moore Paints shows the product (and a happy consumer) in the foreground, with the usage situation—a repainted bathroom—in the background. The ad for Lysol also shows the product in the foreground, with a consumption situation—keeping one's home free from germs and bacteria in order to protect one's family—in the background, and the tag line "Think of it as a security blanket for parents." In both cases, the background provides a relevant context for the product.

Although the situational model may seem simple compared with the descriptions of decision making in Chapters 2, 3, and 4, it is not as simple as it appears. Do consumers attribute behavior to the situation, to the product, or to both? Attributing behavior to the product means that the consumer is loyal to a particular brand and buys it regardless of the situation. Attributing behavior to the situation means that consumers purchase different brands for different situations; the situation rather than the product is the determining factor.

As a result, behavior may be due primarily to loyalty to the product regardless of the situation, or to the situation regardless of the product. But it is more likely that behavior is due to some interaction between product, situation, and the consumer. (The possibility of such interactions is represented in Figure 5.1 by the two-way arrows between situation, product, and consumer.)

CONSUMER ATTRIBUTIONS TO SITUATION VERSUS PRODUCT

A key consideration in the situational model is whether consumers attribute their behavior to the product's characteristics or to the situation. Consumer researchers have used attribution theory to answer this question. **Attribution theory** states that people attribute a cause to their prior behavior.[25] If consumers attribute behavior to the product rather than to the situation, attitudes toward the product are more positive, increasing the likelihood that consumers will purchase the product again.[26] Thus, if consumers attribute the purchase of a cereal to its nutritional content (a product attribute), rather than to the fact that it was on sale (a situational determinant), their attitudes toward the cereal are likely to be positive and they are likely to repurchase it. On the other hand, if attribution is to the situation ("I purchased because it was on sale"), their attitude toward the product is not likely to be as positive.[27] Several principles can be stated in determining whether the product or the situation is a more important influence on consumer behavior.

1. *The greater the degree of brand loyalty, the less important are situational influences.* For example, the loyal Michelob beer drinker makes no distinction between drinking Michelob when alone, with guests, while watching TV, with meals, between meals, or at any other time. This consumer happens to like Michelob, and the consumption situation does not influence purchasing behavior. The product, not the situation, is paramount in determining this consumer's behavior. Conversely, when loyalties are not strong, the consumption situation may be the determining factor in brand choice. A consumer may prefer a certain brand of beer because it is adequate and less expensive than most beers. For social occasions, this consumer may purchase a higher-priced beer. The consumption situation determines what brand the consumer buys.

2. *The higher the level of enduring product involvement, the less likely it is that situational factors determine behavior.* This principle relates to the distinction between enduring and situational involvement cited in Chapter 4. Enduring involvement is an ongoing interest in the product, whereas situational involvement is interest in the product triggered by a need to purchase it. In cases of high enduring involvement, consumers' interest in the product itself influences behavior. In cases of high situational involvement, consumers' need to purchase the product is the motivator for their brand evaluation. Clarke and Belk studied situational and enduring involvement for four product categories.[28] They found that when enduring involvement in the product is low, the situation tends to determine behavior. When enduring involvement is high, the situation is not as important.

3. *When a product has multiple uses, situational factors are less important in determining brand choice.* Conversely, products purchased for a single use are more likely to be influenced by the situation. Such products are most likely to be packaged goods. Studies of soft drinks,[29] snack foods,[30] beer,[31] meat products,[32] and breath fresheners[33] all have shown that the consumption situation directly affects behavior. Consumers tend to purchase these products for particular occasions—for meals, between meals, or social occasions. Products that consumers purchase for multiple uses are more likely to be durable goods. It is unlikely that consumers own different television sets for different viewing occasions or different stereo sets for different listening occasions. In some cases, however, situational effects may be important. For example, many two-car families use one car primarily for work purposes and another for local shopping or evening entertainment. Some camera buffs may have several cameras for different types of situations. Belk concluded that even though situational effects are less likely to be important for durable goods, "there are few if any product and service purchases which are devoid of potential consumption situation influences."[34]

In summary, situational factors tend to be less important when consumers are loyal to a brand, when consumers are involved with the product category on an ongoing basis, and when the product has multiple uses.

PROXIMITY OF SITUATION TO BEHAVIOR

Another issue relevant to the situational model in Figure 5.1 is the proximity of the situation to behavior. If the purchase and the situation are close in time, then the situation is likely to influence brand choice.[35] A consumer who is shopping for food for a big dinner party that evening may buy items not ordinarily purchased. A consumer who sees a sharp reduction in price for a particular brand (a purchase situation) may buy it even though it is not among those brands regularly purchased. In both cases, behavior is situation-specific. On the other hand, the consumer buying food items for normal usage may just be "stocking up" for the future. Situational requirements are not apparent, and the consumer purchases preferred brands. Under such conditions, behavior is due to preferences for the product rather than to the urgency of any situation.

Situational Influences on Product Attitudes, Choice, and Decision Making

The research cited in the previous section has shown that consumers frequently purchase products for particular situations. Research on situational influences has tended to focus on three areas: (1) product attitudes (Shake 'n' Bake chicken may be rated as convenient to prepare for lunch but not for dinner), (2) product choice (Coca-Cola may be purchased for parties rather than for meal occasions), and (3) the consumer's decision process (more product attributes are considered when selecting a hair dryer as a gift than when selecting it for oneself).

INFLUENCE ON PRODUCT ATTITUDES

A number of studies have shown that consumers' attitudes toward products and brands vary depending on the situation.[36] For example, in evaluating fast-food chains, a consumer may rate "convenience" more important for lunch or snack occasions than for dinner, and "good for the family" more important for dinner occasions than for lunch or snacks.

One study of transportation alternatives found that the value consumers placed on certain attributes varied by situation.[37] For example, individuals who avoided riding buses put more emphasis on shorter travel time and comfort when going to work than did bus riders. Such differences in needs and attitudes by situation have important implications for marketing strategy. Encouraging more people to use buses than cars to get to work would require convincing them that the bus can be as fast and as comfortable as a car.

Differences in attitudes by situation might indicate strengths and weaknesses of brands. If consumers rate a certain snack food particularly low on taste for parties and social occasions, the marketer should correct this potential weakness: Is it a problem with the product formulation or with the brand's image? Furthermore, if a brand is stronger in a particular situation, this strength should be exploited. For example, if consumers regard Budweiser as a good beer to have alone, rather than on social occasions, perhaps marketers should emphasize taste benefits for situations when beer drinkers are alone.

Miller and Ginter undertook one of the most comprehensive studies of the situational determinants of product attitudes.[38] They asked consumers to rate eight fast-food restaurants on attributes such as speed of service, variety, cleanliness, and convenience for four situations:

1. Lunch on a weekday
2. Snack during a shopping trip
3. Evening meal when rushed for time
4. Evening meal with the family when not rushed for time

Convenience and speed of service were considered most important for lunch on a weekday and for evening meals when rushed. Variety of menu and popularity with children were most important for evening meals with the family when not rushed for time. Thus, consumers do differentiate product benefits by situation.

Consumers also rated various fast-food outlets by situation. They saw Arby's and Burger King as more convenient for snack occasions during a shopping trip. Burger Chef and McDonald's were more convenient for evening meal occasions.

INFLUENCE ON PRODUCT CHOICE

The final element in the Miller and Ginter study cited in the last subsection was to evaluate the ability of the four situations in the study to predict consumers' restaurant choices. The results are shown in Table 5.1. Miller and Ginter predicted consumers' choices of fast-food restaurants with and without the benefit of knowing the situation. When the consumption situation was included in the prediction, the model correctly predicted a greater proportion of consumers' restaurant choices than a model that did not take account of the situation. For example, the situational model predicted the right choice for lunchtime occasions 41.3 percent of the time, compared with 30.5 percent of the time for the nonsituational model. This result shows the importance of situation in explaining consumer behavior.

Other studies have also found that situational variables better predict product choice. For example, Stanton and Bonner found that situational variables outperformed demographics and attitudes in predicting the choice of a food item.[39] Similarly, Umesh and Cote found that they could better predict choice of soft drinks by including situational variables.[40]

TABLE 5.1

Prediction of choice of fast-food outlets using a nonsituational model versus a situational model

	% Correct Predictions	
Situation	**Nonsituational model**	**Situational model**
Lunch on a weekday	30.5	41.3
Evening meal when rushed for time	38.6	44.0
Evening meal with family when not rushed for time	45.9	49.5
Snack during a shopping trip	31.6	34.7

Source: From Kenneth E. Miller and James L. Ginter, "An Investigation of Situational Variation in Brand Choice Behavior and Attitudes," *Journal of Marketing Research* 16 (February 1979), p. 121. Reprinted with permission.

INFLUENCE ON DECISION MAKING

Studies have focused on the effects of different situations on decision making. It is likely that the number of brands considered, the amount of search, the type of information sought, and the sources of information vary by the consumption and purchase situations. For example, one study found that when a shopper is with friends, he or she visits more stores and makes more unplanned purchases than when shopping alone.[41]

Several studies have examined differences in decision making when consumers buy a product as a gift or for themselves. As mentioned previously, consumers' purchase decisions for gifts tend to be more involving than when buying for themselves. As a result, as Clarke and Belk note, shopping for a gift "increases the overall level of arousal and causes more effort to be expended."[42] It follows that consumers' information search is more extensive when purchasing a gift than when purchasing for themselves.

Studies have found other factors that characterize decision making for gifts:

▌ Consumers are more likely to use in-store information sources (such as salespeople) than out-of-store sources (such as advertising).[43]

▌ Consumers are likely to set a price limit beforehand.[44]

▌ Consumers are likely to shop in higher-quality stores and to buy prestige brands.[45]

▌ Consumers consider stores' policies on return merchandise to be important.[46]

The studies that have been cited evaluated differences in decision making for purchasing situations. Studies have also focused on differences in decision making for consumption situations.

A study by Dhar and Simonson recognized that consumers often use several products for a given consumption occasion—for example, cereal and eggs for breakfast.[47] These researchers evaluated the decision-making implications when such products involve positive and negative tradeoffs (nutritional cereal but high-cholesterol eggs). They point out that a pizza parlor could balance the "sin" associated with eating pizza by offering health foods as well. Similarly, service providers could bundle services for particular occasions to maximize satisfaction—for example, having conferences sponsored by business organizations in plush resorts to provide guilt-free fun.

Use of Situational Variables in Marketing Strategy

Marketers can use situational variables in marketing strategy in two ways: (1) by introducing new usage situations or (2) by targeting existing ones.

INTRODUCING NEW USAGE SITUATIONS

An effective marketing strategy is to influence consumers to use the product for new usage situations. Car wax was introduced in the 1930s when Johnson Products discovered that consumers were using their furniture wax on cars. Similarly, Arm & Hammer expanded the uses for baking soda by first advertising it as a refrigerator deodorizer and then suggesting it could also be used to brush teeth. The company took the next logical step by introducing separate products in these categories—a toothpaste product and a room deodorizer with baking soda as a basic ingredient.

Wansick and Ray examined how advertising can effectively encourage consumers to use a brand in new situations in the context of *usage expansion* strategies.[48] They found that advertising is effective in proposing new uses for a brand as long as the new usage occasion is congruent with the consumer's existing notion of how to use the product. For example, if Campbell Soup Company proposes drinking soup for breakfast, the question is whether this usage is consistent with eating hot cereals for breakfast. Consumers who see a difference between eating hot cereal and drinking soup for breakfast are likely to reject such a usage expansion strategy.

In this context, Johnson's Wax could have advertised using furniture wax on cars ("Get your car as shiny as you get your dining room table") because consumers saw this usage extension as congruent. But Pepsi failed in trying to get consumers to drink Pepsi AM at breakfast because the usage situation was not congruent with the consumers' existing notion of carbonated soft drink usage.

TARGETING EXISTING USAGE SITUATIONS

Marketers can target existing usage situations by (1) segmenting users by product usage, (2) developing new products to appeal to specific usage situations, (3) advertising to position products to particular usage situations, (4) distributing products to satisfy situational needs, and (5) targeting web sites to specific situations.

▌ **Market Segmentation**   Market segmentation often depends on consumers' usage situations. A snack food company, Great Snacks, conducted a study to define consumer segments by similarity in needs. It identified six segments: nutritional snackers, weight watchers, guilty snackers, party snackers, price-oriented snackers, and indiscriminate snackers.

The consumption situation was important in defining five of the six segments. Both nutritional snackers and weight watchers were less likely to eat snacks between meals. Guilty snackers tended to eat snack foods between meals. Party snackers obviously ate and served snacks primarily at social occasions. Price-oriented snackers bought based on the purchase situation rather than the consumption situation, buying snacks primarily when they were promoted by price deals and coupons. The only segment for which situational factors were not important was the indiscriminate snackers who tended to eat snacks in most usage occasions.

The importance of the situation was evident when Great Snacks considered introducing a new chip-type snack made of only natural ingredients. The fact that the target market—nutritional snackers—was unlikely to consume the product during the prime time for snacking (between meals) caused the company to reevaluate the viability of targeting the product to this segment.

▌ **New Product Development**   Companies can develop new products for specific situations. As mentioned at the beginning of the chapter, Timex developed new line extensions of its watches for various sports situations and extended new product introductions to include watches designed for specific business purposes.

Pepsi targeted Pepsi AM to a particular situation, the need for a "pick-me-up" at breakfast. It advertised the brand to baby boomers as a healthier substitute for coffee to provide that caffeine boost in the morning. But the product flopped because consumers could not accept a carbonated cola drink for breakfast.

▌ **Product Positioning**   A study of paper towel usage shows the importance of situational variables in positioning products. Heavy-duty uses included cleaning ovens, washing windows, cleaning cars; light-duty uses involved wiping hands,

STRATEGIC APPLICATIONS

Crest Whitestrips—From the Dentist's Office to Home Use

In July 2000, packaged goods giant Procter & Gamble launched Crest Whitestrips, an over-the-counter kit designed to whiten teeth at home, rather than at the dentist's office (see Exhibit 5.3). The strips are coated with a hydrogen peroxide whitening gel and other enamel-safe whitening agents that dentists traditionally use and are designed to be worn twice a day for thirty-minute intervals over a two-week period.

The product introduction came at a time when P&G had seen loss of market share to other brands in much of its core business. Industry analysts noted that the company had not had a true blockbuster product, akin to Tide or Pampers, in more than two decades. But P&G saw several developments that spelled opportunity. First, 50 percent of people surveyed wanted whiter teeth, but only 5 percent had actually had

their teeth whitened. Second, a greater number of baby boomers, as they reached middle age, were looking for anything to make themselves look or feel younger. Third, the vast majority of consumers could not afford, or did not want to spend, upwards of $500 to have their teeth professionally whitened. The company put these trends together and saw an opportunity to develop a product for a specific situation: a $44 tooth-whitening kit designed for use in the home. In the process, P&G was expected to balloon the size of the fledgling tooth-whitening product industry beyond the $250 million mark.

On introduction of Whitestrips, P&G did not immediately sell through its normal retail distribution channels, but instead started selling directly on its web site. The purpose was not to bypass retailers but to attract early adopters before a full-scale retail rollout. P&G provided detailed information on its web site, as well as recommendations from dentists, to educate consumers before the product became available in stores.

P&G's product launch is an interesting example of the expansion of a usage situation. According to psychologist Carol Moog, "If your teeth aren't straight—or white—it's not just a sign of age but a sign of poverty. People used to talk about eyes as jewels. Now, teeth are jewelry."

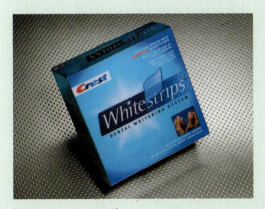

| EXHIBIT 5.3 |

A product targeted to home usage occasions: Crest Whitestrips.

The Procter & Gamble Company.

Sources: "Something to Smile About," *Global Cosmetic Industry* (September 2000), p. 10; "Balancing Act: P&G Shuffles Brands, People," *Brandweek* (March 26, 2001), p. 8; "Marketers Find Internet Opens New Avenues to Customers," *New York Times* (March 26, 2001), p. C.1; "Crest Markets White Teeth to the Masses; Boomers Expected to Bite as $44 Strips Hit Stores," *USA Today* (May 4, 2001), p. B.1; www.dentalcare2.com.

wiping kitchen counters, wiping dishes; and decorative uses were for napkins or placemats.[49] Thus, positioning a paper towel requires recognition of the usage situation. A positioning toward heavy-duty usage should dictate the product's characteristics (multi-ply), the target segment to which the product should be positioned (the heavy-duty user), the promotional appeals (strength and durability), and possibly the media to be used (based on the demographic characteristics of the heavy-duty segment).

▌ Advertising   The usage situation can also dictate promotional appeals. If consumers purchase a soft drink primarily for social occasions, then marketers should advertise it in this context. Similarly, if a certain segment purchases a food processor primarily for cooking for guests, marketers should advertise it in the context of meal preparations for guests rather than for the family. Deighton, Henderson, and Neslin referred to the practice of advertising products in the context of the usage situation as **framing.**[50] That is, the usage situation frames the product in a relevant context for consumers. On this basis, the ad "tells the consumer what to look for in the product-usage experience."

The ad in Exhibit 5.4 frames a product in a usage situation. This ad for Völkl skis declares that the SuperSport ski is "the new all-mountain standard." It shows a skier enjoying the product down the side of a ski slope.

Two other bases for advertising products by situation are gift giving and seasonal usage. Ads for holidays and special occasions are fairly commonplace. An advertising campaign may also reflect seasonal usage—for example, iced tea during the

▌ EXHIBIT 5.4 ▐

An ad that frames a product in a usage situation.

Courtesy Völkl Sport America.

summer and hot soup in the winter. Because consumption of Gatorade is heavier in the summer, the company tries to smooth out demand by advertising Gatorade not only as a summer thirst quencher during active sports activities, but also as a winter fluid replacement for consumers with colds and the flu. General Foods follows a similar strategy for Sanka coffee, but with reversed seasons. Because coffee consumption is heavier in the winter, the company advertises iced Sanka for the summer.

▌ Distribution　　The situation may also influence distribution strategies. One of the competitive advantages of 7-Eleven, the largest chain of convenience food stores in the country, is that it stays open late to cater to unanticipated situations food shoppers face when most supermarkets are closed.

Perrier's distribution strategy is also a function of situational influences. As a carbonated mineral water, Perrier tends to be taken at mealtimes. As a result, more than a third of its bottles are shipped to restaurants, hotels, and bars.[51]

▌ Web Site Development　　The situations in which web sites are used affect their design and purpose. Thus, a site for locating and purchasing gifts is designed and arranged differently from a site that is for personal entertainment.

We have noted that consumers have found the Web to be a good vehicle for searching for and purchasing gifts. In other contexts, sites are built around social situations and social interaction. Some sites, such as talkcity.com and chatweb.net, are designed to act as portals for consumers to locate other consumers who have the same interests or are in similar geographic areas. Others, such as cnn.com's Talk Back live and artistdirect.com, were developed around more specific consumer interest—specifically politics and music. Regardless of the topic, these sites are generally free to users and are supported by advertising. When consumers register with the site, they provide specific information that allows marketers to target them more directly according to their interests. Although there are currently many of these chat-based sites, there is some uncertainty as to how many can be economically viable, as advertising has proven to be a poor source of revenue to maintain these sites.

Many consumers also choose to use the Web for entertainment purposes. Whereas some sites, such as uproar.com, serve as portals to all sorts of games, game shows, and lotteries, others, such as mtv.com, are linked to or affiliated with other forms of media (in this case the television network). In all these cases, web site development is driven by the situational context that the site is targeting.

SUMMARY

The usage situation is an important factor that directly influences consumers' decisions. Marketers have largely overlooked this factor, however. It should influence marketing strategy by affecting how markets are segmented, products are positioned, and brands are advertised and distributed.

Three types of situations have important implications for marketing: the consumption situation, the purchase situation, and the communication situation. The consumption situation refers to the circumstances in which consumers use the product. The purchase situation refers to the conditions under which consumers make a decision (*e.g.,* whether purchasing an item as a gift or for themselves) and the in-store conditions at the time of the purchase. The communication situation refers to the conditions in which advertising exposure occurs (*e.g.,* a radio commercial heard in a car or at home, or TV watched alone or with friends).

Gift giving was cited as a particularly important purchase situation since gifts represent a substantial portion of retail sales. Consumers buying gifts tend to be more involved with the purchase and, as a result, are more likely to see the purchase as risky. The Web is an excellent vehicle for searching and buying gifts because it offers advantages based on selection and direct delivery to the recipient.

The chapter described a simple model of the decision process incorporating situational factors. The model recognizes that a consumer's decision can be a function of the brand, the situation, the consumer's own predispositions, or, more likely, some combination of these factors. Various studies were cited demonstrating that for many products, the most important factor in explaining behavior is the interaction between situation and product. That is, choice of brands is likely to vary by situation. However, the situation is not important in all cases; when a high level of brand loyalty exists or there is enduring involvement with the product, consumers may buy a particular brand regardless of the situation.

Studies have examined the effects of situational influences on product attitudes, product choice, and the nature of consumer decision making. In most cases, situational variables have led to a better understanding of consumer attitudes and a better prediction of consumer choices. Marketers should pay special attention to situational variables to understand how best to develop, position, or extend their brands in the marketplace. The chapter described applications of situational variables to market segmentation, product positioning, new products, advertising, distribution strategies, and web site development.

The next section of the book, Part Three, considers what the consumer brings to the decision process; namely, his or her own individual predispositions in the form of perceptions, attitudes, and needs.

QUESTIONS FOR DISCUSSION

1. A manufacturer of instant coffee considers introducing a new line of continental flavors to be advertised for special occasions. The objective is to gear marketing strategy to the situations that warrant distinctive coffee that can be conveniently prepared.

- For what types of situations should the coffee be positioned?
- What are the implications for (a) defining a target segment and (b) developing an advertising strategy?

2. A product manager for a leading brand of paper towels notices substantial variation in sales performance for the brand among stores in the same trading area. The manager hypothesizes that marked differences in the in-store purchase situation may be causing variation in sales. What differences in in-store purchase situations could be causing differences in sales?

3. A manufacturer of hair dryers identifies two types of purchase situations that lead to differences in brand evaluation: (a) purchase for self and (b) purchase as a gift.

- What are the marketing implications for positioning a product to appeal to each of these purchasing situations?

- What may be the differences in brand evaluation in each condition?

4. How might a large department store try to counteract some of the negative aspects of gift giving cited in the Sherry et al. study on p. 124?

5. Develop a list of communication situations that may affect a consumer's awareness and comprehension of (a) print advertising and (b) television advertising.

6. Under what conditions is brand choice more likely to be influenced by the situation than by product characteristics? Under what conditions is the reverse likely to be true?

7. How does the consumption experience differ in the online versus the offline world? Identify a key difference between them for each of the five situational characteristics.

8. What types of issues must traditional brick-and-mortar marketers concern themselves with as they try to translate their unique situation-specific product attributes onto the Web?

9. A company marketing a leading brand of yogurt has always focused on yogurt's nutritional benefits without considering the possibility of varying its appeal to depend on the usage situation.
   - Could the product benefits consumers see in yogurt vary by the usage situation? Specify.
   - What are the marketing implications of variations in perceived benefits by usage situation?

10. Why are situational influences more important when they are contiguous to behavior? Cite some examples.

11. What are the marketing implications of the Wansink and Ray study (p. 135) for advertising existing products in new usage situations?

12. Market segments can be defined by usage situation for snack foods; for example, there are between-meal snackers and party snackers. What market segments could be identified by usage situation for (a) deodorants and (b) paper towels?

13. What marketing opportunities led P&G to introduce Crest Whitestrips? How were these opportunities situation-specific?

14. What do we mean by the framing effect in advertising? Cite two examples of the framing effect other than that shown in Exhibit 5.4.

15. What are some examples of purchase and consumption situations that might influence distribution strategies?

RESEARCH ASSIGNMENTS

1 Select two product categories that are frequently given as gifts: one that is higher in price (*e.g.*, hair dryers or watches) and one that is lower priced (*e.g.*, compact discs or books). Select a sample of about fifty respondents and ask them (1) how much time they would spend and (2) what information sources they would consult in choosing a particular alternative for the following:

a. a product for themselves
b. a birthday gift for a close friend
c. a wedding gift for a close friend
d. a thank-you gift to repay someone for watching their home or apartment while they were away
e. a birthday gift for a casual friend[52]

- Did respondents spend more time in selecting a product for themselves (a) or as a gift (b–e)?
- Did respondents spend more time in selecting a gift in a high-involvement gift-giving situation (b and c) or in a low-involvement gift-giving situation (d and e)?
- How did sources of information differ when respondents bought for themselves versus buying a gift? when they gave a gift in a high- versus a low-involvement situation?
- Were there any differences in the amount of time respondents spent in searching for a high-priced gift versus a low-priced gift? in the sources of information used in evaluating the higher- versus the lower-priced gift?

2 Select a product category you believe is likely to be affected by the usage situation (soft drinks, paper towels, coffee, snacks, etc.). Conduct several depth interviews with consumers to define (a) the four most frequent usage situations for the category and (b) a vocabulary of evaluative product attributes. Then develop a questionnaire in which consumers are asked to rate the following:

a. The importance of each of the attributes by the four most important situations you defined in the depth interviews (*e.g.,* How important is a soft drink that is refreshing when drinking it alone? when drinking it at a party?)

b. The three leading brands by the vocabulary of product attributes for the four most important situations (*e.g.,* Rate Pepsi on "refreshing" when drinking it alone, drinking it at a party, and so on.)

- What is the variation in importance ratings by usage situation?

- What is the variation in brand ratings by usage situation?

- What are the implications of variations in importance ratings and brand image by situation for (a) positioning a new product, (b) repositioning an existing product, (c) advertising strategy, and (d) definition of a target group?

3 Do a series of depth interviews with consumers to develop a comprehensive situational inventory for snack products. Make sure the inventory contains the five elements Belk defined: physical surroundings, social surroundings, time, task definition, and antecedent states. Submit the inventory to a small sample of consumers (ten to twenty) and determine the frequency with which various snack foods (potato chips, pretzels, cheese, crackers, fruit, cookies) are considered for each usage occasion. What are the implications of your findings for (a) product line strategy, (b) new product development, and (c) advertising?

4 Find examples of two web sites that consumers would use in each of the following situations: gift giving, social interaction, and entertainment.

- How do the sites differ in terms of design and the provisions for consumer interactivity? interface?

- In what ways do each of the sites account for the usage situation?

- What are the different ways in which consumers can customize searches, information, or interests based on specific usage situations on each site?

NOTES

1. Timex Web site at www.timex.com as of March 20, 2000.
2. Ibid.
3. Ibid.
4. Flemming Hansen, *Consumer Choice Behavior* (New York: The Free Press, 1972).
5. See, for example, C. Whan Park, Easwar S. Iyer, and Daniel C. Smith, "The Effects of Situational Factors on In-Store Grocery Shopping Behavior: The Role of Store Environment and Time Available for Shopping," *Journal of Consumer Research* 15 (March 1989), pp. 422–433.
6. "The Teen Market," *Product Marketing* (Spring 1982), p. S26.
7. "Sales Promotion: The Year in Review," *Marketing & Media Decisions* (July 1989), pp. 124–126; and "Ad Spending Outlook Brightens," *Advertising Age* (May 15, 1989), p. 24.
8. Russell Belk, "Gift-Giving Behavior," in J. Sheth, ed., *Research in Marketing,* Vol. 2 (Greenwich, Conn.: JAI Press, 1979), pp. 95–126.
9. Keith Clarke and Russell Belk, "The Effects of Product Involvement and Task Definition on Anticipated Consumer Effort," in William Wilkie, ed., *Advances in Consumer Research,* Vol. 6 (Ann Arbor, Mich.: Association for Consumer Research, 1979), pp. 313–317.
10. A. Ryan, "Consumer Gift-Giving Behavior: An Exploratory Analysis," in Danny Bellinger and Barnett A. Greenberg, eds., *Contemporary Marketing Thought* (Chicago: American Marketing Association, 1977), pp. 100–104.
11. Amanda Joy, "Gift Giving in Hong Kong and the Continuum of Social Ties," *Journal of Consumer Research* 28 (September 2001), pp. 239–256.
12. David B. Wooten, "Qualitative Steps Toward an Expanded Model of Anxiety in Gift-Giving," *Journal of Consumer Research* 27 (June 2000), pp. 84–95.
13. John F. Sherry, Mary Ann McGrath, and Sidney J. Levy, "The Dark Side of the Gift," *Journal of Business Research* 28 (1993), pp. 225–244.
14. Ibid, p. 237.
15. Joseph A. Cote, James McCullough, and Michael Reilly, "Effects of Unexpected Situations on Behavior-Intention Differences: A Garbology Analysis," *Journal of Consumer Research* 12 (September 1985), pp. 188–194.
16. William L. Wilkie and Peter R. Dickson, "Patterns of Consumer Information Search and Shopping Behavior for Household Durables," Working Paper Series (Cambridge, Mass.: Marketing Science Institute, 1985).
17. William O. Bearden and Arch G. Woodside, "Consumption Occasion Influence on Consumer Brand Choice," *Decision Sciences* 9 (April 1978), pp. 273–284.
18. Kenneth C. Gehrt and Mary Beth Pinto, "The Impact of Situational Factors on Health Care Preferences: Exploring the Prospect of Situationally Based Segmentation," *Journal of Health Care Marketing* 11 (June 1991), pp. 41–52.
19. Marvin E. Goldberg and Gerald J. Gorn, "Happy and Sad TV Programs: How They Affect Reactions to Commercials," *Journal of Consumer Research* 14 (December 1987), pp. 387–403.
20. Margaret S. Clark, Sandra Milberg, and John Ross, "Arousal Cues Arousal-Related Material in Memory: Implications for Understanding Effects of Mood on Memory," *Journal of Verbal Learning and Verbal Behavior* 22 (1983), pp. 633–649.
21. Meryl P. Gardner, "The Consumer's Mood: An Important Situational Variable," in Thomas C. Kinnear, ed., *Advances in Consumer Research,* Vol. 11 (Ann Arbor, Mich.: Association for Consumer Research, 1984), pp. 525–529.
22. Russell W. Belk, "Situational Variables and Consumer Behavior," *Journal of Consumer Research* 2 (December 1975), pp. 159.
23. S. Tamer Cavusgil and Catherine A. Cole, "An Empirical Investigation of Situational, Attitudinal and Personal Influences on Behavioral Intentions," in Kenneth Bernhardt et al., eds., *Proceedings of the American Marketing Association Educators' Conference* (Chicago: American Marketing Association, Series No. 47, 1981), p. 161.
24. Donna L. Hoffman and Thomas P. Novak, "Marketing in Hypermedia Computer-Mediated Environments: Conceptual Foundations," *Journal of Marketing* 60 (July 1996), pp. 50–68.
25. D. Bem, "Self-Perception Theory," in L. Berkowitz, ed., *Advances in Experimental Social Psychology* (New York: Academic Press, 1972), pp. 1–62.
26. Brian Sternthal and Gerald Zaltman, "The Broadened Concept: Toward a Taxonomy of Consumption Situation," in Gerald Zaltman and Brian Sternthal, eds., *Broadening the Concept of Consumer Behavior* (Ann Arbor, Mich.: Association for Consumer Research, 1975), p. 144.
27. Ibid.
28. Clarke and Belk, "The Effects of Product Involvement and Task Definition on Anticipated Consumer Effort," in Wilkie, ed., *Advances in Consumer Research,* pp. 313–317.
29. William O. Bearden and Arch G. Woodside, "Interactions of Consumption Situations and Brand Attitudes," *Journal of Applied Psychology* 61 (1976), pp. 764–769.
30. Russell W. Belk, "An Exploratory Assessment of Situational Effects in Buyer Behavior," *Journal of Marketing Research* 11 (May 1974), p. 160; and Louis K. Sharpe and Kent L. Granzin, "Market Segmentation by Consumer Usage Context: An Exploratory Analysis," *Journal of Economics and Business* 26 (1974), pp. 225–228.
31. Bearden and Woodside, "Consumption Occasion Influence," pp. 273–284.
32. Belk, "An Exploratory Assessment," p. 160.
33. Rajendra K. Srivastava, Allan D. Shocker, and George S. Day, "An Exploratory Study of the Influences of Usage Situation on Perceptions of Product Markets," in H. Keith Hunt, ed., *Advances in Consumer Research,* Vol. 5 (Ann Arbor, Mich.: Association for Consumer Research, 1978), pp. 32–38.
34. Russell W. Belk, "A Free Response Approach to Developing Product-Specific Consumption Situation Taxonomies," in Allan D. Shocker, ed., *Analytic Approaches to Product and Market Planning* (Cambridge, Mass.: Marketing Science Institute, 1979), p. 178.
35. Sternthal and Zaltman, "The Broadened Concept," p. 146.
36. See Eric N. Berkowitz, James L. Ginter, and W. Wayne Talarzyk, "An Investigation of the Effects of Specific Usage Situations on the Prediction of Consumer Choice Behavior," in Barnett A. Greenberg and Danny N. Bellenger, eds.,

Proceedings of the American Marketing Association Educators' Conference (Chicago: American Marketing Association, Series No. 41, 1977), pp. 90–94; and William O. Bearden and Arch G. Woodside, "Situational Influence on Consumer Purchase Intentions," in Arch G. Woodside, Jagdish N. Sheth, and Peter D. Bennett, *Consumer and Industrial Buying Behavior* (New York: North-Holland, 1977), pp. 167–177.

37. James M. Daley and James H. Martin, "Situational Analysis of Bus Riders and Non-Riders for Different Transportation Methods," *Logistics and Transportation Review* 24 (June 1988), pp. 185–199.

38. Kenneth E. Miller and James L. Ginter, "An Investigation of Situational Variation in Brand Choice Behavior and Attitude," *Journal of Marketing Research* 16 (February 1979), pp. 111–123.

39. John L. Stanton and P. Greg Bonner, "An Investigation of the Differential Impact of Purchase Situation on Levels of Consumer Choice Behavior," *Advances in Consumer Research*, Vol. 8 (Ann Arbor, Mich.: Association for Consumer Research, 1980), pp. 639–643.

40. U. N. Umesh and Joseph A. Cote, "Influence of Situational Variables on Brand-Choice Models," *Journal of Business Research* 16 (1988), pp. 91–99.

41. Donald H. Granbois, "Improving the Study of Customer In-Store Behavior," *Journal of Marketing* 32 (October 1968), pp. 28–33.

42. Clarke and Belk, "The Effects of Product Involvement and Task Definition," p. 314.

43. Adrian B. Ryans, "Consumer Gift Buying Behavior: An Exploratory Analysis," in Greenberg and Bellenger, eds., *Proceedings of the American Marketing Association Educators' Conference,* pp. 99–104.

44. Ibid.

45. Bruce E. Mattson, "Situation Influences on Store Choice," *Journal of Retailing* 58 (Fall 1982), pp. 46–58.

46. Ibid.

47. Ravi Dhar and Itamar Simonson, "Making Complementary Choices in Consumption Episodes: Highlighting Versus Balancing," *Journal of Marketing Research* 36 (February 1999), pp. 29–44.

48. Brian Wansink and Michael L. Ray, "Advertising Strategies to Increase Usage Frequency," *Journal of Marketing* 60 (January 1996), pp. 31–46.

49. Ptacek and Shanteau, "Situation Determinants of Consumer Decision Making."

50. John Deighton, Caroline Henderson, and Scott Neslin, "Scanners and the Framing Effect," *Marketing & Media Decisions* (October 1989), p. 112.

51. "Perrier Rival Talks of Serendipity," *New York Times,* (February 24, 1990), p. A33.

52. Situational items taken from Russell W. Belk, "Effects of Gift-Giving Involvement on Gift Selection Strategies," in Andrew Mitchell, ed., *Advances in Consumer Research*, Vol. 9 (Ann Arbor, Mich.: Association for Consumer Research, 1982), pp. 408–412.

The Individual Consumer

CHAPTER 6

Consumer Perceptions

One of the key elements of a successful marketing strategy is the development of product and promotional stimuli that consumers will perceive as relevant to their needs. In Chapter 3, consumer **perceptions** were defined as the selection, organization, and interpretation of marketing and environmental stimuli into a coherent picture. In this chapter, consumer perceptions are considered in more detail.

Marketers attempt to influence consumer perceptions by creating an image of a brand that connotes value and reliability. Names such as Coca-Cola, Nike, McDonald's, AOL, and Intel have been successful in establishing and consistently reinforcing positive consumer perceptions over the years.

In this chapter, we first focus on what consumers are perceiving—stimuli. Next, we consider the three processes by which consumers perceive stimuli—selection, organization, and interpretation—and their strategic implications for marketing. We also consider the risks consumers perceive in purchasing decisions and strategies they use to reduce risk. We conclude by examining one of the most important applications of perceptions—consumer perceptions of prices and association of price with product quality.

Pepsi Tries to Change Consumer Perceptions

At times, marketers seek to strengthen a brand's image through change. As one recent example, consumers around the world have watched Pepsi change from its familiar red, white, and blue cans to a blue background with the Pepsi globe. The planned $300 million campaign was designed to create global conformity in design and consistency in brand image. It began in Europe in mid-1996 and slowly made its way around the world to the makeover in the United States in 1998. Pepsi described the decision to revise the well-known packaging as a way for its global brand to "have one look and one feel around the world."[1]

The idea for the change evolved from Pepsi's desire to improve its sales overseas, where Coca-Cola was outselling Pepsi three to one.[2] Often a trip to the beverage section in the local grocery store was met with a sea of red—mostly Coca-Cola with a few Pepsi products sprinkled in. Pepsi decided it wanted to stand out more and differentiate itself from its nearest competitor, as well as provide a global image that was pleasing worldwide. Studying another Pepsi product that was successful overseas, Pepsi Max, and working with image consultants on the color, Pepsi decided that the blue packaging was pleasing to consumers and provided a way to distinguish its cans and bottles from Coca-Cola's. Soon afterward, the electric blue cans were introduced in Europe (see Exhibit 6.1).

Pepsi's move certainly didn't go unnoticed. Critics argued that the move was confusing to consumers, especially since the actual soft drink was not changing its formula in any way.[3] Others called it a waste of money and a risky strategy for the second-most popular soft drink company. However, the company pressed on with its decision and generated substantial fanfare with its initial launch in Europe. In the United Kingdom, Pepsi's huge advertising and promotions during the change, such as coloring the masthead of the *Daily Mirror* (one of the United Kingdom's leading newspapers) blue and using celebrities like Cindy Crawford

and Andre Agassi in its ads, led to close to a 70 percent recognition rate just forty-eight hours after the launch of the campaign.[4] By 1998, two years after the initial launch, Pepsi claimed to have rolled out the blue can in 190 world markets.[5]

Although sales didn't increase significantly immediately following the launch, Pepsi continues to believe that it made the right long-term decision. Pepsi's core consumer group, teens, is increasingly global through access to the Internet, cable channels like MTV, and travel. Uniformity in perceptions among teens has strengthened the brand's image and worldwide position.

Since the Pepsi Blue project stopped making headlines, Pepsi has used a "Joy of Cola" campaign globally, and in early 2001 changed it to the "Joy of Pepsi" to maintain one worldwide message. Domestically, it emphasized the blue can by using former presidential candidate Bob Dole as a spokesperson, extolling his "little blue friend," in TV commercials, a humorous takeoff on Dole's prior appearance as a spokesperson for Viagra with the same tag line.

| EXHIBIT 6.1 |

Pepsi's change to blue packaging.
Pepsi-Cola Company.

Marketing Stimuli and Consumer Perceptions

Stimuli are any physical, visual, or verbal communications that can influence an individual's response. The two most important types of stimuli influencing consumer behavior are marketing and environmental (social and cultural influences). In this chapter, we consider marketing stimuli. Environmental stimuli are considered in Parts Four and Five.

Marketing stimuli are any communications or physical stimuli designed to influence consumers. The product and its components (package, contents, physical properties) are **primary** (or **intrinsic**) **stimuli.** Communications designed to influence consumer behavior are **secondary** (or **extrinsic**) **stimuli** that represent the product either through words, pictures, and symbolism or through other stimuli associated with the product (price, store in which it was purchased, effect of the salesperson).

To survive in a competitive market, manufacturers must constantly expose consumers to secondary marketing stimuli. Continuous advertising is not profitable, however, unless enough consumers buy again. Therefore, the ultimate determinant of future consumer actions is experience with the primary stimulus, the product. At times, manufacturers attempt to introduce such product experience prior to a purchase by giving consumers free samples. This provides consumers a direct and risk-free product experience. However, distributing free samples as a primary stimulus to influence consumers to buy products is the exception. The dominant element in marketing strategy is communication about the product.

The key requirement in communicating secondary stimuli to consumers is the development of a product concept. A **product concept** is a bundle of product benefits that can be directed to the needs of a defined group of consumers through messages, symbolism, and imagery. The product concept represents the organization of the secondary stimuli into a coordinated product position that can be communicated to consumers. For example, Nestlé developed the concept for its freeze-dried coffee entry, Taster's Choice, as a product that provides the convenience of instant but the taste and aroma of regular coffee. Nestlé geared the secondary stimuli to the intended concept. The brand name implied taste, and the advertising demonstrated the taste benefits of a good instant coffee for the head of the family. Nestlé even tested the shape of the jar and determined that a deep square jar would provide more of an image of hefty taste than would the traditional cylindrical jar. Clearly, definition of the product concept must precede development of the secondary stimuli in the marketing plan.

Two key factors determine which stimuli consumers perceive and how they interpret them: (1) the characteristics of the stimulus and (2) the consumers' ability to perceive the stimulus. These two influences interact in determining consumer perceptions. Assume a company producing a leading deodorant subtly changes ingredients to give the deodorant a "cleaner" smell (a stimulus characteristic). If many consumers cannot distinguish between the new and the old smell (a consumer characteristic), the change in stimulus is ineffective. Stimulus and consumer characteristics are considered in the following sections.

Stimulus Characteristics Affecting Perception

Several characteristics of marketing stimuli affect the way consumers perceive products. These characteristics can be divided into sensory elements and structural elements. Both have implications for product development and advertising.

SENSORY ELEMENTS

Sensory elements are composed of sight, taste, smell, sound, and feel.

Sight: Color Perceptions

The most important factor in regard to sight is color. Color has important sensory connotations. Consider the preponderance of red logos or names on packages in the supermarket aisle—Coca-Cola, Nabisco, Campbell's Soup, Colgate, Jell-O, Kellogg's (see Exhibit 6.2). Evidence suggests that red is regarded as warm, sensual, and not intimidating. On a more basic level, red represents the lifeblood.[6] Blue is seen as comforting, possibly one reason why IBM's logo is in blue—an attempt to convey a more friendly image from a company that is often seen as cold and distant.[7]

Research shows there is a close link between color preferences and brand choice. One study tested the same roll-on deodorant packaged in three different colors.[8] Respondents said the product in one color scheme dried quickly and was effective, the product in the second had a strong aroma, and the product in the third was irritating and ineffective. Differences in consumers' reactions to the identical product were caused solely by differences in the color of the packaging.

Mary Kay, the second-largest direct seller of skin care products in the United States, has always associated its products and logo with pink—a color that reinforced an old-fashioned image. To appeal to the contemporary woman, the company has begun to use a more sophisticated off-white.[9] In Spain, a more traditional

EXHIBIT 6.2

Color as a marketing stimulus.

Visuals Unlimited.

country, Mary Kay uses new color schemes to depict a contemporary woman but retains its basic pink as background. In Russia, however, Mary Kay uses pale lavender and soft imagery because most Russian women are not assertive, modern working women as is the case in the United States. It appeals to middle-class housewives or perhaps women who work in low-wage jobs. Even in the United States, Mary Kay is changing with the times. In addition to the traditional pink Cadillac awarded to top salespeople, Mary Kay offers the choice of a white GMC Jimmy, a pink Pontiac Grand Prix, and a red Pontiac Grand Am.[10]

The importance of color perceptions is further illustrated by P&G's attempt to change Prell shampoo from its traditional green to blue. An outcry arose among loyal Prell users and forced the company to change Prell back to its traditional green. One analyst concluded: "Challenging [long-standing] consumer perceptions is very tricky and is generally a mistake."[11]

Color perceptions are likely to differ among countries because of cultural associations. A study by Jacobs et al. of consumers in the Far East and in the United States found that consumers in China and Japan associate purple with expensive products and gray with inexpensive products. The associations are exactly the opposite for American consumers, who associate purple with inexpensive products and gray with expensive ones. In Hong Kong, Marlboro uses cross-cultural differences in color perceptions by depicting the cowboy in a white hat on a white horse because white is culturally significant in China.[12]

▌ Taste   Taste is another sensory factor that conditions consumers' brand perceptions. When PepsiCo introduced Crystal Pepsi to appeal to consumers' desire for light, natural flavorings, it immediately captured 2 percent of the soft drink market, making it a $1 billion brand. But sales quickly slid. Why? They slid because many consumers expected it to taste like regular Pepsi, whereas it had a distinctly lighter taste. Reinforcing the taste problem was the lack of color. Some consumers associate clear with natural and healthy; others simply associate it with water.[13] PepsiCo tried to recoup by advertising "You've never seen a taste like this," but to no avail. The expectation of a cola taste was too strongly ingrained in consumers' minds.

Taste can be an elusive perception. Allison and Uhl found that when consumers were asked to taste three unlabeled brands of beer (research known as a "blind taste test"), they rated all three brands similarly; most consumers could not identify their regular brand.[14] However, when shown the labels, consumers had a strong preference for their regular brand. The result shows that taste is not an objective criterion. It is inextricably linked to the brand's image in the consumer's mind. Without brand identification, the consumer's taste experience is entirely different. This fact was illustrated when Coca-Cola tried to change the formula of its flagship brand. Blind taste tests showed that New Coke was superior to the original. When the company tried to change the formula, however, consumer resistance was so great it had to bring back the original as Coca-Cola Classic. The strong association with a brand that was part of many consumers' heritage went beyond taste.

▌ Smell   Smell is particularly important for cosmetics and food products. In one study, two different fragrances were added to the same facial tissue. Consumers perceived one facial tissue as elegant and expensive and the other as a product to use in the kitchen.[15] Smell can be a factor even in car purchases. Car dealers have been known to use a spray inside cars so they smell "new." Rolls Royce included scent strips in advertisements in *Architectural Digest* to convey the smell of its leather upholstery. In another application, Procter & Gamble used scratch-and-sniff stickers on its detergent packaging so consumers could more easily smell the products in the store.[16]

Smell also has cross-cultural dimensions. The social role of perfumes and colognes in Western society has never been established in Japan. Because of crowding and small living spaces, Japanese consumers value cleanliness and never have felt the need for using these products as a means of avoiding body odor. In fact, many Japanese regard perfumes and colognes as intrusive to other people's privacy.

▮ Sound   Sound is another important sensory stimulus. Advertisers have traditionally used English accent voice-overs to convey status and authority. This is one reason why Commander Whitehead was an effective spokesperson for Schweppes beverage mixers. Advertisers also frequently use music through jingles or as background themes to create positive associations with brands. Marketers must pretest such stimuli to ensure that they create the desired positive associations with a brand. Gorn demonstrated the importance of such associations in an experiment. Consumers were asked to choose among several pens, one of which they saw advertised with background music. Consumers were more likely to choose the pen if they liked the background music.[17]

▮ Feel   The feel of certain products also influences consumers' perceptions. Softness is considered a desirable attribute in many paper products. For example, the former theme "Don't squeeze the Charmin" suggests the importance of feel. Feel is also a means of determining quality. Consumers often use the feel of textile fabrics, clothing, carpeting, or furniture to evaluate quality. For example, a smooth, velvety feel in textile fabrics is considered an indication of quality.

One of the reasons Gap, Inc. began encountering problems in 2000 is that many consumers began associating the feel of the merchandise to lower quality because of their association of Gap merchandise with its less expensive sister stores—Old Navy. Consumers were not convinced that the distinction in quality between the two stores was sufficient, and feel had a lot to do with that perception.[18]

The importance of feeling merchandise has also inhibited the sale of certain products on the Web. Consumers may be reluctant to buy without the security of some sensory interaction with the product. Some marketers have referred to this as a "kick the tires" syndrome; that is, the desirability to experience the feel of the product before buying. Lack of such interaction may inhibit sales of items such as clothing, furniture, appliances, and cars.

STRUCTURAL ELEMENTS

Along with sensory elements, structural elements also affect perception. Structural elements are the physical characteristics of the marketing message. In print ads, such an element is the size of an ad or its position in a magazine. For TV commercials, physical characteristics relate to the length of the ad (thirty- vs. sixty-second

| **EXHIBIT 6.3** |

Attracting attention through novelty.

Chick-fil-A, Inc. © 2001.

Over 30 years ago, the folks at Chick-fil-A® invented the original reason to eat more chicken. Namely, the world's first chicken sandwich. Ever since then, they've been responsible for one tasty chicken creation after another. And because chicken's the healthier choice, one thing's for sure: You'll have no beef with us.

spot), the time of day it is aired, or the use of jingles. A number of findings have emerged from studies of structural elements applied primarily to print advertising. For example:

- The larger the size of the ad, the more likely it is to be noticed.[19]
- A position in the first ten pages of a magazine or in the upper half of a printed page produces more attention.[20] Similarly, a position on the home page of a web site increases the number of users who are exposed to the ad.
- **Contrast** can influence the attention an ad receives. For example, the picture of a product on a stark white background is likely to produce notice.

Novelty is another attention-getting device. The Chick-fil-A ad (see Exhibit 6.3) is an example. Novelty also works on the Web. For example, use of animation in a web ad is likely to produce attention.

Consumer Characteristics Affecting Perception

Two characteristics are important in determining consumers' perception of stimuli: (1) the ability to discriminate between stimuli and (2) the propensity to generalize from one stimulus to another.

STIMULUS DISCRIMINATION

One of the basic questions regarding the effect of marketing stimuli on perceptions is whether consumers can discriminate among differences in stimuli. Do consumers perceive differences between brands in taste, in feel, in price, in the shape of the package?

The ability to discriminate among stimuli is learned. Generally, frequent users of a product are better able to notice small differences in product characteristics between brands. However, in many cases, the consumers' ability to discriminate sensory characteristics such as taste and feel is small. As a result, marketers rely on advertising to convey brand differences that physical characteristics alone do not impart. They attempt to create a brand image that will convince consumers that one brand is better than another.

This concept is especially important in the virtual world of the Internet. Marketers have to determine the extent to which their web site or banner advertising stands out from the crowd and what unique characteristics create identity for them. The frequent web user is able to distinguish one web site from another based on its design, purpose, and informational content. Such a consumer is more likely to have been an early adopter of the Web. As web usage increases, a greater number of less web-savvy consumers will be navigating the Web. They will have to learn how to discriminate key characteristics of web sites to assess their content and relevance.

Clutter on the Web makes discriminating more difficult because so much information is available. For instance, companies have recently tried to influence readers to click through by designing web ads to look like a search engine, opinion poll, or button. However, because clicking only led users to the advertiser's web site, they have learned not to trust such executions.[21]

▌ **Threshold Level**   The ability of consumers to detect variations in light, sound, smell, or other stimuli is determined by their **threshold level.** Some consumers are more sensitive to these stimuli than others. Arthur D. Little, a management consulting firm, has identified expert taste testers for products such as cigarettes and coffee. Since their level of sensory discrimination is much greater than the average consumer's, these experts can detect subtle differences in coffee or cigarette blends and are used by marketers to evaluate various test products and to screen out potential losers. Once these experts identify the best prospective blends, the products are then tested on consumers in standard taste tests.

Just-Noticeable Difference.   A basic principle in determining a consumer's threshold level is that a differential threshold exists in comparing two stimuli. The consumer does not detect any difference between stimuli below his or her differential threshold. The differential threshold, therefore, represents the **just-noticeable difference (JND).** For example, if a private label detergent is five cents below the consumer's regular brand, the consumer may not notice the difference. However, if the private label brand is ten cents below the regular brand, the consumer is likely to notice the difference. Therefore, ten cents is the differential threshold, or JND, for this consumer.

Marketers sometimes seek to make changes in marketing stimuli that will not be noticed (a decrease in package size or an increase in price). A good example of the need to change a marketing stimulus without notice is the periodic updating of existing packaging. For instance, General Mills has subtly changed one of the most enduring symbols in advertising, Betty Crocker, who was first introduced in 1921, to give her a more contemporary look[22] (see Exhibit 6.4).

Most consumers did not notice the more subtle changes (*e.g.,* the ones between 1965 and 1980) because they were below their JND. But the company departed from

an attempt to stay below the JND with its 1986 version of Betty Crocker. This portrayal attempted to show a professional working woman with family responsibilities. The most marked departure from the traditional portrayal occurred in 1996, the year of her seventy-fifth birthday, when the company decided to develop a composite to represent American women across ethnic and age groups. It selected pictures of seventy-five women and developed a composite representation. The new Betty Crocker "will look more like the growing market of blacks and Hispanics. This will let [General Mills] straddle their conservative core and their emerging market."[23] The new Betty Crocker is the last picture in Exhibit 6.4.

Of even more direct application to marketing strategy is the need to differentiate a brand from that of the competition so it is noticed. In this case, the marketer seeks to develop product characteristics and advertising messages that are easily detectable (differences in size, taste, color, ingredients, and so on).

Weber's Law.   As most consumers cannot detect small changes in a product's price, package size, or physical characteristics, a relevant question for marketers is the degree of change required for consumers to take notice. A principle developed by a German physiologist over a hundred years ago, known as Weber's law, provides some insight into this question. **Weber's law** says that the stronger the initial stimulus, the greater the change required for the subsequent stimulus to be seen as different. In marketing terms, this means that the higher the price, the greater the change in price required for consumers to take notice. The price of a $500 stereo set would have to increase more significantly than that of a $100 tape deck to be noticed. Moreover, Weber's law says that the increase in the difference required to reach the differential threshold (the JND) is constant. That is, if price had to increase by a minimum of $10 to be noticed for a $100 tape deck, it must increase by a minimum of $50 to be noticed for a $500 stereo set. In both cases, the JND is a constant 10 percent.

The Federal Trade Commission implicitly recognized the nature of Weber's law when it required that the surgeon general's warning in cigarette advertising had to be a certain size.[24] The bigger the ad, the bigger the warning's typeface had to be to be noticed. If the typeface size fell below the specifications the FTC set, it might have been below the JND for many consumers who would thus not perceive it.

The most direct applications of Weber's law are in regard to price. One important implication is that the higher the original price of an item, the greater the markdown required to increase sales. Thus, the required markdown on a designer suit is greater than that on a regular suit.

Subliminal Perceptions.   The differential threshold was identified as the minimum difference between two stimuli that consumers can detect. Thus, a consumer may be able to tell the difference between two drinks that are 40 proof and 60 proof, but if the difference between the two is smaller, a consumer will not detect it (60 minus 40, or 20 proof, is the JND). There is also an **absolute threshold** below which consumers cannot detect the stimulus at all. Thus, a consumer can detect alcohol in a cordial that is 10 proof, but below that, a consumer can detect no alcoholic content in the beverage. Therefore, the differential threshold is 20 proof, and the absolute threshold is 10 proof.

One of the major controversies regarding consumer perceptions is about whether consumers can actually perceive marketing stimuli below their absolute threshold. **Subliminal perception** is the perception of a stimulus below the conscious level.[25] The absolute threshold level at which perceptions occur is referred to as the **"limen."** Thus, perception below the absolute threshold is *subliminal.* It may seem contradictory that consumers can perceive a message below their minimum level of perception, but experiments conducted in the 1950s suggested that exposure may actually occur without attention and comprehension. That is, consumers do not see the message, but they register it.

Vicary conducted a test in 1957 in which two messages, "Eat popcorn" and "Drink Coca-Cola," were shown in a movie theater for 1/3,000 of a second (well below the absolute threshold) at intervals of every five seconds.[26] Popcorn sales in the theater increased by 58 percent and Coca-Cola sales by 18 percent compared with periods in which there was no subliminal advertising. These results immediately raised serious ethical questions about consumers being influenced by messages without their approval or knowledge. The *New Yorker* magazine said that "minds had been 'broken and entered.' "[27]

The controversy over subliminal advertising proved shallow, however, because there was little continuing proof that it influenced consumer actions.[28] Subsequent attempts to replicate Vicary's findings did not succeed.[29] Although the Federal Communications Commission took an immediate interest in the implications of subliminal advertising, it could not confirm the conclusion that subliminal advertising influences the receiver's responses.[30] In later studies, Moore and Saegert found little influence resulting from subliminal advertising.[31] However, at least one study, by Janiszewski, did find that consumers process advertising information on a subliminal level and that such processing may in fact interfere with communication of the intended advertising message.[32]

The controversy over subliminal advertising has extended to print as well as to TV advertising. Some writers have claimed that print ads use **subliminal embeds;** that is, tiny figures inserted into magazine ads by high-speed photography or by airbrushing.[33] As evidence, a Gilbey's Gin ad was cited in which the ice cubes spell out the word "sex." However, a study by Rosen and Singh found little evidence that such embeds exert a subconscious influence on unaware consumers.[34]

Overall, the evidence suggests it is extremely difficult at best to exert influence through subliminal stimuli. Variations in perceptual ability among consumers, the difficulty of implementing advertising themes at low threshold levels, and the lack of evidence of any effect of subliminal advertising on purchasing behavior have effectively eliminated subliminal advertising as a marketing tool.

▌ **Adaptation Level** **Adaptation level** is the level at which consumers no longer notice a frequently repeated stimulus. An individual walking into an air-conditioned room, a kitchen full of fragrances, or a noisy party does not notice these stimuli after a period of time. **Advertising wearout** is the consumers' adaptation to an advertising campaign over time due to boredom and familiarity. Consumers reduce their attention level to frequently repeated ads and eventually fail to notice them.

Consumers differ in their levels of adaptation. Some tune out more quickly than others. Certain consumers have a tendency to be more aware of the facets of information and communication, even if they are repeated frequently. Because of the advertiser's desire to gain attention and maintain distinctiveness, the typical advertising campaign aims to decrease the adaptation level by introducing attention-getting features. Novelty, humor, contrast, and movement are all stimulus effects that may gain consumers' attention and reduce their adaptation. The most effective means of reducing the adaptation level, however, is to ensure that the message communicates the benefits consumers desire.

Advertising wearout is of great concern to Internet advertisers. During the dot-com boom of the late 1990s, banner ads were touted as a logical extension of a company's promotional mix. Click-through rates became the yardstick for ad effectiveness on the Internet. But as banner ads became more commonplace, consumer adaptation levels increased, and banner ads began to be largely ignored. Click-through rates plummeted until, by 2000, they were well below 1 percent.[35] Web advertisers are trying to adapt by creating more conventional-looking, magazine-type ads, often in pop-up formats, to try to gain attention.[36] They are also introducing new formats such as floating ads; that is, ads that float across a web page.[37] These devices suggest that the emphasis in measuring the effectiveness of web ads is turning from click-through rates to simple exposure and attention; that is, the recognition that a web ad message can sink in without the consumer having to click on the ad to get to the advertiser's web site.

STIMULUS GENERALIZATION

Consumers develop not only a capacity to discriminate among stimuli but also a capacity to generalize from one similar stimulus to another. The process of **stimulus generalization** occurs when two stimuli are seen as similar (contiguous), and the effects of one, therefore, can be substituted for the effects of the other.

Discrimination allows consumers to judge brands selectively and to evaluate one brand over another. Generalization allows consumers to simplify the process of evaluation because they do not have to make a separate judgment for each stimulus. Brand loyalty is a form of stimulus generalization. The consumer assumes that positive past experiences with the brand will be repeated. Therefore, a consumer does not need to make a separate judgment with each purchase. Perceptual categorization is also a form of stimulus generalization. As new products are introduced, consumers generalize from past experience to categorize them. When the automobile was first introduced at the turn of the century, it was called the horseless carriage. People generalized from their experience with the best-known mode of transportation, the horse and carriage, and put the automobile in the same general category.

▮ Strategic Applications of Generalization It may appear that marketers seek to avoid stimulus generalization by consumers because they are attempting to distinguish their brands from those of the competition. However, in some cases, generalization may be a conscious and productive strategy. Heinz uses a strategy of generalization by advertising "57 varieties." The hope is that consumers will generalize the positive experience with one of the company's brands to other brands. General Electric also follows this policy of family branding. On the other hand, Procter & Gamble avoids a policy of generalization, preferring to position each brand in a unique way without reference to the company name. Whereas Heinz and General Electric employ stimulus generalization, Procter & Gamble employs stimulus discrimination.

▮ Brand Leveraging. **Brand leveraging,** that is, extending a well-known brand name to other products, is one of the most direct and popular applications of stimulus generalization in marketing. Companies have utilized the strategy with increasing frequency because of the growing expense of introducing new products and the fact that such introductions are 40 percent to 80 percent less expensive when a product is given an existing name. Aaker and Keller found two perceptual requirements for brand leveraging to work.[38] First, consumers must associate the brand with high quality. Second, there must be a perception of fit between the two products—that is, a logical transference from the old to the new product—so stimulus generalization can take place. A quality name and positive transference through stimulus generalization led Eastman Kodak to introduce a battery line. Research showed that a significant number of consumers thought the company already sold batteries, even before it introduced them.

However, when concept consistency such as that between cameras and batteries is lacking, brand leveraging fails because consumers cannot generalize from one product category to another. When Virgin Airlines tried to move its brand to Virgin Rail, it failed. Consumers could not generalize the Virgin name to trains (which were often shoddy and late) because the category was not consistent with its image as a low-cost trendsetter.[39]

Another danger in leveraging a brand is the possibility of diluting its equity. Bic's failure in leveraging its name to disposable perfumes hurt its brand image because the concept of disposability did not transfer easily to perfumes.

Advertisers also use generalization in positioning brands to compete with the market leader. A brand may be introduced with the same basic benefits but at a

OF CONSUMER BEHAVIOR

WEB APPLICATIONS

Gap Leverages Its Brand Equity on the Web

A key strategic issue for marketers is whether to leverage their brand equity on the Web. For example, Gap, Inc. has established a successful web site by transferring the company's name, image, and product and service offerings to the Web.

Gap's successful Web strategy is based on several factors. First, it created a web site with a recognizable logo directly linking the site with the store and with Gap's national ad campaign. Second, it created synergies between the web site and the store by providing reminders of the web site on shopping bags and on its advertising. Synergy is also created by allowing web purchases to be returned to any Gap store. Third, it organized the merchandise on the Web in the same manner as in the store. It has departments for men, women, and children and merchandise categories that users can click on. Further, the Web provides users with a wider range of size, style, and color alternatives than the typical store.

As a result, the web site has become an extension of the store's boundaries. In many cases consumers who cannot find the product in the store are encouraged by store employees to go online. In other cases, consumers who do not have easy store access or need an item quickly can shop online. In short, the Web has enhanced Gap's ability to get the right product to the consumer at the right time and place.

The downside of Gap's strategy is the possibility that web sales are simply cannibalizing store sales. If most of the online sales would have otherwise occurred in the store, then establishing a web site would not be cost-effective. Although some cannibalization is inevitable, Gap's web site has proved profitable because the site provides additional value to the brick-and-mortar facilities.

Sources: "GAP.COM," *Boston Globe* (July 30, 2001), p. C2; "Online Shopper; Web Totally Slacks," *Los Angeles Times* (May 24, 2001), p. T4; "The Winning Shopping Sites Are . . .," *Target Marketing* (August 2000), pp. 38–40.

lower price or in a larger package. The hope is that consumers will generalize the known benefits of the leading brand to the new entry and thus accept it. Principles of generalization can also be used to encourage new uses for a product, such as eating cold cereals as a snack or using bleach as a cleaner. Wansick found that such usage generalizations are most likely to be accepted by consumers if common attributes are advertised—for example, the desirability of a nutritious cereal and a nutritious snack.[40]

Perceptual Selection

Having described the nature of stimuli and the factors that affect stimulus perception, we can now turn to describing the process of perception. The steps in the perceptual process—selection, organization, and interpretation—are shown in Figure 6.1.

The first component of perception is **selection.** For perceptual selection to occur, the consumer must first see or hear the stimulus and then respond to it. Three processes define such selection: exposure, attention, and selective perception.

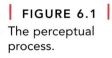
FIGURE 6.1
The perceptual
process.

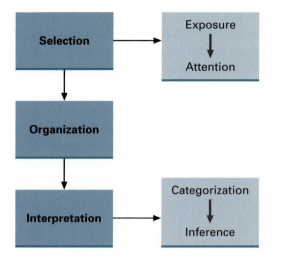

EXPOSURE

Exposure occurs when consumers' senses (sight, sound, touch, smell) are activated by a stimulus. Consumers pick and choose the stimuli they are exposed to. A consumer in the market for a new car is more likely to look for car ads. The consumer shopping for a laptop computer is more likely to ask friends and business associates about their experiences with various brands.

Consumers are also likely to avoid exposure to stimuli that are unimportant and uninteresting. The advent of remote control devices for TV sets has permitted "zapping" of TV commercials by switching channels. Consumers also employ "zipping" (as opposed to zapping) by fast-forwarding through commercials when playing recorded tapes. Some VCRs even remove the need for zipping by automatically removing commercials while recording. Another manifestation of stimulus avoidance is known as the "flush factor." When the first Superbowl game was held between the Green Bay Packers and the Kansas City Chiefs in 1967, at halftime the water pressure in Kansas City reached a record low.

ATTENTION

Attention is the momentary focusing of a consumer's cognitive capacity on a specific stimulus. When consumers notice a TV ad, a new product on a shelf, or a car in a showroom, attention has taken place.

Advertisers can use many of the structural factors described previously to get consumers' attention—for example, size through larger ads, position by placing an ad in the upper half of a page, and novelty by using eye-catching photos or illustrations. These factors apply to in-store stimuli as well. For example, researchers in one study found that brands on the upper shelf in a supermarket received 35 percent more attention than those on the lower shelf and that increasing the number of packages for a particular brand on the shelf from two to four increased attention by 34 percent.[41] Sensory factors can also increase consumers' attention—for example, sound such as the use of a jingle or voice-overs of famous people in a commercial, or smells such as scratch-and-sniff print ads for perfume.

Attention does not always occur after exposure. A consumer may be exposed to an ad but pay little attention to it. Yet some of the information in the ad may be retained. Such **preattentive processing** is most likely in low-involvement situations when the consumer may not be motivated to actively process information.

SELECTIVE PERCEPTION

Consumers perceive marketing stimuli selectively because each individual is unique in the combination of his or her needs, attitudes, experiences, and personal charac teristics. **Selective perception** means that two consumers may perceive the identical advertisement, package, or product very differently. One consumer may believe a claim that Clorox gets clothes whiter than other bleaches; another may regard such a claim as untrue and may believe that all bleaches are the same.

Selective perception occurs at every stage in the perceptual process in Figure 6.1. *Selective exposure and attention* occur because people's beliefs influence what they choose to listen to or read. *Selective organization* occurs because people organize information to be consistent with their beliefs. Also, *selective interpretation* occurs so that perceptions conform with prior beliefs and attitudes. For example, Arm & Hammer's claim that its baking soda toothpaste is healthier for teeth and gums was consistent with consumers' beliefs that the type of toothpaste makes a difference, even though it usually does not. As a result, many consumers chose to believe the claim, despite statements from dentists that baking soda does not affect dental hygiene one way or the other.[42]

▎ **Functions of Selective Perception**   Selective perception ensures that consumers receive information most relevant to their needs. This process is called **perceptual vigilance.** In a marketing study demonstrating the operation of percep tual vigilance, Spence and Engel found that consumers recognized names for pre ferred brands more quickly than they did names for other brands.[43] That is, individuals were more likely to perceive preferred stimuli.

In high-involvement purchases, perceptual vigilance guides consumers to the information that is instrumental in attaining desired benefits. In low-involvement purchases, perceptual vigilance acts by screening out information because con sumers want to minimize information processing. It filters out unnecessary stimuli.

Consumers sometimes perceive information to conform to their beliefs and atti tudes. This second function of selective perception is called **perceptual defense** because it protects the individual from threatening or contradictory stimuli. For example, the cigarette smoker may avoid antismoking advertisements or play down their importance. The recent purchaser of a poorly insulated home may ignore unexpectedly high fuel bills or rationalize the situation by saying fuel costs are high for everyone.

Perceptual defense tends to operate when consumers are involved. Involved con sumers have strong beliefs and attitudes about a brand. In terms of Sherif's social judgment theory, firmly held beliefs reflect a narrow latitude of acceptance.[44] Messages in agreement with the consumers' beliefs are accepted and distorted in the direction of those beliefs (an assimilation effect). Messages that do not conform to the consumers' strongly held beliefs are rejected or distorted to contrast with the consumers' opinions (a contrast effect).[45]

▌**Perceptual Equilibrium** The underlying principle in the operation of selective perception is that consumers seek **perceptual equilibrium**; that is, consistency between the information they receive about a brand and their prior beliefs about that brand. Such consistency ensures that the consumers' psychological set is in equilibrium. Three cognitive theories are based on the principles of selective perception and perceptual equilibrium:

1. *Sherif's social judgment theory* (discussed in Chapter 4) states that consumers process information to ensure consistency either by rejecting contradictory information (contrast) or by interpreting acceptable information to fit more closely with their views (assimilation).[46]

2. *Heider's balance theory* states that when information about an object conflicts with the consumers' beliefs, consumers achieve balance by changing their opinion about the object, about the source of information, or both.[47] The result is a balance in beliefs about the information and the object. For example, if a close friend expresses the view that your favorite camera takes poor pictures, you can doubt the credibility of your friend as a source of information about cameras, form a more negative attitude toward your favorite camera, or do a little bit of both to obtain balance between information and object.

3. *Cognitive dissonance theory* states that when postpurchase conflicts arise, consumers seek balance in the psychological set by seeking supporting information or by distorting contradictory information. An example is heavy smokers discounting the link between cancer and smoking and rationalizing their smoking behavior.

Each of these theories results in consistency between consumers' perceptions of marketing stimuli and their beliefs and attitudes.

Another strategy for achieving perceptual equilibrium is to avoid conflicting situations and seek the status quo. One study found that consumers facing a decision that may have negative consequences (*e.g.,* selecting the best medical insurance coverage) often deal with such decisions by delaying or avoiding them. Perceptual equilibrium is achieved by simply avoiding the possibility of disequilibrium.[48]

▌**Perceptual Disequilibrium** Consumers not only accept information consistent with their beliefs, but they also accept discrepant information about a selected product. If they did not, it would mean that every time a consumer was dissatisfied, he or she would attempt to rationalize the purchase and would never switch brands.

Learning and cognitive dissonance theories predict different outcomes from dissatisfaction. As noted, in *cognitive dissonance,* the consumer seeks balance by discounting negative information. In contrast, *learning theory* says that when a brand does not meet expectations, consumers learn from the negative experience and adjust beliefs and attitudes accordingly. The result is a reduction in the probability of repurchase. For example, even though 90 percent of nonsmokers accept the link between smoking and cancer, well over half of heavy smokers also accept this link. These smokers must be in a state of perceptual disequilibrium. Many will accept this dissonant information and attempt to stop smoking to change their behavior to conform to the information.

SELECTIVE PERCEPTION AND MARKETING STRATEGY

Marketing messages can be clear-cut or ambiguous. If consumers engage in perceptual defense, ambiguous messages are more likely to be effective because the marketer is giving consumers latitude to interpret the message to be in accord with their beliefs about the brand. If consumers engage in perceptual vigilance, then clear-cut messages are more likely to be effective because it is apparent that the information is supportive of or contradictory to the consumers' beliefs.

▌ Using Perceptual Defense   Ambiguity should be used in advertising when the product is important to consumers, but its benefits are not clear-cut. Because consumers are introducing beliefs that are consistent with their needs, the operating principle is perceptual defense. An ad for Microsoft illustrated this principle. Its tag line, "Where do you want to go today?", enabled the consumer to project almost any motive for using Microsoft products. The theme can mean different things to different people. As a result, consumers can selectively perceive a range of applications with a minimum of informational content. Ambiguity, therefore, permits different consumers to perceive a message selectively in line with their needs.

Generally, a moderate amount of ambiguity is optimal. If the message is too explicit, consumers have little room for projecting, and the marketer may be unnecessarily restricting the potential market. On the other hand, if the message is too ambiguous, consumers have difficulty understanding it or relating to it.

▌ Using Perceptual Vigilance   Marketers should be explicit in their advertising if the product's benefits are clear-cut and if the product is targeted to a well-defined segment. In such cases, the informational content of the advertisement dominates and ambiguity is held to a minimum. Industrial advertising tends to be largely unambiguous because it is more heavily balanced toward informational content than toward symbolism. Because consumers are seeking information directed to their needs and avoiding unnecessary information, the operating principle is perceptual vigilance.

Performance-oriented autos use unambiguous ads with straightforward informational content. An ad for the Pontiac Grand Prix refers to a turbocharged V6 engine creating over 200 horsepower, a cross-ram intake, GT14 radial tires, and so on. There is little left to the imagination. The information is clear and readily perceived. It is also easily filtered out by those who are not interested in the intricacies of a car's performance.

SELECTIVE PERCEPTION AND THE INTERNET

Because consumers do not like conflict between what they know (beliefs) and what they see (perceptions), two issues can arise in Internet marketing. First, a potential conflict can occur between offline and online brand perceptions. This might be the result of poorly implemented brand leveraging strategies online. Failure to convey a strong brand image on a firm's web site may undermine brand equity. To be successful, a brand or company's web presence must be consistent with its established image.

Second, as we saw in Chapter 2, conflict between brand purchase decisions and subsequent negative experience with the brand can result in dissonance. The Web can be an effective vehicle for reducing dissonance. Interactivity allows marketers to establish relationships with consumers on a one-to-one basis in an attempt to allay concerns and reinforce positive brand experiences. Saturn, for example, emails consumers to remind them of service requirements, encourages feedback regarding any problems with the car, and responds effectively to consumer inquiries and concerns.

Perceptual Organization

In being exposed to three hundred to six hundred commercials a day, the typical consumer uses some form of perceptual organization of disparate, and at times conflicting, stimuli. **Perceptual organization** means that consumers group information from various sources into a meaningful whole to comprehend it better and to act on it.

The basic principle of organization is **integration,** which means that consumers perceive various stimuli as an organized whole. Such an organization simplifies information processing and provides an integrated meaning for the stimuli. These principles have been derived from **Gestalt psychology.** (*Gestalt* is roughly translated from German as "total configuration" or "whole pattern.") Because they provide a framework for interpreting advertising messages as an integrated whole, principles of Gestalt psychology apply directly to marketing strategy. The advertising campaign, price level, distribution outlet, and brand characteristics are not disparate elements of the marketing plan. Rather, they are viewed in concert and produce an overall brand image. In short, the whole is greater than the sum of the parts.

The principles of perceptual integration are based on Gestalt psychologists' basic hypothesis that people organize perceptions to form a complete picture of an object. Perceptual integration is a process of forming many disparate stimuli into an organized whole. The picture on a television screen is a good example. In actuality, it is made up of thousands of tiny dots, but we integrate these dots into a cohesive whole so that there is little difference between the picture on the screen and the real world.

The most important principles of perceptual integration are those of closure, grouping, and context.

CLOSURE

Closure refers to a perceiver's tendency to fill in the missing elements when a stimulus is incomplete. Consumers desire to form a complete picture, and they derive a certain amount of satisfaction in completing a message on their own. This principle operates when consumers develop their own conclusions from moderately ambiguous advertisements. Heimbach and Jacoby showed that an incomplete ad may increase attention to and recall of the message.[49] They presented one group of consumers with a complete commercial and another group with a commercial cut at the end. The incomplete commercial generated 34 percent more recall than did the complete version.

The principle of closure was shown in an ad for J&B Scotch whisky. In this ad, the letters J and B were left out of "jingle bells." The desire to produce closure caused the viewer to organize the information into the brand name J&B.

GROUPING

Consumers are more likely to perceive a variety of information as chunks than as separate units. They integrate various bits and pieces of information into organized wholes. **Chunking,** or **grouping, information** permits consumers to evaluate one brand over another by using a variety of attributes. Principles of grouping that have emerged from Gestalt psychology are proximity, similarity, and continuity. These principles are represented in Figure 6.2.

The tendency to group stimuli by **proximity** means that one object is associated with another because of its closeness to that object. Because of their horizontal proximity, the twelve dots in Figure 6.2 are seen as four columns of three dots rather than three rows of four dots. Most advertising employs principles of proximity by associating the product with positive symbols and imagery close to the product. For example, an L.A. Gear ad positions sneakers in proximity to a guitar and a picture of James Dean. The attempt is to associate the product with rock music and with a symbol of antiestablishment culture.

Web sites' home pages are designed using the principles of proximity by organizing brand or product category information closely. For example, Disney's home page organizes the site's content into categories consumers can associate with. Under the heading "Entertainment" a user could get information about Disney movies, TV, and videos (see Exhibit 6.5). In addition, the company uses animation, sounds, and pictures to associate the web site with the values Disney portrays offline.

Consumers also group products by **similarity.** The eight squares and four circles in Figure 6.2 are grouped in three sets because of their similarity—two sets of four squares and one set of four circles. Web sites use similarity in the design of their home pages. Disney's home page (Exhibit 6.5) shows a picture of a theme park with a train driving through each of the options the user can click on (entertainment, vacations, shopping, etc.). The intention is to organize the site by similarity of each option provided.

Consumers also group stimuli into uninterrupted forms, rather than into discontinuous contours, to attain **continuity.** The dots in the third part of Figure 6.2 are more likely to be seen as an arrow projecting to the right than as columns of dots. In applying continuity to a retail store, no sharp breaks should occur from one sales station to the next by type of merchandise; the transition should be reasonably continuous. Continuity is impor-

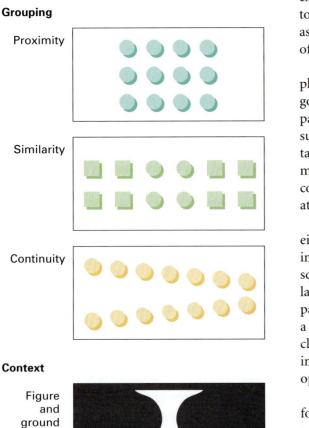

Grouping

Proximity

Similarity

Continuity

Context

Figure and ground

| FIGURE 6.2 |

Principles of organization.

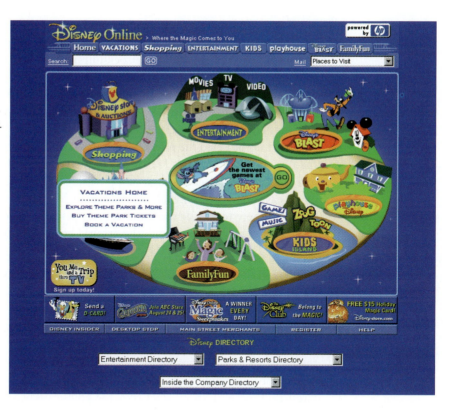

tant in web site development, especially if it is a multicategory web site. Issues such as what brand information to start with and where and how to provide brand name, pricing, and specification information arise. The train in the Disney example cited attains continuity. By showing the categories pictorially and having the train circle through each area, Disney can provide a continuous flow of information.

CONTEXT

Consumers tend to perceive an object by the **context** in which it is shown; therefore the setting of an advertisement influences the perception of a product. For example, consumers may perceive one advertisement quite differently in two different media. In a study by Fuchs, identical advertisements were placed in high-prestige magazines (*Harper's, New Yorker*) and in low-prestige magazines (*True, Detective*). Not surprisingly, consumers rated advertisements in the high-prestige magazines much higher than the identical ads in low-prestige magazines, showing that media context directly influences the perception of the ad.[50]

The most important principle of context is **figure and ground.** Gestalt psychologists state that in organizing stimuli into wholes, individuals distinguish stimuli that are prominent (the figure that is generally in the foreground) from stimuli that are less prominent (those in the ground or background). The lower part of Figure 6.2 illustrates the principle of figure and ground. The picture can be seen as a goblet (figure) with a dark background or as two profiles (figure) with a lighter background. Advertisers seek to ensure that the product is the figure and the setting is the background.

The determination of what part of the whole is the figure and what part is ground greatly affects the way consumers perceive stimuli. Pets.com, a now bankrupt Internet start-up, adopted a sock puppet character as its mascot in an aggressive campaign to build brand recognition. The memorable character—a wisecracking, soda-drinking dog—became a cultural icon printed on T-shirts and interviewed on television talk shows. However, the commercials, although entertaining, failed to describe the advantages of Pets.com's products and services,[51] because they reversed the proper use of figure and ground. One commercial showed the dog drinking a can of Fresca out of a straw, with the Fresca positioned in the foreground and Pet.com's logo barely visible in the background. The commercial could easily have been mistaken for a Fresca ad, with the soda as figure. The ad did little to adhere to a basic communications principle: Product benefits and associations should be the figure, with the ground being a supportive context.

Perceptual Interpretation

Once consumers select and organize stimuli, they interpret them. Two basic principles help consumers interpret marketing information. The first principle involves a tendency to place information into logical categories. **Categorization** helps consumers process known information quickly and efficiently. ("This is another ad for Crest toothpaste. I know what they are going to say, so I don't have to pay much attention.") Categorization also helps consumers classify new information. ("This is an ad for a new breakfast food that is probably like Carnation Slender.")

Inference involves the development of an association between two stimuli. For example, consumers might associate a high price with quality or blue suds in a detergent with cleansing power.

PERCEPTUAL CATEGORIZATION

Marketers seek to facilitate the process of perceptual categorization. They want to make sure consumers recognize a brand as part of a product class but do not want their brand to be a direct duplicate of other brands. **Product positioning** attempts to establish both product categorization and product uniqueness.

Monsanto's Starch-Eze failed because it was not correctly categorized. A starch concentrate, Starch-Eze had to be diluted and was meant to be used only every ten or twelve washings.[52] The product was advertised as a starch, and the name implied it was easy to use. Thus, consumers categorized it as another brand of starch and used it in every wash cycle. The result was a cardboard shirt.

The Monsanto example illustrates the importance of categorizing a new product. One recent study found that advertisers can significantly influence the way consumers categorize new products by the associations made in that product's advertising or by the placement of the product in a store. For example, associating a digital camera with either film or computer graphics in advertising, or placing the product in the camera or computer aisle of an electronics store, will influence whether consumers categorize it as an extension of the camera or computer category.[53]

FIGURE 6.3
Category levels for computers.

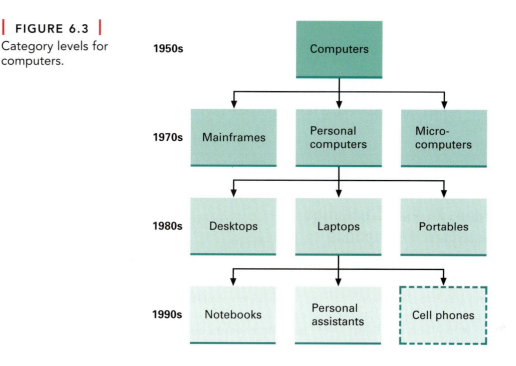

Category Levels   When consumers first learn about a product, they classify it at the most basic level. As they process more information, they then develop a capacity to use refined classifications.[54] For example, when computers were first introduced in the 1950s, they were all in one category. By the 1970s, consumers could distinguish between mainframes, microcomputers, and then later, personal computers (PCs) (see Figure 6.3). By the 1980s, PCs could be categorized into desktops, portables, and laptops. Then, by the 1990s, as laptops became more widespread, they were further categorized as notebooks and personal assistants. In the future, cell phones might develop laptop capabilities.

The more involved the consumer, the greater the likelihood that he or she classifies stimuli at more refined levels. Thus, the typical consumer might say, "I rode to work in my neighbor's car," whereas the car buff might say, "I rode to work in my neighbor's new Chevy Blazer." Categorization based on usage also varies across cultures. Chinese consumers are likely to have many categories for bicycles, but they may view computers as one category. Conversely, most American consumers view bicycles as one category but recognize several categories for computers.

The Process of Categorization   The process of establishing subcategories within a broader product category can be better understood by introducing two concepts—schema and subtyping.

Schema.   When consumers first gather information about a new product like computers, they store bits and pieces of information about the category in their memory.[55] As they gain more knowledge of the category, they recall information in clusters of thoughts, ideas, and symbols known as a **schema**.[56] The consumers' original schema for computers in the 1950s might have equated them to desk calculators and more generally to business machines. By the 1960s, consumers' schema for computers had become more detailed, probably involving ideas and objects such as "punch cards," "mainframes," and "automatic processing." By the 1990s, the schema was transformed to include terms such as "microprocessors," "operating systems," and "workstations."

STRATEGIC APPLICATIONS

OF CONSUMER BEHAVIOR

J.D. Power Expands Its Auto Categories to Conform to Consumer Perceptions

J.D. Power is a company that provides product recommendations to consumers, much like *Consumer Reports*. But whereas *Consumer Reports* develops its product evaluations based on its own expert testing of product performance, J.D. Power rates products based on consumer surveys. The company's consumer satisfaction ratings for automobiles are widely used by consumers to help them select cars and by car companies to help them sell cars. J.D. Power rates car models on a five-point scale, with a 5 meaning the model is among the top 10 percent in consumer satisfaction, a 4 meaning it is in the top 20 percent, and so on. Car models are rated on criteria such as mechanical quality, performance, creature comforts, mechanical reliability and dependability, style, and safety. The company also collects data on the model and type of car owned.

J.D. Power reports car ratings and ownership not only by model, but also by automobile category. Recently, the company expanded its car categories to reflect changes in consumer perceptions and ownership patterns. The car categories the company used in 1996 and 1999 are listed in the table in the first column.

The most striking difference in the change in categories over this three-year period is in the luxury and large car categories. Whereas in 1996 there was one luxury car category, by 1999 J.D. Power had three categories for large-sized/luxury cars. Further, in 1999 it distinguished between compact and full-sized vans.

Why the expanded categories for luxury/large-sized models? This change occurred because in the affluent 1990s, a wider group of consumers were willing to consider luxury cars as an alternative to economy and midsized models. The luxury car category became more mainstream, with companies like Honda and Toyota offering models to challenge the more traditional Cadillacs, Lincolns, and Mercedes. As a result, the distinction between the luxury and large categories became more meaningful, as did (within the luxury category) the distinction between domestic and international. These categories merely reflected those that consumers had developed in their own minds as they became willing to spend more money on automobiles.

1996	1999
1. Compact	1. Compact Premium
2. Economy	2. Compact Entry
3. Midsize	3. Midsize
4. Sports	4. Sporty
5. Luxury	5. Basic Large Vehicle
	6. Domestic Luxury
	7. International Luxury
6. Compact Pickup	8. Compact Truck
7. Full-Sized Pickup	9. Full-Sized Truck
8. SUV	10. SUV
9. Minivan	11. Compact Van
	12. Full-Size Van

Sources: Nielsen Television Index, 1996 and 1999; www.jdpower.com, as of October 2001.

equity, as reflected in the estimate that the Coca-Cola name is worth more than $100 billion exclusive of physical facilities. This estimate is based solely on the value of the brand name.

The key ingredient in influencing consumers' brand image is product positioning. Marketers try to position their brands to meet the needs of defined customer segments. They do so by developing a product concept that can communicate the desired benefits through advertising and by utilizing media that reach the target segment.

Brand image formation is as important online as offline. As mentioned earlier, it is essential for offline firms to reinforce their existing brand image online if their web sites are to be successful. It is more difficult for pure dot-coms to establish a brand image, for the simple reason that they have to start from scratch. Companies that have effectively offered an online value proposition to consumers have been successful. For example, eBay has been effective in filling the need for an online mass auction facility. In contrast, companies that did not have a well-defined value proposition or were ineffective in communicating value have failed online. A company like Pets.com spent millions on magazine and TV advertising. It was successful in creating awareness of its ads, but it did not establish a strong brand image because of its failure to communicate what it was delivering to consumers.

| **Store Image**   Consumers develop store images based on advertising, merchandise in the store, opinions of friends and relatives, and shopping experiences. Store image often influences brand image. Consumers will perceive the identical product differently in Wal-Mart or Kmart than in Nieman-Marcus or Bloomingdale's. In one study, four identical samples of carpet were given to consumers to evaluate.[65] Each sample was labeled with a more and a less prestigious store.

Even when prices were identical, consumers rated the same samples higher in a prestigious store than those in a less prestigious one. A positive store image thus produced a positive brand image, even though product and price were identical.

Retailers have a particular stake in establishing a positive store image, as their image is directly tied to sales results. JCPenney upgraded its image by repositioning its line to higher-quality merchandise.[66] It deleted appliances, garden supplies, and automotive products and put more emphasis on designer clothing.

■ **Corporate Image**   Consumers also organize the variety of information about companies and experiences with a company's products into corporate images. Companies spend millions of dollars to improve their images with the public for several reasons. First, a positive corporate image reinforces positive perceptions of the company's products. Such a link between corporate and brand image is particularly important when the brand name is closely associated with the company. General Electric advertises itself as innovative and forward-looking in the hope that consumers will carry over the association to its brands. Such advertising is not as important for Procter & Gamble, because that company does not link its brands closely to the corporate name.

Companies also seek to maintain a favorable image regarding public issues that may directly affect consumers. For example, Toyota advertised that it invested $5 billion in the American economy through manufacturing facilities in Kentucky and California and the creation of sixteen thousand U.S. jobs. The purpose was to show that Toyota's presence in America is having a positive effect.[67]

PERCEIVED RISK

One important component of perceptual interpretation is **perceived risk.** The perception that a purchase might be risky is an outcome of how consumers perceive the brand and the purchasing process.

■ **Factors Associated with Perceived Risk**   Several factors are likely to increase the risk consumers see in purchasing. Risk is likely to be perceived as greater when

- consumers are highly involved with the purchasing process.
- there is little information about the product category.
- the product is new.
- the product is technologically complex.
- consumers have little self-confidence in evaluating brands.
- there are variations in quality among brands.
- the price is high.
- the purchase is important to consumers.[68]

Perceived risk in purchasing DVD players is high because most of the preceding listed criteria will be met. As the product category is still relatively new for many consumers, they have little experience with alternatives. Moreover, the product is technologically complex, making evaluation more difficult. As a result, consumer confidence in selecting one brand over another is low. Furthermore, substantial variations among brands and incompatible systems heighten risk. A high price also contributes to perceived risk. Finally, such a purchase is probably important to consumers.

Perceived risk is also likely for well-established products. Self-confidence in purchasing products such as cameras, stereo equipment, and carpeting is low because most consumers lack knowledge of the criteria by which to judge variations among brands and price. To reduce risk, consumers tend to rely on sources of information with a high degree of credibility, such as friends who have purchased the brand or impartial sources such as *Consumer Reports.*

■ **Types of Risk**   Consumers may face several different types of risk in purchasing decisions:

1. *Financial risk* is a function of the cost of a product relative to consumers' disposable incomes. For example, the consumer who has saved for four years to buy a high-priced car runs a greater risk than the individual who can buy the same car out of discretionary income every two years.

2. *Social risk* means that a purchase may not meet the standards of an important reference group. Visible items (clothing, cars, household furnishings) and items designed to enhance social attractiveness (cosmetics, mouthwash) are particularly subject to social risk.

3. *Psychological risk* is the loss of self-esteem when the consumer recognizes an error—for example, buying a product and seeing it at a cheaper price a week later, or having difficulty operating a product like a VCR timer.

4. *Performance risk* is associated with the possibility that the product will not work as anticipated, or may fail. It is greatest when the product is technically complex or when ego-related needs are involved.

5. *Physical risk* is the risk of bodily harm as a result of product performance—for example, faulty brakes that could lead to a car crash, or an adverse reaction to a pharmaceutical product.

The Internet lends itself to new kinds of perceived risk in addition to the types just described. Examples of risks consumers perceive in using the Internet include the following:

■ *Security of financial information.* Consumers worry that entering their credit card number online will put them at risk of fraud.

■ *Privacy.* Consumers fear that marketers (or their employers) will be able to see and track their net-surfing behavior.

■ *No direct product contact.* Without being able to see or touch the actual product, consumers worry that the product will not be what they think it is.

■ *Difficulty in navigation.* Consumers fear that difficulty in navigation will cause them to be unable to gather as much information as they would like.

■ *Shipping and handling costs.* These costs are often not disclosed until the end of the sale and are, therefore, generally a reason for lack of completion of intended purchases.

■ *Late delivery, or delivery of damaged or incomplete products.*

■ **Consumer Strategies to Reduce Risk**   The most direct means consumers use to reduce risk is to engage in more extensive information processing to better evaluate alternatives. More detailed brand evaluation can ensure that consumers avoid products that fail. The Internet is a vehicle to reduce risk because it allows the consumer to access more information to identify more alternatives and to better evaluate these alternatives. For example, as discussed in Chapter 2, consumers can go to *www.autobytel.com* as an unbiased source to search for product and service information, pricing information, options available, recall history, warranties, loan information, and more.

Another strategy to reduce risk is brand loyalty. Buying the same brand repeatedly increases the certainty of the purchase outcome because consumers know what to expect from the product. The best way to avoid the possibility of dissatisfaction is to stay with a reasonably acceptable alternative. Many consumers make Internet purchases from the web sites of traditional companies because they are more familiar with their name than that of an Internet-only company. For instance, eToys was the first company to offer sales of toys through the Internet. Analysts expected eToys to change the way people shop for toys, and brick-and-mortar competitors such as Toys "R" Us were afraid that eToys' first-mover advantage would make it hard to compete. Two years after its initial start-up, the e-tailer went bankrupt. The reason cited for the bankruptcy was heavy competition—not from other e-tailers, but from traditional brick-and-mortar companies such as Toys "R" Us, Wal-Mart, and Target.

Other strategies to reduce risk are to buy the lowest-priced item or the smallest size. Obtaining a warranty or guarantee on the product also reduces the consequence of failure. These strategies reduce financial risk but not psychological risk. A strategy for reducing the psychological risk of making the wrong decision is to reduce the level of expectation before making the purchase. Consider a purchaser who decides that cars are a necessary evil that inevitably succumb to mechanical failures and engender repair bills. This purchaser is not going to be terribly disappointed if his or her car does not perform well; he or she expects it.

■ **Marketer Strategies to Reduce Risk**   Marketers can reduce risk to consumers by offering warranties, money-back guarantees, and liberal return policies for defective merchandise. Offering products at lower prices or in smaller packages also minimizes consumers' risk in trying a product for the first time. Free samples also give consumers the opportunity to try new products before making a purchase commitment.

Internet marketers can reduce risk through strategies such as frequent communications to increase confidence, offering online services such as postorder follow-up, minimizing the number of clicks to get information, and providing links in the Internet site to past ads or associations to increase familiarity. A number of firms now specialize in helping consumers be more comfortable with Internet purchasing. One such company is shopsmart.com. This UK company provides consumers with a list of one thousand UK online stores. These stores are reviewed and rated based on ease of use, product range, quality of shopping experience, and customer service. In addition, all stores on the list meet shopsmart criteria of providing secure online transactions and offering contact details for consumers.

Price Perceptions

Consumers' price perceptions may appear to be a simple matter of determining a product's price based on an ad or on observation in a store. However, it is not that simple because consumers (1) have certain expectations about what prices are or should be, and (2) frequently associate price level with the product's quality.

PRICE EXPECTATIONS

When deciding whether to replace an old nineteen-inch color TV set, a consumer may expect to pay about $400 for a comparable set. This price is the consumer's **reference price** (also known as a **standard price**); that is, the price the consumer expects to pay for a certain item. The reference price serves as a standard or frame of reference by which consumers compare prices for alternative brands.[69]

Consumers do not have just one price point when they consider buying a product. Generally, they are willing to accept a range of prices, known as an **acceptable price range,** for a particular product. The reference price and the acceptable price range for the consumer buying a TV set are shown at the top of Figure 6.5. The acceptable price range is from $250 on the lower end to $500 on the higher end. The higher end of the acceptable price range is known as the **reservation price** and is the "upper limit above which an article would be judged too expensive." The lower end of the acceptable price range is the "lower limit below which the quality of the item would be suspect."[70]

One other measure of price expectations is shown in Figure 6.5. The **expected price range** is the range of prices the consumer expects to find in the marketplace.[71] This range is almost always wider than the acceptable price range. In our example, the consumer expects to find nineteen-inch color TV sets priced as high as $600 and as low as $200, but anything above or below the acceptable price range is unlikely to influence the consumer's behavior.

Research has found that consumers typically understate actual prices.[72] That is, if the consumer's expected price range for color TVs is $200 to $600, the actual price range might be from $300 to $750. But when consumers are actively involved in the decision and are collecting product information, the expected and actual price ranges converge.[73]

| FIGURE 6.5 |

Measures of consumers' price expectations.

PRICE-QUALITY RELATIONSHIP

Consumers are most likely to perceive a price-quality association when they do not have sufficient information about product quality. In that situation, they use price as an indication of quality. Because these consumers know little about the product, they are less likely to be involved. Conversely, consumers with information about product characteristics are less likely to make price-quality inferences. These consumers are more likely to be involved with the product category.[74]

Price is also more likely to be a reflection of quality if consumers have confidence in the source of the price information. A study of online shopping found that consumers were willing to pay more for branded merchandise or for goods from retailers they knew well because of the credibility and reliability of the price information. The quality association of a brand name warranted a higher price.[75]

SUMMARY

A product's success depends largely on the way consumers perceive and process marketing stimuli designed to promote it. In this chapter, the nature of marketing stimuli and how consumers perceive them were considered.

Marketing stimuli were classified into the primary stimulus (the product) and the secondary stimuli (symbols, imagery, and information representing the product). A key question is the degree to which consumers can discriminate between marketing stimuli. Marketers attempt to create such discrimination by informing consumers about the differences between their brands and competitors' brands. Consumers also generalize from one similar stimulus to another. By using existing brand names for new products, marketers use strategies of stimulus generalization through brand leveraging. Positive associations with the existing brand help launch the new product. The chapter also recognized that consumers differ in their ability to perceive marketing stimuli.

Selection, organization, and interpretation are the three basic processes underlying consumer perceptions. Selection involves being attentive to stimuli and selectively perceiving them. Selective perception serves two purposes: (1) it guides consumers in selecting information that is relevant and in screening out information that is not relevant to their needs (a process known as "perceptual vigilance"), and (2) it permits consumers to select information that conforms to their beliefs and predispositions about brands, products, and companies (a function known as "perceptual defense").

The organization of marketing stimuli depends on the principle of integration. Integration permits consumers to perceive many different stimuli and to organize them into a cohesive whole. Consumers integrate information by the processes of closure, grouping, proximity, similarity, continuity, and context.

Interpretation of stimuli also depends on two processes: categorization and inference. Categorization simplifies information processing by permitting consumers to classify brands into product categories. Inference is a belief about objects that consumers develop from past associations. Consumers often make product inferences based on the symbols associated with products. The science of semiotics analyzes the meaning consumers give symbols and their association to objects such as brands and products.

Consumers form total perceptions or images of brands, stores, and companies based on inferences. Marketers try to influence brand image by communicating desired product benefits through positioning strategies. The store image also influences the brand image, particularly for brands that are distributed in selective stores. The corporate image affects consumers' purchasing behavior, particularly for brands that are tied to the company name.

Consumer perceptions of prices are particularly important to marketers because they often influence perceptions of quality. Consumers also form expectations regarding price levels that influence their behavior.

Embedded in this chapter were the implications of how consumers perceive brands on the Internet. The chapter discussed the risks firms face in developing web sites, how generalization can affect Internet marketing, how selective perception can be managed on the Internet, and the marketing implications of categorization.

Chapter 7 focuses on how consumers process the information they perceive.

QUESTIONS FOR DISCUSSION

1. What were Pepsi's objectives in launching the Pepsi Blue campaign?

2. Are there likely to be any differences in a blind taste test of Pepsi versus Coke compared with a labeled taste test? Why?

3. What is the likely effect of the ability of consumers to discriminate marketing stimuli on the Web as web usage becomes more widespread?

4. Can you cite applications of the differential threshold to changes in (a) package size and (b) advertising duration and intensity?

5. Some studies have shown that sensory perceptions (taste, smell, etc.) play a minimal role in the selection of major national brands in such categories as tea, coffee, cigarettes, and perfumes. How does Coca-Cola's experience when it had to reintroduce old Coke relate to this finding?

6. What are the implications of the concept of stimulus discrimination for changes in the packaging of Ivory Soap in the hundred-plus years it has been in existence?

7. How has the consumer's adaptation level diminished the effectiveness of banner ads on the Web?

8. What are the implications of the concept of stimulus generalization for (a) GE using its name on refrigerators, (b) Colgate introducing cold tablets and antacids under its name, and (c) Bic introducing perfumes?

9. What are the requirements of successfully leveraging an existing brand's or company's image and equity to an online presence?

10. What is the distinction between perceptual vigilance and perceptual defense? Which is more likely to operate when (a) a consumer buys the same brand of frozen orange juice because of inertia and (b) a consumer buys the same perfume because of brand loyalty?

11. What are the implications of principles of proximity and similarity for (a) product-line policies and (b) in-store product organization?

12. How do the principles of proximity, similarity, and continuity apply to web site design?

13. What are some of the implications of the principle of context for (a) media selection, (b) advertising layout, and (c) positioning of brands to specific usage situations?

14. Do consumers have a schema for brands such as the Macintosh computer as well as categories such as PCs? What is the purpose of a brand-related schema? What might be some logical components of a Macintosh schema?

15. Cite a product category and trace the subtyping that has occurred over time for the category. Why does such subtyping take place?

16. What are the marketing implications of categorization in identifying the logical extensions of a company's businesses?

17. How can a semiotician help a marketer in developing an advertising campaign for a BMW motorcycle in an attempt to challenge Harley-Davidson's dominant position?

18. Why are certain companies that do not sell directly to the final consumer (*e.g.,* pharmaceutical companies) concerned with the corporate image they project to the consuming public?

19. Under what conditions is price likely to be used as an indicator of quality? Are consumers more likely to establish a price-quality association for certain products than for others? If so, what products?

RESEARCH ASSIGNMENTS

1 Pick two closely competing brands in two product categories: a high-involvement category (such as cars) and a low-involvement category (such as toothpaste). Identify a number of consumers who own or regularly use each brand. Ask consumers to rate the two competing brands (their own and the close competitor) on a number of need criteria (for cars it might be economy, durability, and style). If consumers perceive brands selectively, they are likely to rate their own brand much higher than they do the competitive brand. This selective perception should be more likely for the high-involvement than it is for the low-involvement category.

- Do your findings show this to be true? That is, (a) are brand ratings for the consumer's own brand much higher than those of the competitive brand, and (b) are the differences in ratings between the regular and competitive brands greater for the high-involvement product category?

- Do consumers rate their own brand much higher on certain attributes but not on others?

- Do these differences reflect a process of selective perception?

2 Test consumers' ability to discriminate between the taste of alternative brands in one of the following product categories: soft drinks, coffee, or tea. Run the following experiment: Identify three leading brands in the category. (Make sure the brands tested are in the same class for the product; for example, colas or noncolas for soft drinks, regular or instant for coffee.) Select an equal number of respondents who pick one of the three brands as their regular brand. Ask all respondents how often they purchase their regular brand. Then have each respondent taste the three unidentified brands. (Make sure to rotate the order of tasting so the same brand is not always presented first.) Ask the respondent to identify his or her preferred brand. On the basis of chance, one would expect one-third correct identification.

- Was the proportion of correct identification significantly more than chance?

- Were those who correctly identified their preferred brand different from those who did not? Were they more frequent users of the category? Did they use a certain brand?

3 Select two retailers that have an online presence, one being a traditional retailer, the other a pure dot-com. Select a sample of Internet users and have them rate the two sites on criteria such as quality, service, range of merchandise, and adequacy of information.

- How do perceptions of the two sites differ? What are the implications for building brand equity?

- Did the traditional retailer's web site reflect the same brand image as the brick-and-mortar facilities?

4 Select two advertising campaigns that are informationally oriented and two that rely on symbolism and imagery and can be regarded as more ambiguous. Select a sample of consumers and measure (a) unaided advertising awareness for the four brands and (b) awareness of key points in the advertising message.

- Was awareness of the informationally oriented campaign more accurate than that of the more ambiguous campaign?

- Were consumers more likely to project themes and messages not actually in the ads into the more ambiguous communications? If so, what was the nature of these projections?

- Did you detect any misperception or misinterpretation of the advertising messages? Did these misperceptions reflect perceptual defense?

5 Select a frequently purchased consumer good (such as toothpaste, detergents, or analgesics). Select a sample of fifty consumers who buy the product. Determine each consumer's acceptable price range by identifying a standard size and by asking consumers the price below which they would not trust the product's quality and the price above which they would not buy. In addition:

- Ask consumers to identify their regular brand. Then ask them to assume there is a price increase in their regular brand. At what price increase would they switch to a competitive brand?

- Determine the strength of the consumers' preference for the regular brand. Do they think it is the best brand on the market, one of the best brands, or the same as other brands?

- One would expect that the higher the price required for the consumer to switch to another brand, the greater the degree of brand loyalty. Was this confirmed in your study?

NOTES

1. "Pepsi Gets Ready to Roll Out the Blue Cans," *Atlanta Constitution* (September 30, 1997), p. C01.
2. "It's in the Can: Pepsi Enters a Blue Period to Raise World-Wide Sales," *Asian Wall Street Journal* (April 3, 1996), p. 1.
3. "The Point of Saturation," *Marketing Week* (March 11, 1999), p. 40.
4. Ibid.
5. "Pepsi Blue, or Is It White?" *Marketing* (August 6, 1998), p. 3.
6. "Red Symbols Tend to Lure Shoppers Like Capes Being Flourished at Bulls," *Wall Street Journal* (September 18, 1995), p. A9B.
7. Ibid.
8. "Design Research: Beauty or Beast," *Advertising Age* (March 9, 1981), p. 43.
9. "Mary Kay Puts on a New Face," *Adweek's Marketing Week* (July 3, 1989), p. 4.
10. "Mary Kay Fleet Gets Makeover with GM OnStar," *Twice* (February 22, 1999), p. 42.
11. "P&G Discovers a New Look to an Old Product," *New York Times* (January 28, 1993), p. D20.
12. Laurence Jacobs, Charles Keown, Reginald Worthley, and And-Il Ghymn, "Cross-Cultural Colour Comparisons: Global Marketers Beware!" *International Marketing Review,* 8 (1991), pp. 21–30.
13. "Crystal Pepsi, A Clear, Colorless Cola Is Being Launched in 3 Test Markets," *Wall Street Journal* (April 13, 1992), p. B7; and "Coke Hopes to Revive Tab as a Clear Cola," *Wall Street Journal* (December 15, 1992), pp. B1, B8.
14. Ralph I. Allison and Kenneth P. Uhl, "Influence of Beer Brand Identification on Taste Perception," *Journal of Marketing Research* 1 (August 1964), pp. 36–39.
15. William Copulsky and Katherine Marton, "Sensory Cues," *Product Marketing* (January 1977), pp. 31–34.
16. "Finding New Ways to Make Smell Sell," *New York Times* (July 23, 1988).
17. Gerald J. Gorn, "The Effects of Music in Advertising on Choice Behavior: A Classical Conditioning Approach," *Journal of Marketing* 46 (Winter 1982), pp. 94–101.
18. "Gap's Image Is Wearing Out," *Wall Street Journal* (December 6, 2001), p. B1.
19. R. Barton, *Advertising Media* (New York: McGraw-Hill, 1964), p. 109.
20. "Position in Newspaper Advertising: 2," *Media Scope* (March, 1963), pp. 76–82.
21. "New Media: Wallpaper or Banner Ads? Spot the Difference: Rich Johnston on the Panic Over Boring Online Advertising," *The Guardian* (January 8, 2001), p. 78.
22. Last picture of Betty Crocker in "My Years with Betty," *Wall Street Journal* (July 5, 1995), p. A6.
23. "Betty Crocker Plans to Mix Ethnic Looks for Her New Face," *Wall Street Journal* (September 11, 1995), pp. A1 and A6.
24. John Revett, "FTC Threatens Big Fines for Undersized Cigarette Warnings," *Advertising Age* (March 17, 1975), p. 1.
25. For additional references on subliminal advertising, see Timothy E. Moore, "The Case Against Subliminal Manipulation," *Psychology and Marketing* 5 (1988), pp. 297–316; Anthony Pratkanis and Anthony Greenwald, "Recent Perspectives on Unconscious Processing: Still No Marketing Applications," *Psychology and Marketing* 5 (1988), pp. 337–354; Philip M. Marikle and Jim Chessman, "Current Status of Research on Subliminal Perception," in Melanie Wallendorf and Paul Anderson, eds., *Advances in Consumer Research,* Vol. 14 (Provo, Utah: Association for Consumer Research, 1987), pp. 298–302.
26. See "What Hidden Sell Is All About," *Life* (March 31, 1958), pp. 104–114.
27. *New Yorker* (September 21, 1957), p. 33.
28. Timothy E. Moore, "Subliminal Advertising: What You See Is What You Get," *Journal of Marketing* 46 (Spring 1982), pp. 38–47.
29. M. L. DeFleur and R. M. Petranoff, "A Television Test of Subliminal Persuasion," *Public Opinion Quarterly* (Summer 1959), pp. 170–180.
30. "Subliminal Ad Okay If It Sells: FCC Peers into Subliminal Picture on TV," *Advertising Age* (1957).
31. Moore, "The Case Against Subliminal Manipulation," pp. 297–316; and Joel Saegert, "Why Marketing Should Quit Giving Subliminal Advertising the Benefit of the Doubt," *Psychology and Marketing* 4 (Summer 1987), pp. 107–120.
32. Chris Janiszewski, "Preconscious Processing Effects: The Independence of Attitude Formation and Conscious Thought," *Journal of Consumer Research* 15 (September 1988), pp. 199–209.
33. Wilson Bryan Key, *Media Sexploitation* (Englewood Cliffs, N.J.: Prentice-Hall, 1976).
34. Dennis L. Rosen and Surendra N. Singh, "An Investigation of Subliminal Embed Effect on Multiple Measures of Advertising Effectiveness," *Psychology and Marketing* 9 (March/April 1992), pp. 157–172.
35. "New Media: Wallpaper or Banner Ads?" p. 78.
36. "E-Commerce Overview—A Look at the Pros and Cons of Various Types of Web Advertising," *Wall Street Journal* (April 23, 2001), p. 12.
37. "'Out of Banner' Ads Face Skepticism, Poor Timing," *Electronic Commerce* (October 1, 2001), p. 1.
38. David A. Aaker and Kevin Lane Keller, "Consumer Evaluations of Brand Extensions," *Journal of Marketing* 54 (January 1990), pp. 27–41.

39. "Britain's Railways: The Rail Billionaires," *The Economist* (July 3, 1999), p. 57; Thomas K. Grose, "Brand New Goods: European Companies Are Discovering That Licensing a Brand Can Protect Its Trademark, Promote Its Image—And Generate Profits," *Time Inc.* (September 27, 1999), p. 62.

40. Brian Wansink, "Advertising's Impact on Category Substitution," *Journal of Marketing Research* 31(November 1994), pp. 505–515.

41. "Packaging Research Probes Stopping Power, Label Reading, and Consumer Attitudes Among the Targeted Audience," *Marketing News* (July 22, 1983), p. 8.

42. "Tooth-Brushers Take a Shine to Baking Soda," *Wall Street Journal* (March 2, 1992), pp. B1, B6.

43. Homer E. Spence and James F. Engel, "The Impact of Brand Preference on the Perception of Brand Names: A Laboratory Analysis," in David T. Kollat, Roger D. Blackwell, and James F. Engel, eds., *Research in Consumer Behavior* (New York: Holt, Rinehart & Winston, 1970), pp. 61–70.

44. Muzafer Sherif and Carl I. Hovland, *Social Judgment* (New Haven, Conn.: Yale University Press, 1964).

45. Ibid.

46. Ibid.

47. Fritz Heider, *The Psychology of Interpersonal Relations* (New York: John Wiley, 1958).

48. Mary Francis Luce, "Choosing to Avoid: Coping with Negatively Emotion-Laden Consumer Decisions," *Journal of Consumer Research* 24 (March 1998), pp. 409–433.

49. James T. Heimbach and Jacob Jacoby, "The Zerganik Effect in Advertising," in M. Venkatesan, ed., *Proceedings, 3rd Annual Conference* (Provo, Utah: Association for Consumer Research, 1972), pp. 746–758.

50. Douglas A. Fuchs, "Two Source Effects in Magazine Advertising," *Journal of Marketing Research* 1 (August 1964), pp. 59–62.

51. "Death of a Spokespup," *Adweek* (December 11, 2000), pp. 44–46.

52. Kenneth E. Runyon, *Consumer Behavior and the Practice of Marketing* (Columbus, Ohio: Charles E. Merrill, 1977), pp. 302–303.

53. C. Page Moreau, Arthur B. Markman and Donald R. Lehmann, "What Is It? Categorization: Flexibility and Consumers' Responses to Really New Products," *Journal of Consumer Research* 27 (March 2001), pp. 489–498.

54. Joseph W. Alba and J. Wesley Hutchinson, "Dimensions of Consumer Expertise," *Journal of Consumer Research* 13 (March 1987), pp. 411–454. For additional references on categorization, see Mita Sujan and Christine Dekleva, "Product Categorization and Inference Making: Some Implications for Comparative Advertising," *Journal of Consumer Research* 14 (December 1987), pp. 372–378; Joel B. Cohen and Kunal Basu, "Alternative Models of Categorization: Toward a Contingent Processing Framework," *Journal of Consumer Research* 13 (March 1987), pp. 455–472; Craig Thompson, "The Role of Context in Consumers' Category Judgments," in Thomas K. Srull, ed., *Advances in Consumer Research,* Vol. 16 (Provo, Utah: Association for Consumer Research, 1989), pp. 542–547; and Eloise Coupey and Kent Nakamoto, "Learning Context and the Development of Product Category Perceptions," in Michael J. Houston, ed., *Advances in Consumer Research,* Vol. 15 (Provo, Utah: Association for Consumer Research, 1987), pp. 77–82.

55. Bobby J. Calder and Paul H. Schurr, "Attitudinal Processes in Organizations," *Research in Organizational Behavior* 3 (1981), pp. 283–302.

56. For additional references on schema, see Lawrence W. Barsalou and J. Wesley Hutchinson, "Schema Based Planning of Events in Consumer Contexts," in Wallendorf and Anderson, *Advances in Consumer Research,* Vol. 14, pp. 114–118; and Meera Venkatraman and Angelina Villarreal, "Schematic Processing of Information: An Exploratory Investigation," in Thomas C. Kinnear, ed., *Advances in Consumer Research,* Vol. 11 (Provo, Utah: Association for Consumer Research, 1984), pp. 355–360.

57. Mita Sujan and James R. Bettman, "The Effect of Brand Positioning Strategies on Consumers' Brand and Category Perceptions: Some Insights from Schema Research," *Journal of Marketing Research* 26 (November 1989), pp. 454–467.

58. For additional references on perceptual inference, see Jeen-Su Lim, Richard W. Olshavsky, and John Kim, "The Impact of Inferences on Product Evaluations," *Journal of Marketing Research* 25 (August 1988), pp. 308–316; Valerie S. Folkes, Susan Koletsky, and John L. Graham, "A Field Study of Causal Inferences and Consumer Reaction," *Journal of Consumer Research* 13 (March 1987), pp. 534–539; Frank R. Kardes, "Spontaneous Inference Processes in Advertising," *Journal of Consumer Research* 15 (September 1988), pp. 225–233; and Gary T. Ford and Ruth Ann Smith, "Inferential Beliefs in Consumer Evaluation," *Journal of Consumer Research* 14 (December 1987), pp. 363–371.

59. See Arthur Asa Berger, *Signs in Contemporary Culture: An Introduction to Semiotics* (New York: Longman, 1984.)

60. Teresa J. Domzal and Jerome B. Kernan, "Reading Advertising: The What and How of Product Meaning," *Journal of Consumer Marketing* 9 (Summer 1992), pp. 48–64.

61. See David Mick, "Consumer Research and Semiotics: Exploring the Morphology of Signs, Symbols, and Significance," *Journal of Consumer Research* 13 (September 1986), pp. 196–213.

62. "PepsiCo Bases Water Ads on 'Nothing'," *Wall Street Journal* (June 25, 2001), p. B10.

63. "Firms' Eye-Catching Logos Often Leave Fuzzy Images in Minds of Consumers," *Wall Street Journal* (December 5, 1991), pp. B1, B8.

64. For a fuller understanding of the relationship of a consumer to a brand, see Susan Fournier, "Consumers and Their Brands: Developing Relationship Theory in Consumer Research," *Journal of Consumer Research* 24(March 1998), pp. 343–373.

65. Ben M. Enis and James E. Stafford, "Consumers' Perception of Product Quality as a Function of Various Informational Inputs," in Phillip R. McDonald, ed., *Marketing Involvement in Society and the Economy,* Proceedings of the American Marketing Association (Chicago: American Marketing Association, Series No. 30, 1969), pp. 340–344.

66. "Penney Moves Upscale in Merchandise but Still Has to Convince Public," *Wall Street Journal* (June 7, 1990), pp. A1, A8.

67. "A Corporate Campaign Tries Selling Toyota's U.S. Presence," *New York Times* (July 21, 1993), p. D24.

68. James R. Bettman, "Perceived Risk and Its Components: A Model and Empirical Test," *Journal of Marketing Research* 10 (May 1973), pp. 184–190.

69. See Robert Jacobson and Carl Obermiller, "The Formation of Expected Future Price: A Reference Price for Forward-Looking Consumers," *Journal of Consumer Research* 16 (March 1990), p. 420; and James E. Hegelson and Sharon E. Beatty, "Price Expectation and Price Recall Error: An Empirical Study," *Journal of Consumer Research* 14 (December 1987), p. 379.

70. Andre Gabor and C. W. J. Granger, "Price as an Indicator of Quality: Report on an Enquiry," *Economica* 46 (February 1966), pp. 43–70.

71. See Joel E. Urbany, William O. Bearden, and Dan C. Weilbaker, "The Effect of Plausible and Exaggerated Reference Prices on Consumer Perceptions and Price Search," *Journal of Consumer Research* 15 (June 1988), pp. 95–110.

72. E. Scott Maynes and Terje Assum, "Informationally Imperfect Consumer Markets: Empirical Findings and Policy Implications," *Journal of Consumer Affairs* 16 (Summer 1982), pp. 62–87.

73. Dhruv Grewal and Howard Marmostein, "Market Price Variation, Perceived Price Variation, and Consumers' Price Search Decisions for Durable Goods," *Journal of Consumer Research* 21 (December 1994), pp. 453–460.

74. Donald R. Lichtenstein, Peter H. Bloch, and William C. Black, "Correlates of Price Acceptability," *Journal of Consumer Research* 15 (September 1988), pp. 243–252.

75. "The Online Price Just Wasn't All That Right," *U.S. News & World Report* (February 12, 2001), p. 39.

Consumer Information Acquisition and Processing

To make purchasing decisions, consumers acquire and process information from advertising, the Web, friends and neighbors, and their own experiences with products. Acquiring information means that consumers must gather information from various sources based on their needs. Processing requires that consumers perceive information by selecting, organizing, and interpreting it, areas reviewed in Chapter 6. However, processing also requires that consumers go beyond these perceptual processes; consumers must retain information in memory and retrieve it when evaluating brands.

Marketers have a direct interest in the way consumers acquire and process information. If **consumer information processing** does not result in positive brand evaluation and purchase behavior, companies can lose millions of dollars on ineffective marketing.

Nike Facilitates Online Information Search

A web strategy is likely to fail if the company's site increases the complexity of the consumers' information search. Nike learned this lesson when it introduced Nike.com. When Nike first launched its site in 1996, it was designed simply as an extension of its advertising campaign—a marketing tool to support its efforts at the Atlanta Summer Olympics. The site, which lasted for just fifty-six days before being pulled for a complete overhaul, was thought to lack the innovation and creativity for which Nike is known.[1] For a long time, Nike's marketing team worried that if they tried to do too much online, they would directly conflict with their distributors and retailers. So, from 1996 through 1998, Nike's online presence consisted of old-fashioned advertising and investor information. Sports enthusiasts and other brand-loyal Nike consumers went to the site looking for information about the latest design in running shoes or aerobics apparel and were disappointed to find nothing more than what looked like a magazine advertisement.

In February 1999, Nike expanded its web site to include an online store called Niketown *(www. niketown.nike.com),* which sells footwear and apparel directly to consumers. This decision reflected the company's new understanding that an online store can be used as much as a source of information as a means of purchasing products. As Nike's director of U.S. sales pointed out, "a large percentage of consumers who check out the Internet are more interested in getting product information before buying the product in person than in placing an order online."[2] This perspective is reflected in Niketown's current home page (see Exhibit 7.1). The site, which allows consumers to shop for men's, women's, and children's products and identifies the most popular models, makes the information search easier and more convenient for consumers. Because of this focus on information rather than online purchasing, Nike avoids conflict with its retail outlets.

Recently, Nike developed an integrated marketing campaign that added unusual web components to capture eyeballs and user interests, mostly of the 18- to 24-year-old crowd that lives and breathes all things on the Web. For example, the company developed ads for Nike's Air Cross Trainer that featured American sport stars like Olympic runner Marion Jones, baseball icon Mark McGwire, and snowboarder Rob Kingwell. The sport-star TV spots featured cliffhanger endings and directed viewers to continue the action at "whatever.nike.com." Users were then able to choose from several endings via

EXHIBIT 7.1

Nike facilitates information search on its web site.

The Nike name, swoosh design, and product names are trademarks of Nike, Inc. and its affiliates. Copyright © 2002 Nike, Inc. All rights reserved.

streaming media technology.[3] These actions allow Nike to leverage its TV investments directly into promoting online traffic. It is not yet clear how greatly online sales have been impacted by the campaign.[4]

Nike also has developed content that appeals to specific areas of the world, with separate Internet sites for different countries, such as Canada, Japan, Korea, and Taiwan. These sites tailor content that is appropriate for the local culture. For example, the Canadian site includes an entire section for hockey. Information can be found regarding the game, equipment, and local retailers that carry Nike hockey gear. Nike also has developed links to local sporting event interests. For example, when one visits the soccer section of its site, links can be found to brazilfutbol.com and teams from other countries that wear the Nike logo.

Nike is selling more than just basic sneakers online. The site features a place for sports teams to customize shoes or apparel, create music videos, and purchase high-tech gadgets like distance monitors or two-way radios.[5] Customers can also enter the "design your own shoe" section that will enable consumers to select the style, color, measurements, and personalized characteristics of their new athletic shoes.

In this chapter, we extend our discussion of perception by focusing on how consumers process information. We first discuss how information is acquired from marketing and nonmarketing sources. We then consider information processing, with particular emphasis on the role of memory and the limitations consumers face in processing information. We conclude by considering the strategic and societal implications of information processing.

Consumer Information Acquisition

Consumers must acquire information before they can process it. The role of information acquisition in consumer decision making is shown in Figure 7.1.

Consumers acquire information from their environment—from ads, salespeople, word-of-mouth communications with friends and neighbors, impartial sources such as *Consumer Reports,* and so forth. In addition, more than ever, consumers perform their information searches online. In fact, according to a recent study by *Ad Age,* consumers utilize the Web more as a source for finding information about products than as a means of purchasing. In fact, a majority of consumers say they will not make a major purchase unless they first research the product or service on the Web. The Web is now so ubiquitous that many consumers view it as being as trustworthy and reliable as other more traditional sources of information.

Consumers acquire information offline and online in various ways. The method used is largely dependent on the consumer's level of involvement with the product. Table 7.1 shows that consumers use four different processes for acquiring such external information, with each process being related to the consumer's involvement with the product.

1. *Ongoing search.* This might characterize the consumer with enduring involvement in the product. For example, the computer buff who subscribes to com-

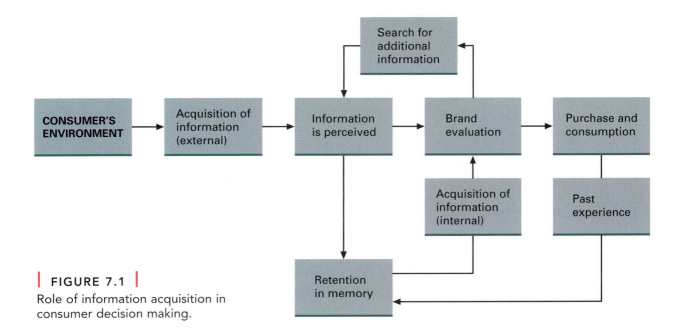

| FIGURE 7.1 |

Role of information acquisition in consumer decision making.

puter magazines is aware of a wide variety of options. Or alternatively, a consumer who actively participates in the stock market might subscribe to *Barron's* or *Investor's Daily,* and research stocks on *www.etrade.com* or *www.stocks.com* numerous times each day. Such ongoing searches are *directed* in that users focus on specific areas or product categories and know the direction their search will take.

2. *Directed purchase-specific search.* This type of search is characteristic of the consumer with situational involvement who collects information when making a purchase decision. For example, if a consumer is in the market for a minivan, she might visit a dealer or ask the advice of a friend who owns one. In this case, before visiting a dealer, the consumer might first acquire information from an **infomediary;** that is, a site designed to provide product information. Two such sites for cars are Kelley's Blue Book *(www.kbb.com),* and J.D. Power's ratings of car models *(www.jdpower.com/auto).* After getting information on specific models, a consumer might then go to a **BOT;** that is, a site designed to help a consumer make a decision. These sites serve as *recommendation agents* by asking consumers their needs and priorities (*e.g.,* the importance of safety,

TABLE 7.1
Processes for acquiring external information

Acquisition process	Type of involvement
1. Directed ongoing search	Enduring involvement
2. Directed purchase-specific search	Situational involvement, prior knowledge
3. Nondirected purchase-specific search	Situational involvement, little prior knowledge
4. Passive acquisition	Low involvement

style, performance, economy) and their price range. On this basis, BOTS will recommend models. Examples of such BOTS are *http://hotbot.lycos.com* and *http://shopping.yahoo.com.* The consumer might also go directly to a company's web site, such as *www.volvo.com,* for information about specific models.

3. *Nondirected purchase-specific search.* This type of search is most often done by a consumer who needs general information. For example, a consumer may need a new computer but is unsure what kind of computer she is looking for. The Web is a particularly good vehicle for starting such a search because of the existence of **search engines** (*e.g., www.google.com* and *www.altavista.com*). These sites are designed to identify other relevant web sites based on keywords. Choosing from among these sites, consumers begin the early stages of what will be a high-involvement search. The benefits of such a nondirected search are primarily educational; it helps the consumer identify the most important product attributes and identify brand and price alternatives.

4. *Passive acquisition of information.* This minimal search characterizes the uninvolved consumer. Information is acquired in passing, with little effort on the consumer's part. The benefits of actively acquiring additional information are not worth the cost. In the case of low-involvement products and services, the cost may be too great to engage in any kind of active information search. A consumer looking for a low-calorie cereal might simply examine several packages for nutritional information, look at prices, and wind up buying Product 19 because it is produced by Kellogg. The total time expended might be less than thirty seconds. There are ways in which consumers can passively gather information on the Web. A consumer can follow links on a web site letting the sequence of links control him or her instead of actively searching out information by controlling the search.

The Web is also a good vehicle for making simple decisions. In the case of a low-involvement situation, the consumer might simply want to buy the least expensive item or most popular brand. For example, an uninvolved consumer who wants to find the lowest-priced computer can quickly identify the lowest price alternative on most BOTS. To make shopping over the Internet easier, many shopping sites offer links to the lowest-priced or most popular item for specific product categories.

After acquiring information from the online or offline environment, consumers perceive it; that is, they organize and interpret it. In the course of processing the information, consumers may believe more information is necessary to evaluate alternative brands or to determine product features (see Figure 7.1). In seeking additional information about product or price alternatives, consumers reduce the risk of making a poor choice. They retain the more important information in memory to retrieve in the process of brand evaluation.

Consider the business school student who is in the market for a laptop computer. She is most concerned about the laptop's screen size, keyboard flexibility, and capacity of the hard drive. She stores in memory information on these three attributes for each brand being considered and retrieves it when she compares the brands. Figure 7.1 shows one other type of information stored in memory: past purchase and consumption experiences. These are also recalled in the process of brand evaluation. In this way, consumers learn from past experience.

Figure 7.1 shows that retrieving information from memory is regarded as *internal information acquisition* because the source of information is the consumer. The four types of information search in Table 7.1 represent *external information acquisition* in that consumers acquire new information.

DETERMINANTS OF INFORMATION SEARCH

A key component of information acquisition in Table 7.1 is whether the process is active or passive. Several factors encourage consumers to actively acquire more information:

1. *High consumer involvement.* As we saw in Chapter 4, the higher the level of involvement, the greater the amount of information acquired. That is, information search is greater if consumers' self-images are tied to the product, if the product has emotional appeal or badge value, or if consumers have ongoing interest in the product.

2. *High perceived risk.* The higher the perceived risk in purchasing, the greater the amount of information search. Locander and Hermann found that when risk was high, consumers searched for more information from neutral sources such as *Consumer Reports* and from personal sources such as friends and neighbors.[6] Murray also found that perceived risk increases information search, particularly for services compared to products. This is because services tend to be harder to evaluate, and collecting more information on them is instrumental in reducing risk.[7]

3. *Product uncertainty.* The more uncertain the consumer is about brand choice, the greater the product search. Moorthy and his colleagues found that when consumers were uncertain about which brand was best, they were more likely to search for information.[8]

4. *Little product knowledge and experience.* In a study of purchases of TVs, VCRs, and home computers, Beatty and Smith found that consumers with less knowledge of these products were more likely to search for information.[9] Conversely, Srinivasan and Ratchford found that past experience with a product reduced information search because consumers with experience learned how to search for information more efficiently.[10] However, if past experience is negative, it may increase the search for information.[11]

5. *Clear goals.* Information search is likely to be greater when consumers have clear goals that identify the features they want—for example, a goal of auto safety can be promoted with air bags and shatterproof glass. Huffman and Houston found that such clear goals direct a consumer to acquire specific information on product attributes.[12]

6. *Less time pressure.* Time pressure to make a decision discourages information search. Beatty and Smith found that if consumers have more time available, their information search increases.[13] This is probably true for high- rather than low-involvement products.

7. *High price.* The higher the price, the greater the information search. This was found to be true for women's apparel, appliances, and cars.[14] A higher price means that the economic benefits of information search are greater; therefore,

consumers are more likely to devote more effort to search. A higher price also means that consumers are more motivated to search so as to learn how to lower future search costs.[15]

8. *More product differences.* Searching for information has a higher payoff when substantial differences exist between brands. Claxton, Fry, and Portis found that furniture and appliance buyers who saw more differences between brands visited more stores.[16]

9. *Cost-effectiveness of information search.* Another determinant of information search is its cost. Monetary and nonmonetary costs are associated with information search. For example, information search frequently involves the monetary costs of traveling to various retail stores. Another cost is the time involved in traveling, shopping, reading advertisements, asking the advice of friends, and so on. Consumers must weigh search time against alternatives such as leisure or business pursuits. A third cost is psychological. Information search may not be desirable to individuals who dislike shopping.

SOURCES OF INFORMATION

Consumers can utilize several sources of information from their environment. Figure 7.2 shows these sources categorized on two dimensions: (1) personal versus nonpersonal sources and (2) marketer-controlled versus non-marketer-controlled sources. Figure 7.2 shows both offline and online sources categorized by these two dimensions.

In evaluating alternative laptop computers, our student utilizes all four types of sources shown in Figure 7.2. She talks to salespeople in retail stores about alternatives, prices, and peripherals, or after searching for information online, she receives emails from online retailers (personal marketer-controlled sources). She is aware of advertising in magazines for laptops and views online banner advertisements (nonpersonal marketer-controlled sources). She also talks to friends and business associates about their experiences with laptops and enters an online chatroom regarding laptops (personal non-marketer-controlled sources). Finally, she uses neutral sources such as *Consumer Reports* magazine, a publication that impartially tests and rates

FIGURE 7.2
Sources of consumer information off- and online.

	Personal	Nonpersonal
Marketer-controlled	• Salespeople • Telemarketing • Trade shows • email	• Media advertising • In-store displays • Sales promotions • Packaging • Internet advertising
Non-marketer-controlled	• Word of mouth • Professional advice • Experience from consumption • Chatrooms	• Publicity • Neutral sources (e.g., *Consumer Reports*) • Infomediaries • BOTS

products, to determine its evaluation of laptop brands, and online infomediaries such as J.D. Power, which impartially rates various models based on consumer satisfaction ratings (nonpersonal, non-marketer-controlled sources). Our consumer thus employs on- and offline sources for each of the alternatives in Figure 7.2.

Figure 7.2 shows the sources of information for external search. As we noted, consumers also undertake a process of internal search by retrieving information from memory. In trying out several laptop models her friends own, our consumer stores her experiences in memory and retrieves them in the process of brand evaluation.

The consumers' stage in the decision process affects their use of information sources. Marketer-controlled sources tend to be more important in the early stages of decision making when consumers are obtaining information on product alternatives. The opinions of friends and associates and the consumers' own experiences become more important as they move closer to the final decision because they regard these sources as more trustworthy.

Use of information sources also varies according to the conditions for information search. In their study of VCRs, TVs, and home computers, Beatty and Smith found that consumers with little product knowledge were more likely to rely on friends and associates for information because they are regarded as more credible than a salesperson.[17] On the other hand, more knowledgeable consumers are likely to rely on their past experiences because they are confident of their evaluations and judgments.

AMOUNT OF INFORMATION SEARCH

Despite consumers' reasons for undertaking a search for information, their amount of information search for all but the most expensive products is very limited.[18] In subscribing to principles of **cognitive economy,** consumers often consider the search for additional information not worth the time and effort involved.

Jacoby and his colleagues illustrated the limited nature of consumer search in an experiment.[19] They presented consumers of breakfast cereals with information in a matrix of sixteen brands by thirty-five product characteristics—560 pieces of information in all. On average, consumers selected eleven pieces of information, or less than 2 percent of the information available, before making a decision.

Other studies have focused on the number of retail stores consumers visited.[20] Most purchasers of toys and small appliances visit only one store. Purchasers of refrigerators and furniture are more likely to visit three or more stores. Half of the purchasers of cars and major appliances, however, visit only one showroom. The amount of shopping for these products is not as great as one might expect, given the risks involved. Similar behavior is found on the Web. Studies find that searches are often limited to one or two sites because it is often not worth the time and effort to go to more sites.[21]

Studies have also considered the number of alternative brands. One study found the following proportions of consumers considering more than one brand:[22]

∎ 59 percent for refrigerators
∎ 53 percent for cars and household appliances[23]
∎ 39 percent for washing machines
∎ 29 percent for vacuum cleaners

These figures suggest that the number of brands consumers consider is typically small. Although the evidence points to limited information search, this does not mean buyers are uninvolved. A prospective consumer may be entering the decision-making process with a large amount of past experience and purchase information stored in memory.[24] Therefore, for such consumers, the necessity for extensive information search may be low.

LIMITS OF INFORMATION ACQUISITION

Some consumer advocates and government agencies assume that consumers should be supplied with as much information as possible to permit a comparison of brand alternatives. The same assumption underlies economic theory: Optimal choice requires access to information on all alternatives. The reality, however, is that consumers rarely seek all of the available information. They find the cost of search and the complexity of processing just too great to attempt to consider all brand alternatives. Therefore, more information is not necessarily better. In fact, too much information may create **information overload;** that is, confusion in the decision task, resulting in an ineffective decision.

Jacoby, Speller, and Kohn found that information overload exists.[25] They provided consumers with a range of eight to seventy-two items of information on alternative laundry detergents by varying the number of brands consumers could consider and the number of pieces of information per brand. They then related the amount of information to the effectiveness of brand choice. Effectiveness of choice was determined by the degree to which consumers chose brands that were similar to their ideal laundry detergent. If consumers used up to twenty-four pieces of information, the "more is better" notion seemed to hold. However, more than twenty-four pieces of information seemed to cause consumers to choose brands that were not similar to their ideal. Thus, having too much information and too many brands to choose from complicated the consumers' decision task and resulted in less effective choices.

Similarly, in a study of supermarket shoppers, two displays were set up, one with thirty varieties of jam, the other with six. When consumers were offered a discount coupon to purchase jam, only 3 percent bought from the display with thirty items, while over 30 percent bought from the display with six items.[26]

Consumers react by filtering out information and looking only at the most important information in the context of their needs. The possibility that at some point too much information may have negative consequences on decision tasks suggests that both advertisers and public agencies must be careful not to provide consumers with irrelevant information. The problem is aggravated by the sheer number of commercials on the air. Simplifying information on complex decisions would be a step in the right direction.

Information overload is a particular problem on the Web. Consumers sometimes face a large number of web sites or a confusing set of choices within individual sites. They logically react by limiting the time spent on the Web because of frustration, confusion, and time constraints.

Another factor contributing to information overload is the large number of alternative brands available to consumers. A decade ago, the average supermarket carried nine thousand items; today, it carries over forty thousand. American consumers buying cereal face a choice of more than two hundred products. Further, the number of variations of existing products (known as brand extensions) has increased tremendously because marketers are finding it safer and cheaper to rely on such extensions rather than on new products. As a result, there are sixteen flavors of EGGO waffles, nine variations of Kleenex tissues, and nineteen Pert Plus shampoos and conditioners. Originally, Pert Plus was introduced as one product, a combination shampoo and conditioner.[27]

INFORMATION ACQUISITION FOR UTILITARIAN VERSUS HEDONIC PRODUCTS

In Chapter 2, we saw that consumers can view products as primarily utilitarian, as serving some functional purpose, or hedonic, as creating pleasure and encouraging fantasy. Thus, a Saturn car or a Harley-Davidson motorcycle can be a utilitarian product for one consumer and a hedonic product for another.

The nature of information acquisition is likely to differ in each case, as shown in Table 7.2. In evaluating utilitarian products, consumers logically seek information on product performance. Product attributes, therefore, are the focus of a consumer's information search. In evaluating hedonic products, consumers seek out sensory stimuli that might trigger pleasure or fantasy. In such cases, symbols and imagery may be more important than hard information on product performance. The consumer buying a Harley for transportation seeks information on acceleration, gas mileage, comfort, and other product attributes. The consumer buying a Harley as an extension of his or her self-image is more sensitive to images and symbols in ads that connote the "feel" of the product or the "pleasure" of sitting on one. These consumers do not ignore performance information. Rather, performance is a requirement for considering the product. The basic decision hinges on more emotive criteria.

As a result, when we talk of information acquisition, consumers may be acquiring information regarding the product's potential for sensory stimulation as well as information on product attributes.

Table 7.2 also suggests that when consumers evaluate hedonic products, information search is likely to be ongoing, whereas when they evaluate utilitarian products, information search is apt to be purchase-specific. This is because products purchased for pleasure and fantasy are likely to be involving on an ongoing basis. Products purchased for utilitarian purposes are likely to be relevant to the specific purchase situation.

In addition, consumers purchasing products for pleasure and fantasy are more likely to seek the advice of those with similar experiences because of the emphasis

TABLE 7.2

Information acquisition for hedonic versus utilitarian products

Hedonic products	Utilitarian products
1. Sensory stimuli dominate	Product attribute information dominates
2. Ongoing information search	Purchase-specific information search
3. Personal sources most important	Nonpersonal sources most important
4. Symbols and imagery most effective	Product information most effective

WEB APPLICATIONS

Hedonic Surfers: Achieving a Flow State on the Web

Web surfers, that is, those who undertake a nondirected search, can be divided into two broad groups, utilitarian and hedonic surfers. A *utilitarian surfer* is concerned with cognitive economy and only continues to surf the Web as long as the incremental benefits of the search outweigh the costs. Utilitarian surfers do not inherently enjoy surfing the Web. They are engaged in a nondirected search in an attempt to find information that lets them become more directed—for example, the consumer searching for travel ideas. These surfers cut back on the time and energy it takes to continue the search if they can.

A *hedonic surfer* is one who enjoys the act of surfing in and of itself. Utilitarian surfers are situationally involved with the Web; that is, they view the Web as a vehicle for specific purposes. Hedonic surfers are involved with the Web on an ongoing basis.

The highest level of enjoyment with the process of surfing is known as attaining a "flow state." Hoffman and Novak first proposed the existence of a flow state and described it as a situation where "consumers are so acutely involved in the act of network navigation that . . . nothing else seems to matter" (p. 57). When hedonic surfers are in a flow state they are so focused on navigating the Web and attain such a high level of involvement that they lose their sense of time and place: "Irrelevant thoughts and perceptions are screened out and the consumer focuses entirely on the interaction [with the Web]" (p. 58).

The key point is that these surfers are having fun. But in so doing, they are learning which types of web activities give them the most pleasure and satisfaction. Further, these surfers are likely to be web opinion leaders. In being involved on an ongoing basis, they are likely to talk about their web activities and the best sites for information and entertainment.

What are the implications for marketers? First, if these hedonic surfers can be reached, they are more likely to interact with marketers by stating their opinions and preferences regarding new and existing products and promotional campaigns. Second, as web opinion leaders, if they can be influenced, they are likely to exert a disproportionate amount of influence on others since their opinions regarding web sites have credibility.

Some people may get their kicks from champagne, but an increasing number are likely to get their kicks from the Web.

Sources: Donna L. Hoffman and Thomas P. Novak, "Marketing in Hypermedia Computer-mediated Environments," *Journal of Marketing* 60 (July 1996), pp. 50–68; "What Is This Thing Called Flow?", *Los Angeles Times* (July 6, 1998), p. 3.

on the experiential aspects of the product. As a result, they rely on personal nonmarketing sources—friends, relatives, and owners of the product, as well as their own past experiences. The prospective Harley owner is likely to rely on the experiences of others in evaluating the potential for the bike to be an extension of his or her self-image. Consumers purchasing utilitarian products are more likely to rely on nonpersonal sources for product attribute information.

STRATEGIC IMPLICATIONS OF INFORMATION ACQUISITION

The way consumers acquire information has direct implications for marketing strategy. Such implications depend on the type of search (active or passive), the type of product (utilitarian or hedonic), and the cost of information search to the consumer.

TABLE 7.3
Strategic implications of passive versus active information search

Passive information search	Active information search
1. Use repetitive advertising	Vary message content frequently
2. Use TV	Use print
3. Emphasize price promotions	Emphasize advertising
4. Emphasize in-store marketing stimuli	Emphasize marketing before entering store

▌**Type of Information Search: Passive versus Active**   The type of information search—passive or active—also has important ramifications for marketers. The strategic implications of passive versus active information search are summarized in Table 7.3.

If the product is in a low-involvement category, marketers realize that consumers acquire information passively, and marketers must support such passive receipt of information. For example, in introducing a new product, they might use repeat advertising on TV to establish a sufficient level of awareness. Television is the best medium to ensure passive acquisition because consumers' exposure to TV commercials does not require information search. The Web may also be a good vehicle for passive information acquisition through banner and pop-up ads. Web surfers are likely to notice these ads in passing since they are a means to gain exposure rather than to stimulate active information processing.

Passive acquisition points to the importance of trial as a means of obtaining information.[28] It may actually be cheaper for consumers to buy an inexpensive product for trial than it is to search for additional information. Marketers who recognize the limits of information search may decide to put more money into inducing trial than in trying to convey information to consumers. That is, it might be more cost-effective to put additional dollars into free samples and price promotions than to increase advertising budgets.

Passive information search also means that in-store stimuli are more important. Consumers are unlikely to have searched for information before entering the store; therefore, displays, shelf position, and price promotions are likely to make consumers take notice of the brand and serve as a reminder effect.

If information search is active, marketers are likely to change message content more frequently to provide fuller information. Print ads are more likely to be used than TV because of the importance of communicating product features. Dollars are more likely to be spent on advertising than in-store promotions because consumers are more likely to search for information prior to entering the store. Such marketers are also more likely to establish web sites as informational adjuncts to offline sales, Nike being one example as noted earlier.

▌**Type of Product: Hedonic versus Utilitarian**   The distinction between hedonic and utilitarian products has a direct bearing on the type of information that marketers convey. Information for hedonic products is likely to be conveyed through symbols and imagery, whereas information for utilitarian products is more likely to rely on the written word.

| EXHIBIT 7.2 |

Hedonic versus utilitarian appeals in advertising.

(top) Schwinn/Pacific Cycle; (bottom) Bell Sports, Inc.

Read poetry. Make peace with all except the motor car.

DOES YOUR KID HAVE HUNDRED DOLLAR FEET AND A TEN DOLLAR HEAD?

The ad for Schwinn bicycles in Exhibit 7.2 was meant to reestablish the company's image with bike enthusiasts after it emerged from bankruptcy. The symbol of a biker challenging cars on the road is likely to hit an emotive chord with this group. The ad is practically all image, with little text. In contrast, the ad for bicycle helmets is almost all text. A bicycle helmet is unlikely to arouse pleasure and fantasy. It is a product designed for a utilitarian purpose, protection. As a result, the ad is designed to communicate product information.

Cost of Information Acquisition   There are different costs of information searches. First, and most obvious, is the opportunity cost of spending time searching on the Web. Slow Internet access and lengthy delays in downloading software cost the searcher time. The consumer may also experience monetary costs from the search. For example, a consumer may have to pay a fee to obtain access to information on a web site or may have to become a member of some organization to access the needed information. There are psychological costs that can come from frustration with further searching or boredom in the search. Plus, there are possible delays in decision making from gaining excessive information in the search. The inability to try products as a means to gain experience can also be a cost of information search on the Web.

Marketers must consider ways to reduce the costs of information search for consumers. Changes necessary to reduce information costs on the Web include faster access through broadband, search engines, affiliations and partnerships to make access to related sites easier, and improved web site organization and simplicity. In addition, web site providers can facilitate trial by providing product coupons on the Web.

Offering free samples is another method of reducing search costs by providing consumers product experience. Apple Computer's past advertising campaign to "Test drive a Macintosh" offered consumers direct experience with the product in-store to avoid the need for additional search costs. When AOL offers free startup software and usage minutes, it has a similar objective—to provide consumers with direct experience to reduce the need for additional information. Intensive distribution of products is also a means of reducing information search, as consumers do not have to travel as far to inspect products. For marketers who can identify prospects and provide relevant information directly, direct mail is another way to reduce the costs of information search. In-store information can also reduce search costs. Unit pricing has helped some consumers reduce the time spent in in-store brand comparisons.

Marketers might also try to direct product information more effectively to groups who have higher costs of information search. For instance, AT&T realized that the groups who were taking the best advantage of off-peak rates were higher-income, better-educated consumers. As a result, AT&T directed its message to the lower-income groups to facilitate information acquisition. Because the marginal cost of information is higher for low-income consumers, AT&T's strategy was designed to lower the cost of search by directing information more effectively to this segment.

Consumer Information Processing

Once they acquire information, consumers must process it. Marketers are interested in information processing because it determines which information consumers remember, which information they use in the process of brand evaluation, and how they use it.

AN INFORMATION-PROCESSING MODEL

Figure 7.3 presents a model of information processing as an extension of Figure 7.1. Let us continue the example of the business school student in the market for a laptop computer. Figure 7.3 shows that processing takes place as information is acquired. In the process of information search, our consumer notices an ad for a Toshiba, decides to visit several stores to try one out, and realizes the speed of the machine is faster than anticipated. This information is perceived in that it receives the consumer's attention, is organized, and interpreted.

| FIGURE 7.3 |

A model of information processing.

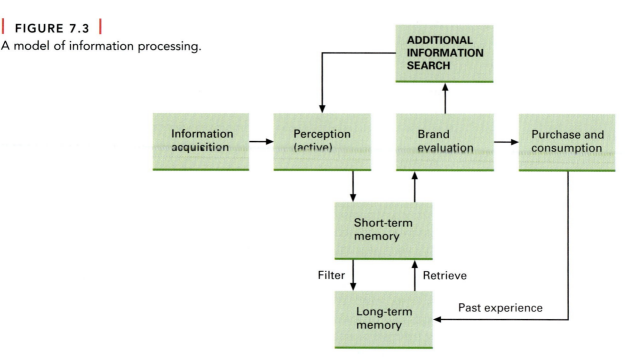

The next step in processing is determining what information will be retained in memory to be retrieved in the process of brand evaluation. Our consumer first processes information in her **short-term memory,** which acts as a filter to determine the information she stores and the information she ignores. Such a filter is necessary because no consumer can retain everything that is seen (and no consumer would want to). The principle of **selective retention** states that only the most important and relevant information to the brand decision will be stored in long-term memory.

Our consumer is interested in information obtained on the Toshiba from advertising, from several salespeople, and from the Web. She organizes information on the Toshiba and other laptops by product features to facilitate future comparison (*i.e.*, she compares brands by speed, by price, etc.). She uses a BOT such as *www.activebuyersguide.com* to help her make these comparisons. Once she states what is most important and the desired attributes of the laptop, the BOT provides a side-by-side comparison of recommended brands. She retains the information on the Toshiba's speed, microprocessor, and price in **long-term memory.** However, other information such as the size of the screen and necessary attachments to the printer are passed through short-term memory and not retained.

Our consumer retrieves information in long-term memory in the process of brand evaluation. Information on the Toshiba causes our consumer to change her beliefs about the characteristics of the brand and to develop a more positive attitude toward it and thus increase the chance that she may select it.

In the process of brand evaluation, consumers determine whether they need additional information to make a decision. An important factor in determining whether additional information search is warranted is the degree of risk involved in the purchase. Such perceived risk may be because of high price, product complexity, the importance of the product to the consumers' peer groups, or the consumers' emotional attachment to the product. Such risk encourages consumers to seek additional information before making a purchase decision. Our student sees both financial and performance risks in the purchase of the laptop. As a result, she continues her information search by obtaining information on two additional brands identified by frictionless.com, Compaq and NEC, to ensure that she is not overlooking better or more economical makes than the Toshiba.

Our student decides to buy the Toshiba. She has collected much of the information for her decision online, but she decides to purchase it at a retail store that provides a service warranty. Once a purchase is made and the product is used, consumers remember and learn from the purchase and usage experience. Thus, after our student's purchase, she stores her experience with the machine in long-term memory and may use this information if and when she decides to upgrade to a more powerful PC. She also stores her experiences in deciding on the Toshiba in memory. This information will be useful when she goes back into the market for another machine. Based on these experiences, she will be a more effective information searcher, shopper, and brand evaluator.

▌ Involvement and Information Processing   The way consumers process information depends largely on their level of involvement with the product decision. As we saw, when consumers are involved in a product, they actively search for information and analyze it to assess alternative brands effectively. For low-involvement products, consumers are more likely to receive and process information passively.

Our business school student processed information actively. She carefully interpreted the information and evaluated it in the context of her needs. Brand evaluation was fairly extensive. Further, since perceived risk was high, our consumer actively searched for additional information.

Low-involvement information processing differs in at least four respects, as shown in Table 7.4. First, because consumers process information passively, they can store this information in memory, with little attention to it.[29] For instance, the consumer seeing an advertisement for Diet Pepsi may remember two things: the brand name and a theme such as "The Joy of Pepsi." However, the theme has little immediate meaning, although the message that Pepsi makes you feel good may sink in eventually. The next time the consumer goes to the store, the sight of Pepsi's can on the shelf may evoke an association with "The Joy of Pepsi" and may remind the consumer of a need to purchase a diet soft drink.

TABLE 7.4
High- versus low-involvement information processing

High involvement	Low involvement
1. Active processing	Passive processing
2. Extensive brand evaluation	Minimal brand evaluation
3. Additional information seeking is likely	Additional information seeking is unlikely
4. Rely more on product information	Rely more on past experience

A second contrast with the high-involvement model is that here, brand evaluation is minimal. The consumer's belief that Pepsi makes you feel good may lead to a decision to buy without formation of any strong brand attitudes. The sequence is consistent with the low-involvement hierarchy in Chapter 4: beliefs leading to behavior with the possible development of brand attitudes after the fact.

The third difference is that since perceived risk is low, consumers probably will not seek additional information to make a brand choice. It is not worth the time and effort to do so.

A further contrast is that less involved consumers are likely to be satisfied with relying on their past experiences to make brand judgments. More involved consumers are likely to seek and use product information. Park and Hastak found that as the level of consumer involvement increases, the use of specific product information also increases.[30]

MEMORY PROCESSES

In both the high- and the low-involvement cases, processing information requires that

1. information is filtered through short-term memory,
2. it is stored in long-term memory, and
3. it is retrieved for purposes of brand evaluation.

▌ **Filtering Information through Short-Term Memory**   When consumers perceive information, they briefly evaluate it in short-term memory to determine whether to store it in long-term memory or to filter it out as unimportant or undesirable information. Consumers decide whether to retain information or to filter it out by relating it to information they already have stored in memory. If the information is important enough, then consumers store it.

Short-term memory has a limited capacity to process information. Short-term memory capacity is usually limited to an average of seven pieces of information at any one time, and processing occurs in seconds. Individuals react to this restriction by *chunking* information. For example, a social security number is composed of nine figures; but people usually chunk it into three groups of figures to recall it more easily. Similarly, a phone number has ten digits, but people chunk it into three groups, the area code, exchange, and number. A brand image represents the beliefs consumers associate with a brand and is an information chunk. It may be composed of twenty different components, but it can be retrieved as one general impression.

Once consumers filter the information through short-term memory, they either store it in long-term memory or choose not to retain it. Most information is not retained for a variety of reasons: It might be irrelevant, not important enough, confusing information that is difficult to interpret, or undesirable information that consumers choose to ignore.

▌ **Storing Information in Long-Term Memory**   Information in long-term memory is stored as images that reflect our memory of past events (**episodic memory**) or as words and sentences that reflect facts and concepts we remember (**semantic memory**).[31]

Consumers' memories of brands are in the form of both words and images. The word "Nike" may evoke other ideas such as "Just Do It" and physical exertion during sports. It also may evoke images learned from advertising and from past experience, such as the "swoosh" (Nike's symbol) and famous endorsing athletes. Words and images in long-term memory are linked to other words or images in an information network. Each word or image in long-term memory is called a **node.** For example, a consumer may link Nike (a node) to other nodes such as running, playing sports, sweating, working hard, professional athletes, athletic apparel, "Just Do It," and the "swoosh." These nodes represent beliefs about Nike in the consumer's mind.

As we saw in Chapter 6, such a cluster of beliefs is called a **schema.** In the context of memory processes, a schema occurs when a certain node (such as a brand) elicits a cluster of other nodes.[32] In marketing terms, such a schema is a consumer's brand or company image. Nike is a schema because when the word "Nike" is activated by an ad, a sporting event, or in conversation, a group of associated nodes is elicited in the consumer's mind.

Marketing strategy has two important objectives in the context of long-term memory: first, establishing linkages between the brand and other positive nodes, and second, activating these linkages once they are established. As we saw in Chapter 3, positive associations are established through consumer learning. The most important element in establishing associations in memory is consumers' experience with the product, but advertising has a key role in maintaining positive linkages over time.

Repetitive advertising for Nike has been successful in establishing such linkages. Its past theme, "Just Do It," was the basis for communicating an image of rugged sports and hard physical activity values, important nodes in Nike's schema. The high level of awareness of the campaign and the positive associations it produced meant that consumers were likely to retain it in long-term memory.

In contrast to Nike, Reebok has had a long-standing problem in maintaining such positive linkages because of a lack of consistent advertising over time. In 1997, its newly appointed worldwide director of advertising, John Wardley, commented on this problem. "The key thing I will have to develop is consistent brand imagery. Our brands have been represented in many different ways in many different markets. This can confuse the consumer as to whether we are a fashion brand or a sports performance brand. In fact, we are a sports brand with superior technology to anyone else, and we must get this across to consumers."[33] Reebok has attempted to establish a more consistent image with its global "Defy Convention" advertising campaign, which premiered on Superbowl Sunday in 2001.[34] (See Exhibit 7.3.)

| EXHIBIT 7.3 |

Reebok's attempt to establish a consistent brand image.

Reebok International Ltd/Chris McPherson © 2001.

▌ **Retrieving Information for Purposes of Brand Evaluation**   Once consumers filter information through short-term memory and store it in long-term memory, it is available for retrieval. When retrieving information from long-term memory, consumers briefly store it in short-term memory and use it to evaluate brands (see Figure 7.3). In evaluating a brand, consumers activate some key pieces of information. The activation of the schema for Nike and its related nodes determines how consumers evaluate Nike relative to Reebok or Adidas.

In this respect, marketing strategy in branding has two important objectives: (1) to establish positive associations of brands in long-term memory and, once these associations are established, (2) to facilitate *retrieval* of the brand from memory.

Factors Encouraging Retrieval.   Three factors are required for retrieval of information from long-term memory: activation, placement and transfer. The linkages between nodes must be *activated* for retrieval to take place. For the consumer in Figure 7.3, Nike advertising activates various nodes associated with the Nike schema. Sporting teams and star athletes play an important role in such **activation** for Nike. Michael Jordan invokes strong association with "Air Jordan" shoes, which have cult popularity with certain groups. More indirectly, any of the nodes in the Nike schema—for example, the words "Just Do It"—might activate it. Keller found that when consumers were provided with cues related to a brand (such as a picture of the swoosh), recall for the brand increased.[35] The brand's schema could be activated by these related nodes without the brand name.

A second process necessary for retrieval is **placement,** which determines to which other nodes consumers will connect the activated node. The student buying a laptop computer may connect Toshiba to processing speed based on new information.

A third factor required for retrieval is a **transfer** process that determines the information consumers will retrieve from long-term to short-term memory. Generally, consumers transfer information that is most important in making a decision—that is, information with the highest potential utility.

Factors Inhibiting Retrieval.   Certain factors inhibit retrieval. The four most important are forgetting, interference, inconsistency, and extinction. **Forgetting** is the inability to retrieve information from long-term memory. A consumer who does not retrieve information for a period of time may forget it, and any subsequent attempt to do so may fail.

Interference occurs when a related information node blocks the recall of the relevant information. An advertisement by Reebok for its new tennis shoe, featuring DMX technology and tennis star Venus Williams, may cause a consumer to lose the connection in long-term memory between sports shoe performance, famous athletes, and Nike. This could happen due to the strength of the Reebok-DMX-Venus Williams tennis shoes connection.[36] Competitive advertising often causes consumers to be unable to recall advertising for a related brand. At times, consumers confuse one brand with another. Some consumers may even recall an advertisement for NFL football sporting apparel as a Nike ad because of the strength of the Nike schema in their long-term memory. In the first case, interference hurt Nike; in the second case, interference helped it.

Inconsistency in the information delivered to the consumers can also inhibit activation or retrieval of a brand. Confusion is created for consumers if varying

STRATEGIC APPLICATIONS

Advertising Repetition Can Work for or against You

One proven method to increase retention of messages in consumers' long-term memory is repetition. Long-lasting symbols such as Betty Crocker, the Pillsbury Doughboy, and the Marlboro Cowboy are examples of the benefits of repetition.

When companies lose sight of the benefits of repetition, they can run into trouble. Heineken is an example. It slashed its advertising budget by 80 percent in the space of two years in the face of intense competition from brews such as Corona. Ads on network radio and television were cut entirely. The result? Market share went down from 38 percent to 23 percent. The moral? "Out of sight, out of mind." The company has since increased advertising expenditures to remain competitive.

However, repetition has several risks. One risk is that consumers learn to expect an advertising theme after many repetitions and pay less attention to it. Such advertising wearout takes its toll by decreasing consumers' attention level to repetitive ads.

A second risk of repetition is that it creates such strong linkages in consumers' long-term memory (*i.e.,* the schema associated with the brand node) that any subsequent attempt to change these linkages is difficult. An example is Oldsmobile cars. Its image, originally reinforced by repeated advertising and editorial content, was that of a car for older adults. The brand's very name reinforced this image and inhibited Oldsmobile from selling to younger consumers. To combat this problem, General Motors redesigned many of its Oldsmobile models to give them a more "hip" design. The company also initiated a new advertising campaign to attract younger consumers. The campaign, entitled "Not Your Father's Olds" (see Exhibit 7.4), only compounded the problem by reminding younger consumers that the car was once "your father's Olds." The cost of an ingrained image and Olds's failure to change it was GM's decision in 2001 to eliminate the division.

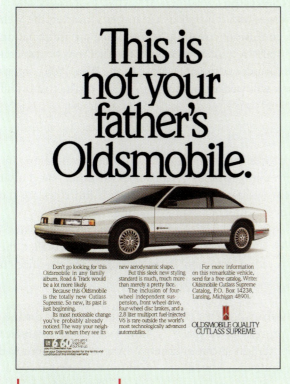

This is not your father's Oldsmobile.

Don't go looking for this Oldsmobile in any family album. Road & Track would be a lot more likely.
Because this Oldsmobile is the totally new Cutlass Supreme. So new, its past is just beginning.
Its most noticeable change you've probably already noticed. The way your neighbors will when they see its new aerodynamic shape.
But this sleek new styling standard is much, much more than merely a pretty face.
The inclusion of four-wheel independent suspension, front wheel drive, four-wheel disc brakes, and a 2.8 liter multiport fuel-injected V6 is rare outside the world's most technologically advanced automobiles.
For more information on this remarkable vehicle, send for a free catalog. Write: Oldsmobile Cutlass Supreme Catalog, P.O. Box 14238, Lansing, Michigan 48901.

OLDSMOBILE QUALITY
CUTLASS SUPREME

| EXHIBIT 7.4 |

The risks of repetition: Olds's attempt to change its image. Courtesy of Oldsmobile.

Sources: "Making Room in the Junkyard," *Advertising Age* (April 9, 2001), p. S8.; Ronald C. Goodstein, "Category-Based Applications and Extensions in Advertising: Motivating More Extensive Ad Processing," *Journal of Consumer Research* 20 (June 1993), pp. 87–99; "The Message, Clever as It May Be, Is Lost in a Number of High-Profile Campaigns," *Wall Street Journal* (July 27, 1993), pp. B1, B4; "Heineken Learns the Pitfalls of Cutting Advertising Expenditures," *Forbes* (February 8, 1988), pp. 128–130.

OF CONSUMER BEHAVIOR

messages or ideas are communicated to the consumer about the brand. For example, Amazon.com is known as an online retailer for books and music. However, if it expands too far from the core values associated with the brand, it could lead to consumer confusion. McDonald's launched an "Arch DeLuxe" campaign that tried to create more adult images for McDonald's. This endeavor only served to confuse consumers because of the conflict with the brand's core values of family and fun.

Whereas forgetting, interference, and inconsistency result in consumers' inability to recall linkages in long-term memory, **extinction** is a change in these linkages due to negative information about the product. Assume that a consumer reads that Nike athletic shoes have been criticized for being of poor quality. For this consumer, the linkage between Nike and quality athletic products is broken. The Nike schema also changes. As we saw in Chapter 3, the FTC may order corrective advertising to create extinction so as to correct past erroneous linkages that misleading advertising establishes, such as Listerine's former claim that it fights colds.

Whether the Web is a plus or minus in creating strong brand associations depends on a company's ability to integrate and effectively communicate its message online. The Web is a good vehicle for reinforcing existing associations and encouraging information retrieval because consumers are active processors, and it is easier to establish stronger linkages and multiple associations. However, the Web can also increase clutter and confusion, creating interference in information retrieval. As many pure dot-com startup companies have realized, it may be difficult to establish images from scratch. As more companies move to the Web, Web content may become a commodity, which will weaken attempts to create distinctive brand associations.

BRAND EVALUATION

The final step in information processing in Figure 7.3 is brand evaluation. Information on brands comes from many sources. As a result, consumers need a set of guidelines or decision rules for evaluating brands. These decision rules are the information-processing strategies consumers use in evaluating brands.

Consumers use a variety of such strategies, depending on the level of involvement with the brand, amount of knowledge about the brand, and whether the information is new or already stored in memory. These strategies are classified in Figure 7.4.

▌ **Evaluative versus Nonevaluative Processing**   The most basic distinction is whether an evaluative process takes place or not. **Evaluative strategies** require the organization of information about alternative brands. **Nonevaluative strategies** involve the use of a simple decision rule to avoid the necessity of evaluating brands—for example, buying the most popular brand, the cheapest brand, the same brand as your best friend, or the brand a salesperson recommends. The Web is a good vehicle for nonevaluative strategies in identifying the least expensive or most popular brand. In each case, brand evaluation is avoided.

Gardner and her colleagues found that consumers most likely use evaluative strategies when involvement is higher and nonevaluative strategies when involvement is lower. People using a nonevaluative strategy try to avoid the effort involved in active information processing. They do not actively seek brand information.

| FIGURE 7.4 |

| FIGURE 7.4 |
Processing strategies for
brand evaluation.

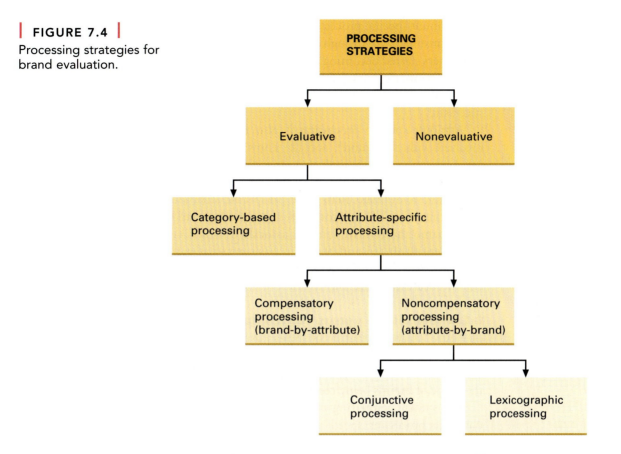

When they view ads, they do not focus on message content; rather, they might view
ads for enjoyment or curiosity.[37]

▌ Category-Based versus Attribute-Specific Processing

Evaluative
strategies can be divided into category-based strategies and attribute-specific strategies.[38] A **category-based strategy** involves evaluation of a brand as a totality rather
than on specific attributes. Such brand evaluation requires development of a
schema for the brand so that consumers can retrieve a set of associations as a whole
from long-term memory. On this basis, they can quickly compare brands and establish a preference. On the other hand, an **attribute-specific strategy** requires comparison of each brand alternative on specific attributes such as quick service, good
taste, or nice atmosphere; then consumers decide which brand to choose.

When are consumers most likely to use category-based processing? They use it
when they have an overall image (schema) of the brand that they can call up readily from memory. For example, consumers who objected to Coca-Cola's withdrawal
of old Coke did not base their objections on an analysis of specific attributes but on
an overall feeling about the brand. Consumers also use category-based processing
as a means of simplifying complicated decisions.[39] For example, a "nontechie" lost
in the maze of criteria for selecting a computer may simply decide to evaluate two
or three brands based on their overall brand image rather than specific product
attributes.

Attribute-specific processing is required when a new product is introduced or when consumers go through a more extensive process of comparing brands. When consumers started becoming aware of the effects of tartar and plaque on teeth, they began to move from category to attribute processing in evaluating toothpaste. This processing shift is one reason new tartar- and plaque-fighting toothpastes are successful.

Attribute-specific processing is also more likely when the consumer is (1) involved with the brand[40] and (2) knowledgeable about the product category[41] Involved consumers are unlikely to be satisfied with an overall judgment of brands based on past information. They are likely to seek additional information about brands and to evaluate them based on specific attributes.

If consumers use category-based processing, marketers should emphasize the brand name and positive symbols associated with it, such as the McDonald's arch or the Pepsi-Cola red-and-blue logo. In doing so, they trigger the schema associated with the brand. If processing is attribute-specific, marketers should focus more on communicating specific information on product characteristics.

▎ Compensatory versus Noncompensatory Processing   The bottom of Figure 7.4 shows that if consumers use attribute-specific evaluation, two additional strategies are possible. Consumers can evaluate brands one at a time across a range of attributes (**compensatory evaluation**) or evaluate specific attributes across the range of brands being considered (**noncompensatory evaluation**).

The student comparing various laptop models could consider a Toshiba by evaluating its processing speed, memory capacity, screen display, keyboard, and other attributes and come up with an overall evaluation. Such a compensatory method of evaluation is additive: The evaluation of the Toshiba is the sum of all the attributes; a good rating on one attribute, such as processing speed, can *compensate* for a poor rating on another attribute, such as screen display.

The student could also consider one attribute at a time and evaluate all brands being considered by each attribute. In this case, the student compares the Toshiba, NEC, and Compaq models on processing speed, then on price, then on memory capacity, and so on until she has evaluated each brand on all important attributes. This strategy is noncompensatory because a consumer can eliminate a brand as a result of a deficiency on one attribute. If the student finds the NEC to be significantly more expensive than the Compaq or Toshiba, she might rule it out even before she considers the brand on other attributes. In the compensatory approach, the student would consider the NEC on all attributes before making a decision.

Use of compensatory strategies requires marketers to communicate a broad set of product attributes to allow consumers to make comparisons between brands. If consumers use noncompensatory strategies, the marketer can focus on a few key attributes that consumers are likely to use in brand evaluation.

Consumers often use a noncompensatory strategy first to screen out brands, especially when a large number of brands are being considered, and then use a compensatory strategy to evaluate the remaining candidates.[42] Lussier and Olshavsky found that consumers frequently use this processing strategy.[43] This is a good strategy for reducing the number of brands under consideration and ensuring that the amount of information to be processed is manageable.

A study of the strategies consumers use in selecting stereo systems supported this dual strategy.[44] Consumers first eliminated systems that were not competitively priced and did not have a knowledgeable sales force to back them up. Consumers then evaluated the remaining makes by considering attributes such as quality, style, warranty, and other product features on a compensatory basis.

Figure 7.4 splits noncompensatory strategies into two types. These are further described in Table 7.5. Assume our consumer rates four laptop brands on three attributes. She uses a seven-point scale, with 7 being the best rating. Using a **conjunctive strategy,** a consumer considers a brand only if it meets acceptable standards on key attributes. Assume an acceptable rating is one that scores 5 or higher. In this case, NEC is eliminated because our consumer rated it below the acceptable level on processing speed, and Compaq is eliminated because of a poor rating on keyboard/display features and on storage capacity. The choice is then between the Toshiba and the IBM. Since they are both tied on storage capacity, the consumer then chooses IBM based on keyboard display. Alternatively, after eliminating NEC and Compaq, the selection between the Toshiba and Compaq then might be made on a compensatory basis by evaluating each brand across all attributes. The consumer selects the make that is rated best.

Using a **lexicographic strategy,** consumers first evaluate brands on the most important attribute. If there is a tie, consumers next evaluate brands on the second most important attribute, and so on until a brand is selected. Assume the most important attributes are listed in the same order as in Table 7.5. Toshiba and Compaq are tied for first based on ratings on the most important criterion, processing speed. The consumer then goes to the second most important criterion, storage capacity, and chooses Toshiba over Compaq on this basis.

TABLE 7.5
Noncompensatory processing strategies

	NEC	Toshiba	Compaq	IBM
Processing speed	2	7	7	5
Storage capacity	6	6	4	6
Keyboard/display	7	5	3	7

Conjunctive processing

- NEC is eliminated because of poor rating on processing speed
- Compaq is eliminated because of poor rating on keyboard/display and on storage capacity
- Select between Toshiba and IBM

Lexicographic processing

- Assume most important attributes are listed in same order as in table above.
- Toshiba and Compaq are tied for first. Go to next most important attribute and select Toshiba on this basis.

INFORMATION PROCESSING FOR UTILITARIAN VERSUS HEDONIC PRODUCTS

As with information acquisition, information processing varies depending on whether the product is regarded primarily as utilitarian or hedonic. Both the nature of information retrieval and brand evaluation vary on the continuum from hedonic to utilitarian products.

▌ Information Retrieval

The nature of the information retrieved from long-term memory differs depending on whether the product is viewed as functional or pleasure-seeking and emotive. Information for utilitarian products is likely to be based on actual experiences and past events. Consumers may recall information they have seen regarding a motorcycle helmet or remember their experiences in wearing a particular brand.

Information for hedonic products may be based on past experiences, but they may also be based on fantasy. As Hirschman and Holbrook note:

> The colors and shapes that are seen, the sounds that are heard, and the touches that are felt have never actually occurred, but are brought together in the particular configuration for the first time and experienced as mental phenomena."[45]

The prospective purchaser of a Harley-Davidson may visualize himself as the modern version of the lonely rider of frontier days; the prospective purchaser of a Starter jacket may see himself in the batting lineup for the Tigers. In both cases, the imagery has little to do with reality but may directly influence the purchase.

▌ Brand Evaluation

The processing strategies used to evaluate brands also differ for utilitarian versus hedonic products. Consumers evaluating utilitarian products are likely to use attribute-specific strategies. Product information is sought to allow the consumer to evaluate a brand's performance. Consumers might evaluate alternative makes of cars on gas mileage, interior roominess, trunk space, acceleration, durability, and price.

Consumers are likely to evaluate hedonic products by category-based strategies; that is, as a totality rather than on particular product attributes. Consumers are apt to associate the product with a set of experiences or fantasies. In this respect, the Harley-Davidson motorcycle may conjure up a set of images, moods, or emotions that are foreign to utilitarian products. In such cases, marketers should emphasize symbols and imagery that encourage positive emotional associations with the product. Such symbols and imagery are meant to create an overall impression rather than to impart specific product information.

Strategic Implications of Information Processing

This chapter has described two key components of information processing—storing information in memory and evaluating brands. Important marketing implications emerge in these areas.

MEMORY PROCESSES

A primary objective of advertising strategy is to ensure that consumers retain the message in memory. The most obvious means of increasing retention is through repetition of the advertising message. Ray and Sawyer found that advertising recall almost tripled as the number of repetitions went from one to six.[46] The study also showed the diminishing returns of additional repetitions. As advertising is repeated, the incremental gains in consumer retention become smaller. There is another problem with frequent advertising repetition: a wearout effect. Consumers may become so familiar with an ad campaign that they no longer notice it. The campaign can be revitalized only by introducing new and fresher ideas to communicate product benefits. Constant repetition, in fact, may irritate consumers.

Another important implication of memory processes is for marketers to develop sets of associations with a brand that lead to a positive and consistent brand image. In establishing a positive image, advertising must link the brand to nodes with positive associations in consumers' memory.[47]

Once consumers establish a strong brand image, marketers should reinforce it by all elements of marketing strategy. This is best achieved by a marketing campaign that coordinates advertising, packaging, and in-store stimuli. McDonald's marketing strategy promotes a strong image because various elements of its campaign such as Ronald McDonald, playgrounds, sales promotions, and in-store decor promote the image of good service and family values. Elements at variance with an established image cause confusion and a weakening of associations in consumers' memory, as when Cadillac introduced a medium-sized car.

BRAND EVALUATION

The manner by which consumers evaluate brands also has strategic implications. Evaluative processing, which suggests a more involved consumer, requires the marketer to develop a message closely related to consumer needs. Nonevaluative processing suggests a less involved consumer. Here, advertisers can use simpler themes and peripheral cues and rely primarily on TV to communicate them.

The types of evaluative processing consumers use also have strategic implications. If consumers evaluate brands on an attribute-specific basis, advertising should be informational and present product characteristics that consumers can evaluate easily. As we saw, category-based evaluation lends itself more to image-oriented advertising since consumers evaluate the brand as a whole. Symbols and images such as the Marlboro Cowboy or the Apple Computer logo can be used as a shorthand for the brand. These symbols evoke the brand image without having to specify particular attributes of the brand.

Societal Implications of Information Processing

Consumers have the right to adequate information to give them the capability to make reasonable decisions. Three societal issues emerge in this regard. First, should consumers be given more information? This is what consumer activists propose. Or, in some cases, should consumers be given less? Some researchers who have found that consumers are subject to information overload have proposed this. Second, do consumers sometimes use poor strategies to process complex brand information, and if so, can anything be done to encourage them to use more optimal strategies? Third, evidence of less efficient information processing among younger and older consumers, particularly on the Web, raises the question of whether government and/or business organizations have a role in increasing the information processing capabilities of these two groups.

MORE OR LESS INFORMATION?

Several studies have found that, for some product categories, more information increases consumer confusion and leads to less efficient choice. This may suggest that product information should be limited and kept simple.

Consumer activists would argue that product information such as ingredients, nutritional content, performance, and price should be made available to consumers on a uniform basis, and consumers should then decide how much information to use. These activists believe it is better to run the risk of too much information and consumer confusion than too little information and a poor choice.

Government is taking an increasingly activist view in supporting additional information. The Food and Drug Administration has established rules requiring more information on ingredients and nutritional value and clearer warning labels on packaging. More states are requiring unit pricing information in stores and open dating of perishable items. Business organizations are also showing more willingness to supply detailed product information in ads, brochures, and by direct mail. Some retailers such as Jewel and Shop-Rite stores have introduced in-store consultants to inform shoppers of price and brand alternatives.

There are several compelling reasons to support this trend to more information. First, some consumers use such information. Unfortunately, older and less-educated consumers are least likely to use product information. Government and business can do more to increase information acquisition by these groups—for example, by providing comparative price information for key product categories such as pharmaceuticals and improving transportation to shopping areas.

Second, when consumers use information, they often make more efficient purchases. Several studies have found that consumers who use unit pricing information shift their purchases toward lower-priced goods.[48] Third, providing more information increases consumer confidence. One study found that although only 10 percent of consumers used credit information in buying a durable good, 54 percent said they felt better about knowing the rates and charges.[49]

COMPENSATORY OR NONCOMPENSATORY PROCESSING?

A second issue is whether consumers use adequate processing strategies, regardless of the amount of information available. Hutchinson and Alba found that in selecting stereo speakers, most consumers used only two or three criteria, despite the availability of a full complement of product information.[50] Unless consumers are knowledgeable about the product category, such noncompensatory strategies may lead to suboptimal decisions, particularly for expensive and high-risk items like stereo speakers and appliances.

A strong case could be made for encouraging consumers to use a wider set of criteria in making decisions for expensive, high-risk products, particularly if consumers lack knowledge and confidence in their choices. Companies can do more to educate consumers in criteria for comparing brands by product features. For example, a computer company can provide prospective buyers an informational brochure explaining how to use criteria such as memory, capacity, and speed in selecting a computer.

AGE-RELATED INFORMATION PROCESSING

Sufficient evidence of reduced processing capacities among the very young and very old raises some serious societal issues. The information capabilities of preschoolers are limited and improve by the early elementary school years.[51] Young children generally fail to understand the purpose of commercials and often cannot distinguish between TV programming and commercials. Responsible actions by business are needed to avoid taking advantage of children based on their reduced processing abilities.

There are also well-founded concerns about children's use of the Web. Many children eight and under are sufficiently computer-savvy to have Internet access. Research has demonstrated that such children often fail to distinguish between advertising and program content on TV, and they are more likely than adults to be influenced by ads.[52] Children are even less likely to distinguish between commercial and informational content on the Web given the integration of banner and pop-up ads with on-screen content.

Evidence also indicates that older consumers process information less efficiently. Studies have found that older consumers cannot retain as many alternative advertising claims or brand alternatives in memory as younger consumers and tend to use fewer attributes in evaluating brand alternatives.[53] One study found that elderly consumers had poor memory of advertising claims and tended to assume that repetitive claims were more truthful, even when this was not warranted.[54] Another study found that when elderly consumers were instructed to select a cereal according to specific nutritional criteria, they were less likely than younger consumers to search for information and to select a cereal based on their needs.[55]

How elderly consumers process information could be responsible for the age divide on the Internet. A recent Pew study found that 56 percent of Americans go online. But among those 65 and over, only 15 percent go online.[56] Lack of Internet access is a serious informational constraint for senior citizens.

SUMMARY

An important part of any consumer's decision process is the acquisition and processing of information. Consumers acquire more information about products if they are involved in the purchase, see risk in purchasing, have little product knowledge, and see differences among products. Information acquisition is limited by the amount of information consumers can reasonably process. Studies have shown that consumers sometimes are subjected to information overload—that is, too much information—which results in confusion.

We discussed the ways in which consumers acquire information, such as ongoing search, directed purchase-specific search, nondirected purchase-specific search, and passive acquisition of information. In such cases, information acquisition can take place on- or offline. Increasingly, the Web is being used as an information resource rather than a means of purchasing products. The amount of information obtained and the level of information about product attributes was discussed.

To a large extent, the level of information search is a function of the level of consumer involvement. Information search is also likely to be greater if purchase risk is high, the consumer has little knowledge of the product category, and the consumer is under time pressures.

Once consumers acquire information, they must process it. To process information, consumers must be able to retain it in and retrieve it from memory. The memory process has short-term and long-term components. Short-term memory acts as a filter to determine what information is retained in long-term memory. Information stored in long-term memory is organized into schemas, which represent the sets of associations consumers have with brands, products, or companies. Such schemas are the basis for brand or company images.

Consumers retrieve information from long-term memory to evaluate brands. Brand evaluation requires a set of decision rules for comparing brands. Using category-based processing, consumers evaluate brands as a whole and make judgments based on associations in long-term memory. Attribute-specific processing requires consumers to compare brands according to specific attributes.

A distinction was drawn between information acquisition and processing for hedonic versus utilitarian products. Consumers buying hedonic products are more likely to seek symbols and imagery rather than specific product information. They are also more likely to retrieve fantasy-like imagery from memory rather than actual experiences, and they process information as a whole rather than on an attribute-by-attribute basis.

Strategic applications were developed from the two key components of information processing—storing information in memory and evaluating brands. The chapter concluded by considering the societal implications of information processing. Three issues were considered. First, should more information be provided to consumers, and if so, what should be the role of government and business in providing such information? Second, can consumers be encouraged to use processing strategies that evaluate brands on a wider set of criteria? Third, given the reduced processing abilities of the very young and very old, can business or government play a role in improving their abilities?

In Chapter 8, we consider the results of information processing; namely, the formation of consumer attitudes toward brands and products.

QUESTIONS FOR DISCUSSION

1. What are Nike's objectives in establishing its web site? What risks does Nike face in having a visible web presence?

2. Which of the following situations would you describe as either (a) ongoing search, (b) purchase-specific search, or (c) passive information acquisition? Why?

- A consumer listening to a radio ad for life insurance
- A consumer shopping for a suit to wear to a job interview
- A consumer reading several magazines dealing with antique furniture

- A consumer surfing on the Web for vacation ideas

3. What is the difference between a search engine and a BOT? How are consumers likely to use each tool in searching the Web for product information?

4. What types of sources of information are most likely to be important for each of the following consumers and why?
   - A business school student close to a final decision in purchasing a laptop computer
   - An industrial buyer purchasing electrical cable
   - A consumer first considering various alternatives in selecting life insurance

5. What are the limits of consumers' ability to acquire and process information? Are these limits likely to be greater on the Web? Why or why not?

6. How can marketers attempt to overcome the limits you cited in Question 5 above, both off- and online?

7. Consider these two purchasing situations:
   - A consumer regards cereals as a source of bran and other nutritional ingredients and is aware of brand alternatives and their ingredients. This consumer regards the brand decision for cereals as important, as it is related to health and fitness.
   - Another consumer sees little difference among brands of cereal and buys primarily for taste. This consumer has a low level of information regarding brand alternatives and ingredients and does not associate the purchase of cereals with health and fitness.

   A new brand of cereal containing raisins and nuts and advertised as a product with all-natural ingredients is introduced. What differences might occur between the two consumers in acquiring and processing information on the new cereal?

8. What is the difference between a utilitarian surfer and a hedonic surfer?

9. What are the costs of information acquisition offline and online? Is online processing likely to reduce the costs of information acquisition? If so, what type of costs and why?

10. How does short-term memory operate for (a) the prospective car buyer who first becomes aware of GM's new Saturn models and (b) the consumer who sees an ad for Pampers disposable diapers while watching a quiz show?

11. Cite an example of how certain factors might inhibit retrieval of brand information from the Web.

12. Cite an example of a conjunctive and a lexicographic processing strategy in making a decision about a car.

13. What are the differences in information acquisition and processing for products consumers regard as hedonic versus utilitarian? What are the strategic implications of these differences?

14. What are the pros and cons of providing consumers with more information? Under what circumstances should business and government be encouraged to provide consumers with more information?

15. What are the societal issues regarding age-related differences in acquiring and processing information? What are the public policy implications of these differences?

RESEARCH ASSIGNMENTS

1 Review notebook computers on the following web sites: (1) *http://shopping.yahoo.com* and (2) *www.activebuyersguide.com*.

a. For shopping.yahoo, select a product category and click on "buyer's guide." Then click on "select by feature" and fill out the specifications.

b. For activebuyersguide.com, follow the procedures online and review notebook computers.

- Does each site have a screening procedure using a noncompensatory model of evaluation?

- Does each site have a compensatory model that provides brand recommendations based on desired attributes?

- What are the advantages and disadvantages of each site in producing brand recommendations?

2 Develop an information board for automobiles and another information board for cereals. The boards should list at least four brands or models across the top and eight attributes down the side. Show the boards to about ten consumers for each product category. Ask consumers to describe aloud their process of evaluating the brands on each board. On this basis, try to determine if processing is by category or by attribute and, if by attribute, whether it is compensatory or noncompensatory processing.

At the end of the process of evaluation, ask consumers to complete a short questionnaire to determine (a) demographics, (b) selected lifestyle items, (c) brand or model used, and (d) frequency of usage or number of miles driven in a year.

- What are the differences in evaluation between the cereals and the autos? Specifically, are consumers more likely to evaluate autos and cereals by category-based or by attribute-based processing? If the latter, are consumers more likely to evaluate each product category by compensatory or noncompensatory processing?

- Are there differences in evaluation between types of consumers? That is, are certain consumers more likely to evaluate by category whereas others evaluate by attribute? If so, are there differences in the characteristics of category versus attribute evaluators?

NOTES

1. "Nike Picks Up the Pace in Race to Harness Web," *Advertising Age* (March 6, 2000), p. S4.
2. "Internet Swoosh," *Traffic World* (February 22, 1999), p. 17.
3. "Picture This," *Adweek* (December 4, 2000), pp. 26–30.
4. "Standing Out Online: The 5 Best e-marketing Campaigns," *Sales and Marketing Management* (January 2001), pp. 51–57.
5. Ibid.
6. William B. Locander and Peter W. Hermann, "The Effect of Self-Confidence and Anxiety on Information Seeking in Consumer Risk Reduction," *Journal of Marketing Research* 16 (May 1979), pp. 268–274.
7. Keith B. Murray, "A Test of Services Marketing Theory: Consumer Information Acquisition Activities," *Journal of Marketing* 55 (January 1991), pp. 10–25.
8. Sridhar Moorthy, Brian T. Ratchford, and Debabrata Talukdar, "Consumer Information Search Revisited: Theory and Empirical Analysis," *Journal of Consumer Research* 23 (March 1997), pp. 263–277.
9. Sharon E. Beatty and Scott M. Smith, "External Search Effort: An Investigation Across Several Product Categories," *Journal of Consumer Research* 14 (June 1987), pp. 83–95.
10. Narasimhan Srinivasan and Brian T. Ratchford, "An Empirical Test of a Model of External Search for Automobiles," *Journal of Consumer Research* 18 (September 1991), pp. 233–241.
11. Peter D. Bennett and Robert M. Mandell, "Prepurchase Information Seeking Behavior of New Car Purchasers—The Learning Hypothesis," *Journal of Marketing Research* 6 (November 1969), pp. 430–433.
12. Cynthia Huffman and Michael J. Houston, "Goal-Oriented Experiences and the Development of Knowledge," *Journal of Consumer Research* 20 (September 1993), pp. 190–207.
13. Beatty and Smith, "External Search Effort," pp. 83–95.
14. W. P. Dommermuth and E. W. Cundiff, "Shopping Goods, Shopping Centers, and Selling Strategies," *Journal of*
Marketing* 31 (October 1967), pp. 32–36; and Joseph W. Newman and Richard Staelin, "Prepurchase Information Seeking for New Cars and Major Household Appliances," *Journal of Marketing Research* 9 (August 1972), pp. 249–257.
15. Brian T. Ratchford, "The Economics of Consumer Knowledge," *Journal of Consumer Research* 27 (March 2001), pp. 397–411.
16. John D. Claxton, Joseph N. Fry, and Bernard Portis, "A Taxonomy of Prepurchase Information Gathering Patterns," *Journal of Consumer Research* 1 (December 1974), pp. 35–42.
17. Beatty and Smith, "External Search Effort," pp. 83–95.
18. Howard Beales, Michael B. Mazis, Steven C. Salop, and Richard Staelin, "Consumer Search and Public Policy," *Journal of Consumer Research* 8 (June 1981), pp. 11–22.
19. Jacob Jacoby, Robert W. Chestnut, K.C. Weigl, and W. Fisher, "Pre-Purchase Information Acquisition," in Beverlee B. Anderson, ed., *Advances in Consumer Research*, Vol. 3 (Atlanta: Association for Consumer Research, 1975), pp. 306–314.
20. Compiled from five studies by David L. Loudon and Albert J. Della Bitta, *Consumer Behavior* (New York: McGraw-Hill, 1979), p. 463.
21. "When Some Choose Not to Choose," *Brandweek* (June 19, 2000), p. 14.
22. W. P. Dommermuth, "The Shopping Matrix and Marketing Strategy," *Journal of Marketing Research* 2 (May 1965), pp. 128–132.
23. Newman and Staelin, "Prepurchase Information Seeking," pp. 249–257.
24. Girish Punj, "Presearch Decision Making in Consumer Durable Purchases," *Journal of Consumer Marketing* 4 (Winter 1987), pp. 71–82.
25. Jacob Jacoby, Donald E. Speller, and Carol A. Kohn, "Brand Choice Behavior as a Function of Information Load,"

Journal of Marketing Research 11 (February 1974), pp. 63–69.

26. "Too Many Choices," *Wall Street Journal* (April 20, 2001), pp. B1, B4.

27. Ibid.

28. C. Whan Park and Henry Assael, "Has the Low Involvement View of Consumer Behavior Been Overstated?" working paper, University of Pittsburgh, 1983.

29. Herbert E. Krugman, "Memory Without Recall, Exposure with Perception," *Journal of Advertising Research* 17 (August 1977), pp. 7–12.

30. Jong-Won Park and Manoj Hastak, "Memory-Based Product Judgments: Effects of Involvement at Encoding and Retrieval," *Journal of Consumer Research* 21 (December 1994), pp. 534–547.

31. Elo A. Tulving, "Episodic and Semantic Memory," in E. Tulving and W. Donaldson, eds., *Organization of Memory* (New York: Academic Press, 1972).

32. See Joan Meyers-Levy, "The Influence of a Brand Name's Association Set Size and Work Frequency on Brand Memory," *Journal of Consumer Research* 16 (September 1989), pp. 197–207.

33. "Sporting Chance for Honest John," *Marketing Week* (November 6, 1997), pp. 36–37.

34. "Reebok defies convention with new campaign," *Adweek* (January 22, 2001), p. 11.

35. Kevin Lane Keller, "Memory Factors in Advertising Evaluations," *Journal of Consumer Research* 14 (December 1987), pp. 316–333.

36. "Reebok's Pick-up Game," *Brandweek* (May 15, 2000), pp. 42–46.

37. Meryl P. Gardner, Andrew A. Mitchell, and J. Edward Russo, "Low Involvement Strategies for Processing Advertisements," *Journal of Advertising Research* 14 (1985), pp. 4–12. See also Wayne D. Hoyer, "An Examination of Consumer Decision Making for a Common Repeat Purchase Product," *Journal of Consumer Research* 11 (December 1984), pp. 822–828.

38. For a similar distinction, see Mita Sujan, "Consumer Knowledge: Effects on Evaluation Strategies Mediating Consumer Judgments," *Journal of Consumer Research* 12 (June 1985), pp. 31–46; see also John G. Lynch, Jr., Howard Marmorstein, and Michael F. Weigold, "Choices from Sets Including Remembered Brands: Use of Recalled Attributed and Prior Overall Evaluations," *Journal of Consumer Research* 15 (September 1988), pp. 169–184.

39. "The Influence of Task Complexity on Consumer Choice: A Latent Class Model of Decision Strategy Switching," *Journal of Consumer Research* 28 (June 2001), pp. 135–148.

40. Sujan, "Consumer Knowledge," pp. 31–46.

41. Douglas M. Stayman, Dana L. Alden, and Karen H. Smith, "Some Effects of Schematic Processing on Consumer Expectations and Disconfirmation Judgments," *Journal of Consumer Research* 19 (September 1992), pp. 240–255.

42. James R. Bettman, Mary Frances Luce, and John W. Payne, "Constructive Consumer Choice Processes," *Journal of Consumer Research* 25 (December 1998), pp. 187–217.

43. For example, Dennis A. Lussier and Richard W. Olshavsky, "Task Complexity and Contingent Processing in Brand Choice," *Journal of Consumer Research* 6 (September 1979), pp. 154–165.

44. Naelm H. Abougomaah, John L. Schlacter, and William Gaidis, "Elimination and Choice Phases in Evoked Set Formation," *Journal of Consumer Marketing* 4 (Fall 1987), pp. 67–73.

45. Elizabeth C. Hirschman and Morris B. Holbrook, "Hedonic Consumption: Emerging Concepts, Methods and Propositions," *Journal of Marketing* 46 (Summer 1982), pp. 92–101.

46. Michael L. Ray and Alan G. Sawyer, "Repetition in Media Models: A Laboratory Technique," *Journal of Marketing Research* 8 (February 1971), pp. 20–29.

47. John Deighton, "How to Solve Problems That Don't Matter: Some Heuristics for Uninvolved Thinking," in Thomas C. Kinnear, ed., *Advances in Consumer Research,* Vol. 11 (Provo, Utah: Association for Consumer Research, 1984), pp. 314–319.

48. Clive W. Granger and Andrew Billson, "Consumers' Attitudes Toward Package Size and Price," *Journal of Marketing Research* 9 (August 1972), pp. 239–248; and J. Edward Russo, Gene Dreiser, and Sally Miyashita, "An Effective Display of Unit Price Information," *Journal of Marketing* 39 (April 1975), pp. 11–19.

49. George S. Day, "Assessing the Effects on Information Disclosure Requirements," *Journal of Marketing* 40 (April 1976), pp. 42–52.

50. Hutchinson and Alba, "Ignoring Irrelevant Information," pp. 326–345.

51. Jennifer Gregan-Paxton and Deborah Roedder John, "Are Young Children Adaptive Decision Makers? A Study of Age Differences in Information Search Behavior," *Journal of Consumer Research* 21 (March 1995), pp. 567–580.

52. Ronald S. Rubin, "The Effects of Cognitive Development on Children's Responses to Television Advertising," *Journal of Business Research* 4 (1974), pp. 409–419; Nancy Stephens and Mary Ann Stutts, "Preschoolers' Ability to Distinguish Between Television Programming and Commercials," *Journal of Advertising Research* 11 (April–May 1982), pp. 16–25.

53. Irving Janis and Leon Mann, *Decision Making* (New York: Free Press, 1977); and Charles Schaninger and Donald Sciglimpaglia, "The Influence of Cognitive Personality Traits and Demographics on Consumer Information Acquisition," *Journal of Consumer Research* 8 (September 1981), pp. 208–216.

54. Sharmistha Law, Scott A. Hawkins, and Fergus I. M. Craik, "Repetition-Induced Belief in the Elderly: Rehabilitating Age-Related Memory Deficits," *Journal of Consumer Research* 25 (September 1998), pp. 91–107.

55. Catherine A. Cole and Siva K. Balasubramanian, "Age Differences in Consumers' Search for Information: Public Policy Implications," *Journal of Consumer Research* 20 (June 1993), pp. 157–169.

56. *Pew Internet and American Life Project Survey,* November–December 2000.

CHAPTER 8

Attitude Development and Change

Chapters 6 and 7 dealt with how consumers perceive and process information. In this chapter, we explore how consumers develop beliefs about and preferences for brands based on the information they have processed. These beliefs and preferences define consumers' attitudes toward a brand. In turn, their attitudes toward a brand often directly influence their brand evaluation and determine whether they buy it.

We first consider the nature of brand attitudes and their relationship to purchasing behaviors. We also review attitude models that provide a basis by which marketers can evaluate a brand's strength or weakness relative to consumer needs, and the strategic implications for advertising and product positioning. In this regard, a key strategic consideration is whether marketers should reinforce attitudes or change them. The term "repositioning" has been widely used in marketing to connote the need to change a brand's image by changing consumer attitudes. Key principles of attitude change are also examined.

Benetton Attempts to Change Consumer Attitudes

Benetton's repositioning strategy in the United States illustrates a recent attempt at changing consumer attitudes. Long identified as a company that touted a social consciousness through often quirky ads dealing with social issues, in 2001 Benetton decided to shift gears and become a mainstream fashion retailer. Gone are the ads featuring death row inmates, smooching clergy, and AIDS patients. For the first time in almost twenty years, the company is focusing on fashion with Gap-like ads featuring "exuberant models frolicking in colorful knitwear."[1]

Why the change? Benetton's sales shrunk by 50 percent from 1993 to 2001 in the United States. In addition, the number of its stores decreased from 600 in 1987 to 150 in 2001.[2] Part of the problem was that it opened too many stores too fast and was slow in adopting more fashionable merchandise. But basically, its "in-your-face" socially conscious advertising was starting to turn off many consumers.

The campaign started in 1983 with an innocent "United Colors of Benetton" theme that featured models of different races so as to promote racial harmony. After that, Benetton's campaigns began to focus on ads meant to serve as controversial social statements. One particularly memorable ad in 1992 showed an AIDS patient moments before his death. Increasingly, consumers began to lose the connection between Benetton and fashion.

Things came to a head in 2000 with a campaign, "We on Death Row," showing prison inmates sentenced to death. Relatives of the victims sued the company, claiming Benetton was using the victims' fate for its own purpose and had misrepresented itself to gain access to inmates.[3] As a result of the campaign, Sears pulled the company's new line of sportswear off its shelves.

At that point, Benetton realized its advertising was hurting its bottom line. The company hopes its new ads change consumer attitudes toward the store by restoring the link between Benetton and fashionable merchandise. Some people would have preferred to keep the controversial advertising and criticize the new campaign as bland. In England, where the campaign broke earlier, ads were described as "so innocuous as to be invisible."[4] But the criticism speaks more to advertising execution than to the need for attitude change. It was becoming increasingly obvious that the company had to reposition itself through a campaign of attitude change if it was to remain viable in the U.S. market.

Any campaign of attitude change like Benetton's is risky. Although the company alienated many consumers with its ad campaigns, it had still sustained a core market in the United States. The risk now is that in attempting to attain a wider audience, the company may alienate its core market and be left with even less than before it attempted to change attitudes.

The Nature of Consumer Attitudes

More than fifty years ago, Gordon Allport formulated the most frequently used definition of attitudes. He wrote: "Attitudes are learned predispositions to respond to an object or class of objects in a consistently favorable or unfavorable way."[5] **Brand attitudes** are consumers' learned tendencies to evaluate brands in a consistently favorable or unfavorable way; that is, consumers' evaluation of a particular brand on an overall basis from poor to excellent.

Attitudes toward brands are based on the schema of a brand consumers store in long-term memory. (Recall that a *schema* is a cluster of thoughts and ideas about a brand or company.) A schema of AT&T as being stodgy and old-fashioned has led many younger consumers to choose other long-distance providers. Older consumers, however, are more likely to have a schema of the company associated with reliability, security, and good service. Because these attributes constitute the beliefs many older consumers have about AT&T, they are likely to lead to a positive evaluation of the company and to selection of AT&T as the long-distance provider. As a result, brand beliefs (AT&T provides good service) lead to brand evaluations (I like AT&T) and thus to intended behavior (I plan to use AT&T for my long-distance service).

THREE COMPONENTS OF ATTITUDES

Cognitive component
Brand beliefs

Affective component
Brand evaluation

Behavioral component
Intention to buy

Purchase decision

| **FIGURE 8.1** |
Three components of attitudes.

The link among brand beliefs, evaluations, and intended behavior is a main focus of this chapter. *Brand beliefs, brand evaluations,* and *intention to buy* define the three components of attitudes shown in Figure 8.1. Brand beliefs are the **cognitive** (or **thinking**) **component** of attitudes; brand evaluations, the **affective** (or **feeling**) **component;** and intention to buy, the **behavioral component.** Because these three attitudinal components play such a central role in marketing strategy, a fuller understanding of each of them will be helpful.

▌ **Beliefs: The Cognitive Component**   Consumers' beliefs about a brand are the characteristics they ascribe to it. Through marketing research, marketers develop a **vocabulary of product attributes and benefits** similar to the vocabulary a large food company develops for a beverage (see Table 8.1). These types of vocabularies are based on the results of a series of depth or focus-group interviews with consumers. Once marketers establish a vocabulary of product attributes and benefits, they include it in a questionnaire and conduct a consumer survey in which they ask respondents to rate brands utilizing the vocabulary. Thus, a study of soft drinks may involve asking consumers to rate various brands on the criteria listed in Table 8.1.

The vocabulary of beliefs for a soft drink in Table 8.1 shows both attributes and benefits. Consumers are asked to rate soft drinks on attributes such as sweet and carbonated, and on benefits such as nutritional and thirst-quenching. Such ratings provide the marketer with the means to identify the strengths and weaknesses of the company's brand relative to that of the competition. For example, beliefs may show that teenagers regard Pepsi as a sweeter and more carbonated beverage than Coke. If beliefs show weakness, then the marketer might consider a repositioning strategy,

TABLE 8.1
Vocabulary of brand beliefs for a soft drink product

Product attributes	Product benefits
Caloric content	Restores energy
Vitamin content	Nutritional
Natural ingredients	Good for the whole family
Sweetness	Gives a lift
Aftertaste	Good at mealtimes
Carbonation	Thirst-quenching

similar to what AT&T is doing in attempting to strengthen attitudes among younger consumers.

Such vocabularies also help consumers in their brand evaluations. A study by West and her colleagues found that giving consumers a vocabulary like that in Table 8.1 to rate brands helps them better understand the nature of their beliefs about brands and produces more consistent and well-defined brand preferences over time.[6]

The vocabulary of attributes and benefits in Table 8.1 provides the marketer with only part of the equation in understanding beliefs. A consumer may rate a soft drink as very sweet, but this rating does not mean the consumer wants a sweet drink. Therefore, marketers must determine the value consumers place on attributes such as sweet and refreshing and benefits such as nutritional and thirst-quenching. Two consumers can rate a soft drink "very sweet," but one may put a high value on sweetness, whereas the other may not. As a result, the first consumer will have a more positive attitude toward the brand compared with that of the second consumer, despite similar beliefs.

What consumers value is important in segmenting them, because this shows what they want. In this case, it is logical to define a "sweet" or a "nutritional" segment in the soft drink market.

▮ Overall Brand Evaluation: The Affective Component

The second attitude component, the affective (feeling) component, represents consumers' overall evaluation of the brand. Beliefs about a brand are multidimensional because they represent the brand attributes consumers perceive. The affective component, however, is one-dimensional. Consumers' overall evaluation of a brand can be measured by rating the brand from "poor" to "excellent" or from "prefer least" to "prefer most." If we accept the basic attitudinal model in Figure 8.1, brand evaluations result from brand beliefs. For example, assume teens believe that Pepsi is a sweeter drink. Because most teens put a high value on sweetness, they would then have a positive attitude toward Pepsi.

Of the three components, brand evaluation is central to the study of attitudes because it summarizes consumers' predisposition to be favorable or unfavorable to the brand. Brand beliefs are relevant only to the extent that they influence brand evaluations, which are the primary determinants of intended behavior. In fact, brand evaluation conforms to the definition of brand attitudes as a "tendency to evaluate brands in a favorable or unfavorable way." As a result, consumer researchers treat brand evaluations as synonymous with attitudes (as we do later in this chapter). But it is important to know that attitudes (*i.e.,* brand evaluations) are formed by beliefs and influence intention to buy.

▮ Intention to Buy: The Behavioral Component

The third attitude component, the behavioral dimension, is consumers' tendency to act toward an object, which is generally measured in terms of intention to buy. Measuring buying intent is particularly important in developing marketing strategy.

Marketing managers frequently test the elements of the marketing mix—alternative product concepts, ads, packages, or brand names—to determine what is most likely to influence purchase behavior. Tests of these alternatives are conducted under artificially controlled circumstances that try to hold all factors constant except the marketing stimuli being tested. Consumers viewing alternative ads or trying various product formulations are asked about their intentions to buy after experiencing these marketing stimuli. Marketers regard the alternative producing the highest buying intent as the best choice. In the absence of actual buying behavior, management uses the closest substitute, intention to buy, to determine the effectiveness of the marketing mix components.

Marketers can try to appeal to this third component of attitudes without necessarily influencing the other two. A sharp reduction in price or a special coupon offer may be inducement enough for consumers to try a less favored brand. Beliefs and attitudes about the chosen brand do not have to change for consumers to establish an intention to buy if the economic inducement is large enough.

ATTITUDES AND THE HIERARCHY OF EFFECTS

The relationship between the three components of attitudes is known as the **hierarchy of effects.** The three different hierarchies are as follows:

1. A high-involvement hierarchy
2. A low-involvement hierarchy
3. An experiential hierarchy

Table 8.2 describes these hierarchies based on the three components of attitudes.

❚ High- versus Low-Involvement Hierarchy   When consumers are involved, they first develop beliefs about the brand through a process of active information search. On this basis, they evaluate the brand, develop definite brand attitudes, and make a purchase decision accordingly. In the low-involvement hierarchy, consumers form beliefs passively. They make a purchase decision with limited information because it is not worth the time and trouble to engage in active information search and processing. Brand evaluations and attitudes are formed after the fact and are likely to

TABLE 8.2
Three hierarchies of effect

Type of hierarchy	Sequence	Nature of information processing
HIGH-INVOLVEMENT	Beliefs Evaluation Behavior	Active, purchase-specific processing
LOW-INVOLVEMENT	Beliefs Behavior Evaluation	Passive, purchase-specific processing
EXPERIENTIAL	Evaluation Behavior Beliefs	Active, ongoing processing

be weak. This means that consumers often buy low-involvement products without forming a definite attitude about the brand. As a result, attitudes do not predict behavior as well in low-involvement purchases as in the high-involvement case because well-defined attitudes do not generally precede behavior.

Although the attitudes consumers form after a low-involvement purchase may be weakly held, they may still influence future purchases. A consumer who tries a new paper towel and decides it is not as good as his or her regular brand is unlikely to buy it again. This overall evaluation is important information for the marketer, even if this consumer is not very involved with the brand.

▌ The Experiential Hierarchy   Our focus on hedonic as opposed to utilitarian products in past chapters leads to a third hierarchy of effects, an *experiential hierarchy*.[7] The experiential hierarchy is based primarily on a consumer's emotional response to the brand.

As Table 8.2 suggests, consumers first evaluate a brand on an overall basis by relying on their feelings, emotions, and fantasies and then act on this basis. Beliefs about the attributes and characteristics of a brand may be formed after the fact. The consumer's primary purchase motive is the anticipated *experience* of enjoying the brand, not the projected performance of the brand based on evaluative product criteria. A teen may buy a Shaq Attack basketball sneaker because of the desire to be like Shaquille O'Neal on the basketball court, not because of any specific performance or comfort criteria. The teen may determine the degree of comfort only after buying them.

The experiential hierarchy has important implications for marketing strategy when compared with the traditional high-involvement hierarchy. In the experiential hierarchy, consumers are likely to be more aware of stimuli such as symbols and imagery that shape their feelings about a brand. Given their emotional involvement, search for such stimuli is apt to be ongoing. In contrast, in the high-involvement hierarchy, consumers are more likely to be aware of brand attributes and search is more likely to be purchase-specific.

Sealy Corporation initiated a repositioning strategy that effectively shifted its focus from a high-involvement to an experiential hierarchy. Its traditional positioning was as a high-quality mattress maker, and its ads touted the product attributes that made a Sealy mattress comfortable and luxurious. Then in 2001 it launched a $20 million campaign to reposition itself as a "sleep-wellness provider." It is attempting to associate its products with a good night's sleep and good health. Rather than advertising specific product attributes, the campaign shows Dot Richardson, a surgeon and Olympic athlete, experiencing one of her typical hectic days that ends on a Sealy mattress with the tag line "I love this bed."[8] The ad is purely experiential.

ATTITUDE DEVELOPMENT

To understand the role of attitudes in consumer behavior, we must understand how they develop and the functions they play. Attitudes develop over time through a learning process affected by family influences, peer-group influences, information and experience, and personality.

▌Family Influences   The family is an important influence on purchase decisions. Regardless of children's tendency to rebel in the teenage years, their attitudes correlate highly with those of their parents. As Bennett and Kassarjian note, "Attitudes toward personal hygiene, preferences for food items, attitudes toward boiled vegetables or fried food, and beliefs about the medicinal value of chicken soup are similarly acquired (from parents)."[9]

This influence is demonstrated in some advertising themes. For instance, Johnson & Johnson once advertised its baby powder by portraying a mother using it on her daughter's wedding day and tearfully reminiscing about its earlier use. Parental influence is especially apparent in attitudes toward candy. If parents used candy as a punishment or reward for their children, in later years those children as adults have subconscious guilt feelings about eating candy. Thus, some advertising tries to alleviate guilt feelings by making positive associations with candy.

▌Peer-Group Influences   Many studies have shown pervasive group influence on purchasing behavior. Katz and Lazarsfeld found peer groups to be much more likely than advertising to influence attitudes and purchasing behavior.[10] Coleman found that socially integrated doctors who valued peer-group norms accepted a new drug faster.[11] Arndt found that socially integrated consumers accepted a new coffee product sooner.[12] In each of these studies, group norms influenced product attitudes.

▌Information and Experience   Consumers' past experiences influence their brand attitudes. According to learning theory, such experiences condition future behavior. Information is also an important attitude determinant. For example, knowing that a pain reliever has a newer, faster-acting formula may result in a more favorable evaluation of the brand and may induce consumers to switch.

▌Personality   Consumers' personalities affect their attitudes. Traits such as aggression, extroversion, submissiveness, or authoritarianism may influence attitudes toward brands and products. For example, an aggressive individual may be likely to be involved in competitive sports and buys the most expensive equipment in an attempt to excel. In such a case, attitudes toward sports equipment are a function of personality.

FUNCTIONS OF ATTITUDES

Understanding the **functions of attitudes** means understanding how they serve the individual. Daniel Katz proposed four classifications of attitude functions:[13]

▌ Utilitarian
▌ Value-expressive
▌ Ego-defensive
▌ Knowledge

▌Utilitarian Function   The utilitarian function of attitudes guides consumers in achieving desired benefits. For example, a consumer who considers safety and immediate relief the most important criteria in selecting a pain reliever is directed to brands that fulfill these benefits. Conversely, in their utilitarian role, atti-

EXHIBIT 8.1

Ads depicting the utilitarian and value-expressive functions of attitudes.

(left) Reebok International Ltd.; (right) Aerosoles. Model: Siew Longhorn/Flutie Entertainment;
Aerosoles, a division of Aerogroup International, Inc.

tudes direct consumers away from brands unlikely to fulfill their needs. Auto advertising reflects the utilitarian function of attitudes when it features performance characteristics.

Exhibit 8.1 shows examples of advertising's use of the functions of attitudes. The ad for Reebok sneakers is an example of the utilitarian function. For the active person who values comfort, style, and flexibility while jogging, doing aerobics, or participating in other sports activities, the ad's appeal enhances the brand's utility.

Value-Expressive Function   Attitudes can express consumers' self-images and value systems, particularly for a high-involvement product. The self-image of an individual purchasing a sports car, for example, may be of a hard-driving, domineering person who likes to gain the upper hand. Aggressiveness may manifest itself in purchasing a car that fits this image. Likewise, the individual who dresses conservatively like everyone else where he or she works has accepted the values of conservatism and wealth as expressions of success.

Advertisers often appeal to the value-expressive nature of attitudes by implying that use or purchase of a certain item leads to self-enhancement, achievement, or independence. In this manner, advertisers appeal to a large segment of consumers who value these self-expressive traits. The Aerosoles ad in Exhibit 8.1 says that the wearer has a wild or rebellious side, suggesting a confident, self-aware woman who isn't afraid to go out on the edge every so often.

▌ **Ego-Defensive Function**   Attitudes protect the ego from anxieties and threats. Consumers purchase many products, like mouthwashes, to avoid anxiety-producing situations. Most individuals use mouthwashes to avoid bad breath rather than to cure it. Advertising capitalizes on the fears of social ostracism by demonstrating greater social acceptance through use of certain products. As a result, consumers develop positive attitudes toward brands associated with social acceptance, confidence, and sexual desirability. A United Kingdom ad for Mercedes Benz was an example. The tag line "Make Your Learjet Jealous" projected thoughts about social status. By purchasing this vehicle, drivers could feel they exemplified an air of status, power, social acceptance, and influence.

▌ **Knowledge Function**   Attitudes help consumers organize the mass of information they are exposed to daily. Consumers sort all of the messages, ignoring the less relevant information. The knowledge function also reduces uncertainty and confusion. Advertising that provides information about new brands or new characteristics of existing brands is valuable for the information it provides. An ad for Ortho Tri-Cyclen informed women that it was not only over 99 percent effective as a birth control pill, but it also reduced acne to maintain clearer skin.

In summary, attitudes have different functions. The function that is served affects the individual's overall evaluation of an object.[14] For example, two individuals having equally favorable attitudes toward Listerine mouthwash vary markedly in the nature of these attitudes, depending on whether they reflect a utilitarian function (Listerine freshens my mouth) or an ego-defensive function (Listerine avoids bad breath). Trying to influence the utilitarian consumer that Listerine avoids bad breath would be as ineffective as trying to influence the ego-oriented consumer that Listerine freshens one's mouth.

The Role of Attitudes in Developing Marketing Strategy

Marketers define and measure attitudes toward their brands because attitudes help them (1) identify benefit segments, (2) develop new products, and (3) formulate and evaluate promotional strategies.

IDENTIFY BENEFIT SEGMENTS

Market segments are identified by the benefits consumers desire. These benefits define the key product attributes marketers should use to influence consumers. The benefits consumers desire are measured by attribute evaluations. For example, consumers who rate nutrition, taste, or economy as most important in buying cereals belong to one of these three benefit segments. In the car market, segments can be defined by economy, performance, and luxury. Marketers attempt to influence consumer attitudes in the performance segment by citing key features such as acceleration, horsepower, and fuel efficiency; price and service costs are the primary criteria to emphasize for the economy segment.

DEVELOP NEW PRODUCTS

Attitudes are crucial in evaluating alternative positionings for new products. For example, at one time Nabisco conducted a benefit segmentation study of the snack food market to identify opportunities for a new product. The largest segment in the study was identified as "nutritional snackers"—snackers who identified nutrition and natural ingredients as the most important attributes in selecting a snack.

On this basis, Nabisco decided to test consumer reactions to a new product intended to be positioned to this segment, a mixed chip, nut, and fruit snack. It confirmed that nutritional snackers rated the brand positively on the two key attributes of nutrition and natural ingredients and were likely to buy the product as a result.

FORMULATE AND EVALUATE PROMOTIONAL STRATEGIES

Attitudes are important in developing promotional strategies. If snack purchasers emphasize nutrition and natural ingredients as desired benefits, these are the appeals marketers must emphasize in advertising and promotions to create favorable attitudes among the target group. Communication of these benefits as well as their subsequent fulfillment by the product will result in positive attitudes toward Nabisco's fruit-and-nut snack product. Advertising's role is to communicate the benefits the brand can deliver.

Attitudes are also important in evaluating the effectiveness of advertising messages. Television commercials and print ads are frequently judged by how large and how favorable an attitude shift they produce. Brand attitudes are measured before and after exposure to a commercial in a controlled environment. Marketers use any changes in brand attitudes to evaluate the commercial's effectiveness.

Marketers also use attitudes to evaluate advertising campaigns over time to determine whether the attitudes are being maintained or whether they are changing favorably or unfavorably. Advertising campaigns may have attitude change as a specific objective. Consider the **perceptual map** in Figure 8.2 showing the position of

| FIGURE 8.2 |

Using attitudes to evaluate a department store's position.

Source: "Image and Attitude Are Department Store's Draw," *New York Times* (August 12, 1993), p. D1. Copyright © The New York Times. Reprinted with permission.

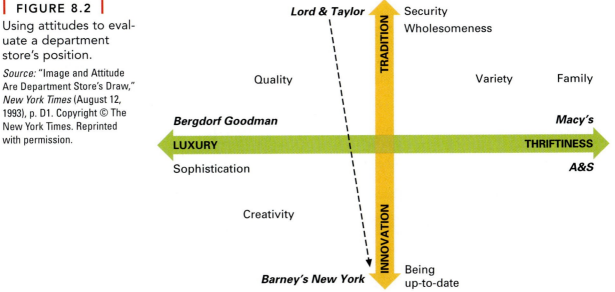

Lord & Taylor department stores. Lord & Taylor is associated with security and tradition, which is a positioning that may be strong among older consumers. But Lord & Taylor recognizes that it must begin to appeal to the under-40 set. As a result, it should consider a repositioning strategy that would move its stores down the vertical axis toward a combination of tradition and innovation (see the dotted line in Figure 8.2 for desired attitude shift). An advertising campaign with this objective would measure attitudes toward Lord & Taylor before and after the campaign to determine the degree to which attitudes reflect a shift to a more innovative and up-to-date image. In this case, changes in brand attitudes are used to evaluate an advertising campaign's effectiveness.

Relationships of Beliefs, Attitudes, and Behavior

The key concern of marketers is the relationships among the three components in Figure 8.1—beliefs, attitudes, and behavior.[15] These relationships are important to marketers because they indicate the success of marketing strategies. If advertising is successful in establishing positive beliefs about a brand, consumers are more likely to evaluate the brand positively and to buy it. Satisfaction with the brand strengthens positive attitudes and increases the probability that consumers will repurchase it.

THE RELATIONSHIP OF BELIEFS AND ATTITUDES

Two theories focus on the relationship among beliefs and attitudes: Heider's balance theory and Fishbein's multiattribute theory (later modified to the theory of reasoned action).

■ **Heider's Balance Theory**   Heider's **balance theory** is so named because it maintains that people seek balance between their thoughts (beliefs) and feelings (evaluations).[16] A good illustration of how balance theory operates occurred when JCPenney attempted to upgrade its image by contracting to carry Halston's designer line of clothes. Many consumers had a positive image of Halston but a negative image of Penney (as shown in the left-hand triangle in Figure 8.3). When Halston began selling at Penney (represented by a plus between Halston and Penney), this relationship created an imbalance (a positive object linked to a more negative object). Two pluses and a minus produce a minus, leaving an imbalance in con-

| **FIGURE 8.3** |
Illustration of balance theory.

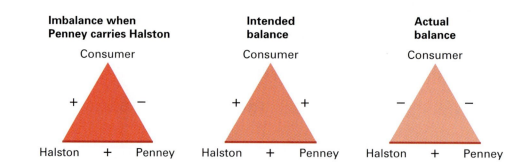

sumers' minds. Penney hoped that consumers would resolve this imbalance by developing a more favorable image of its stores (middle triangle). What actually happened was that many consumers maintained their image of Penney but developed a more negative image of Halston (right-hand triangle). This image shift created balance in consumers' cognitive system (two minuses and a plus produce a plus), but not the balance Penney intended.

As the Penney example suggests, marketers use balance theory to link their brand or company to symbols, brands, or persons with more positive images. This was Kmart's intent when it used Martha Stewart as a spokesperson. It hoped that her stylish image would rub off on Kmart.

Balance theory conforms to a basic behavioral principle of **cognitive consistency,** which states that consumers value harmony between their beliefs and evaluations. If one is inconsistent with the other, consumers change their attitudes to create harmony in their cognitive structure. Research supports the idea that consistency exists between beliefs and brand evaluations. In a study of six consumer goods, Sheth and Talarzyk found that brand ratings on specific attributes such as taste, price, nutrition, and packaging were closely related to overall evaluation of the brand.[17] Other studies have also found a link between brand beliefs and overall evaluations.[18]

▌ Fishbein's Multiattribute Model

Fishbein's **multiattribute model** of attitudes[19] describes attitude formation as a function of consumer beliefs about the attributes and benefits of a brand. Fishbein's model allows marketers to diagnose the strengths and weaknesses of their brands relative to those of the competition by determining how consumers evaluate brand alternatives on important attributes. In so doing, marketers can apply multiattribute models directly to vocabularies of attributes used to evaluate specific brands.

As shown in Figure 8.4, consumers start with the evaluation of certain attributes (a medicinal-tasting mouthwash is good for you). Consumers then form beliefs as to whether an object has that attribute (Listerine has a medicinal taste). Attitudes toward the object are the sum total of beliefs and values for not just one attribute, but for all relevant attributes. Thus, a consumer might rate Listerine more favorably because it has a medicinal taste and gives the mouth a fresh feeling, both of which this consumer considers desirable attributes. At the same time, the consumer might rate Listerine less favorably on certain other important attributes, such as irritation to the gums.

As a result, Fishbein's model is a compensatory model of brand attitudes. That is, consumers can compensate for the weakness of a brand on one attribute by the strength on another. The fact that Listerine is rated positively based on its medicinal taste and refreshing feeling but negatively because of irritation to the gums should produce a somewhat positive overall evaluation of the brand. Fishbein's model also states a linkage between brand evaluations and intended or actual

Evaluation of product attributes — Mouthwashes with a medicinal taste are good for you.

Brand beliefs — Listerine has a medicinal taste.

Overall brand evaluations — I like Listerine because of its medicinal taste and fresh feeling, but it irritates my gums.

Intention to buy — I intend to buy Listerine.

Behavior

│ FIGURE 8.4 │
Fishbein's multiattribute model.

behavior: A positive (negative) attitude toward a brand increases (decreases) the likelihood that consumers intend to buy it.

Fishbein's model suggests that marketers identify the key attributes that are likely to influence brand attitudes and emphasize these attributes in advertising. In the preceding example, if Listerine can convey the benefits of a strong, effective mouthwash that freshens the mouth without irritation, it is likely to result in positive brand attitudes and a greater likelihood of purchasing.

▌ **Fishbein's Theory of Reasoned Action**   A consumer may have a very positive attitude toward a Rolls-Royce but may be unlikely to buy because of the high price. In this and other similar cases, product attitudes do not lead to behavior, contradicting Fishbein's multiattribute model. In an attempt to explain this discrepancy, Fishbein modified his multiattribute model. The resulting **theory of reasoned action** proposes that to predict behavior more accurately, it is more important to determine the person's *attitude to that behavior* than to the object of the behavior.[20] That is, it is more important to determine an individual's attitude toward buying a Rolls-Royce than it is to measure attitudes toward the brand itself. The consumer's act of purchasing and, ultimately, consuming the product determines satisfaction. The attitude toward the object may not be a valid basis for gauging attitudes. A consumer may have a very positive attitude toward a Rolls-Royce but a negative attitude toward buying one because of the price.

Fishbein introduced a second modification to his model. He concluded that since family and peer groups are likely to influence consumer attitudes toward brands, the model must account for such social influences. As a result, he introduced a key social element, *normative beliefs,* based on the degree to which consumers think they are complying with the wishes of family or friends. Fishbein weighted his attitudinal measures based on the degree to which (1) consumers think they are complying with the wishes of friends or family, and (2) their motivation to comply with these norms.

Studies have found that the theory of reasoned action predicts intentions and behavior better than does the original multiattribute model. Wilson, Matthews, and Harvey measured intentions and behavior for toothpaste purchases using the original and extended Fishbein models.[21] They found that attitudes toward the purchase of a brand were more closely related to behavior than were attitudes toward the brand. A study by Knox and Chernatony of buyers of mineral water confirmed that attitudes toward purchasing served as good predictors of subsequent behavior.[22]

THE RELATIONSHIP OF INTENTION TO BUY TO BEHAVIOR

Positive attitudes toward a brand lead to a greater likelihood consumers will express an intention to buy it. Intention to buy in Fishbein's attitudinal models is an intervening variable between attitudes and behavior (see Figure 8.4). Both marketers and economists have used intention to buy to predict future behavior—marketers to evaluate alternative new product concepts and advertising themes, and economists to predict future economic trends.

Marketers should confirm the relationship between intention and subsequent behavior if purchase intention is to be regarded as a valid measure of action tendency. The Survey Research Center at the University of Michigan has provided the most extensive confirmation of the relationship between intentions and purchase. George Katona, founder of the Center, used consumer buying intentions to forecast economic trends. He reported on the close relationship between intentions and behavior in buying automobiles.[23] Among those consumers who said they planned to or might buy a new car, 63 percent bought in the next year. Among those consumers who did not intend to buy, 29 percent purchased a new car. Katona's studies showed that the majority of consumers who intended to buy a product fulfilled their intentions.

Katona conducted his studies before 1970. Since then consumer intentions have proved to be a less reliable predictor of behavior. Energy shortages and two severe recessions in the early 1980s and early 1990s made the relationship between intentions and behavior less certain. The economic downturn that began in 2000 is likely to reinforce this trend. During the energy crisis, most consumers said they would cut back on driving but did not. After the stock market crash of 1987, many consumers said they would cut back on purchases of high-ticket items but did not. Interestingly, the Survey Research Center now asks consumers not what they intend to buy, but what their expectations are regarding their economic situation.[24] The latter measure seems to be more predictive of total consumer expenditures.

Another factor inhibiting the fulfillment of consumer intentions is a long repurchase cycle. The University of Michigan study interviewed consumers to determine actual car purchases one year after determining intentions. Many factors, such as a change in needs, economic circumstances, or alternatives available, can intervene in the space of a year to change intentions.

THE RELATIONSHIP OF BEHAVIOR TO ATTITUDES

Not only do consumer attitudes influence behavior, but behavior can also influence subsequent attitudes. Three situations are likely to result in behavior influencing attitudes: cognitive dissonance, passive learning, and a disconfirmation of expectations.

Theories of cognitive dissonance, passive learning, and disconfirmation of expectations have reduced the importance of attitudes in explaining consumer behavior by showing that attitude change is not a necessary condition for a change in purchasing behavior.

■ **Cognitive Dissonance**   According to dissonance theory, consumer attitudes sometimes change to conform to previous behavior, thus reducing postpurchase conflict. Several studies have confirmed these relationships. For example, Knox and Inkster interviewed bettors at a racetrack before bets on a horse were made.[25] On the average, bettors gave their horse little better than a fair chance of winning. The researchers then interviewed the same bettors after they made their bets but before the race. Predictions about the performance of the horse became substantially more positive after they made the decision. Apparently, bettors sought to reduce the potential for postdecisional conflict by enhancing the evaluation of the chosen alternative. This finding indicates that individuals tend to reinforce their decision after the fact by changing their attitudes in favor of the chosen brand.

■ **Passive Learning**   The theory of passive learning provides another basis for downplaying the importance of consumer attitudes as determinants of behavior.[26] As we have seen, under conditions of low involvement, a change in attitude is not necessary to influence a change in behavior. The awareness of a new brand may be sufficient reason for consumers to switch in a search for variety, and consumers may form attitudes toward the new brand after using it. Ginter's study of a low-involvement category, household cleaning products, found that consumers tended to rate brands more favorably after they made the purchase.[27]

■ **Disconfirmation of Expectations**   When expectations regarding product performance are not met, such **disconfirmation of expectations** may give consumers more negative attitudes toward the product after the purchase. According to **assimilation/contrast theories,** when consumers are only slightly disappointed, attitudes adjust to expectations because the experience is accepted and assimilated. When consumers are very disappointed, however, a negative change in attitudes is likely to occur after the purchase, and they may exaggerate this change.

Advertising may promote a disconfirmation of expectations by overselling brands. Frequent claims that a brand is "the highest quality" or "the best value," or that it "will guarantee satisfaction," may result in consumers feeling the claims were not met. The risks of such disconfirmation were the main reason Mars candy bars decided to scale down the benefits it claimed for its brand. Mars had gone through a series of campaigns over the years promoting claims from taste to nutrition. But research showed that consumers associated the brand with "a temporary break, a little bit of relaxation, a little moment for yourself," rather than more grandiose benefits. As a result, the company decided on a campaign centered on little moments of pleasure.[28] Limiting the scope of the message to attainable benefits minimized the risk that consumers would be disappointed when consuming the product.

FACTORS INHIBITING THE RELATIONSHIPS OF BELIEFS, ATTITUDES, AND BEHAVIOR

Marketers must recognize occasions when consumer attitudes are unlikely to be related to behavior. The following conditions may cause a lack of association among beliefs, attitudes, and behavior:

1. *Lack of involvement.* As we saw in Chapter 4, consumer attitudes are less likely to be related to behavior for low-involvement products.

2. *Lack of purchase feasibility.* Consumers may have a very positive attitude toward the brand, but it may not be one of the brands consumers can feasibly purchase. For example, a consumer may evaluate a Rolex very positively, but the watch is not a realistic alternative for most consumers because of its price. As a result, attitudes are not related to behavior.

3. *Lack of direct product experience.* A study by Berger and Mitchell found that when consumers have direct product experience, their attitudes are more likely to be related to subsequent behavior.[29] Lack of product experience may result in weakly held attitudes that are not related to behavior.

4. *Lack of relation between values and beliefs.* Attitudes are unlikely to be related to behavior if brand beliefs are not tied to consumer values. The fact that con-

sumers believe a brand of cereal has fewer calories is not going to predict behavior of those consumers with no interest in losing weight.

5. *Changing market conditions.* An increase in the price of the favored brand may cause consumers to switch with no change in attitudes. Special price promotions or better credit terms for competitive brands may cause consumers to buy a less preferred brand. The unavailability of the preferred brand may lead consumers to purchase a less preferred brand with no change in attitudes.

6. *Poor attitude accessibility.* As we saw in Chapter 7, consumers retain brand beliefs in memory as schema representing their associations with the brand. For these beliefs to affect brand evaluations, they must be accessible from memory. Fazio and his associates suggest that lack of a relationship between attitudes and behavior may be due to the fact that some attitudes are so weakly held that they are not accessible.[30] If consumers have strongly held attitudes, they often spontaneously retrieve them when they encounter the object. If a consumer has a strong positive attitude toward McDonald's, for example, the consumer could spontaneously retrieve the McDonald's schema by the mere mention of a Big Mac or by the sight of the golden arches.

Attitude Reinforcement and Change

Marketers can use their knowledge of consumer attitudes to develop two types of strategies. One strategy reinforces existing attitudes; another tries to change them. In this section, we show how marketers use consumer attitudes to develop strategies of attitude reinforcement and change. To understand this process, we consider the conditions required to change consumer attitudes and the strategies marketers use to implement attitudinal change.

There is no question that reinforcing existing attitudes is easier than changing them. Most advertising for well-known brands attempts to maintain and reinforce positive attitudes. Successful themes such as Chevrolet's "Like a Rock" or Miller Lite's "Less Filling/Tastes Great" reinforced consumer attitudes through long-running campaigns.

Strategies that reinforce attitudes may be easier to implement, but an attempt to change attitudes may be necessary to change a brand's or a company's image. (See the example of Kmart's attempt to change its image in the Strategic Applications box.)

CONDITIONS FOR ATTITUDE REINFORCEMENT AND CHANGE

Several studies show that when communications conform to, rather than contradict, existing brand attitudes, consumers are more easily influenced. McCullough, MacLachlan, and Moinpour found that communicating toothpaste attributes known to be important to consumers was more effective than attempting to change the importance of these attributes.[31] A study by Raj found that reinforcing users' positive attitudes toward a brand was more effective in increasing consumption of the brand than trying to change the attitudes of nonusers.[32]

Kmart Tries to Change Its Image from "The Polyester Palace"

Kmart (originally Kresges 5 and 10 cents stores) was doing great before the 1980s as it transitioned into the number-two mass merchandiser in the United States behind Sears. But in the 1980s, Kmart came up against the baby-boom generation. These consumers wanted greater quality and value than Kmart was giving them. Kmart could not afford to ignore this group, given their numbers and purchasing power. The trouble was that many baby boomers viewed Kmart as a purveyor of low-quality merchandise. These negative attitudes earned Kmart the nickname "The Polyester Palace."

In 1987, a new management team embarked on a strategy to reposition Kmart as a high-fashion discount store and thereby change negative attitudes of baby boomers. The company introduced a high-quality clothing line, the Jacklyn Smith Signature Collection, by using the former star of the TV show "Charlie's Angels" to promote the line. In a further attempt to leave its polyester image behind, Kmart signed on Martha Stewart, an icon of stylishness, as its spokesperson in its advertising.

By 1990, flat sales were showing Kmart the difficulty of changing its polyester image. So management initiated a five-year, $3 billion chainwide store renovation program to improve its in-store decor. Then, in 1993, it embarked on a new advertising campaign to try to get working women to think of Kmart as a source of fashion. The campaign used a "soft-image" approach to try to show that Kmart is in tune with consumers' feelings. One ad showed a working mother relaxing, with the copy: "You put yourself through a lot. Between the kids, the home, and your job, it seems there's no time left for you."

But these efforts did not produce results, demonstrating the difficulty of changing ingrained attitudes about a company. From 1987 to 1995, Kmart's share of total discount sales fell from 34.5 percent to 22.7 percent. A new management team fared no better after 1995, and Kmart's performance continued to decline.

The new millennium saw yet another management change. The new management team began putting more focus on products and services targeted to Hispanics and African Americans because of projections that these groups would be the company's two largest future segments. Further, management initiated a micromarketing strategy in an attempt to do a better job at getting the right product to the right customer at the right time. In late 1999, it revamped its web site, *www.BlueLight.com* to institute everyday low prices, expand selections, and improve service. In 2000 it also began installing thirty-five hundred kiosks in eleven hundred stores to allow shoppers to connect directly to the Bluelight site to purchase items that cannot be found in Kmart stores or that are on sale but out of stock. Of equal importance, the company sought to improve product availability and in-store service to consumers through better personal sales help.

But by 2001, it became clear that these strategies were too little, too late. Targeting minorities and improving the web site were insufficient to sustain revenues. Kmart's efforts failed to alter ingrained attitudes. As a result, in January 2002 the company filed for bankruptcy and began closing many of its stores.

The Kmart experience shows the difficulty of changing attitudes once they are deeply ingrained. Despite Martha Stewart and an improvement in service, Kmart continued to be the Polyester Palace to many consumers.

Sources: "Kmart's Shopping List for Survival," *Business Week* (March 25, 2002), p. 38; "Kmart Marketing: Urban/Ethnic Strategy Remains Pillar of Competitive Advantage," *DSN Retailing Today* (March 5, 2001), pp. 44–46; "Conaway Begins to Execute at Kmart," *Home Textiles Today* (May 21, 2001), pp. 1, 4; "Customer Initiatives Top Kmart's Agenda," *DSN Retailing Today* (June 4, 2001), p. 7; "Kmart Installs 3,500 Shopping Kiosks Nationwide," *Direct Marketing* (April 2001), p. 11; "For Big or Small, Image Is Everything," *Adweek* (March 8, 1993), pp. 28–29; and "Loss Leader: How Wal-Mart Outdid a Once-Touted Kmart," *Wall Street Journal* (March 24, 1995).

Given the greater difficulty in changing consumer attitudes than in reinforcing them, marketers must know when attitude change is feasible. Under what conditions should changes in attitudes be attempted? A number of conditions reflecting the product category, market environment, and nature of consumers make it easier to produce changes in attitudes through marketing strategies. These principles may change consumer beliefs about a brand, brand attitudes (evaluations), or intention to buy:

1. *Beliefs are easier to change than desired benefits.* Marketers can seek to change beliefs about a brand. They can also attempt to change the benefits consumers desire by changing the value consumers place on brand attributes. Desired benefits are more enduring, ingrained, and internalized than beliefs because they are more closely linked to consumer values.[33]

2. *Attitudes are easier to change when there is a low level of involvement with the product.* Attitudes toward uninvolving products are easier to change because consumers are not committed to the brand. Sherif's theory of social judgment supports this view.[34] When consumers have a high level of involvement with a product, they accept messages only if the messages agree with their beliefs. When involvement is low, consumers are more likely to accept a message even if it does not agree with prior beliefs.

3. *Weak attitudes are easier to change than strong ones.* If consumer brand attitudes are not strong, marketers can more easily establish new associations with the brand product. When company or brand attitudes are strongly held, as with Rolls-Royce and Kmart, they are much more difficult to change.

4. *Attitudes held by consumers who have less confidence in their brand evaluations are easier to change.* Consumers who are unsure of their evaluation of a brand will be more receptive to the informational content of advertising and more subject to attitude change. Confusion about the criteria to use in evaluating a brand can cause consumers to lack self-confidence in making a decision. A number of years ago, the Carpet Institute hired a research firm to study the purchasing process for rugs and carpets. They concluded, "There is a great deal of confusion and misconception about the characteristics, features and terminology in carpeting. Even the terms rug vs. carpet, the type of rug construction vs. company names are confused."[35]

   In a case like this, consumers would be receptive to a brand that provides information on a few key product attributes. The strategy would be to change beliefs about the product category and to capitalize on these attitudinal changes by associating them with the manufacturer's brand name.

5. *Attitudes are easier to change when they are based on ambiguous information.* Consumers faced with ambiguous claims about competitive products or with highly technical information they cannot assess seek clarifying information. This clarifying information may cause a change in attitudes. One study found that high informational ambiguity consistently produced greater attitude change over a wide variety of products.[36]

   By presenting a clear-cut message of the user-friendly nature of its machines, Apple was successful in introducing its personal computers to schools in the late 1970s. At that time, PCs were in a product category that first-time users found highly technical and ambiguous. For many students, the symbolism of the Apple was meant to alleviate the uncertainty of using a PC.

ATTITUDE CHANGE BEFORE A PURCHASE

Given the frequency with which marketers try to change consumer brand and product attitudes and the frequent difficulty in doing so, a fuller understanding of the attitude change process is warranted. Marketers can attempt to change consumer attitudes before they make a purchase to influence them to buy, or they can change attitudes after a purchase to reduce any postpurchase dissonance. Three attitudinal theories described earlier provide a basis for influencing pre-purchase attitudinal change; namely, (1) Fishbein's multiattribute models, (2) Katz's functional theory of attitudes, and (3) Heider's balance theory.

▍ Fishbein's Multiattribute Models and Attitude Change   In Fishbein's multiattribute models (see Figure 8.4), consumer beliefs about brands and the value placed on these beliefs influence the overall evaluation of the brand, which, in turn, influences behavioral intent and, ultimately, behavior.

On this basis, marketers can consider four strategies to influence behavior based on the multiattribute models:

1. Change beliefs.
2. Change the values placed on particular product attributes.
3. Change the overall brand evaluation—that is, brand attitudes.
4. Change behavioral intentions.

Change Beliefs.   By far, the most common strategy is one that attempts to change consumer beliefs about brands through product and advertising strategies. The important point is to ensure that the beliefs being changed induce favorable changes in consumer brand evaluations and intention to buy. Quaker Oats tried to change consumer beliefs about Quaker Rice Cakes.[37] Typical comments from consumers in consumer research indicated that rice cakes taste like Styrofoam or cardboard. The introduction of flavored rice cakes brought back some past users. However, Quaker had to attract nonusers who generally had negative attitudes. It did so with an effective campaign showing a foam cup with a piece bitten out and with the headline "If this is what you think of rice cakes, wait till you taste them now" (see Exhibit 8.2).

Change the Values Placed on Particular Product Attributes.   This strategy requires convincing consumers to reassess the value of a particular attribute—for example, convincing consumers that bad taste is a good quality in mouthwash. Any attempt to change the values placed on product attributes must rely on prior research showing that a certain segment of the market would be receptive to such a change.

Values based on deep-seated social and cultural norms are the most difficult to change. The values consumers place on the taste of a mouthwash may be changed, but it is doubtful that advertising could influence a change in values related to social attractiveness, security, or status.

Change Brand Attitudes (Evaluations).   Marketers also try to influence consumer brand attitudes directly without specific reference to product attributes. This

| **EXHIBIT 8.2** |

Changing beliefs about rice cakes.

Reprinted with the permission of the Quaker Oats Company.

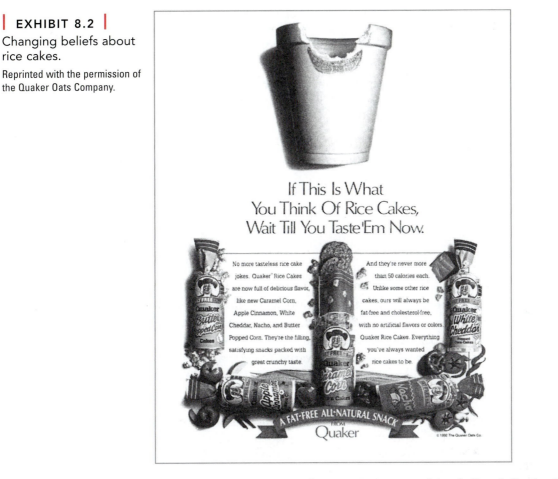

shortcut strategy may involve associating a positive feeling (affect) with product usage. As noted, this strategy can be used to try to establish a more hedonic perception of a brand, one based on emotion and fantasy. For example, Philip Morris was successful in changing attitudes toward Miller High Life from a beer promoted to the elite based on the theme "the champagne of bottled beer" to a more emotion-laden theme depicting blue-collar beer drinkers in interactive sports or social situations. The music and the theme "Miller Time" changed attitudes in a more hedonic direction without referring to specific brand attributes.

Marketers are putting more emphasis on changing consumer attitudes through symbols and imagery to create uniqueness in increasingly standardized product categories.

Change Behavioral Intentions or Behavior. Another change strategy is to induce consumers to purchase a brand that is not preferred—that is, to induce attitude-discrepant behavior. The assumption is that some inducement to try an unpreferred brand (possibly by lowering the price or by offering a deal or a coupon) may change consumers' brand attitude after the purchase to conform to their behavior.

For example, an individual may purchase a pain reliever with a 25-cents-off coupon. Assume there is little difference in effectiveness between the regular brand and the new brand. To justify the purchase, the consumer might decide that the new brand provides immediate relief and, therefore, decides to buy it again, even when the price returns to normal. This strategy makes use of the theory of cognitive dissonance. According to Festinger, the magnitude of such inducements to switch should not be large; otherwise, consumers could always say the only reason for a brand switch was the obvious price difference.[38] The tendency then would be to switch back to the regular brand when the price of the less preferred brand returns to normal. However, if the difference is a relatively small price change, but one sufficient to cause a saving, consumers will have to find a reason other than price to justify the purchase.

▌ Katz's Functional Theory and Attitude Change

Another model that has implications for strategies of consumer attitude change before a purchase is Katz's functional theory of attitudes.[39] As noted, Katz believes that attitudes serve four functions: the utilitarian, value-expressive, ego-defensive, and knowledge functions. Marketing strategies can attempt to change attitudes serving each of these functions.

Changing Attitudes through the Utilitarian Function. One way to influence a positive change in brand attitudes is to show how the product can solve a utilitarian goal consumers may not have previously considered. For example, Arm & Hammer began advertising various utilitarian uses of baking soda in an attempt to increase sales. According to the Arm & Hammer package, the product

- soothes minor skin irritations (insect bites, sunburn, etc.).
- absorbs carpet odors ("helps eliminate all types of odors in a safe, effective way").
- is a pure, natural skin conditioner ("for a relaxing bath and soft, smooth feeling skin").
- is an antacid (to alleviate heartburn, sour stomach, and/or acid indigestion).
- is a bleach booster (when using liquid chlorine bleach, add baking soda).

This array of uses for a traditional cooking and baking product may induce a favorable change in consumers' attitude toward the brand. These uses satisfy a set of utilitarian functions.

Changing Attitudes through the Value-Expressive Function. Advertising that attempts to influence the value-expressive function deals with personal values that may be difficult to change. By advertising its benefits to baby boomers, Miami Beach, the epitome of retirement communities, attempted to change an image that only the elderly and infirm live there. The campaign did not persuade baby boomers and alienated older residents. The town council would have been wiser to continue to appeal to older residents but to use youthful themes more in accord with the personal values of potential retirees, rather than targeting a new segment with ingrained beliefs about the community.

Changing Attitudes through the Ego-Defensive Function. Research has consistently shown that the more ego-defensive the attitude, the less subject it is to outside influence. The heavy drug user is likely to ignore information about the dangers of drug use. Avoiding painful information is an ego-defensive reaction. Thus, advertising should accept and adapt to ego-defensive attitudes rather than try to change them. This means that rather than taking a negative approach by showing the dangers of drug use, advertising should instead show what steps the user can take to decrease usage.

Changing Attitudes through the Knowledge Function. The knowledge function organizes and classifies information, facilitating consumers' information-processing task. It is important for marketers to provide a clear and unambiguous positioning for their product to ensure favorable attitudes.

A good example of a clear and unambiguous positioning is Carnation Instant Breakfast. The company clearly positioned the product as a breakfast food directed to nutritionally oriented consumers who did not have time to prepare a traditional breakfast. Had the product tried to reach a broader market by being positioned as a nutritional pick-me-up at any time of the day, it probably would have failed. Although this positioning would be directed to a greater number of usage situations, it would have been more likely to confuse the consumer. Consumers could have seen the product as a breakfast food, a nutritional snack, or a dietary supplement. Such an ambiguous positioning might have led to a less favorable evaluation of the brand.

▌ **Heider's Balance Theory and Attitude Change**   Heider's balance theory also provides direct implications for attitude change. Balance theory says that attitudes change to avoid conflict between beliefs and evaluations.[40] Marketers implicitly use balance theory to create attitudinal conflicts in the hope that the resultant change in consumer brand attitudes will be positive. Thus, Gallo's link to Waterford crystal created conflict because of the luxury image of Waterford and the economy image of Gallo. Balance theory predicted that either Waterford's image would suffer because of the linkage, or Gallo's image would improve. Both Waterford and Gallo obviously believed the latter to be more likely than the former.

ATTITUDE CHANGE AFTER A PURCHASE

Marketers may seek to change consumer brand attitudes after as well as before a purchase. Such a strategy may attempt to counter competitive advertising that creates doubts in consumers' mind about the purchase, or it may attempt to counteract negative experiences with the product. Three theories provide strategy implications for attitude change after the purchase: dissonance theory, attribution theory, and the theory of passive learning.

▌ **Dissonance Theory**   Dissonance theory suggests that marketers should seek to reduce dissonance by supplying consumers with positive information about the brand after the purchase. Runyon cites five strategies to provide supporting information after the purchase and, thus, to reduce dissonance:

1. Provide additional product information and suggestions for product care and maintenance through brochures or advertising.

2. Provide warranties and guarantees to reduce postpurchase doubt.

3. Ensure good service and immediate follow-up on complaints to provide postpurchase support.

4. Advertise reliable product quality and performance to reassure recent purchasers of product satisfaction.

5. Follow up after the purchase with direct contacts to make sure the customer understands how to use the product and to ensure satisfaction.[41] A study by Hunt showed that such postpurchase reassurances from a seller were effective in reducing consumer dissonance after purchase of a refrigerator.[42]

All these strategies are relevant for high-risk, high-involvement product categories. They are designed to change consumer attitudes toward the product by reducing postpurchase doubts.

▌ **Attribution Theory**   **Attribution theory** states that consumers seek to determine causes (or attributions) for events, often after the fact.[43] Attribution theory implies that advertisers should give consumers positive reasons for the purchase after they have bought the product. For example, a consumer buys a brand of coffee on sale and attributes the purchase to the fact the brand is cheaper. Such an attribution is unlikely to win long-term converts to the brand. However, if the manufacturer's advertising could convince the consumer that the brand makes a richer, heftier brew, the consumer is likely to buy again. The important point is that the manufacturer is trying to convince the consumer of the claim after the purchase.

Based on attribution theory, a marketing strategy for low-involvement products is to demonstrate potentially significant product differences that consumers can use after the fact as a rationale for having purchased. Such differences give consumers a reason for buying again. Marketers cannot rely solely on price promotions to influence consumers to buy uninvolving products. They must use advertising to provide a nonprice rationale to buy the same brand again.

▌ **Passive Learning**   Krugman's passive learning theory states that consumers learn about brands with little involvement and purchase with little evaluation of alternative brands.[44] Therefore, attitudes are more likely to be formed after, rather than before, a purchase.

Krugman's theory is most relevant for developing strategies to increase the level of consumer involvement after the purchase. Marketers seek to increase involvement with their brand because a higher level of commitment means that true, rather than spurious, brand loyalty is more likely to result. In Chapter 4, the following strategies for increasing involvement were cited:

1. Link the product to an involving issue.
2. Link the product to an involving personal situation.
3. Link the product to involving advertising.
4. Change the importance of product benefits.
5. Introduce an important characteristic in the product.

STRATEGIES FOR CHANGING ATTITUDES

Based on the preceding theories, we can consider strategies that attempt to change consumer attitudes. Such strategies generally require repositioning an existing brand; that is, changing the set of attributes and benefits communicated to consumers to influence them to buy. Marketers can direct such repositioning strategies to existing users to improve the brand's image or target them to nonusers to influence them to switch to the brand.

■ **Changing Attitudes of Existing Users**   Companies faced with declining sales often attempt to reposition their offerings to existing users. Arrow Shirts has been successful in repositioning itself. The company's image as a purveyor of conservative white shirts was restricting sales in an increasingly fashion-oriented market, so Arrow expanded its offerings with a wider line of sports shirts and casual wear.

JCPenney is another company that attempted a repositioning strategy targeted to existing users. It now touts itself as a fashion leader, with Vanessa Williams, the singer and actress, narrating spots that feature trendy shirts and pants targeted to Penney's core market, women 35 to 54 years old.[45] Each spot ends with the tag line "Look Who."

Very often, attempts at repositioning to reverse downward demand trends are undertaken on an industrywide basis through a cooperative advertising effort. The campaign of the National Fluid Milk Processor Promotion Board is an example. The industry was successful in positioning milk as the fitness drink of the 1990s because its appeals conformed to the emphasis on health and nutrition.

In the past, cooperative campaigns to reverse downward demand trends were run for men's hats and for sterling silverware. Both campaigns failed because they were swimming against, rather than with, the consumer tide. The campaign for men's hats tried to bring back a conservative look that contradicted the trend toward youth and vigor. The campaign for sterling silverware failed because it tried to bring back the custom of giving sterling silverware as a wedding present, which contradicted the trend toward greater informality.

■ **Changing Attitudes of Nonusers**   In an attempt to appeal to new segments of the market, companies often strive to change attitudes among nonusers. Often these changes are necessary for the company to ensure future sales. AT&T is trying to change its image among younger consumers who are using alternative services. Kmart is having difficulty changing its image among more fashion-oriented, affluent working women. In both cases, younger consumers view these companies as conservative and old-fashioned.

Mercedes is trying to expand its market to younger car buyers by reducing the size and price of its luxury cars. In 2001, it rolled out a $26,000 two-door hatchback with cloth seats.[46] In repositioning itself to incorporate lower-priced "luxury" models for a younger crowd, the company runs the risk of alienating its older core market prepared to spend much more on a luxury car.

Changing Attitudes Toward Social Issues

So far, we have discussed changes in consumer attitudes regarding brands and companies. Marketing also has a role in changing consumer attitudes toward social issues. An example is an advertising campaign to correct the many misconceptions about AIDS. The campaign, sponsored by the U.S. Department of Health, was designed to eliminate some of the fears about contracting AIDS, and in so doing, to encourage the public to become less fearful of and more tolerant toward those who have contracted the disease.

Changing attitudes toward social issues such as AIDS is a difficult task, because such attitudes are almost always deep-seated. Often people reject the message because it conflicts with strongly held beliefs. Another factor creating difficulty is that such attempts are generally public-service campaigns that rely on free media time. As such, TV time is relegated to off-peak hours, and exposure is minimal.

Some successes have occurred in changing consumer attitudes through marketing communications. Both the American Cancer Society and the American Heart Association have used advertising to increase awareness of the risks of smoking. Such advertising has been successful over the years in a supportive role in conjunction with information from government sources (*e.g.*, the Surgeon General's Office).

STRATEGIC APPLICATIONS

OF CONSUMER BEHAVIOR

Changing Attitudes Toward a Social Issue

One of the most successful campaigns to change attitudes toward a social issue has been mounted by the Partnership for a Drug-Free America. The Partnership is composed of advertising agencies and media companies engaged in a cooperative effort to reduce drug use. The target is nonusers and occasional drug users, as well as their parents. If attitudes toward drug use can be changed among this broad-based group, then peer group and family pressure might discourage drug use among heavier users. The Partnership relies on time donated by the TV networks, space donated by national magazines, outdoor advertising, and ads on web sites.

Starting in the late 1980s, the Partnership initiated an intensive effort to change attitudes toward drugs. Some three hundred ads were created for all the major media and run without charge. Because of this intensive effort, the organization was highly successful. In markets where the ads were run most frequently, more teens said there is a greater risk in using marijuana and more preteens spoke to teachers about drugs. Further, the use of cocaine went down during this period. Although these changes could not be solely attributed to the campaign, the increase in antidrug attitudes and the decreased use of drugs in markets with more advertising suggest the ads were highly effective. A current ad sponsored by the Partnership is shown in Exhibit 8.3.

The efforts of the consortium of companies that continue to support the Partnership show that both business and government can play a constructive role in changing consumer attitudes toward social issues.

Sources: Media-Advertising Partnership for a Drug-Free America, *What We've Learned About Advertising* (New York: American Association of Advertising Agencies, 1990); "TV Antidrug Messages Are No Scandal," *Wall Street Journal* (January 19, 2000), p. A22; "Fletcher Martin Hits Home in Anti-Drug Messages," *Adweek* (April 10, 2000), p. 8; and "Dive-Bomber in the War on Drugs," *Business Week* (November 21, 1998), p. 8.

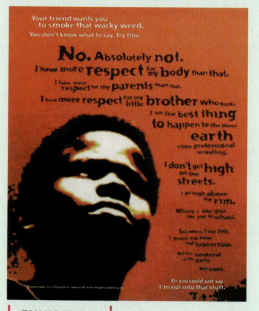

| **EXHIBIT 8.3** |

Changing attitudes toward a social issue.
Partnership for a Drug-Free America.

SUMMARY

This chapter focused on one of the most important consumer thought variables—attitudes. In a marketing context, attitudes are predispositions toward specific brands, products, or companies that cause consumers to respond favorably or unfavorably toward them. The development and function of attitudes were discussed.

Brand attitudes are composed of consumer beliefs about a brand, an overall evaluation of the brand, and an action tendency. A hierarchy of effects links these three components in a sequence leading to purchase behavior. This sequence differs depending on whether the purchaser is involved with the product and whether the product is purchased on a utilitarian or experiential basis.

The relationships between brand beliefs and brand attitudes and between brand attitudes and behavior were also highlighted in this chapter. Two theories best describe the link between brand beliefs and attitudes. Heider's balance theory posits that consumers always strive for cognitive balance between beliefs and evaluations. Fishbein's multiattribute model describes attitudes as a function of beliefs that a brand has certain attributes and the desirability of these attributes.

The link between brand attitudes and behavior was also examined. Fishbein's theory of reasoned action proposes that the appropriate focus of research is consumer attitudes toward the purchase of a brand rather than attitudes toward the brand itself. Research suggests that such a focus increases the strength of association between attitudes and behavior.

The chapter also considered various factors that might inhibit the relationships among consumer beliefs, attitudes, and behavior and the role of attitudes in developing marketing strategies.

A key consideration in the chapter was the principles of attitude change. Attitudes are easier to change when they are weakly held, when consumers are not involved with the product, when consumers have little confidence in evaluating the brand, and when information is ambiguous. Various attitudinal theories discussed previously were considered in the context of changing consumer attitudes before a purchase. Marketers may also seek to change consumer attitudes toward a brand after a purchase. Three theories provide strategic guidelines in this respect. Dissonance theory suggests that advertisers should provide consumers with positive information after they purchase a product, to reduce dissonance. Attribution theory suggests that marketers supply consumers with a reason for purchasing after the fact. The theory of passive learning suggests that inertia can be translated into brand loyalty by increasing consumers' commitment to the brand.

The chapter also discussed various strategies to change consumer attitudes by either repositioning products to strengthen the brand among existing users or by attracting new users.

The chapter concluded by considering attitude change for social issues. Marketing has an important role in changing consumer attitudes toward key issues such as preventive health care, perceptions of AIDS, smoking, and environmental protection.

In Chapters 6, 7, and 8, we have considered how the consumer's mindset—namely, perceptions and attitudes—influences purchase decisions. In Chapters 9 and 10, we consider the consumer's characteristics—demographics, personality, and lifestyles—as influences on consumer behavior.

QUESTIONS FOR DISCUSSION

1. Why did Benetton initiate a strategy of attitude change? What are some of the problems it might face as a result?

2. Why are attitudes more closely related to behavior for consumers who are involved with the purchase? Does this mean that consumer attitudes play no strategic role for low-involvement products? Explain.

3. What are the strategic implications of an experiential hierarchy of effects for advertising?

4. Two manufacturers of men's clothing launch a national advertising campaign. One directs the campaign to value-expressive attitudes toward men's clothing. The other directs advertising to ego-defensive attitudes.

- What differences may result from the two campaigns?
- To what types of consumers would each ad appeal?

5. Which of the four functions in Katz's functional theory of attitudes do the ads in Exhibit 8.1 reflect? How do they reflect these functions?

6. A consumer has a positive attitude toward his gas-guzzling car and values environmental protection. Apply balance theory in resolving this apparent conflict.

7. A food company is considering introducing an artificial bacon product that is leaner and has less cholesterol than bacon. How can it use Fishbein's multiattribute model to evaluate the new product? What strategic implications might it derive by applying the model?

8. One study linking attitudes to behavior suggested that an ongoing marketing information system designed to track changes in attitudes may benefit management. Of what use would a system that tracks consumer attitudes be for (a) new product development and (b) evaluating advertising effectiveness?

9. Consider the statement: "Consumer attitudes toward the act of using or purchasing a brand are more closely related to behavior than are consumer attitudes toward the brand itself." Assume you are a marketer considering repositioning a breakfast food so that it will also appeal to the snack market. What are the implications of the statement for repositioning strategy?

10. Under what circumstances is consumer behavior likely to influence subsequent attitudes? What are the strategic implications of attitude change occurring after behavior?

11. Under what circumstances are consumer brand attitudes unlikely to be related to purchase behavior? If attitudes are not related to behavior, should marketers continue to measure them? Why or why not?

12. Why is it easier to implement strategies reinforcing rather than changing attitudes?

13. Which of the following companies might find it most difficult to change consumers' attitudes toward its products and why?
- Manufacturer of breakfast cereals trying to attract the adult market
- Specialty retailer introducing a line of designer clothes
- Low priced, no frills airline that decides to expand its routes, add services, and increase fares
- Fast-food outlet that decides to open a chain of low-priced restaurants

14. Which of the companies cited in Question 13 do you think would find it easiest to change consumer attitudes? Why?

15. What problems might the Department of Transportation face in mounting an advertising campaign to influence people to switch from automobiles to mass transit?

16. When Cadillac introduced a medium-sized car, it could have developed a reinforcement or a change strategy in communicating this basic change in its line. What focus could advertising have taken in following (a) a reinforcement strategy and (b) a change strategy?

17. What are the differences among (a) dissonance theory, (b) attribution theory, and (c) the theory of passive learning in explaining attitude change after a purchase?

18. A producer of ready-to-eat cereals conducts a survey and finds that consumers who rate the company's brand high on nutrition are more likely to buy it. These consumers tend to be younger and more affluent. The advertising manager decides to direct a major portion of the advertising budget to nonusers (older, less-affluent consumers) to try to convince them of the cereal's nutritional content. The manager reasons there will be a higher payoff in attempting to change attitudes of nonusers than in reinforcing attitudes of users. What are the pros and cons of this argument?

19. What role can marketing play in changing consumer attitudes toward social issues? Why are such attempts more difficult than changing attitudes for products and brands?

RESEARCH ASSIGNMENTS

1 An important aspect of the Internet is the ability to provide feedback to manufacturers regarding your brand attitudes. Visit *www.planetfeedback.com* and explore some of the categories and companies to whom you can send feedback to express your opinions and attitudes, both positive and negative. Now visit an individual company's web site (*e.g.,* visit *www.ual.com.* and click on "Contact United," then on "Email," and then on "Customer Relations"). Compare the methods for feedback provided by the site.

- Which method is better?
- Were there any problems in providing feedback to the company?
- Does Planetfeedback provide any advantage in offering one place to supply feedback to companies?

2 According to the theory of cognitive dissonance, recent purchasers of important items such as cars or appliances are more likely to have positive attitudes toward their brands than those who have owned the brand for a longer period of time. The reason for this is that once they make a purchase, recent purchasers are likely to seek positive information about the brand to reinforce the choice they have made.

Test this hypothesis by selecting both recent purchasers of a major durable good (car, stereo set, microwave oven) and consumers who have owned the item for a longer period of time. Measure (a) beliefs about the brand utilizing a vocabulary of need criteria and (b) overall evaluation of the brand.

- Do recent purchasers have more positive attitudes?
- Are there differences in beliefs about brands between recent purchasers and longtime owners?
- What are the strategic implications of your findings, particularly for (a) advertising and (b) service policies?

3 Select a particular brand to study (preferably a consumer packaged good). You would like to evaluate the strengths and weaknesses of the brand relative to the competition. To do so, you decide to utilize a multiattribute approach.

Conduct a number of depth interviews with consumers to develop a vocabulary of attributes that consumers use in evaluating brands. Construct scales to measure (a) how consumers evaluate each attribute in the vocabulary and (b) beliefs about the brand under study and two or three other key competitive brands, based on the vocabulary of attributes. Select a sample of users of the product category so that at least one-third of your sample uses the brand under study.

- What are the brand's strengths and weaknesses based on a comparison of the brand to (a) desired attributes and (b) competitive brands?
- How do brand ratings differ between users and nonusers of the brand?
- What are the implications of your findings for (a) possible repositioning strategies for the brand, (b) identification of unmet needs, and (c) formulation of new product concepts to meet consumer needs?

4 Some marketers believe that a significant proportion of consumers develop images of brands based on the advertising rather than on product experience. If this is true, one would expect beliefs about brands to reflect advertising themes. Select a product category in which different advertising themes can be associated with brands (*e.g.,* pain relievers, airlines, paper towels). Construct a vocabulary of product attributes, including the advertising themes. Ask consumers to rate the brands in the product category utilizing the vocabulary.

- Are brands rated higher on criteria used in the brand's advertising?
- Do both heavy and light users of the product category rate brands in accordance with the advertising themes? Do both users and nonusers of the brand?

5 Select a frequently purchased product for study (such as a soft drink, coffee, or a detergent). Select a sample of about one hundred product users.

a. Develop a description of a fictitious brand and give it to consumers. The description should come from a neutral source such as a government agency.
b. Ask the consumer to rate the brand from poor to excellent.

c. Split the sample into three groups: Group 1 receives an ad reinforcing the prior brand description (a reinforcement strategy); Group 2 receives an ad meant to change beliefs about the brand ("Brand X is much tastier or much more effective than previously described"); and Group 3 receives an ad attempting to change values (*e.g.,* an ad saying brands with low sudsing ability are more effective).

d. Ask consumers to rate the brand again after they see one of the three ads.

If a reinforcement strategy is more effective, one would expect the first ad to produce the most positive attitudes. Furthermore, of the two change strategies, one would expect the ad attempting to change beliefs to produce more positive effects than the ad attempting to change values. Do your findings conform to these expectations?

6 Principles of attitude change suggest that attitudes are easier to change when consumers are less confident in their evaluations of a brand. Pick a product category and ask consumers to rate three of the leading brands on (a) an overall basis and (b) a vocabulary of product attributes. In addition, ask consumers to (c) rate their degree of confidence in making judgments about brands in the category and (d) rate the degree to which they think the product is important to them.

Present consumers with ads for each of the three brands in a dummy magazine format. Have consumers rate the brands once again on an overall basis and on the vocabulary of product attributes.

- Do overall brand ratings for those consumers who have less confidence in their brand evaluations shift more than those of consumers who have a greater degree of confidence?

- Do ratings shift in the direction of the advertised claims?

- Attitude theory also suggests that those who rate the product category as less important are more likely to change attitudes. Do your findings support this?

NOTES

1. "About Face," *Forbes* (March 19, 2000), pp. 178–180.
2. Ibid.
3. "Benetton Settles Suit Over Use of Inmates In Its Campaign," *Wall Street Journal* (June 18, 2001), p. B11
4. "About Face," pp. 178–180.
5. Gordon W. Allport, "Attitudes," in C. A. Murchinson, ed., *A Handbook of Social Psychology* (Worcester, Mass.: Clark University Press, 1935), pp. 798–844. For a good review of attitudinal theories, see Richard J. Lutz, "The Role of Attitude Theory in Marketing," in Harold H. Kassarjian and Thomas S. Robertson, eds., *Perspectives in Consumer Behavior* (Glenview, Ill.: Scott, Foresman, 1991).
6. Patricia M. West, Christina L. Brown, and Stephen J. Hoch, "Consumption Vocabulary and Preference Formation," *Journal of Consumer Research* 23 (September 1996), pp. 120–135.
7. See Michael Solomon, *Consumer Behavior* (Englewood Cliffs, N.J.: Prentice-Hall, 1966), pp. 162–163.
8. "A Campaign to Turn a Mattress Maker into a Wellness Provider," *New York Times* (June 8, 2001), p. C9.
9. Peter D. Bennett and Harold H. Kassarjian, *Consumer Behavior* (Englewood Cliffs, N.J.: Prentice-Hall, 1972), p. 81.
10. Elihu Katz and Paul F. Lazarsfeld, *Personal Influence* (New York: The Free Press, 1955).
11. James S. Coleman, Elihu Katz, and Herbert Menzel, *Medical Innovation: A Diffusion Study* (Indianapolis: Bobbs-Merrill, 1966).
12. Johan Arndt, "Role of Product-Related Conversations in the Diffusion of a New Product," *Journal of Marketing Research* 4 (August 1967), pp. 291–295.
13. Daniel Katz, "The Functional Approach to the Study of Attitudes," *Public Opinion Quarterly,* 24 (Summer 1960), pp. 163–204.
14. Richard J. Lutz, "A Functional Theory Framework for Designing and Pretesting Advertising Themes," *Attitude Research Plays for High Stakes* (Chicago: American Marketing Association, 1979), pp. 37–49; and William B. Locander and W. Austin Spivey, "A Functional Approach to Attitude Measurement," *Journal of Marketing Research* 15 (November 1978), pp. 576–587.
15. For research on attitude formation and structure, see Mark P. Zanna, "Attitude-Behavior Consistency: Fulfilling the Need for Cognitive Structure," in Thomas K. Srull, ed., *Advances in Consumer Research,* Vol. 16 (Provo, Utah: Association for Consumer Research, 1989), pp. 318–320; Michael D. Johnson, "On the Nature of Product Attributes and Attribute Relationships," in Srull, *Advances in Consumer Research,* Vol. 16, pp. 598–604; Morris B. Holbrook and William J. Havlena, "Assessing the Real-to-Artificial Generalizability of Multiattribute Attitude Models in Tests of New Product Designs," *Journal of Marketing Research* 24 (February 1988), pp. 25–35; Punam Anand, Morris B. Holbrook, and Debra Stephens, "The Formation of Affective Judgments: The Cognitive-Affective Model Versus the Independence Hypothesis," *Journal of Consumer*

Research 15 (December 1988), pp. 386–391; Michael D. Johnson and Claes Fornell, "The Nature and Methodological Implications of the Cognitive Representation of Products," *Journal of Consumer Research* 14 (September 1987), pp. 214–228; and Robert E. Smith and William R. Swinyard, "Attitude-Behavior Consistencies: The Impact of Product Trial Versus Advertising," *Journal of Marketing Research* 20 (August 1983), pp. 257–267.

16. See Fritz Heider, *The Psychology of Interpersonal Relations* (New York: John Wiley, 1958).

17. Jagdish N. Sheth and W. Wayne Talarzyk, "Perceived Instrumentality and Value Importance as Determinants of Attitudes," *Journal of Marketing Research* 9 (February 1972), pp. 6–9.

18. See Richard J. Lutz, "An Experimental Investigation of Causal Relations Among Cognitions, Affect, and Behavioral Intentions," *Journal of Consumer Research* 3 (March 1977), pp. 197–208; Jagdish N. Sheth, "Brand Profiles from Beliefs and Importances," *Journal of Advertising Research* 13 (February 1973), pp. 37–42; Frank M. Bass and William L. Wilkie, "A Comparative Analysis of Attitudinal Predictions of Brand Preference," *Journal of Marketing Research* 10 (August 1973), pp. 262–269; and David E. Weddle and James R. Bettman, "Marketing Underground: An Investigation of Fishbein's Behavioral Intention Model," in Scott Ward and Peter Wright, eds., *Advances in Consumer Research,* Vol. 1 (Urbana, Ill.: Association for Consumer Research, 1973), pp. 310–318.

19. Martin Fishbein, "An Investigation of the Relationships Between Beliefs About an Object and the Attitude Toward That Object," *Human Relations* 16 (1963), pp. 233–240. For a good review of multiattribute models, see William L. Wilkie and Edgar A. Pessemier, "Issues in Marketing's Use of Multiattribute Models," *Journal of Marketing Research* 10 (November 1983), pp. 428–441.

20. Martin Fishbein, "Attitudes and the Prediction of Behavior," in Martin Fishbein, ed., *Readings in Attitude Theory and Measurement* (New York: John Wiley, 1967), pp. 477–492.

21. David T. Wilson, H. Lee Matthews, and James W. Harvey, "An Empirical Test of the Fishbein Behavioral Intention Model," *Journal of Consumer Research* 1 (March 1975), pp. 39–48.

22. S. Knox and L. de Chernatony, "The Application of Multiattribute Modeling Techniques to the Mineral Water Market," *Quarterly Review of Marketing* (Summer 1989), pp. 14–20.

23. George Katona, *The Powerful Consumer* (New York: McGraw-Hill, 1960), pp. 80–83.

24. "Recession Coming? Ask the Consumer," *New York Times* (April 4, 1990), p. D6.

25. Robert E. Knox and James A. Inkster, "Post-Decision Dissonance at Post Time," *Journal of Personality and Social Psychology* 8 (1968), pp. 319–323.

26. Herbert E. Krugman, "The Impact of Television Advertising: Learning Without Involvement," *Public Opinion Quarterly* 29 (Fall 1965), pp. 349–356.

27. James L. Ginter, "An Experimental Investigation of Attitude Change and Choice of a New Brand," *Journal of Marketing Research* 11 (February 1974), pp. 30–40.

28. "Mars and Other Marketers Offer Scaled-Down Spots Based on the Simple Pleasures in Life," *New York Times* (April 1, 2002).

29. Ida E. Berger and Andrew A. Mitchell, "The Effect of Advertising on Attitude Accessibility, Attitude Confidence, and the Attitude-Behavior Relationship," *Journal of Consumer Research* 16 (December 1989), pp. 269–279. See also Smith and Swinyard, "Attitude-Behavior Consistencies," pp. 257–267.

30. Russell H. Fazio, Martha C. Powell, and Carol J. Williams, "The Role of Attitude Accessibility in the Attitude-to-Behavior Process," *Journal of Consumer Research* 16 (December 1989), pp. 280–288.

31. James McCullough, Douglas MacLachlan, and Reza Moinpour, "Impact of Information on Preference and Perception," in Andrew Mitchell, ed., *Advances in Consumer Research,* Vol. 9 (Ann Arbor, Mich.: Association for Consumer Research, 1982), pp. 402–405.

32. S. P. Raj, "The Effects of Advertising on High and Low Loyalty Consumer Segments," *Journal of Consumer Research* 9 (June 1982), pp. 77–89.

33. Richard J. Lutz, "Changing Brand Attitudes Through Modification of Cognitive Structures," *Journal of Consumer Research* 1 (March 1975), pp. 49–59.

34. Muzafer Sherif and Carl E. Hovland, *Social Judgment* (New Haven, Conn.: Yale University Press, 1964).

35. Neil H. Borden and Martin V. Marshall, *Advertising Management: Text and Cases* (Homewood, Ill.: Richard D. Irwin, 1959), p. 126.

36. Benjamin Lipstein, "Anxiety, Risk and Uncertainty in Advertising Effectiveness Measurements," in Lee Adler and Irving Crespi, eds., *Attitude Research on the Rocks* (Chicago: American Marketing Association, 1968), pp. 11–27.

37. "Resorting to Blandishments to Fight Image of Blandness," *New York Times* (August 10, 1992), p. D7.

38. Leon Festinger, *A Theory of Cognitive Dissonance* (New York: Harper & Row, 1957).

39. Daniel Katz, "The Functional Approach to the Study of Attitudes," *Public Opinion Quarterly* 24 (Summer 1960), pp. 163–204.

40. Heider, *The Psychology of Interpersonal Relations.*

41. Kenneth B. Runyon, *Consumer Behavior and the Practice of Marketing* (Columbus, Ohio: Charles E. Merrill, 1977), p. 287.

42. Shelby D. Hunt, "Post-Transaction Communications and Dissonance Reduction," *Journal of Marketing* 34 (July 1970), pp. 46–51.

43. D. Bem, "Attitudes as Self-Descriptions: Another Look at the Attitude-Behavior Link," in A. Greenwald, T. Brock, and T. Ostrom, eds., *Psychological Foundations of Attitudes* (New York: Academic Press, 1968). For applications of attribution theory to consumer behavior, see Bobby Calder, "When Attitudes Follow Behavior—A Self-Perception/Dissonance Interpretation of Low Involvement," in John C. Maloney and Bernard Silverman, eds., *Attitude Research Plays for High Stakes* (Chicago: American Marketing Association, 1979), pp. 25–36.

44. Herbert E. Krugman, "The Impact of Television Advertising: Learning Without Involvement," *Public Opinion Quarterly* 29 (Fall 1965), pp. 349–356.

45. "In the Fall Fashion Season, J.C. Penney Leads the Way with a Sweeping Campaign," *New York Times* (September 27, 1999), p. C16.

46. "Class Meets the Mass," *Forbes* (May 14, 2001), pp. 205–206.

CHAPTER 9

Demographics and Social Class

Demographic characteristics such as age, income, family size, and employment status are the objective descriptors of individuals and households. The consumer thought variables we considered in Chapters 6 to 8—primarily perceptions and attitudes—are cognitive processes that are specific to a product; that is, perceptions and attitudes are formed in consumers' minds regarding brands and products. In contrast, demographics are objective characteristics (age is age, income is income) that are not product-specific. One's age and income can affect purchases from autos to deodorants. **Social class,** one's ranking in society based on power and prestige, is defined primarily by demographic characteristics; namely, occupation, income, and education.

In this chapter, we focus on the nature of demographics and social class and their applications to marketing strategy. Specifically, we consider demographic trends that have changed the shape of American society and of the global marketplace; namely, population growth, changing age distributions, socioeconomic changes affecting purchasing power and patterns of consumption, and changes in household composition.

We then discuss the nature and importance of social class distinctions in societies worldwide and how they help shape consumer purchases. The chapter also considers applications of demographics and social class to marketing strategy in two areas: (1) defining target segments and (2) *micromarketing;* that is, using demographic and social class information to reach individual consumers rather than broader market segments.

In discussing strategic applications, we will see that marketers now define more specific demographic segments than in the past. Whereas ten years ago marketers might have defined the increasing proportion of working women as a target for autos or clothing, today they might split that group by occupation (professional, white-collar, blue-collar) or more broadly by social class (upper, middle, lower). The prerequisite is understanding their needs and attitudes.

BMW Targets Emerging Demographic Groups

Luxury automakers have stumbled badly in their attempt to target working women because the market has been traditionally male-dominant. Marketers had spent so many decades using scantily clad models to entice men that they seemed to have no idea what professional women wanted. At first, they tried placing women in the same product ads they had always produced for men. With women responsible for 46 percent of car sales, it quickly became clear that a more dramatic approach was needed, especially when the automobile showroom remained a place where women were treated like second-class citizens.

The demographic research was revealing. BMW had thought that professional women wanted a car designed specifically for them, but focus groups showed that they share the same desires as men: They want a car that is safe, reliable, and durable. Likewise, conventional wisdom held that women tended to buy with their children in mind. However, a survey conducted by the Condé Nast magazine group found that women are "more likely to purchase cars for themselves" while men are "more likely to buy cars for the family."[1]

Although BMW has shied away from creating a "woman's commercial," it has used these data to stress style and performance in its appeals to women. In 1993, for instance, the company invited women journalists to view video testimonials from female BMW owners discussing road feel and driving excitement. The hope was that the writers would convey the testimonials to their audience, thereby creating interest among prospective women customers. In 1994, BMW started seminars for women on subjects such as traction control and braking systems and invited them to take a BMW out for a test drive.[2] In explaining why car companies must stop talking down to women drivers, one BMW executive said: "Women under 40 grew up driving, not sitting in the passenger seat." To reach the 25- to 50-year-old professional women with an active lifestyle who it believes are its ideal customers, BMW

| **EXHIBIT 9.1** |
BMW targets a demographic group: young affluents.
Topham/The Image Works.

underwrites rock climbing competitions, biking events, marathons, and even triathlons.

Recently, BMW has tried to direct the brand toward another demographic segment—young affluents, the same segment that Mercedes is trying to capture.[3] BMW plans to offer in 2004 a small, less expensive car, the 1-series, in an attempt to target this group.[4] Despite entry into less expensive autos,

BMW executives still focus on vehicles that sell at high margins with relatively low volumes.[5] BMW has reintroduced the Mini, an updated version of the 1960s-era British classic (see Exhibit 9.1). According to Jack Pitney, general manager of Mini's U.S. division, the vehicle will target affluents aged 24 to 34 who like to experiment with new products.[6]

The 1990s and early 2000s have seen many major demographic changes that have had an impact on American society. Baby boomers (the group born in the two decades after World War II) are now entering the mature market (those over 50), which is growing rapidly as a result. Further, nontraditional households are becoming the norm as a result of later marriages, more divorces, and more singles. The effect of these changes has been to further fragment an already diverse American market place.

The Demographic Fragmentation of the American Market

Demographics have long been used to target consumers. Demographics have been used in three periods, representing three distinct approaches: the *mass market era* (pre 1970), the *market segmentation era* (post 1970), and the *micromarketing era* (post 1990). In the mass market era, marketers targeted broad demographic groupings because consumer needs and purchases tended to be more similar. For example, GM relied on its traditional socioeconomic division of the market by targeting Chevrolet to lower-income consumers, then moving up the income scale from Chevrolet to Pontiac to Oldsmobile to Buick to Cadillac in broad socioeconomic sweeps. Pepsi targeted teens with its flagship brand without having to worry about expanding its product line to compete with New Age beverages. Campbell Soup simply targeted families with children. Levi Strauss targeted a broad youth market for its jeans.

After 1970, several changes occurred that made such a mass market approach infeasible. The proportion of working women accelerated, the traditional family of a married couple with children under 18 fragmented, increased immigration from Asia and Latin America developed into regional clusters of Asian- and Hispanic Americans, and age groups such as baby boomers and Generation Xers (those born between 1965 and 1977) became defined as subgroups with distinct norms and values. These changes resulted in differences in needs, attitudes, and purchasing behavior that marketers could not ignore. One could no longer talk about a youth market without distinguishing between specific age categories, one could no longer refer to the needs of working women without considering socioeconomic differences, and one could no longer talk about families without distinguishing between married couples and unmarried couples with and without children.

This fragmentation gave rise to a focus on market segmentation. GM could still position Chevrolets as its lowest-priced cars, but it now needed to target different models to younger consumers with families, singles, or white-collar working women with the common denominator being price consciousness. Campbell began targeting its soups to specific ethnic groups on a regional basis with new flavors such as nacho cheese soups in Texas and Creole soups in the South, a far cry from selling tomato and chicken soup to a mass market. Levi introduced different jeans to older baby boomers, younger baby boomers, Generation Xers, teens, and even preteens.

After 1990, marketers began to recognize the feasibility of going even further than market segmentation and began to talk about **micromarketing;** that is, reaching individual consumers based on their demographic and social class characteristics. Micromarketing is an extension of market segmentation in breaking down the market to more discrete components. Whereas market segmentation was brought about by the demographic fragmentation of the marketplace, micromarketing is the result of technological developments that make it easier for marketers to reach these fragments.

Three technological and data-related developments make micromarketing feasible. First, interactive technologies such as the Internet and interactive TV make it possible for advertisers to target individual consumers with messages. Second, databases have been established through credit card usage or car registration that can identify the individual's demographic characteristics, allowing targeting through direct mail. Third, as discussed later, **geodemographic analysis** allows marketers to identify the demographic characteristics of zip code areas (or even zip code + four areas). Research companies such as Claritas have grouped together zip code areas with common demographic and socioeconomic characteristics such as the suburban elite, upwardly mobile young influentials in urban areas, and single-parent families in inner cities. Claritas has identified sixty-two such segments, allowing marketers to target them with direct mail or by regional promotions.

Demographic Trends in the American Marketplace

Marketers define users and prospective users of their brands by demographic characteristics so as to target them with promotional, product, pricing, and distribution strategies. Developing such profiles requires an understanding of demographic trends in the marketplace. The increasing proportion of working women on professional career paths was a trend that led BMW to realize that this group was a natural target market for luxury cars.

The 2000 census was essential in providing marketers with the latest demographic information on the characteristics of U.S. consumers and changes that took place in the last decade. In this section, we consider the demographic trends that define the American marketplace. We start with the broadest demographic trend: changes in population growth.

POPULATION GROWTH

The U.S. population has increased steadily since this country was formed. There were 281.1 million people in the United States according to the 2000 U.S. Census, a 13.2 percent increase from the 1990 census.[7]

Three factors determine population growth: birthrate, life span, and immigration. Immigration was instrumental in fueling growth until 1920. A high birthrate has fueled growth at various periods in our history and is often tied to economic prosperity. For example, the birthrate was at a low during the Depression and World War II, and then it more than doubled after the war. More recently, a rise in the birthrate, increased life expectancy, and increases in immigration have fueled population growth. Let us consider these three factors further.

▎**Birthrate** Substantial swings have occurred in the birthrate since World War II (see Figure 9.1). The birthrate increased by 50 percent from 1940 to its highest point in 1957 and then decreased to a historic low in 1976. The period from 1946 to 1964 is known as the "baby-boom period," a term that reflects the higher birthrate at the time. From 1965 to 1976, the birthrate steadily decreased. Some call this period the "baby-bust period." From 1976 to 1985, the birthrate increased slightly, largely as a result of the baby-boom generation entering its childbearing years. As a result of this "baby boomlet," by 1991 there were 15 percent more preschoolers than in 1980.[8]

The somewhat higher birthrate held steady through the mid-1990s, as 30-something baby boomers, new immigrants, and professionals in their 40s who delayed having families began having babies. The number of births in the United States has remained relatively flat since 1995. More notably, the birthrate among

▎ **FIGURE 9.1** ▎

Birthrate in the United States: 1940 to 2000.

Sources: U.S. Department of Health and Human Services, *Monthly Vital Statistics Report* (June 7, 1990), Table I-1, pp. 1–7; U.S. Department of Commerce, Bureau of the Census, *Statistical Abstract of the United States, 1990,* p. 63, Table 821; U.S. Department of Commerce, Bureau of the Census, *Statistical Abstract of the United States, 2000.*

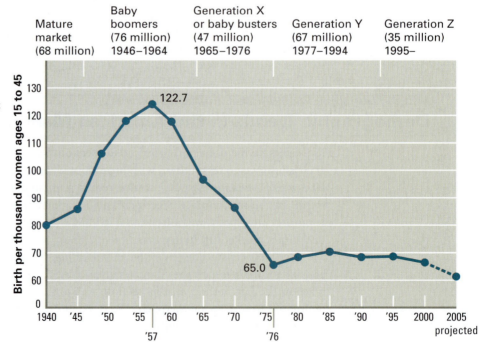

teenagers has declined by about 20 percent from 1990 to 2000.[9] The overall birthrate is expected to continue dropping as the baby boomers leave their childbearing years and the smaller baby bust group (also known as "Generation X") enters theirs. However, this trend is partially offset by more women having children later in life. In fact, in 1999, the birthrate for women aged 40–44 reached the highest level reported and is expected to continue to increase.[10]

Gerber illustrates the impact of variations in the birthrate on marketing strategy. Declining baby food sales in the late 1960s and 1970s led the company to seek growth elsewhere. It unsuccessfully tried to diversify into foods for the elderly, life insurance, and transportation. The increase in the birthrate in the early 1990s provided an opportunity for the company to revert to the business it knows best—baby products.[11] In 1993, it introduced a microwavable line of foods for toddlers called Gerber's Graduates, after lending its name to children's clothing and toys. It financed this growth by selling off some of its ventures into adult products.[12] And, in 1997, Gerber introduced the Tender Harvest line in response to consumer demand for more healthful, natural, and organic baby foods and to competitors such as H. J. Heinz, which acquired the leading organic baby food manufacturer, Earth's Best, in 1996. In 2000, Gerber began targeting the exploding birthrate among Hispanic Americans by introducing its first ad campaign aimed at a specific ethnic group.[13]

Gerber's expansion into organic foods and a larger array of baby products reflects the baby boomers' willingness to spend more on their children. Because many boomers marry and have children relatively late in life when they are more financially secure, they are willing to spend more on baby clothes and toys, thus creating a more lucrative market.

▌ Life Expectancy

Due to medical improvements, life expectancy has increased consistently in recent years. Advances in combating heart disease and cancer have been instrumental in increasing longevity. Of equal importance has been the American public's awareness of how to better care for themselves. The percentage of smokers has declined steadily since the Surgeon General first linked smoking to cancer in 1965. The fact that Philip Morris makes substantially more money from cigarettes than from its ownership of General Foods, Kraft, and Miller combined is due to overseas cigarette sales. (Greater health awareness seems to be more of an American and Western European phenomenon than it is a worldwide trend.)

Americans are also more conscious of what they eat. The desire to reduce cholesterol intake has caused a shift away from red meat and dairy products. The combined effects of better medical care and greater health awareness have resulted in increased longevity in the past twenty years. Life expectancy in the twentieth century increased more than twenty-seven years, from 49.2 years in 1900 to 76.5 years in 1999. The greatest contribution has been from mortality reductions among children. Mortality reductions among those under 20 have contributed about 58 percent of the twenty-seven-year gain.[14] Because of continued improvements in medical care, the number of people aged 85 and older will grow from 4.2 million in 1999 to a projected 6.8 million by the year 2020 and 19.4 million by 2050.[15] Increased longevity due to lower mortality rates is also evident in other industrialized countries, in some cases outdistancing the United States. From 1985 to 1995, the U.S. death rate showed a 0.4 percent average annual decline compared with an annual overall drop of 1.5 percent in France and 1.2 percent in Japan.[16]

It should be noted that there are substantial differences in longevity by race and social class. Longevity for African Americans, which averages six years less than for whites, reflects poorer health care and less access to health-care facilities.

▌Immigration   The third factor affecting population growth is immigration. Immigration was a significant factor in creating the American "melting pot," with successive waves from the English-speaking countries, western Europe, China, and eastern European countries up to 1920. More recently, it has had an equally significant effect on the nation's population growth. The greatest immigration has occurred from Mexico, the Caribbean, and Central America, as well as from China, Korea, the Philippines, and Vietnam.[17] Estimates project that by the middle of this century, the U.S. population will include 82 million people who arrived in this country after 1991 or who were born to parents who did. This group will account for one out of every five Americans.

Marketers like Bank of America and IBM have successfully targeted immigrant groups in the United States. Bank of America targets immigrants from Vietnam, Cambodia, and Laos in newspapers in their own language with ads to overcome their natural mistrust of banks. IBM is implementing a $600 million campaign to promote its e-commerce products to immigrant groups.[18]

CHANGING AGE COMPOSITION

Figure 9.1 identifies three age groups that are the focus of most marketing strategies: (1) baby boomers, born between 1946 and 1964 and representing about 76 million consumers; (2) baby busters (or Generation Xers), born between 1965 and 1976 and representing about 47 million consumers; and (3) the baby boomlet (or Generation Y—teens and preteens), born from 1976 to 1994 and representing about 67 million consumers. Children born after 1994 represent 35 million people. A fourth group that has become increasingly important but is not fully shown in Figure 9.1 are those born before 1946, representing 56 million consumers.

Figure 9.1 presents age by generational groups. We can refer to the Depression-era generation (born before 1935), the World War II generation (born 1935–1945), the Woodstock generation (the older baby boomers), and the Vietnam generation (the younger baby boomers). These labels represent the defining moment for each generation in their youth. As such, these groupings are known as **age cohorts;** that is, people of similar ages who have gone through similar experiences.

As a result of these experiences, many individuals in age cohorts also share common values and needs that have not changed much since adolescence. Baby boomers have been described as independent types who see themselves stretching society's bounds.[19] Generation Xers have been described as cynical, pessimistic, and alienated as a result of a bleak economic outlook and resentment for having to pay the future bill for an unbalanced budget and a polluted environment. Although this is a generalization that may not accurately reflect the views of most Xers, such descriptions may be useful in painting age groups in broad strokes. Levi Strauss's strategy reflects an age cohort perspective as it followed the aging baby boomers by

FIGURE 9.2

Projections for two key age groups: 1970 to 2050.

Source: U.S. Department of Commerce, Bureau of the Census, *Statistical Abstract of the United States, 2000.*

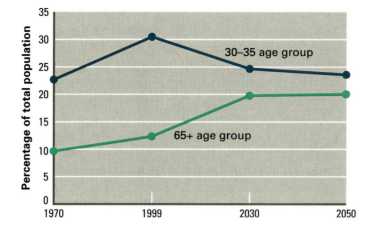

moving them from jeans to Dockers to adapt to their expanding waistlines, and, more currently, by introducing Slates, a new line of slacks to meet their growing need for casual wear in the office.

Another important perspective on age is to project future age distributions. Figure 9.2 effectively portrays the future "graying of America." It shows that the fastest-growing age group will be the 65+ group (the older mature market). In 1970, this group represented one out of every ten Americans. By 2030 one out of five Americans will be over 65. This increase represents the weight of baby boomers moving into the mature market and increased life expectancies. By 2011, the first baby boomers will be 65, with steady growth in this segment after that date. The marketing implications of the graying of America are enormous. In the past, marketers have not effectively targeted the 65+ segment, but as it grows, they will have to. Everything from autos to furniture to clothing will have to be designed with the 65+ group in mind. Further, a major redistribution in purchasing expenditures will occur as more money goes to health care.

Figure 9.2 also shows that the proportion of Americans who are 30–50 will decline significantly from 1999 to 2050. This group grew rapidly from 1970 to 1999, reflecting the weight of the baby boomers, but the graying of America will mean proportionately fewer consumers in this broad age group.

Given the importance of the age cohorts in Figure 9.1, we consider each of them in Chapter 12, "Subcultural Influences and Age Cohorts."

CHANGING HOUSEHOLD COMPOSITION

The American household is becoming a smaller, less cohesive unit. (A household is simply a residential unit composed of one or more people.) As a result, traditional definitions of family are being remolded to match reality more closely. This means shifting the definition of the family as mother, father, and child/children to include unmarried couples living together, single-parent families, same-sex relationships, and multigenerational families. Subaru recognized this shift and decided to include marketing to gays and lesbians in some of its advertising campaigns. Subaru chose the openly gay, former women's professional tennis player Martina Navratilova as a pitchwoman for its cars.[20]

Further, marriage rates are at an all-time low, and Americans are marrying later and having fewer children. In 2000, only 23.5 percent of American households represented the traditional picture of a married couple with children under 18 living at home, a startling drop from 45 percent in 1960.[21] During the 1990s, the number of married couples with children grew by slightly under 6 percent, whereas households with children headed by single mothers grew by 25 percent and comprised nearly 7 percent of all households.

In fact, nontraditional households (married couples who never had children, single parents, unmarried couples, singles) now represent the majority of all households. In 1998, 56 percent of the adult population were married and living with their spouse compared with 72 percent in 1970. Among people aged 25–34, 34.7 percent had never been married compared with only 17 percent in 1970.[22] The 2000 census showed that the number of unwed couples living together almost doubled since 1970.[23] The number of single dads increased by 50 percent in the same period.[24]

A major factor in the decline of the traditional family is an increasing divorce rate. Half of all marriages today end in divorce, triple the rate in 1970. In 1998, 19.4 million adults, or 9.8 percent of the adult population were currently divorced and did not remarry.[25] As a result, today 28 percent of all children live in single-parent households.[26] As one might expect, single-parent homes are likely to have lower incomes. Forty-five percent of households with a female head with children at home live in poverty, as do 19 percent of households headed by a male with children. In contrast, just 8 percent of married couples with children live in poverty.[27]

Another effect of high divorce rates is the number of people living alone. Approximately 26 percent of households were comprised of single persons in 2000, and their numbers are growing 2.5 times faster than the overall population. The number of single women living alone represents 13.1 percent of all households, almost double what it was in 1970.[28]

The marketing impact of these trends is significant. Singles and childless couples spend more on travel, leisure products, and investments. Single persons, for example, spend 50 percent of their food dollars dining out, compared with 37 percent for two-person households.[29] Smaller households also have led some companies to emphasize foods and toiletries in smaller sizes and to introduce kitchen appliances and furnishings in smaller models. Singles are also more willing to buy on credit and to spend more on restaurants and entertainment.

Marketers have been either slow or reluctant to appeal to this lucrative market, because they have not figured out how. They are reluctant to appeal to single moms, for example, unless ads clearly show how a product empowers these groups.[30] Part of the problem is the lack of magazines, TV programs, and other media targeted to divorcees or single parents.

Charles Schwab Corporation is successful in targeting nontraditional households, particularly households headed by single moms, by showing how its products can empower them. In January 2001, it debuted a television ad featuring Sarah Ferguson, former wife of Prince Andrew and one of the world's most famous single working mothers. Her voice is heard telling a little girl a bedtime fairy-tale story with the expected happy ending; however, the ad ends with a twist. Sarah Ferguson warns, "Of course, if it doesn't work out, you'll need to understand the difference between a P/E ratio and a dividend yield, a growth versus a value strategy," referring to Schwab's online stock research service.[31]

Some marketers are looking at the changes in family composition outside the United States. With 22 million babies born in China each year (six times the number in the United States), Heinz, for instance, saw an opportunity for introducing baby products. In 1990, it began marketing an instant rice cereal for babies and almost immediately saw a profit. The cereal is precooked and instant and appeals to the 70 percent of Chinese women who work.[32]

Changes in household formation and the impact of the increasing number of nontraditional households are considered in Chapter 15 when household influences on purchasing decisions are discussed.

REGIONAL DIFFERENCES

One of the most common demographic characteristics marketers use in analyzing purchasing behavior is region. Differences in consumer purchasing habits and tastes by region have led many marketers to vary their marketing strategies on a regional basis. For instance, the auto industry spends more money on regional and local "spot" advertising than on national campaigns. Much of it has gone to California, where cars are seen as important lifestyle indicators.

The regional strategy is particularly important to national retailers. Sears maintains a master database of all the items sold in its stores and tailors the stock in each according to local preferences. For instance, it caters to the differences in tastes of Mexican Americans in Los Angeles and in San Antonio. In Los Angeles, Mexican Americans prefer styles in black, whereas in San Antonio they prefer them in red. Black is a more subdued color, reflecting a greater level of assimilation among Mexican Americans in Los Angeles compared with those in San Antonio.

❚ Geodemographic Analysis   Differences in consumer tastes and purchases can cut across regions and be identified by specific localities. *Geodemographic analysis* identifies demographic targets by region. Claritas *(www.claritas.com),* the market research firm that pioneered geodemographic analysis, uses census data to define groups of zip code areas that are similar in age, income, or family composition. In its database called PRIZM, it has defined sixty-two such groupings. One group, identified as "Blue Blood Estates," includes Chappaqua, New York, and Winnetka, Illinois. This group is described as "America's wealthiest socioeconomic neighborhoods, populated by established managers, professionals, and heirs to old money."

Such analysis can be used to determine whether similarities in demographic characteristics translate into similarities in purchasing behavior. For example, Dannon Yogurt could determine average yogurt consumption in each of the sixty-two clusters defined by Claritas based on scanner data (checkout scanners that record in-store sales) tabulated by zip code. Dannon could then use this data to distribute products to clusters that have higher-than-average yogurt purchases. The company also could distribute coupons or mailers to those clusters that represent the heaviest purchase groups.

❚ Global Geodemographic Analysis   Recently attention has been given to creating global geodemographic categories by regional similarities. Experian, based in Nottingham, England, maintains a vast database of cluster systems that analyze consumers in nineteen countries from Australia and Belgium to South Africa, Peru, and the United States. These data are linked into a single segmentation system called Global MOSAIC. Experian's computers have boiled down 631 different MOSAIC types in the various countries to come up with fourteen common lifestyles, classifying 800 million people, who produce roughly 80 percent of the world's gross domestic product.[33] For example, affluent urban dwellers or retirement communities could identify segments with common demographics and lifestyle characteristics globally.

In a variation of MOSAIC's approach, GfK Marktforschung of Germany divides European shoppers into sixteen "Euro-style" categories by regional similarity, including "Euro-Protest" for neighborhoods with a heavy concentration of purchases of environmentally friendly products, and "Euro-Gentry" for affluent areas with a concentration of large-ticket items.[34]

SOCIOECONOMIC TRENDS

Key demographic variables that define consumers' current and future purchasing power are socioeconomic factors; that is, consumers' occupational status, income, and education. We next describe the most important occupational trend in the past forty years, the increasing proportion of working women, and additional trends in income and educational status in the United States.

▌ Occupational Status: Increase in the Proportion of Working Women   Changes in occupational status directly affect purchasing power. For instance, increased unemployment and underemployment (a decrease in time devoted to the job or taking a lesser job to avoid unemployment) during both the 1990–1991 recession and the recession that began in 2000 restricted purchasing power.

The farthest-reaching change in occupational status has been the increasing proportion of working women. Figure 9.3 shows that the proportion of women in the labor force went from 33 percent in 1950 to 61 percent in 2000. The increase in the proportion of working wives has also been dramatic, going from 24 percent in 1950 to 61 percent in 2000. Among mothers with children from ages 6 to 13, close to 70 percent are employed. However, even these figures understate the impact of working women, because many women work on a part-time basis. Among women from ages 18 to 49, fully 90 percent were part of the labor force at some time in the past two years. Further, women are closing the gap in educational attainment between the sexes.[35] By 2000, an equal number of men and women had attained bachelor's degrees.

Figure 9.3 shows that the rapid rise in the proportion of working women in America is projected to tail off by 2010, with 63 percent of women (about half of all workers) expected to be in the labor force.

An important effect of the greater proportion of working women is the increased affluence of dual-earner households. In 2000, the median income of the family with a full-time working husband and wife was $72,930 compared with $48,514 for families with only a husband working.[36] A Bureau of Labor Statistics study found that differences between families with and without working wives

FIGURE 9.3

Percentage of women in the labor force.

Sources: "Employed Persons with Single and Multiple Jobs by Sex," *Monthly Labor Review* (May 1982), Table 1, p. 48; "A Portrait of the American Worker," *American Demographics* (March 1984), p. 19; *Handbook of Labor Statistics* (June 1985), Tables 1, 6, and 20; Monthly Labor Review (February 1986), Table 1; U.S. Department of Commerce, Bureau of the Census, *Statistical Abstract of the United States, 1990,* p. 378, Table 625; U.S. Department of Commerce, Bureau of the Census, *Statistical Abstract of the United States, 1966* (Springfield, Va.: National Technical Information Service, 2000).

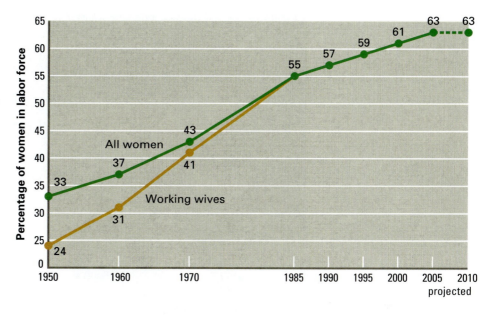

extend beyond income. Dual-earner families are younger, better educated, and less likely to have children. They are more secure about the future and less likely to delay purchases, as evidenced by the fact that they save less.

Another dimension not shown in Figure 9.3 is the even greater rise in professional women. In 1997 approximately 57 percent of master's degrees and 41 percent of doctorate degrees were awarded to females in the United States, compared with only 40 percent of master's degrees and a mere 14 percent of doctorate degrees in 1971.[37] Consider the proportions of women that made up the following professional categories in 1960 and 1990:[38]

	1990 (%)	1960 (%)
Accountants	50.8	16.4
Financial managers	44.3	11.9
Lawyers and judges	20.8	3.3
Physicians	19.3	7.0
Architects	18.4	2.5

The proportion of women in each category is likely to be even greater today.

Companies are starting to target women with ads citing detailed specifications for women. Subaru was the first automaker to mount a coordinated strategy to target working women. It used women sports stars in its ads portraying ruggedness and athleticism with assertive tag lines like "Subaru is a proud sponsor of women who kick butt" (see Exhibit 9.2). Similarly, office electronics companies have begun to target their products to women executives based on studies that found women own 32 percent of the nation's sole proprietorships and that 75 percent of women managers have a role in buying office equipment.[39]

A direct impact of these trends is the time crunch working women face. Despite their increased job responsibilities, they are still the primary homemaker. In 1975, 45 percent of working women believed they had enough leisure time. By 1990, only 35 percent believed they had enough time. Food companies have adapted

| EXHIBIT 9.2 |

Targeting working women.

Subaru of America, Inc.

to the time crunch working women face by emphasizing easy-to-prepare foods. Campbell's Chunky soups, for example, are advertised as the perfect light meal that even a husband can fix for his working wife.[40] Food concerns have also hedged their bets by buying fast-food outlets. General Mills, General Foods, and Quaker Oats are all mindful of statistics that show that working wives average 7.4 meals out per week.[41]

▌ Income   A direct correlation exists between income level and the purchasing power of a household. As a result, marketers segment consumers by income level and frequently allocate greater effort to the more affluent segments.

Although most Americans like to think that their country promotes economic equality, the fact is that the period from 1970 to 2000 saw greater inequality in income between rich and poor. Consider the following data:[42]

	Average income 1970	*Average income 1998*	*Percentage change 1970–1998*
Top 5 percent by income	$95,708	$145,199	+52 percent
Bottom 20 percent by income	$20,128	$21,600	+ 7 percent

WEB APPLICATIONS

The Demographics of Web Usage

Demographics are important descriptors of web site visitors. Traditional brands and companies that develop web sites use demographics to determine whether visitors to their sites are the same as visitors to their stores.

Demographic characteristic	1996 Online users	2001 Online users	Incidence in U.S. population
Males	62%	49%	49%
Females	38%	51%	51%
Average household income	$62,700	$49,800	$40,816
Adults 18–49	88%	76%	63%
Adults 50+	12%	24%	37%

Retailers like Barnes & Noble and the Gap use demographic analysis in this way to assess the potential for cannibalization of store sales by their web sites. Ideally, web site purchasers would represent a different demographic profile, possibly higher income and better educated than typical in-store customers, thereby expanding the company's market base. Demographics are also used for brand-specific sites such as Crest.com or Tide.com. P&G did not establish these sites to sell products on the Web but to provide services and information for buyers of their brands in-store. Here, P&G hopes that the demographics of visitors to its web sites are the same as those of its brand purchasers, because the sites are meant to establish a closer relationship with their existing customers.

Demographic profiles of site visitors also are used to sell advertising space on a site much the same way that magazines sell space. The site describes its demographic profile to potential web advertisers in the hope that these demographics match the targets the advertiser seeks to reach. For example, assume the demographic profile of visitors to ivillage.com, a site geared to the interests of women, is females 25–54 with children and a household income of $75,000 plus. Range Rover might decide to advertise on the site because these demographics match the target profile for one of its SUV models.

Demographics have also been used to describe Internet users in general since its inception. When the Internet was introduced, analysts described a gender gap, an age gap, and an income gap based on the fact that early Internet users tended to be young, technically adept, higher-income males. More recently, as Internet usage has become more widespread, these gaps are disappearing. The table above shows Internet usage in 1996, shortly after the Internet started becoming available on a widespread basis, and in 2001. It compares usage incidence by demographic group to the incidence of that group in the population based on the 2000 census.

The figures show that the gender gap totally disappeared in the five years between 1996 and 2001. Now, the incidence of web usage is the same as the incidence of men and women in the general population. Further, the income gap has almost disappeared. Whereas income of web users was much higher than average in 1996, it was only slightly higher in 2001. This leveling of income among web users is supported by the fact that the fastest-growing group for Internet access in 2000 was blue-collar workers. The age gap is also decreasing. Adults 50 and over were twice as likely to use the Web in 2001 as they were in 1996, although web usage among this group is still below average.

This demographic profile belies a frequently heard criticism of the Internet, that it does not reach the average consumer. The data shows that as web usage becomes more widespread, web users are logically reflecting the general demographic makeup of the American consumer.

Sources: "Dot-Coms Head Down-Market for Dollars," *Wall Street Journal* (July 10, 2001), pp. B1, B8; "Online Consumers Now the Average Consumer," Cyberatlas.com/bigpicture/demographics, as of 2001; *Insight Express,* 2001; U.S. Bureau of the Census, 2000.

OF CONSUMER BEHAVIOR

The data show that the rich have become richer while the poor have lost ground when accounting for inflation.

The social consequences of these changes are likely to be significant, particularly in urban areas. The infrastructures of some cities are decaying, with a shrinking tax base and fewer support services available. One reflection of this decay has been the decrease in retail facilities in center cities. The long-term shift of department stores and mass merchandisers to the suburbs and the development of shopping malls indicate that retailers are "moving to where the money is."

Added to the greater disparities in income are the underlying disparities associated with race and ethnic origin. In 1998, median income was $49,023 for whites, versus $29,404 for African Americans. Disparity also exists between Hispanic Americans and whites.[43]

Because marketers tend to allocate resources by purchasing power, it is not surprising that they pay more attention to the affluent end of the market. The increasing proportion of working women and the greater number of single-member households have increased purchasing power for many consumers, which further spurs interest in the high-priced end. In 1998, 25 percent of all households earned more than $75,000, spurring a superpremium price niche in many categories from ice cream to beer.[44]

▌ Education   Education is directly related to purchasing power, as there is a high correlation between education and income. The educational level of Americans has been rising rapidly. In 1940, only 25 percent of American adults had completed high school; by 1999, 84 percent had done so. The proportion of college-educated Americans also increased, from 5 percent in 1940 to 25 percent in 1999.[45]

Education affects the way consumers make decisions. Evidence suggests that less educated consumers do not have the same amount of information on brand and price alternatives as do better educated consumers. For example, in making decisions, the less educated are not as likely to use unit price information in stores. However, consumers using such information are more aware of lower-priced alternatives.[46] Furthermore, poor and less educated consumers often do not have the means to comparison-shop. This relationship also translates onto the Web, as poorer consumers usually do not have Internet access and are unable to obtain price or product information from that source. The net result is that the underprivileged have restricted choices and often pay more than necessary.

Demographic Trends Worldwide

Given the growing globalization of marketing activities, companies and marketers are looking at demographic trends outside the United States to help them understand and better serve markets abroad, many of which represent large, untapped opportunities. The same factors are influencing marketing strategies abroad as in the United States; namely, population trends, changing age and household compositions, and the increasing proportion of working women.

POPULATION

World population grew substantially over the last century, with especially high growth during the 1970s and 1980s. In the early twentieth century, the world population was 1.5 billion. By 1960, the population had grown to 3 billion, and today it is just over 6 billion. Most of this growth has come from economically underdeveloped countries, which make up 80 percent of the world population (or 4.8 billion people). The highest growth came from Africa, Asia, Latin America, and the Caribbean. Africa has nearly tripled in size since the 1960s. Asia, Latin America, and the Caribbean have all doubled in size since that time.[47] This is in sharp contrast to high-income countries, which have seen their population growth slow and stabilize over the same time period.

Many companies are also expecting future profits to come in these fast-growing geographic regions. Levi Strauss, for example, has developed advertising directed at numerous Latin American countries and even supports their products with country-specific web sites for Argentina, Brazil, Chile, Mexico, Peru, and Uruguay.[48]

As noted earlier, three key factors account for most population growth: birthrate, life expectancy, and immigration. Birthrates are tied to economic development, with the lowest birthrates in countries with advanced economies. Current projections are that birthrates will decline in the next twenty-five years.[49] According to the U.S. Census Bureau, eighty-three countries will have birthrates below replacement levels.[50] Birthrates have declined most rapidly in Latin America, although these regions still have relatively high fertility rates. Japan has the lowest number of children per household and Africa has the highest (see Figure 9.4). Declines in birthrates are due to greater access to contraception, education about family planning, and overall improved opportunities for women (education levels, work force, social status, etc.). Government policy is another factor in reducing birthrates. China has instituted severe penalties on families who have more than one child in an attempt to contain population growth.

Companies like Gerber Products, the maker of baby foods, realize the importance of statistics like these and continue to expand into international markets. Gerber, which is already in eighty countries, is planning to enter the Chinese and Indian markets. Based on continued decline in birthrates in North America, Gerber

| FIGURE 9.4 |

Average number of children per household (fertility rates).

Source: United Nations web site, average rates for 1995–2000, http://www.un.org/depts/unsd, as of 2/27/2000.

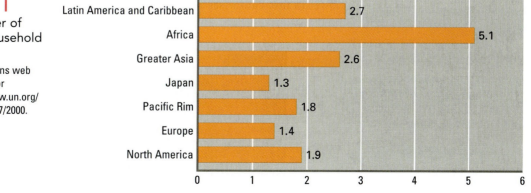

expects more than half of the company's revenues to come from countries outside the United States.[51]

In addition to a declining birthrate, overall life span has increased. Since World War II the average worldwide life expectancy has increased from 46 years to 66 years and is projected to be 76 by 2050.[52] Aging adults worldwide could be a marketing opportunity for some companies. The Body Shop has tried to appeal to the older consumer globally by introducing a new line of skin care products, New Skin, that is designed specifically for aging skin.[53]

Life expectancy varies widely from country to country. In sub-Sahara Africa, the rampant spread of AIDS has actually decreased life expectancy rates in the last decade. In other countries, like eastern European and former Soviet Union countries, an increase in poverty, poor nutrition, and inadequate health care has also led to decreased life spans.

Regarding immigration, movement has historically been from less to more developed countries. Asia and Latin America have the highest number and percentage of migrants leaving the country, with Africa the next highest. About 10 percent of the total population in Europe is composed of non-European immigrants, compared with about 12 percent in the United States.[54] With low fertility rates in Japan and Europe, these regions will be faced with a smaller labor force that will threaten economic growth. Countries like Germany have loosened immigration laws to allow a greater number of immigrants to fill the work force. The United States has increased the number of immigrants to more than one million per year since 1990 to offset declining birthrates.[55]

CHANGING AGE COMPOSITION

Most of the world population growth has occurred at opposite ends of the age spectrum. There are more young people aged 15–24 in the world than ever before (1 billion), and more older people, especially more of the "older old." By 2050, the number of people aged 65–84 will triple to 1.3 billion, the number of people 85+ will increase sixfold to 175 million, and the number of people 100+ will grow sixteenfold to 2.2 million.[56] There are striking differences, however, between developed and developing countries. In many high-income countries, like the United Kingdom and Japan, the older population is growing, whereas middle-aged and younger people account for a smaller percentage of the total population. Africa, on the other hand, has the youngest demographic profile because life expectancy is much lower in the region (see Figure 9.5).

| **FIGURE 9.5** |

Aging of the population—percentage over 60 years of age.

Source: United Nations web site, http://www.unfpa.org/swp/1999/chapter2.htm, as of 2/27/2000.

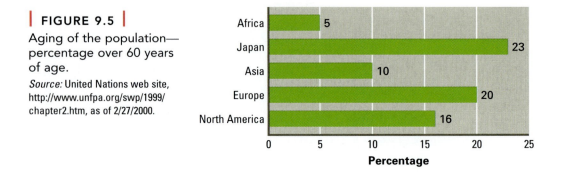

Economic conditions in a country are often partly the result of changing age profiles. Some say that Japan's recent economic crisis could have been forecast by one of the highest life expectancy rates in the world, resulting in a growing number of older Japanese and a declining working age population. This sparked a government response to increase taxes to offset the expected decline in productivity and led the country into recession.

CHANGING HOUSEHOLD COMPOSITION

Nontraditional households have been increasing abroad as well as in the United States, particularly in Northern Europe. In Norway, 49 percent of all births were to unwed parents in 1999, and in England, 38 percent. Even in more conservative Ireland, the figure was 31 percent. Marriage may be less relevant for many couples in these countries, but children remain as important as before. As one unwed parent said, "We have little commitment to the institution of marriage, but we do have a commitment to parenthood."[57]

Another factor regarding household composition abroad is the importance of multigenerational families. In most developing nations, like India, China, Korea, and the Philippines, multigenerational families are commonplace. Parents raise their children and then expect their children to care for them as they age. Nearly 80 percent of Chinese households live in this type of generational arrangement. About 50 percent of South American households fit this description. For the most part, as countries become more developed, multigenerational households are less commonplace. One exception is Japan, where 40–50 percent of the population lives in multigenerational families.[58] Yet this is also changing as more newly married couples are starting to live alone.

SOCIOECONOMIC FACTORS

Worldwide socioeconomic factors reflect the increasing percentage of working women and persistent disparities in buying power between developed and underdeveloped countries.

■ **Percentage of Working Women**   As in the United States, the number of working women, as well as the number of married working women and working mothers, has increased in most countries, with an average of about 40 percent of females in the work force worldwide. Figure 9.6 shows that the percentage of women in the labor force varies from 27 percent in the Middle East and North Africa to 47 percent in Europe and Central Asia, meaning that every region of the world has a significant proportion of working women. The increasing proportion of working women is particularly apparent in Asian and Latin American countries as the stigma against married working women is easing.

A gender gap exists between countries or regions with more progressive cultures and attitudes toward women and those with more restrictive attitudes. The lowest proportions of females in the work force are in Saudi Arabia (14 percent), United Arab Emirates (14 percent), Iraq (19 percent), and Oman (15 percent).[59] This is in contrast to the current figure of 61 percent in the United States.

The greatest difference when comparing the status of working women between countries is the percentage of women in professional versus blue-collar jobs. The

| **FIGURE 9.6** |

Percentage of global
female work force.

Source: World Bank web site,
http://www.worldbanklorg/data,
as of March 4, 2000. Reprinted
by permission of The World
Bank.

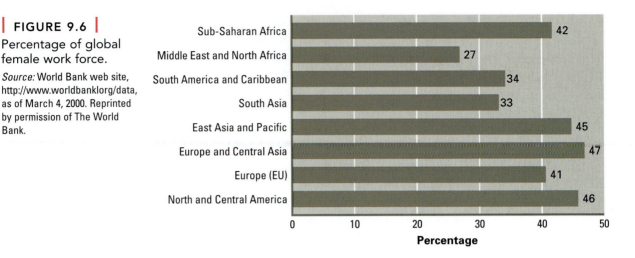

percentage of professional women is significantly higher in European Union (EU)
countries and in North America than in other countries. This is important because
women in professional jobs have greater discretionary income. One reason that
financial services companies, like Bank of America, created marketing programs
targeted specifically at professional women is that they have more control over
household finances.

■ **Income** The average income for a full-time worker worldwide is $4,890 (in
U.S. dollars). The per capita income is $520 in underdeveloped countries, $2,950 in
less developed countries, and $25,510 per person in highly developed countries. The
disparity in buying power between the richest and the poorest groups can be measured by the proportion of goods consumed and is most evident for less developed
countries. In Brazil, for example, the richest 10 percent consume 48 percent of all
goods and services; the poorest 20 percent consume only 2.5 percent. But sharp disparities also occur in highly developed countries. In the United States, the richest 10
percent of the population consume 28.5 percent of all goods and services while the
poorest 20 percent consume 4.8 percent.[60]

Using Demographics to Develop Marketing Strategy

Marketers use demographics to describe and better understand existing and potential users of their products. In this section, we consider using demographics to identify *market segments* and to identify individual consumers using databases of their
characteristics, an application known as *database marketing*.

IDENTIFYING MARKET SEGMENTS

Marketers use demographics to identify a target group for their brand or product
category. A demographic description of a brand's target group helps in media selection, advertising, and product development. It helps in media selection by deter-

| EXHIBIT 9.3 |

Mercedes targets its C Class to a younger segment.

Visuals Unlimited.

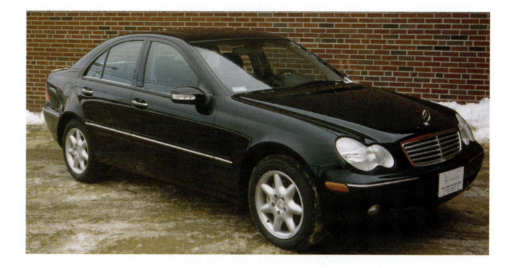

mining the magazines prospective buyers read or the TV shows they watch. For example, if the professional woman is likely to read *Business Week* or *Vogue,* then BMW might advertise in these magazines to target this segment. A demographic profile also can guide advertising strategy by setting the appropriate scene to appeal to a demographic group. Pepsi has targeted teens since the mid-1960s, taking on the mantel of the Pepsi Generation. For example, in 2001, pop star Britney Spears appeared in a television commercial aimed at promoting Pepsi to teens.

Demographic segmentation is the basis for Kodak's decision to shift from product-driven to age-driven marketing. Now, instead of selling its film to all audiences with a general campaign, the company is creating different commercials for different age groups. One of the ads, for example, aims at teenage girls by showing how photos provide a good record of one's adolescent years. Demographics were also the key factor in Mercedes-Benz's recent push to obtain younger, higher-income consumers. Mercedes targeted its C class autos toward this younger audience (see Exhibit 9.3). Mercedes found that this demographic group has an individualistic streak but has ties to family and tends to be serious about its future. Therefore, the company tailored its ads to reflect those sentiments.

Segmenting with demographic data is also critically important for international marketers. For example, one U.S. bleach firm that was interested in selling to developing countries found that women in Kenya, Bangladesh, Algeria, and Pakistan tended to have five or more children whom they were unable to furnish with proper medical attention. So it positioned its bleach as a disinfectant, and because literacy rates are low, it advertised its use with pictures.[61]

DATABASE MARKETING

Whereas marketers typically segment consumers into groups such as higher versus lower income or baby boomers versus Generation Xers, **database marketing** allows them to identify individual consumers and customize product, service, or promotional offerings to meet their specific needs. The Internet is an excellent vehicle for identifying the demographics of site visitors and web purchasers, assuming that users are willing to provide the information. Databases rely on broader sources of information than the Web. Other sources used to identify individual consumer characteristics are sweepstake entries, coupon redemptions, credit card bills, or telephone bills. In each case, demographic data on individual consumers are available, providing the basis for micromarketing.

Marketers use demographic data to target emails, coupons, and ads to individual consumers. Assume that United Airlines determines that frequent purchasers of airline tickets on the Web are business executives between 35 and 54 living in urban areas with yearly income over $100,000. It could target these individuals directly by email, promoting frequent flier miles and travel discounts. It could also determine web sites that are most likely to be visited and magazines that are most likely to be read by this group. Pop-up ads on web sites and print ads in magazines would then be targeted based on the demographic profile of the frequent business traveler.

Companies also create their own databases. For example, Levi Strauss gives its customers the ability to place alteration instructions in computers that then order tailor-made jeans. In so doing, customers provide Levi Strauss with demographic information the company can use to reach these same customers with direct-mail promotions.[62]

In addition to reaching individual customers and customizing offerings, database marketing has been used to solidify the relationship between a company and its customers. For example, Bloomingdale's identifies heavy purchasers in its stores from billing data and provides services such as sending reminders to spouses to buy birthday or anniversary presents or taking orders by fax.[63] Such **relationship marketing** strategies are an attempt to win customer loyalty in an increasingly competitive market.

An issue that arises in the use of databases is the customer's right to privacy. If a customer does not want personal information on the Internet or in credit card or telephone bills used for promotional purposes, he or she should have the right to block the use of this information. We consider relationship marketing further in Chapter 18 when we discuss micromarketing strategies.

Social Class Influences

Marketers use three socioeconomic factors—occupation, income, and education—to identify another important dimension of consumer behavior, social class. Social class defines the ranking of people in a society into a hierarchy of upper, middle, and lower classes based on their power and prestige. In American society, power and prestige are generally equated with one's occupation, income, and education. Therefore, social class is based on demographic variables.

THE NATURE OF SOCIAL CLASS

To understand how social class affects purchasing behavior, we must understand *social stratification, status symbols,* and *social mobility.*

❚ Social Stratification   Social class is defined by **social stratification,** that is, "the ranking of people in society by other members into higher and lower positions so as to produce a hierarchy of respect or prestige."[64] The classifications of consumers into upper, middle, or lower class imply that certain members of society rank higher than others in prestige and power. Although contrary to the American creed that all people are created equal, social stratification suggests that some people are more equal than others.

What criteria are used to define this social hierarchy? Not only income, education, and occupation but more intangible factors like lifestyles, ties and connections, political power, and public service are used. One study using these criteria found that physicians, scientists, government officials, and college professors rate highest on the social scale.[65] Thus, although a young college professor may be making less than a factory foreman, she may rank higher in social status.

Because the basis for defining power and prestige varies from one society to another, the composition of upper, middle, and lower classes is also likely to vary. Social stratification depends on the ideals and values of the society. In Europe, for example, artists and writers probably would be rated higher than in the United States.

Social class status is likely to indicate common values and similar purchasing patterns. For example, studies have shown that individuals in the upper-middle class emphasize education, are fashion oriented, and are less likely to be brand loyal than other groups. Such similarity in norms, values, and purchasing patterns means that social classes serve as a frame of reference for the purchasing behavior of consumers in a particular social class.

▌ **Status Symbols**　Another indicator of social class is our possessions—the clothing we wear, the houses we live in, and the cars we drive. When Thorstein Veblen wrote of conspicuous consumption in the early 1900s, he was referring to the tendency of affluent consumers to demonstrate upper-class membership through their possessions. In other words, homes, clothing, and other visible signs of wealth were signs of achievement, or *status symbols*. At a time when robber barons were producing unimaginable wealth, and class divisions were sharper, Veblen referred to the demonstration of these symbols of "new wealth" as *conspicuous consumption*. Among the aristocratic "old wealth," there was a reverse tendency to take possessions for granted and downplay them as indicators of affluence.[66]

Status symbols do not have to be associated with wealth. A **status symbol** is a symbol of one's status in society. Thus, the policeman's uniform or the CEO's pin-stripe suit are status symbols.

▌ **Social Mobility**　**Social mobility** refers to the movement of an individual or household from one social class to another. Since the turn of the century individuals and households have moved up the social ladder, expanding the ranks of the middle class as the American standard of living has increased. One study of eight hundred households has supported a pattern of upward social mobility. In almost two-thirds of households, the husband or wife had a higher social status than their parents. In only 8 percent of households was the social status lower.[67]

Yet recessions in the early 1980s and 1990s have partially reversed this trend. The recession in the early 1980s was a *blue-collar recession,* thrusting some working-class families into poverty income levels. The recession in the early 1990s was a *middle management recession* due to the effects of the information revolution and corporate downsizing to reduce costs. Managers often had to settle for jobs at half their former salaries. As a result, the social status of many middle-class families declined.

The recession that began in 2001 is likely to further affect social identification. One outcome is the pessimistic economic prospects perceived by many Generation Xers, causing them to be the first age cohort to believe that their economic status may be lower than that of their parents.

These trends show that social class is a dynamic concept, resulting in changes in social stratification over time.

SOCIAL CLASS CATEGORIES IN THE UNITED STATES

As noted earlier, one's position on the social hierarchy is defined primarily by socioeconomic factors related to occupation, income, and education. These factors are combined into an index of social status that serves to define a consumer's social class.

▌ Warner's Index of Status Characteristics

The most widely used index at one time was W. Lloyd Warner's **Index of Status Characteristics.**[68] Warner developed his index in a study of social class lines in a midwestern city in the early 1940s.[69] The ISC is based on the following socioeconomic indicators:

- ▌ Occupation (ranging from unskilled workers to professionals)
- ▌ Source of income (ranging from public relief to inherited wealth)
- ▌ House type (rated from very poor to excellent)
- ▌ Dwelling area (ranging from slums to "gold coast" areas)

Warner identified seven social class categories from low to high based on these four demographic characteristics.

▌ Coleman-Rainwater Social Standing Hierarchy

The fact that Warner's index was developed right before World War II led two sociologists, Richard Coleman and Lee Rainwater, to update it. The resulting groupings, shown in Table 9.1 and known as the **Coleman-Rainwater Social Standing Hierarchy,** are similar to Warner's, but they more directly reflect the power and prestige associated with each group.

Because it focuses on power and prestige, the Coleman-Rainwater Hierarchy draws social class lines more sharply than does Warner's index. Whereas Warner refers to the next to lowest group as on private relief and living in semislum conditions, Coleman and Rainwater describe the group as portraying behavior that others judge as "crude" and "trashy," thus reflecting the severe judgments by upper- and middle-class Americans of the lower classes. In so doing, the Coleman-Rainwater Hierarchy better reflects the tensions between social groups.

Another advantage of the Coleman-Rainwater Hierarchy over Warner's is that it distinguishes between a middle class and a working class. Although the middle class tends to be white-collar and the working class blue-collar, the distinction reflects the values of each group as well as occupation. For example, Coleman describes working-class Americans as "family folk, depending heavily on relatives for economic and emotional support."[70] The values of working-class Americans are

TABLE 9.1

Categories in the Coleman-Rainwater Social Standing Hierarchy

Upper Americans

Upper-Upper (0.3%)—The "capital S society" world of inherited wealth, aristocratic names

Lower-Upper (1.2%)—The newer social elite, drawn from current professional, corporate leadership

Upper-Middle (12.5%)—The rest of college graduate managers and professionals; lifestyle centers on private clubs, causes, and the arts

Middle Americans

Middle Class (32%)—Average pay, white-collar workers and their blue-collar friends; live on "the better side of town," try to "do the proper things"

Working Class (38%)—Average pay, blue-collar workers; lead "working-class lifestyle" whatever the income, school background, and job

Lower Americans

"A lower group of people but not the lowest" (9%)—Working, not on welfare; living standard is just above poverty; behavior judged "crude," "trashy"

"Real Lower-Lower" (7%)—On welfare, visibly poverty-stricken, usually out of work (or have "the dirtiest jobs")

Source: From *Social Standing in America* by Richard P. Coleman and Lee P. Rainwater. Copyright© 1978 by Basic Books, Inc. Reprinted by permission of Basic Books, a member of Perseus Books, L.L.C.

reflected in their preference for local rather than national news, for vacationing with relatives at local resorts, and for buying American. In contrast, middle-class Americans tend to buy based on their perception of the norms and values of the upper class. They want to do the right thing and buy what is popular. Their upward mobility distinguishes them from the working class.

The values of each of these groups are reflected in what they buy, what they wear, and who they look up to. A survey by *Fortune* magazine of three of Coleman and Rainwater's groups, the working, middle, and upper-middle classes (representing over 80 percent of households) reflected these differences as shown in Table 9.2. Research into the social classes in Table 9.1 makes it possible to further detail their norms, values, and lifestyles.

The Old Wealth. The mere presence of wealth is not sufficient to get into this class. This group (upper-upper class; .3 percent of the population) represents the social elite based on inherited wealth. They dress conservatively and well and avoid ostentatious purchases. They emphasize self-expression, buy quality merchandise, and reflect an ideal of "spending with good taste." Members are part of a closed society of townhouses, country homes, and social gatherings. They are expected to engage in philanthropy and public service.

The New Wealth. This group (lower-upper class; 1.2 percent of the population) is likely to be composed of the influentials in society—business leaders and the professional elite. They are self-made individuals who are apt to be active in

TABLE 9.2
Differences in fashions and tastes for three social class groups

		CLASS DISTINCTIONS: You are what you choose		
		Working class	**Middle class**	**Upper-middle class**
Car	1980s	Hyundai	Chevrolet Celebrity	Mercedes
	1990s	Geo	Chrysler minivan	Range Rover
Business shoe	1980s	Sneakers	Wingtips	Cap toes
(men)	1990s	Boots	Rockports	Loafers
Business shoe	1980s	Spike-heel pumps	Mid-heel pump	High-heel pumps
(women)	1990s	High-heel pumps	Dressy flats	One-inch pumps
Alcoholic beverage	1980s	Domestic beer	White wine spritzer	Dom Perignon
	1990s	Domestic lite beer	California Chardonnay	Cristal
Leisure pursuit	1980s	Watching sports	Going to movies	Golf
	1990s	Playing sports	Renting movies	Playing with computers
Hero	1980s	Roseanne Barr	Ronald Reagan	Michael Milken
	1990s	Kathie Lee Gifford	Janet Reno	Rush Limbaugh

Source: "Class in America," from *Fortune* (February 7, 1994). Copyright © 1994 Time Inc. All rights reserved.

community affairs and public issues. Although not a target for the mass marketer, this group would make an excellent market for specialty items such as expensive clothing, jewelry, furniture, or boats.

Occasionally, members of this group have been derisively referred to as the *nouveau riche*. The name implies an ostentatious display of new wealth without taste. The phenomenon is apparent in former communist countries where the transition to capitalism has created a new class of wealthy entrepreneurs who seek the means to display their newfound wealth but are often frustrated by the lack of availability of luxury goods.

Upper Middle Class. This group (12.5 percent of the population) is also composed of successful professional and business people, but it does not have the wealth or status of the upper class. Combined with the two upper-class categories, the upper-middle class possesses most of the wealth in the United States. These three groups own two-thirds of the securities and almost two-thirds of the real estate in this country, even though they represent only 14 percent of the population.[71] The upper-middle class is career oriented and achievement motivated. Members of this group emphasize education; most are college graduates. Because they are well educated, this group is more likely to appraise product alternatives critically. They emphasize quality and value and good taste, rather than status, in their purchases. Women in this group are more likely to be employed, active, and more self-expressive than women in other groups.

Middle Class. This group (32 percent of the population) is represented by white-collar workers, owners of small businesses, and highly paid blue-collar workers. There is a split in this group between those who emphasize traditional norms and those who subscribe to more modern values.[72] Traditionalists are more home and family oriented. Women in this group pride themselves on their role of mother and homemaker. Their orientation is toward traditional, conservative benefits such as pride in meal preparation and satisfaction in the upbringing of their children.

The nontraditional consumers in this group reflect the values of the upper-middle class because they are upwardly mobile. Compared with the traditionalists, wives are more likely to work, husbands and wives are more likely to make joint decisions, and parents are more likely to emphasize a college education for their children. Timesaving benefits in food preparation and appliances that are likely to appeal to the nontraditionalist middle-class families are unlikely to appeal to the traditionalists.

Because they seek the trappings of wealth of the upper-middle class, nontraditionalists are more likely to buy based on status considerations. They are more likely to own credit cards, top-of-the-line electronic equipment, and designer clothes.

The middle class is perhaps the most international social class grouping. Middle classes have begun to emerge in developing countries, particularly in the Pacific Rim and Latin America. A new prosperity combined with access to global television has communicated Western products from jeans to breakfast cereals and resulted in demands for similar lifestyles. Because of a global outlook and acceptance of American lifestyles, middle-class families are "increasingly looking, living, and even talking more like each other."[73]

Working Class. The working class (38 percent of the population) consists primarily of blue-collar workers. People in the working class depend on friends and relatives for emotional support and escape from uncreative jobs. The narrow dimensions of and lack of self-expression in their jobs lead to a pattern of impulse purchasing to escape from the dull routine. This group would rather buy for today than plan for tomorrow; therefore, advertising appeals to fantasy and escape are likely to be successful.

Their view of life tends to reflect traditional values. The husband is likely to be the breadwinner and the decision maker; the wife, the traditional homemaker. Whereas over one-half of middle-class women work, only about one-third of working-class women are employed.[74]

Lower Class. This group (16 percent of the population) represents the unskilled, poorly educated, and socially disadvantaged. They earn only one-fifth the income of the average American.[75] Lower-class consumers often live in poverty, frequently are on welfare, and are more likely to have a female head of household. Lower-class families often have difficulty moving up the social hierarchy. As a result, they are frustrated and angry about their economic status and inability to share in the "American Dream."

The bulk of the lower-class consumer's income goes to rent and heat. This group also spends a disproportionate amount of their income on food and medicine, reflecting a lower income level. They often pay higher prices for goods than do other groups because they are restricted to poor, inner-city areas and do not have the means or mobility to comparison-shop.[76]

IS THE UNITED STATES BECOMING A CLASSLESS SOCIETY?

A key question that may inhibit the use of social class in consumer behavior studies is whether social class lines are becoming more blurred. The universal ownership of television sets means everyone is exposed to the same mass communications. The rise of mass merchandising and the standardization of consumer packaged goods means that most people buy similar brands. The universal ownership of automobiles means greater mobility. Increased access to the Internet means more equal product and price information across age and income groups.

GLOBAL APPLICATIONS OF CONSUMER BEHAVIOR

Social Class in China

Class divisions occur worldwide. There are differences in the definition of social classes because of differences associated with power and prestige in various societies. For example, age promotes status in some Asian countries but not in Western society. Education is given more weight in Europe than in the United States. Occupation and income seem to be more universal measures of social status.

China is a good example of the role of occupation and income in defining social class. Despite having a communist government, sharp social disparities exist. A report in the *China Business Review* categorized China's consumers into four social class segments: the nouveau riche, yuppies (young, urban professionals), salary men, and working poor.

The *nouveau riche* group is primarily entrepreneurs, businesspeople, celebrities, and government officials who make more than $5,000 (U.S. dollars) per year. They are likely to use status products, like credit cards, cell phones, and foreign-made goods. This group is a minute part of China's population, estimated to be between 200,000 and 2 million people, less than one-tenth of 1 percent of the total population. It includes government officials with various perks such as staying at luxury guest houses.

China's *yuppies* are younger workers who have some education or technical training and tend to live in urban areas. The average age range of a yuppie is 25 to 45, and the average household income is $1,800 to $5,000. Consumers in the yuppie group tend to experiment more than the other groups and are more receptive to new products and ideas, including foreign goods. These are the members of the emerging middle class, estimated at 5 percent of the population, about 60 million consumers. This is the favored class outside the nouveau riche group, because the government favors industrial over agricultural development, and this group has the technical expertise to run industry. This group is beginning to afford cars, bringing a vast change in social attitudes and habits because of their greater mobility.

China's *salary men* are the white-collar workers of Chinese society. They make an annual household income between $1,150 and $1,799 and often work for the government. Many of the salary men aspire to be in a higher social class and occasionally purchase luxury goods, but they are highly constrained by their income. This group represents 27 percent of China's population, or nearly 330 million people.

The largest social group in China is the *working poor*, China's blue-collar workers and farmers. Most of the consumers in this group have low education levels and training and are working in manual labor in small companies. Most of China's peasants and retired people are included in this group, representing 67 percent of the population, or about 800 million people.

Sources: "Emerging Middle Class Hits the Road in China," *New York Times* (October 7, 2001), p. A27; "The Different Faces of the Chinese Consumer," *China Business Review,* (July/August 1997), p. 34; "At One Resort in China, Two Distinct Worlds," *New York Times* (August 10, 2001), p. A1; "The Rural-Urban Divide: Economic Disparities and Interactions in China," *Journal of Asian Studies* (February 2001), p. 169.

However, recent evidence suggests that social class lines are becoming sharper. The deep recession of 1990–1991 drove many middle-class consumers a notch lower on the social scale. At the same time, opportunities for managers and professionals in high-technology and service areas have provided the means for many middle-class consumers to move into the upper class.[77] The result has been more pronounced distinctions between the upper and lower classes. The information revolution has contributed to these distinctions. Former secretary of labor Robert Reich estimates that about 20 percent of American workers have been able to keep up with the new technologies. The other 80 percent—assembly-line workers, data processors, retail salespeople, cashiers, and blue-collar workers—are facing insecure job prospects.[78] This is reflected in surveys that have shown the vast majority of American workers feeling insecure about their current jobs. The recession that began in 2001 has increased this sense of insecurity and may further sharpen class divisions.

As a result of these trends, one writer described an erosion of the American egalitarian spirit and a reemergence of the class system as a result of these trends.[79] Social class in America is still very much a reality and a component to be considered in explaining consumer behavior.

Applications of Social Class to Marketing Strategy

Marketers have found social class measures important because of substantial differences in behavior between classes. As a result, social class characteristics have been related to every aspect of marketing strategy.

ADVERTISING

Social class values can give direction to advertisers. Members of a social class must understand the language and symbols used in advertising; otherwise, communication will not be achieved. For example, working- and lower-class consumers are more receptive to "advertising that is strongly visual in character, that shows activity, ongoing work and life, impressions of energy, and solutions to practical problems in daily requirements."[80] In contrast, upper-class consumers are more open to subtle symbolism, to approaches that are more "individual in tone . . . that offer the kinds of objects and symbols that are significant of their status and self-expressive aims."[81]

The ad for the Lincoln LS automobile in Exhibit 9.4 is linked with upper-class symbols of Madison Avenue, Broadway theater, and luxury. An example of an appeal to working-class values would be an ad that HUD ran for financing homes, showing a working-class family in the foreground and a home in the background. It reflected the focus on a solution to a very practical problem, guaranteeing home ownership with financial security.

Power is a frequently used symbol of social class. The ads in Exhibit 9.5 show power themes directed to upper- and upper-middle-class values. The ad for the Concorde, targeting professionals and managers, is based on economic power and cites a "power upgrade" to business class. The Motorola ad is directed to the upper-middle-class professional woman who is trying to successfully balance work and

family. To direct a power theme to working-class customers, an ad for Power Line vacuum cleaners associates the product to a power theme through the brand name.

MARKET SEGMENTATION

The substantial differences among social classes in the purchases of clothing, furniture, appliances, leisure goods, financial services, and food products provide marketers with a basis for segmenting consumers. For example, upper classes are likely to emphasize style and color in purchasing appliances, whereas lower-class consumers emphasize appliances that work.[82] In each case, different product lines for different social class segments would be appropriate. Some companies are adapting to social class influences abroad. For example, Nestlé recognizes the emerging middle class in developing countries. It has sought to establish manufacturing facilities for many of its packaged goods in countries such as Egypt, India, and Pakistan to facilitate the targeting of its goods to middle-class consumers. Former communist countries such as Poland are also on the list.[83]

DISTRIBUTION

Social classes frequently differ in store patronage. Lower-class consumers are more likely to shop in discount stores and in neighborhood stores where they feel most comfortable and can rely on friendly salespeople for information. Upper-class consumers are more likely to shop in regular department stores for products they consider risky and in discount stores for products with little risk.[84]

| EXHIBIT 9.5 |

Power themes directed to upper- and upper-middle-class consumers.

(left) Air France; (right) Reproduced with permission from Motorola, Inc.

These findings suggest that social class characteristics can provide guidelines for distribution strategies. If the target market is more likely to be in the lower socioeconomic group, neighborhood stores should be used rather than downtown shopping centers. More emphasis should be placed on sales personnel and a friendly store environment. Middle- and upper-class target groups suggest the use of regular department stores, with primary emphasis on the nature and variety of merchandise.

PRODUCT DEVELOPMENT

Social classes may react differently to product characteristics and styles. For example, a study by AT&T examined the style and color preferences for telephones among various social groups.[85] Lower-class consumers were not interested in a decorative or modern phone; they just wanted one that worked. The working class placed the greatest emphasis on phones of different designs and colors. These findings demonstrate that the lower-class group would be a poor target for decorative phones, but the working class is a surprisingly good target. Had AT&T assumed that higher socioeconomic groups were the best target for high-style phones, it might have missed an important target group.

SUMMARY

Demographic trends in the U.S. market have had a direct impact on marketing strategies. Several basic trends were considered in this chapter:

- Population growth in the postwar period, resulting in the baby boom, a subsequent decline in the birthrate, and a baby boomlet since 1977 as baby boomers had children

- The effect of population growth on the changing age composition of the U.S. population, particularly in the senior segment

- Socioeconomic trends, particularly the increase in the proportion of working women

- Changes in household composition such as increases in the divorce rate, decreases in family size, and increases in single-parent households, resulting in an increase in nontraditional households

- Growing access to and use of the Internet among women, seniors, and lower-income households

The effects of these changes on purchasing and consumption behavior were also considered. For example, the increase in the proportion of working women has resulted in changing purchasing and consumption roles within the family, less time for shopping, and greater patronage of fast-food establishments.

Demographic changes worldwide and their implications for marketing were also discussed. These changes included a growing world population at both ends of the age spectrum, the growing number of working women worldwide, the widening income disparity between the haves and have-nots, and growing Internet usage worldwide.

Marketers segment markets by demographic characteristics to identify the best media to reach prospective users and to give them guidelines for advertising and product strategies. An increasingly important use of demographics is in micromarketing—that is, the use of databases that identify the demographic characteristics of individual consumers, allowing marketers to target these consumers through direct mail and interactive technologies.

The chapter also considered the use of demographics in two key strategic areas: (1) identifying market segments for purposes of media selection and advertising development and (2) the use of databases to identify individual consumers and target them through a strategy of micromarketing.

The chapter concluded by describing social classes. Social class refers to consumers' positions on a social scale based on three key demographic factors—occupation, income, and education. Consumers are classified by these criteria into social class groupings. The most frequently used classification is a five-part designation of upper-, upper-middle-, middle-, working-, and lower-class consumers. Each of these groups has distinctive norms, values, family roles, and patterns of purchasing behavior. On this basis, social classes vary markedly in the purchase of such items as clothing, furniture, leisure goods, and even food. These differences permit marketers to use social class criteria to identify market segments, select the language and symbols used in advertising, develop in-store strategies, and indicate appropriate product characteristics and styles.

In Chapter 10, we consider two key descriptors that further influence purchase behavior: consumer personality and lifestyles.

QUESTIONS FOR DISCUSSION

1. How does BMW use demographics in developing its markets?

2. What is micromarketing? Why has it become more feasible in recent years?

3. A large food producer is considering directing a wide range of packaged food products specifically to the singles market. How do the needs of single-person households differ from those of multiple-person households? What are the implications for the marketer?

4. What is meant by geodemographic analysis? How can marketers use it to target geographic segments?

5. What are the marketing implications of the greater emphasis working women put on time-saving conveniences?

6. How have marketers adjusted to the increasingly influential role of working women in buying decisions that men used to dominate? Provide specific examples.

7. Why have more working women stayed home to rear children in the last five years? What are the marketing implications?

8. How do changing demographics of web users affect companies' marketing strategies?

9. What are some of the major demographic trends worldwide? How do they compare with those found in the United States? What are the implications for marketers?

10. Two companies produce different lines of furniture. One directs its line toward upper-middle-class consumers; the other, to working-class consumers. What are likely to be the differences in (a) product styles and features, (b) print media used, and (c) distribution and in-store environment?

11. A magazine publisher decides there are sufficient differences in the orientation, role, and purchasing behavior of working women in different social classes to segment the magazine market by introducing three different magazines: one directed to the working woman in the upper-middle class, another to the working woman in the working class, and a third to the working woman in the lower class. Do you agree with the publisher's premise? Specifically, how might each magazine differ in (a) editorial content and (b) advertising?

12. A company is introducing a new line of instant baking products designed to facilitate the preparation of more-complicated recipes for breads, cakes, and pies. Should the company segment its line so that one set of products is directed to higher social classes and another to lower social classes? How would the advertising campaigns to each group differ?

13. Some researchers believe that sports and leisure-time activities serve a different purpose for the upper and lower classes. For the upper class, sports activities may be a compensation for a more sedentary existence as most of these activities involve active movement. For the lower class, sports and leisure-time activities are more of an escape from the dull routine of jobs. What are the implications of this finding for a large producer of sporting equipment?

14. What trends are being noticed in large companies' efforts with relation to the higher levels of growth in less developed geographic areas outside the United States? How are marketers reaching these new audiences?

15. What implications may social class have for marketers in foreign countries such as China?

RESEARCH ASSIGNMENTS

1 Visit the following web sites: *www.bananarepublic.com, www.oldnavy.com, and www.gap.com.*

- Do the three sites appeal to different socio-economic segments from high to low?
- Do the sites appeal to different age cohorts?
- Do they appeal to different life styles?

2 Select a group of working women and nonworking women (approximately thirty to forty women in each group). Select two food products requiring preparation (*e.g.,* cake mix, coffee). Ask respondents to rate various need criteria in selecting brands (such as importance of time saving, ease of preparation, good taste, good for the whole family) and to identify their favorite brand in each category.

- Do the needs of working and nonworking women differ?
- Do they prefer different brands?
- Do the results conform to your expectations about differences between working and non-working women? In what ways?

3 A study by a large electronics firm determined the demographic characteristics of purchasers of personal digital assistants (PDAs). These purchasers tended to be under 40, in the higher-income group ($75,000 and over), and in professional or managerial occupations.

a. Try to obtain a copy of a Simmons Report or another readership service like MRI. (It is all right if the report is somewhat dated). Analyze ten or twelve magazines to determine their relative efficiency in reaching the target group identified earlier. Incorporate cost-per-thousand data for each magazine if they are available. If not, analyze the magazines solely on their ability to reach the target group.

b. If data are also available for TV shows, do the same analysis for a selected number of shows as well.

4 Visit web sites that are targeted to women. Start with *www.ivillage.com,* which is a content information site designed for women. How are the messages different from other sites that are less targeted? Check other sites such as *www.women.com.*

5 Visit web sites that are targeted for high-income consumers for luxury goods, such as *www.ashford.com.* How do such sites attempt to attract this segment?

NOTES

1. "Subaru, GMC Top Push to Win Over Women," *Advertising Age* (April 3, 1995), p. S-24.
2. "BMW Tailors for Women," *Brandweek* (April 11, 1994), p. 4.
3. "A Battle for the Autobahn—Renewed BMW Plans to Push at High and Low Prices While Mercedes Struggles," *Wall Street Journal* (February 26, 2001), p. B1.
4. "BMW and Mercedes are Expecting; The Babies Will Visit America," *New York Times* (March 4, 2001), p.12.1.
5. "A Battle for the Autobahn" p. B1.
6. "BMW Expects Edge for Mini," *Advertising Age* (January 29, 2001), p. 49.
7. "Population Change and Distribution," Census 2000 Brief, April 2001.
8. U.S. Department of Commerce, Bureau of the Census, *Current Population Reports, 1991* (Washington, D.C.: U.S. Government Printing Office, 1991), Series P-25, No. 1045.
9. "National Vital Statistics Reports," from the Centers for Disease Control and Prevention, August 8, 2000.
10. Ibid.
11. "Gerber Childrenswear," *Home Textiles Today* (January/February 2000), p. 6.
12. "Gerber Stumbles in a Shrinking Market," *Wall Street Journal* (July 6, 1993), p. B1; and "Gerber: Concentrating on Babies Again for Slow, Steady Growth," *Business Week* (August 22, 1993), p. 52.
13. "Gerber Aims at Latino Birth Explosion," *Advertising Age* (March 6, 2000), p. 8.
14. "Annual Summary of Vital Statistics, Trends in the Health of Americans During the 20th Century," *Pediatrics* 106 (December 2000), pp.1307–1317.
15. *Statistical Abstract of the United States, 2000,* U.S. Census Bureau.
16. "Scientists Say Longevity Promoters Are Dead Wrong; Numbers Suggest We May Reach an Expectancy of 100 in the 26th Century," *Washington Post* (March 6, 2001), p. WH.6.
17. *Statistical Abstract of the United States, 2000.*
18. "IBM Targets Eight Niche Groups in Multimillion-Dollar Campaign," *Editor & Publisher* (March 6, 2000), pp. 30–32.
19. "Selling by Evoking What Defines a Generation," *Wall Street Journal* (August 13, 1996), pp. B1, B5.
20. "Martina Navratilova Enters the National Mainstream Market in a Campaign for Subaru," *New York Times* (March 13, 2000), p. C14.
21. Vanessa O'Connell and Jon E. Hilsenrath, "Advertisers Are Cautious as Household Makeup Shifts," *Wall Street Journal* (May 15, 2001), pp. B1, B4.
22. "Current Population Reports, Population Characteristics—Marital Status and Living Arrangements: March 1998," U.S. Department of Commerce, October 29, 1998.
23. O'Connell and Hilsenrath, "Advertisers Are Cautious," pp. B1, B4.
24. "Single Dads Wage Revolution One Bedtime Story at a Time," *New York Times* (June 17, 2001), pp. 1, 16.
25. "Current Population Reports, Population Characteristics—Marital Status and Living Arrangements: March 1998."
26. *Statistical Abstracts of the United States, 1996,* Table 82, p. 66.
27. "Single Parents," *American Demographics Desk Reference* (July 1992), p. 12.
28. *Statistical Abstracts of the United States, 1996,* Table 66, p. 58, and *Statistical Abstracts of the United States, 2000.*
29. "Rise in Never-Marrieds Affects Social Customs and Buying Patterns," *Wall Street Journal* (May 28, 1986), p. 1.
30. O'Connell and Hilsenrath, "Advertisers Are Cautious," pp. B1, B4.
31. Ibid.
32. "Feeding China's 'Little Emperors,'" *Forbes* (August 6, 1990), pp. 84–85.
33. "Parallel Universe," *American Demographics* (October 1999), pp. 58–64).
34. "Reaching the Real Europe," *American Demographics* (October 1990), pp. 38–43.
35. "Educational of Population Age 25 and Over by Sex," U.S. Census Bureau, March 2000.
36. *Statistical Abstracts, 2000,* Table 749, p. 472.
37. Ibid., Table 321, p. 195.
38. "Imperfect Picture," *Wall Street Journal* (April 24, 1995), p. R7.
39. "PC Makers, Palms Sweating, Try Talking To Women," *Business Week* (January 15, 1990), p. 48; and "Women Start Younger at Own Business," *Wall Street Journal* (February 15, 1993), p. B1.
40. "Eating Habits Force Changes in Marketing," *Advertising Age* (October 30, 1978), p. 30.

41. "Campbell's New Soup-to-Go Ads Are Directed at Working Women," *Wall Street Journal* (November 18, 1999), p. B4.

42. *Statistical Abstracts of the United States, 2000,* Table 745, p. 471.

43. Ibid., Table 744, p. 470.

44. Ibid., Table 743, p. 470.

45. Ibid., Table 250 p. 157.

46. Reed Moyer and Michael D. Hutt, *Macromarketing* (New York: John Wiley, 1978), pp. 123–141; Clive W. Granger and Andrew Billson, "Consumers' Attitudes Toward Package Size and Price," *Journal of Marketing Research* 9 (August 1972), pp. 239–248; and J. Edward Russo, Gene Dreiser, and Sally Miyashita, "An Effective Display of Unit Price Information," *Journal of Marketing* 39 (April 1975), pp. 11–19.

47. United Nations web site, http://www.unfpa.org/swp/1999/chapter2d.htm, as of February 27, 2000.

48. http://www.levi.com/lar/index-flash.html, as of April 17, 2001.

49. "The New Trend: A Population Bust," Washington Post (March 18, 2001), p. B.07.

50. Ibid.

51. "Gerber Products Goes Global: Foreign Ownership Puts Fremont in a Different Scenario," *Detroit News* (July 26, 1998), p. C4.

52. United Nations web site, http://www.unfpa.org/swp/1999/chapter2c.htm, as of February 2, 2000.

53. "Marketing in Europe to the Consumer over Age Fifty," *Marketing News* (August 4, 1997), p. 18.

54. "The Global Aging Crisis: Gray Dawn Transforming Our Future," *Denver Post* (February 7, 1999), p. J-01; and National Center for Policy analysis, www.ncpa.org/pd/immigrant, as of 2001.

55. "Population-Loss Trends Cited; Economic Growth of Japan, Europe at Risk, U.N. Report Says," *The Washington Post* (Mar 22, 2000), p. A28.

56. United Nations web site, http://www.unfpa.org/swp/1999/chapter2.htm, as of February 27, 2000.

57. "For Europeans, Love, Yes; Marriage, Maybe," *New York Times* (March 24, 2002), pp. 1, 18.

58. http://www.undp.org/popin/popdiv/untech/untechdocs.htm, paper by J. Sokolovsky, "Living Arrangements of Older Persons and Family Support in Less Developed Countries," as of February 28, 2000.

59. World Bank web site, http://www.worldbank.org/data, Figure 2.3, Labor Force Structure, 1999 World Development Indicators, as of March 4, 2000.

60. World Bank web site, http://www.worldbank.org/data/wdi/pdfs/tab2_8.pdf, Figure 2.8, Distribution of Income or Consumption, 1999 World Development Indicators, as of March 4, 2000.

61. Del I. Hawkins, Roger J. Best, and Kenneth A. Coney, *Consumer Behavior* (Homewood, Ill.: Irwin, 1992), p. 33.

62. "Digital Blue Jeans Pour Data and Legs into Customized Fit," *New York Times* (November 8, 1994), p. A1.

63. "Chains Start to Tune in on Frequency," *Brandweek* (March 21, 1994), pp. 36–38.

64. Bernard Berelson and Gary A. Steiner, *Human Behavior: An Inventory of Scientific Findings* (New York: Harcourt, Brace & World, 1964), p. 453.

65. Robert W. Hodges, Paul M. Siegel, and Peter H. Rossi, "Occupational Prestige in the United States 1925–1963," *American Journal of Sociology* 70 (November 1964), pp. 290–292.

66. Thorstein Veblen, *The Theory of the Leisure Class* (New York: Macmillan, 1912).

67. Terence A. Shimp and J. Thomas Yokum, "Extensions of the Basic Social Class Model Employed in Consumer Research," in Kent B. Monroe, ed., *Advances in Consumer Research,* Vol. 8 (Ann Arbor, Mich.: Association for Consumer Research, 1981), pp. 702–707.

68. W. Lloyd Warner, Marcia Meeker, and Kenneth Eells, *Social Class in America: Manual of Procedure for Measurement of Social Status* (New York: Harper & Row, 1960).

69. W. Lloyd Warner and Paul S. Lunt, *The Social Life of a Modern Community, Yankee City Series,* Vol. 1 (New Haven, Conn.: Yale University Press, 1941).

70. Richard P. Coleman, "The Continuing Significance of Social Class to Marketing," *Journal of Consumer Research* 10 (December 1983), p. 270.

71. "New Boundaries of Affluence," *Marketing Communications* (February 1986), p. 33.

72. Coleman, "The Continuing Significance of Social Class to Marketing," p. 272.

73. "The Emerging Middle Class," *Business Week, 21st Century Capitalism* (2001), pp. 176–193.

74. "Women's On-the-Job Attitudes," *Research Alert* (February 5, 1988), p. 3.

75. "Reaching Downscale Markets," *American Demographics* (November 1991), p. 40.

76. Andre Gabor and S. W. J. Granger, "Price Sensitivity of the Consumer," *Journal of Advertising Research* 4 (December 1964), pp. 40–44; David Caplovitz, *The Poor Pay More* (New York: The Free Press, 1963); and Frederick E. Webster, Jr., "The Deal-Prone Consumer," *Journal of Marketing Research* 1 (August 1964), pp. 32–35.

77. "The Middle Class Comes Undone," *Ad Forum* (June 1984), pp. 32–39.

78. "Class in America," *Fortune* (February 7, 1994), pp. 114–126.

79. Florence Skelly, "Prognosis 2000," speech before New York Chapter of the American Marketing Association, December 15, 1977.

80. Sidney J. Levy, "Social Class and Consumer Behavior," in Joseph W. Newman, ed., *On Knowing the Consumer* (New York: John Wiley, 1966), pp. 146–160.

81. Ibid.

82. A. Marvin Roscoe, Jr., Arthur LeClaire, Jr., and Leon G. Schiffman, "Theory and Management Applications of Demographics in Buyer Behavior," in Arch G. Woodside, Jagdish N. Sheth, and Peter D. Bennett, eds., *Consumer and Industrial Buying Behavior* (New York: North-Holland, 1977), pp. 74–75.

83. "Nestlé Courts the LDC Middle Class," *Wall Street Journal* (June 4, 1990), p. A13.

84. V. Kanti Prasad, "Socioeconomic Product Risk and Patronage Preferences of Retail Shoppers," *Journal of Marketing* 39 (July 1975), pp. 42–47.

85. Roscoe, LeClaire, and Schiffman, "Theory and Management," p. 74.

Lifestyle and Personality

The demographic characteristics described in Chapter 9 are the surface descriptors of consumers. They answer the *who* of consumer behavior, but not necessarily the *why.* Two higher-income baby boomers living in urban areas may not buy the same brands or have similar possessions. Lifestyle and personality characteristics may provide us with the reasons why. **Lifestyles** are consumers' modes of living as reflected in their attitudes, interests, and opinions. **Personality** is defined as patterns of individual behavior that are consistent and enduring. Lifestyle and personality variables are known as **psychographic characteristics** because they are psychologically oriented variables that can be quantified.

In this chapter, we first discuss consumer lifestyles, because they are more directly applicable to marketing strategies than personality. We describe the lifestyle trends that are changing the face of marketing today and the measurement of lifestyle variables. We then examine the strategic applications of lifestyle variables. Personality variables are considered next, despite their limited applications, because they are especially relevant when deep-seated purchasing motives are involved. Various personality theories that have been used to understand consumer behavior are described.

When researchers first began to study consumer behavior, they turned to existing personality theories to explain motivations. First among these theories was Freud's psychoanalytic approach, which stresses subconscious drives. However, theories designed to explain childhood conflicts, adult neuroses, and social disorders are unlikely to explain consumer behavior. Researchers turned to lifestyle variables as factors that more closely reflect consumers' day-to-day interests and, therefore, are more likely to explain consumer purchases.

ConAgra's Healthy Choice Encounters Conflicting Lifestyles

Marketers have viewed the lifestyle trends of the last ten years with particular interest because these trends have affected every facet of marketing strategy. ConAgra, for instance, introduced its hugely successful Healthy Choice frozen food line because of lifestyle research that found increasing concern among consumers with salt and cholesterol in foods. The idea for Healthy Choice came from ConAgra's CEO, Charles Harper. For most of his 57 years, Harper had not given a second thought to smoking two packs of cigarettes a day, routinely drinking fifteen cups of coffee, or eating an artery-hardening diet of beef and fudge. However, that all changed in 1987, when Harper was felled by a massive heart attack and had to curb his diet.

While recuperating at home, Harper invited a company executive to a lunch of freshly made chili. Watching his guest rave about the healthy meal his wife had cooked, Harper realized that there had to be millions of men out there just like him, all desperate for tasty foods that suited their diets.[1] Subsequent research proved Harper's thesis. The only problem was that most consumers rejected the idea of low-salt, low-cholesterol dinners as being tasteless and associated them with "sick people's food."

Agreeing that a tasty product and a strong name would be needed to combat these impressions, ConAgra began a program that eventually resulted in a method of reducing fat and salt in frozen foods while retaining the taste. In 1989 a fourteen-item line was rolled out under the name Healthy Choice, backed by ads that evoked family values (a grandfather with his kids under the tag line "Listen to Your Heart"). Healthy Choice caught on like wildfire, capturing a quarter of the frozen foods market. By 1995, Healthy Choice was a three-hundred-item product line representing $1.3 billion in sales.[2] And it was an early entrant on the Web, establishing a site offering health management programs that track food intake and exercise and the opportunity to exchange email messages with a registered dietician.

But by 1995, Healthy Choice's sales started to slip because it began to encounter a countervailing lifestyle, the trend to self-indulgence. Although Healthy Choice was better than most low-fat foods on taste, it was not good enough to satisfy the emerging desire for the good things in life, including taste. Referring to ConAgra's declining sales, one industry analyst said:

> While consumers never wanted to compromise taste, the importance of taste has increased significantly to the point where [consumers] are not willing at all to compromise taste or nutrition.[3]

ConAgra was slow to recognize the need for better-tasting products to satisfy this lifestyle trend, but by 1998, it began to adapt. Its first move was to reformulate its frozen dinners and entrees with improved taste, using contemporary ingredients and bold flavors. It launched this reformulation with a $20 million ad campaign themed "feel good food." In 2000, it reformulated its cheese and ice cream lines to improve taste by adding a little more fat without compromising nutritional benefits[4] (see Exhibit 10.1). And in 2001 it introduced extensions of its Healthy Soup line by emphasizing ingredients to enhance flavor such as more clams and herbs in its clam chowder.[5]

ConAgra was first successful with Healthy Choice by targeting it to an important lifestyle trend. It then adapted Healthy Choice to respond to a subsequent lifestyle trend. ConAgra's continued success will depend on its ability to stay attuned to the lifestyles of the marketplace.

EXHIBIT 10.1

Healthy Choice repositions itself to a more self-indulgent segment.

Visuals Unlimited.

The Nature of Lifestyles

Lifestyle variables are defined by how people spend their time (activities), what they consider important in their environment (interests), and what they think of themselves and the world around them (opinions). Some activities, interests, and opinions that define lifestyles are listed in the following table:

Activities	Interests	Opinions
Work	Family	Personal relations
Hobbies	Home	Social issues
Social events	Job	Politics
Vacation	Community	Business
Entertainment	Recreation	Economics
Club membership	Fashion	Education

Lifestyle factors are relevant to marketers on two levels. First, broad lifestyle trends such as changing male/female purchasing roles have altered the habits, tastes, and purchasing behavior of American consumers. Second, lifestyles can be applied on a product-specific basis. For example, ConAgra might develop an inventory of activities, interests, and opinions specifically designed to identify the health-oriented consumer to better understand the needs of this group.

In the following sections, we consider various approaches to measuring lifestyle characteristics and the broad lifestyle trends that are changing American consumers today.

Measuring Lifestyle Characteristics

The previous section described lifestyles in general terms. But lifestyle characteristics specific to certain consumers and product categories must be defined and measured if they are to be useful to marketers. For instance, it would be relevant for a food company to identify a dieter segment or a clothing company to identify a fashion-conscious segment. The researcher must define such lifestyle characteristics, in contrast to demographics, because there are no fixed definitions such as age, income, or occupation. As a result, marketers must devise methods to measure lifestyles.

AIO INVENTORIES

The most common method for measuring lifestyles is to develop an inventory of activities, interests, and opinions (an **AIO inventory**). Marketers develop such inventories by formulating a large number of questions regarding consumer activities, interests, and opinions and then selecting a smaller number of questions that best define consumer segments.

Table 10.1 shows an AIO inventory with eleven lifestyle categories. These categories were based on three hundred AIO statements with which a sample of consumers was asked to agree or disagree on a six-point scale.[6] Typical statements were "I like to be considered a leader" and "I usually keep my home very neat and clean."

TABLE 10.1

Sample lifestyle categories based on perceived activities, interests, and opinions

Price-conscious	Compulsive housekeeper
I shop a lot for specials. I find myself checking the prices in the grocery store even for small items. I watch the advertisements for announcements of sales. A person can save a lot of money by shopping for bargains.	I don't like to see children's toys lying about. I usually keep my house very neat and clean. I am uncomfortable when my house is not completely clean. Our days seem to follow a definite routine such as eating meals at a regular time, etc.
Fashion-conscious	**Self-confident**
I usually have one or more outfits of the very latest style. When I must choose between the two I usually dress for fashion, not comfort. An important part of my life and activities is dressing smartly. I often try the latest hairdo styles when they change.	I think I have more self-confidence than most people. I am more independent than most people. I have a lot of personal ability. I like to be considered a leader.
Homebody	**Self-designated opinion leader**
I prefer a quiet evening at home over a party. I like parties with lots of music and talk. (Reverse scored) I would rather go to a sporting event than a dance. I am a homebody.	My friends or neighbors often come to me for advice. I sometimes influence what my friends buy. People come to me more often than I go to them for information about brands.
Community-minded	**Information seeker**
I am an active member of more than one service organization. I do volunteer work for a hospital or service organization on a fairly regular basis. I like to work on community projects. I have personally worked in a political campaign or for a candidate or an issue.	I often seek the advice of friends on which brand to buy. I spend a lot of time asking friends about products and brands.
	Dieter
Child-oriented	I drink low-calorie soft drinks several times a week. I buy more low-calorie foods than the average housewife. I have used Metrecal or other diet foods at least one meal a day.
When my children are ill in bed, I drop most everything else to see to their comfort. My children are the most important things in my life. I try to arrange my home for my children's convenience. I take a lot of time and effort to teach my children good habits.	**Financial optimist**
	I will probably have more money to spend next year than I have now. Five years from now, the family income will probably be a lot higher than it is now.

Source: Adapted from William D. Wells and Douglas J. Tigert, "Activities, Interests and Opinions," *Journal of Advertising Research* 11 (August 1971), p. 35. Reprinted by permission of the Advertising Research Foundation.

These statements were then reduced to the eleven lifestyle dimensions in Table 10.1 by a statistical technique known as **factor analysis,** a method for grouping items that are highly correlated. The factor analysis showed, for example, that consumers who agreed with the statement "I shop a lot for specials" also tended to agree with the statements "I find myself checking prices," "I watch advertisements for sales," and "A person can save a lot by shopping for bargains." People who agreed with these statements were classified as price-conscious consumers. By using responses to the three hundred statements, consumers can be described as price-conscious, fashion-conscious, child-oriented, and so on.

These lifestyle dimensions can be used in the same manner as demographics to describe and segment consumers. One study using these dimensions found that users of eye makeup tended to agree with the items defining fashion consciousness, whereas nonusers did not. The heavy user of shortening liked housekeeping, was more child oriented, and was more of a homebody than was the nonuser.

We must recognize that lifestyles are constantly changing. The financial optimist and the compulsive housekeeper segments in Table 10.1 are smaller today than when these categories were developed, and the price-conscious segment is larger. Furthermore, new lifestyle trends develop. For example, any AIO inventory developed today would identify a health-conscious segment, an environmentally aware segment, and a techno-savvy segment.

CONSUMER SURVEYS

Another approach to measuring lifestyles is to conduct consumer surveys to identify consumer activities, interests, and opinions, and then to develop lifestyle categories on this basis.

▌ **Value and Lifestyle Survey (VALS)**   The Value and Lifestyle Survey (VALS), which the Stanford Research Institute (SRI) developed in 1978, reflects a survey-based approach. VALS conducts yearly surveys of twenty-five hundred consumers and has identified groups such as actualizers, strivers, and strugglers based on common lifestyles and values. For example, actualizers have a high level of self-esteem, are open to change, and buy the finer things in life. They are good targets for laptop computers, adult education courses, or the latest in sound systems. They can best be targeted through upscale magazines rather than television. Such lifestyle profiles help marketers target products to specific consumer groups. That helps explain why the VALS system is the most widely used method of assessing cultural and lifestyle values. More than 150 companies subscribe to its findings on a yearly basis.

The VALS Segments.   The VALS system (known as VALS 2 because it is a revision of an earlier lifestyle grouping, VALS 1) identifies eight groups, as shown in Figure 10.1. The groups are split on two dimensions. The vertical dimension represents consumers' resources—not only money, but also education, self-confidence, and energy level. Actualizers have the most resources; strugglers, the least. The horizontal dimension represents three different ways consumers see the world. Principle-oriented consumers are guided by their views of how the world is or should be and are represented as either fulfilleds or believers. Status-oriented consumers (achievers and strivers) are guided by others' opinions. Action-oriented consumers (experiencers and makers) are motivated by a desire for activity, variety, and risk taking. Of the two groups in each sector, one has abundant resources and one minimal resources.

Application of VALS to Marketing Strategy.   The most direct applications of lifestyles to marketing strategies have been through the use of the VALS groups in

FIGURE 10.1

The VALS 2 consumer segments.

Source: "Markets with Attitudes," *American Demographics* (July 1994), p. 25.

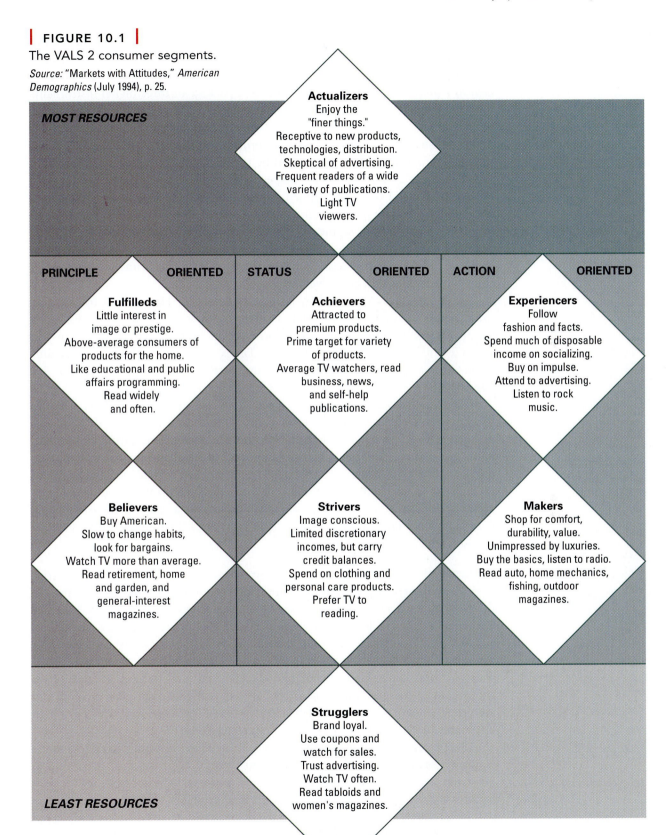

MOST RESOURCES

Actualizers
Enjoy the "finer things."
Receptive to new products, technologies, distribution.
Skeptical of advertising.
Frequent readers of a wide variety of publications.
Light TV viewers.

PRINCIPLE   ORIENTED   **STATUS   ORIENTED**   **ACTION   ORIENTED**

Fulfilleds
Little interest in image or prestige.
Above-average consumers of products for the home.
Like educational and public affairs programming.
Read widely and often.

Achievers
Attracted to premium products.
Prime target for variety of products.
Average TV watchers, read business, news, and self-help publications.

Experiencers
Follow fashion and facts.
Spend much of disposable income on socializing.
Buy on impulse.
Attend to advertising.
Listen to rock music.

Believers
Buy American.
Slow to change habits, look for bargains.
Watch TV more than average.
Read retirement, home and garden, and general-interest magazines.

Strivers
Image conscious.
Limited discretionary incomes, but carry credit balances.
Spend on clothing and personal care products.
Prefer TV to reading.

Makers
Shop for comfort, durability, value.
Unimpressed by luxuries.
Buy the basics, listen to radio.
Read auto, home mechanics, fishing, outdoor magazines.

Strugglers
Brand loyal.
Use coupons and watch for sales.
Trust advertising.
Watch TV often.
Read tabloids and women's magazines.

LEAST RESOURCES

Figure 10.1. Marketers have used VALS to develop market segmentation, media, and advertising strategies.

A good example of the application of lifestyles is Timex's use of VALS 2 data to *identify segments* for a new line of products, a package of three digital instruments for home use (a weight scale, a thermometer, and a blood pressure monitor) under the name Healthcheck. The company believed that consumer attitudes toward health maintenance and home diagnostic products were likely to be value based and that demographic segmentation would be insufficient. Timex subscribed to VALS and ranked the VALS groups by the degree to which they used high-tech and health-related products. Two target segments were identified for Healthcheck: achievers and fulfilleds. Despite the fact that one group was status oriented and the other was principle oriented, both segments showed a concern with health and were better educated than other groups. This identification of the primary target segments drove all subsequent marketing strategy for the Healthcheck line, particularly as regards media selection and advertising.

Timex used the VALS typology in *media selection* for Healthcheck by targeting the achievers and fulfilleds. VALS data showed that these two segments do not watch much TV. As a result, Timex used print advertising. When these groups do watch TV, it is generally news programs. Timex scheduled its introductory campaign during early and late news programs, with no prime-time or daytime TV advertising.

The basic *advertising theme* Timex used to promote Healthcheck was "Technology—where it does the most good." Models in the ads gave off "the self-satisfied vibes achievers can relate to."[7] Clothing had to appear natural looking and be in muted tones to appeal to the fulfilleds, but "statusy enough" to appeal to achievers. Models also were featured outside, often riding bicycles, playing tennis, or doing a similar activity. Both the ads and the package provided information to appeal to the factual needs of the two target groups. As a result of these strategies, the Healthcheck line moved to the top spot in its market within four months of its introduction.

Forrester's Technographic Segments   Forrester Research has contributed to lifestyle segmentation by applying consumer activities and interests to the Web. Forrester's model is based on two dimensions as shown in Figure 10.2. The horizontal axis is divided into primary motivations—family, career, entertainment, and status. The vertical axis reflects attitudes toward technology (optimistic or pessimistic) and disposable income. The segments include career-focused "hand-shakers," who have high disposable income and are technology pessimists; entertainment-focused "mouse potatoes," who have higher disposable incomes and are proponents of technology; and status-oriented "cyber-snobs," who have high disposable income and are optimistic about technology.[8]

These categories can help marketers when they have a specific need to address consumer segments about technology-related products or services. According to Forrester, "fast forwards" and "techno-strivers" make rational connections between features and benefits when buying technological products, and they are prime targets for products that can link features to superior performance—for example, cell phones with computer connections.

FIGURE 10.2

Forrester's Technographic segments.

		Family	Career	Entertainment	Status
TECHNOLOGY OPTIMISTS	**High disposible income**	Neo heartminders	Fast forwards	Mouse potatoes	Cyber-snobs
	Low disposible income	Neo heartminders	Techno strivers	Gadget grabbers	X-techs
TECHNOLOGY PESSIMISTS	**High disposible income**	Traditionalists	Handshakers	Media junkies	Country clubbers
	Low disposible income	Sidelined citizens			

Changing Lifestyle Trends of American and Global Consumers

Changes in the lifestyles of American consumers are due partially to changes in their demographic characteristics and partially to changes in their values. Seven broad changes in lifestyles have occurred in the last ten years:

1. Changes in male/female purchasing roles
2. Evolving view of health and nutrition
3. Increasingly home-oriented lifestyles
4. Greater time pressures
5. Growing consumer self-awareness
6. A more frugal and value-oriented lifestyle
7. Larger role of the Internet in affecting lifestyles

CHANGES IN MALE PURCHASING ROLES

The 2000 census showed an increase in the number of women working outside the home and in single-parent households, which has meant a shift away from the traditional roles of a working male and a stay-at-home female. The change in the male's purchasing role is most apparent in increased responsibilities for shopping and childcare and in more involvement with cooking and housecleaning—all traditional female roles. The trend became evident in the early 1990s, with one survey finding that 35 percent of men buy all the food for their homes, about 30 percent buy all the cleaning supplies and housewares, and about 67 percent buy all their own personal items.[9] When they do shop, men do not act that differently from women. They tend to spend the same amount of time preplanning purchases, checking prices, and redeeming coupons.

In particular, men are taking an increasing role in parenting. A University of Maryland study found that fathers reported spending an average of 4 hours a day with their children in 2000, compared to 2.7 hours in 1965.[10] Internet sites such as babycenter.com's "Dad Zone" are devoted to fathering. In June 2000, *dad* magazine was launched as "the lifestyle magazine for today's father," with an initial circulation of two hundred thousand.[11] Contributing to this trend is the growing number of fathers who are single parents, a role that prescribes shopping and household chores by necessity. By 2000, 8 percent of all fathers were in this category.[12]

The changing male role is not a function of demographics only. It is also a result of changes in male values. Increasingly, males do not feel the need to conform to a "macho" image. Research has shown that some males are more willing to buy products that at one time might have been dismissed as too feminine—jewelry, skin care products, moisturizers, and cosmetics. In 1999, L'Oreal started marketing a line of hair color (Feria) to younger, image-conscious men and planned to expand its appeal to men with other hair and skin care products.[13] By 2000, *Advertising Age* magazine was pointing to greater competition in the workplace and dress-down casual Fridays as other contributing factors to changing male sensitivities.[14]

In marketing these products, advertisers have had to depict males in a way that is very different from the traditional strong, masculine image of the Marlboro Cowboy or in the typical beer commercial. A new concept of masculinity has emerged—the sensitive male who is as vulnerable in many ways as his female counterpart, a target identified as SNAGS (Sensitive New Age Guys). An ad for Lauder Pleasures for Men is a good example. The nurturing image of a father rolling on the ground with his son and a puppy conveys the message that this cologne is "for the best times in life," which are now more oriented to spending time with family than with a career or other individual pursuits.

The net result of the greater involvement of men in shopping and housekeeping activities and their willingness to shed a traditional male image has led consumer researchers to note a merger of male and female purchasing roles (see Exhibit 10.2). Today, it is as shortsighted for a marketer conducting a survey of paper towels, disposable diapers, or frozen foods to restrict the sample to the "woman of the house" as it is for a marketer of financial services or automobiles to restrict the sample to the "man of the house."

CHANGES IN FEMALE PURCHASING ROLES

Today's woman has greater affluence, independence, and self-confidence than in the past, creating a substantial change in women's purchasing roles. As women's purchasing power has increased, they have flexed more muscle in just about every product category, leaving almost no enclave a male preserve anymore. As we saw in Chapter 9, women are responsible for 46 percent of car sales. They are also more likely to be the chief financial officer of the family. A 1999 survey by SRI found that "women managed financial affairs in 40 percent of the homes surveyed, while men were responsible for financial decisions in 33 percent of homes."[15]

Women's increasing independence suggests a desire for an identity beyond a traditional homemaking role. With over 60 percent of wives working full-time, most women combine job and homemaking throughout their lives. As a result, women no longer identify with ads that tell them how to clean their floors to please

EXHIBIT 10.2

The traditional male image has shifted.

Don and Pat Valenti/Stone/Getty Images.

their husbands. The problem is creating ads they do identify with. The advertising industry does not have an illustrious track record in this regard. Reviewing the portrayal of women in the last thirty years, the National Advertising Review Board found that until the late 1970s, women were typically depicted as "stupid [and] too dumb to cope with familiar everyday chores unless instructed by children or a man." In the early 1980s, many advertisers went to the other extreme, creating a "superwoman" model, which one ad executive described derisively as

> . . . that disgustingly perfect specimen who serves her family a bountiful, hot breakfast, dashes off to run a corporation all day, and then glides in at 6 P.M. to create a lavish gourmet meal while at the same time changing diapers, leading Cub Scouts, and carrying on stimulating conversation with her husband.[16]

In the 1990s, campaigns targeting women were more likely to identify with their professionalism and reinforce their self-esteem. For example, Avon abandoned its old-fashioned image with appeals to contemporary women such as "After all, you have more on your mind than what's on your lips. And Avon thinks that's beautiful."[17] By 2000, this focus began to be extended abroad. A Nike campaign for the Taiwanese market with the tag line "My No. 5" shows a woman glistening with sweat in Nike workout gear. It is aimed at active, assertive women who define themselves less by alluring evening attire, complete with a spritz of Chanel No. 5, than they do by their personal achievement.

A GLOBAL PERSPECTIVE ON MALE/FEMALE ROLES

Male and female roles differ greatly among cultures. The relative equality between the sexes in North America and Western Europe is the exception, globally. Most cultures are male-dominant. One extreme example is the Taliban's imposition of a very restrictive culture in Afghanistan, in which women were prohibited from working and were required to be covered from head to foot when seen in public. In Japan, wives are expected to stay home and care for children, and they traditionally walk two steps behind their husbands. In Latin America, women are frequently portrayed as sex objects or blonde goddesses in ads and the media. Hispanic communities in the United States are traditionally bound by a more macho-oriented culture.

In some parts of Asia, however, the tide is beginning to shift. More women are joining their Western counterparts and are attempting to juggle the dual lives of career women as well as attentive mothers. The cultural view of the traditional lifestyle is not easy to break down. Many Asian husbands have yet to embrace the role of many Western men of assisting in household duties and childcare. The perception is often that women are secondary or supplementary wage earners and not that they are involved in self-affirming careers.[18] As one women executive in Singapore said, "You're damned by pro-family lobbyists if you eschew marriage and children to climb the corporate ladder, and you're damned by your peers for not maximizing your potential if you exchange your power suit for infant formula-stained happy coats."[19]

The ad for Bijan perfumes in Exhibit 10.3 appeared in the Spanish edition of *Vogue* magazine and portrays the many conflicting cultural roles of women. The first picture shows a woman in Islamic garb with the copy that women should be quiet, composed, obedient, modest, submissive, and very, very serious. The second shows a woman as more of a sex object and says women should be sophisticated,

EXHIBIT 10.3

Portraying women's roles in different cultures.

Bijan Fragrances; Art Director, Cynthia Miller.

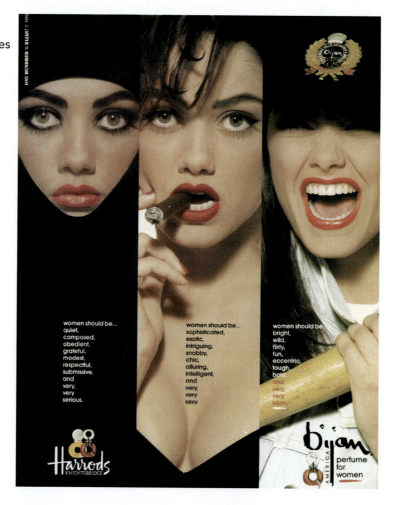

exotic, mysterious, chic, seductive, and very, very sexy. The third pictures a more independent and liberated woman and says women should be bright, wild, fun, tough, bold, and very, very Bijan. The perfume obviously wants to be associated with this last image of the more independent woman.

STRATEGIC APPLICATIONS

OF CONSUMER BEHAVIOR

Can Anheuser-Busch Build Bridges to Women?

Since they began advertising on television, beer companies have used provocatively clad women to titillate their male customers, with the two leading beer companies, Miller and Anheuser-Busch, being frequent participants. So when Stroh's Brewery decided to sell its Old Milwaukee beer by showing a giggling band of blond bombshells called the Swedish Bikini Team parachuting into a campsite of sex-starved men, no one at the company figured it would cause a ripple. However, in December 1991, Stroh's female employees filed a suit against the beer maker claiming the ads were degrading and encouraged sexual harassment.

The Stroh's controversy forced the entire beer industry into a state of reexamination. Though women buy 35 percent of all domestic beer and 45 percent of light beer, few companies have seen a need to talk directly to them. By the time Stroh's pushed the envelope too far, women had become used to macho beer advertising. As a result, they either bought brands *in spite* of their advertising or chose unadvertised selections.

In an attempt to turn that liability into an asset, Anheuser-Busch tried building new bridges. In 1991 it shot ads for Bud Dry from a woman's point of view. They featured five different nightmare date scenarios—including a nerd who talks about his mother's meatloaf and a grating yuppie who keeps interrupting conversation to talk on his cellular phone. The spoofs adopted a gender-oriented slant and used humor to diffuse old hostilities.

More recently, in an award-winning 2000 ad for Bud Light, Anheuser targeted its low-cal beer directly to women by appealing to a personal situation that many women face, that of having to wear an awful bridesmaid dress. In the ad, the consolation is that there is an open bar after the

wedding, where presumably the bridesmaid can forget the dress by downing a few Bud Lights.

But Anheuser seems to be developing a split personality regarding its attitudes toward women. When it comes to its flagship brand, primarily targeted to men, Anheuser appears to be returning to ads that portray women as sex objects. In one commercial, a woman in a tight, sheer top saunters into a barroom, turning heads in slow motion. Anheuser's main competitor, Miller Brewing, has followed suit, running ads with scantily clad women. In a recent Miller commercial, several men sit at an empty bar on a rainy night and rub their eyes in boredom. While the men have their eyes closed, two scantily dressed women walk in to dry off and leave before the men notice.

Over ten years after the lawsuit against Stroh's for the Swedish Bikini Team ads, why are so many beer companies using sex-laden ads to attract male beer drinkers? Apparently, beer companies believe that when targeting a male market, they still have to portray women as sex objects. As one marketing consultant explains, "For a while, it was dogs, cats and penguins [in beer advertisements]. Now they're reverting back to sex sells. It's an attention grabber." Maybe, when it came to learning the lessons from the Stroh experience, Anheuser-Busch really didn't get it.

Sources: "Sex Appeal Slipping Back into Beer Ads: 'Risqu' TV Leads to More Liberal Promotions," *USA Today* (March 15, 2000), p. 20B; "It's Miller Time Again in Brewer's New Ads," *Wall Street Journal* (March 6, 2000), p. B10; "Bud Light Aims to Knock Beer Sector into Shape," *Marketing* (February 25, 1999), p. 17; "It's Again True: This Bud and Babe Are for You," *Advertising Age* (October 31, 1994), p. 3; "Michelob Ads Feature Women—And They're Not Wearing Bikinis," *Marketing News* (March 2, 1992), p. 2; "This Bud's for You. No, Not You—Her," *Business Week* (November 4, 1991), p. 86; and "A-B Cranks up Michelob Ads, Accents Light," *Advertising Age* (July 17, 2000), p. 4.

EVOLVING ATTITUDES TOWARD HEALTH AND NUTRITION

Research shows that American consumers are among the most devoted in the world to maintaining their health and fitness, as reflected in the initial success of ConAgra's Healthy Choice line. But in the mid-1990s, awareness and concern regarding health and fitness began to level off.

▌ The Health- and Fitness-Conscious American Consumer

American consumers are highly aware of the effects of dietary habits on health, as well as the effects of cholesterol and salt levels, caffeine content, and food additives. At least one-half of the U.S. adult population is trying to lose weight at any given time.

This awareness has been translated into a change in consumer purchasing patterns. Estimates indicate that almost half of the adult population takes vitamin supplements and over one-third of adults use low-calorie foods and beverages. Consumption of certain products has also decreased. Per capita consumption of cigarettes, liquor, and coffee has steadily decreased since 1980. Consumers have been switching from red meats to poultry because of cholesterol concerns, and their purchase of some dairy products has declined, with a switch to low-fat products such as skim milk and yogurt.

As a result of these concerns, there is hardly a food company that does not have at least one line of diet or nutritionally oriented products. Companies that repositioned existing products to health-conscious consumers have posted strong profits. For example, Tums saw its sales grow by 50 percent when it repositioned itself as a calcium supplement targeted to women concerned about bone disease later in life, even though calcium was always part of the product. Bertolli successfully repositioned its olive oil as a means of avoiding saturated oils with the tag line "Eat well, live long, and be happy."

Health concerns have translated into more involvement with fitness-related activities. Although some Americans are not as obsessive about working out to achieve the perfect, sculpted body, by 2000 some marketers noted a cultural shift wherein fitness is no longer viewed as a niche activity but is now part of a broader lifestyle.[20] Companies are creating "mini-fusion workout centers" to make exercising more accessible. People like the opportunity to work out in places they have to go anyway, such as airports, laundromats, and even supermarkets. For example, in 2000 Kroger started putting Cardio Express centers in some of its Georgia supermarkets.[21] Food and beverage companies are positioning products to appeal to this ethic. The ad for V8 in Exhibit 10.4 touts the health benefits of the juice (fights free radicals)

EXHIBIT 10.4

Appealing to fitness.

Campbell Soup Company; Agency, Young and Rubicam.

while juxtaposing it with boxing gloves—a stand-in for fitness as it has become a more recognized part of a consumer's lifestyle, even if he or she does not make it to the gym every day.

▌A More Self-Indulgent Lifestyle

A countertrend to the dominant health and fitness orientation of American society is a more self-indulgent lifestyle. In particular, the diet crazes that characterized the last twenty years have begun to fade. A marketing study in 2000 noted that the high-pressure lives of many consumers have led them to look to snacks as more of a reward that offers taste gratification.[22] They may still be concerned about their overall health, but when they indulge, consumers want the real thing—the taste, mouth feel, and flavor of high-fat products. A more self-indulgent attitude has also carried over to fitness. A study by the Centers for Disease Control and Prevention found that in 2001, only 25 percent of the U.S. population was getting enough exercise.[23]

As a result of these trends, marketers are positioning fewer products to the health segment. Companies introducing light versions of their products have not always fared well. Frito-Lay, for example, reported disappointing results after introducing light versions of Cheetos and Doritos.

Consumers also rejected products with P&G's fat-free Olestra. Some contend that P&G missed the shift from diet-based concerns to more of a focus on taste in the late 1990s; that is, a shift from utilitarian to more hedonic motives.[24] These trends suggest that Americans are more willing to accept the bodies they have and resent advertisers who make them feel anxious about it.

This greater self-indulgence seems to be a worldwide trend. A 2000 Worldwatch Institute study found that obesity is an increasing health problem among richer nations. "The number of those overfed and overweight around the world has climbed to 1.1 billion, rivaling the number of those who are underweight and under-nourished."[25] The Institute found that 61 percent of adults in the United States are overweight; 54 percent in Russia; 51 percent in the United Kingdom; and 50 percent in Germany.

A MORE HOME-ORIENTED LIFESTYLE

Consumers are spending more time at home for at least two reasons—leisure and working at home.

Today, research shows that consumers are more likely to stay at home for leisure and entertainment than they were in the past. One marketing survey found that 25 percent of American households have a home theater and 37 percent have a thirty-plus-inch TV screen.[26] The stay-at-home trend is particularly apparent for baby boomers and Generation Xers. As baby boomers have aged, they have become more traditional stay-at-home types. They are more likely to embrace homespun values and peace of mind as they enter middle age. Some have referred to this trend as "cocooning."[27] Generation Xers are also staying at home more, but for different reasons. They are more likely to be economically strapped and simply cannot afford to go out. Further, many stay home as a form of escapism by eating comfort foods and watching TV and home videos, thereby avoiding issues such as pollution and AIDS. The September 11, 2001, terrorist attacks reinforced this trend. Many consumers felt safe staying at home among friends and relatives rather than traveling or going to entertainment events.

A second dimension of a more home-oriented consumer is the greater opportunities for working at home spawned by the information revolution, making it easy for home-based entrepreneurs to operate as if they worked in a corporate office. All that is needed is a fax machine, a copier, and a personal computer.

According to the 2000 census, about 9 percent of the work force is self-employed.[28] The fastest-growing group in the segment are 50-something white males with managerial and administrative experience—the prime victims of the corporate layoffs due to the recession that began in 2000. These highly educated, white-collar executives often find that their skills no longer fetch the price they once did. They find their best course is to become independent operators, even though they are likely to earn less than they did in the corporate world. This is a prime reason why most of the new businesses started at home tend to involve consulting, graphic design, computer maintenance, and personnel. These areas have suffered from corporate downsizing, but at the same time require minimal start-up capital.

Not all home-based workers are self-employed, however. Many companies now allow their employees to work from home via computer hookups to save time and to free employees from nonproductive office distractions. Baxter Health Care, American Express, Apple Computer, IBM, Sears, and JCPenney are just a few of the firms with work-at-home policies. This trend is not isolated to the United States. The United Kingdom's Institute for Employment Studies estimates that in 2000, 7 percent of the Canadian and Swedish work force worked from home at least part of the week, which compares to 6 percent in the United States and 5.5 percent in the United Kingdom.[29] The biggest problem with telecommuting and working from home is that "human beings are social animals" with a "need to be in touch with others: the need to communicate and feel involved with [the] head office."[30] So, although technology is making it increasingly simpler to work from remote locations, the social fabric of working in an office is not under immediate attack.

Marketers have responded to this trend by trying to serve the rapidly expanding niche of home-based workers. Computer software designers such as Lotus and Borland are leading the way with programs that enable individuals to create elaborate graphics packages and presentations. However, they are by no means alone. Apple, IBM, Canon, Fujitsu, and other companies are all appealing to the home-based entrepreneur, all through personalized versions of office machines.

GREATER TIME PRESSURES

Time pressures in American society have been increasing in the last thirty years. Americans are twice as likely to say they have less free time than they said ten years ago. The primary reason is increased stress levels, as the American consumer's life has been getting more frenzied. The problem is compounded by the fact that the Americans who are doing the best materially are spending more hours at work and fewer with their families. A study by the Council of Economic Advisers estimated that by 2000, parents had twenty-two hours less a week to spend with their children than they did thirty years before.[31] This problem does not seem to be as serious in Europe, where there are more restrictions placed on the number of hours an employee can work.

An ad for Eddie Bauer tries to capture the desire on the part of many American consumers to "Stop the world; I want to get off." It shows a photo of a man skipping a stone across a lake, accompanied by the words, "Deep inside each of us is someone striving to do absolutely nothing." In 2000, a study by the National Leisure Travel Monitor concluded that time poverty in U.S. travel planning meant that "In many households the time available to take a vacation has become a more important consideration than the actual cost when planning a vacation."[32] Consequently, marketers have focused more on the rejuvenating and relaxing aspects of a getaway, rather than the low cost.

The most direct effect of greater time pressures is the increasing emphasis consumers are placing on timesaving conveniences. As a result, some marketers have concluded that "time has come to rival money in importance to many consumers. The focus on timesaving convenience has created two trends in consumption—grazing and refueling.

"Grazing" is the need to eat on the run. People eat breakfast in the car on the way to work, munch on a sandwich while walking, or eat lunch at their desks. This trend, also known as "multitasking,"[33] is the result of the demise of sit-down breakfasts and lunches in most households. The need for quick food has led many marketers to repackage their products into food bars to suit grazers' dietary needs. The advent of snack bars, energy bars, nutrition bars, breakfast bars, and diet bars led to an increase in products in this category from 25 in 1990 to 426 in 2000.[34] "Refueling" refers to less time spent in preparing and eating dinner. Because of this trend, ConAgra introduced Healthy Choice Bowl Creations in 1999, a line of meals targeted to time-pressed consumers "because they are easily carried, have bite-size pieces that require one utensil for eating, and don't involve messy cleanup at the office."[35]

Service-oriented organizations have also launched offerings that acknowledge the crunch for time. For example, many U.S. and European banks have recognized that time is becoming more valuable and have launched online banking services.[36] The Web has become a vehicle to reduce time poverty for many consumers. Search engines and infomediaries help consumers make sense of the bewildering array of choices available. Services that have expanded online to help ease time poverty include car purchasing (autobytel.com, autoweb.com), travel arrangements (travelocity.com, expedia.com), and financial services (schwab.com, csfbdirect.com, e*trade.com).

GROWING CONSUMER SELF-AWARENESS

The last decade has seen an increase in the demand for products and services that offer a sense of personal achievement, such as sports equipment, home electronics, and educational products. Two prerequisites for a more self-aware lifestyle are the money required to pursue self-satisfying activities and the time to do so. However, time pressures conflict with a desire for a more self-aware lifestyle. One resolution to this conflict is an increasing emphasis on activities that can be mastered easily, provide high rewards in a short time period, and can be accomplished at or near home—namely, activities such as surfing the Web, exercising, or simply reading.

Another trend that has developed is that age 50+ adults are not ready to ease into quiet hobbies. The aging baby boomers in the United States and in Western Europe are into self-development and creativity and want to engage in diverse and varied social lives. One British study projects that by 2010 many baby boomers over 60 will be pursuing an actively hedonistic lifestyle.[37] Marketers will have to evaluate the messages they send to this group to reinforce their desire for accomplishment and self-actualization.

Consumers have also been able to take charge of how they plan and lead their lives through the use of technology. On a global basis, consumers find information on the Web more quickly and connect with communities of other consumers with similar interests. As the number of Internet users worldwide increases, Web communities increase in size, contributing to a more interconnected and knowledgeable consumer.

A MORE FRUGAL AND VALUE-ORIENTED LIFESTYLE

The recession of 1990–1991 and the one that began in 2000 created a marked trend toward frugality among consumers. Among the signs are fewer expenditures on luxury items, renewed demands for quality, and the loosening of brand loyalties. The market for luxury products has suffered because consumers now frame their lives in terms of survival and security instead of success and acquisition. As one researcher observed:

> People today are more concerned about money, less concerned about 'having it all.' Needs are more basic—less luxury, less concern with the trendy [and] less faith in their ability to fulfill the American dream.[38]

A desire for quality has gone hand in hand with the trend toward economy, creating a *value orientation.* Consumers may be buying less expensive products, but they are seeking the same level of quality. This value orientation has resulted in a loosening of brand loyalties and an increase in the purchase of private label and lower-priced brands. Shoppers are more secure with themselves and no longer need to impress others with expensive purchases. They are more interested in quality merchandise at bargain prices than they are in brand names.

Consumers are using the Internet in their search for value. With shopping BOTS, it has become easier to compare prices and other metrics across products in order to find the best value available.[39]

THE ROLE OF THE INTERNET IN AFFECTING LIFESTYLES

Internet access is changing consumers' lifestyles because of the amount of time spent on the Web. A UCLA survey of two thousand households conducted in 2001 found that Internet users watched 12.3 hours of TV a week compared with 16.8 hours for non-Internet users. Internet users also spent significantly fewer hours reading books, magazines, and newspapers.[40] Clearly, the Internet is competing with more traditional pastimes, and winning.

The Internet is not only changing lifestyles because of the time devoted to it, it is also changing lifestyles because of involvement with the medium. Many consumers are beginning to view the Internet as a lifestyle. Chapter 7 noted that heavy web users often surf the Web for entertainment and enjoyment (hedonic surfers) and, in so doing, achieve a "flow state." Flow is described as a "psychological state of high involvement, skill and playfulness . . ." that "happens during network navigation. When you are completely focused on the activity at hand and your skills are perfectly attuned to the challenges of the online environment, there is a loss of consciousness about what's happening in the external world."[41]

At the extreme, such involvement can become compulsive, as when the video game player or day trader begins to devote more time to these activities than to family or friends. "Life becomes a continuous stream organized around the Internet."[42] A more typical and healthier scenario is a consumer who may be highly involved with Internet surfing but integrates it as part of a lifestyle with other interests and activities.

Personality

An individual's personality represents another set of characteristics that contributes to an understanding of consumer behavior. These personality characteristics can be valuable guides to marketers. For example, knowing that users of a brand of headache remedies are more likely to be compulsive led one company to advertise the product in an orderly setting that described a fixed routine. Another company found that an important segment of users of artificial sweeteners tended to be compliant and to accept guidance from others, especially medical experts, in an attempt to lose weight. This finding suggested advertising these products through an authority figure.

Marketers have used four personality theories to describe consumers: (1) psychoanalytic theory, (2) social-cultural theory, (3) self-concept theory, and (4) trait theory. These four theories vary greatly in their approach to personality measurement. The psychoanalytic and social-cultural theories take a qualitative approach to evaluating personality variables; trait theory is the most empirical; and self-concept theory is somewhere in between qualitative and quantitative in its orientation.

Extensions of psychoanalytic theory have been widely used in marketing in developing qualitative insights into why consumers buy. Insights from psychoanalytic theory are particularly relevant when purchase motives are deep-seated. Such motivational research derives from both psychoanalytic concepts related to the resolution of childhood conflicts and from psychoanalytic techniques that rely on depth interviews. Self-concept theory is also relevant for marketers because it focuses on how an individual's self-image affects his or her purchasing behavior. It recognizes that what we buy and own is a reflection of who we are.

Psychoanalytic theory is described first because it underlies much of the framework for other personality theories, particularly social-cultural theories of consumer behavior and self-concept theory.

PSYCHOANALYTIC THEORY

Freud's **psychoanalytic theory** stresses the unconscious nature of personality as a result of childhood conflicts. These conflicts are derived from three components of personality: id, ego, and superego. The **id** (or the **libido**) controls the individual's most basic needs and urges such as hunger, sex, and self-preservation. The source of all innate forces that drive behavior, the id operates on one principle—directing behavior to achieve pleasure and to avoid pain. The id is entirely unconscious, with no anchor in objective reality. A newborn baby's behavior, for example, is governed totally by the id.

The **ego** is the individual's self-concept and is the manifestation of objective reality as it develops in interaction with the external world. As manager of the id, the ego seeks to attain the goals of the id in a socially acceptable manner. For example, rather than manifest a basic need to be aggressive in antisocial ways, an individual may partially satisfy this need by buying a powerful sports car.

The **superego** is the leash on the id and works against its impulses. It does not manage the id but restrains it by punishing unacceptable behavior through the creation of guilt. Like the id, it operates in the unconscious and often represses behavior that would otherwise occur based on the id. The superego represents the ideal rather than the real. It motivates us to act in a moral way.

According to Freud, the ego manages the conflicting demands of the id and the superego. The way the child manages these conflicts (particularly sexual conflicts) determines the adult personality. Conflicts that are not resolved in childhood result in **defense mechanisms** (strategies that the ego uses to reduce tension) and frequently influence later behavior in a manner that the adult is unaware of.

■ **Motivational Research**   Psychologists applying Freud's theories to marketing believe the id and superego operate to create unconscious motives for purchasing certain products. Although these motives are extremely hard to determine, they might be central to explaining certain purchasing behaviors. Because the focus is on developing the means to uncover these unconscious motives, applications of psychoanalytic theory to marketing are known as **motivational research.**

Motivational researchers believe that deep-seated purchasing motives can best be determined through indirect methods by researching a small number of consumers. Two techniques derived from psychoanalytic theory and applied to marketing—depth interviews and projective techniques—have been used frequently in marketing studies.

Depth Interviews.   **Depth interviews** are interviews with individual consumers designed to determine deep-seated or repressed motives that structured questions cannot elicit.[43] Consumers are encouraged to talk freely in an unstructured interview, and their responses are interpreted carefully to reveal motives and potential purchase inhibitions. An offshoot of the depth interview is the **focus-group interview,** in which eight to twelve consumers are brought together under the direction of a moderator to discuss issues that may reveal deep-seated needs or unconscious motives. The advantages of focus groups are that they are likely to stimulate discussion because of the group context, and they may elicit thoughts and motives that individual depth interviews do not.

The foremost proponent of depth and focus-group interviews was Ernest Dichter, acknowledged as the father of motivational research. A Freudian psychologist by training, Dichter came to the United States in the late 1930s and began applying psychoanalytic theory to advertising. One of his first applications was for Procter & Gamble in 1940. The company asked Dichter if there was some way to revitalize Ivory soap. Based on depth interviews with teenagers, he found that they considered bathing as almost a ritual, especially before a date. It was a means of "getting rid of all your bad feelings, your sins, your immorality, and cleansing yourself."[44] On this basis, Dichter developed the slogan "Be smart, get a fresh start with Ivory Soap . . . wash all your troubles away." Dichter used depth and focus-group interviews in numerous studies that have provided actionable findings; for example:

▌ Consumers want a sense of freedom and power when they get behind the wheel of a car. They look for that surge of acceleration to free themselves of the mundane aspects of everyday life. If you want to advertise gasoline, go along with this feeling and advertise the "tiger in your tank" (see Exhibit 10.5).

▌ Men resist giving blood because they equate it with a loss of potency. The Red Cross would be smart to advertise to potential donors that they are lending rather than giving their blood, because blood is regenerated in a short period of time.

▌ Candy consumption is a source of guilt because of childhood associations with reward and punishment. Any attempt to market candy to adults should emphasize the fact that they deserve the rewards associated with candy consumption.

| EXHIBIT 10.5 |

An appeal based on motivational research.

Exxon Mobil Corporation.

Projective Techniques.   **Projective techniques** compose the second set of methods derived from psychoanalytic theory and applied to marketing. Like depth interviews, these techniques are designed to determine motives that are difficult to express or identify. Because consumers may not be aware of their motives for buying, researchers cannot ask direct questions consumers may not be able to answer. Instead, consumers are given a situation, a cartoon, or a set of words and asked to respond. They project their feelings and concerns about products to this less threatening or less involving situation.

Projective techniques ask consumers to complete sentences (Someone who buys Brand X is . . .), to complete bubbles in cartoons (husband changing a diaper with a bubble over his head to designate what he is saying), or to personify brands or products with human or animal traits. In each case, the consumer is projecting his or her feelings regarding a product or situation without being asked a direct question. In one application of personification, when consumers were asked to imagine long-distance carriers as animals, many described AT&T as a lion, MCI as a snake, and Sprint as a puma. Sprint's ad agency used this insight to position its service as the one that could "help you do more business" rather than taking the savings-oriented approach of the other carriers.[45]

▌ **Criticisms of Motivational Research**   Motivational research has been criticized for relying primarily on the researcher's qualitative judgments without any hard data. Some have also questioned whether advertising could or should influence deep-seated motives. The psychoanalytic approach may be "touchy, feely," but motivational researchers were the first to argue that consumers are "complex, devious, difficult to understand and driven by mighty forces of which they are unaware."[46] In this respect, motivational research has made a significant contribution in understanding behavioral drives for more complex and involving products.

SOCIAL-CULTURAL THEORIES

A number of Freud's disciples shifted from his view of personality in two respects. First, they thought that social and cultural variables, rather than biological drives, are more important in personality development. Second, Freud's understanding of personality focused primarily on observations of emotionally disturbed people. His disciples subsequently believed that insights into personality development should also rely on observations of people who function normally in the social environment.

Carl Jung and Alfred Adler, the foremost students of Freud, took the psychoanalytic approach in separate directions. Jung believed that one's culture created an accumulation of shared memories from the past—nurturing female, heroic warrior, old wise man. Jung called these commonly shared memories **archetypes.** Jung's archetypes are sometimes depicted in ads that attempt to capitalize on the positive shared meanings in our culture. For example, one advertiser equates Betty Crocker with the Great Mother of ancient myth, and the Bud Man as the hero in the Homeric tradition.[47]

Alfred Adler was the foremost proponent of a social orientation. Rather than focus on the importance of sexual conflicts, as did Freud, or culturally shared meanings, as did Jung, Adler emphasized the individual's striving for superiority in a

GLOBAL APPLICATIONS

Why Do U.S. Consumers Want Their Cheese to Be Dead?

Clotaire Rapaille is a French-trained cultural anthropologist who decided to apply his talents to motivational research and became the most successful practitioner since Ernst Dichter. Rapaille has gone several steps beyond Dichter, however, in searching for the recesses of the consumer's mind that will reveal purchase motives.

Consider the work he did for a large French food manufacturer to determine how Americans viewed cheese. Rather than gather consumers together for a series of depth interviews, Rapaille follows a three-step process. He first takes a group of about twenty people through a series of word-associations, in this case related to cheese. He then asks his respondents to create childlike stories based on the associations they have with the words. In the final step, he asks his subjects to lie on the floor while droning massage music plays in the background for twenty minutes. As respondents approach a sleeplike state he asks them to recall their earliest memories. He then asks them to write down their memories. When he sees repetitive patterns in the stories, he knows he has found basic motivational associations. Consider what he found out about cheese in his own words:

In France, the code for cheese is "alive." It is young, mature or old. You smell it to tell the age. When you go to America, cheese is "dead." The first impression in America is that smell doesn't matter. Cheese is put in the refrigerator. In France, never. You would not put a cat in the refrigerator because it is alive. But in America, you put cheese in plastic like a body bag. It is legally dead.

The French company selling the cheese had a French commercial showing a woman smelling the cheese, opening it, poking it, touching the Camembert. You could see fingerprints on it. A love affair. Americans saw this commercial in a test and thought it was disgusting. Americans want safety. They want their cheese dead.

The obvious conclusion was that the French company could not advertise cheese in the same emotional context it used in France. Cheese advertising in the United States would have to be hygienically correct.

In another application of his methods, Rapaille persuaded the Timber Association of California to change its name because "timber" reminded people of the logger's cry resulting in the death of trees. One of the Association's ads showed a man carrying a sapling (a baby) by the branches (the hair) and planted it by stomping it with his boots. The ad was replaced by a Rapaille creation—a woman cradling a burlap diaper of a sapling, planting it with her hands, watering it, and promising to return.

If Rapaille's methods seem remote, consider his corporate roster of clients—AT&T, P&G, General Mills, Ford, and Seagram. Ernst Dichter's methods are alive and well in a new form, and many companies have a fuller understanding of their consumers as a result.

Source: "Does the Smell of Coffee Brewing Remind You of Your Mother?" *New York Times Magazine* (May 7, 2000), pp. 71–74. Reprinted with permission.

---

social context. He stressed that children develop feelings of inferiority, and their primary goal as adults is to overcome these feelings.

Karen Horney was another social theorist. She believed that personality is developed as an individual learns to cope with basic anxieties stemming from parent–child relationships. She hypothesized three approaches to coping with this anxiety: *compliance*, a strategy of moving toward people; *aggressiveness*, moving against people; and *detachment*, moving away from people.

In one study relying on **social-cultural theories** of personality to explain purchase behavior, Joel Cohen developed a compliance-aggressiveness-detachment (CAD) scale based on Horney's work.[48] Cohen measured CAD using a thirty-five-item inventory. In applying the CAD scale, Cohen found that compliant types used more mouthwash, toilet soaps, and Bayer aspirin; aggressive types used more cologne and after-shave lotion and bought Old Spice deodorant and Van Heusen shirts; and detached types drank more tea and less beer. These findings suggest advertising the use of mouthwash or toilet soap as a means of social approval, advertising colognes and after-shaves as a means of social conquest, and advertising tea as a means to enjoy life in a traditional and subdued context.

Measures such as Cohen's CAD scale are important because they were constructed for marketing applications and have a theoretical base in personality theory. In such cases, the researcher begins a study with defined hypotheses of which personality variables to measure.

SELF-CONCEPT THEORY

Self-concept (or **self-image**) **theory** holds that individuals have a concept of self based on who they think they are (the **actual self**) and a concept of who they think they would like to be (the **ideal self**). Self-concept theory is related to two key concepts of psychoanalytic theory, the ego and the superego. Since the ego is a reflection of one's objective reality, it is similar to the actual self. The superego is defined by the way things should be and is therefore a reflection of the ideal self. To determine one's self-concept, consumers are asked to describe how they see themselves (actual) or how they would like to see themselves (ideal) on various attributes such as the following:

Happy	Serious
Dependable	Self-controlled
Modern	Successful
Practical	Sensitive
Energetic	Aggressive

Self-concept theory is governed by two principles: the desire to attain self-consistency and the desire to enhance one's self-esteem. Attaining self-consistency means that individuals act in accordance with their concept of actual self. For example, a consumer may see himself as a practical and self-controlled individual. He buys conservative suits, drives a large four-door sedan, and spends quiet evenings at home. Deep down, however, he would like to be more carefree and reckless. If he were to act more like his ideal self, he might own a small sports car, dress in jeans and sportshirts, and go to rock clubs.

■ **Actual Self**   There is no one actual self. Consumers have various "role identities"—wife, mother, working woman, volunteer for AIDS organizations. One of these roles is dominant in specific situations; the particular role affects the style of dress and behavior of the individual. The amalgam of the individual's roles makes up the actual self.

Applied to marketing, the concept of "actual self" says that the image consumers have of themselves influences their purchases. They attain self-consistency by buying products they perceive as similar to their self-concept. That is, there is congruence between brand image and self-image.

Several studies have confirmed that consumers buy products related to their self-concept. Dolich studied this relationship for beer, cigarettes, bar soap, and toothpaste.[49] He found that respondents tend to prefer brands they rate as similar to themselves. Several studies have shown the same relationship for automobiles.[50] An owner's perception of his or her car is consistent with self-perception. Furthermore, the consumer's self-image is similar to his or her image of others with the same automobile.

▌ Ideal Self   The concept of the "ideal self" relates to one's self-esteem. The greater the difference between the actual self and ideal self, the lower an individual's self-esteem. In a marketing context, dissatisfaction with oneself could influence purchases, particularly for products that could enhance self-esteem. Thus, a woman who would like to be more efficient, modern, and imaginative may buy a different type of perfume or deodorant or tend to shop at different stores than a woman who would like to be more warm and attractive.

Richins found that advertising themes and images often increase the discrepancy between the real and ideal selves.[51] Advertising that portrays beautiful models or luxurious lifestyles creates an idealized world that is unreachable. As a result, consumers are left with a sense of inadequacy based on a comparison of their real self with these idealized images. For example, the average female fashion model is five feet nine inches and weighs 123 pounds; the average U.S. woman, on the other hand, is five feet four inches and weighs 144 pounds.[52] In acting to increase the disparity between the real and ideal selves, advertising tends to lower consumers' self-esteem.

The desire for both self-consistency and self-esteem could be conflicting. Consumers who buy in accordance with their actual self-concept may be achieving consistency but may not be enhancing self-esteem. Generally, consumers buy products that conform to their actual self-image. But if they are lower in self-esteem (*i.e.*, if there is greater disparity between the actual and ideal selves), they are more likely to buy based on what they would like to be rather than on what they are. As a result, these consumers are more likely to be swayed by appeals to fantasy that portray an idealized self—the alluring woman, the lone biker on his Harley-Davidson, the well-dressed man who attracts women's attention.

Buying to achieve an unrealizable self-image can lead to compulsive purchasing behavior. Frequent purchasing is a means to overcome the discrepancy between the real and ideal selves and to relieve a sense of low self-esteem.[53]

▌ Consumption and the Extended Self   Another dimension of self-concept theory is applicable to consumers. Not only does our self-image influence the products we choose, but also the products we choose frequently influence our self-image. Certain products have symbolic (badge) value. They say something about us and the way we feel about ourselves. For example, when we buy a certain suit or dress, we may anticipate that it will enhance our self-esteem.

On this basis, there is an **extended self** as distinct from the actual self. The extended self incorporates some of our more important possessions into our self-concept, because what we own reflects our personality. In simple terms, we are what we wear, and we are what we use. As Belk notes, "People seek, express, confirm, and ascertain a sense of being through what they have."[54] Belk cites various occasions when it is apparent that possessions are an extension of self. Consider the following statements:

- (A college student whose bike was stolen): "It hurts to think that someone else is selling something that for me is more precious than money."

- (By an elderly consumer pawning possessions to make ends meet): "I stand in that hock shop, and I tell myself that my entire life is being sold."[55]

- (By Saul Bellow after his treasured car was vandalized): "I felt a . . . rip at my heart. . . . I had allowed the car to become an extension of my own self."

Research based on the concept of extended self examines the constellation of products a consumer owns and tries to equate these groups of products to the consumer's self-concept. This type of research is very different from looking at a single product and determining if it is related to a consumer's actual or ideal self-concept. It seeks to understand the symbolic role that groups of products play in shaping the consumer's self-concept.

Marketers have understood the symbolic role of product constellations in projecting an image. Advertising for jewelry might show fashionably dressed models or expensive automobiles, and ads for clothing might show jewelry. The increasing importance of cobranding also reflects an acceptance of the concept of product constellations. Many marketers are finding other products to link up with in joint advertising and promotional efforts. These products must be seen as complementary by consumers. In the car market, for example, the Lincoln Town Car offers a version fitted out by Cartier jewelers; Chrysler's Jeep Grand Cherokee links up with Orvis, the marketer of outdoor gear for fishing and hunting; and VW offers a Trek bike and bike rack to link itself with a rugged, fun lifestyle.[56] In each case, the two products blend together in projecting a consistent image.

TRAIT THEORY

Trait theory states that personality is composed of a set of traits that describe general response predispositions. Trait theorists construct personality inventories and ask respondents to respond to many items, perhaps agreeing or disagreeing with certain statements or expressing likes or dislikes for certain situations or types of people. These items then are statistically analyzed and reduced to a few personality dimensions. This method does not predetermine personality traits and is unlike psychoanalytic and social theories, which have specific hypotheses about the traits that affect behavior (*e.g.*, compulsiveness, aggressiveness, and detachment in Horney's theory).

A number of studies have used personality traits to segment markets. A study of smoking behavior found that heavy smokers scored higher on heterosexuality, aggression, and achievement and lower on order and compliance (all personality traits in standard personality inventories).[57] Heavy smokers are more likely to be oriented toward power and competitiveness and may be more influenced by sexual themes and symbols. They are not as compulsive or submissive as nonsmokers.

Because of this emphasis on power and competitiveness, it is not surprising that one of the most successful cigarette campaigns has been the Marlboro Cowboy.

Personality measures specifically developed for consumer behavior applications, rather than generalized inventories, have more strategic marketing applications. For example, Gottlieb hypothesized that compulsive and punitive consumers would be more frequent users of antacids.[58] Compulsiveness and punitiveness were measured by agreement or disagreement with a set of predetermined statements such as "I like to set up a schedule for my activities and then stick to it" (compulsiveness) and "Discipline is the single most important factor in building children's character" (punitiveness). As expected, high compulsives tended to consume more antacids; but punitive respondents actually consumed less. Because of these results, the advertising for the brand under study emphasized a specific routine and regimen to appeal to the compulsive segment. The results also suggested that it was not necessary to make antacids taste bad to appeal to the punitive segment, as was originally thought.

Limitations of Personality Variables

Consumer behavior researchers have seen drawbacks in using personality characteristics to explain purchasing behavior. Personality theories are meant to describe enduring patterns of behavior. Quite often, the focus is on aberrant, rather than typical, behavior. To apply measures developed for these purposes to consumer behavior assumes that consumers are motivated to buy based on deep-seated drives. As we have seen, however, most consumer behavior is a mundane, day-to-day affair. Kassarjian summarized the limitations of personality measures:

> Instruments originally intended to measure gross personality characteristics such as sociability, emotional stability, introversion, or neuroticism have been used to make predictions of the chosen brand of toothpaste or cigarettes. The variables that lead to the assassination of a president, confinement in a mental hospital, or suicide may not be identical to those that lead to the purchase of a washing machine, a pair of shoes, or chewing gum. Clearly, if unequivocal results are to emerge, consumer behavior researchers must develop their own definitions and design their own instruments to measure the personality variables that go into the purchase decision.[59]

The limited capability of personality theories to explain more mundane, day-to-day consumer behavior led researchers to look elsewhere for an understanding of such behavior. The investigation of consumer lifestyles was largely motivated by these limitations of personality variables.

SUMMARY

Two consumer characteristics of importance to marketers are lifestyle and personality. Lifestyles are the activities, interests, and opinions of an individual that define day-to-day living. Personality characteristics, which are enduring and deep-seated, reflect consistent patterns of response developed since childhood. Lifestyle and personality characteristics make up a richer set of descriptors than do demographics because they represent the psychological makeup of consumers.

Marketers have used lifestyle characteristics in studies by developing inventories to measure consumers' activities, interests, and opinions. Another approach is to conduct consumer surveys to determine lifestyles. The most widely used consumer lifestyle survey—the Value and Lifestyle Survey (VALS)—identifies eight lifestyle segments based on their values and economic resources.

Marketers use VALS as well as Forrester's Technographics to identify market segments, develop advertising strategies, and provide guidelines for media selection.

The chapter examined the following important changes in lifestyles in American society in the last decade:

- Changes in male/female purchasing roles
- Evolving view of health and nutrition
- Increasingly home-oriented lifestyles
- Growing consumer self-awareness
- Greater time pressures
- A more frugal and value-oriented lifestyle
- An emerging Internet lifestyle

Personality variables are more difficult to use in marketing because they are not as closely related to brand usage as are lifestyles and demographics. Because marketers continually use personality variables, several personality theories were reviewed:

- Psychoanalytic theory stresses the unconscious nature of consumer motives as determined in childhood by the conflicting demands of the id and the superego. Marketers have applied psychoanalytic theory by using depth and focus-group interviews and projective techniques to uncover deep-seated purchasing motives. These applications are known as motivational research.

- Social-cultural theory emphasizes environmental variables in personality development. It goes beyond psychoanalytic theory in examining conscious, goal-directed behavior and considering individuals who function normally in a social environment.

- Self-concept theory suggests that individuals have an actual self-image based on who they think they are and an ideal self-image based on who they would like to be. Marketers have applied this theory in the belief that a congruence may exist between consumers' self-image and their image of the brand. An extension of this theory realizes that the symbolic properties of groups of products and brands can influence people's self-image based on the assumption that we are what we use.

- Trait theory seeks to measure personality traits by the development of personality inventories. Trait theory is the most widely applied of the personality theories in marketing because specific personality variables can be measured and related to consumer usage.

In Chapter 11, we shift our focus from the individual to society as a whole by considering how culture influences consumers.

QUESTIONS FOR DISCUSSION

1. What are the marketing implications in using any of the lifestyle groups cited in Table 10.1 for describing users (or prospective users) of the following?
   - A new detergent that advertises that it makes washing easier
   - Personal care appliances such as curling irons or facial care appliances
   - A new magazine designed to provide up-to-date marketing and financial information to the working woman
   - A new breakfast cereal for the diet-conscious and active adult

2. Based on Figure 10.1, which VALS group or groups might be the best targets in marketing the following?
   - Ecologically oriented products
   - Weight-lifting equipment
   - A new family-oriented magazine

3. What are the marketing implications of a merger of male and female purchasing roles?

4. An ad for a leading detergent manufacturer depicts a woman using the product and being praised by her husband for getting his clothes clean.
   - What are the potential problems with this positioning?
   - What alternative positionings might you suggest to reflect the changing role of women in today's society?

5. An executive for a food company has said, "There has been some talk around here about repositioning some of our existing products to promote health and nutritional benefits. I see companies promoting beans as having fiber and tuna packed in spring water. I am against such repositionings because consumers are just going to see them as a ploy to get on the nutritional bandwagon. It is much better to introduce new products for health and nutritional benefits than to reposition existing products." Do you agree with the executive's position? Why or why not?

6. What evidence is there that concerns about health and fitness leveled off in the 1990s?

7. What is the relationship between the information revolution and a more isolate American consumer? What are the marketing implications of this link?

8. American consumers are feeling more time pressures despite the fact that they have more leisure time than in the past. What are the marketing implications of this trend?

9. Define "grazing" and "refueling." How are these trends reflected in consumers' behavior? What are the marketing implications of each trend?

10. In what ways is the Web a vehicle to alleviate the problems of consumers with time poverty?

11. What are the marketing implications of a more value-oriented lifestyle?

12. Because it deals with deep-seated needs and motives derived from childhood conflicts, psychoanalytic theory has been criticized for having little relevance to marketing.
    - Do you agree?
    - For what types of product categories might psychoanalytic theory provide insights into consumer purchasing motives?

13. How have marketers used depth interviews and projective techniques to better understand consumer behavior? Provide specific examples of marketing applications.

14. A working woman sees herself as efficient, competitive, and achievement-oriented. Ideally, she would like to combine these traits with greater warmth and understanding.
    - How would her behavior differ if she governed her purchases based on her actual self-image versus her ideal self-image?
    - Under what circumstances might she be more likely to buy based on her ideal self rather than on her actual self?

15. What is meant by the extended self?

RESEARCH ASSIGNMENTS

1 Visit the following web sites: *www.carsmart.com* and *www.womanmotorist.com.*

- Should there be a separate web site for women for the purchase of a new car?
- The womanmotorist web site is sponsored by carsmart. Why does the company need two web sites?
- How does the "women's interest" section on the carsmart site differ from the "womansmotorist" site's approach?

2 Select a sample of teenagers and Generation Xers. Ask consumers in each group to rate the importance to them of a wide variety of products (life insurance, automobiles, jeans, banking services, do-it-yourself products, phosphate-free detergents, cameras, deodorants, cereal, etc.). Ask respondents for their (a) demographic characteristics, (b) view of their economic future, (c) political preferences, and (d) level of price consciousness (see Table 10.1).

- What are the similarities and differences between the two age groups on the variables you measured? Explain these similarities and differences.

- Can you identify a more and a less price-conscious group in each age segment? Are these differences related to demographics? To economic outlook?

3 Using lifestyle criteria, you would like to distinguish users of natural food products (granola, wheat germ, yogurt, etc.) from nonusers. You plan to use lifestyles to position a new line of natural food products and to develop guidelines for advertising.

a. Conduct a number of depth interviews with users of natural foods. On this basis, develop a lifestyle inventory designed to identify natural food users.

b. Submit the inventory to a sample equally divided between users and nonusers of natural foods.

- Does the lifestyle inventory discriminate between the two groups? If so, what are the distinctive lifestyle characteristics of natural food users?

- What are the implications of these lifestyle characteristics for (a) advertising and (b) new product development?

4 Select one or two U.S. and one or two non-U.S. web sites in the same general product category. Identify how they differ and compare across one or more of the following criteria:

- The change in male/female purchasing roles. Do the sites appeal to a male or female consumer, or do they try to appeal to both? Does the appeal match the existing product focus, or is the company trying to branch out to new consumers?

- Attitudes toward health and/or fitness. Does the product category make an appeal to health or fitness? Does it treat health/fitness as an assumed part of the consumer's lifestyle or is it making a stretch?

- Social versus isolate lifestyle. Does the web site promote social activity, or is it making it easier for the consumer to lead a more isolate lifestyle?

- Value-orientation. Does the site make it easy for consumers to compare prices with other sites? Is additional value added by purchasing online? Is the product supported by any offline infrastructure?

- Appeal to consumer empowerment. Does the product focus on a consumer's personal achievement?

5 Self-concept theory suggests that the disparity between a consumer's actual and ideal self-images could predict the purchase of brands or products related to the consumer's identity.

a. Select ten or fifteen adjectives like those on page 300. Submit these items to a sample of consumers and ask respondents to rate themselves on both actual and ideal selves. Ask the same respondents to identify brands they regularly purchase for products such as perfume, clothing, magazines, automobiles, or any other items that may be related to self-image.

b. Determine the disparity between actual and ideal self-images by summing across the differences for each item in the scale. Are these differences related to brand or product ownership?

NOTES

1. "How a Heart Attack Changed a Company," *New York Times* (February 26, 1993), pp. C1, C6.

2. "Healthy Choice Invades Bread Aisle," *Brandweek* (October 2, 1995), p. 6.

3. "Healthy Choice Sets Site On Adventure; Bristol's 'Beauty Central,'" *Brandweek* (November 27, 1995), p. 14.

4. "Healthy Choice Needs Help," *Advertising Age* (September 25, 2000), pp. 32–36.

5. "ConAgra Expands Healthy Choice," *Brandweek* (October 29, 2001), p. 4.

6. William D. Wells and Douglas J. Tigert, "Activities, Interests and Opinions," *Journal of Advertising Research* 11 (August 1971), pp. 27–35.

7. See Arnold Mitchell, *Changing Values and Lifestyles* (Menlo Park, CA: SRI International, 1981).

8. http://www.forrester.com/ER/research/report, as of 2001.

9. "The Brave New World of Men," *American Demographics* (January 1992), p. 40.

10. "Make Room for Daddy," *American Demographics* (June 2000), pp. 34–36.

11. Ibid.

12. Bureau of the Census, *Statistical Abstract of the United States, 2000.*

13. "L'Oreal Hopes Young Men Go for Color," *Wall Street Journal* (June 8, 1999), p. B10.

14. "Vanity, Thy Name Is . . . Man?" *Advertising Age* (April 17, 2000), p. 24.

15. "For Richer & for Poorer," *American Demographics* (July 2000), pp. 59–64.

16. *Advertising Age* (July 26, 1982), p. M13; *Advertising Age* (April 2, 1984), p. M10.

17. "Avon Products Is Abandoning Its Old-Fashioned Image in an Appeal to Contemporary Women," *New York Times* (April 27, 1993), p. D21.

18. "The Burden of Being Woman," *New Straits Times— Management Times (Malaysia)* (November 21, 2000); and "The Drudgery of Disadvantage," *New Straits Times— Management Times (Malaysia)* (September 11, 2000).

19. "Checking Out Her Options," *Business Times (Singapore)* (November 3, 2000), pp. 1, EL 2.

20. "Health and Fitness Trend Blossoms into a Way of Life," *Advertising Age* (March 13, 2000), pp. S14–S16.

21. "Crunched for Time? Workout on Aisle 3," *New York Times* (July 18, 2000), p. F8.

22. "Snack Food Resurgence Puts Kabash on Health Trend," *DSN Retailing Today* (October 2, 2000), pp. 48–50.

23. "Americans' Waistlines Have Become the Victims of Economic Progress," *New York Times* (March 22, 2001), p. C2.

24. "Olestra Sales Prove Leaner than Expected: Public No Longer as Fat Conscious," *Times-Picayune* (October 24, 1999), p. F16.

25. "Obesity a Global Threat," *Associated Press* (December 19, 2000).

26. "Drawn to the Hearth's Electronic Glow," *New York Times* (January 24, 2002), pp. G1, G7.

27. "The Future's Paying Off Nicely for a Trend Spotter," *New York Times* (June 6, 2001), p. B2.

28. Bureau of the Census, *Statistical Abstract of the United States,* 2000.

29. "Survey—The Work Life Balance: Chats Over Coffee Hard to Replace," *Financial Times* (May 8, 2000), p. 1.

30. Ibid.

31. "United States: Got the Time?" *The Economist* (June 26, 1999), pp. 32–35.

32. "Ten Trends Shaping the Future of Leisure Travel," *Hotel and Motel Management* (November 6, 2000), pp. 26–27.

33. "Snacking Today: Any Time and Anywhere," *New York Times* (July 30, 1999), pp. A1, A15.

34. "Kellogg, General Mills Battle Over Bars," *Wall Street Journal* (March 26, 2001), p. B10.

35. "New Life in the Freeze Case," *Supermarket Business* (February 1999), pp. 34–36.

36. "Banks Found Lacking in Online Advertising," *Advertising Age International* (December 14, 1998), p. 28.

37. "Fifty-Somethings of 2010 Will Be 'Active Hedonists,'" *Independent* (November 20, 2000), p. 6.

38. "The QRCA Trends Project: How Qualitative Researchers See the Consumer of the 1990s," *Marketing Review,* p. 10.

39. "Curiouser and Curiouser," *Business Line* (January 25, 2001).

40. "Survey Suggests Internet Use Affects TV-Viewing Habits," *Wall Street Journal* (November 29, 2001), p. B11.

41. "What Is This Thing Called Flow? Think Nirvana on the Web," *Los Angeles Times* (July 6, 1998), p. 3.

42. "Internet Surfing Can Cut into 'People Time,'" *UPI News* (February 16, 2000).

43. See Sidney J. Levy, "Interpreting Consumer Mythology: A Structural Approach to Consumer Behavior," *Journal of Marketing* 45 (Summer 1981), pp. 49–61.

44. Rena Bartos, "Ernest Dichter: Motive Interpreter," *Journal of Advertising Research* 26 (February/March 1986), p. 20.

45. "The Frontier of Psychographics," *American Demographics* (July 1996), pp. 38–43.

46. William D. Wells and Arthur D. Beard, "Personality Theories," in Scott Ward and Thomas S. Robertson, eds., *Consumer Behavior: Theoretical Sources* (Englewood Cliffs, N.J.: Prentice-Hall, 1973), pp. 142–199.

47. *American Demographics* (July 1996), pp. 38–43.

48. Joel B. Cohen, "An Interpersonal Orientation to the Study of Consumer Behavior," *Journal of Marketing Research* 4 (August 1967), pp. 270–278.

49. Ira J. Dolich, "Congruence Relationships Between Self-Images and Product Brands," *Journal of Marketing Research* 6 (February 1969), pp. 80–85.

50. For example, Al E. Birdwell, "Influence of Image Congruence on Consumer Choice," in *Proceedings, Winter Conference, 1964* (Chicago: American Marketing Association, 1965), pp. 290–303; and Edward L. Grubb and Gregg Hupp, "Perception of Self-Generalized Stereotypes and Brand Selection," *Journal of Marketing Research* 5 (February 1968), pp. 58–63.

51. Marsha L. Richins, "Social Comparison and the Idealized Images of Advertising," *Journal of Consumer Research* 18 (June 1991), pp. 71–83.

52. *American Demographics* (January 1993), p. 56.

53. See "Compulsive Buying: A Phenomenological Exploration," *Journal of Consumer Research,* 16 (September, 1989),
pp. 147–157; and Alice Hanley and Mari S. Wilhelm,
"Compulsive Buying: An Exploration into Self-Esteem and
Money Attitudes," *Journal of Economic Psycholog,* 13 (1992),
pp. 5–18.

54. Russell W. Belk, "Possessions and the Extended Self,"
Journal of Consumer Research 15 (September 1988), pp.
139–168, at p. 146.

55. Ibid.

56. "In a Marryin' Mood," *Brandweek* (September 2, 1996),
pp. 22–28.

57. Arthur Koponen, "Personality Characteristics of
Purchasers," *Journal of Advertising Research,*1 (September
1960), pp. 6–12.

58. Morris J. Gottleib, "Segmentation by Personality Types," in
Lynn H. Stockman, ed., *Advancing Marketing Efficiency,
Proceedings of the 1959 Conference* (Chicago: American
Marketing Association, 1960), pp. 148–158.

59. Harold H. Kassarjian, "Personality and Consumer Behavior:
A Review," *Journal of Marketing Research* 8 (November
1971), pp. 409–419.

Group and Cultural Influences

CHAPTER 11

Cultural Values

T he broadest environmental factor affecting consumer behavior is "culture," as reflected by the values and norms society emphasizes. Culture affects purchasing behavior because it mirrors the values consumers learn from society—values such as individuality, independence, achievement, and self-fulfillment. As historian Daniel Boorstin said, Americans affiliate themselves less by their political or religious beliefs than by what they consume. As a result, the purchases and possessions of consumers are a reflection of culture.

In this chapter, we consider

▋ the nature and characteristics of cultural values.

▋ how cultural values are identified.

▋ how cultural influences manifest themselves through products in the form of symbols, myths, and ritual.

▋ recent changes in cultural values.

▋ societal issues relating to the effects of cultural values on consumer behavior.

Cultural values are more enduring and deep-seated than the lifestyle values described in Chapter 10. For example, describing someone as a sports enthusiast reflects a component of his or her lifestyle. A more deep-seated cultural value that might drive one's interest in sports is the desire for an exciting life or the self-fulfillment one might feel in being involved in a challenging sports activity. Because cultural values are enduring, attempts to change them have generally failed—for example, the attempt on the part of sterling silver manufacturers to revive the use of formal dinnerware in the face of a general cultural trend to informality.

McDonald's: A Strategy to Reflect Cultural Values

Marketers almost always attempt to swim with, rather than against, the cultural tide. One company that has successfully done so is McDonald's. In the 1970s, its campaign "You deserve a break today" implied the deep-seated American belief that the work ethic deserves its rewards. In the early 1980s, the company's advertising theme "McDonald's and You" reflected a shift away from the work ethic to a "me" orientation; that is, a desire to avoid self-sacrifice and to live for today. By the mid-1980s, there was a general shift to a "we" orientation as reflected in a more traditional focus on family values. McDonald's advertising shifted accordingly by moving from the focus on the individual consumer to family-oriented themes. Its campaign "It's a Good Time for the Great Taste of McDonald's" was effective in communicating food and fun in the context of family values. The creation of the Ronald McDonald character and the introduction of kiddie playgrounds in many McDonald's outlets further strengthened the family image. The success of McDonald's strategy was confirmed by a study that found that people saw the company as friendly and nurturing. In contrast, its prime rival, Burger King, was described as aggressive, masculine, and distant.[1]

The deep recession in the early 1990s produced another cultural change and a parallel shift in McDonald's strategy. Many consumers became less optimistic about the future, more insecure about the traditional American dream, and more price sensitive—a trend referred to later in the chapter as "the new reality." In 1991, McDonald's instituted a series of price cuts, introduced numerous price promotions, and emphasized value as the dominant theme in its advertising. As the economy came out of recession and economic insecurities lingered, McDonald's adopted a more nurturing theme, "Have You Had Your Break Today?". The slogan reflected a shift to more hedonic values in implying the right to a break.

Finally in the booming late 1990s, McDonald's altered its slogan yet again to "We Love to See You Smile," reflecting good times. The theme suggested that customer satisfaction is tantamount to a positive experience at the restaurant. With more competition in the market, and consumers looking for value, the intangible benefit of being happy with the experience takes McDonald's to a new level. It will be interesting to see if McDonald's alters this theme in the wake of the economic downturn that began in early 2001 and the 2001 terrorist attacks, events that have substantially altered the optimism of the late 1990s.

The one constant in these adaptations to cultural trends has been McDonald's strong focus on attracting kids to its franchise. In a mirror of the times, the company is now trying to attract preteens on the Internet. The company developed a new web site designed to "empower" kids by giving them a chance to create personalized newspaper headlines on the screen so they can develop fantasies like teaming up with Michael

| **EXHIBIT 11.1** |

McDonald's web-based global appeal to kids.

Jordan to beat the bad guys. McDonald's knows that the creation of such myths and fantasies helps kids fulfill a basic cultural value—the drive to individualism. McDonald's has also created a site for kids at *www.ronald.com* with links to 56 countries. The home page (see Exhibit 11.1) has links to "Ronald McMagic" (magic tricks), "coloring with clowns," and a fun fact quiz that offers kids a "Super Surfer Certificate."

McDonald's not only reflects American culture at home, it also exports it overseas. The golden arches have been accepted as an American icon of service and good food abroad as the fast-food craze has become global. With more than 25,000 restaurants in 119 countries, McDonald's has learned to adapt its menu to local tastes.[2] Most restaurants carry the standard burger and fries fare, perhaps spiced with curry in Asia or served with avocados in South America, but many also carry additional items that appeal specifically to locals.

Adapting to local tastes often means offering a radically different menu. The first kosher McDonald's opened in Israel, offering everything on the menu cooked according to kosher preparations. And in India, McDonald's adapted to a country with a 40 percent vegetarian population by providing vegetarian burgers that are prepared in a separate area in the kitchen using separate utensils. This diversity is recognized on McDonald's web site with separate pages for forty-one countries. Each country's page gives information on McDonald's outlets, products, and community involvement.

McDonald's has also started to recognize changing consumer tastes and preferences on a regional basis in the United States. For example, in 2000, franchisees in southern California introduced a new Fiesta Menu, featuring half a dozen Mexican-style menu items designed to appeal to the large Latino community.[3] Other regional differences include bratwurst in Minnesota, lobster sandwiches in Maine, and Quarter Pounders in Nebraska topped with mushrooms and Swiss cheese.

Culture is a set of socially acquired values that society accepts as a whole and transmits to its members through language and symbols. As a result, culture reflects a society's shared meanings and traditions. Cultural values are similar to lifestyles in reflecting a consumer's attitudes and opinions; however, they differ in being more enduring, widespread, and deep-seated. A consumer's desire to travel frequently may reflect a lifestyle, but the more basic drive to achieve a sense of freedom and independence through travel reflects cultural values typical of American society.

Culture Influences and Reflects Consumer Behavior

A culture's values are likely to influence its members' purchases and consumption patterns. For example, one consumer may place a high value on achievement and may demonstrate success with symbols of luxury and prestige. Another consumer may have a culturally derived desire to appear young and active, may buy cosmetics that advertise a "younger look," and may enroll in an exercise program. In either case, the marketer must define the consumer's value orientation and determine the symbols that reflect these values.

Culture not only influences consumer behavior, it reflects it. The preponderance of exercise machines, fitness clubs, skin care lotions, diet foods, and low-fat products reflects the emphasis American culture places on youth and fitness. Culture is therefore a mirror of both the values and possessions of its members.

CULTURE INFLUENCES AND REFLECTS MARKETING STRATEGIES

Marketing strategies rarely attempt to change cultural values because of the simple fact that advertising, sales promotions, salespeople, and packaging are not sufficiently powerful forces to influence consumers' core values. For example, no matter how much the men's hat industry advertised, it could not reverse the trend toward informality and the demise of the man's business hat. When President Kennedy went around hatless in the early 1960s, the association of hat manufacturers appealed to him and he agreed to walk around with a hat in hand, but never on his head. This did little to help the industry—it was facing an irreversible cultural trend.

Although marketing strategies are unlikely to change cultural values, when viewed in the context of the mass media, marketing does influence culture as well as culture influencing marketing. An advertising agency, a music company, a fashion design house, and a book publisher are all *producers of culture.* In total, they can be regarded as a **culture production system,** that is, the individuals and organizations responsible for creating and producing products designed to meet cultural goals.[4] The products, songs, books, and clothing that emerge from such a culture production system influence the desire to be slim, independent, beautiful, secure, or socially recognized. Thus, in a broader context, marketing and culture are interactive.

CROSS-CULTURAL AND SUBCULTURAL INFLUENCES

The increasing importance of international trade in the 1990s and 2000s makes it essential for marketers to understand the value systems of other cultures as well as their own. Such **cross-cultural influences** form the basis for marketing strategies abroad. Understanding that the greater emphasis on health and nutrition was not just an American phenomenon, Kellogg correctly saw that appeals to health could change breakfast eating habits abroad, thus increasing demand for packaged cereals. On the other hand, Gerber failed to recognize that the strong emphasis on family values in Brazil would cause many mothers to reject processed baby foods. These mothers' attitude was that only they can prepare food for their babies.

Not everyone in a particular country holds cultural values to the same degree. For example, although values of comfort and social recognition are widely held in American society, differences in these values between groups provide marketers with a basis for developing different strategies within as well as across countries. Frequently, strategies are targeted to particular **subcultures;** that is, broad groups of consumers with similar values that distinguish them from society as a whole.

Subcultures can be defined by age, region, religious affiliation, or ethnic identity. Older baby boomers might be considered a subculture because many of them experienced a shift in values from acquisitiveness to personal development. Many consumers in New England might constitute a subculture because they demonstrate traditional Yankee values of stubborn individualism. In a broad sense, African-

American, Hispanic-American, and Asian-American consumers are subcultures because they demonstrate certain similarities in tastes and purchasing behavior.

We consider subcultural influences in Chapter 12 and cross-cultural influences in Chapter 13. In this chapter, we focus on the effects of societal values on consumer behavior in a given culture.

A Definition of Cultural Values

Rokeach defined **cultural values** as beliefs that a general state of existence is personally and socially worth striving for.[5] Some cultural values Rokeach defined are shown in the first column in Table 11.1. **Value systems** are the relative importance cultures place on these values. For example, many Asian cultures might place more emphasis on "inner harmony," whereas Western cultures might put more stress on "individual accomplishment." A value such as "a world at peace" is likely to be more universally accepted across cultures.

Rokeach considered cultural values such as inner harmony or individualism as **terminal values,** or goals to be attained and developed. Rokeach also defined another category of values, **instrumental values,** which are the means of achieving

TABLE 11.1
Cultural values, consumption, specific values, and product attributes

Cultural (terminal) values	Consumption-specific (instrumental) values	Product attributes
A comfortable life	Prompt service	Service quality
An exciting life	Reliable advertising claims	Reliability
A world at peace	Responsiveness to consumer needs	Performance
Equality	Accurate information	Safety
Freedom	Elimination of pollution	Ease of use
Happiness	Free repair of defective products	Durability
National security	Convenient store locations	Economy
Pleasure	No deceptive advertising	Convenience
Salvation	Courteous and helpful salespeople	Styling
Self-respect	Low prices	
Social recognition	Solutions to urban decay and	
A world of beauty	unemployment	
Wisdom	Legislation to protect the consumer	
Family security	No product misrepresentation	
Mature love		
Accomplishment		
Inner harmony		

Sources: Cultural values from Milton J. Rokeach, "The Role of Values in Public Opinion Research," *Public Opinion Quarterly* 32 (Winter 1968), p. 554; Consumption-specific values from Donald E. Vinson, Jerome E. Scott, and Lawrence M. Lamont. "The Role of Personal Values in Marketing and Consumer Behavior," *Journal of Marketing* 41 (April 1977), p. 47.

the desired goals. A value such as "ambition" is a guidepost for action to attain a desired end state such as "accomplishment"; it is not a goal in itself. Other instrumental values might be "friendliness," "logic," and "independence."

Applying Rokeach's classification to purchasing behavior, terminal values are the ultimate purchasing goals, and instrumental values are the consumption-specific guidelines to attain these goals. We can go a step beyond consumption-specific values and also cite product attributes and benefits that can attain these values. Thus, in consumer behavior terms (1) product attributes are the means for attaining (2) consumption-specific (instrumental) values, which are the vehicle for attaining (3) cultural (terminal) values (see Table 11.1). The ad for the Columbia Sportswear jacket in Exhibit 11.2 is an example of instrumental values—warmth and protection to gain an end, namely self-preservation. The ad for the Chevy Cavalier is an example of terminal values, because it represents an end in itself—family protection.

EXHIBIT 11.2

Advertising instrumental and terminal values.

(left) Courtesy Columbia Sportswear Co.; (right) Courtesy General Motors Corporation, Chevrolet Motor Division, and Campbell-Ewald.

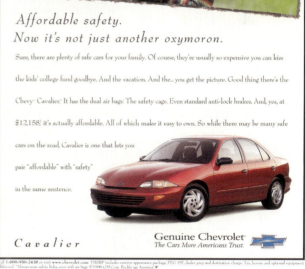

WOULD YOU LIKE TO KEEP ALL YOUR APPENDAGES?

■YES. ■NO. IF YOU ANSWERED YES, PLEASE READ ON.

There are times when frost doesn't just bite, it devours. In these situations, a Titanium Alloy Tri-Form Shell™ is the best way to make sure your body parts remain attached. Waterproof, breathable Omni-Tech™ Tri-Ply Micro-Rip™ fabric stretches in critical areas to provide increased movement and comfort while keeping the bad stuff out. A spacious fit leaves plenty of room for layering. A zip-off storm hood is there when you need it. And radial vents keep you from steaming up inside. Okay, you can stop reading now. For a dealer near you call 1-800-MA BOYLE.

Chairman Gert Boyle

Few marketing studies have utilized cultural values as descriptors of consumer behavior because most marketing studies operate on a brand-by-brand basis, whereas cultural values are more likely to influence broad purchasing patterns. But it can be argued that a better understanding of the motivation behind brand purchases can be gained by understanding culturally derived purchasing values.

Characteristics of Cultural Values

Five characteristics are common to all cultural values:

1. *Cultural values are learned.* Children are instilled with cultural values at an early age. The process of learning the values of one's own culture from childhood is known as **enculturation.** Learning the values of another culture is known as **acculturation.** Cultural learning can occur by informal learning (a foreigner copying local customs), formal learning (a child taught by family members how to behave), and technical learning (a child taught in a school environment).

   Enculturation takes place through a process of instilling values from key institutions, particularly the family, schools, and religious institutions. The family is particularly important because it is the vehicle for passing values from one generation to the next. Advertising also has a role in enculturating consumers through informal learning. The use of spokespersons (*e.g.,* Michael Jordan for Nike sneakers) encourages consumers to imitate these role models or experts and to adopt certain products or styles.

   Consumer acculturation occurs when a person from another country adapts to the consumption values and behavior of the adopted country. Such adaptation occurs by observation, by word-of-mouth communication, and through communication from the mass media. The process of acculturation is particularly important for businesspeople in foreign markets, because an understanding of the local culture is necessary before they can develop product and advertising plans.

   Hair and Anderson studied the process of acculturation among immigrants to America.[6] They found that consumers from developed countries were more quickly acculturated than were those from developing countries. One explanation is that the heritages and lifestyles of consumers from developed countries are closer to those of American consumers. In a study of Mexican immigrants, Penaloza found that their rate of consumer acculturation was rapid because they became familiar with many American products and retail establishments while still in Mexico.[7]

2. *Cultural values are guides to behavior.* Cultural values guide and direct an individual's behavior through the establishment of **cultural norms.** Such norms establish standards of behavior regarding proper social relations, means of ensuring safety, eating habits, and so forth. If behavior deviates from the cultural norm, society may place sanctions or restrictions on behavior.

3. *Cultural values are enduring.* Cultural values endure as parents pass them on to children. When values are passed on in this manner, they represent enduring

cross-generational influences. Schools and religious groups also are important in maintaining cultural values. The emphasis on values such as freedom, self-respect, and individuality has not changed substantially over time in the United States.

4. *Cultural values are dynamic.* Culture is also dynamic; values must change as society changes. Basic changes in values have taken place in American culture during the past 60 years. The Depression, wars, and economic dislocation have drastically changed traditional values such as the work ethic, materialism, and respect for authority figures.

Yankelovich's Monitor service, described in Chapter 10, found some important differences in values between the 1980s and subsequent years, largely as a result of the recession in the early 1990s and consequent concerns among younger consumers about whether they can achieve the same level of well-being as their parents.[8] The deep recession that began in 2001 and resulting dislocations are likely to reinforce these concerns. The following changes have occurred:

1980s	*1990–2002*
Belief in the American dream	A new reality
Live to work	Work to live
Be a winner	Do not be a loser
Family, religion	New alternatives
Home as a cocoon	Home as a resource center
Control the environment	Manage the environment
Control technology	Adapt to technology
Conspicuous consumption	Prudent purchasing

These important societal changes are explored later in the chapter. They are rich in their strategic implications. For example, the greater pessimism regarding the future cited in the last paragraph and embodied in the "new reality" suggests that many luxury goods may be on the decline in a more austere environment in the decade of the 2000s. Further, the change in the perspective of the home from a focus on love and nurturing to a resource center for work and entertainment is intriguing. It reflects the extension of work from office to home with the use of cellular phones, fax machines, and personal computers, as well as an increasing proportion of consumers who work at home full-time based on this flexible technology.

5. *Cultural values are widely held.* Each culture has certain widely held and commonly accepted values that differentiate it from other cultures. Individuality and youthfulness are widely shared values in the United States, whereas conformity to the group and respect for the aged are widely shared values in many Asian countries.

The sharing of values is facilitated by a common language. In multilingual countries such as Canada, India, and the Soviet Union, the lack of a single cultural bond through language has led to divisiveness. In the United States, the mass media have facilitated the sharing of cultural norms. When two out of three households with television sets view a particular program at the same time, they must share values.

Traditional American Values

Four widely held traditional values in American society are materialism, individualism, youthfulness, and a work ethic.

MATERIALISM

Materialism, a reflection of the accumulation of wealth and objects, is manifested in two ways. One is the attainment of goods to achieve a desired goal—for example, buying a new computer to increase storage capacity and speed or acquiring a cellular telephone to provide mobile communications. Using Rokeach's classification, this is known as "instrumental materialism" because the acquisition of such goods is instrumental in attaining cultural values. A second manifestation of materialism is owning items for their own sake. This is known as "terminal materialism" because the acquisition of such goods is directly motivated by cultural values rather than by some intermediate goal. Buying a piece of jewelry for its beauty and acquiring an automobile for its status rather than its functional benefits, would be examples of terminal materialism.

Research by Richins suggests that consumers who hold strong material values place their possessions at the center of their lives and value them as a means of achieving happiness.[9] These consumers view their possessions as an indicator of their own success. Such material values are likely to be dominant in the more advanced economies of North America, Europe, and Japan. Consumers who do not emphasize material values are more hedonically oriented. They are more likely to view their possessions as sources of pleasure and comfort than as symbols of status and wealth. In some societies, spiritual as opposed to material values may be emphasized, even to the extent of encouraging members to renounce worldly wealth.

INDIVIDUALISM

Themes focusing on individualism and "standing apart from the crowd" are often seen in advertising. For example, an ad for the Lincoln Navigator exhorts the consumer to "Define luxury for yourself." It is an attempt to associate the Lincoln with independence and freedom of thought.

YOUTHFULNESS

Most Americans are preoccupied with trying to look and act young, regardless of their age. As will be discussed in Chapter 12, advertising to the mature market is trying to portray older Americans as active, vital, and younger looking than their age. Advertising to baby boomers is also focused on maintaining their youth through face creams, moisturizers, exercise machines, and health clubs. Even though the fitness craze has been moderated to accommodate a more self-indulgent consumer, advertisers still extol fitness as a means to stay young.

WORK ETHIC

A work ethic has been a traditional value in American society as a means of personal achievement and attainment of material rewards. Thus, advertisers often seek to promote their products as a reward for work. McDonald's former theme, "You Deserve a Break Today," is an example.

The Yankelovich Monitor suggests that the nature of the work ethic in American society may be changing. The "live to work" orientation of the 1980s meant that people saw work as its own reward, a means of personal achievement and self-gratification. However, severe recessions in the early 1990s and 2000s promoted a skepticism that has been translated into people's viewing work as a means of acquiring the necessities of life ("work to live"), and the ability to retire in comfort. This means the ethic behind work has changed. Rather than being a terminal goal (work is rewarding), work has become an instrumental goal (work is a means of getting what I want).

But Americans are having to work harder to get what they want. The average workweek is still around 50 hours, and unlike European and Australian counterparts, U.S. workers are afforded less vacation with which to recharge their batteries.[10]

OTHER CORE VALUES

Other core values in the United States are progress, freedom, and activity. "Progress" is reflected in people's belief in technology and continued improvement in the standard of living. The Yankelovich Monitor suggests that the belief in progress might have been partially undermined by greater skepticism in the economy. The result has been a shift from conspicuous consumption and an emphasis on status in the 1980s to a current emphasis on more prudent purchasing behavior and value.

"Freedom" is another traditional American value that is reflected in people's ideals of equality and freedom of expression for all. In marketing terms, this value has been translated into an emphasis on consumer rights: the right to choose, the right to be informed, the right to be heard, and the right to safety. This emphasis on freedom was manifested in the last decade in an increasingly independent and well-informed consuming public. Consumers are more skeptical of advertising claims and more willing to look at a wider range of product alternatives than in the past.

"Physical Activity" is another traditional value, probably originating with the establishment of frontier farming communities in colonial times. This value seems to have been transformed in an urban setting into a hectic lifestyle that many societies regard as peculiar to American culture. The "grazing" phenomenon cited in Chapter 10 and the popularity of fast-food chains are means of facilitating an active lifestyle.

Cross-Cultural Values

Understanding variations in cultural values in different societies is a necessary prerequisite to successful marketing abroad. It is shortsighted for any marketer to assume that core American values are universal. In this section, we consider the meaning of core values abroad.

MATERIALISM

The obvious materialism that is so pervasive in American and, to a lesser extent, other developed countries' cultures is not found throughout the rest of the world.

In fact, much of the rest of the world is concerned that U.S. culture will be spread via the global reach of cable TV channels such as MTV, Hollywood films, and the Internet (as it is a predominantly English-language medium).[11] In some studies, researchers are finding that above a certain point, wealth does not increase happiness. For example, the inhabitants of Mexico and Brazil consider themselves to be happier than residents in some developed countries, such as the United Kingdom, Germany, France, Japan, and Italy.[12]

INDIVIDUALISM

The rest of the world does not generally share the American view of the individual's needs overriding those of the collective group. In most parts of Asia, Latin America, and the Middle East, achievement is most often acknowledged when the group benefits. These societies emphasize connectedness with others and social relationships, whereas American society emphasizes separateness and the uniqueness of the individual.[13] In Japan there is a traditional desire to subjugate individuality in favor of group and societal conformity. Such themes as "McDonald's and You" would not reflect this dominant value. But recent evidence suggests that the traditional Japanese value system is changing among the young who have a greater desire for American-made goods. For example, L.L. Bean's first retail store outside of its home base in Maine opened in Japan in 1992. Bean's outdoor look is strongly identified with American individualism, reflecting the adoption of key American values by Japanese youth.[14]

YOUTHFULNESS

The penchant for youthfulness is not universal. In Asian countries, the aged are more revered than they are in the United States. Whereas in the United States, youth dominates almost all ads, in Asian countries, the elderly are portrayed more frequently and with greater respect. An elderly spokesperson is more likely to be accepted in these countries as an expert or a role model. But here again, American values seem to be taking hold abroad. Japanese women are increasingly turning to the same products as American women to keep them looking young. For example, Dior's Svelte and Estee Lauder's Thigh Zone, both creams designed to reduce cellulite and make women's thighs look firmer and thinner, are selling at a rapid rate in Tokyo department stores and being grabbed up by Japanese tourists abroad.[15]

WORK ETHIC

Europeans in general take a different view of the separation of work and leisure than do most Americans. Whereas many corporate workers in the United States may eat at their desks, this would be considered an affront to most Europeans. Richard Miniter of the *Wall Street Journal* describes the separation as "aggressive leisure" that has come down through "an aristocratic cultural heritage." To Europeans, "it [aggressive leisure] is a sense of entitlement to pleasure for itself, as an activity with a special claim on our attention."[16] This is carried over into the common practice of Europeans enjoying far more vacation time per year than their average American counterparts.

Japan is closer to the United States in accepting a work ethic as a traditional value. Interestingly, it seems to be experiencing the same shift to a view of work as a means to an end rather than as an end in itself. One aspect of the desire for L.L. Bean clothes among younger Japanese consumers is to look more relaxed and casual as a manifestation of this trend.

Identifying Cultural Values

The changes in American values between the 1980s and 2000s demonstrate the need to identify cultural values over time. Researchers have used several methods to track cultural values; namely, (1) field studies (known as "ethnographic research"), (2) cultural value inventories such as Rokeach's classification, (3) research services such as the Yankelovich Monitor, and (4) content analysis of a society's literature and media.

ETHNOGRAPHIC STUDIES

An increasingly important method to identify consumer values is in-depth studies of small groups of consumers by researchers through "participant observation." As noted in Chapter 1, such in-depth observations are known as **ethnography,** a field borrowed from cultural anthropology. Anthropologists determine cultural values through field studies in which they live with a group or a family in a culture and observe their customs and behavior. Similarly, consumer researchers may spend months living with or observing groups of consumers in their natural environment to study their values and purchasing behavior. The purpose is to understand the role of the product in a cultural context.

A study by Belk, Sherry, and Wallendorf of the behavior of buyers and sellers at swap meets illustrates the use of ethnographic methods.[17] "Swap meets" are markets in which buyers and sellers exchange goods for other goods or for money. A swap meet is distinct from a flea market in that downscale consumers generally frequent swap meets, and barter is the more prevalent mode of exchange. The researchers used both observation and open-ended qualitative interviews to try to develop an understanding of the participants' value system and the cultural underpinnings of swap meets.

In studying one swap meet, Belk et al. concluded that freedom is an important motivation for buyers and sellers. Participants enjoy being free from the institutional constraints of buying in retail stores, yet they accept the social order inherent in swap meets such as establishing and running stalls, adhering to opening and closing times, and following certain rules such as not allowing dogs. The researchers also found that male-female roles were sharply defined, with men responsible for setting up booths and displays and women acting as clerks and salespersons. Other findings related to the mutual values participants held, the nature of bargaining, and the symbolism associated with what is bought and sold.[18]

CULTURAL INVENTORIES

Researchers develop cultural value inventories by studying a particular culture, identifying its values, and then determining whether these values are widely held. The best-known inventory is the Rokeach Value Survey. The cultural values identified by the survey are based on a study of American culture and are in the left-hand column in Table 11.1.

Kahle, Beatty, and Homer developed another widely used cultural inventory, the List of Values (LOV).[19] LOV was developed as an alternative to Rokeach's value inventory because the terminal values that Rokeach identified were too abstract and difficult to apply to marketing situations. The LOV inventory measures nine values:

1. Self-fulfillment
2. Excitement
3. Sense of accomplishment
4. Self-respect
5. Sense of belonging
6. Being well-respected
7. Security
8. Fun and enjoyment
9. Warm relationships with others

A study by Homer and Kahle, which utilized the LOV scale, found that purchasers of natural foods are more likely than others to emphasize self-fulfillment, excitement, and accomplishment.[20] These values reflect a desire to control one's life as reflected in an emphasis on health and nutrition. Consumers who emphasized belonging and security were least likely to buy natural foods because they were more likely to let others control their lives.

RESEARCH SERVICES

In an attempt to identify changes in cultural values, several research services conduct periodic surveys of consumers. VALS 2, discussed in Chapter 10, identifies values as well as lifestyles. Categories such as actualizers, achievers, and strivers not only reflect a particular lifestyle, but they also suggest the terminal values driving these groups.

For example, family security is most important to makers, social recognition to strivers, and accomplishment to achievers. These end-state values are manifested in the lifestyles described for each group in Figure 10.1.

Like VALS, the Yankelovich Monitor service (see p. 317) determines changes in values measured by a series of multiple-choice questions. The trends found in Monitor surveys have direct implications for major companies. For example, General Electric cited the greater value placed on beauty in the home and concern about the environment (two trends that Monitor identified) to produce more stylish yet energy-efficient appliances. CBS considered two other trends identified by the service—toward personal creativity and physical fitness—to justify daytime TV programming aimed at self-improvement (*e.g.,* cooking, exercise, and art programs).

CONTENT ANALYSIS

Content analysis measures cultural values as they are reflected in a culture's media and literature. Researchers employing content analysis review a culture's literature and mass communications to identify repetitive themes. In his famous study, McClellan identified the degree to which achievement motivated cultures by conducting a content analysis of the themes in children's stories.[21]

When Belk applied content analysis to investigate how materialistic values are portrayed in comic books, he found that wealthy characters were portrayed ambivalently. On the one hand, some were portrayed as selfless and honest, while others were portrayed as spendthrifts. Overall, Belk concluded that these portrayals had a positive socializing influence on children by holding the work ethic in high esteem.[22] Content analyses also have been performed to determine whether the portrayal of African Americans and females in advertising is an accurate reflection of their role in society.

Linking Cultural Values to Consumer Behavior: The Means–Ends Chain

Marketing strategies generally attempt to reflect core cultural values of American society. Several behavioral theories attempt to clarify this link between cultural values and consumer behavior.

UNDERLYING THEORIES

Gutman has described the role of cultural values in influencing consumer behavior as a **means–ends chain,** in that the means (product attributes) are the vehicle for attaining cultural values (the ends) with consumption goals as an intermediary between them (see Figure 11.1).[23] As such, product attributes are a reflection of cultural values.

This conceptualization relies on two theories. First is Rokeach's distinction between cultural (terminal) values and consumption (instrumental) goals shown in Figure 11.1. Gutman makes Rokeach's conceptualization more applicable to marketing by adding another factor, product attributes, as a means of attaining consumption goals.

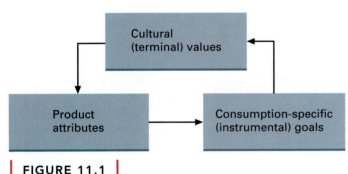

| FIGURE 11.1 |

The means–end chain.

The second theory underlying the means–end chain in Figure 11.1 is Rosenberg's expectancy-value theory.[24] Rosenberg posits that consumers evaluate products based on the degree to which they are instrumental in achieving cultural values. Consumers evaluate the projected consequences of their actions and buy products that achieve the desired consequence. Thus, a consumer who values a world of beauty (a terminal value) favors product attributes such as biodegradability because the consequence of buying a biodegradable product is to help preserve the environment. Applying Rosenberg's theory, the means–ends chain leading to the purchase of the product is:

- product attribute: biodegradability

- consumption consequence: helping to preserve the environment

- cultural (terminal) value: a world of beauty

LADDERING

Reynolds and Gutman applied the means–end chain to the development of marketing strategies through a process they called **laddering**.[25] Laddering involves a series of consumer interviews to move up the means–ends chain by determining the links among product attributes, consumption goals, and cultural values. Consumers are "helped up the ladder" through a series of probes that start with concrete product attributes and then uncover more abstract consumption goals and even more abstract cultural values. As an example, a consumer might state a preference for fruit-flavored cottage cheese. Probes show that she favors this product attribute because it makes cottage cheese more palatable, causing her to eat less fatty foods, lose weight, and look better (consumption goal). This results in greater self-esteem (a terminal value).

Marketers can then use the three components of the means–end chain in the ladder to develop marketing strategy as follows:[26]

1. *Message elements:* the specific product attributes to be communicated in advertising. In the preceding cottage cheese example, advertising would focus on flavor and taste as key elements.

2. *Consumer benefits:* the positive consumption consequences of using the product. The key requirement in the preceding example is to link the product attributes to a tastier product and the benefit of weight control.

3. *Leverage point:* the way advertising attempts to associate the attributes and benefits to the terminal values and to activate them. The executional requirement in the advertising is to show that weight loss as a result of product consumption creates greater self-esteem. This can be done by portraying self-confident and attractive consumers in the advertising or by showing greater peer-group acceptance as a result of product usage.

Once the marketer develops advertising, it is evaluated based on its ability to climb up the means–ends ladder from message element to consumer benefit to leverage point.

In the next two sections, we consider the two main cultural interfaces in Figure 11.1—the impact of culture on the product and on consumption.

The Cultural Meaning of Products

The cultural meaning of products and services is often expressed in symbolic form. As we saw in Chapter 2, consumers frequently buy products for their symbolism rather than for their utility. Marketers try to establish symbols that equate the product with positive cultural values. The McDonald's golden arches are meant to be a reflection of fun and family values; the Marlboro Cowboy is a portrayal of rugged individualism and independence; the Mercedes emblem is meant to portray status and security.

A symbol sometimes takes on a meaning of its own beyond its association with the product and comes to represent the culture. McDonald's golden arches, Levi's jeans, and the Coca-Cola logo have become global symbols of Western culture.

Before the fall of communism, youths in Eastern Europe valued Levi's jeans as a representation of Western culture and independence. Wearing Levi's was a safe way to protest against a police state.

ROLE OF PRODUCT SYMBOLISM

Tharp and Scott have identified five symbolic roles of products that reflect cultural values:[27]

1. *Products are a means of communicating social status.* As we saw in the discussion of social class in Chapter 9, products often connote a consumer's status in society. Symbols of status may be a Gucci scarf, a Mercedes car, or a Rolex watch. In the inner cities, an equally important symbol of status might be a pair of Air Jordan sneakers. Marketers try to establish their products as symbols of prestige, whether aiming at affluent business executives or inner-city kids.

2. *Products are a means of self-expression.* Products reflect the values that are most important to consumers. Marketers try to associate their products to these values. The ad in Exhibit 11.3 uses the tag line "Seek Out" to link Timberland boots to self-expressive values that would appeal to a youth market that wants to avoid the "organizational box" depicted and subscribes to values of individualism, freedom, and personal development.

3. *Products are a means of sharing experiences.* Products often provide a basis for sharing experiences. Food and drink on social occasions, flowers for happy or sad events, and gifts are all a means of sharing social events. In this respect, products have an important symbolic role, since the nature of the product defines the occasion. Serving beer or wine at a party, sending roses or carnations for a special occasion, and giving a pen or a piece of jewelry as a graduation present all have very different meanings. The ad for Freixenet, a Spanish

| EXHIBIT 11.3 |

Appealing to the desire for self-expression.

sparkling wine, in Exhibit 11.4 implies that you do not need a defined holiday to share an experience or some good news to enjoy the company's product. You can enjoy it "on any occasion."

4. *Products are hedonic.* That is, they often have aesthetic or sensual qualities that give the consumer pleasure. Examples might be jewelry, perfume, foods, clothing, furniture, and works of art. The emphasis on the hedonic as opposed to utilitarian qualities of a product reflects consumers' values. Various cultures might tend to emphasize one or the other for certain products. Harley-Davidson puts more value on the hedonic in both its ads and the design of its motorcycles. Japanese motorcycle companies tend to place more value on the utilitarian. The French fashion industry has traditionally placed more emphasis on the hedonic value of clothing, whereas American styles are more likely to emphasize the utilitarian.

5. *Products are experiential.* That is, they remind consumers of past experiences. On a personal level, an engagement ring is experiential, as is an old photo album or a record or CD that triggers memories of past events. Marketers sometimes attempt to project the experiential value of products. An ad for the Honda S2000 captures a consumer's memories of being awed by cars as a kid with the tag line "The last time you had this much fun driving a car it cost a quarter and gyrated in front of the supermarket." Honda is effectively associating its products with this positive experience.

EXHIBIT 11.4

Products as a means of sharing experiences.

Courtesy Dave Sanchez, Red Wagon Advertising & Design, and Freixenet USA.

Your boss told his boss you have boss potential.

Freixenet
BRUT
SPARKLING WINE · FERMENTED IN THIS BOTTLE · CAVA SAN SADURNI
ORDON NEGRO

Pick an Occasion. Any Occasion.
www.freixenetusa.com

SEMIOTICS

People often develop shared meanings from signs and symbols as a reflection of their cultural values. Consumer researchers have applied the field of semiotics to the study of product signs and symbols to better understand how people derive such meaning (see Chapter 6 for a description of semiotics). For example, when Lever introduced a new fabric softener with the symbol of a huggable teddy bear named Snuggle, it used semiotics to evaluate the symbolism of a bear. It found that the bear connotes aggression, but a teddy bear is seen as a softer and nurturing side of that aggression. The teddy bear is a logical symbol of tamed aggression and a good representation of a fabric softener that tames rough clothing.

Such a semiotic analysis is based on three components: a sign (the symbol of a teddy bear), an object (Snuggle), and an interpretant (the consumer interpreting the symbol).[28] These three components represent the same interface between culture and consumer behavior as in Figure 11.1. Lever's analysis showed that the symbolism of the teddy bear was *instrumental* in attaining a *terminal* value (controlling nature) through a *consumption goal* (softening rough clothes) based on Snuggle's product attributes.

Because it demonstrates the different meanings various cultures place on the same signs and symbols, semiotics is an important tool in cross-cultural analysis. For example, in American society, animals are accepted as symbols of speed (jaguar) and freedom (eagle). However, in many Asian countries, animal symbolism is rejected since animals are seen as a lower life form.

PRODUCTS AS MYTHS AND FANTASIES

Marketers sometimes establish product symbols in the form of fantasies and myths to better link the product to cultural values. **Myths** are stories or character representations in fantasy form that attempt to portray cultural values. Advertising has a role in creating and maintaining such myths. For example, McDonald's advertising has created a mythical world of food, fun, and fantasy. As one advertising executive said, "McDonald's advertising [portrays] a wondrous, magical place where everyone is welcome, safe, happy, loved, kind, sharing, caring and forever young at heart. The McDonald's that exists in the consumer's mind is a microcosm of everything America is supposed to be."[29] The golden arches are a universally recognized symbol of American culture, attracting foreign consumers as an American icon and providing a recognizable haven for American tourists.

Mythic images are also associated with imaginary characters—the Pillsbury Doughboy, who conveys a user-friendly image; Betty Crocker as the great mother image, representing the security of family and home-cooked meals; Mr. Goodwrench, the repairman General Motors once used to represent safety, security, and dependability.

Marketers also create mythologies around places. Pepperidge Farm's advertising takes us back to a time of farming communities and old-fashioned values. Similarly, advertising for Maxwell House 1892 coffee creates a mythology of a less harried time when coffee tasted better.[30]

These mythical images are not limited to U.S. marketers. The French Michelin Man is one of the top ten worldwide advertising icons. The character, known as Bibendum and inspired by the shape of a stack of Michelin tires, represents safety, dependability, and quality to consumers throughout the world.[31]

| **EXHIBIT 11.5** |

Linking a brand to story-telling on the Web.

© Abbe Don Interactive, Inc.
Visit Bubbe's Back Porch
@ http://www.bubbe.com.

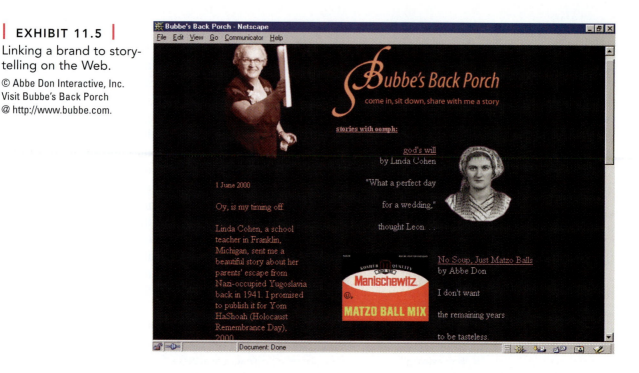

Marketers are also using the Internet to encourage consumers to communicate experiences and stories about their brands. Apple Computers and Coca-Cola do so on their web sites. An annual digital storytelling festival on the Internet (*www.dstory.com*) provides consumers with a venue for translating product experiences into myths and fantasies. One site, *www.bubbe.com,* mixes traditional stories from a Jewish grandmother with Manischewitz products (see Exhibit 11.5).

Culture and Consumption

Culture not only influences the way products are portrayed; it also influences the way they are consumed. In particular, culture is important in defining the ritualistic role of consumption for many product categories.

CONSUMPTION RITUALS

A **ritual** is a series of symbolic behaviors that occur in sequence and are repeated frequently.[32] *Grooming* is a ritual for most people, because it involves a series of behaviors (showering, brushing teeth, using deodorants, brushing hair) that occur in sequence and are repeated frequently. Marketers try to link their products to these rituals—for example, brush your teeth twice a day or shampoo frequently.

Gift-giving is also a ritual that requires a sequence of events; namely, acquiring a gift, exchanging gifts, and then evaluating the receiver's reaction. The exchange of gifts, the types of gifts exchanged, and the occasions are all fairly well prescribed in our society. Some industries rely primarily on gift giving for sales. Gift giving at Christmas alone represents close to $40 billion in sales and is a substantial portion of yearly business for most retailers.

Holidays also involve ritual behavior in addition to gift-giving rituals. Christmas rituals prescribe the consumption of special foods and drink. Holidays may additionally involve vacation rituals such as going to the same vacation spot and being involved in the same activities every year. Students also take part in rituals in *school-related social activities.* Going to a prom, joining a fraternity or sorority, moving into a dorm, and graduating all require certain patterns of behavior that occur in sequence and are predictable.

Each of these types of ritual behavior has three things in common. First, they involve **ritual artifacts,** often in the form of consumer products. Colored lights, mistletoe, wreaths, and Santa Claus representations are all artifacts associated with Christmas rituals; corsages are associated with proms; and caps and gowns are associated with graduation. Second, rituals involve a **script** that prescribes how, when, and by whom products will be used. The use of the ring, cake, and photographs at weddings is fairly well scripted by society, for example. Third, rituals require that **performance roles** be prescribed for certain individuals.[33] The roles of the bride, groom, best man, and bridesmaids are all well defined at weddings. The roles of students, faculty, deans, and parents are well defined at graduation ceremonies.

Marketers try to promote their products as artifacts in the process of ritual consumption. An ad for The Diamond Trading Company portrays a diamond ring as an artifact in a prewedding ritual, the engagement, with the tag line "How can you make two months' salary last forever?" (see Exhibit 11.6). Marketers can also portray the sequence of behaviors in rituals. An ad for Lubriderm lotion, for example, shows a brushing, cleaning, and moisturizing sequence in portraying a grooming ritual.

Rituals vary across cultures as a reflection of the predominant values of that culture. For example, gift-giving rituals in Japan emphasize the gift as a reflection of one's duty to others in one's social group; thus, gift giving is viewed as a shared moral imperative through which reciprocal obligations are fulfilled. For example, on Valentine's Day only men receive chocolates from women, whereas the women have to wait a month, until White Day on March 11, to receive candy. This ritual was divined by Japan's confectionary industry after World War II in an attempt to increase sales.[34] In the United States, gift giving is of a more personal nature. Although there is often a sense of obligation in gift giving, it is more in the context of personal rather than group obligations.

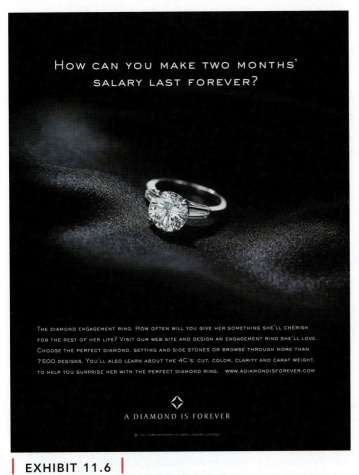

EXHIBIT 11.6

A product with a ritualistic role.

Copyright J. Walter Thompson USA and The Diamond Trading Company.

SACRED AND SECULAR CONSUMPTION

Culture also influences the way goods are consumed. An important distinction in this respect is between sacred and secular consumption.[35] **Sacred consumption** is the consumption of goods that promote beauty, the preservation of nature, and cooperation. Consumers who seek the sacred aspects of consumption are attracted to natural imagery or appeals to family ties. They favor food products with natural ingredients and fashions with simple styles.

Hirschman cites campaigns that reflect such a sacred orientation to consumption, as follows:[36]

■ *Gallo wines.* Accompanied by soft music, the opening visuals show the homecomings of family members for Christmas. Imagery includes snow on evergreens, wooden porches, red plaid flannel shirts, and down jackets. The gathered, multigenerational family sits at a wooden table laden with a turkey, yams, bread, and bottles of wine.

■ *Tropicana orange juice.* A young woman, dressed in jeans and a cotton shirt, stands in an orange grove. She recalls eating oranges from her father's grove as a young girl. Her hands and face would get sticky from the sweet, delicious juice; and her mother would help her wash up when she returned home. [The announcer says] "Tropicana is natural and pure, just the way the rain and sun make it. . . . It comes fresh from nature, without any artificial additives."

WEB APPLICATIONS

The Sacred and Secular Dimensions of Consumption on the Web

Web sites can reflect the sacred and secular dimensions of consumption; some orient themselves around the reverence with which people treat certain products. Harley-Davidson tries to reflect the sacred dimension of consumption on its web site through streaming frames that show the words "Freedom," Passion," and "It's a Way of Life" on its home page. The viewer is then transported into the next frame with the tag line "The Road Starts Here. It Never Ends," with links to Harley products and dealers.

The site reflects the reverence with which many bikers treat their motorcycles. For the serious biker, it is strictly taboo to touch another person's Harley without permission. The process of cleaning a Harley is an elaborate ritual involving careful washing and polishing. The garage or shed in which the motorcycle is kept is regarded almost as a shrine. The kinship with others (bikers call each other "bro") verges on a religious order. And when the Harley is ridden, it is in a sacred context in which the riding experience is "magical or otherworldly."

On the other side of the coin, marketers are using the Web to attract consumers who seek the secular aspects of consumption by promoting technology. Oakley, Inc., which entered most consumers' consciousness through its sale of sunglasses, has expanded into watches, apparel, and footwear and touts the technical superiority of its products on its web site (*www.oakley.com*). Clinique, Inc. (*www.clinique.com*) uses its vaguely technical-sounding name and white-lab-coat-attired "consultants" to sell its products that promise to defy aging and promote healthier skin.

Sources: References to web sites as of July 2002; John W. Schouten and James H. McAlexander, "Subcultures of Consumption: An Ethnography of the New Bikers," *Journal of Consumer Research* 22 (June 1995), pp. 43–61.

These two ads emphasize natural food, natural settings, a rural environment, and family. Implicitly, nature is viewed as nurturing and life-giving.

Another aspect of sacred consumption is the fondness and even reverence with which some consumers treat certain products. For example, a piece of jewelry given on a special event or a suit or dress associated with business or social success is worn in a more sacred fashion. The study of the Harley-Davidson subculture describes the reverence with which bikers treat their motorcycles[37] (see the Web Applications box).

Secular consumption is the consumption of goods that promote technology, the conquest of nature, and competition. Consumers who seek the secular aspects of consumption are attracted to products that improve control over one's life.

Hirschman also cites campaigns that reflect such a secular orientation to consumption, as follows:[38]

▌ *Static Guard.* A woman enters a restaurant in an elegant dress. When she removes her coat, static cling (an undesirable natural event) causes the dress to rumple unbecomingly. She is embarrassed. A technological product (Static Guard) is sprayed on the offending natural phenomenon and conquers it.

▌ *Oil of Olay.* An attractive woman states, "I don't intend to grow old gracefully. I intend to fight it every step of the way. I'm going to be 40 and wonderful." The announcer states, "Oil of Olay beauty fluid helps to replenish the fluids your skin loses with time."

The two commercials just cited emphasize control over nature through the use of manufactured products—in one case, to overcome an unwanted event; in another, to conquer aging. Here, nature is viewed as potentially harmful and the focus is on controlling it.

Depending on the values they wish to convey through the product or service, marketers emphasize the sacred or the secular. Both Gallo and Tropicana use sacred imagery because they want to convey the natural aspects of their products. Static Guard and Oil of Olay use secular imagery because they want to portray their products as vehicles for controlling nature.

The two ads in Exhibit 11.7 reflect the same dichotomy. The ad for United Airlines captures the image of a child sleeping on his grandfather's shoulder. Although the image is clearly from another culture, it emphasizes values of tranquility and family. The ad for Oakley shoes places the product in the more secular domain by describing the technical mastery that went into creating the product. The purpose is to confer this technical mastery to the consumer who, it is implied, will be able to wield more control over his or her environment.

Changes in Cultural Values in the United States and Abroad

Several significant and interrelated changes occurred in the American consumer's value system in the last decade. One, cited earlier in the chapter, is a *new reality* about the limits of prosperity and the attainment of the American Dream. This change occurred largely as a result of two severe recessions in the early 1990s and

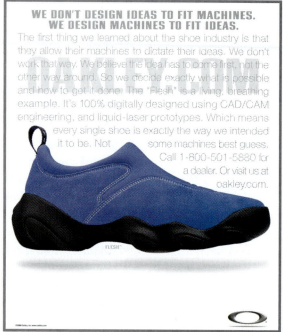

EXHIBIT 11.7

Ads reflecting the sacred and secular dimensions of consumption.

(left) Courtesy United Airlines and National Geographic Society Image Collection; (right) Courtesy Oakley.

early 2000s. Three other changes reflected in the values of consumers in the 1990s and 2000s are as follows:

1. A shift from *valuing youth to valuing youthfulness*
2. *Greater traditionalism,* as reflected in a shift in focus from a "me" to a "we" orientation
3. Emergence of a *new materialism*

NEW REALITY

The **new reality** has had a profound effect on American consumers and their spending patterns. Many have come to realize that there are limits to growth in the American economy and that these limits translate into restricted future purchasing potential. As a result, consumers have become more price conscious and value oriented. As we have seen in previous chapters, consumers are less likely to be brand loyal and more likely to buy lower-priced private brands and to comparison-shop. A major change in buying motives is from prestige to value. Purchasing based on status is out; purchasing based on quality and performance is in.

The Yankelovich Monitor identified several dimensions of the new reality. One is a decline in commitment to organizational values and a greater willingness to explore other options. Despite the risks, starting one's own business or freelancing has gained new legitimacy as an alternate course to climbing the organizational ladder. As a result, the home is increasingly viewed as a work as well as a family center. Another dimension is a more constrained view of technology and the environment. People have shifted from a strong belief in technology and science as a means of conquering the environment to a belief in technology as a means of managing and preserving the environment. A manifestation of this shift is the greater emphasis consumers place on environmental protection. The bursting of the dot-com bubble in the stock market beginning in April 2000 has reinforced a recognition of the limits of technology.

This more sober consumer view is likely to continue. Marketers have adjusted by placing more focus on quality merchandise at lower prices. The acronym EDLP—everyday low prices—reflects a more common marketing strategy. These changes reflect not only an economic shift, but also a more basic shift in cultural values from achievement to security and from environmental control to environmental management.

YOUTHFULNESS RATHER THAN YOUTH

As baby boomers have aged, there has been a significant change in the emphasis put on the traditional American value of youth. Increasingly, beauty and attractiveness are no longer the province of the young. Advertising is using models in their 40s and even 50s for beauty products—Isabella Rosellini as a spokeswoman for Lancôme and Lauren Hutton for Revlon. In fact, when one survey asked women to rank today's top twenty beauties, sixteen were over 40.[39] As a result, the cultural emphasis seems to have shifted from youth to youthfulness; that is, retaining the feeling of youth as one gets older. Advertisers are subscribing to this shift by portraying the mature market in more vibrant and youthful pursuits.

GREATER TRADITIONALISM

The shift to traditionalism represents a greater emphasis on family and patriotic values. Until the mid-1980s, a "me" orientation was fairly pervasive, especially among baby boomers and the youth segment. It reflected a need to live life "my way" and a fierce desire to live for today without concern for the more restrictive values that society or family might impose. The me orientation was a reaction to the self-sacrifice imposed on Americans by the Vietnam War, the disillusion brought on by Watergate, and subsequent economic dislocations. It started in the early 1970s, gained momentum through the early 1980s, and then began to wane by the end of the 1980s as many consumers began to de-emphasize self-gratification.

The shift to a "we" orientation is reflected in a more traditional focus on family values, patriotism, and the work ethic. Early evidence of this shift was a study of baby boomers that found that 69 percent said they are more family-oriented than they thought they would be when they were younger.[40] Why this greater traditionalism? Baby boomers have shifted away from the drive for affluence to a greater focus on personal development. An important component of personal development is the need to balance the competing demands of work, home, and recreational pursuits.

This we orientation has continued into the 1990s and early 2000s. It is reflected in the greater traditionalism of Generation Y, a result of baby-boomer parents having passed on some of this traditionalism to their children. A recent poll suggests that "in some ways [Gen Y is] as wholesome and devoid of cynicism as the

generation that wore saddle shoes." This corresponds to admiration for their parents, trust in government, a belief that it is possible to start out poor and become rich, and a fairly conservative stance on sexual matters.[41]

Two broad groups share a greater emphasis on traditionalism. The "new traditionalists" integrate family values with the modern lifestyles reflected in the focus on personal development and self-actualization. "Old traditionalists" subscribe to traditional beliefs without acceptance of new lifestyles. Marketers have captured this old traditionalism by focusing on patriotic appeals such as Wal-Mart's "Buy American." The terrorist attacks in 2001 created a reemergence of patriotic values and reinforced the old traditionalism.

The two ads in Exhibit 11.8 reflect the new and the old traditionalism. The ad for Memorex DVDs emphasizes family togetherness, but in the context of a lifestyle that embraces new technology. The ad for Union Pacific epitomizes the "old" traditionalism, with a portrayal of Union Pacific as linking America together.

NEW MATERIALISM

Greater emphasis on self-fulfillment might suggest a decrease in the traditional focus on materialism in American society, but this is not the case. The United States remains a materialistic, consumption-driven society. However, the nature of materialism has changed. In the past, affluence was desired as a means of enhancing one's social status through "conspicuous consumption." Today, the emphasis on wealth as a means of status is not as important. Wealth is seen as a means of expressing individualism rather than group conformity. Consumers are less defined by traditional social dimensions. For example, a consumer may drive a luxury automobile and search for the cheapest service station. Another may buy designer suits from an exclusive retailer and $3 socks from a discount store.

Affluence is seen not only as a means of expressing individualism, but also as a means of enhancing personal development. Booming expenditures on adult education, recreation, and travel reflect the focus on personal development. The ad for GMAC in Exhibit 11.9 reflects the new materialism. The main theme is that the rewards for sound money management are family fun and togetherness rather than higher social status.

THE GLOBALIZATION OF AMERICAN CONSUMPTION VALUES

Most of the top global brands, including McDonald's, Coca-Cola, and Nike, originated in the United States and have spread throughout the world, capturing the imagination, and the wallets, of consumers. McDonald's, for example, opened with great fanfare in Moscow in 1990 and offered a distinctly different service experience from dysfunctional, Soviet-run state agencies. Today, company officials claim that the original outlet in Pushkin Square is the busiest restaurant in the world.[42] Coca-Cola has made a strong push into China, the world's largest consumer market, and controls roughly a third of the carbonated beverage market there. The Chinese government, however, is openly reluctant to allow Coke to have free rein in expanding its soft-drink empire.[43]

But many countries throughout the world worry about the pervasive presence of American culture and values. For example, when the Disney Corporation opened

| **EXHIBIT 11.9** |

The new materialism.

Courtesy General Motors Acceptance Corporation and Campbell-Ewald.

STRATEGIC APPLICATIONS

The Effects of September 11 on Consumer Values: A Shift to Traditionalism

It is rare that a single event can cause a shift in deep seated cultural values. But September 11 was that type of event. A survey of one thousand respondents conducted by Market Facts, a leading research firm, two weeks after the event found that more than three-quarters of respondents said spending time with their family mattered more in the aftermath of the attacks. Not surprisingly, there was also a surge in patriotism. About two-thirds of the respondents said that serving their country had taken on a greater significance. About 73 percent said that helping others had become more important. Another survey of one thousand college students found a similar shift in values toward patriotism and volunteer work, leading these students to "reorder their priorities [and] change their core values."

The emphasis on family, patriotism, and helping others reflects a reinforcement of the core values of traditionalism and the we orientation that have become more dominant in the last ten years. Yet marketers must tread lightly if they are to refer to September 11. The majority of respondents in the survey of college students felt it would be inappropriate to refer to the terrorist attacks in advertising and said any such reference would make them less likely to buy the advertiser's products. The survey found that teens and college students were extremely skeptical of companies that do good works just for public relations purposes.

One analyst interpreting these results said:

Advertisers should can the hype and provide a sense of connection. . . . Consumers are searching for brands they can trust, brands that are successfully coping with the events of 9/11, not taking advantage of them.

A good example of providing a "sense of connection" is a TV ad for ESPN that included news footage from the attacks, pictures of rescue workers, and video of baseball players singing "God Bless America." The ad was more like a documentary than a commercial and gave consumers a sense of "security and community that comes from emotional linkages with a brand."

The shift to greater traditionalism as a result of September 11 means that appeals to family, community and patriotism are likely to achieve new resonance.

Sources: "Research Offers Insights on the Mood of College Students Since Sept. 11," *New York Times* (November 27, 2001), p. C8; "Shifting Careers," *American Demographics* (December 2001), pp. 39–40.

EuroDisney in 1991, it had to counteract the contention by many in France that it was creating a "cultural Chernobyl" and that this marked the invasion of American culture. Clotaire Rapaille, the motivational researcher cited in Chapter 10, used his methods to study the French consumer's aversion to EuroDisney. He found that the French, who put great emphasis on liberty without prohibition, viewed Disney as a place for unwanted prohibitions—no alcohol, no pets, no earrings or miniskirts for the staff. In response to Rapaille's findings, Disney established special areas for pets and for drinking and relaxed its dress code for employees.[44]

Other groups are doing everything they can to counteract the consumption-driven pace of life brought about by American-inspired globalization. For example, the "slow city" movement has been founded in Italy to preserve the pace of life in the Tuscan and Umbrian regions and to defend against all cities becoming homogenized versions of one another.[45] Many view the spread of American culture via movies, brands, and other pop paraphernalia as an attack on more traditional values, such as spending time with family, enjoying a nice meal, or taking in a locally produced entertainment option. With the increased globalization of culture, mostly driven by dominant U.S. firms, there may be even more backlash in the future.

Societal Implications of Cultural Values

Cultural values can have both positive and negative effects on society. The increasing global value placed on the preservation of the environment will have positive consequences in protecting the limited natural resources of this planet for future generations. The shift in values reflected in the new reality in the 1990s is also likely to be positive in the long run. In putting more emphasis on product value, consumers are becoming more efficient shoppers. With the increasing adoption of the Internet, price comparisons and product search have been simplified and made more efficient. Similarly, manufacturers are learning to do more with less by increasing their productivity and decreasing costs, partly due to the increased price transparency resulting from Internet searches. This has enabled them to deliver the value that consumers seek.

The impact of cultural values on society also has negative consequences. For example, although materialism may increase our standard of living, it also encourages the accumulation of wealth and the creation of a greater gap between the haves and have-nots. On a global scale this is becoming more and more of an issue as the wealthiest countries increase the divide between themselves and the developing world.

The emphasis on youthfulness may promote an active and vibrant society, but it also encourages society to ignore the needs of the aged. This problem will become magnified with the aging of the American population into the next century. The emphasis on individualism may reflect America's pioneering spirit, but it has also created barriers to teamwork. Such barriers put many American companies at a disadvantage in competing with more group-oriented societies.

Cultural values also may produce undesirable consumption consequences. Consider addictive consumption. Although drug and alcohol consumption are the most serious abuses, addictions develop for many other products. The negative consequences of addiction to cigarettes are now widely recognized, even among lifelong smokers. Addictions can also develop for more mundane products such as chocolates, diet sodas, and snack foods. Compulsive purchasing behavior can be as socially undesirable as compulsive consumption. One result of addictive shopping is that consumers run up large debts that they may not be able to repay.

Cultural values such as materialism may also encourage antisocial behavior such as theft, shoplifting, or insurance fraud. By one estimate, loss of merchandise due to shoplifting has increased prices by an estimated $300 per year for a family of four.

Overall, cultural values have a positive impact on consumers by directing their behavior in constructive ways. However, it is also important to recognize the negative consumption consequences of some cultural values.

SUMMARY

This chapter introduced the broadest environmental influence on consumer behavior—culture. Cultural influence is transmitted through societal values, which are learned from childhood through socialization and form permanent guides to understanding consumer behavior. Cultural values are terminal values or desirable end states to be attained. Another category of values, instrumental values, are the means of achieving these end states.

Cultural values have five key characteristics: (1) they are learned; (2) they are guides to behavior; (3) they are enduring; (4) they are dynamic; and (5) they are widely held by members of society. Four such widely held values in American society are materialism, individualism, youthfulness, and the work ethic.

There are various means of identifying cultural values, including cultural inventories such as Rokeach's Value Survey, research services that conduct consumer surveys to determine changes in values such as the Yankelovich Monitor, field studies and observation, and content analysis of a society's mass media and literature.

In marketing terms, consumers seek to attain cultural values through a means-end chain in which (1) product attributes are a means for achieving (2) consumption goals that are instrumental in attaining (3) cultural values. The effect of culture on consumer behavior is reflected in its impact on the way products are portrayed and consumed. The means of portraying products in cultural terms is through symbols such as McDonald's golden arches. Marketers sometimes attempt to create myths and fantasies for products to strengthen their symbolism. The symbolism and mythology surrounding a product are enhanced with the use of the Internet as a pervasive medium that is not defined by geographic boundaries.

Culture is also important in defining a ritualistic role for many products. Consumers often purchase and consume products associated with grooming, gift giving, and holidays in a series of symbolic acts that reflect cultural values. Many American holidays are gaining increased significance in global markets as a means of promoting consumption. One perspective in better understanding the impact of culture on consumption is to view consumption as sacred or secular. Sacred consumption emphasizes beauty and the preservation of nature, whereas secular consumption emphasizes technology and the conquest of nature.

Several significant changes have occurred in the American consumer's value system in the last decade. The most important is a new reality that modifies the American dream of unimpeded growth and recognizes future limits on purchasing power and spending. Other changes are (1) a shift in values from emphasizing youth to emphasizing youthfulness among older consumers; (2) a new traditionalism, reflected in a shift from a "me" to a "we" orientation; and (3) the emergence of a new materialism that views wealth as a means of enhancing self-fulfillment rather than social status.

Cultural values can have both positive and negative effects on consumers and society. Some of the negative effects are addictive consumption, compulsive purchasing behavior, and antisocial behavior such as shoplifting or insurance fraud. Overall, cultural values have a positive impact on consumers by directing their behavior into constructive channels.

In Chapter 12, we focus on more specific components of culture—how subcultures and age cohorts influence consumer behavior.

QUESTIONS FOR DISCUSSION

1. In what ways has McDonald's been successful in reflecting cultural changes over time?

2. Why is it rare for a marketing strategy to try to change cultural values?

3. What is meant by a "culture production system"? Cite some examples of such a system and how it might influence cultural values.

4. What is the distinction between terminal and instrumental values? What terminal and instrumental values might influence the purchase of a designer suit? A sports car?

5. What are the strategic implications of the cultural trend in the last decade identified as the "new reality" for (a) advertising fax machines and (b) selling luxury goods?

6. What is the difference in the value placed on individualism within American and Japanese societies?

7. What changes have occurred in the work ethic in American society in the last decade? What are the strategic implications of these changes?

8. How does the differing view of work between American and European societies affect the marketing of
   (a) luxury goods,
   (b) personal computers, and
   (c) vacation packages?

9. What are the theoretical underpinnings for Gutman's concept of a means–end chain?

10. What is the relationship between laddering and the means–end chain? How can marketers use laddering to develop advertising strategies?

11. What might be the role of product symbolism for the following products: a pair of designer jeans; a motorcycle; an engagement ring?

12. Why is semiotics useful in analyzing cultural influences on consumer behavior? Why is it particularly important to marketers in evaluating cross-cultural influences?

13. What do all consumption rituals have in common? How can marketers use these components in developing marketing strategy?

14. A manufacturer of plastic wrap is considering using the sacred dimensions of consumption to advertise the company's brand. A competitor decides to use the secular dimensions of consumption. How would each advertising campaign differ on this basis?

15. Assume a manufacturer of personal hair care appliances (hair dryers, setters, etc.) wants to introduce two different lines: one directed to new traditionalists; the other, to old traditionalists. What type of appeals could the manufacturer use to appeal to each segment?

16. What do we mean by the "new materialism"? In what way does the ad in Exhibit 11.9 reflect the new materialism?

RESEARCH ASSIGNMENTS

1 Identify two web sites (other than those listed in the text) that reflect sacred values and two sites that reflect secular values.

- What are the differences in each site distinguishing it as sacred or secular?

- How do the sites differ in (a) layout, (b) informational content, and (c) design?

- What is the target audience for each site? Do the target audiences for the sacred and secular sites vary by level of involvement with the product or subject reflected in the web sites?

2 A study of automobile purchase preferences identified two segments based on cultural values: a self-enhancement segment and a social-recognition segment.[46] The two segments had very different need criteria for automobiles, different purchasing patterns, and different emphases on social issues. The self-enhancement group placed more emphasis on durability, environmental controls, and ease of repair. The social-recognition segment put more emphasis on luxury, prestige, and spaciousness. Regarding social attitudes, the self-enhancement group put more emphasis on equality, logic, and intellect; the social-recognition segment, on national security and law and order.

a. Use the attitudes toward the following five items to identify these two segments: (1) law and order, (2) national security, (3) religion, (4) individual freedom, and (5) logic. (The self-enhancement segment would place less emphasis on the first three items and more emphasis on the last two; the social-recognition segment would do the reverse.)

b. Select a sample of respondents and place them into one of the two segments based on their responses. (You may wish to form a third segment composed of those who do not clearly fit into one of the two segments.) Ask the respondents about the criteria they emphasize in purchasing a particular durable good (a car, a stereo set, furniture, etc.). Determine particular brands or models owned.

- What are the differences in (1) need criteria emphasized and (2) brand ownership between the self-enhancement and the social-recognition segments?

3 Choose three different types of products (*e.g.*, clothing, cars, personal electronics) and find two U.S.-based web sites and two non-U.S.-based web sites promoting these products. Compare and contrast the sites based on the elements of materialism, individualism, youthfulness, and the work ethic. Do the sites focus on only one or on more than one of these values? Does the site's emphasis match what you would expect for both the product category and the culture to which it is marketed?

NOTES

1. "Advertisers Put Consumers on the Couch," *Wall Street Journal* (May 13, 1988), p. 21.
2. From McDonald's web site, www.mcdonalds.com/surftheworld, as of April 9, 2000.
3. "Beyond Burgers: New McDonald's Menu Makes Run for the Border," *Los Angeles Times* (August 13, 2000), p. C.1.
4. Richard A. Peterson, "The Production of Culture: A Prologomenon in the Production of Culture," in Richard A. Peterson, ed., *Sage Contemporary Social Science Issues* (Beverly Hills: Sage, 1976), p. 722.
5. Milton J. Rokeach, "The Role of Values in Public Opinion Research," *Public Opinion Quarterly* 32 (Winter 1968), pp. 547–549; and Milton J. Rokeach, "A Theory of Organization and Change Within Value-Attitude Systems," *Journal of Social Issues* 24 (January 1968), pp. 13–33.
6. Joseph F. Hair, Jr., and Rolph E. Anderson, "Culture, Acculturation and Consumer Behavior: An Empirical Study," in Boris W. Becker and Helmut Becker, eds., *Combined Proceedings of the American Marketing Association, Series No. 34* (Chicago: American Marketing Association, 1972), pp. 423–428.
7. Lisa Penaloza, "*Atravesando Fronteras*/Border Crossings: A Critical Ethnographic Exploration of the Consumer Acculturation of Mexican Immigrants," *Journal of Consumer Research* 21 (June 1994), pp. 32–54.
8. Adapted from "Rewriting the Book on Buying and Selling—Angry and Anxious Americans Seek Out New Values," *Adweek* (November 30, 1992), pp. 20–23.
9. Marsha L. Richins, "Special Possessions and the Expression of Material Values," *Journal of Consumer Research* 21 (December 1994), pp. 522–533.
10. "Are American Workers Vacation Deprived?" *Incentive* (September 2000), p. 9.
11. "Hollywood Goes Global," *The World & I* (February 2001), pp. 263–275.
12. "Lead a Happy Life Without Big Bucks," *San Francisco Chronicle* (January 14, 2001), p. S.6.
13. Jennifer L. Aaker and Durairaj Maheswaran, "The Effect of Cultural Orientation on Persuasion," *Journal of Consumer Research* 24 (December 1997), pp. 315–328.
14. "Japan to Get L.L. Bean's Outdoor Chic," *New York Times* (March 5, 1992), p. D3.
15. "Smoothing Away Age Time," *Advertising Age International* (September 1996), p. 144.
16. "Taste—de Gustibus: Work? Non! The Effortless Pursuit of Pleasure," *Wall Street Journal* (September 1, 2000), p. W.13.
17. Russell W. Belk, John F. Sherry, Jr., and Melanie Wallendorf, "A Naturalistic Inquiry into Buyer and Seller Behavior at a Swap Meet," *Journal of Consumer Research* 14 (March 1988), pp. 449–470.
18. Ibid.
19. Lynn R. Kahle, Sharon Beatty, and Pamela Homer, "Alternative Measurement Approaches to Consumer Values: The List Values (LOV) and Values and Life Style (VALS)," *Journal of Consumer Research* 13 (December 1986), pp. 405–409.
20. Pamela Homer and Lynn R. Kahle, "A Structural Equation Test of the Value-Attitude-Behavior Hierarchy," *Journal of Personality and Social Psychology* 54 (April 1988), pp. 638–646.
21. David C. McClellan, *The Achieving Society* (Princeton, N.J.: Van Nostrand, 1961).
22. Russell W. Belk, "Material Values in the Comics," *Journal of Consumer Research,* 14 (June 1987), pp. 26–42.
23. Jonathan Gutman, "A Means-End Chain Model Based on Consumer Categorization Processes," *Journal of Marketing* 46 (1982), pp. 60–72.
24. Milton J. Rosenberg, "Cognitive Structure and Attitudinal Affect," *Journal of Abnormal and Social Psychology* 53 (1956), pp. 367–372.
25. Thomas J. Reynolds and Jonathan Gutman, "Laddering Theory, Method, Analysis, and Interpretation," *Journal of Advertising Research* 28 (February/March, 1988), pp. 11–31.
26. Thomas J. Reynolds and Alyce Byrd Craddock, "The Application of the Meccas Model to the Development and Assessment of Advertising Strategy: A Case Study," *Journal of Advertising Research* 28 (April/May 1988), pp. 43–59.
27. Mary Tharp and Linda M. Scott, "The Role of Marketing Processes in Creating Cultural Meaning," *Journal of Macromarketing* (Fall 1990), pp. 47–60.
28. Charles Sanders Pierce, *Collected Papers,* ed. Charles Hartshorne, Paul Weiss, and Arthur W. Burks (Cambridge, Mass.: Harvard University Press, 1931–1958); and David Glen Mick, "Consumer Research and Semiotics: Exploring the Morphology of Signs, Symbols, and Significance," *Journal of Consumer Research,* 15 (September 1986), pp. 196–213.

29. "Advertising as Myth-Maker: Brands as Gods and Heroes," *Advertising Age* (November 8, 1993), p. 32.

30. These examples are from "The Power of Mythology Helps Brands to Endure," *Marketing News* (September 28, 1992), p. 16.

31. "Michelin Man—Fighting Fit," *New Straits Times* (April 26, 1998).

32. Dennis W. Rook, "The Ritual Dimensions of Consumer Behavior," *Journal of Consumer Research* 12 (December 1985), pp. 251–264.

33. Ibid., p. 253.

34. "Buzzwords of Love in Japan—With a Sting," *Christian Science Monitor* (February 11, 1999), p. 1.

35. Elizabeth C. Hirschman, "The Ideology of Consumption: A Structural-Syntactical Analysis of 'Dallas' and 'Dynasty'," *Journal of Consumer Research* 15 (December 1988), pp. 344–359; and Elizabeth C. Hirschman, "Point of View: Sacred, Secular, and Mediating Consumption Imagery in Television Commercials," *Journal of Advertising Research* 31 (December 1990/January, 1991), pp. 38–43.

36. Ibid.

37. John W. Schouten and James H. McAlexander, "Subcultures of Consumption: An Ethnography of the New Bikers," *Journal of Consumer Research* 22 (June 1995), pp. 50–51.

38. Hirschman, "The Ideology of Consumption," pp. 344–359, and "Point of View," pp. 38–43.

39. "Door Ajar to Women of All Ages in Ads," *Advertising Age* (October 4, 1993), pp. S-2, S-4.

40. "Double Standards of Post-War Adults," *Research Alert* (June 24, 1988), p. 1.

41. "Teen-Age Poll Finds a Turn to the Traditional," *New York Times* (April 30, 1998), p. A20.

42. "That Golden Touch to the Arches in Russia McDonald's Is Unsung Bearer of Western 'Civilization,'" *Christian Science Monitor* (March 4, 1997), p. 1.3.

43. "Coke Expects Sales in China to Grow at a Strong Pace," *Wall Street Journal* (September 2, 1998).

44. "Does the Smell of Coffee Brewing Remind You of Your Mother?" *New York Times Magazine* (May 7, 2000), pp. 71–74.

45. "Preserving 'la dolce vita' in Italy," *USA Today* (October 13, 2000), p. D1.

46. Donald E. Vinson, Jerome E. Scott, and Lawrence M. Lamont, "The Role of Personal Values in Marketing and Consumer Behavior," *Journal of Marketing,* 41 (April 1977), pp. 44–50.

12

Subcultural Influences and Age Cohorts

Individuals in a society do not all have the same cultural values. Certain segments may be identified as **subcultures;** that is, groups of people who have norms, values, and behaviors that are distinct from the culture as a whole. The individual who identifies closely with a certain religious, ethnic, or national subculture accepts the norms and values of that group. As a result, members of a subculture frequently buy the same brands and products, read the same magazines and newspapers, and shop in the same types of stores. Subcultures can be defined not only by race and religion, but by age as well. Common values among teenagers that set them apart from an adult-dominant society define a "teen subculture."

The religious, ethnic, national, and lifestyle diversity in American culture makes it distinct from most other societies. The vast majority of people in most European countries are of the same race and religion. In Japan, most people consider themselves of common ancestry. It is rare to find a country where ethnic minorities represent over one-fourth of the population and no one religion dominates. Because of this diversity in American society, subcultural analysis is more important both from the standpoint of understanding consumer behavior and in attempting to influence it.

In this chapter, we consider the two most important subcultural groupings—those based on age, and those based on ethnic or national identity. We focus on the characteristics of the three largest minority groups in the United States based on ethnicity and national identity—African Americans, Hispanic Americans, and Asian Americans. Regarding age, we consider the key age cohorts described in Chapter 9—the mature market, baby boomers, Generation X, and Generation Y. We also examine subcultures of consumption; that is, groups that revolve around product owner-ship or activities, such as motorcycle owners or mountain climbers. Individuals often view such products and activities in a lifestyle context and share common norms and values as a result.

Metropolitan Life Recognizes the Value of Diversity

Metropolitan Life has recognized the diversity in American society. Its strategy has been to target particular ethnic groups with specific campaigns geared to their needs and values. For African Americans, it focuses on the importance of family and the ability to have a safety net for the future (see Exhibit 12.1). In appealing to Hispanic Americans, the company dispensed with Snoopy, its cartoon character mascot, in favor of more family-oriented ads placed in Spanish-language media because the company wanted to be more in touch with this segment's values. But Met Life kept Snoopy in ads targeting Chinese Americans, garbing him in traditional Chinese apparel (again see Exhibit 12.1). Apparently, the company felt that Snoopy was more in touch

with Chinese Americans' values than with those of Hispanic Americans.[1] Met Life promotes its services to the Chinese-American community through coupons, and Chinese-language newspaper ads as well. It also offers brochures and seminars in an attempt to educate Chinese immigrants in banking procedures and services.[2]

In each case, the company has recognized that themes directed to the broad American market must be adapted to the differing values and tastes of particular subcultures. Metropolitan is a trailblazer in targeting Asian Americans in particular, because many companies consider the 10.6 million Asian Americans too small a target.

| EXHIBIT 12.1 |
Met Life ads targeted to ethnic groups.
PEANUTS © United Feature Syndicate, Inc.

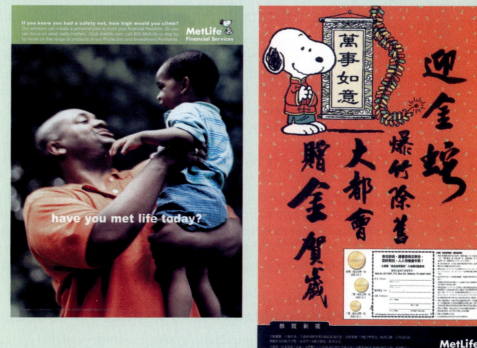

The Influence of Subculture on Consumer Behavior

The influence of a subculture on consumer behavior depends on several factors:

▮ *Subcultural distinctiveness.* The more a subculture seeks to maintain a separate identity, the greater its potential influence. The Hispanic-American subculture is distinctive because many of its members have maintained their language as a means of cultural identification.

▮ *Subcultural homogeneity.* A subculture with homogeneous values is more likely to exert influence on its members. Hispanic Americans are a diverse subculture composed of Mexicans, Cubans, Puerto Ricans, and individuals from South American countries, so some might consider each of these groups separate subcultures. However, in general, it is appropriate to talk of a Hispanic-American subculture because of common threads among all of these groups; namely, strong family and religious ties, conservatism, male dominance, and a common language.

▮ *Subcultural exclusion.* At times, subcultures have sought exclusion from society or have been excluded by society. The Amish communities in Pennsylvania, Ohio, and Indiana have purposefully sought exclusion to maintain and protect their beliefs. African Americans have at times been excluded from a white-dominant society through the denial of educational and occupation opportunities. Exclusion tends to strengthen the influence of subcultures by isolating them from society and, thus, encouraging the maintenance of subcultural norms and values.

THE UNITED STATES: MELTING POT OR SALAD BOWL?

Distinctiveness, homogeneity, and exclusion interact to maintain subcultural identity separate from the general culture. In many subcultures, an individual is torn between maintaining a distinctive subcultural identity and integrating into the general society. The traditional path of immigrants in this country has been integration into the American "melting pot."

More recently, pressures to acculturate by accepting traditional, American middle-class values have lessened. For example, many Hispanic and Asian immigrants have a strong desire to maintain their language and heritage. This desire to maintain subcultural values led one marketer, writing in the late 1980s, to view America not as a melting pot but as a salad bowl "brimming with a polyglot, multi-hued potpourri of people who mix but don't blend. These immigrant groups have a need to maintain their separate identities rather than to meld into a cultural mainstream."[3] The challenge for marketers is to appeal to the separate identities of these subcultural groups while also appealing to the broader market.

THE KEY STRATEGIC ISSUE:
SHOULD MARKETERS APPEAL TO SUBCULTURES?

A key strategic question is whether marketers should appeal to these groups with the same strategy they use for the general market or whether they should design specific campaigns targeted to particular subcultures. When it comes to insurance, two of the largest companies have taken diametrically opposite views on this question. As we saw, Met Life targets the three key ethnic groups based on research that shows distinct differences in values and perceptions that affect their attitudes toward insurance. John Hancock, however, has found it more cost-effective *not* to target ethnic groups because as one spokesperson said, "Fundamental financial needs don't vary that much for each ethnic group."[4] As a result, in 1999 it rolled back previous efforts at ethnic targeting. For example, it decided to cease efforts to specifically target the Chinese-American community, forgoing its adopted Chinese name "The Everlasting Health and Happiness Mutual Life Company" in favor of the same name and advertising as in the national market.

Given subcultural diversity, many financial institutions, such as Bank of America and American Express, are following Met Life's strategy of targeting subcultures; they would probably disagree with John Hancock that financial needs do not vary sufficiently to warrant targeting.

Another issue in targeting minorities is sensitivity to their needs and values. At times, marketers do not research ethnic subcultures sufficiently and therefore make blunders. Despite its focus on ethnic subcultures, for instance, Met Life did not research the Korean market in California well enough to effectively target it. Its ads portrayed customers in traditional Chinese rather than Korean dress.[5] There is also the issue of taking advantage of disadvantaged minorities by targeting them with potentially harmful products. This issue is addressed later in the chapter when the efforts of cigarette and beer companies in targeting minorities are discussed.

Types of Subcultures

Subcultures in the United States vary by geography, religion, lifestyles, age, and ethnic identification.

GEOGRAPHIC SUBCULTURES

Geographic groups can be identified as subcultures. One purpose of geodemographic analysis, cited in Chapter 9, is to identify such subcultures. For example, residents of retirement communities, whether in Florida, Arizona, or New Jersey, might be identified as a subculture because of common values regarding housing, medical care, and retirement benefits. Another regional grouping might be residents of college communities, from Chapel Hill, North Carolina, to Madison, Wisconsin, based on the similarities in tastes and expenditure patterns of two subcultures, college students and faculty.

Marketers target their products to regions based on differences in tastes and preferences. For example, Campbell targets its soups to regional tastes with a heavier dose of advertising and distribution of chicken noodle and tomato soups to Northeasterners, cream of mushroom soups to Californians, and nacho cheese soups to Southwesterners. And, as we saw in Chapter 11, McDonald's varies its menu regionally, offering Mexican-style items in the West, bratwurst in the Midwest, and lobster sandwiches in New England.

RELIGION

Religious groups can also be regarded as subcultures as a result of traditions and customs tied to their beliefs and passed on from one generation to the next. As an example of differences in values, Catholics tend to be more traditional with an emphasis on strong family ties, Protestants tend to value the work ethic as the avenue for success, Jews tend to emphasize individual responsibility for their actions and self-education, and Muslims tend to be more conservative with an emphasis on adherence to family norms.[6]

Traditions and customs are reflected in purchasing behavior. Jews are less likely to eat pork and shellfish, Mormons are less likely to smoke tobacco and drink liquor, and Catholics are more likely to eat fish on Friday. The nonmaterialistic values of born-again Christians make them poor targets for credit cards but good targets for fast foods and do-it-yourself products.[7]

At times, religious groups take a more active part in influencing the purchasing behavior of their members. For example, the Southern Baptist Convention encouraged its members to boycott Disney products and theme parks because the company provides employee health benefits for same-sex couples.[8] To lift the boycott, the group wants Disney to stop cooperating with any gay activities and causes.[9] More globally, in April 2001, many Arab countries sponsored a boycott of American products because of the U.S. government's support for Israel. Fast-food outlets such as Kentucky Fried Chicken and McDonald's saw a sharp drop in traffic in these countries.

NONTRADITIONAL SUBCULTURES: THE GAY COMMUNITY

Subcultures can also be grouped around nontraditional lifestyle choices—for example, the gay community. Approximately 4 percent to 6 percent of the adult population is gay.[10] As this subculture grew more politically and economically visible in the last twenty years, advertisers began actively courting it, mindful that gay couples tend to have more discretionary income than the average American, high-end tastes, and fierce brand loyalty.

Financial service firms have targeted gays because of their upscale profile. In 2001, Prudential Securities created both gay and lesbian versions of an ad touting its expertise in financial planning for unmarried couples, such as estate planning.[11] Similarly, American Express advertises domestic partner financial planning in gay magazines such as *Out* and *The Advocate.* Carmakers are also targeting gay consumers.[12] A Subaru ad for the popular Outback model directs its message to the gay community by indicating "It's Not a Choice. It's the Way We're Built" (see Exhibit 12.2).

Gays also have an active communications network with more than two hundred web sites to communicate about issues and to spread the word about companies that have the courage to target them. The Web is an excellent vehicle for reaching gays because it can target small segments. The number of gay-specific magazines is limited, and TV is too inefficient to target gays.[13]

One issue marketers face is whether targeting gays may alienate a portion of their straight customers. The *Wall Street Journal* noted that DuPont "retreat[ed] swiftly at the first hint of controversy," when it targeted gays in 2001. An ad for the

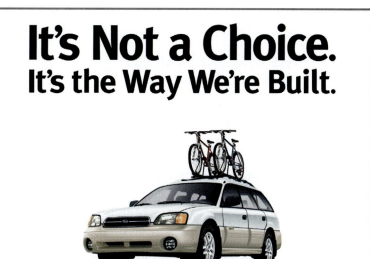

company's HIV drug Sustiva showing two grooms arm in arm appeared in general circulation medical journals and consumer magazines. After receiving some negative reaction, DuPont restricted the ads to gay media.[14]

The remainder of this chapter is devoted to the two most important designations for subcultures: age cohorts and ethnic groups.

Age Cohorts

Although some may debate whether age cohorts have sufficiently homogeneous and distinctive values to constitute a subculture, marketers have tended to identify the age groups cited in Chapter 9 as subcultures—Generation Y, Generation X, baby boomers, and the mature market. These groups are identified as **cohorts** because of similar values and life experiences; for example, Vietnam and Watergate for older baby boomers. Despite similar experiences, these age cohorts may be too broad to be defined as subcultures. More specific designations, such as younger versus older baby boomers or the young old versus the very old, do a better job of defining age groups with homogeneous norms and values.

Next, we consider age cohorts from oldest to youngest and cite the values that are sufficiently common to some of these age groups to qualify them as subcultures.

THE MATURE MARKET (OVER 55 YEARS OLD)

The 59 million Americans who are over 55 (21 percent of the population)[15] are often divided into the following four subsegments:

1. The *bridge generation* (55 to 64), labeled as such because they bridge the attitudes of their parents and mainly Gen X children. This group represents about half of the mature market.
2. The elderly (65 to 74).
3. The aged (75 to 84).
4. The very old (85-plus).

As a result, those over 55 cannot be described as a single subculture, although they do have certain values in common. Mature consumers want to lead active lives; to be self-sufficient; to look and act youthful; to reap the benefits of their past savings by enjoying new experiences; and to give back something to society, perhaps in the form of volunteer work or monetary contributions.

The emphasis on these values changes over time, however, depending on which of the four age groups an individual is in. For example, as one ages, self-sufficiency becomes a much more important value than enjoying new experiences. Even though their purchasing power and income decrease with age, discretionary income continues to rise because these consumers have fulfilled obligations like mortgages and children's education.

Overall, this age cohort represents the most powerful buying group in the American economy. Although they are one-fourth of the U.S. population, they control half its discretionary income and three-fourths of its assets. Despite the fact that many in this group are retired, their earning power is almost as great as that of baby boomers. Further enhancing the desirability of marketing to this group is the fact that the mature market represents the majority of all expenditures for leisure travel.

Given this group's tremendous purchasing potential, it is curious that marketers target so few products and ads to this group. According to a large ad agency, only 6 or 7 percent of TV commercials target the mature market, and only a handful of products or services are tailored to their needs. Of the few commercials targeted to older consumers, almost all suffer from what some call the Methuselah Syndrome; that is, portraying the 55-plus consumer as frail, cutesy, and prunelike. As one executive quipped, "Everyone in the world of advertising seems to move straight from 32 to 75-plus."[16]

There are three probable reasons why marketers have not targeted the mature market. First, most marketers are under 40 and do not understand how to appeal to older consumers. Many of these media buyers and agency staffers are in a life phase wherein they look for ads that are hip, cool, and award-winning, rather than ones that may target the majority of the marketplace. If this disconnect continues it may cost marketers sales.[17] Second, older consumers do not like to be reminded of their age. The general approach to the mature market has been to advertise a product to, say, Generation Xers or baby boomers using youthful models in the expectation that a portion of the mature market will also buy it. This approach has some validity because, in general, mature consumers think of themselves as 15 years younger than their actual age.[18] As a result, mature consumers prefer to identify with younger spokespersons.

Third, marketers prefer to target a younger demographic because if they can gain the loyalty of Generation X or Y, these consumers may make a lifetime commitment to the brand. But marketers may be spending disproportionately to reach younger consumers at the expense of the mature market. One study found that ads on TV programs targeting the 18- to 34-year-old group cost 75 percent more than ads on programs targeting the mature market.[19] This is despite the fact that the 50+ group spends more per capita. As a result, there is a disconnect between the purchasing potential of the mature market and the allocation of marketing dollars to this group.

Marketers are beginning to be more sensitive to the mature market, possibly because baby boomers are starting to enter this group. Because baby boomers were the generation that marketers and the media focused on, it is little wonder that the perspective on aging is beginning to change. Baby boomers are starting to redefine the worship of a youth culture in American society, and advertisers are portraying them as more youthful and vital. This is illustrated in a new campaign inaugurated by the AARP in 2001 to appeal to older baby boomers about to enter the mature market. The left-hand ad in Exhibit 12.3 portrays a vital, energetic 66-year-old who is still active as opposed to a less active "mature" adult.

EXHIBIT 12.3

Two different portrayals of the mature market.

(left) Courtesy AARP and Della Femina Agency; (right) Kellogg's® POP-TARTS PASTRY SWIRLS® are registered trademarks of Kellogg Company. All rights reserved. Used with permission.

The conclusion is that strategies to the mature market based on negative stereotypes are inappropriate. The ad for Kellogg's Pastry Swirls in Exhibit 12.3 is a more traditional portrayal of an older consumer, with the humorous tag line "Few things come with a money-back guarantee." Depending on the product category, marketers might want to emphasize vitality or maturity. Marketers who emphasize vitality rather than age are more likely to be successful, as in the AARP ad.

BABY BOOMERS (BORN BETWEEN 1946 AND 1964)

Marketers have focused on the baby-boom generation more than any other group. The reason is not hard to find: This group is 70.5 million strong, or 26 percent of the U.S. population.[20] Most are in their prime spending years, with over $1 trillion in income. Further, as they move into their 50s, their discretionary income increases, making them the cohort with the largest amount of purchasing power.

The greater purchasing power of baby boomers is also a result of their high level of education. In addition, they are less likely to marry; but if they do, they are more likely to be in dual-income households and to delay parenthood, factors that combine to create higher discretionary income. Additionally, roughly 30 percent of baby boomers were empty nesters in 2000, and the remainder with children will enter this phase over the next decade. This will further increase discretionary income.[21]

Most marketers have come to believe that their products' success depends on how they adapt to this generation's transition to the mature market. Alitalia, the Italian state airline, attempts to tap into this generation's propensity for indulgence and self-discovery by targeting empty nesters to "have a renaissance to rediscover your passion for each other and for life." The AARP, which runs the largest-circulation magazine in the United States, *Modern Maturity,* launched a new magazine in 2000, called *My Generation,* to baby boomers over 50. The organization wants to ease the boomers into their senior years without making them feel older than necessary. Additionally, it plans to break its flagship magazine, *Modern Maturity,* into two demographically targeted editions, one for the 56-to-65 crowd and the other for readers 66 and up.[22]

Changes in values will also cause baby boomers to spend more money on home improvements, travel, education, recreation, and other facets of self-development. As a result, companies developing new products and services in these areas are likely to benefit most from the growing affluence of baby boomers.

▮ **Older Baby Boomers** Given the eighteen-year span defining the baby-boom market, it would be misleading to treat it as one age cohort with similar tastes and values. Broadly speaking, there are two cohorts of baby boomers, the older baby boomers (those born in the first half of the baby-boom generation from 1946 to 1954) and the younger boomers (those born from 1955 to 1964).

The older baby boomers went through a transition from the rebellious 1960s and early 1970s of Vietnam and Watergate to a more materialistic lifestyle in the 1980s to a more inward and less materialistic outlook in the 1990s. The defining moment for this group was on January 1, 1996, when the first boomers reached 50. Older boomers are best described by a trend toward self-fulfillment—redefining priorities from the importance of money to the importance of personal self-

enhancement and meaningful work. This group has caught the attention of marketers and shaped the definition of what baby boomers want and value.

Marketers have begun to direct their attention to mature baby boomers, recognizing that as they reach 50, they will redefine the meaning of aging, just as they have redefined every other life stage they have been through.[23] For example, L'Oreal exhorts older baby boomers to "cultivate your gray chic." Similarly, the ad for Olay's Provital, targeted at women over 50, says: "It's not just about looking younger, it's about looking wonderful" (see Exhibit 12.4). Older boomers are simply unlikely to accept the tendency of marketers to ignore consumers over 50.

▌ Younger Baby Boomers   Younger baby boomers represent the majority of boomers. They are not the antiestablishment generation that was molded by the Vietnam War and Watergate. They tend to be more conservative than their older siblings and did not go through the change from materialism to personal development described in the last section. Not having gone through the societal upheavals of their older siblings, younger baby boomers are somewhat more conservative and materialistic. They can best be described by a trend mentioned in Chapter 11, greater traditionalism; that is, a greater focus on family values, patriotism, and the work ethic.

Appeals to the older baby boomers do not always catch the attention of the junior group. If anything, younger baby boomers resent the older group because they had to compete in a tight job market during the 1990–1991 recession and often found their way blocked by older boomers.

Marketers must fine-tune their ads to distinguish between the older and younger groups or develop a theme that is relevant to all. For example, Amex targets younger baby boomers with its Optima card, since they are likely have younger children and to need the financial security of a debit card like Optima

GENERATION X
(BORN BETWEEN 1965 AND 1976)

Generation X is composed of 49.8 million consumers, or 18 percent of the population.[24] They tend to feel neglected by a marketing establishment that has been distracted by the higher-profile boomers, leading to their designation as the anonymous "Generation X." They are hard to pin down with easy labels, reinforcing this designation. They are both liberal and conservative, optimistic and pessimistic, ready to spend and tightfisted. The group is also known as the "baby bust" generation since they were born in a period of the lowest birthrate in this century. The result is fewer young adults today than ten or fifteen years ago. Despite their numbers, consumers in their late 20s and 30s are responsible for $125 billion in spending each year.[25] About a quarter of their annual spending comes from discretionary income, making Gen Xers prime customers for restaurants, alcoholic beverages, clothing, and electronics.

Xers have been described as more multicultural, media-savvy, techie oriented, and cynical about their future than baby boomers. They are also more self-reliant and save a larger proportion of their incomes than baby boomers, anticipating an old age with no social security and soaring health costs. Many Xers came of age in the economically depressed early 1990s, and the recession in the early 2000s reinforced their view of a precarious economic future. As a result, they have been described as being more cynical and alienated than other age groups, with income levels well below their expectations.[26]

Xers blame their elders for leaving them the check after a decade of free spending. They are also more concerned than their elders about environmental issues, drugs, and the AIDS epidemic. This group is best described by the "new reality" in Chapter 11—the realization that they may not achieve the income potential of their parents and some resentment for having to pay the future bill for an unbalanced budget and the need for greater pollution control. Gen Xers also have some resentment toward their older baby-boomer sisters and brothers for capturing better jobs and, in many cases, blocking their path to achievement.

Although this paints a somewhat depressing picture, a survey of women in their 20s found that this description of cynicism and alienation fits about 40 percent of Generation Xers in one way or another.[27] Research by 7UP, however, found a downbeat profile of Xers to be exaggerated. Many actually think positively about life and take a more practical and pragmatic approach to purchasing decisions than baby boomers.[28] As a result, Toyota targeted Xers in a 1999 campaign that combined hip-hop music with Xers at play in Toyota's new Echo compact to show a positive spirit.[29]

These results point to one of the basic problems of using age as a subcultural definition—common values often describe a minority of an age group. Other Xer subgroups were described as those who found fulfillment in their careers and those who were more traditional and family oriented. As a result, it is probably more appropriate to talk about three Generation X subcultures rather than one.

Marketers have tried targeting Xers by appealing to their pragmatism and by creating ads that are stripped of glitz. The ad for Sharp high-definition TV in Exhibit 12.5 takes a similar approach in conveying a sense of empowerment. The tag line "be uplifted" illustrates the adoption of new technologies and suggests control over one's environment. Marketers are also taking a more hedonistic approach in targeting this age cohort, trying to convey a message that there is nothing wrong with being self-indulgent. The ad for Lycos in Exhibit 12.5 tries to encourage Gen Xers to shop on the Web by conveying fun and just a little bit of glitter.

GLOBAL APPLICATIONS

In Japan the Xers, Not the Boomers, Are the Movers and Shakers

Whereas in the United States, the baby boomers were the defining generation for styles and fashion, in Japan they were something of a yawn. Japan also had a postwar baby boom. But it peaked in 1949, eight years earlier than in the United States, and as a result, boomers were a smaller part of the population.

It was not smaller numbers, however, that defined the lack of impact of boomers in Japan. Because boomers in Japan accepted the norms and values of their parents, and there was no hint of rebellion in their attitudes toward family or institutions, marketers took them for granted, correctly assuming that what worked for boomer parents would work for their children.

Boomers' attitudes toward cars is an example. Growing up in a devastated postwar Japan, they saw a car as a status symbol rather than an expression of self, and they wanted a fancy sedan, a reflection of their parents' tastes.

The group that has played the role of change agents in Japan is the equivalent of Generation Xers, young adults in their late 20s and early 30s. They have broken the old rules and established new ones. They were the first to break with the traditionalism and male dominance of Japanese society. In the car market, they were the first to lead the move out of sedans and into minivans and sport-utility vehicles. They are the first group where more than 50 percent of women have a driver's license. And they are the first group to show the beginnings of a feminist movement as younger women begin demanding some semblance of equality in the workplace.

If Generation Xers have the same impact in Japan as boomers had in the United States, that tradition-bound country is going to change in a big way. Many U.S. marketers have taken notice of the highly influential youth market in Japan, many of whom are enamored of U.S. brands and culture. A new web portal called *www. thinkamerican.com* is attempting to bring smaller U.S. brands to the attention of Japanese Xers without each company having to develop a site in Japanese all by itself. So far the site has assembled a few boutique brands, such as Cynthia Rowley and Searle, but it hopes to bring heavy hitters such as Abercrombie & Fitch and Steve Madden to trendy Japanese consumers.

Sources: "'Cultural Portal' Could Translate Way to Profit," *Wall Street Journal* (February 12, 2001), p. B6; "Thirty-somethings Dominate Japan's Market Direction," *Advertising Age* (April 1, 1996), p. S18.

GENERATION Y (BORN BETWEEN 1977 AND 1994)

Consumers born between 1977 and 1994 have been designated Generation Y for the simple reason that they followed Generation X. They are a more racially diverse group, with 36 percent being minorities compared with 28 percent for the U.S. population as a whole.[30] Like baby boomers, they fall into two distinct age cohorts, the older Gen Ys composed of teens and young adults, and the younger Gen Ys composed of preteens.

▍**Older Generation Ys**   The older wave of this cohort was born between 1977 and 1988. They have certain distinct values. They are not easily hyped and are hard to shock. They are more environmentally aware and health conscious than past youths. They are concerned not only about everyday woes like acne and bad hair, but by real-world problems like AIDs and gang violence. They are more cyberliterate than even Xers and are comfortable with any new technology.

There are 42.06 million teens and young adults in this age group, representing 16 percent of the population.[31] They have $150 billion in purchasing power per year.[32] According to a Nickelodeon/Yankelovich Monitor survey, this generation is distinct from Xers in having great expectations for the future regarding material comforts.[33] Over 90 percent expect to be as well off as their parents or better.

Because these are the "latchkey" kids (young children who fend for themselves when they come home from school because their parents work) of the older baby boomers, today's teens and young adults have spent more hours outside their parents' influence than any generation before. In addition, they have taken on more family responsibilities, such as food shopping. Despite this independence, the Yankelovich Monitor found that the majority say they learned how to shop and save from their baby-boom parents.[34] Not surprisingly, advertisers such as General Foods, Castle & Cooke, Kraft, and Lipton have begun targeting magazines such as *Seventeen*. Fortune 500 companies such as AT&T have used a number of other teen market magazines—from *Details* to *YM* to *Sassy*—to get their messages across in the hopes that teens will be able to influence their parents' behavior.

Teens and young adults are also major consumers of media. They watch an average of 5.25 hours of MTV a week, see 2.5 motion pictures a month, are heavy FM radio listeners, and are the largest group of regular prime-time TV viewers.[35] Because of their media consumption and the fact they are willing to experiment with new products, teens form a very attractive market for manufacturers looking to develop long-term loyalty, especially because many establish lifelong brand loyalties at this age.

Another characteristic of teens is "multitasking"; that is, the ability to do three or four things at once. The computer and the Internet have enhanced multitasking.[36] Teens can work on a term paper while checking email, listening to music, and searching the Web for information. Marketers must recognize that multitasking is going to limit the attention span of the average teenager, so marketing messages must be short and to the point to get across.

As adolescents, teens have in common a self-consciousness and search for identity that affects their purchasing behavior. Adopting a "funky" look, skateboarding, and hip-hop music are manifestations of a search for identity. Part of this search in the teen culture is a key conflict between the need to rebel and be independent from family and society, and the need to be accepted for support and nurturance.

Gen Y consumers receive much more information via the Web about what is hot at a faster pace than any preceding group. Because of this trend, fashions have become more varied and faster changing. "Young consumers have shown that they'll switch their loyalty in an instant to marketers that can get ahead of the style curve."[37] Tommy Hilfiger has done an impressive job of paying attention to this influential group of consumers by sending researchers into music clubs to see how these young customers wear their clothes as well as by recognizing its customers' passion for video games. It not only sponsored a Nintendo competition but also put Nintendo terminals into many of its stores. Gen Y rewarded Hilfiger's attentiveness by recognizing it as their No. 1 brand in an American Express survey.[38]

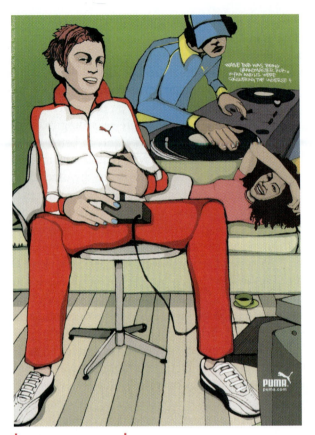

| EXHIBIT 12.6 |

Puma targets young adults.

PUMA.

The ad in Exhibit 12.6 from Puma's 2002 print media plan targets older Gen Ys with an appeal to fun and camaraderie.

Another trend that several prominent marketers have capitalized on is the use of a hybrid catalog-magazine, or "magalog," that combines stories on trends, celebrities, music, travel, and so on, with more typical product information. The bet is that a brand can retain favor with the elusive teen market by reflecting how teens live and not just how they dress. Some of the more successful brands to employ this strategy are Skechers, Abercrombie & Fitch Company, and Target Corporation.[39]

The youth experience has been one of America's most successful exports, making teen demographic marketing a global phenomenon. Like their American peers, Japanese teens are ruggedly individualistic and have rebelled against flashy advertising. As a result, value-oriented products such as L.L. Bean are popular, and the environmentally sensitive cosmetics that The Body Shop makes sell better in Japan than those from Chanel.[40]

■ **Younger Generation Ys** This preteen group (also known as "tweens") was born between 1989 and 1994 and represents 19.8 million people.[41] They are important to marketers as much for their potential as future consumers as for their current purchasing power. Estimates of their pocket money range as high as $31.7 billion.[42] Most preteens live in dual-earning households. Between 1976 and 2000, the number of dual-earning households with children under 12 increased over 50 percent.[43] Preteens are increasingly likely to live in nontraditional households—single-parent households or with stepparents. Demographers now predict that more than half of the youngsters born in the 1990s will spend at least part of their childhood in a single-parent home.[44]

Many baby-boom parents, especially single parents, feel guilty for not spending more time with their children and assuage this guilt by being more willing to buy what children want. The combination of parents' expenditures plus their own money makes preteens an area of opportunity for many product categories. One survey found that this age group influences up to $565 billion of their parents' purchases.[45] This makes kids spending one of the fastest-growing sectors of the American economy.

As a result, marketers of foods that kids enjoy continue to directly target their messages to these preteens rather than to their parents. Heinz launched a campaign in August 2001 in conjunction with ESPN's X-Games to target its Ore-Ida Hot Bites frozen snacks to the preteen market. The campaign features X-Games champion Tony Hawk with the hope of appealing to a younger audience that will help the Hot

Bites franchise to continue to grow.[46] The goal of these marketers is to create brand loyalty with kids early on so they can develop long-term relationships with these customers. Marketers are doing this by trying to build kid appeal for a product while also attracting the parent's attention.[47] Quaker Oats, for example, targets kids with Dinosaur Eggs, brown-sugar-flavored hot oatmeal that includes "eggs" that "hatch." But it also appeals to moms through its emphasis on the nutritional value of the cereal in TV and print ads, which are supported by coupons and an in-store presence. As a result of these types of activities, a new niche of magazines has emerged to cater to children. Two of the best known are Time Warner's *Sports Illustrated for Kids* and the Walt Disney Company's *Disney Adventures.*

Preteens are almost as cyberliterate as their teenage siblings. Some are beginning to call this group the "Net generation," given their skills with the Internet and new technologies. As a result, computer and consumer electronics companies, both traditionally adult categories, now also target their products to preteens. For example, Eastman Kodak is actively marketing its Max One-Time Use camera to preteen girls based on research that showed that girls had a strong interest in taking pictures.[48]

Preteens are also a target for web sites. One such site, *www.bestbuy.com,* actively targets this group because it expects them to influence the purchase decisions of parents and older siblings. These retailers recognize that the younger members of the household heavily influence most of the consumer electronics purchases that families make.

Preteens in China are very different from those in the United States. Because of China's one-child-per-family policy, preteens earn the full attention of parents, grandparents, and marketers. The number of preteens in China, 380 million, is greater than the total population of the United States, and this group is targeted with products from toothpaste to basketball sneakers. Nike targets what has come to be known as the "little emperor" segment with ads showing Chinese kids scoring points on the playground. The ads play into the pressure to succeed that is the dominant ethic among the little emperor segment.[49]

Ethnic Subcultures

One of the most important subcultural entities in the United States is defined by ethnic origin, particularly by race and/or national origin. Consumers in a particular racial or national group are considered part of a subculture when they have a common heritage or environment that influences values and purchasing behavior.

Three key ethnic groups—African-, Hispanic-, and Asian Americans—represent roughly 29 percent of the U.S. population. But this figure understates their importance, because by the year 2050 they are projected to represent one-half of all Americans due to a combined growth rate of approximately 130 percent, more than triple the growth rate of 38 percent for the general population[50] (see Figure 12.1).

As with age, geographic, or religious groups, we might consider these three ethnic groups to be too diverse to constitute subcultures. For example, the diversity that exists among lower-, middle-, and higher-income African Americans is probably as great as that for white consumers. However, as one African-American writer

| FIGURE 12.1 |

Population projections
for key minority groups,
2001–2050.

Sources: Bureau of the Census,
*Statistical Abstract of the United
States, 2000,* Table 18; "Hispanics
Largest Minority Maybe," *Denver
Post,* January 22, 2003, p. A6.

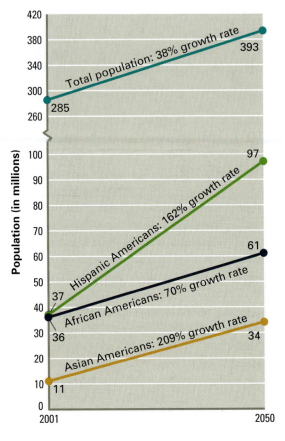

noted fifteen years ago, before marketers began paying attention to this group,
"Regardless of income brackets, African Americans have a unique culture, and the
African-American community has a distinct personality."[51]

THE AFRICAN-AMERICAN SUBCULTURE

More African Americans tend to identify with their ethnic group than whites do
with theirs. This ethnic identity, plus the fact that African Americans differ in many
ways from whites in their tastes and purchases, justifies characterizing them as a
subculture. In this section, we first review differences in characteristics and purchasing behavior and then consider how companies direct marketing strategies to
the African-American market.

■ Demographic Characteristics   The 36.2 million African Americans made
up 12.7 percent of the total population in the United States in 2001 and accounted
for $533 billion in purchasing power in 2000.[52] The median income of African-
American households is less than two-thirds that of whites. Disparities in educational level parallel those in income.[53] Only 15.4 percent of African-American
adults had college degrees in 1999, compared with 25.9 percent of whites; and 77
percent had high school degrees, compared with 84.3 percent of whites.[54]

Lower income and educational levels among African Americans are the result of
decades of discrimination. As barriers to equality have decreased, however, income

and educational levels of African Americans have improved, resulting in a growing middle class. In the past twenty years, the rate of growth in annual income for African Americans has been about the same as for whites. About 23 percent of African-American families have an income that exceeds $50,000, compared with over 40 percent for whites.[55]

Educational levels have improved as well. Since 1960 the proportion of whites finishing high school increased by 49 percent, whereas that of African Americans increased by 74 percent, making them the fastest-growing group to earn high school diplomas in the country.[56] Still, despite these positive trends, this country has a long way to go to achieve income and educational equality.

Another demographic factor that indicates increasing purchasing potential for African Americans is age. The average African-American consumer is six years younger than the average white consumer,[57] which means that a larger proportion have entered their prime spending years in the 1990s as compared with whites.

Some people might conclude that as the African-American middle class grows, it will lose its cultural identity. This is not the case. One study found that the greatest cultural affiliation occurs among affluent African Americans rather than among the underprivileged.[58]

▌ **Purchasing Patterns**   Differences exist in purchasing patterns between African Americans and whites. African Americans spend proportionately more than whites for cosmetics, toiletries, and children's clothing; and whites spend more on medical care, entertainment, and insurance. These differences are largely the result of lower-income levels among African Americans, as lower-income households spend proportionately more of their dollars on necessities.

Because African Americans spend a greater proportion of money on necessities, marketers might believe they spend substantially less on discretionary items. This assumption ignores the growing African-American middle class. One survey found that a larger proportion of African Americans own CD players than do whites. As for purchase intentions, the survey found that African Americans are more likely to purchase cars, furniture, home appliances, jewelry, and computers than are whites in the next year.[59]

These findings put to rest the misconception that the African-American market is a poor economic target. As a result, companies producing major appliances and electronics increasingly target African-American consumers.

▌ **Web Usage**   Web usage is growing for African Americans. In the early days of the Internet, there was a significant racial divide in web usage, with Internet access and incidence of usage for African Americans at levels less than half those for whites. According to *www.thestreet.com,* by 2000, the growth rate in web usage among African Americans was 42 percent a year, compared with 28 percent for whites. As a result, the divide has almost disappeared. Web usage among African Americans is now 40 percent according to thestreet.com, compared with 44 percent for whites.[60]

One reason web usage is increasing is that the Web is becoming more relevant for African Americans. For example, there are now search engines for African Americans *(www.netnoire.com; www.woyaa.com).* Sites also are geared to the specific interests of African Americans; *www.everythingblack.com* claims that it is "the place to find anything and everything black on the Net." And there is a site, African village, that provides an all-inclusive virtual community *(www.africanvil-lage.com)*. There are also sites devoted to news *(www.afroam.org; www.tbwt.com)* and to entertainment *(www.msbet.com)*.

MARKETING TO AFRICAN-AMERICAN CONSUMERS

Viewing African-American consumers as a homogeneous subculture can lead to over-simplified marketing strategies. Marketers can use most of the same demographic, lifestyle, and value criteria to segment the African-American market as they use to segment the white market. As a result, specific advertising, media, and product development strategies are required when selling to the African-American market.

■ **Advertising**   Marketers have significantly changed their view of advertising in the African-American market. In the past, nonethnic advertising campaigns rarely depicted African Americans. With the growth of the African-American and Hispanic-American markets, general advertising can no longer ignore these minorities. As one advertiser said, "In the old days, 'general' was a code word for "white." For any general program to be effective [today], you have to be aware of the sensitivities [of minorities.]"[61] This means that marketers are more likely to develop all-inclusive campaigns that depict minorities rather than target them separately.

As an example, the ad for Verizon in Exhibit 12.7 appeared in *Sports Illustrated,* a general-circulation magazine. The ad makes the same appeals to African Americans as to whites.

Companies also target African Americans for products designed to foster ethnic identification. For example, the ad for CREME OF NATURE®, also in Exhibit 12.7, takes an ethnically aware approach by emphasizing the distinctive hairstyles of African-American women and fosters African-American identity.

Despite greater ethnic awareness, marketers still occasionally make gaffes by failing to sufficiently research the African-American market. Greyhound discovered this when it bought time on African-American radio stations and aired a commercial with a country music soundtrack that few of the hoped-for customers could relate to. To prevent such gaffes, Fortune 500 companies are using African-American ad agencies to get it right. Chrysler used one such agency, Don Coleman & Associates, to advertise its Neon in an attempt to reverse a long-term loss in market share to imports in the African-American market. The print ads combined a view of the car with "jazzy visuals" designed to appeal to African Americans.

■ **Media**   Hundreds of radio stations and magazines are directed to African Americans across the country. Radio is particularly effective, because African Americans listen to radio 20 percent more than the general public. The one weak spot is television. The United States has few African-American TV stations, despite the fact that African Americans spend 44 percent more time than whites watching TV. An exception is the Black Entertainment Television Network (BET). In 1999, the Network established BET.com to provide content on BET's TV programming and magazines, which reach over half of African-American households.[62] The site also serves as a direct seller of Afrocentric products.

| **EXHIBIT 12.7** |

Depicting African Americans in general, versus targeted campaigns.

(left) Joel Baldwin for stocklandmartel.com; (right) © Reprinted with the permission of Colomer U.S.A., Inc. CREME OF NATURE is a registered trademark of Colomer U.S.A., Inc.

PRIORITIES KEPT STRAIGHT
WITH THE HELP OF PAGING ✓ VOICE MAIL ✓ MOBILE WEB ✓

Not all services available in all areas
©2003 Verizon Communications

WE PUT TOGETHER THE WORLD'S MOST POWERFUL TECHNOLOGIES IN WAYS THAT HELP YOU DO WHATEVER YOU WANT, WHENEVER YOU WANT. LOCAL CALLING PLANS • LONG DISTANCE WIRELESS SERVICES • CALLING SERVICE PACKAGES • ONLINE DSL • NATIONAL 411 • VOICE MAIL SUPERPAGES.COM • MOBILE WEB SERVICE • CALLER ID • ADDITIONAL LINES • VISIT VERIZON.COM.

How to get life done.

Joel Baldwin for stocklandmartel.com

■ Product Positioning

Cultural factors also play a large part in the positioning of products to African Americans. As African-American buying power has increased, many of the luxury carmakers have started to market luxury vehicles coming off lease to more affluent members of this community. According to Charles Wimbley of the Wimbley Group, an African-American advertising agency, "African-Americans like to trade up to luxury as fast as possible, and one point of entry is used vehicles."[63] Additionally, Jaguar has partnered with filmmaker Spike Lee to market its cars to African Americans, with a special interest in developing awareness for the launch of its more affordable X-type.[64]

Even more mundane consumer goods are being targeted to African Americans in different ways. To reach African-American youths who are often leery of or unreachable by mainstream media, Coke and Pepsi have outfitted vans and trucks to market their products from the streets. Not only is this viewed as more authentic by the target audience, it is also cheaper than sponsoring events or putting up billboards on a local basis.[65]

▌ **Product Development**   Products have also been designed for African Americans. As African-American women emerged as a force in the workplace, they looked for cosmetics that suited their skin tones. A handful of African-American–run companies, such as Fashion Fair, filled the void until the major cosmetics companies estimated that the ethnic cosmetics market was worth at least $100 million in sales. As a result, Maybelline developed a line called Shades of You; Revlon, a line called Color Style.[66] Product development is also required to meet the needs of the African-American community in general. JCPenney met this need by opening boutiques in twenty markets that carry African-style clothing, housewares, and art.[67]

THE HISPANIC-AMERICAN SUBCULTURE

Because they have largely maintained their language and customs, Hispanic Americans are a distinct subculture. One survey found that almost 90 percent of Hispanics say that the Spanish language is the most important aspect of their culture.[68] More than two-thirds prefer to speak Spanish at home, and one-fifth do not speak English.

In this section, we examine the challenges and opportunities posed by the strong cultural identity of this fast-growing subculture.

▌ **Demographic Characteristics**   In 2001, Hispanic Americans became the largest minority group in the United States, surpassing the African-American population.[69] As of 2001, there were 37 million Hispanics in the United States, representing 13 percent of the population and over $430 billion in purchasing power.[70] The Hispanic-American segment grew by almost 40 percent in the 1990s.[71] As shown in Figure 12.1, the Hispanic population should almost triple by 2050.

Among Hispanics, Mexicans represent more than 60 percent of the total, with most of the remainder being people of Puerto Rican and Cuban origin. Many are immigrants (one-third have come to the United States since 1981), and all are united by a common language and family bonds that make them nurture their heritage.

Hispanics tend to be younger, with a median age of 27, as compared with 38 for the white population.[72] Their median income is about two-thirds that of the average American, and educational levels are well below average. However, both income and education are rising rapidly. Hispanic family size is also larger, with about 3.5 persons per household, as compared with 2.6 for the general population.[73] Hispanics are also more likely than whites or African Americans to live in metropolitan areas. Over 60 percent live in the top ten urban areas in the United States.

Hispanics have traditional and conservative values, which are shown in the respect they give their elders and a strong commitment to family. Hispanics also have a generally male-dominant culture. The views of one Hispanic-American writer expressed over twenty years ago are probably true today: "Machismo is still strong and women's lib has a long way to go in Hispanic communities." This writer predicted that as a result of these values, "The Spanish market will cling to its language, customs, and cultural background and will not, like other ethnic groups, be absorbed into the melting pot tradition of the U.S."[74]

These differences in values and customs justify defining the Hispanic market as a separate subculture, despite differences among Mexicans, Cubans, and Puerto Ricans.

▌ Purchasing Patterns   Hispanic Americans are a highly brand-loyal segment of the market. One survey found that 62 percent of Hispanics buy the same food, beverage, and household items on a regular basis. Hispanics are also more likely to believe that advertising represents an honest and helpful portrayal of products.[75] They demonstrate faith in the quality of well-advertised national brands and are less likely to buy private brands and generic products.

Because of their large family sizes, Hispanics also spend twice as much money per week as non-Hispanics on soft drinks, coffee, canned goods, household cleaners, and beauty aids. The brands they are loyal to also differ. For example, market share of the following brands among Hispanics is at least 20 percent higher than that for whites:

- ▌ Colgate toothpaste
- ▌ Dove and Zest bar soaps
- ▌ Coors and Budweiser beers
- ▌ Avon and English Leather colognes
- ▌ Alberto and Head & Shoulders shampoos[76]

▌ Web Usage   Like African Americans, Hispanic Americans experienced a gap in web usage compared with whites. And also like African Americans, web usage has largely caught up. According to thestreet.com, the level of usage among Hispanic Americans is 43 percent compared with 44 percent for whites.[77]

There are now many more Spanish-language sites relevant to Hispanic Americans than in the early days of the Web. Several search engines serve the needs of this group *(www.cibercentro.com/busqueda; www.mundolatino.org)*. One site provides a wide range of health information offered in Spanish *(www.graciasdoctor. com)* and another, free Internet access to Spanish-speaking customers *(http:// quepasa.com)*. CNN, the cable news channel, has a site specializing in news from Latin America *(http://cnnenespanol.com/latin)*, and several sites provide information on Spanish culture *(http://spanishculture.miningco.com; http://polyglot. lss.wisc.edu)*.

MARKETING TO HISPANIC-AMERICAN CONSUMERS

The commitment of consumer-goods companies to target the Hispanic-American market in the form of advertising and new products is increasing. In 2000, Hispanic media took in about $2 billion in U.S. ad spending compared with $953 million in 1994.[78] But ad spending on Hispanic Americans represents only 1 percent of the total, even though this group is 12 percent of the population.

Although the Hispanic market is made up of various nationalities, marketers have generally avoided segmenting it because the small budgets allocated to Hispanics preclude preparation of separate campaigns for individual segments. Frito-Lay treats Hispanic Americans as a single market because, in the words of one executive, the company tries to project a "consistent national image."[79]

However, differences in customs and language among various Hispanic groups warrant separate strategies for Mexicans, Cubans, and Puerto Ricans. Donnelley Marketing Information Services developed a model that splits the market into eighteen components. The model is so finely tuned that one segment is described as "higher income, younger Puerto Ricans living in single-family homes."[80]

One company that recognizes such differences is Anheuser-Busch. It has followed a segmentation approach for Budweiser, the leading beer among Hispanics, by using different advertising for Mexican, Cuban, and Puerto Rican consumers. The purpose is to ensure that its campaigns pick up on the differences in values between these groups Thus, a Puerto Rican commercial might be set in a disco featuring salsa rhythms, a Mexican commercial in a rodeo with mariachi music, and a Cuban commercial on a private boat because Cubans are the most affluent Hispanic group.

As a result of such targeted efforts, companies are directing advertising, product, and distribution strategies to Hispanic segments.

▌ Advertising   Marketers must be aware of the norms, values, and language nuances of the Hispanic market. In failing to recognize these factors, some companies have made classic blunders. For example, Coors was left red-faced when its slogan "Get loose with Coors" translated into Spanish as "Get the runs with Coors."

Companies use two basic approaches in advertising to Hispanics. One uses the same ads as those in English-language media; the other adapts the campaign to the specific values of the Hispanic market. Exhibit 12.8 shows both approaches. The ad for Perry Ellis fragrances has appeared in Hispanic magazines such as *Vanidades* and in general-circulation magazines. The danger with such an approach is that it may not reflect Hispanics' specific needs and values. That is, given the strong cultural identity of Hispanic Americans, they may not identify with a fragrance called America and an ad that pictures the vastness of the United States.

Advertising approaches to the Hispanic market should reflect its conservative values and emphasis on family and children. This is better illustrated in the ad for Wal-Mart, also in Exhibit 12.8. The ad appeals to the family ties and emotions of Hispanic consumers by showing an older sibling taking care of a younger one. It appeals to basic family values that Hispanic Americans can easily identify with, without being a "tearjerker." Similarly, MasterCard's well-known "priceless" campaign was targeted to the Hispanic market in 2000, with several ads appearing in Spanish. One TV commercial shows a father diapering and dressing his newborn, all the while showing the prices of diapers, booties, and a baby carriage. The point is to show that the feeling of being a father is priceless. Since fewer Hispanics use credit cards than the balance of the U.S. population, this is a chance to build awareness and relevancy for MasterCard in the minds of Hispanic consumers.[81]

▌ Media   Hundreds of radio stations and magazines are targeted to Hispanic Americans. Because a network of Spanish-speaking television stations exists, the Hispanic-American market is easier to target than the African-American market. There are well over a hundred local Spanish TV stations plus two national Spanish networks, Univision and Telemundo. In 2002, a third national network was established, Telefutura, reflecting the growing importance of the Hispanic-American market.[82] Radio is almost as effective as TV in reaching Hispanics, with about 125 Spanish-language stations nationwide.

| EXHIBIT 12.8 |

Taking a general approach versus targeting the Hispanic identity.

(left) Courtesy Perry Ellis; (right) Courtesy Wal-Mart.

Television and radio are effective in this market because Hispanics are more likely than the general population to tune into these media, and half of the time they tune into Spanish-speaking stations. Thus, the major networks are beginning to target Hispanic-American households. In 2001, CBS wrote several Latino characters into the script of "The Bold and the Beautiful" to accompany the patrician characters on the program. CBS also dubs the soap opera in Spanish in Hispanic markets.[83]

Spanish-language magazines and newspapers are also becoming more important. *Vista,* a Sunday magazine newspaper supplement, reaches over 1 million Hispanic households. *Vanidades* magazine is aimed at Hispanic women in their late teens and early twenties, whereas *Cosmopolitan en Espanol* is targeted to the young, modern Hispanic woman. *Miami Mensual* is designed to reach affluent Hispanic audiences.

▌ Product Development In the product development area, Estee Lauder designs makeup shades for Hispanic-American women. Faberge also has developed shampoos and conditioners specifically designed for the Hispanic woman's typically long and thick hair.

In the food category, General Mills has introduced a line of cereals called Para su Familia ("For Your Family"), which includes Frosted Corn Flakes, Frutis, Cinnamon Corn Stars, and Raisin Bran, all in packages with bilingual labels. This is an attempt to capitalize on Hispanics' interest in nutritious meals.[84]

In electronics, Gateway launched a Spanish-language PC line including software, Internet services, and a targeted ad campaign.[85]

■ **Distribution**   Hispanics tend to favor large supermarkets and department stores. Many also shop in *bodegas,* small grocery stores that specialize in Hispanic foods and serve as a place for socializing. Hispanics value the personal interaction with friends and shop owners in the bodegas as well as the selection of foods with which they are familiar, such as certain ethnic foods they cannot find in larger supermarkets.[86] One reason Goya Foods has been a successful marketer of Hispanic products is that it has cultivated strong relationships with bodega owners. Similarly, by establishing strong distribution through bodegas, P&G has been successful as the largest marketer of Hispanic products. The company has a bilingual sales and distribution force that caters to bodegas in key metropolitan areas such as New York and Miami. To reinforce this presence, P&G spent $64 million in the first half of 2000 on Spanish-language television alone.[87]

THE ASIAN-AMERICAN SUBCULTURE

Asian Americans are the third-largest minority group, with 11 million people representing about 4 percent of the U.S. population, and accounting for approximately $228.5 billion in yearly purchasing power.[88] The reason for identifying Asian Americans as a subculture is the same as that for African Americans and Hispanic Americans: strong ethnic identity. The Asian-American population grew by 43 percent in the 1990s, the most rapid growth of any minority group.[89] Growth was mainly due to immigration, with 50 percent of Asian Americans having arrived in this country during the past twenty years.[90] The greatest growth due to immigration has occurred among Vietnamese Americans, a group that grew by 83 percent in the 1990s.[91]

Asian Americans are more varied than Hispanic- and African Americans, accounting for twenty-nine distinct ethnic groups. Chinese represent the largest group, followed closely by Filipinos, and then by Japanese, Vietnamese, and Koreans. Despite this diversity, Asian Americans hold some values in common. They value close-knit family ties, put a high premium on education, and emphasize a strong work ethic.

They tend to be brand loyal and like to buy status-oriented products. But because many are recent immigrants, Asian Americans are not always familiar with brand names. For example, one survey found that 32 percent of Chinese residents in Los Angeles did not know what brand of laundry detergent they use, and 35 percent did not know what brand of soft drink they last purchased.[92]

■ **Demographic Characteristics**   Asian Americans are the most highly educated and affluent minority group. About 42 percent have college degrees, compared with 25 percent for the general population, and their median income is 20 percent higher than that of other Americans. The average age of this group is four years younger than that of the general population.[93] As Figure 12.1 shows, the Asian-American segment is projected to increase threefold over the next half century, primarily because of a high rate of immigration. About 93 percent live in highly urbanized areas, with 55 percent living in the West, mostly in California.[94]

▍ Web Usage   Asian Americans are the most wired group in the United States. Thestreet.com estimates that 68 percent of Asian Americans have web access, compared with 44 percent of whites.[95] Jupiter Research estimates that this figure will jump to 84 percent in 2005.[96]

Asian Americans have an assortment of sites to choose from. Most are targeted to the Asian-American market in general. For example, *www.aarising.com* is an offshoot of the magazine by the same name offering human interest stories targeted to Asian Americans. A competitor in the same area is *www.aOnline.com.* Asian Americans also have an online news service, *www.Click2Asia.com.* A site targeted to Generation Y Asian Americans from 15 to 25 is *www.AsianScene.com.*

Given the diversity of the Asian-American market, many sites are starting to target specific nationalities. For example *www.Ona.com* targets Japanese women, while *www.AsiaDera.com* targets the Filipino market in the United States.[97]

MARKETING TO ASIAN-AMERICAN CONSUMERS

Because the Asian-American market is small, few marketers direct advertising strategies to it. Their philosophy is that Asian Americans need no special marketing effort and that general advertising campaigns also attract this segment. These marketers also find targeted marketing difficult because of the community's diversity and range of native tongues. One survey determined that most Asian Americans speak their native language at home, particularly Koreans (94 percent) and Chinese (90 percent).[98]

As a result, Asian Americans are poor media consumers. On average, they watch about 12 hours of English-language television a week, well below the national average. They are also below average in radio exposure. One survey found that about half those polled did not read English-language magazines.[99] In addition, there is no national Asian cable TV network.

Some companies are beginning to target Asian Americans, however, because their youth and greater affluence make them an attractive market. Sears was one of the first major retailers to target Asian Americans in 1994 when it hired an ad agency to develop an ad campaign aimed at this segment.[100] Nordstrom and Gap use outdoor and point-of-purchase ads to attract Asian Americans in California. These attempts to target the Asian-American market are the exception, however. For most companies, it is difficult to implement such campaigns due to the diversity of the Asian-American market.

Specific Asian nationalities can be more easily targeted because they tend to live in the same areas. For example, in 2001, General Motors aired ads, showing three generations of a Chinese family riding in a Buick Rendezvous, on Chinese-language TV stations in New York, Los Angeles, and San Francisco—cities with the largest Chinese populations.[101] The heavy concentration of immigrants from Southeast

California: On the Cutting Edge of Catering to Ethnic Identity

In 1999, California became the first state in the United States where African-, Hispanic-, and Asian Americans constituted a majority of the population. As a result, marketers are pulling out all the stops to woo ethnic customers, whom they largely ignored just a decade ago. In the process, they are learning that selling to ethnic shoppers requires considerably more effort than just putting an Asian or a Latino actor in an English commercial.

These efforts are felt most in the Hispanic community, which accounts for a quarter of the state's population, and the Asian community, which is 10 percent of the state's total. Banks, phone companies, TV stations, and supermarket chains are all quickly learning about the diversity, nuances, and perceptions of these communities so they can apply a strategy that one consultant calls "international marketing within your own borders." This means that just as American strategies may not work abroad, marketers cannot assume that strategies designed for a homogeneous U.S. market will work in ethnic enclaves. New immigrants often are mystified by American norms, and those who have assimilated frequently retain their cultural identity.

Some of the worst marketing blunders have occurred because California marketers have not been sensitive to ethnic cultures. Coors was roundly criticized for sexual stereotyping during the 1988 Chinese New Year when it erotically portrayed a Chinese woman in the folds of a silk dragon. And, when Pepsi tried aiming its "Choice of a New Generation" campaign at Chinese Americans, it suffered a major embarrassment when the slogan was unintentionally translated into "Come and wake up your dead ancestors."

Bank of America showed more ethnic sensitivity in dealing with the fact that most of the new Latino residents in California had never set foot in a bank. It embarked on a massive education campaign, including a slick soap-opera video that followed a Latino couple through marriage, having children, and buying their first home—with explanations at each juncture about how a bank can help. The Bank gives these videos to various outreach groups that socialize new Americans.

Asians pose more difficulties than Hispanics for California marketers because of the variety of languages they speak—Vietnamese, Cantonese, Mandarin, Korean, Tagalog (spoken by Filipinos), or Cambodian. One strategy for bridging the gap is to rely less on mass-market tools such as television and use the growing list of ethnic newspapers. Companies such as the Bank of America follow this strategy. Another strategy is to use members of a targeted ethnic group to help market products or services. In 1996, many HMOs in California (Oxford, Kaiser, and others) recruited Cantonese- and Spanish-speaking doctors to better target Chinese and Hispanic consumers.

It is often said that California leads the rest of the United States. As minorities become the majority in state after state, California's ethnic marketers will surely have much to teach the rest of the nation.

Sources: "Ground Shifts in California," *Advertising Age* (September 25, 2000), p. 78; "Health: HMOs Say 'Hola' to Potential Customers," *Wall Street Journal* (November 30, 1995), p. B1; "Catering to Consumers' Ethnic Needs," *New York Times* (January 23, 1992), pp. D1, D8; "Solutions: Making a Connection," *Adweek* (October 7, 1991), p. 46; "California's Asian Market," *American Demographics* (October 1990), pp. 34–37.

Asia in California made it possible for Bank of America to be among the first to target Asian Americans selectively. The Bank targeted immigrants in the central valley of California by advertising in newspapers in Vietnamese, Cambodian, and Laotian. The ads urged readers to "come see us," as these recent immigrants mistrusted banks. The ad in Exhibit 12.9 is another example of the Bank's selective targeting, in this case, a campaign aimed at Chinese Americans in California.

Subcultures of Consumption

So far, we have identified subcultures based on consumer characteristics—age, race, national identity, religion. Subcultures also can be formed around product interests or activities. These are known as **subcultures of consumption.** Subcultures of consumption are defined by four characteristics related to a product category's central role in the subculture: The product (1) serves as a total lifestyle focus, (2) defines a common value system, (3) has a social hierarchy generally related to expertise with the product, and (4) generates intense interest and enduring involvement.

THE HARLEY SUBCULTURE: AN EXAMPLE

Based on the four points just cited, owners of Harley-Davidson motorcycles conform to a subculture of consumption. First, the Harley represents a total lifestyle focus. There are the hard-core "outlaw" bikers and the "weekend warriors," both resentful of each other, but both viewing the Harley as their main vehicle for socialization. Second, the Harley defines a common value system. The outlaw bikers value the "freedom to"; that is, the license to do whatever they want outside the bounds of social norms. The weekend warriors value the "freedom from"; that is, the liberation in getting away from the day-to-day routine of office and home. Third, a clear social hierarchy is manifested by the riding formation and the status symbols related to Harley paraphernalia. And fourth, bikers are involved with their Harleys on an ongoing basis.

Harley-Davidson supports its product as a subculture of consumption by cultivating the mystique and reverence paid to the product "through means such as supplying a steady stream of information geared to the needs of newcomers and providing a full range of clothing, accessories, and services that function as involvement-enhancing side bets and exit barriers."[102] As a result, the Harley subculture represents an "identifiable, hierarchical social structure; a unique ethos, or set of shared beliefs and values; and unique jargons, rituals, and modes of symbolic expression."[103]

Other product-specific activities or interests that might result in subcultures of consumption based on these characteristics are sports-related activities, music, automobiles, and travel.

TARGETING SUBCULTURES OF CONSUMPTION

Targeting a subculture of consumption has implications for each component of the marketing mix. The *product* must have characteristics that are easily related to an owner's self-identity. The size of a Harley connotes power as do the roar of the engine and the speed on the open road. Further, the company recognizes the commitment of riders by leveraging these associations to various product and clothing accessories. A Harley jacket is a must to many riders.

Advertising should employ symbols that are related to the owner's self-identity and that portray the desired lifestyle. It is little surprise that the typical motorcycle ad depicts the freedom of the open road and a rider at one with his bike. Part of the promotional program should be a *relationship marketing* strategy that maintains strong ties with the owner over time. Harley has promoted and fostered Harley Owners' Groups (HOGS) to maintain such a relationship, sponsoring meets and publishing *HOGS* magazine.

Media should employ specialized magazines to satisfy the interests of the involved owner. Motorcycle, car, and ski magazines are examples of media that meet the needs of the enduringly involved consumer. *Retailers* should be highly knowledgeable to gain the respect of the prospective purchaser. Further, retailers should also have a relationship marketing program to provide product service and to ensure repurchase of the product.

Many companies have found the Internet a valuable tool in marketing to subcultures of consumption. By supporting and monitoring chatrooms, firms help direct discussions and provide information about products that are of value to core consumers. Additionally, the Internet can reach a large group of interested consumers with sites devoted exclusively to specific products. Some examples of sites that help support specific subcultures of consumption include *www.dead.net.com* for followers of the Grateful Dead; *www.starwars.com* for devotees and fans of the Star Wars series of movies; and *www.extremesports.com* for devotees of rugged sports activities.

Societal Implications of Subcultural Influences

The nature of **subcultural influences** creates a number of societal issues regarding age cohorts, particularly the very young and very old, and minorities. As we saw in Chapter 7, issues arise in targeting the very young (those under 8, beginning to be referred to as Generation Z) because of their lack of ability to adequately process promotional messages; thus, the potential for taking advantage of this group must be monitored and controlled. As for the very old, the issues are their diminished capacities and the need to assist them in processing information and in designing products to meet their needs.

Regarding minorities, the issue is one of consumer rights. Minority consumers should have the same rights as others without being at a disadvantage. However, this is not always the case. Minority consumers in lower socioeconomic groups are often at a disadvantage when it comes to adequate brand alternatives, fair prices, and the assurance of product safety.

Another issue is the attempt to target potentially harmful products to minorities. R.J. Reynolds targeted Uptown cigarettes specifically to African Americans. Before Uptown came along, cigarette companies had devoted part of their advertising budget for their existing brands to African Americans and Hispanics, but none had ever developed a product with the intent of targeting it to a minority segment. Reynolds's plans provoked an outcry that was successful in getting the company to withdraw the product. However, apparently the lesson did not fully sink in. Shortly after it withdrew Uptown, Reynolds considered marketing a cigarette called Dakota to blue-collar women under 21. Although there was no evidence Reynolds planned to introduce Dakota, the issue remains—attempting to target underprivileged consumers with potentially unsafe products. This issue is considered further in Chapter 19 when issues of social responsibility are discussed.

SUMMARY

Subcultures are important to marketers because they represent groups with distinct values, customs, and purchasing habits. The more distinctive and homogeneous a subculture, the greater will be its influence on consumer purchases.

Subcultures in the United States can be identified on the basis of five things: age, geography, race, religion, or national origin.

Age cohorts, including baby boomers, Generation X, Generation Y, and the mature market, are all important segments to which marketers must pay specific attention. Each group has different values and life experiences resulting in different strategic implications. Of particular significance is the aging of the baby boomers and the consequent adjustment of the perspective on youth. As a result of this phenomenon, more attention is likely to be paid to the mature market, a group that has received insufficient attention by marketers. The chapter also considered Generation X and Y as important targets with very different values and perspectives regarding the future.

Another key subcultural dimension considered is ethnic subcultures. The three most important ethnic subcultures for marketers are African Americans, Hispanic Americans, and Asian Americans, who together represent nearly 30 percent of the U.S. population. These subcultures also represent significant purchasing power—close to $1 trillion a year—and are profitable markets because they tend to be brand loyal.

Marketers have increasingly directed strategies to these groups. The African-American consumer market has seen more cosmetic and toiletry products directed to its specific needs. In addition, marketers have directed ads to African Americans through African-American magazines and radio, and ad campaigns have frequently attempted to foster Afro identity. Targeting marketing strategies to Hispanics is facilitated by greater homogeneity in values. Companies such as Anheuser-Busch and Polaroid have developed Spanish-speaking ad campaigns for their national brands. However, companies find targeting ad campaigns to Asian Americans difficult because of the diversity of nationalities and languages within this broad segment. Overall, marketers have a long way to go in recognizing the potential of the African-, Hispanic-, and Asian-American markets and adequately targeting marketing efforts to these groups.

The chapter also considered subcultures of consumption; that is, subcultures that are formed around lifestyle interests or activities centered on products. Examples might be consumers who are highly involved with motorcycles, music, travel, or sports-related activities.

The chapter concluded by considering some societal implications of cross-cultural and subcultural influences; namely, the desirability of being sensitive to the informational needs of the very young and the very old, and the need to protect the rights of underprivileged consumers.

In Chapter 13, we consider another environmental factor: cross-cultural influences; that is, how consumer needs and values vary globally.

QUESTIONS FOR DISCUSSION

1. What are the characteristics that identify a subculture? Would you identify residents of retirement communities as a subculture? Why or why not?

2. What are the marketing implications of America becoming more of a "salad bowl" than a "melting pot"?

3. What types of companies might find it economically attractive to target the gay community? What sort of risks might a firm encounter in openly targeting this segment?

4. Why are so few ads and products targeted to the mature market? Is this lack of attention to the mature market likely to change in the future? Why or why not?

5. How would you describe the prevalent norms and values of Generation Xers? What are the marketing implications of your description?

6. Why is the role of baby boomers and Generation Xers different in Japan compared with the United States?

7. What are the different values and needs of younger versus older baby boomers? What are the strategic implications of these differences?

8. Can a marketer target Generation X as a single age cohort? Why or why not?

9. On what basis could you support identification of the African-American consumer market as a subculture? On what basis could you argue against such an identification? What are the marketing implications of each position?

10. A company is considering three alternative strategies in marketing a hair-care line to African-American consumers:

   a. Introduce two lines: one positioned to those who seek Afro identity; the other, to those who identify with white middle-class values.

   b. Introduce one line to appeal to both segments mentioned in alternative (a).

   c. Introduce one line to appeal only to those seeking Afro identity.

   What are the pros and cons of each strategy? Which would you select? Why?

11. Hispanic Americans have been described as a more homogeneous ethnic subculture than African Americans. Why? What are the marketing implications of a greater level of homogeneity?

12. An ad for a household cleanser targeted to Hispanic women uses an appeal showing the husband's approval when entering a sparkling clean home. Do you think such an appeal would be successful among Hispanic women? Among the general population? Why or why not?

13. What are the pros and cons of targeting Asian-American consumers as one segment?

14. Provide an example of a subculture of consumption (other than the Harley subculture). What are the strategic implications of targeting this group?

15. What are the pros and cons of having allowed R.J. Reynolds to target Uptown to African Americans?

RESEARCH ASSIGNMENTS

1 Identify a web site that reflects a "subculture of consumption"; that is, a site that revolves around a product or set of products with the characteristics in the following list:

a. The product serves as a lifestyle focus.

b. Social interactions revolve around the product.

c. The product defines a common value system among users or owners.

d. Interest in the product results in a social hierarchy related to expertise.

In what ways does the site you selected reflect the preceding characteristics? What are the implications for marketing strategy?

2 Identify an ethnic group that can be regarded as a subculture (whether by race, religion, or national origin). Interview thirty people in this group and thirty people in the general population. Ask respondents to (a) rate their agreement with lifestyle items such as those in Table 10.1 and (b) indicate how frequently they purchase products such as cosmetics, household cleaners, and soft drinks.

- Do your findings justify identifying the group you selected as a subculture? Specifically, what are the differences in values, lifestyles, and purchases between the subcultural group and the general group? Is the subcultural group more homogeneous in lifestyles and values than the general group?

- What are the implications of your findings for developing (a) products and (b) advertising strategies for the subcultural group?

NOTES

1. "Ethnic Population Too Big to Ignore," *USBanker* (June 2000), pp. 65–68.
2. "Marketers Greet Newcomers," *Advertising Age* (November 29, 1999), p. S14.
3. "Reaching the New Immigrants," *Adweek's Marketing Week* (September 11, 1989), p. 24.
4. "Ethnic Population Too Big to Ignore," pp. 65–68.
5. "Ground Shifts in California," *Advertising Age* (September 25, 2000), p. 78.
6. Elizabeth Hirschman, "American Jewish Ethnicity: Its Relationship to Some Selected Aspects of Consumer Behavior," *Journal of Marketing* 45 (Summer 1981), pp. 102–105.
7. "Bringing in the Sheaves," *American Demographics* (August 1988), pp. 28–32.
8. "Baptist Leader Mixes Preaching, Politics," *St. Louis Post-Dispatch* (March 23, 2002), p. A16.
9. "Southern Baptists Wish Upon a Star," *The Advocate* (July 17, 2001), p. 19.
10. "Out of the Closet," *Marketing Review* (March 1996), pp. 21–23.
11. "As Same-Sex Households Grow More Mainstream Businesses Take Note," *Wall Street Journal* (August 8, 2001), pp. B1, B4.
12. "Cracking the Gay Market Code—How Marketers Plant Subtle Symbols in Ads," *Wall Street Journal* (June 29, 1999), p. B1.
13. "Gay Market Power," *American Demographics* (June 1999), pp. 32–34.
14. "As Same-Sex Households Grow More Mainstream," pp. B1, B4.
15. Bureau of the Census, *Statistical Abstract of the United States, 2000,* Table 14.
16. "A Never-Say-Old Generation Can't Outrace the Clock Forever," *New York Times* (December 3, 2000), pp. 3, 12.
17. Henry Assael and David F. Poltrack, "Debunking the Myth of the Older Consumer," *STERNbusiness* (Summer 2000,) pp. 20–23.
18. "Ads for Elderly May Give Wrong Message," *Wall Street Journal* (December 31, 1991), p. D4.
19. Assael and Poltrack, "Debunking the Myth of the Older Consumer," pp. 20–23.
20. Bureau of the Census, *Statistical Abstract of the United States, 2000,* Table 14.
21. "The Joy of Empty Nesting," *American Demographics* (May 2000), p. 50.
22. "AARP Puts Boomers First with New 'My Generation,'" *Advertising Age* (September 25, 2000), p. 15.
23. "A Never-Say-Old Generation," p. 3.
24. Bureau of the Census, *Statistical Abstract of the United States, 2000,* Table 14.
25. "The X-files," *Catalog Age* (May 2000), p. S4.
26. "Generation X, Still Undecided," *New York Times* (June 17, 2001), p. C10.
27. *The Mademoiselle Report: Redefining a Generation* (New York: Mademoiselle, 1994).
28. "Generation Xers' Reinvented 'Traditionalism,'" *Brandweek* (June 5, 2000), pp. 28, 30.
29. "Toyota, Seeking Younger Drivers, Uses Hip Hop, Web, Low Prices," *Wall Street Journal* (September 9, 1999).
30. "Tally of Students Equals Number at Boomer Peak," *New York Times* (March 23, 2001), p. A17.
31. Bureau of the Census, *Statistical Abstract of the United States, 2000,* Table 14.
32. Mark Alch, "The Echo-Boom Generation: A Growing Force in American Society," *The Futurist* (September/October 2000), pp. 42–46.
33. "Spending It, Investing It—Coming on Strong: The Children of the Baby Boomers Are Affecting Spending and Investing as Significantly as Their Parents Did; The Similarity Ends There," *Wall Street Journal* (November 29, 1999), p. R, 12:1.
34. Ibid.
35. "The Child Research, Custom, Consulting and Qualitative Divisions," MSW Newsletter.
36. "Teenage Overload, or Digital Dexterity?" *New York Times* (April 12, 2001), pp. G1, G5.
37. "Generation Y: Today's Teens—the Biggest Bulge Since the Boomers—May Cause Marketers to Toss Their Old Tricks," *Business Week* (February 15, 1999), p. 84.
38. Ibid.
39. "To Reach the Unreachable Teen: Retailers Are Trying a Whole-Lifestyle Approach to Win Gen Y," *Business Week* (September 18, 2000), p. 78.
40. "Asian Teens Get Cultural Cues from Japan, Not U.S.; Hello Kitty Is In, Mickey Mouse Is on the Retreat," *Houston Chronicle* (February 10, 2000), p. 22.
41. Bureau of the Census, *Statistical Abstract of the United States, 2000,* Table 14.
42. "'Superstars' of Spending," *Advertising Age* (February 12, 2001), pp. S1, S10.
43. "Families with Both Parents Employed Are Now a U.S. Majority," *Work & Family Life* (January 2001), p.1.
44. "Unmarried, with Children," *Newsweek* (May 28, 2001), p. 48.
45. "'Superstars' of Spending," pp. S1, S10.
46. "Heinz Rolls Out New Hot Bites," *Advertising Age* (April 16, 2001), p. 37.
47. "Brand Loyalty Begins Early," *Advertising Age* (February 12, 2001), p. S2.
48. "Tweens Mesh Latest Fads, Moms & Dads," *Advertising Age* (February 14, 2000), p. 40.
49. "Target: 380 million Chinese Emperors," *Advertising Age* (April 12, 1999), p. 26.
50. Bureau of the Census, *Statistical Abstract of the United States, 2000,* Table 18.
51. "Madison Avenue Blindly Ignores the Black Consumer," *Business and Society Review* (Winter 1987), p. 11.
52. "Hispanics Largest Minority Maybe," *Denver Post,* January 22, 2003, p. A6; and "Minority Purchasing Power Tops $1.1 Trillion," *Houston Chronicle* (May 27, 1999), p. 4.
53. Ibid.
54. Bureau of the Census, *Statistical Abstract of the United States, 2000,* Table 249.
55. Ibid., Table 736.
56. Ibid., Table 249.
57. Ibid., Table 19.
58. *Adweek's Marketing Week* (May 6, 1991), p. 18.

59. "Motorola Gets Signal on Blacks' Pager Use," *Wall Street Journal* (June 24, 1996), p. B6; and *Adweek's Marketing Week* (May 6, 1991), p. 18.

60. http://abcnews.go.com, "Online Rhumba," as of December 20, 2000.

61. "Blending into the Mainstream," *Advertising Age* (July 17, 1995), p. S2.

62. "The Battle to Usher Blacks Onto the Web," *Wall Street Journal* (August 12, 1999), p. B1.

63. "Automakers Step Up Used-Vehicle Ads," *Advertising Age* (August 14, 2000), pp. 3, 39.

64. "Spike Lee's Jaguar Ads Begin First Test Mailing," *Advertising Age* (December 18, 2000), p. 18.

65. "Urban Warfare," *Advertising Age* (September 4, 2000), pp. 16–17.

66. "Mining the Non-White Markets," *Brandweek* (April 12, 1993), p. 29.

67. "Buying Black," *Time* (August 31, 1992), p. 52; and "J.C. Penney Finds Profit," *American Demographics* (November 1992), p. 12.

68. "Publishers Shout Over the Din," *Advertising Age* (February 12, 1990), p. S12.

69. "Hispanics Largest Minority Maybe," p. A6.

70. Ibid.; and "Mas Appeal," *Adweek* (December 18, 2000), pp. 44–46.

71. "Hispanic and Asian Populations Expand," *New York Times* (August 30, 2000), p. A16.

72. Bureau of the Census, *Statistical Abstract of the United States, 2000*, Table 18.

73. Ibid., Table 62.

74. "Cultural Differences Offer Rewards," *Advertising Age* (April 7, 1980), p. S20.

75. "Poll: Hispanics Stick to Brands," *Advertising Age* (February 15, 1993), p. 6.

76. "What Does Hispanic Mean?" *American Demographics* (June 1993), p. 50; and C. Webster, "The Effects of Hispanic Subcultural Identification on Information Search Behavior," *Journal of Advertising Research* 32 (September/October 1992), pp. 54–62.

77. http://abcnews.go.com.

78. "Mas Appeal," pp. 44–46; and "Brand Loyalty Wavers; Private Label Gains," *Advertising Age* (January 23, 1995), p. 32.

79. "What Does Hispanic Mean?" p. 50.

80. Ibid., p. 48.

81. "MasterCard Is Shifting Its Efforts to Market to Hispanics to a New Level and Another Language," *New York Times* (August 30, 2000), p. C6; and "'Priceless' a Hit with Hispanic Audiences," *Marketing News* (January 15, 2001), pp. 5–6.

82. "Univision Seeks a Bigger Pie for Spanish TV," *New York Times* (January 15, 2002), pp. B1, B3.

83. "CBS Gives 'Bold and Beautiful' a Spanish Accent," *New York Times* (April 17, 2001), pp. B1, B6.

84. "Food for Thought," *American Demographics* (May 2000), p. 40.

85. "Gateway Marketing Effort Has a Latin Pitch," *Wall Street Journal* (September 30, 1999), p. B10.

86. "Spanish-Speaking Hispanics Prefer Neighborhood Shops," *Discount Store News* (October 4, 1999), p. 4.

87. "P&G Reaches Out to Hispanics—Marketing for Secret, Pampers and Cover Girl Take on a Distinctly Latin Flavor," *Wall Street Journal* (October 13, 2000), p. B1.

88. Bureau of the Census, *Statistical Abstract of the United States, 2000*, Table 18; and "Minority Purchasing Power," p. 4.

89. "Hispanics and Asian Populations Expand," p. A16.

90. Bureau of the Census, *Statistical Abstract of the United States, 2000*, Table 7.

91. "U.S. Asian Population Grew and Diversified, Census Shows," *Wall Street Journal* (May 15, 2001), p. B4.

92. "Asian-Americans: The Three Biggest Myths," *Sales & Marketing Management* (September 1993), pp. 86–101.

93. Bureau of the Census, *Statistical Abstract of the United States, 2000*, Table 22, Table 249, and Table 737; and "Ethnic Population Too Big to Ignore," pp. 65–68.

94. Bureau of the Census, *Statistical Abstract of the United States, 2000*, Table 26; and "A New Look at Asian Americans," *American Demographics* (October 1990), p. 30.

95. http://abcnews.go.com, as of December 20, 2000.

96. "Eyeing Asian American E-Shoppers," *San Francisco Chronicle* (June 19, 2000), p. G1.

97. Ibid.

98. "Taking the Pulse of Asian-Americans," *Adweek's Marketing Week* (August 12, 1991), p. 32.

99. "Poll: Hispanics Stick to Brands," p. 6.

100. "Sears Targets Asians," *Advertising Age* (October 10, 1994), p. 1.

101. "Chrysler's Latest Ads for Minivans Stress Multicultural Over Motherly," *Wall Street Journal* (December 18, 2001), p. B9.

102. John W. Schouten and James H. McAlexander, "Subcultures of Consumption: An Ethnography of the New Bikers," *Journal of Consumer Research* 22 (June 1995), pp. 43–61.

103. Ibid.

Cross-Cultural and Global Influences

Chapter 12 focused on the ways cultural values influence consumer purchasing behavior, primarily in the United States. In this chapter, we consider **cross-cultural influences** (*i.e.,* differences in values across countries) and describe marketing strategies that adapt to local differences. A counterpoint to cross-cultural influences is **global influences,** which reflect common needs and values across countries. We also examine strategies that allow companies to market "world brands"—brands such as Coca-Cola and McDonald's that are marketed similarly worldwide—based on globally shared values, needs, and wants.

Nestlé Stays Local and Levi Strauss Goes Global

Switzerland-based food manufacturer Nestlé closely follows cross-cultural trends and adapts its marketing strategies to local differences. With approximately 98 percent of revenues generated outside of Switzerland, Nestlé recognizes the importance of foreign markets. It operates with a highly decentralized strategy, offering more than eighty-five hundred products in seventy countries, in order to appeal to the individual needs and cultures of each market. Nestlé uses regional management structures to oversee its efforts in different parts of the world.[1] As the world's largest food company, Nestlé knows that consumer behavior is driven largely by cultural customs and values. This country-specific view is all the more important because most of Nestlé's brands are food items, and tastes and customs for food differ across countries. For example, Germans like a sweet pasta sauce whereas Britons like a more acidic sauce. As one Nestlé executive said, "In the food area, local understanding is fundamental."[2] As a result, only 10 percent of Nestlé's products are sold in more than one country.

Even when the underlying product is similar, like mineral water, Nestlé uses different brands in different regions because the brands are often associated with a particular region and image that doesn't cross over well to another area. So Nestlé offers thirteen mineral water brands, including Vittel, Calistoga, San Pellegrino, and Perrier. It has also recently launched a low-cost bottled-water brand, Pure Life, for developing countries.

Nestlé's chocolate and confectionary group is another good example of its locally oriented strategy. Nestlé offers a wide range of chocolate and confectionary products, ranging from chocolate bars to sweet biscuits. The Willy Wonka candy line, which includes candy like Nerds, Gobstoppers, and Fun Dip, has been popular among children in the United States and the United Kingdom. High-end chocolates, like After Eight, have been popular in Europe and the United States, whereas Italians prefer Baci chocolates. Biscuits are popular in Latin America, where Nestlé offers São Luiz, McKay, and La Rosa biscuits. People in China and India prefer a sweet chocolate wafer snack.[3]

EXHIBIT 13.1
LEJ: A global brand.
Courtesy Bartle Bogle Hegarty, London.

In contrast to Nestlé, Levi Strauss has adopted a world branding strategy because jeans reflect more universal values among a global Generation Y culture. This strategy is aided by the fact that world cultures are becoming closer in many respects. For example, the company recognizes that tastes in music, fashion, and technology among the young are becoming more similar across the world with greater facilities for travel, Internet communications, and the global reach of cable TV channels such as MTV. It has also recognized the increasing Americanization of consumption values abroad as more consumers crave American goods. Levi's® jeans are the only U.S. apparel label that can be called a world brand. The company has achieved world brand status by marketing the Levi's® brand as an enshrined piece of Americana. Teenagers wearing Levi's® jeans portray common values whether in Bangkok, Leningrad, Paris, or Rio.

Most recently, in response to lagging global sales among its core teenage market, Levi Strauss launched a new sub-brand of jeans, Levi's® engineered jeans® (LEJ), which features trademarked twisted seams. The marketing campaign reflects and supports the company's global brand strategy. Targeted toward the 15- to 19-year-old market, LEJ advertisements feature teenagers in various situations based on the theme of "twisted to fit" (see Exhibit 13.1).

Although Levi Strauss's strategy is global, it adapts its American roots to each country through the actions of local managers. In France it associates its jeans with the freedom of the global teenager. In Indonesia, managers selected a TV commercial showing teenagers clad in Levi's® jeans cruising around Dubuque, Iowa, in a 1960 convertible. In Japan, local managers use past movie stars such as Marilyn Monroe because of the obsession for American movie icons among Japanese youth. The company also is finding fertile ground in Eastern Europe and Russia since consumers in these countries hunger for any symbol of Americana, from McDonald's arches in Moscow to Coca-Cola cans in Warsaw. As a result, Levi Strauss exemplifies the adage "think global, act local," by following a global strategy that is adjusted at the local level.

Nestlé and Levi Strauss illustrate that some companies can effectively exploit differences in cultural norms and values, while others can take advantage of a trend to more common values worldwide.

The International Dimensions of Consumer Behavior

Marketing abroad has become an increasingly important part of American business. Today, three out of four manufacturing jobs are linked to products sold abroad, directly or indirectly. American companies such as Procter & Gamble, Colgate-Palmolive, Kellogg, Coca-Cola, IBM, Gillette, and Johnson & Johnson earn more of their revenue abroad than in the United States. Many foreign-owned companies, such as Nestlé, Lever, and Shell Oil, which are often mistaken for American companies, earn a significant percentage of their revenues in the United States.

As foreign markets emerge and offer global opportunities for growth, marketing abroad is likely to increase in importance. American firms are finding opportunities in Eastern Europe and Russia with the development of free-market systems. For example, Procter & Gamble is introducing Russian consumers to brands that offer relief from the dismal hardships of everyday life, such as dandruff control products and skin moisturizing creams. On gift-giving occasions, Russian consumers wrap bars of Camay soap and bottles of Pert Plus shampoo to give to loved ones. Before Camay was introduced (at a cost eight times that of Russian soaps), the only soaps available were coarse bars wrapped in brown paper.

China, the world's largest market, is becoming more consumption oriented with the establishment of free-trade zones in Southeast China. The turnover of Hong Kong to the Chinese government in 1997 spurred the trend among Chinese consumers to become more brand oriented. The regular appearance of American brands such as Coca-Cola, Contac cold capsules, and Head and Shoulders shampoo on Chinese TV is further evidence of the development of a consumer society.[4] Coca-Cola figures that if the Chinese drink half as much Coke as Americans, the additional income will far exceed the company's total revenues.

Such global considerations apply equally to foreign companies. For example, Netherlands-based Heineken NV. markets its Heineken beer to other European countries, the United States, Asia, and parts of Africa. L'Oreal is headquartered out of Paris, France, and promotes its cosmetics and skin care products to countries around the world, as do other beauty care companies such as Japan-based Shiseido. People around the world are familiar with European clothing design houses such as Chanel, Valentino, and Armani, which sell their clothes and accessories to all major world markets. Another Netherlands-based company, Philips NV, sells its consumer electronics products globally, as does Japan-based Sony.

Companies have also been successful in marketing abroad by adapting global perspectives to local differences in consumer needs and customs. To do so, such companies have had to acculturate themselves by learning local consumers' needs and values. Thus, despite McDonald's world brand status, it varies its offerings by selling beer in Germany, wine in France, mango milk shakes in Hong Kong, mutton pie in Australia, and McSpaghetti in the Philippines to compete with local noodle houses.

Companies face dangers in assuming that what works at home will work abroad. Such companies take an **ethnocentric** view of foreign consumers; that is, they assume foreign consumers have the same norms and values as domestic consumers. Such an ethnocentric view is bound to fail. For example, in 1990 P&G misstepped when it assumed that a campaign for Camay soap in Europe would also be successful in Japan. The campaign depicted a Japanese husband who walked in on his wife as she sat in a bathtub and complimented her on her complexion. Although the basic premise of the campaign—that women want to be attractive to men—is universally correct, the campaign flopped. Unlike most Europeans who considered the campaign sexy, the Japanese regarded it as bad manners to intrude on a woman's privacy.[5]

Cross-Cultural Influences on Consumer Behavior

International marketers subscribing to an acculturated view of foreign markets are affected by two crosscurrents. First, they recognize differences in customs and values between countries and understand the need to adapt marketing strategies to these differences. Second, they also recognize that a commonality of cultural values has grown between countries as the result of global communications through TV, more frequent travel, and increasing access to the Internet.

Cross-cultural differences require companies to develop localized strategies on a country-by-country basis, whereas global influences provide them an opportunity to standardize strategies. In this section, we consider cross-cultural variations that influence consumer behavior. In the next section, we consider global influences.

At least five cross-cultural factors influence marketing strategies abroad: (1) consumer customs and values, (2) product preferences, (3) language, (4) symbols, and (5) economic environment.

CONSUMER CUSTOMS AND VALUES

American businesspeople often take an ethnocentric view by assuming the values of American consumers are universal. However, the traditional American values of achievement, materialism, individualism, and youthfulness are not nearly as important in other parts of the world. For example, in many Asian countries, acceptance of one's place in society and compromise is more important than individual initiative in influencing behavior.[6] Differences in the perspective of time also exist. Americans structure their day into times for work and pleasure based on business, family, and individual needs. In many South American and European countries, however, people are more likely to mix business with pleasure, and being late for an appointment may be the norm.

Such differences in cultural values affect consumers' purchasing behavior, and a failure to account for these differences is likely to spell trouble for the foreign marketer. Campbell Soup Company failed to account for cultural values when it introduced its line of condensed soups in Britain. It was not sensitive to the fact that English consumers preferred ready-to-eat soups and were unaware of the condensed soup concept. Campbell's cans were at a disadvantage in the store because English consumers considered them small. In addition, the variety of flavors was not tailored to English tastes. Several years of low sales occurred before the company became aware of the difficulties and made the required adjustments.

U.S. companies are not the only ones who misread cultural differences. A recent public service advertisement for breast cancer awareness proved highly successful in Japan but failed in France due to cultural differences.[7] The ad showed an attractive woman in a sundress drawing attention from men along the sidewalk with the voice-over, "If only women paid as much attention to their breasts as men do." The Japanese thought it was a lighthearted way to highlight an important women's health issue; the French, in contrast, were offended, as they viewed breasts to be life-affirming, healthy sexual objects and believed the commercial presented a serious health issue in an inappropriate manner.

When companies marketing internationally have accounted for foreign consumers' norms and values, they have been effective. Ford recognized a growing independence among Japanese women. In a traditionally male-dominated society, many more women were working full-time. In the 1990s, Ford targeted its Festiva car to single, young Japanese working women. In the past, Japanese carmakers had assumed Japanese women would have deferred to fathers, husbands, or brothers in the purchase decision for a car. Another example is Taco Bell's entry into Singapore.

The company launched its Asian debut without Gidget, the ubiquitous Chihuahua in U.S. commercials for the fast-food franchise, because Muslims, who comprise a large portion of Singapore's population, consider touching a dog taboo.[8]

PRODUCT PREFERENCES

Product preferences are likely to differ sharply across countries. The five brands with the strongest image in the United States are Coca-Cola, Campbell, Disney, Pepsi, and Kodak. Yet none of these brands make it among the top five in Japan, which are Sony, National, Mercedes-Benz, Toyota, and Takashimaya.

A lack of awareness that product preferences are culturally based can lead a company into trouble. When companies recognize and adjust to local tastes, they are successful. Consider the following examples:

- Frito-Lay had to introduce new flavors for its Cheetos snack in China when focus groups showed that the Chinese did not like the cheesy taste. This revelation resulted in new flavors such as Savory American Cream and Zesty Japanese Steak.[9]

- Pillsbury began marketing in India with a packaged wheat blend, Pillsbury Chakki Fresh Atta, recognizing that Indians consumed the second-highest amount of wheat per year behind top-ranked China. However, Pillsbury faces an uphill battle, as Indian housewives culturally prefer fresh wheat for their home-made breads over packaged wheat, believing packaged wheat to be inferior in taste and nutrition.[10]

- Parmalat's Long Life brand of nonrefrigerated, shelf-stable milk is trying to overcome American's culturally ingrained belief that fresh milk must be refrigerated.

LANGUAGE

Language provides the means of communicating the customs and beliefs of a culture. Therefore, marketers must be aware of the meaning and subtleties of languages and dialects when selling in foreign markets. Many marketing blunders have resulted because of a lack of awareness of language.

- When Coca-Cola was introduced in China, shopkeepers made their own signs in calligraphy with the words "ke kou ke la," which translated into "bite the wax tadpole," an association that is not likely to encourage sales. When the company discovered this, it researched forty thousand Chinese characters and came up with "ko kou ko le," which not only sounds more like the real thing, but also means "may the mouth rejoice."[11]

- PepsiCo had to change its slogan "Come alive with Pepsi" in certain Asian countries because the theme translated into "Bring your ancestors back from the dead."

- General Motors discovered it could not use the name "Nova" on its models worldwide because in Spanish-speaking markets the name translated into "won't go."

- In the U.S. market, the Ford Probe experienced strong sales where the name conjured up images of adventure and space exploration. In contrast, sales were slow in the United Kingdom where the word "probe" evoked images of doctors' waiting rooms and unpleasant medical examinations.[12]

SYMBOLS

Symbols in a culture also influence purchasing behavior. Companies must be particularly sensitive to the use of color in advertising. Pink is associated with femininity in the United States, but yellow is considered the most feminine color in much of the rest of the world. Many Latin American countries disapprove of purple because it is associated with death. In contrast, purple connotes quality in China.[13] The Marlboro Cowboy is shown in a lighter-colored hat in Hong Kong and China than in the rest of the world because of the positive cultural significance of the color white in China.

Symbols other than color also influence behavior. Two elephants are a symbol of bad luck in many parts of Africa. This forced Carlsberg to add a third elephant to its label for Elephant Beer. A moon appears frequently in Chinese ads because it is a traditional symbol of good luck in that country. The word for the number four in Japanese also means death, so Tiffany sells glassware and china in sets of five in that country. Nike withdrew its flame logo when it received protests from the Arabic markets that noted that the logo resembled the Arabic symbol for Allah. To make matters worse, the symbol was associated with shoes. In Arab countries, the foot and sole are viewed as unclean.[14]

ECONOMIC ENVIRONMENT

A country's economic environment influences consumer behavior. Three factors are particularly important: a country's standard of living, its economic infrastructure, and its economic policies.

The high standard of living in the United States, one of the most advanced industrial nations in the world, allows for widespread ownership of electronics, appliances, and automobiles. Underdeveloped countries do not approach the level of ownership of TVs and telephones in the United States (over 95 percent) or home computer ownership (over 40 percent).[15]

When Kellogg introduced its cereals into Southeast Asia, it knew it would have to try to change breakfast eating habits to influence Asian consumers to accept cereals. It also knew that a TV campaign would not be an effective way to do so because of limited TV ownership. Similarly, marketing researchers investigating consumer attitudes and behavior abroad cannot rely on collecting information by telephone in many countries because only upscale households own phones. Hence, in countries such as India, door-to-door personal interviews are more effective ways to conduct marketing research.

The facilities a country uses to conduct business—media, telecommunications, transportation, and power—are known as the country's *economic infrastructure*. Media, telecommunications, and distribution facilities in many underdeveloped countries are primitive. For example, although consumers in Russia and Eastern Europe crave American goods, difficulties abound in marketing them because of archaic distribution networks and limited facilities for advertising. Marketers cannot take for granted basic requirements such as good road networks and warehousing facilities. Companies targeting less developed countries face similar limitations in implementing marketing strategies. L'Oreal launched Maybelline New York in India in 2000.[16] Despite the company's success in other Asian markets, it faces significant challenges in distribution because of the country's dependence on small corner stores.

A country's economic policies also influence consumer behavior. Many countries have instituted tariff barriers against imports to protect domestic industries, thus limiting their consumers' access to foreign goods. Although tariffs have been reduced substantially in the last twenty years as exemplified by the North American Free Trade Agreement and the lifting of trade tariffs by several South American countries, they still remain as barriers to consumer choice in many countries.

Global Influences on Consumer Behavior

Supporters of global strategies in international marketing cite increased similarity in tastes and values across countries. Improvements in transportation and communication have resulted in distribution of products and transmission of advertising messages on a worldwide basis. The increasing availability of the World Wide Web provides a further spur to global communications. As a result of these trends, brands such as Coca-Cola and Levi's jeans and fast-food outlets such as McDonald's and Pizza Hut can be regarded as world brands.

Certain values, such as materialism, desire for beauty, nurturing of children, and security exist in most countries. If consumers associate these values with a product category, a standardized marketing strategy across countries may be possible. For example, Polaroid developed a single global campaign based on the theme of pictures as a universal language. The campaign was successful because a theme of communicating through pictures is relevant to most cultures.[17]

WORLDWIDE COMMUNICATIONS

The most significant spur to globalization has been the increase in worldwide communications. The growing use of the Internet as a global communications vehicle, availability of common TV programs from global cable networks, and the consequent impact on the values of teenagers worldwide have made world brand strategies more viable.

▌ The Role of the Internet in Global Communications   One recent study predicts that global Internet usage will reach 1 billion by 2005, up from 40 million worldwide in 1996.[18] Currently, 275 million people globally are on the Internet. However, Internet usage remains highly concentrated in a few countries, leading one analyst to remark, "[T]he Web has much more ground to make up before it can claim to be a truly worldwide medium on the scale of television."[19] The study shows that the United States ranks first in total Internet users (108 million) and home PC ownership (107 million). Despite these numbers, the United States now represents only 39 percent of worldwide Internet usage. Other "leading edge" countries include Canada, Sweden, the Netherlands, Finland, Switzerland, and Australia. Eastern- and Southern European countries have low PC penetration and

Internet usage. Three of the top ten areas of Internet penetration are in Asia: Hong Kong (35 percent), Japan (33 percent), and Singapore (33 percent).[20]

As these statistics infer, the United States has significantly influenced the development of "Web cultures" worldwide, ranging from web site designs to electronic commerce. A few key statistics tell us why. U.S. corporations earn 85 percent of all online revenues, according to one estimate.[21] In addition, English is the primary language, and the "Net" culture of individualism, informality, and decentralization mirror what many consider to be core attributes of American culture. With the current U.S. dominance of the Internet, it is not surprising that the Web has become a conduit for spreading American fashions, trends, and tastes in everything from music to clothes.

Conversely, several observers argue that the Internet also contributes to underscoring differences across cultures and countries, and that these differences will become more pronounced as Internet access and usage explode, particularly in Europe and Asia. As several U.S.-based Internet companies have learned, underlying cultural norms and ways of doing things continue to drive consumer behavior. For example, Schwab.com started a web site for clients in Great Britain in 1998, which generated a disappointingly low fifteen thousand new accounts in the first year. The reason was that British customers were accustomed to exchanging paper stock certificates in each transaction, which Schwab.com did not provide for its online customers.[22]

■ **Mainstreaming**   One communications theory proposes that individuals tend to see the world around them largely based on information from the mass media. Therefore, heavy viewers of TV develop similar perceptions of reality because they are exposed to similar stimuli. This effect, known as **mainstreaming,**[23] means that global TV networks are promoting similar norms and values on a global basis.

Mainstreaming is a worldwide trend primarily because of the advent of global cable TV channels such as CNN and MTV, channels that number their worldwide audience in the hundreds of millions. Because of such global media facilities, marketers can more easily create world brands by advertising them across many countries with a single theme. The Internet further reinforces mainstreaming by providing a global communications medium to transmit common tastes and preferences, particularly among Gen Y consumers.

UNIVERSAL DEMOGRAPHIC TRENDS

In Chapter 9, we described key demographic trends in the United States, such as the increasing proportion of women working outside the home, the greater proportion of single-member households, rising divorce rates, later marriages, and fewer children per household. The chapter showed that these trends are not restricted to the United States; they apply to most of the developed countries of the world—from France to Taiwan.

These common trends encourage global marketing strategies. For example, the rising divorce rate in France, Japan, Sweden, Russia, and the United States was one factor behind the global success of Toys "R" Us. The company realized that parents who separate are more likely to give toys to their children.[24]

Perhaps the most significant global demographic trend for marketers is the growth in working women in developing countries, particularly in Asia. In Japan, the number of working women has increased by 20 percent over ten years.[25] In Hong Kong, women comprise 40 percent of the work force, an increase of 20 percent in five years, and in Malaysia nearly 47 percent of women work.[26] This trend has led business owners and marketers to change their strategies to reflect this shift. For example, supermarkets stay open longer to accommodate working women's needs for later shopping hours, and advertisements for household and other products now show men performing many traditionally female roles. For example, HSBC Holdings unit, Hong Kong Bank, targeted working women in an ad campaign that shows a husband bringing tea to his wife as she works on her laptop computer and then seeing her off at the airport. He has a list of chores to do while she's traveling—vacuuming, dishes, and grocery shopping.

Similarly, the increasing proportion of working women in Thailand, Malaysia, and Hong Kong led Jusco, a Japanese supermarket chain, to open stores in these countries. Although most women in these countries shop in open-air markets and small grocery stores, Jusco recognized that working women no longer have the time to shop in traditional ways and want the timesaving convenience of supermarkets.[27]

DECREASE IN TRADE BARRIERS

Trade barriers in the form of tariffs and quotas are decreasing worldwide, facilitating the flow of goods among nations and the consequent emergence of common tastes and values. The worldwide effort to eliminate trade barriers started following World War II when in 1947, the United States and twenty-two other countries signed the General Agreement on Tariffs and Trade (GATT). The goal of the GATT was to reduce tariffs in stages, which it did seven times by the early 1990s. In addition to global agreements, regional agreements have also developed to reduce trade barriers. Among the most prominent is the North American Free Trade Agreement (NAFTA). NAFTA has facilitated the flow of goods between the United States, Canada, and Mexico by reducing tariffs to zero. In another such effort, the European Community (EC) eliminated trade barriers among member nations, passed directives to standardize marketing and product safety regulations, and introduced a single currency (the euro) in 2002.

The elimination of trade barriers among the twelve nations of the EC and the adoption of the euro has led many to believe that a **Euroconsumer** will emerge; that is, one who has many shared values with consumers in neighboring European countries. As one European manager for Lever said, "Europeans share yearnings for odor-free underarms; fresh-smelling breath; and soft, easy-to-wash clothing."[28] As a result, companies are trying to sell products the same way across Europe, leading to the development of a **Eurobrand;** that is, a brand with several languages on the same package under the same brand name. Sara Lee has developed a Eurobrand for socks, underwear, and lingerie under a "Dim" name. Using a common strategy, Sara Lee can sell these products to the EC under the Dim name.

Others argue that a Euroconsumer is unlikely to develop because of differences across European cultures and that marketers should adapt their strategies accordingly. BMW's attempt to launch its Series 7 line with a single ad campaign for Europe proved a reminder of these differences. Consumers outside of Germany

GLOBAL APPLICATIONS

The Global Teenager: A Result of Mainstreaming

Mainstreaming has encouraged the development of "global teenagers"; that is, teens with similar values across countries. One major reason for the mainstreaming of teens is television. As teens across the world watch the same television shows and similar commercials, they begin to develop similar consumption patterns. This does not necessarily mean that teenagers around the world are of one mind; there are certainly differences in each country based on religion, values, and national identities. But there is a growing commonality among global teens regarding media and spending habits.

MTV has been the most adept at building a worldwide culture of consumption among youth, while still preserving some of their local preferences. MTV aired its first global show in 1989 because it decided that teen tastes and attitudes were sufficiently similar to warrant a global reach. It mixes global music and commercials with some local programming to appeal to teens in every country. MTV currently reaches teen viewers in more than sixty countries.

So, if television is creating a global teen consumer, what do these teens look like? According to the New World Teen study, teens around the world live in a "parallel universe. They get up in the morning, put on their Levis and Nikes, grab their caps, backpacks, and Sony personal CD players, and head for school" ["Can TV Save the Planet," *American Demographics* (May 1996),

p. 47]. They also seem to enjoy many of the same activities. Teens in the United States, Europe, Latin America, and the Far East find being with friends and watching TV to be the most enjoyable ways to spend time.

Another medium encouraging mainstreaming among global teens is the Web. Teens worldwide are becoming increasingly wired, and chatrooms and bulletin boards are not restricted to national boundaries. For example, *www.loquesea.com* is targeting Hispanic teens in Latin America and the United States with irreverent fare on fashions, dating, and music. Loquesea executives recognize a shift in time spent by teens from TV to the Web, and the site is targeted to the wired Hispanic teen market.

Television and the Web are not the only factors that have encouraged the development of the global teenager. Greater travel, better global communications, and increased access to the Web have spurred the development of common norms and values among teens worldwide. As the director of MTV in Europe said, "Eighteen-year-olds in Paris have more in common with 18-year-olds in New York than with their own parents. They buy the same products, go to the same movies, listen to the same music, sip the same colas" ("Can TV Save the Planet," p. 47).

A growing number of marketers now target the global teenager. Major teen brands like Coca-Cola, McDonald's, Nintendo, Swatch, Sony

OF CONSUMER BEHAVIOR

reacted negatively because the car was shown with German license plates.[29] Such nationalistic tendencies support an emphasis on a local rather than a pan-European perspective. The United Kingdom's "Buy British" campaign serves as an illustration.

AMERICANIZATION OF CONSUMPTION VALUES

The globalization of communications, decreasing trade barriers, and the demise of Communism have spurred the acceptance of American consumption values across the globe. Consumers in all parts of the world crave American goods as status symbols. In so doing, they adapt American consumption values to be consistent with local language, meaning, and beliefs, a process known as **co-optation.**[30] One author

Discman, and Nike understand the importance of marketing to teens worldwide. Nike is one company that has specifically focused on growing sales to teenagers outside the United States. As a premier brand among teenagers worldwide, Nike customizes its message to appeal to kids in different countries. In the United States it uses basketball stars like Michael Jordan, and in Brazil soccer stars like Ronaldo. It also sponsors major sports events like the World Cup and the NBA playoffs, as well as numerous local sports teams around the globe, to appeal to elusive and trend-conscious teens.

Swatch uses its ProTeam, a group of athletes from youth-oriented trend sports, as one way to reach the global teen. Sports like skateboarding, snowboarding, and surfing not only appeal to teens who participate in these sports, but also affect the language they speak, the fashions they wear, and the music they listen to. Swatch ProTeam athletes like Shaquille O'Neal, Andy MacDonald, and Conan Hayes, among others, are leaders in their disciplines and therefore create a positive resonance for Swatch with this group of global trend-setting consumers (see Exhibit 13.2).

Even companies like Polaroid are beginning to understand the importance of global youth markets. Polaroid traditionally marketed to the 30-plus age segments, but in October 1999, the company launched the i-zone camera for the 7- to 17-year-old segment. Now the world's best-selling camera, it comes in funky colors and takes minipictures that can be stuck on telephones and T-shirts.

EXHIBIT 13.2

Targeting the global teenager.

© Copyright by Swatch LTD.

Sources: "Philip Knight of Nike—Just Do It," *Institutional Investor* (January 2000); "Targeting Youth: Loquesea Hopes to Snag Investors," *Advertising Age Global* (March 2000), pp. 1, 32; "Can TV Save the Planet?" *American Demographics* (May 1996), pp. 45–48; "Global Ad Campaigns, After Many Missteps, Finally Pay Dividends, *Wall Street Journal* (August 27, 1992), pp. A1, A8.

has coined the term "McWorld" to describe the co-optation of American consumption values.[31] Consider the following examples:

▌ In Russia, youthful consumers have turned to Western goods to maintain their traditionally disheveled look. They wear Chicago Bears and Los Angeles Lakers T-shirts, knockoff high-top basketball sneakers, and baseball caps. The taste for fast foods has caught on like wildfire, with an *Amerikanski gamburgeri* and a Budweiser being on the top of the list for chic.[32]

▌ Japanese consumers insist on American labels. For example, the L.L. Bean label is associated with a ruggedly functional American look that is now regarded as a status symbol, if not an icon, in Japan.[33]

■ In Brazil, one executive attributed the failure of the Jack-in-the-Box chain to the fact that, unlike McDonald's, "There was nothing in them to evoke for Brazilians 'the American way of life.'"[34]

■ In Holland, an Amsterdam taxi driver points out a pedestrian dressed in a New York Yankee jersey, blue jeans, and green-striped Air Jordans. "I can smell an American anywhere," he says, "but that's a Dutchman." ("Why?" asks his passenger.) "Because he looks too much like an American."[35]

American companies are taking advantage of this trend by using American themes, American celebrities, and American slogans in their advertising. However, this does not mean that American companies are being ethnocentric. These companies are actually following the desires of foreign consumers rather than assuming American values can be imposed on them. Further, companies do adjust American-

WEB APPLICATIONS

When It Comes to the Internet, Japanese Consumers March to a Different Drummer

Japan may illustrate the Americanization of consumer values in many ways. But the Internet is not one of them. For one thing, in one of the most technologically adept countries in the world, Internet usage is about one-half that in the United States. One of the reasons is that Japanese consumers do not like to use credit cards; credit card charges in Japan are less than one-third those in the United States. In addition, when Japanese consumers do use the Internet, most access it by cell phone.

To accelerate Internet usage, Japanese marketers are turning to convenience stores. That may seem a strange marriage to American consumers. But one must understand the role of convenience stores in Japan to understand that buying a book on the Internet at, say, a 7-Eleven web site makes perfect sense.

Japan adopted the convenience store concept from the United States in the early 1970s, naming them *conbinis.* But the Japanese transformed conbinis into more than convenience stores. They became centers of community life, functioning as everything from town halls to culture clubs. Further, the conbini pioneered the use of retail technology to make the best use of cramped space, introducing, for instance, ATM machines on the premises, as well as offering

products beyond food. It is no surprise then that 7-Eleven, the largest convenience chain, saw the Internet as another vehicle for expanding sales.

On July 1, 2000, 7-Eleven launched an online virtual mall, selling everything from CDs to flowers to tour packages. And in October, it introduced in-store Internet kiosks. The key is that consumers can then pick up the product at a 7-Eleven store. This is important because consumers can thus avoid paying by credit card and use cash, and half the Japanese population lives within five minutes from a convenience store. Thus, with eighty-two hundred stores in Japan, 7-Eleven offers Internet accessibility as well as convenient delivery. The company has also adapted to the Japanese consumers' penchant to log on by cell phone by creating a web site designed for a tiny screen.

Some traditionalists in Japan complain of the loss of culture and community in buying online. But sales via the Internet are picking up. In making 7-Eleven the Japanese equivalent of Amazon.com, the Japanese consumer is indeed marching to a different Internet drummer.

Sources: "Online at the 7-Eleven: Japan Begins Embracing Internet Commerce Its Own Way," *Boston Globe* (August 26, 2000), p. C1; "In Japan, the Hub of E-Commerce Is a 7-Eleven," *Wall Street Journal* (October 21, 1999), p. B1.

OF CONSUMER BEHAVIOR

oriented ads to local needs and tastes. For example, when Reebok advertised in France, it deleted a boxing theme from Planet Reebok commercials because of French consumers' aversion to any depiction of violence.[36]

Although American consumption values pervade the world, some argue that the effect is less significant than one might expect. Americans dominate in film and television. However, local companies continue to dominate their markets in most other areas, such as books, sport, music, food, drink, and fashion. As one writer noted, "the debate on whether there is cultural homogenization remains open . . . there are no surveys showing that people are becoming alike."[37] Regarding the Internet, U.S. influence on content development in Europe has been strong.[38] For this reason, the first wave of Internet and digital magazines in Europe attempted to emulate the look and feel of the U.S.-based magazine *Wired*. Recently, however, web designers have developed a more distinct style to accommodate the tastes of European consumers.

Strategic Applications of Cross-Cultural and Global Influences

The distinction between a cross-cultural and a global perspective is key in developing international marketing strategies. Whether to sell on a localized basis, a global basis, or somewhere in between is perhaps the most important decision a marketer selling abroad must make. Such a decision must be based on the extent of cultural differences across countries and on the degree to which common norms, tastes, and values justify a more global approach. At one extreme, a company could follow a completely localized strategy by adapting product characteristics, advertising, and distribution requirements to the particular needs of each country it serves. Such a strategy may be infeasible because of the costs of running a separate campaign in every country. Nestlé comes close to achieving a completely localized strategy because its food products are geared to local tastes. Yet even here, 10 percent of its products are sold across national boundaries.

At the other extreme, a company could follow a completely global campaign. Coca-Cola comes close to achieving world brand status through its objective of "one look, one sight, one sound," meaning that its advertising message is being constantly reinforced, whether consumers see it at home or abroad. Although such an approach may achieve a universal image and important economies of scale, some adjustment to local conditions is almost always necessary.

Companies rarely follow a completely global strategy. Some degree of adaptation to local consumer needs is required. Such a mixed approach is reflected in the "think globally, but act locally" strategy employed by Levi Strauss. This strategy is referred to as **flexible globalization;** that is, an attempt to standardize marketing strategies across countries but to be flexible enough to adapt components of the strategy to local conditions. Such strategies are becoming the norm due to the shortcomings of a strictly local or global approach.

Because some companies follow a more localized approach and others more global strategies, we consider these two approaches first. We then examine the increasingly common strategy of flexible globalization, which is designed to achieve the advantages of both local and global strategies.

LOCALIZED STRATEGIES

Because of substantial differences between countries in tastes, customs, and product usage, many companies opt to localize their marketing strategies abroad. For example:

▮ Domino's Pizza follows a localized strategy by varying its pizzas with what it calls "cultural toppings." For example, pizzas are topped with sweet corn in the United Kingdom, salami in Germany, and prawns in Australia. In Japan, Domino's offers a chicken teriyaki gourmet pizza for $15.[39]

▮ McDonald's markets the Maharaja Mac in India (two all-mutton patties, special sauce, lettuce, cheese, pickles, onions on a sesame-seed bun), knowing that most Indians consider cows to be sacred.[40]

▮ U.S.-based Internet companies, such as Yahoo!, have entered European markets with country-specific content. As one observer notes, "A strong brand in the U.S. may not carry you if your goal is to be, say, the Internet company of France. You need global vision, but you also need a local touch."[41]

Many companies also take a localized approach to online and offline advertising because of differences in needs or customs between countries. Web sites for companies such as Harley-Davidson, Sony, and McDonald's offer customized pages for different countries.

In the case of offline advertising, Maytag advertises its refrigerators differently worldwide because of differences in the role of a refrigerator and features consumers consider important (see Exhibit 13.3). The Australian ad emphasized the ability of the refrigerator to keep food fresh, particularly seafood. In Arabic countries, refrigerators and major appliances may be viewed more in the context of gift giving, thus the hearts and the reference to a wedding list above the Maytag repairman. In the United Kingdom, Maytag advertises its upscale line of refrigerators with a sleek look since refrigerators are normally regarded almost as commodity items and need some clear point of differentiation. Maytag introduced new TV commercials in thirty-two cities across China that feature dolphins as symbols of freedom from household chores, capitalizing on the Chinese affinity for these mammals.[42]

In another example of localized advertising, Renault advertised its Clio differently to various European countries because of differences in the features consumers consider most important in a car. The company emphasized road performance and features in Portugal, security and safety in France, self-image in Spain, style in Italy, and "new" in Belgium.

THE LIMITS OF LOCALIZED STRATEGIES

The limitation of a localized international strategy is the inability of management to recognize the need to adapt to local tastes and customs (see Exhibit 13.4). Marketers have often attempted to export domestic strategies abroad and have gotten into trouble as a result.

For example, when Snapple was first sold in Japan, ads declared that "The Snapple Phenomenon Has Landed," and Japanese consumers grabbed it up as part

PERFORMANCE YOU CAN DEPEND ON

COOL PERFORMANCE

Available from · Allders · Harrods · House of Fraser · John Lewis · Selfridges and
your local quality electrical dealer. For more information please
visit www.maytag.co.uk or call 01737 231 090

MANUFACTURERS OF AMERICAN REFRIGERATION · WASHING MACHINES · TUMBLE DRYERS · DISHWASHERS

| **EXHIBIT 13.3** |

Localized ad campaigns:
Maytag worldwide.

(above) Courtesy Maytag International,
INC. and Alistair Clarke, Leo Burnett,
Australia; (right) Courtesy Maytag
International, INC. and Dynamite Idea,
United Kingdom; (below) Courtesy
Maytag International, INC. and Linkers
Distribution, Lebanon.

of their obsession for American products. But sales quickly dried up because consumers did not buy again. Why? Japanese consumers like a clear, unsweetened tea. Snapple had a cloudy appearance, a sweet fruit-juice flavor, and fruit sediment in the bottle. Despite the evidence, Quaker (owners of Snapple) would not change the drink to suit local tastes. As one Japanese marketer said, "For all the talk about the Americanization of lifestyles here, Japanese taste buds remain traditional."[43] This need for greater adaptation provides support for a more localized strategy.

GLOBAL STRATEGIES

The cross-cultural differences cited earlier suggest that companies should vary their strategy for a product from country to country. However, in some cases, a company can use the same promotional campaign and positioning in each country if the product has a more global appeal. That is, there may be compelling reasons for following a more global strategy. The resulting standardization in marketing strategies across countries saves millions of dollars as a result of economies of scale for companies such as Coca-Cola and Levi Strauss. Certain conditions are necessary for the successful implementation of a world brand strategy. Using Levi's jeans as an illustration of these criteria, they include the following:

- Similarities in consumer needs and values worldwide. (Consumers want to be perceived as fashionable and seek brands that help them fill this need.)

- Common usage patterns. (Consumers worldwide wear Levi's jeans for casual, stylish wear.)

- Standardized product. (Levi Strauss designs and markets the same jeans products worldwide—with little or no modification, creating economies of scale in production.)

- A global brand strategy that is not based upon a single domestic perspective. (Levi Strauss's marketing campaigns emphasize the shared values and common traits of teenagers worldwide. It does not simply export its U.S. strategy.)

- Use of consistent positioning and universal symbols and imagery. (Levi Strauss's logo and positioning as the "hip" brand for teenagers are used throughout the world, resulting in economies of scale in marketing.)

- Substantial brand equity. (Levi's is consistently ranked as one of the world's most recognized brands.)

▮ Corporate name is used as the brand name. (Levi's brand name is the same as its corporate name, facilitating brand recognition. The same is true for Coca-Cola, Pepsi, Sony, McDonald's, and Harley-Davidson.)

Avon and Master Card, two disparate companies, conform to many of these criteria. Both cosmetics and credit cards have common usage patterns and reflect common needs and values. Both companies have substantial brand equity. In both cases, their corporate and brand names are the same. And both companies have recently embarked on world brand strategies that reflect "consistent positioning and universal symbols and imagery."

In 2000, Avon launched its "Let's Talk" campaign simultaneously in twenty-six markets. The campaign was designed to reflect Avon's mission to be "the company for women [worldwide]," and the universal need for female camraderie.[44] Similarly, in 1998 Master Card launched its "Priceless" campaign on a global basis when it sponsored the World Cup soccer matches. The campaign emphasizes the things that really matter in life that can't be bought, a theme recognized universally.[45]

LIMITS OF GLOBAL INFLUENCES

The focus on global influences might suggest that a company can market one standardized product with a uniform, worldwide advertising campaign. This is rarely the case. No matter how universal the product is, some adaptation to local customs and language is necessary. Even the most universal of brands, Coca-Cola, does not follow a strictly global approach. It makes variations in the brand's formula in certain countries, and though Coca-Cola uses a global theme, it creates variations in its advertising for each country. When the company launched its General Assembly campaign in 1987, showing children of the world singing the Coke jingle in one big assembly, each country's ads focused on a close-up of a local youngster. Thus, a unifying theme was adapted to different countries. Similarly, Avon's "Let's Talk" campaign uses local models, and sales brochures and related web sites are locally designed.[46]

As mentioned, when a company follows a strictly global approach with little adaptation to local needs, it runs into trouble. Parker Pen tried to standardize every component of its marketing strategy in 154 countries in the mid-1980s but paid inadequate attention to local differences—its global advertising campaign overlooked the fact that Scandinavia is a ballpoint pen market, whereas consumers in France and Italy want fancier pens.[47]

Another limitation to global strategies is the development of a backlash to the Americanization of consumption values. Japanese consumers, in their current recession, seem to be shifting from their obsession with American products to a return to more traditional products. In some ways, this trend mirrors the "new reality" in American culture described in Chapter 11, because both trends reflect greater restraint in spending due to economic uncertainty.

A third limitation to a global strategy is that consumers frequently prefer local brands to imports, particularly in product categories for which the home market enjoys a good reputation, such as automobiles and beer in Germany. Western manufacturers of vodka have faced difficulty in gaining acceptance in Russia, which represents the largest market for vodka in the world. Due to trade liberalization in the early 1990s, foreign spirits manufacturers such as Absolut and Smirnoff perceived an opportunity to export branded vodka to the Russian market, hoping to capitalize on the growing demand for Western products and brands. However, Russians ultimately have shown a preference for local brands, considering vodka to be uniquely Russian.[48]

FLEXIBLE GLOBALIZATION

The trend in international marketing has been to implement global strategies with adaptations to local needs, which we have referred to as "flexible globalization." This compromise requires the company to establish an overall marketing strategy but to leave implementation to local executives who are aware of national traits and customs.

Fiat faced the need for flexible globalization when it launched its restyled Palio model globally early in 2001. A key market region was Argentina and Brazil, but the company was faced with economically depressed conditions in these countries, particularly in Argentina. Fiat decided on a campaign centered on the theme "change of concept," communicating the idea that as times change, Fiat changes to adjust. Critics of the campaign said it would be difficult to sell cars in a steep recession, but the campaign succeeded in increasing Fiat's sales by 50 percent in a short period in these countries. Thus, Fiat succeeded in adapting a global launch to local economic conditions.[49]

Dell Computer offers an example of flexible globalization in the service sector. The company has web sites targeted to eighty-five different countries and territories. Renowned for its direct-to-customer method of selling computers, Dell creates a common technology platform for each of its global web sites to ensure a consistent user experience across sites. However, the company then allows the local team to manage the rollout and employs local customer service staff so that customers always deal with someone local.[50]

Societal Implications of Influencing Consumers Abroad

The nature of cross-cultural and global influences creates a number of societal issues that bear on consumer rights in the marketplace. Consumers in foreign markets have the right to safe products, full information, and adequate choice. This should be true whether consumers live in developed or in developing countries. One of the most contentious issues in international marketing is that consumers in Third-World countries do not have adequate protection when it comes to product safety or full disclosure of product contents and performance. Some companies have even been charged with selling products that have misled and harmed consumers in underdeveloped countries.

The most widely publicized case in this regard was Nestlé's infant formula products. A worldwide boycott of Nestlé products ensued in the late 1970s when many infants died in Third-World countries because the formula was often mixed with contaminated water from local sources. The company attempted to resolve the issue by following guidelines the United Nations set for promotion and distribution of infant formula. As a result, the boycott was lifted. The issue arose again in 1989 when Nestlé was charged with distribution of infant formula that did not conform to the spirit of the U.N. guidelines.[51] The issue has still not been fully resolved.

Another issue drawing increasing attention is American cigarette companies targeting brands to consumers in less developed countries. As U.S. legislation continues to impose domestic advertising and marketing restrictions, tobacco companies increasingly look abroad for future growth opportunities. These companies appear to be succeeding, as revenues from non-U.S. markets rose from $15.7 billion in 1993 to $26.3 billion in 1997.[52] In Spain, a Madonna concert is broadcast as a "Salem Madonna" concert, and in Romania pedestrians and drivers can see the Camel logo silhouetted inside traffic lights when the lights turn green.

Consumer advocates believe that it is unethical to encourage smoking, especially in countries where famine and disease are prevalent. A World Health Organization study found that marketing campaigns by U.S. cigarette companies have "caused immediate jumps in consumption among women and teens, traditionally nonsmoking groups in less-developed economies."[53] This trend becomes even more alarming when, according to the World Health Organization, 3.5 million deaths a year worldwide are blamed on smoking, with almost half occurring in developing countries.[54]

SUMMARY

Differing cultural norms and values result in different patterns of purchasing behavior in various countries. These cross-cultural influences require companies to adapt their marketing strategies to the local conditions of various countries. Four important cross-cultural factors influence marketing strategy: consumer customs and values, language, symbols, and the economic environment.

These cross-cultural factors encourage companies to adapt to local conditions. However, several factors are creating common tastes and purchasing preferences on a global basis. These include (1) global communications; (2) demographic trends across countries, such as the greater proportion of working women; (3) a reduction in trade barriers worldwide; and (4) the Americanization of consumption values.

Based on these influences, three types of international marketing strategies were discussed. A localized strategy is important in adjusting to differences in norms and customs in various countries. A globalized strategy achieves economies of scale and a universal image but may fail to adapt to differences in needs and purchasing habits across countries. A company following flexible globalization thinks globally but acts locally by establishing a standard strategy but allowing countries to vary details to meet local needs and customs.

The chapter concluded by considering some societal implications of cross-cultural influences, particularly the need to protect consumer rights in developing countries.

In Chapter 14, we consider another environmental factor: the influence of reference groups on consumer behavior.

QUESTIONS FOR DISCUSSION

1. What are the dangers of an ethnocentric view in marketing abroad? Provide some examples of these dangers.
2. What impact has the Internet had in promoting cultural similarities across borders? In what ways has the Internet promoted differences?
3. How has the decrease in trade barriers affected global branding strategies? In particular, what are the arguments for and against a global brand strategy for the European Community countries?
4. What is meant by "mainstreaming"? How has mainstreaming contributed to the development of a global teenager? How does it facilitate the establishment of world brands?

5. What is the evidence that there is a global teenage market? How might a producer of designer jeans target the global teenager?

6. The chapter noted that many of the demographic trends that have occurred in the United States—an increasing proportion of working women, higher divorce rates, smaller families, and later marriages—have also occurred in most of the developed nations of the world. What are the strategic implications of these trends for (a) a car manufacturer in Japan considering a marketing campaign directed to women, (b) a large toy manufacturer in the United States considering exporting its products, and (c) a manufacturer of household cleaning products considering a worldwide advertising campaign for its line?

7. What are the advantages and disadvantages of a globalized marketing strategy? What are the limits of implementing a truly standardized marketing strategy worldwide? When are such strategies most likely to work?

8. Localization of marketing strategies was suggested as a way to adjust to conditions in specific countries. What are the pros and cons of using a localized strategy?

9. What is meant by "flexible globalization"? Why is it becoming a more common strategy in international markets? Cite examples of (a) product strategies and (b) advertising strategies that have followed this approach.

10. To what extent are the following brands candidates for a global strategy based on the criteria listed in the chapter?
    - Campbell's soup
    - Nescafé coffee
    - Harley-Davidson motorcycles

11. What ethical issues might arise in marketing to foreign consumers, especially in less developed countries?

RESEARCH ASSIGNMENTS

1 How do IBM, Levi Strauss, and Pepsi adapt their web sites to different cultures or countries? What strategies do these sites reflect? Identify other web sites that customize pages for different country or regional markets.

2 Interview at least ten marketing executives in multinational companies. The companies can be large or small, manufacturers or distributors, product or service companies. The important objective is to talk to managers with experience in marketing abroad. Ask these managers to provide their perspectives on the following:

- Do they think tastes and values are becoming more similar worldwide? If so, is this trend likely to facilitate globalized marketing strategies in the future?

- Will decreasing trade barriers affect the company's operations? If so, in what ways? If not, what general opportunities do they think these events will create for American businesses?

- Under what circumstances do they believe globalized strategies are more effective? When are localized strategies more effective? For what types of product categories or services?

- What products or services have they been involved with abroad? What types of strategies did they use?

- Did they adapt strategies to the customs and values of specific countries? How?

Once you have collected this information, summarize the views of the executives you have interviewed. Consider the following:

- What differences in views emerged regarding the issues you investigated?

- Were there differences in views by type of company (*e.g.,* product versus service companies, producers of packaged goods versus durable goods)? If so, why do you believe these differences in views emerged?

3 Select a company's web site (*e.g., www. pampers.com*) and access different countries from the home page. What differences in content, links, style and format do you perceive on these sites? Do you think they accurately reflect the cultural differences that may exist across these countries?

NOTES

1. "'Hometown,' Yet Global," *Dairy Foods* (October 1998), pp. 18–21.
2. "Nestlé Sticks to Strategy of Broad Categories of Brands—Despite Some Urgings to Slim Down, No Large-Scale Overhaul Is Planned," *Wall Street Journal* (September 24, 1999), p. B4.
3. Nestlé web site www.nestle.com, as of April 20, 2000.
4. "The International Agenda," *Marketing* (July 1, 1995), p. 142; and "The Awakening Chinese Consumer," *New York Times* (October 11, 1992), p. F1.
5. "Global Ad Campaigns After Many Missteps, Finally Pay Dividends," *Wall Street Journal* (August 27, 1992), pp. A1, A8.
6. Donnel A. Briley, Michael W. Morris, and Itamar Simonson, "Reasons as Carriers of Culture: Dynamic versus Dispositional Models of Cultural Influence on Decision Making," *Journal of Consumer Research* 27 (September 2000), pp. 157–178.
7. "Sex-Themed Ads Often Don't Travel Well," *Wall Street Journal* (March 31, 2000).
8. "US Multinationals," *Ad Age International* (January 11, 1999), pp. 13–16.
9. "Not Quite Gobal: Marketers 'Discover' the World but Still Have Much to Learn," *Marketing News* (July 3, 1995), p. 1.
10. "Pillsbury Presses Flour Power in India," *Wall Street Journal* (May 5, 1999), p. B1.
11. *Business Marketing* (July 1984), p. 112.
12. "Cultural Quandaries Can Lead to Misnomers," *Marketing News* (November 23, 1998), p. 9.
13. David A. Ricks, *Big Business Blunders* (Homewood, Ill.: Dow Jones-Irwin, 1983), p. 65.
14. "Burnett Tracks Shifts in Norms Shaping China," *Ad Age International* (March 1997), p. 132.
15. Bureau of the Census, *Statistical Abstract of the United States, 2000,* Table 1373.
16. "Indian and Far Eastern Influences are Seen in Exotic Makeup," *St. Louis Post Dispatch* (March 27, 2000), p. L43.
17. Teresa J. Domzal and Larry L. Unger, "Emerging Positioning Strategies in Global Markets," *Journal of Consumer Marketing* 4 (1987), p. 29.
18. "The Digital Divide," *CMA Management* (July/August 2000), p. 57.
19. Ibid.
20. Ibid.
21. "Internet Businesses May Find the Global Village Dauntingly Native," *New York Times* (May 22, 2000), p. C.15.
22. "Global Ad Campaigns After Many Missteps," pp. A1, A8.
23. Thomas C. O'Guinn, Ronald J. Faber, Nadine J. Curias, and Kay Schmitt, "The Cultivation of Consumer Norms," in Thomas K. Srull, ed., *Advances in Consumer Research*, Vol. 16 (Provo, Utah: Association for Consumer Research, 1989), pp. 779–785.
24. "A New Mass Market Emerges," *Fortune* (Fall 1990 Special Issue), p. 51.
25. Matsuko Segawa, "Businesses Targeting Night Owls," *Nikkei Weekly* (February 14, 2000), p. 1.
26. "Depicting Men Doing Housework Can Be Risky for Marketers in Asia," *Wall Street Journal* (August 14, 1998), p. B6.
27. "A New Mass Market Emerges," p. 51.
28. "In Pursuit of the Elusive Euroconsumer," *New York Times* (April 23, 1991), p. B1.
29. "Chasing the Global Dream," *Marketing News* (December 2, 1996), pp. 1, 2.
30. Eric J. Arnould and Richard R. Wilk, "Why Do the Natives Wear Adidas?" in Thomas C. Kinnear, ed., *Advances in Consumer Research,* Vol. 11 (Provo, Utah: Association for Consumer Research, 1984), pp. 748–752.
31. "Jihad vs. McWorld," *New York Times Book Review* (August 20, 1995), p. 8.
32. "Depicting Men Doing Housework," p. B6.
33. "Den Fujita, Japan's Mr. Joint-Venture," *New York Times* (March 22, 1992), pp. F1, F6; and "Moose-Hunting in Japan?" *New York Times* (February 28, 1993), Section 9, p. 4.
34. "Fast-Food Franchises Fight for Brazilian Aficionados," *Brandweek* (June 7, 1993), p. 20.
35. "Pushing U.S. Style, Nike and Reebok Sell Sneakers to Europe," *Wall Street Journal* (July 22, 1993), pp. A1, A8.
36. Ibid.
37. "The 20th Century: Semi-Integrated World," *The Economist* (September 11, 1999), pp. S41–S42.
38. "Europe Defines Itself Against US on the Internet," *Wall Street Journal* (April 2, 2001), p. B9F.
39. "Pizza in Japan Is Adapted to Local Tastes," *Wall Street Journal* (June 4, 1993), p. B1.
40. "Chasing the Global Dream," pp. 1, 2.
41. Christopher Cooper and Stephanie Gruner, "US Internet Firms Must Hustle to Catch Up in Europe—AOL and Others Confront a Raft of Cultural Barriers," *Wall Street Journal* (November 15, 1999), p. A25:3.
42. David Osterhout, "Maytag Name Missing in China Ad Effort," *Advertising Age International* (May 2000), p. 2.
43. "Snapple in Japan: How a Splash Dried Up," *Wall Street Journal* (April 15, 1996), pp. B1, B3.
44. "Avon Talks Globally to Women," *Advertising Age Global* (October 2001), p. 43.
45. "Priceless Campaign Proves Its Value," *Advertising Age Global* (October 2001), p. 40.
46. "Avon Talks Globally," p. 43.
47. "Parker Pen," *Advertising Age* (June 2, 1986), p. 60.
48. "Absolut Frustration: Why Foreign Distillers Find It So Hard to Sell Vodka to the Russians," *Wall Street Journal* (January 15, 1998), p. A1.
49. "Fiat Rolls with the Changes to Become Market Leader," *Advertising Age Global* (October 2001).
50. "Internet Businesses May Find the Global Village Dauntingly Native," p. C15.
51. Carol-Linnea Salmon, "Milking Deadly Dollars from the Third World," *Business & Society Review* (Winter 1989), pp. 43–48.
52. "Tobacco Companies Look to Overseas as Americans Snuff Out Habit," *Houston Chronicle* (April 19, 1998), p. 29.
53. "Even Overseas, Tobacco Has Nowhere to Hide," *Adweek's Marketing Week* (April 1, 1991), p. 4.
54. Ibid.

CHAPTER 14

Reference-Group Influences

One of the most important environmental influences on consumer behavior is the face-to-face group. A consideration of the influence of groups is based on the **reference group;** that is, a group that serves as a reference point for individuals in forming their attitudes and behavior. This chapter

- describes various types of reference groups,
- evaluates the roles they play,
- explores the ways they influence the individual consumer, and
- considers the marketing strategy implications of reference-group influences.

Marketers frequently advertise their products in a group setting—the family eating breakfast cereals, friends having a soft drink after a game of touch football, a neighbor admiring a new car. The purpose is to mirror the influence that friends and relatives have on consumers. The implication is that the product is accepted by the group and enhances their interaction. Another strategy is for marketers to use "typical consumers" in testimonials for the product. The typical consumer reflects the purchaser's norms and values and acts as a representative of the consumer's reference group. For example, in a print ad campaign for Dove soap, six women cite the benefits of the product under the tag line "Women from Scranton to Sacramento will tell you Dove is better."

Marketers also use celebrities as spokespersons to try to mirror group influence. In this case, the celebrity represents a member of a group the consumer admires at a distance rather than an actual member of the consumer's reference group. The assumption is that consumers are likely to be influenced by these individuals because they want to identify with them.

Reebok's Pyramid of Group Influence

Reebok is an example of a company relying on peer-group influence in developing its marketing strategy. Reebok used celebrity spokespersons in the early 1980s based on a concept it called the "pyramid of group influence." Industry experts segment athletic shoe consumers into serious athletes, weekend warriors who use their shoes for sports but are not zealous athletes, and causal wearers who use athletic shoes primarily for street wear. The pyramid of influence posits that the serious athlete is a very small segment at the top of a "pyramid" that influences those below—weekend warriors and casual wearers. Reebok advertised its shoes using celebrities whom weekend warriors and casual wearers could identify with. Reebok also used noncelebrity spokespersons at the top of the pyramid—coaches, fitness trainers, members of sports clubs—by giving them free Reeboks to generate "buzz" about the brand.

The concept worked at first because athletic shoes were relatively new as a category, and opinion leaders were important in getting the word out about Reeboks. But by the late 1980s, as the athletic shoe market matured, the pyramid concept was not as relevant. Reebok's continued reliance on the "pyramid" led to a decline in sales. It then switched gears with its UBU campaign, stressing freedom of expression and the individuality one could achieve by wearing a pair of Reeboks. The ads featured zany vignettes of people expressing their individual styles in their Reebok shoes.[1] In effect, Reebok switched from using personal influence in its ads to imagery.

The switch in gears was only moderately successful. After a series of campaigns that were less than memorable in the 1990s and continued sales declines, Reebok went back to using celebrities in 2001.[2] It began using Venus Williams, the number one ranked woman tennis player in 2001, in its widely recognized "Defy Convention" campaign[3] (see Exhibit 14.1). The campaign celebrates individuals who have defied the odds, people who encounter difficulties and find the wherewithal to succeed despite those challenges. In extending the campaign to celebrities like Venus Williams, Reebok hopes that people recognize that celebrities also have to overcome the odds, just like the everyday consumer—and that they made it.[4] Whereas Reebok's ads in the early 1980s used celebrities as "experts" to spread the word about the brand, the current campaign uses celebrities as "referents"; that is, individuals whom prospective purchasers can identify with based on their personal circumstances.

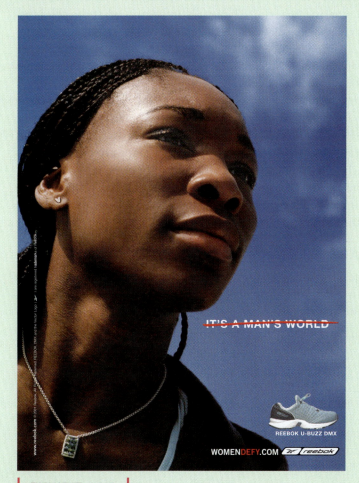

IT'S A MAN'S WORLD

REEBOK U-BUZZ DMX

WOMENDEFY.COM reebok

EXHIBIT 14.1
Venus Williams as a spokesperson for Reebok.
© Reebok International Ltd. and Tony Kaye.

Although marketers often try to influence reference groups, sometimes reference groups influence marketers. If the group is sufficiently visible and cohesive, it can influence marketing strategy. For example, Harley-Davidson owners adopted jeans, black boots, T-shirts, and black leather jackets as the "Harley-Davidson uniform." The company did not initiate this association, but once it was established, Harley-Davidson cultivated it by coming out with a full line of clothing and accessories with the Harley-Davidson logo.[5] Other examples of groups that have affected marketers are the hot-rod groups that influenced car designs during Detroit's "muscle car" era in the 1950s and 1960s, and skydivers and surfers who largely have determined equipment and clothing for these categories.

When Do Reference Groups Exert Influence?

Reference groups provide us with roles and standards of conduct that directly influence our needs and purchasing behavior. The family influences what the child eats for breakfast; the peer group, what the teenager listens to on the radio and watches on TV; and the organizational group, what the adult wears to work. In each case, the group provides the individual with information on how to act and often pressures the individual to conform to group norms.

In adapting to group norms, we not only subscribe to the values established by the family, peer group, or organization, but we also define ourselves.[6] In fact, one essential element of self-concept is how we think others see us. This influence, referred to as the "looking glass self," means that reference groups provide the points of comparison by which we evaluate our own attitudes and behavior.

The influence a group exerts on an individual's purchasing behavior depends on three factors: (1) the individual's attitude toward the group, (2) the nature of the group, and (3) the nature of the product.

ATTITUDE TOWARD THE GROUP

A study by Bearden and Rose found wide variations in an individual's susceptibility to group influence.[7] An individual's purchasing behavior is more likely to be influenced by the group if he or she

- *views the group as a credible source of information* about the product or service.[8]
- *values the views and reactions of group members* regarding purchasing decisions.[9]
- *accepts the rewards and sanctions meted out by the group* for appropriate or inappropriate behavior.

Consider a new member of a Harley-Davidson bikers' group. He (most members are males) relies on other members for information and advice regarding servicing, maintenance, and product performance. Group members accept the rewards and sanctions of the group. In their ethnographic study of Harley-Davidson groups, Schouten and McAlexander report that as an individual gains more respect and authority in the group, he moves up further in the riding pack, with the group leader also leading the pack on the road.[10] New members ride farther back in the pack. If they do not conform to the values and behavior of the group, they may be shunned and ridiculed as "weekend warriors."

THE NATURE OF THE GROUP

As for the nature of the group, reference groups are more likely to influence a member's behavior[11] if they are

- *cohesive,* in that members have similar norms and values.

- *frequently interacting,* thus creating more opportunities to influence members.

- *distinctive and exclusive,* in that membership in the group is highly valued.

Harley-Davidson biker groups have each of these characteristics. The group is closely knit, with an increasing level of commitment by bikers over time. For many members, biking becomes an obsession, almost a full-time hobby. As a result, opportunities for interaction and influence increase. Further, membership becomes exclusive, with members referring to each other as "brothers" and outsiders as "citizens."

THE NATURE OF THE PRODUCT

The third factor that determines the degree of influence a group has on an individual is the nature of the product. Groups are more likely to be influential for (1) visible products such as clothing, cosmetics, and furniture and (2) exclusive products that might connote status.[12]

Motorcycles are visible, and the Harley-Davidson is the necessary mark of status for group membership. Of more interest, however, are the visible indicators associated with the product. Each Harley group has its own distinct signs of membership, such as tattoos, sew-on patches, pins proclaiming various accomplishments at rallies, and most important, varying styles in customizing the bike.[13]

Before we consider the nature of these group influences in more detail, the types of reference groups consumers can belong to are discussed.

Types of Reference Groups

Reference groups provide points of comparison by which to evaluate attitudes and behavior. A consumer can either be a member of a reference group, such as the family, or aspire to belong to a group (*e.g.,* a tennis buff might aspire to associate with tennis pros). In the first case, the individual is part of a **membership group;** in the second, the individual is part of an **aspiration group.**

Reference groups can also be viewed negatively. For example, an individual may belong to or join a group and then reject the group's values. This type of group would be a **disclaimant group** for the individual.[14] Moreover, an individual may regard membership in a particular group as something to be avoided. Such a group is a **dissociative group.**

These four types of reference groups are shown at the top of Figure 14.1. Advertisers rarely appeal to the desire to avoid or disclaim a group, but they do appeal to the desire to be part of a group. Even appeals to nonconformity are made on the positive note of being different from everyone else, not on the negative note of dissociating oneself from certain groups. Marketers, therefore, tend to focus on positive reference groups; namely, membership and aspiration groups.

FIGURE 14.1

Types of reference groups.

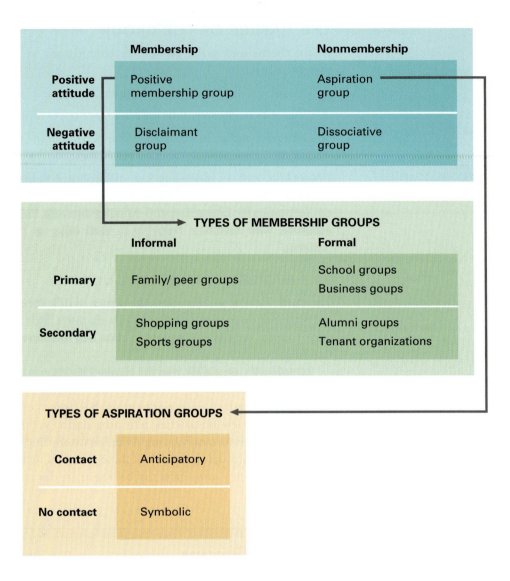

MEMBERSHIP GROUPS

Because positive reference groups are important, Figure 14.1 further breaks down membership and aspiration groups. In the middle of Figure 14.1, positive membership groups are classified as primary or secondary and informal or formal. If a person has regular contact with certain individuals, such as family, friends, and business associates, those individuals are a "primary group." Shopping groups, political clubs, and fellow skiers or joggers constitute a person's "secondary groups," because he or she has less frequent contact with them. Primary groups are more important to the consumer in developing product beliefs, tastes, and preferences and have a more direct influence on purchasing behavior. Reingen and his colleagues found that members of groups with the greatest contact in a variety of situations (*i.e.,* primary groups) were more likely to buy the same brands.[15] Because of their influence, these groups are more interesting to the marketer.

Groups also can be divided by whether they have a *formal* structure (a president, secretary, and treasurer) with specific roles (fundraising, teaching, transmitting

EXHIBIT 14.2

Ads portraying primary formal and informal groups.

(left) Courtesy Hard Tail; (right) Courtesy Firecom.

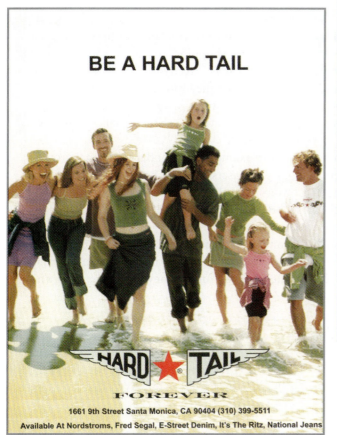

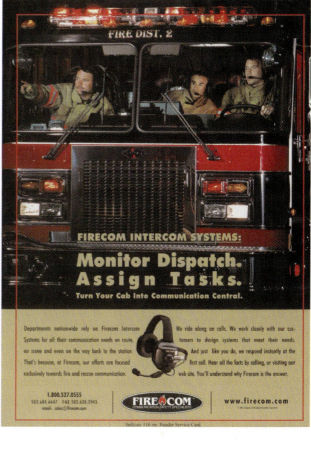

information) or an *informal* structure. The structures and roles of informal groups are implicit. This classification produces four types of membership groups as shown in Figure 14.1.

Primary Informal Groups   The family and peer groups represent **primary informal groups,** which are by far the most important groupings because of the frequency of contact and the closeness between the individual and group members. As a result, advertisers frequently portray consumption among friends and family. For example, by showing a group of family and friends, the Hard Tail ad in Exhibit 14.2 tries to convey that the Hard Tail clothing line is acceptable for the whole family.

Primary Formal Groups   Primary formal groups have a more formal structure than do family, friends, and peer groups. The consumer comes into regular contact with these groups, but not as frequently as primary informal groups. Examples are school class groups assigned to a project or business groups working together on a daily basis. Advertisers portray membership in such groups as a means of winning product approval. For example, Firecom associates its wireless communications devices with the safety of firefighters. By showing firefighters using the product on a fire call, Firecom is appealing to the firefighters' code of ensuring the safety of not only the people they rescue but also their fellow firefighters. The indirect message is that just like a firefighter, Firecom will always be there for you (see Exhibit 14.2).

▌ Secondary Informal Groups   **Secondary informal groups** have no formal structure and meet infrequently. Examples are shopping groups or sports groups that get together once in a while. Such groups may directly influence purchases. In his study of shopping groups, Granbois examined the influence of secondary informal groups.[16] He found that when an individual shops in a group of three or more persons, compared with a smaller group, there is twice as much chance that he or she will purchase more than originally planned.

Chatrooms on the Internet are another example of secondary informal groups. For example, amazon.com encourages purchasers to write book reviews and recommendations enabling potential buyers to make more informed purchase decisions.[17] People identify with these book reviews because they allow them to associate with others shopping on Amazon.

Exhibit 14.3 shows the use of a secondary informal group in advertising. The ad for Head & Shoulders shows a group of waiters at a Chicago restaurant, an informal work group, in a friendly pose, with the tag line "You can never spot the ones who use Head & Shoulders."

▌ EXHIBIT 14.3 ▌

Depicting secondary group influence.

© The Procter & Gamble Company. Used by permission.

▌Secondary Formal Groups **Secondary formal groups** are the least important to the consumer and, therefore, to the marketer, as they meet infrequently, are structured, and are not closely knit. Examples include alumni groups, business clubs, and tenant organizations. Although marketers of specialized products (such as travel agents or developers of executive programs) may have some interest in these groups, marketers of national brands generally do not portray or appeal to these groups.

ASPIRATION GROUPS

Two types of aspiration groups, anticipatory and symbolic, are classified at the bottom of Figure 14.1. **Anticipatory aspiration groups** are those that an individual anticipates joining at a future time and, in most cases, with which he or she has direct contact. The best example is a group higher in the organizational hierarchy that an individual wishes to join. This desire is based on the rewards that have been generally accepted to be most important in Western culture: power, status, prestige, and money. Marketers appeal to the desire to enhance one's position by climbing to a higher aspiration group. Clothing and cosmetics are frequently advertised within the context of business success and prestige.

Manufacturers of men's clothing and fragrances traditionally have used such themes; and women's products increasingly rely on appeals to organizational aspirations because of the growing number of women in the work force. A good example of an appeal to aspiration group norms is the 1988 ad for Johnnie Walker Black Label, shown in Exhibit 14.4. The ad appeals to those who hope to arrive at the top of the

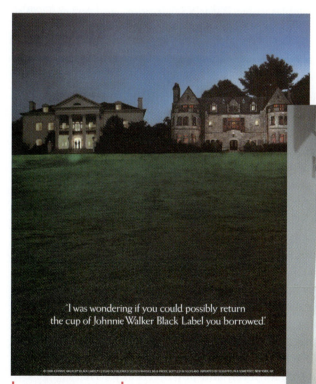

"I was wondering if you could possibly return the cup of Johnnie Walker Black Label you borrowed."

No matter how much I have on my plate I always make room for proper nutrition.

EXHIBIT 14.4

Appealing to anticipatory and symbolic aspirational group norms.

(left) Schieffelin and Somerset, Importers of Johnnie Walker blended scotch whisky; (right) Copyright 2001 EAS, Inc.

socioeconomic ladder, as depicted by drinkers of Johnny Walker. The purchase of the product represents an acceptance of aspirational group norms.

Symbolic aspiration groups are those that the individual admires but is not likely to belong to, despite acceptance of the group's beliefs and attitudes. Fisher and Price found that purchasing a product linked to the aspiration group is a means of establishing a vicarious connection with this group[18]—for example, a football fan buying a sports jacket or a jersey with the team's logo prominently displayed. An important condition for such influence is that the product is visually obvious, as is the case with team-sponsored clothing.

Marketers appeal to symbolic aspirations by using celebrities to advertise certain products. The ad for AdvantEdge nutrition bars featuring Cindy Crawford (see Exhibit 14.4) is an example. Crawford's appearance in the ad is based on her fame as a supermodel, not on her nutritional expertise. Anyone who vicariously associates with supermodels and their slim figures might be influenced to buy AdvantEdge nutrition bars.

The Nature of Reference Groups

Reference groups have certain characteristics that affect their influence on consumers. They establish norms, values, roles, status, socialization, and power. Each of these characteristics operates in the Harley-Davidson biker groups and is described below.

NORMS

Norms are the (generally undefined) rules and standards of conduct the group establishes. Group members are expected to conform to these norms, which may relate to the appropriateness of clothes, eating habits, makes of cars, or brands of cosmetics. Norms in Harley groups are fairly well defined regarding dress, maintenance requirements, assistance given to bikers within the group, and forms of addressing bikers outside the group. These norms are not documented, but they are clearly understood.

VALUES

Values are shared beliefs among group members as to what behaviors are desirable and undesirable. As we saw in Chapters 11 and 12, values are largely defined by cultures and subcultures, but they do vary substantially by family and peer group. One family may place more value on social status, the family next door on personal enhancement independent of status.

The typical Harley rider's values include a strong dose of personal freedom, and the bike as the means to achieve it. This emphasis on freedom and liberation from the constraints of society is as true for mom-and-pop bikers as for Hell's Angels. In addition, most biker groups demonstrate patriotic values, particularly since Harley-Davidson was the sole survivor of the American motorcycle industry. They regard owning a Japanese bike as unpatriotic. American flags abound at rallies, and many bikes and clothing carry pro-USA messages.[19]

ROLES

Roles are functions that the individual assumes or that the group assigns to the individual to attain group objectives. In group purchasing behavior, marketers can identify specific roles in an attempt to offer the best available brand or product category. The following roles have been identified in family decision making: the influencer, the gatekeeper (the individual who has the most control over the flow of information into the group), the decision maker, the purchasing agent, and the consumer. These roles are considered more thoroughly in Chapter 15.

STATUS

Status refers to the position the individual occupies within the group. High status implies greater power and influence. A chairperson of the board has the highest status within an organization but may be the weakest member of a weekly bridge club. Symbols of dress or ownership are frequently associated with both high and low status. For example, the chairperson's oak-paneled office symbolizes status, but so does the janitor's uniform. Status in Harley rider groups is "conferred on members according to their seniority, participation and leadership in group activities, riding expertise and experience, [and] Harley-specific knowledge."[20] Such status is represented by an informal hierarchy based on these factors.

Consumers sometimes purchase products to demonstrate status in a broader societal sense so that the message is one of wealth and implied superiority. The elegant dress and expensive car may be status symbols; but in some groups, symbolism operates in exact reversal to one's wealth and position. Jeans and small cars may be the norm among wealthy suburbanites, and large cars and more expensive clothes may be status symbols among lower socioeconomic groups.

SOCIALIZATION

The process by which an individual learns the group's norms and role expectations is called **socialization.** The individual moving from one job to another must learn the informal rules and expectations from primary work groups along with the organization's formal rules and expectations.

Consumer socialization is the process by which consumers acquire the knowledge and skills necessary to operate in the marketplace. The two most important types are the socialization of children and the socialization of new residents in a community. (The socialization of children is considered in more detail in Chapter 15.)

Based on their experiences with a Harley rider group, Schouten and McAlexander describe their own process of consumer socialization as learning "models for appropriate consumption behavior from a variety of sources including other bikers and the media."[21] Because of an arm's-length attitude of veteran riders, newcomers tend to rely on Harley promotional literature, catalogs, and corporate magazine for initial instruction regarding the appropriate "look." These commercial sources of information are reinforced by the new rider's attempts to emulate role models within the group and by pressures for conformity from the group.

POWER

The influence that a group has on an individual is closely related to the group's power. Various sources of group influence have been identified,[22] but three are particularly relevant for marketing strategy: expert power, referent power, and reward power.

■ **Expert Power**   To have **expert power,** an individual or group must have experience and knowledge. A consumer may accept a friend's purchase recommendation if the friend is regarded as knowledgeable or experienced with the product. A sales representative also may be regarded as an expert source as long as the salesperson has established credibility with the consumer.

■ **Referent Power**   The basis for **referent power** is the individual's identification with members of the group. The greater the similarity between the individual's beliefs and attitudes and those of group members, the greater the group's referent power. The individual either is a member of a group or may aspire to belong to a group because of common norms and values.

■ **Reward Power**   **Reward power** is based on the group's ability to reward the individual. The business organization can reward an employee with money and status. The family can reward the child with praise and approval. Social groups can also provide rewards in purchasing behavior. Compliments on clothes or looks provided by a relevant group member reinforce the consumer's choice.

Groups that have reward power may also have coercive power over the individual. That is, the group "giveth and taketh away." The greater the importance of the group, the greater its power to express disapproval and even punishment. The organization has the power to fire an individual, parents to punish a child, and social groups to exclude individuals for deviant behavior.

These three sources of group influence are not mutually exclusive. Harley rider groups, for example, exert all three forms of influence on members. Veteran riders exert expert power over new members in the process of consumer socialization by demonstrating the right look, riding techniques, maintenance procedures, and language. The group exerts referent power through imitation by new members of veteran riders. And the group exerts reward power through demands for conformity and rewards members with greater status within the group for such conformity.

The Nature of Web Communities

The Internet has served as a vehicle for socialization at a distance. Web communities emerge because people have shared values, beliefs, and interests. These are "grassroots" communities formed by Internet users initially searching for information and finding others interested in the same subject. These people form groups and discuss and share information and experiences based on their common interests. Such communities are formed in three ways. First, surfers can find each other on the Web, primarily through email, and draw other interested parties into their correspondence. Second, web marketers can sponsor sites. Sites such as Yahoo!'s Web Ring provide surfers the ability to determine whether a community already exists for interests as remote as nineteenth-century French military music. If a community does not exist, Web Ring provides the means of forming one. Third, communities can be formed through the development of portals such as *www.iVillage.com,* a site geared to topics of interest to women. The site provides women with a sense of community by matching their shared interests in diverse topics such as health care, fashions, parenting, and women's rights.

Web communities thus imply a sense of belonging among members. The sense of community on the Internet is manifested and reinforced by precisely tailored content, brand preferences among like-minded users, ability to interact with others on the Web, opportunity to shape the development of a web site, and mutual benefits of participants.[23] This section describes the types of communities and discusses the elements of web communities as they relate to establishing norms, values, roles, status, socialization, and power.

TYPES OF COMMUNITIES ON THE WEB

There are four types of communities on the Internet; transaction, interest, fantasy and relationship.[24] **Communities of transaction** primarily facilitate the buying and selling of products and services and deliver information related to those transactions. An example of a web site tailored to the transaction community is a French-based site, *www.clust.com.* The site brings various buyers together interested in purchasing a particular product—for example, a Rolex watch—and attempts to gain the advantages of group buying at a discount. The advantage to consumers is that there is no need to commit to a purchase until it is known at what discount the product can be purchased.

Communities of interest bring together participants who interact extensively with one another on specific topics. These communities involve a higher degree of interpersonal communication than do communities of transaction. For instance, Garden Web is a site where visitors can share ideas with other gardeners through forums, post requests for seeds and other items on the Garden Exchange, and post queries on electronic bulletin boards. Garden Web also provides direct electronic links to Internet gardening resources, including directories of sites relating to gardening.

The Internet also allows people to live out their fantasies in **communities of fantasy,** where users create new environments, personalities, or stories. For instance, on ESPNet, an Internet-based sports community, participants can indulge their need for fantasy by creating their own sports teams (using the names of real players), which then compete against teams created by other participants. Winners are determined based on the performance of the real players during the season.

Finally, there are **communities of relationship.** Groups of people come together in communities of relationship because they share certain life experiences. For instance, the Cancer Forum on CompuServe provides support for cancer patients and their families. Participants talk about how they deal with the disease and exchange information on medical research, pain medication, test results, and protocols.[25] As noted earlier, iVillage is such a site, devoted to forming a community of relationships for women based on areas of common interest.

The type of marketing needed to reach consumers varies for each of the four communities. In a transaction community, users are looking for product information. Marketers are more successful in advertising to communities of interest and relationship if the advertising comes in the form of advice, rather than traditional advertising. An example is Scott's advice on how to care for your lawn. Users can sign up for a service on Scott's web site *(www.scotts.com)* that sends email reminders of when to plant seeds, fertilize, and so on. Although Scott's sells all of the products needed to care for lawns, consumers do not see this as advertising because they like the benefit of being reminded about how and when to care for their lawn. Similarly, Polaroid gets extra mileage on ParentSoup by advising parents that taking pictures

WEB APPLICATIONS

Identifying and Targeting Web Communities

Every day, the Internet gives birth to hundreds of web communities, which are focused on everything from collecting antique cameras to hunting for mushrooms to motorcycle maintenance. By 2000, there were an estimated four hundred thousand such sites on the Web. Forrester Research estimates that community members make up 27 percent of the online audience.

Yahoo!'s Web Ring (formerly Geo Cities) is the largest facilitator in forming web communities. Web Ring provides a facility for surfers to link up with others with similar interests for free. Yahoo! can identify these communities, giving marketers the capability to target them. What if a community is not on Web Ring? IBM has developed a method of identifying any community on the Web through a method called "community mining." If the subject is antique cameras, community mining software finds communications on the subject in multiple related links. The method might initially trace three or four links in iterative fashion until a host of other links are found identifying a community of interest on the subject.

Marketers are interested in targeting web communities because members are highly involved with the subject. Smirnoff, for example, might want to advertise on a site formed by vodka aficionados; Harley-Davidson, on a site devoted to motorcycle maintenance. But communities also represent opportunities to small marketers. A small company producing gardening implements might find it feasible to reach hundreds of thousands of gardening enthusiasts, whereas before the Web it would have been economically unfeasible.

Targeting web communities has a downside, however—offending them with marketing efforts. To avoid offending communities, marketers must get members to buy in before they are bombarded with ad messages. As one expert web marketer said, "Much of what you need to do with communities is permission-based." How can marketers get communities' permission to market to them? Give them value. If you are Harley-Davidson, offer the motorcycle maintenance community a service like free troubleshooting advice or a free magazine on maintenance. Find out how members of the community communicate and help them do so by tying in Harley groups with web access.

Ultimately, effective targeting is not just advertising to a community, but trying to be part of it.

Source: "Cracking the Niche," American Demographics (June 2000), pp. 38–40.

OF CONSUMER BEHAVIOR

with an instant camera can increase a child's self-esteem.[26] In communities of fantasy, advertisers may be more successful if they endorse and sponsor special events on the web site;[27] for example, ESPNet could create a promotional event to reward winning fantasy sports teams.

CHARACTERISTICS OF WEB COMMUNITIES

Like other groups, web communities also can be defined by their norms, values, roles, status, socialization, and power.

▍ **Norms**   Norms may differ based on the type of community to which a user belongs. To feel part of a genuine community, users need to know that there is a critical mass of similar people using the site. For instance, Salon's "Mothers Who Think" *(www.salon.com)* is a forum targeted at intelligent, fairly affluent mothers who were previously working and are now looking after their children. The typical user is more isolated from peers than at previous life stages and has a desire for the exchange of cultural and intellectual stimulation not available from their home environment.[28] The norms of this web site would differ widely from that of ESPNet, where users are engaged in acting out their sports fantasies.

▍ **Values**   Values also differ by type of web community. For instance, in a transaction community, users expect ethical behavior; that is, they assume that others are giving truthful and unbiased advice. For instance, when a user seeks advice from a wine expert or reviews a wine rating on *www.wine.com,* it is expected that the advice is truthful and unbiased. In interest groups, users talk only about topics they have in common with others; personal information is not shared. For instance, on a gardening web site, users would only talk about gardening. They do not discuss their families, work, or even other interests. On the other hand, in relationship communities, users share very personal experiences. Therefore, they discuss not only what is happening to them, but also how they feel about it and how they are handling it.

▍ **Roles**   As with non-Internet groups, people involved in web communities form roles that define their position in the community. For instance, on the British Gardening Online web site *(www.oxalis.co.uk),* the questions on the bulletin board focus on detailed plant and garden product information. For individual problems, the group's expertise provides specific answers. Users can post questions—specific or general—on the bulletin board, and other users provide answers for them. Participants recognize the niche expertise of particular members. For the community as a whole, the composite of such expertise increases each member's knowledge. This means that all site visitors increase their knowledge about plants and gardening through the content provided by the host (the cumulative knowledge of all members). Independent retailers and suppliers who frequent the site have an opportunity to provide word-of-mouth publicity, but in the form of advice rather than advertising.[29]

▍ **Status**   As users become active members of their online communities, they develop positions within the group. Burson-Marstellar and Roper Starch Worldwide have identified a group of men and women who are much more active than other Internet users in terms of their online influence. Representing about 8 percent of the Internet population, about 9 million users, this group, known as "e-fluentials," influences more people on more topics than other online users. And although extremely influential in the online world, this group's influence does not stop there. Many e-fluentials spread their views in the offline world as well. These people tend to be opinion leaders on a wide range of topics. They are three times as likely as the typical online user to be asked for advice; thus, they are the elitists of the Internet. They are asked about everything from finding the best values on products to current events, new technologies, education, hobbies, and family issues.[30] E-fluentials and influentials are discussed in greater detail in Chapter 16.

▌ **Socialization**   Personal relationships can and do develop online, but more slowly because development of trust and communication of intimacy take longer than in face-to-face communication. Studies show that in the process of social interaction online, trust and intimacy in computer-mediated groups gradually increase to a level approaching that of face-to-face groups.[31] However, on the Internet, users have the option to be anonymous. They can join a discussion group and just sit back and watch as typed messages go back and forth. Users can use typed materials to learn about the group's norms and role expectations before participating.

Anonymity on the Web can spur socialization. Over one hundred years ago, sociologist Georg Simmel posited that anonymity may allow individuals to divulge information to strangers, almost as a catharsis, in a way they could not be divulged in face-to-face groups. Such interactions are much more likely to take place on the Web, often encouraging intimacy. Some online interactions have even led to marriage proposals. But anonymity on the Web also has a darker side, as was evident when one chatroom participant divulged a crime anonymously and eventually was identified and apprehended.

▌ **Power**   To have expert power, an individual or group must have experience and knowledge. An example of expert power on the Internet is iVillage.com's use of experts in the areas of women's health and parental care. The experts used are professionals with solid credentials in these areas.[32]

The basis for referent power is the individual's identification with members of the group. For instance, parents value other parents' advice over expert advice on many parenting issues. Therefore, ParentSoup on iVillage.com offers dozens of topical and free-form chats every day. This allows parents to talk to one another to share experiences and exchange advice.[33]

Reward power is based on the group's ability to reward as well as to punish members on the Web. Accepting the marketer as part of a web community in a broad sense, consumers can "punish" marketers by airing their complaints on the Web. Certain sites have been formed for this purpose. For instance, eComplaints.com has billed itself as "Your chance to fight back."[34] After unsuccessful attempts to reconcile problems with a company, consumers can turn to the Internet. And many times, a company deals with a consumer's issues only after the consumer posts a complaint on the Internet.[35]

Reference-Group Influences on Consumers

The three types of group power suggest the ways reference groups influence consumer choice.[36] First, expert power suggests **informational influence.** An expert's testimonial in an advertisement or a knowledgeable friend's experiences are informative communications. Second, referent power suggests that groups have **comparative influence** in permitting a comparison of the individual's beliefs, attitudes, and behavior to those of the group. As referents, groups provide the consumer with the basis for evaluating one's self-image. Third, reward power suggests that reference groups have **normative influence** by directly influencing attitudes and behavior based on group norms and encouraging compliance with these norms.

Table 14.1 shows each type of influence within the context of consumer behavior by citing the type of influence exerted on the consumer, the objectives for the consumer, the basis for group influence, and the effects on behavior.[37]

INFORMATIONAL INFLUENCE

A consumer accepts information from a group if he or she considers the group a credible source of information and expertise and if he or she believes the information enhances knowledge about product choices.[38] As we saw in the Harley rider's socialization process, information can be obtained directly from group members the consumer regards as knowledgeable or by observing the behavior of group members.

Consumers are more likely to seek expert advice from personal sources such as friends and neighbors than from commercial sources such as advertising because they regard personal sources as more trustworthy. That is, consumers may regard a manufacturer's advertising claim with suspicion because of the company's vested interest in promoting the product.

TABLE 14.1

Types of influence exerted by reference groups

Nature of influence	Objectives	Perceived characteristics of source	Type of power	Behavior
Informational	Knowledge	Credibility	Expert	Acceptance
Comparative	Self-maintenance and enrichment	Similarity	Referent	Identification
Normative	Reward	Power	Reward or coercion	Conformity

Source: Material adapted from Burnkrant and Cousineau, "Informational and Normative Social Influence in Buyer Behavior," *Journal of Consumer Research* 2 (December 1975), p. 207. Reprinted with permission from The University of Chicago Press.

▌ The Nature of Informational Influence   Table 14.1 illustrates the nature of informational influence by describing the consumer's objectives as obtaining knowledge, the condition for accepting information as credible, the source of power as expertise, and the final behavior as acceptance of influence. Table 14.2 lists various types of statements that illustrate informational, comparative, and normative influences. Park and Lessig used the statements in a study to determine the relative importance of these three influences in the selection of twenty products.[39] Statements 1 and 2 reflect the objective of seeking information from expert sources or friends and neighbors with reliable information. In addition, observation (Statement 3) is regarded as an important source of information.

Informational influence is likely to be most important in two conditions. The first is when there is social, financial, or performance risk in buying the product.[40] A consumer buying a car seeks information from knowledgeable friends, relatives, or salespeople because of the social visibility of a car, the costs of buying, and possible mechanical failures. In this case, the advice of an expert is probably more

TABLE 14.2
Conditions reflecting informational, comparative, and normative influences

Informational influence

1. The individual seeks information about various brands of the product from an independent group of experts, or from those who work with the product as a profession.
2. The individual seeks brand-related knowledge and experience (such as how Brand A's perfume compares to Brand B's) from those friends, neighbors, relatives, or work associates who have reliable information about the brands.
3. The individual's observation of what experts do influences his or her choice of a brand (such as observing the type of car that police drive or the brand of TV that repair people buy).

Comparative influence

4. The individual feels that the purchase or use of a particular brand will enhance the image that others have of him or her.
5. The individual feels that the purchase of a particular brand helps show others what he or she is or would like to be (such as an athlete, successful businessperson, etc).
6. The individual feels that those who purchase or use a particular brand possess the characteristics that he or she would like to have.
7. The individual sometimes feels that it would be nice to be like the type of person advertisements show using a particular brand.

Normative influence

8. The individual's decision to purchase a particular brand is influenced by the preferences of people with whom he or she has social interaction.
9. The individual's decision to purchase a particular brand is influenced by the preferences of family members.
10. The desire to satisfy the expectations that others have of him or her has an impact on the individual's brand choice.

Source: Material adapted from Park and Lessig, "Students and Housewives: Differences in Susceptibility to Reference Group Influence," *Journal of Consumer Research* 4 (September 1977), p. 105. Reprinted with permission from The University of Chicago Press.

important than that of a referent. Second, if the individual has limited knowledge or experience regarding the product, informational influence is likely to be most important. A consumer with little knowledge of technical products such as computers, cellular phones, or fax machines is likely to seek expert advice.

▌ Informational Influence on the Web   The Internet also provides a means of getting information from personal sources. For example, consumers get information about products from email, newsgroups, bulletin boards, chatrooms, and web sites dedicated to providing consumer opinions. As an example of the latter, epinions.com obtains consumer opinions on a variety of products and services. Users go onto the web site either to post their opinions or to obtain the opinions of others on products, services, or stores.[41] iVillage.com serves as a large chatroom to allow women to share information and experiences about common problems. The web site is successful because it provides consumers with information from people with whom they can relate.[42]

E-commerce sites also provide expert advice. As noted earlier, wine.com has experts on staff to give advice on which wines to buy. This has been successful because consumers value the depth of information, the wide range of alternatives, the prompt response to inquiries, and the education they get about wine.[43] Although many of the wines are not available in local stores, consumers do not see the advice as pushing any one product. Instead, they feel they are learning about different wines and enjoy the interaction with the experts.

COMPARATIVE INFLUENCE

Consumers constantly compare their attitudes to those of members of important groups. In so doing, they seek to support their own attitudes and behavior by associating themselves with groups with which they agree and by dissociating themselves from groups with which they disagree. As a result, the basis for comparative influence is in the process of comparing oneself to other members of the group and judging whether the group would be supportive.

For example, if a family moves into a new home and meets new neighbors, the parents might compare the neighbors' attitudes toward political issues, education, and child rearing with their own. The parents also identify brands and products the neighbors purchase. New residents naturally are attracted to neighbors who are similar to themselves because those neighbors reinforce existing attitudes and behavior. This is the main reason that neighborhoods are made up of people with similar social and economic characteristics.

▌ The Nature of Comparative Influence   Table 14.1 shows that comparative influence is a process of self-maintenance and enrichment. The individual's objective is to enhance his or her self-concept by associating with groups that provide reinforcement and ego gratification. The source of power is referent power, and the individual's behavior toward the group is one of identification. Table 14.2 shows that the conditions relating to comparative influence deal with the enhancement of an individual's self-image through membership in a group (Statements 4 and 5) or identification with other people who are liked and admired as members of an aspiration group (Statements 6 and 7).

Comparative influence implies that those being influenced should have characteristics similar to those doing the influencing. A study by Moschis found that consumers are likely to seek information from friends viewed as similar to themselves and to regard such sources as credible.[44] The study concluded, therefore, that advertisers should try to use spokespersons whom consumers perceive as being similar to themselves (*i.e.*, "typical consumers"). The notion of similarity between influencer and influencee also extends to customer-salesperson interactions. Several studies have found that when a customer sees the salesperson as similar in terms of tastes, attitudes, and even religion, the salesperson is likely to be effective.[45]

Comparative influence may also be due to proximity. Several studies have shown that influencers and influencees tend to live close to each other.[46] For example, one study of elderly residents of a retirement community found that 81 percent of the exchange of information and advice about a new product occurred between persons who live on the same floor.[47]

▌ Comparative Influence on the Web   The Internet provides a means for companies to influence consumer purchases by using a technology called "collaborative filtering" to make product recommendations based on people with similar preferences to the purchaser. The collaborative filtering technology makes recommendations to customers based on their purchasing behavior by comparing it with the behavior of other customers with similar tastes. Both Barnesandnoble.com and Amazon.com use this technology to make book recommendations to users. The system compares a person's demographic profile and the books that person purchased in the past with other people's profiles and purchases stored in the site's database. It then makes recommendations as to books the person may be interested in buying. This is useful in influencing purchase decisions because the technology matches people with similar demographic and reading preferences.[48]

Chatrooms and various targeted web sites have similar effects on influencing purchases. Consumers voluntarily go to chatrooms and web sites to share information with people they perceive as having similar tastes, attitudes, and preferences. Word-of-mouth communication through these vehicles is likely to be effective because people feel they can relate to others in the chatroom or on the web site.[49]

NORMATIVE INFLUENCE

Normative influence refers to the influence a group exerts to conform to its norms and expectations.

▌ Conformity in Consumer Behavior   Conformity to group norms is the ultimate goal of normative influence, as it means that consumers will buy the brands and product categories the group approves. Marketers are interested in such imitative behavior because it implies a snowball effect once the most influential members of a group accept products. The idea of "keeping up with the Joneses" reflects imitative behavior.

Various studies have confirmed that individuals do imitate group behavior. These studies have been largely experimental and were inspired by social psychology studies demonstrating individual conformity to group norms. One of the most famous of these experiments brought groups of seven to nine college students together to judge the length of lines drawn on a card.[50] All group members but one were instructed to give the same incorrect response. The subject, who was not aware of the experiment, was confronted with the obviously incorrect choice of a unanimous group. In 37 percent of the cases, the subject went along with the group, even though the choice appeared to contradict his or her senses.

In an experiment by Venkatesan, three identical men's suits labeled "A," "B," and "C" were described to respondents as being of different quality and manufacture.[51] Three of four students in each group were told to pick Suit B. In the majority of cases, the fourth student also picked Suit B.

▌ The Nature of Normative Influence

According to Table 14.1, normative influence is based on the individual's desire to receive the rewards of the group. The basis for power is reward or coercion; the resulting behavior toward the group is conformity and compliance. Table 14.2 indicates that conditions reflecting normative influence deal with a desire to conform to group preferences (Statements 8 and 9) and to satisfy the expectations of group members (Statement 10).

▌ Conditions for Conformity

When is a consumer likely to be motivated to conform to the norms and behavior of the group? The motivation to conform is apt to occur when

- ▌ *the individual is committed to the group and values membership in it.*[52] In general, Harley owners are highly committed to their biker groups. The less committed the individual, the less he or she feels pressure to comply. Groups identified with disdain by regular bikers, such as the RUBs (rich urban bikers) and SEWERs (suburban weekend riders), are less likely to have the close-knit structure of some outlaw groups and committed mom-and-pop bikers. As a result, there is less pressure to comply to modes of dress or to accept the status hierarchy of the group.

- ▌ *the group provides significant rewards for compliance and punishment for lack of compliance.* The primary reward for compliance with group norms is acceptance. One study found that consumers used friends and relatives as sources of information for products because they provided positive social interaction.[53] The greater the commitment to the group, the greater the importance of rewards and punishment. Moving up in the pack would be much more important to the highly committed biker than to the RUB or SEWER. Similarly, being ignored by the group for wearing what is regarded as nerdy clothes or making ingratiating remarks is going to be less devastating to the RUBs and SEWERs than to the hard-core bikers.

- ▌ *the individual's behavior in conforming is visible to members of the group.*[54] Such rewards are more likely if the behavior is visible. A group can exert normative influence in the purchase of clothes, furniture, and appliances because these items are visible. Whyte demonstrated the importance of visibility in his study of a Philadelphia suburb's purchase of air conditioners when they were first introduced.[55] Research indicated the direct influence of friends and neighbors in purchasing the product, but the most apparent influence was seeing an air conditioner in a neighbor's window. Normative influence may also occur for items such as mouthwash and denture adhesive, even though the items themselves are not visible, because of fear that lack of use may be apparent (bad breath, loose dentures).

Visibility is less important in exerting informational and comparative influence because, in these cases, the objective is not conformity but knowledge and self-enhancement. The consumer could obtain information from the group and gain satisfaction in identifying with the group without any overt action.

■ **Conformity on the Web**   There is conformity on the Internet as well. Members of web communities influence others' purchases by discussing and sharing product and service information with fellow group members. Users may feel compelled to try different products or services so they can retain their feeling of belonging to a special interest community.

A need to conform to the norms and values of a web community also exists. For instance, monopolizing conversations in a chatroom is unacceptable; it is expected that everyone will get a chance to talk. Because people are not face-to-face, however, they are more forceful in making others conform. Anonymity may contribute to such assertiveness—people are less inhibited in saying what they think on the Web.[56] In face-to-face communications, people are likely to be more sensitive in seeking conformity.

■ **The Social Multiplier Effect**   The desire to emulate the behavior of a group often leads an individual to buy the same brand or product. Such imitative behavior reflects a **demonstration principle.** First formulated by economist James Duesenberry,[57] the demonstration principle states that with American consumers' increased mobility and purchasing power, they increasingly come into contact with new products and have the purchasing power to buy them. For example, when cell phones were first marketed, once one individual bought one, friends and neighbors came into contact with the product. Because these people were likely to have the same level of purchasing power, many of them purchased cell phones as well. In turn, other individuals increasingly came into contact with cell phones, and the pattern of ownership spread. The demonstration principle is similar to the idea of "keeping up with the Joneses" because of the element of social pressure to own new products. This concept is referred to as the **social multiplier effect,** because ownership increases in multiples as a function of group influence and product visibility.

One of the best examples of the social multiplier effect is a 1928 ad for Victrola (see Exhibit 14.5). The headline "Keeping Up with the Joneses" was probably the origin of the phrase and the main appeal for buying the new phonograph player. The copy illustrates the social multiplier in action: "The day it came, we celebrated by having the neighbors come over."

The social multiplier effect illustrates the volatility of group influence in the American economy. Certain brands or product categories may be highly visible today and representative of group norms; but five or ten years from now, such influence may become minimal. Because of the social multiplier effect, products that once were considered a luxury (refrigerators, automobiles, air conditioners) are now considered a necessity. Others such as portable computers (the precursor of laptops) and record players have become obsolete due to technological advances. To

| EXHIBIT 14.5 |

A 1928 example of the social multiplier effect.

Photo courtesy of Thomson, Inc.

a large degree, the social multiplier effect has powered the American economy to higher standards of living.

▎ Rejection of Conformity   Many individuals react to group pressures for conformity by rejecting them. As we will see, rejection of group pressures to conform has major societal implications, particularly for teenagers. If society could increase teenagers' willingness to reject peer pressures to smoke, drink, and take drugs, it could save millions of lives and billions of dollars in medical expenses. The likelihood of rejecting pressures to conform depends on

- *the strength of the individual's value system.* If the group sanctions behavior that contradicts deep-seated norms and values, group pressures are likely to be rejected. The teenager who believes that cigarettes are life-threatening and has seen a parent die of lung cancer is unlikely to accept peer pressures to start smoking.

- *the intensity of group pressures to conform.* When group pressures become too intense, consumers may reject group norms and demonstrate independence. In the experiment where all but one respondent purposely misjudged the length of a line, when pressure was put on the individual to go along with the others, the chances of conforming actually went down. Students reacted negatively to such pressure. This situation, known as **reactance,** suggests that consumers conform to group pressures only to a certain point.[58]

▌ *the commitment of the individual to the group.* As noted, the greater the individual's commitment to the group, the greater the likelihood he or she will conform to group norms. Conflict arises, however, if the group is highly important to the individual, yet the group's norms contradict the individual's value system. According to "balance theory," to resolve this conflict, the individual either reduces commitment to the group and maintain his or her values, maintains commitment to the group and modifies values so as to conform, or does some combination of the two. The teenager cited in this list's first point is unlikely to yield to pressures to smoke and will probably reduce commitment to the group.

▌ *the value placed on individuality.* Many people place a high value on individuality and lack of conformity. They like to stand apart from the crowd, yet may not be totally divorced from group membership. Simonson and Nowlis cite a need for uniqueness among many consumers; that is, a tendency to select unconventional choices in preferring uniqueness over conformity.[59] Schouten and McAlexander cited an example of a member of the Hell's Angels encountered in Amsterdam who clearly desired to stand apart from the traditional mode of dress and behavior of the group. This individual unabashedly rode his chopper in full colors (*i.e.,* wearing his official club insignias) over a white T-shirt, flowered Bermuda shorts, and red converse sneakers, instead of the uniform black T-shirt, greasy blue jeans, and black boots of the outlaw biker.[60] Most Harley riders wouldn't be caught dead in this outfit. This biker was obviously unwilling to compromise his independence in the interest of conformity. Some advertisers seek to identify their products with such independence and lack of conformity.

INFORMATION, COMPARISON, OR CONFORMITY

Is group influence on consumer purchasing behavior due primarily to the information supplied by groups, the identification with groups, or the pressure that groups bring to bear on individuals? The obvious answer is that all three components influence consumers. The type of influence that is most important, however, may be a function of the type of product being evaluated.

▌ **Type of Influence by Product**   Park and Lessig measured the relative effects of informational, comparative, and normative influence in the purchase of twenty products.[61] They asked a sample of college students to rate the twenty products by the statements listed in Table 14.2. The types of products most likely to be subject to informational influences are those that are technologically complex (*e.g.,* autos, computers, DVD players) or require objective informational criteria for selection (*e.g.,* insurance, physicians, medication). The products most subject to comparative influence are those that serve as a means of self-expression and identity (*e.g.,* autos, clothing, furniture). Automobiles and clothing are also subject to normative influence because they are visible and are, therefore, a means of conforming to group norms. Schouten and McAlexander found that motorcycles and related clothing were subject to all three influences—informational because of the technical complexity of motorcycles, comparative because of self-identity with the product, and normative because of the visibility of motorcycles and clothing as a means of identifying conformity.[62] The same could be said about the purchase of automobiles.

▌ Influence by Product Category versus Brand

Over forty years ago, Bourne studied the influence groups exert on the ownership of products and/or brands.[63] His findings are relevant today. Bourne focused on two product characteristics—product exclusivity and visibility. He determined that groups would be more likely to influence the *product decision* for exclusive products such as yachts or sports cars because owning such products would in itself make a statement. If the product was visible but not exclusive (a watch), groups would be more likely to influence the *brand decision,* such as buying a Rolex watch. In this case, it is the visibility of the brand rather than the product that makes it subject to group influence. If the product is not exclusive or visible, consumers make purchase decisions based on product attributes alone. Energy efficiency or size is more likely to influence the choice of a refrigerator rather than a neighbor's comments.

▌ What Is the Most Important Component of Group Influence?

The studies of comparative and normative influence suggest that consumers use groups as a means of identification and reward, but they may well use groups more for the information supplied. Ward and Reingen supported the importance of groups as sources of information rather than of conformity. They found that group members moved toward the group's position not because of pressures to conform to group norms, but because of discussions and "shared knowledge that leads to a change in beliefs."[64] Similarly, Park and Lessig found that informational influence was more important to college students than comparative or normative influence for most of the products studied.[65] Summarizing these studies, Kaplan and Miller concluded that "in general, informational influence produces more frequent and stronger shifts (in beliefs) than does normative influence."[66]

These findings suggest that marketers should place more emphasis on the group as a source of information than as a source of compliance. Ads should picture typical consumers citing their experiences and providing information on relevant product attributes. Rather than picture friends and neighbors marveling at a sparkling floor (compliance to group norms of cleanliness), ads might be more relevant if they show group members transmitting information on the product to the prospective buyer. Such an approach shifts the emphasis from conformity to information.

▌ Group Influence versus Product Evaluation

If group influence is such an important source of information, does it supplant objective product evaluation? That is, do many consumers say, "Since most of my friends recommend it, I may as well use it because it must be good," and as a result forgo a process of brand evaluation? In many cases, yes; *reference-group influence can be a substitute for brand evaluation.*

Rosen and Olshavsky's study supports the likelihood that group recommendations often supplant brand evaluation.[67] They studied brand selection for two disparate product categories—pizza and stereos. They considered three possibilities:

that consumers will (1) go along with the group's recommendations without evaluating brand alternatives, (2) evaluate alternative brands, or (3) rely on group recommendations to narrow the choice to a few brands and then evaluate these brands.

They found that group recommendations outweighed brand attribute evaluations for both product categories. That is, in most cases, consumers either totally relied on the group's recommendations or used these recommendations to narrow the field to a few brand alternatives. Surprisingly, this was as true for high-risk products like stereos as for low-risk products like pizza. Based on such evidence, Moschis concluded that as a result of relying on peers for information, "consumers often choose products without evaluating them on the basis of objective attributes."[68]

Strategic Applications of Reference-Group Influences

Advertising and promotional strategies have been used to portray the three types of group influence: informational influence through expert spokespersons, comparative influence by portraying typical consumers, and normative influence by showing the rewards of using a product or the risks of not using it.

PORTRAYING INFORMATIONAL INFLUENCE

Marketers try to convey informational influence through advertising as a counterweight to the dominant influence of friends and relatives. In this effort, they attempt to exert informational influence by using expert spokespersons to communicate product features and performance.

Marketers typically use two approaches to portraying expert spokespersons. One is to portray the role the expert plays—a doctor for a medical product, an engineer for a technical product. A second approach is to show a celebrity who has expertise in the product area—a tennis star's testimonial for a tennis racket, for example. In a tongue-in-cheek ad for Benadryl, kids are portrayed as doctors, but the message is clear: the medical profession stands behind Benadryl as a safe and effective allergy medication for children.

The second approach uses celebrities to provide product testimonials. Such testimonials are accepted only to the degree that consumers view the spokesperson as being an expert on the product. Exhibit 14.6 shows Michael Jordan in an ad for Nike basketball shoes with the tag line "In your dreams." Consumers are likely to view a testimonial from Jordan for the product category as credible.

Advertisers also create their own experts. General Motors has established Mr. Goodwrench as an expert in car maintenance. General Mills created Betty Crocker in 1921, and she has become "a sort of 'First Lady of Food,' the most highly esteemed home service authority in the nation."[69] Also, Reuben H. Donnelley, the leading source of direct-mail coupons, has established Carol Wright as the expert spokesperson on how to achieve value through coupon redemptions.

PORTRAYING COMPARATIVE INFLUENCE

Advertisers can portray comparative influence by using two types of referents. One is an "actual referent" in the form of a "typical consumer" to persuade consumers

Conveying informational influence through expert testimonials.

Courtesy Nike.

You soar above the court, above the competition, above the crowd with the cushioning, support, fit and comfort of the Air Jordan® by Nike—a shoe designed for the best player in the world. Welcome to the dream team.

that people like themselves have chosen the advertised product. The typical consumer is a referent because, by citing common needs and problems, he or she is portrayed as similar to the prospective purchaser. The Schwab ad in Exhibit 14.7 is an example. The individual pictured is a typical consumer who is a Schwab investor. A consumer looking for a credible source of investment advice could easily identify with this consumer. Avon also used a typical consumer approach when it introduced a line of beauty and cosmetic products in 2002 called *Becoming*. The company decided to use real consumers rather than famous models and celebrities because Avon research found that prospective buyers "find less famous personalities easier to relate to."[70] The individuals pictured in the campaign are typical consumers. The ads also invite consumers to visit the brand's web site, *www.ibecome.com*, where they can share their own photos and stories with other consumers.

A second approach is to use a "symbolic referent"; that is, a celebrity whom the consumer empathizes and identifies with because he or she is likable or attractive. Elizabeth Taylor is an effective aspirational referent for her own brand of perfume

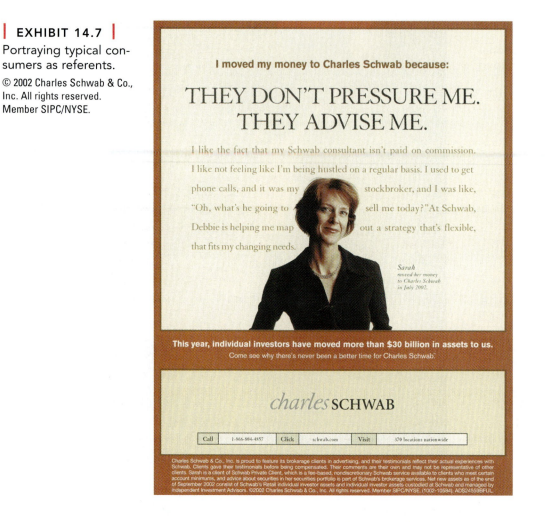

because to many women she evokes empathy as a result of her "struggles with weight control, substance abuse, and men. Women figured if Liz can get control of her life, why can't I? That forged a very strong bond."[71] The same degree of empathy would be unlikely if Taylor were used as a spokesperson for pain relievers or investment services because these products do not evoke the intimacy of perfume.

Whereas Avon depicts referents as part of a consumer's membership group, Elizabeth Taylor perfumes show a referent as part of the consumer's aspiration group. In the case of Avon, consumers consider themselves similar to the referent; in the case of Elizabeth Taylor, consumers would like to identify with the referent. Because most consumers realize they will never meet Elizabeth Taylor, she is portrayed as a symbolic referent.

A darker side of a comparative influence strategy has come to be known as "undercover marketing"; that is, planting paid company confederates to tout a product as "regular" customers. For example, a "consumer" talks up the benefits of a computer or DVD in an electronics store.[72] A form of undercover marketing on the Web is to have paid confederates talking up products in chatrooms as regular consumers. Ethical questions obviously arise when such confederates pose as regular consumers.

PORTRAYING NORMATIVE INFLUENCE

Marketers have tried to portray normative influence by showing group approval in advertising. Praise for a good cup of coffee, a shiny floor, glorious hair, good sherry, and a quiet and comfortable ride are all examples of advertising's simulation of social approval. In each case, an individual who is important to the consumer (spouse, neighbor, friend, business associate) has expressed approval of the consumer's choice. The Johnny Walker ad in Exhibit 14.4 presented earlier shows reward power by associating the product with the rewards for achievement based on socioeconomic status.

Marketers have also used normative influence to show the potential results of not using the product. For example, Poligrip uses the fear of social disapproval due to loose dentures, and Dial demonstrates the fear of group ostracism due to body odor. In each case, use of the product changes disapproval to approval—which demonstrates the fact that coercive power and reward power are linked. Such appeals use the fear of a group's coercive power to gain compliance to group norms.

Societal Implications of Reference-Group Influences

The portrayals of reference-group influences in this chapter have been generally positive—reference groups can be influential as sources of information, means of self-identification, and sources for rewards for conformity. But as we saw, at times group pressures may conflict with an individual's value system, or pressures to conform may be intense.

These issues become most important when it comes to the consumption of potentially harmful products—drugs, cigarettes, and alcohol. Two issues arise in this respect: (1) trying to discourage peer group pressures to use these products and (2) marketers' responsibilities in portraying peer-group influence.

DISCOURAGING CONFORMITY

Teenagers are particularly susceptible to peer-group pressures to conform because of typical stages of adolescent rebellion from parental authority and a search for self-identity. Fears of disapproval and rejection for not conforming to the group are common. If the use of drugs, cigarettes, or alcohol are compatible with group values, pressures to conform by using these products may be severe.

Rose, Bearden, and Teel examined how pressures to conform influence illicit drug and alcohol consumption among high school and college students.[73] To demonstrate the strength of peer pressures, even for harmful products, more than two-thirds of the students in the study were concerned about the implications of accepting or rejecting drugs and alcohol in the eyes of their peers. The researchers felt that if they could find ways to encourage young people to seek explanations for a peer group sanctioning illicit drug and alcohol use, then the pressure to conform might be reduced. That is, if group members could explain why their peer group sanctions such illicit use, then they might find it easier to reject group pressure.

Rose and his colleagues used "attribution theory" to examine students' explanations for their group's acceptance of illicit drug and alcohol usage.[74] As we saw in Chapter 5, attribution theory says that consumers seek to attribute causes to events (*i.e.*, why does the group encourage drug usage?). When an individual could attribute reasons for a group's use of drugs and alcohol, such as saying "they just want to get high" or "they don't think they will get caught," such attributions encouraged the individual to dissent from the group's actions. Such attributions provide a rationale for the potential dissenter to refuse to go along with the group.

The implication is that if plausible reasons for the group's deviant behavior are provided, that makes it easier to dissent. Current public service campaigns based on the slogan "Just Say No," or Bob Dole's theme to discourage drug use in the 1996 presidential elections—"Just Don't Do It"—may stress assertiveness, but they do not really provide an attribution for rejecting group pressures. Rose, Bearden, and Teel's research suggests that campaigns should emphasize themes like "If your

STRATEGIC APPLICATIONS

When Should Advertisers Use Celebrities as Experts or Referents?

Use of celebrities in ads has become more frequent in the last ten years, with celebrities making about 5 percent of their income from endorsements. Celebrities are best used as "experts" when consumers see them as being knowledgeable about the product category and conveying legitimacy in their message. Tiger Woods is an effective spokesperson for Nike golf balls; Venus Williams, for Reebok tennis sneakers; Michael J. Fox, for Parkinson's disease awareness; and Charles Barkley, for Nike basketball sneakers. Expert spokespersons do not necessarily have to represent products associated with their professions. Consumers see Dorothy Hamill as an expert spokesperson for arthritis because consumers believe that an aging sports star knows what she is talking about when it comes to relieving aches and pains. The Duchess of York, Sarah Ferguson, is an effective spokesperson for Weight Watchers because of her difficulties in losing weight. The ability of overweight people to relate to Ferguson helps them tackle their own dieting challenges. Similarly, B.B. King, the famous blues musician, is an effective spokesperson for One Touch Ultra, a means of testing for sugar levels in the blood,

because he has been suffering from diabetes for over ten years (see Exhibit 14.8).

Celebrities have been used as referents when they come across as likable and attractive; that is, someone with whom many consumers would like to identify. The product has to be one that lends itself to identification with the celebrity as a referent, however. Regis Philbin is an effective referent for Phillips-Van Heusen button-down shirts and ties because he is well known for his stylish dressing habits and he actually wears Van Heusen clothing on a regular basis on TV. People can relate to his endorsement of Van Heusen not because he is an expert in the fashion industry, but because he is likable and dresses well. George Foreman is an effective referent for his Fat-Reducing Grilling Machine because of his strong emotional bond with his fans. He is a self-proclaimed hamburger lover, has been very active in the marketing of his grills, and genuinely believes in them. Some of the grills' design elements are his suggestions; for example, enlarging one of the grills to accommodate two burgers at once. His likable personality, combined with his love for food, makes his endorsement successful.

OF CONSUMER BEHAVIOR

friends want to get high, that doesn't mean you have to," or "Fitting in with your friends is no reason to drink." In each case, the reason for the group's actions is directly addressed.

MARKETERS' PORTRAYAL OF PEER-GROUP INFLUENCE

Marketers frequently portray peer groups in social situations in print ads for cigarettes and alcohol, implying that the product is "in" with the group. In most cases, the groups portrayed are young adults. A key issue is whether such advertising is socially responsible. In fostering group identity with their brands, marketers are encouraging liquor and cigarette consumption among young adults. The decision by some liquor companies to lift the self-imposed prohibition against TV advertising is likely to magnify concerns about portrayals of peer groups in commercials.

On the other side of the coin, it could be argued that young adults are subject to group influence for a wide variety of products and should be free to choose the

When advertisers stray from the principles that experts must communicate knowledge and legitimacy and that referents must communicate likability and attractiveness, they get into trouble. Bill Cosby bombed as a referent for E.F. Hutton, the brokerage house, because his good guy image did not convey any special expertise or credibility for financial services. When Cosby intoned the tag line "When E.F. Hutton talks, everybody listens," one observer quipped, "When Cosby talked, nobody listened," meaning that celebrities can serve to reflect group influence only when they are relevant role models for the product.

Of even more concern, the use of referent spokespersons can backfire if they lose their appeal. O.J. Simpson's value as a referent spokesperson for Hertz was lost overnight with the allegation that he murdered his ex-wife. Similarly, Marky Mark's value as a spokesperson for Calvin Klein apparel dissipated when it was discovered that he had made a series of racial slurs in his younger days. These risks have led companies like Diet Coke, Hershey, and Levi Strauss to use deceased celebrities such as Humphrey Bogart, Marilyn Monroe, and James Dean as referent spokespersons. They are sure to remain likable and to stay out of trouble.

Sources: "Star Power," Sales and Marketing Management (April 2001), pp. 52–58; "Marketers Are Always Looking for Good Pitchers," Brandweek (February 26, 1996), p. 27.

| **EXHIBIT 14.8** |

Use of a credible spokesperson in a nonexpert role.

Courtesy LifeScan, Inc., a Johnson & Johnson Company.

brands and products they want to consume. But liquor and cigarette commercials are seen by teenagers and young children and are likely to make an impression.

Overall, marketers of cigarettes, liquor, and beer must be sensitive to portraying group acceptance of their products, especially among younger consumers.

SUMMARY

This chapter focused on reference-group influences on consumer behavior. Reference groups can be classified into membership groups and aspiration groups. Membership groups can be classified further into formal and informal groups and primary and secondary groups. By far, the most influential groups are informal primary groups, represented by family and peer groups. Aspiration groups can also be divided into groups in which the consumer anticipates membership (anticipatory groups) and groups that the consumer admires at a distance (symbolic groups).

These group designations are important, because advertisers frequently portray group influences directly (*e.g.,* one friend advising the other) or employ spokespersons to influence consumer aspirations.

Reference groups serve a number of important functions. They provide norms of conduct, assign roles within the group to individuals, designate status positions within the group, and are a vehicle for consumer socialization. They also influence individuals by exerting three types of power: expert, referent, and reward.

These three types of power correspond to three types of influence. Groups exert informational (expert) influence, comparative (referent) influence, and normative (reward) influence. Informational influence depends on the credibility of the source of information; comparative influence, on the degree of similarity between the consumer and influencer; and normative influence, on the levels of reward or punishment meted out by the group. Normative influence results in conformity to group norms. Conformity is most likely when products are visible and related to group norms. Such conformity may produce a social multiplier effect: One consumer buys a product, and others come into contact with

the consumer and are influenced to buy. Their purchase in turn results in a spread of ownership throughout the group and, eventually, to other groups.

Web communities play an important role in reference groups. There are four types of web communities: transaction, interest, fantasy, and relationship. The sense of community on the Internet is manifested and reinforced by precisely tailored content, identification with the brand, awareness of like-minded users, ability to interact with others on the Web, opportunity to shape the development of a web site and mutual benefits of participants. This chapter related web communities to the important functions of referent groups; that is, norms, values, roles, status, socialization, and power.

Although comparative identification with groups and conformity with their norms are important, studies have shown that information is the most important influence that groups exert on individuals. This is because such information is considered more credible than information from marketer-controlled sources.

Marketers have used informational, comparative, and normative influence in establishing advertising strategies. Informational influence is portrayed through expert spokespersons, comparative influence through typical consumers, and normative influence by showing the rewards of using a product or the risks of not using it.

Reference-group influences raise certain issues regarding the potential negative effects of groups in influencing individuals to consume potentially harmful products like cigarettes, drugs, and alcohol. Public service advertising should develop campaigns that would encourage rejection of peer-group norms that sanction use of harmful products. Cigarette and liquor advertisers should also avoid ads that portray acceptance of these products in a group context.

In Chapter 15, we consider one of the key sources of group influence: the household.

QUESTIONS FOR DISCUSSION

1. When are reference groups most likely to exert influence?

2. What is meant by the "looking-glass self"? How does this concept affect consumer behavior?

3. What is the distinction between aspiration groups and membership groups? Are both types of groups relevant for marketers? In what ways?

4. How do Harley rider groups reflect the key characteristics of reference groups in regard to norms, values, roles, status, and socialization?

5. How are expert, referent, and reward power translated into informational, comparative, and normative influences?

6. What do we mean by "reactance"? Cite some examples. Is a marketer likely to illustrate reactance in advertising? Why or why not?

7. What do we mean by the "social multiplier effect"? What conditions are required for the social multiplier to take effect? Cite some examples of the workings of the social multiplier.

8. What types of products are most likely to be subject to informational influence, comparative influence, and normative influence? Why?

9. What are the purposes of the four types of communities on the Internet?

10. Discuss how the characteristics of reference groups apply to web communities.

11. How are informational, comparative, and normative influence shown on the Web?

12. How has collaborative filtering technology been useful to marketers?

13. Under what conditions should an advertiser use a spokesperson as a referent? As an expert? What are the risks of each strategy?

14. What are the advertising implications of the research by Rose, Bearden, and Teel cited on p. 425 for attempting to discourage conformity to negative group influences such as drug, alcohol, and cigarette consumption?

RESEARCH ASSIGNMENTS

1 Visit the e-fluentials web site at *www.efluentials.com.* Click on e-fluentials on the left. Then click on charts to see a profile of the e-fluentials.

- Can e-fluentials be targeted by marketers of high technology products? How?
- What means other than advertising can be used to influence e-fluentials?

2 Visit *www.bizrate.com* and *www.gomezadvisor.com.*

- How does each site differ in rating retail stores?
- Which site is more likely to be viewed as credible by consumers?
- Which site is more likely to reflect reference-group influences? Why?

3 Ask a group of students to evaluate four identical unlabeled cans of soda. Four students should do the evaluation at the same time. Have three students act as "ringers" and ask them to state a preference for the same can of soda. The fourth student will be an actual respondent. Conduct about twenty such tests so that there are twenty actual respondents. In one-half of the cases, the ringers should express a preference in a low-keyed manner. In the other half, they should be adamant about their preference (*e.g.,* "Wow, this soda is much better!"). One would expect that on a random basis, the fourth student would agree with the other three 25 percent of the time.

- Is the proportion who conform significantly greater than the 25 percent chance expectation?
- Is there a difference in acceptance between those who were subjected to a low-keyed preference and those who were subjected to a more definite preference?

Once the taste test is completed, ask the actual respondents to rate themselves on (a) self-confidence and (b) predisposition to take risk (*e.g.,* "I like to try new and different things"). Do those who conformed differ from those who did not on these two characteristics?

NOTES

1. *Reebok International Ltd.,* Harvard Business School Case, November, 1999.
2. "Reebok's Pickup Game," *Brandweek* (May 15, 2000), pp. 42–45.
3. Reebok Press Release, "Reebok Signs Venus Williams," December 21, 2000.
4. "Reebok Defies Convention with New Campaign," *Adweek* (January 22, 2001), p. 11.
5. John W. Schouten and James H. McAlexander, "Subcultures of Consumption: An Ethnography of the New Bikers," *Journal of Consumer Research* 22 (June 1995), pp. 43–61.
6. William O. Bearden, Richard G. Netemeyer, and Jesse E. Teel, "Measurement of Consumer Susceptibility to Interpersonal Influence," *Journal of Consumer Research* 15 (March 1989), pp. 473–481.
7. William O. Bearden and Randall L. Rose, "Attention to Social Comparison Information: An Individual Difference Factor Affecting Consumer Conformity," *Journal of Consumer Research* 16 (March 1990), pp. 461–471.
8. See also Paul W. Miniard and Joel B. Cohen, "Modeling Personal and Normative Influences on Behavior," *Journal of Consumer Research* 10 (September 1983), pp. 169–180.
9. See also Bobby J. Calder and Robert E. Burnkrant, "Interpersonal Influences on Consumer Behavior: An Attribution Theory Approach," *Journal of Consumer Research* 4 (June 1977), pp. 29–38.
10. Schouten and McAlexander, "Subcultures of Consumption," pp. 43–61.
11. James H. Leigh and Terrance G. Gabel, "Symbolic Interactionism: Its Effects on Consumer Behavior and Implications for Marketing Strategy," *Journal of Consumer Marketing* 9 (Winter 1992), p. 30.
12. Francis S. Bourne, "Group Influence in Marketing and Public Relations," in Rensis Likert and Samuel P. Hayes, Jr., eds., *Some Applications of Behavioral Research* (Paris: UNESCO, 1957).
13. Schouten and McAlexander, "Subcultures of Consumption," p. 49.
14. Leon G. Schiffman and Leslie L. Kanuk, *Consumer Behavior* (Englewood Cliffs, N.J.: Prentice-Hall, 1978), p. 214.
15. Peter H. Reingen, Brian L. Foster, Jacqueline Johnson Brown, and Stephen B. Seidman, "Brand Congruence in Interpersonal Relations: A Social Network Analysis," *Journal of Consumer Research* 11 (December 1984), pp. 771–783.
16. Donald H. Granbois, "Improving the Study of Customer In-Store Behavior," *Journal of Marketing* 32 (October 1968), pp. 28–33.
17. Chris Mole, Miriam Mulcahy, Kevin O'Donnel, and Ashok Gupta, "Making Sense of Virtual Communities," PriceWaterhouseCoopers Report, 2000.
18. Robert J. Fisher and Linda L. Price, "An Investigation into the Social Context of Early Adoption Behavior," *Journal of Consumer Research* 19 (December 1992), pp. 477–486.
19. Schouten and McAlexander, "Subcultures of Consumption," p. 53.
20. Ibid., p. 49.
21. Ibid., p. 56.
22. John R. French and Bertram Raven, "The Bases of Social Power," in D. Cartwright, ed., Studies in Social Power (Ann Arbor, Mich.: Institute for Social Research, 1959), pp. 150–167.
23. Mole et al., "Making Sense of Virtual Communities."
24. Arthur Armstrong and John Hagel III, "The Real Value of On-line Communities," *Harvard Business Review* 74 (May/June 1996), pp. 134–141.
25. Ibid., pp. 134–141.
26. "Web 'Communities' a Target Marketers Dream," p. 2.
27. Armstrong and Hagel, "The Real Value of On-line Communities," pp. 134–141.
28. Mole et al., "Making Sense of Virtual Communities."
29. Ibid.
30. "The e-Fluentials," Burson-Marstellar 2000, www.efluentials.com.
31. "Developing Personal and Emotional Relationships Via Computer-Mediated Communication," *CMC Magazine* (May 1998).
32. Armstrong and Hagel, "The Real Value of On-line Communities," pp. 134–141.
33. "Web 'Communities' a Target Marketers Dream," *Marketing News* (July 7, 1997), p. 2.
34. "I Scream, You Scream: Consumers Vent Over the Net," *New York Times* (March 4, 2001), pp. 3, 13.
35. Ibid.
36. Herbert C. Kelman, "Processes of Opinion Change," *Public Opinion Quarterly* 25 (Spring 1961), pp. 57–78.
37. Robert E. Burnkrant and Alain Cousineau, "Informational and Normative Social Influence in Buyer Behavior," *Journal of Consumer Research* 2 (December 1975), pp. 206–215.
38. Ibid., p. 207.
39. C. Whan Park and V. Parker Lessig, "Students and Housewives: Differences in Susceptibility to Reference Group Influence," *Journal of Consumer Research* 4 (September 1977), pp. 102–110.
40. Margaret L. Friedman and Gilbert A. Churchill, Jr., "Using Consumer Perceptions and a Contingency Approach to Improve Health Care Delivery," *Journal of Consumer Research* 13 (March 1987), p. 503.
41. "About Epinions," Epinions.com–Company Information: About Epinions, www.epinions.com, as of April 30, 2001.
42. "Web 'Communities' a Target Marketers Dream," p. 2.
43. Armstrong and Hagel, "The Real Value of On-line Communities," pp. 134–141.
44. George P. Moschis, "Social Comparisons and Informal Group Influence," *Journal of Marketing Research* 13 (August 1976), pp. 237–244.
45. F. B. Evans, "Selling as a Dyadic Relationship—A New Approach," *American Behavioral Scientist* 6 (May 1963), pp. 76–79; and Timothy C. Brock, "Communicator-Recipient Similarity and Decision Change," *Journal of Personality and Social Psychology* 1 (June 1965), pp. 650–654.
46. See William H. Whyte, "The Web of Word of Mouth," *Fortune* (November 1954), pp. 140–143; and Sidney P. Feldman, "Some Dyadic Relationships Associated with Consumer Choice," in Raymond M. Haas, ed., *Proceedings of the American Marketing Association, Series No. 24* (Chicago: American Marketing Association, 1966), pp. 758–775.

47. Leon G. Schiffman, "Social Interaction Patterns of the Elderly Consumer," in Boris W. Becker and Helmut Becker, eds., *Combined Proceedings of the American Marketing Association, Series No. 34* (Chicago: American Marketing Association, 1972), p. 451.

48. "Firefly Network," *Inter@ctive Week* (Board of Trustees of the Leland Stanford Junior University), March 3, 1997.

49. "Developing Personal and Emotional Relationships."

50. Solomon E. Asch, "Effects of Group Pressure upon the Modification and Distortion of Judgments," in Harold Geutzkow, ed., *Groups, Leadership and Men* (Pittsburgh, Penn: Carnegie Press, 1951).

51. M. Venkatesan, "Experimental Study of Consumer Behavior Conformity and Independence," *Journal of Marketing Research* 3 (November 1966), pp. 384–387.

52. Park and Lessig, "Students and Housewives," pp 102–110.

53. Henry Assael, Michael Etgar, and Michael Henry, "The Dimensions of Evaluating and Utilizing Alternative Information Sources," working paper, New York University, March, 1983.

54. Park and Lessig, "Students and Housewives," pp. 102–110.

55. Whyte, "The Web of Word of Mouth," pp. 140–143.

56. "Developing Personal and Emotional Relationships."

57. James Duesenberry, *Income, Savings and the Theory of Consumer Behavior* (Cambridge, Mass.: Harvard University Press, 1949).

58. Asch, "Effects of Group Pressure."

59. Itamar Simonson and Stephen M. Nowlis, "The Role of Explanations and Need for Uniqueness in Consumer Decision Making: Unconventional choices Based on Reasons," *Journal of Consumer Research* 27 (June 2000), pp. 49–68.

60. Schouten and McAlexander, "Subcultures of Consumption," p. 56.

61. Park and Lessig, "Students and Housewives. . . ," pp. 102–110.

62. Schouten and McAlexander, "Subcultures of Consumption," p. 56.

63. Bourne, "Group Influence in Marketing and Public Relations."

64. James C. Ward and Peter H. Reingen, "Sociocognitive Analysis of Group Decision Making Among Consumers," *Journal of Consumer Research* 17 (December 1990), pp. 245–262.

65. Park and Lessig, "Students and Housewives," pp. 102–110.

66. Martin Kaplan and Charles Miller, "Group Decision Making and Normative Versus Informational Influence: Effects of Type of Issue and Assigned Decision Role," *Journal of Personality and Social Psychology* 53 (1987), pp. 306–313.

67. Dennis L. Rosen and Richard W. Olshavsky, "The Dual Role of Informational Social Influence: Implications for Marketing Management," *Journal of Business Research* 15 (1987), pp. 123–144.

68. Moschis, "Social Comparisons," p. 240.

69. Julian L. Watkins, *The 100 Greatest Advertisements* (New York: Dover, 1959), p. 205.

70. "Advertising: Using Real Women and Believable Promises," *New York Times* (February 22, 2002), section C.

71. "Doesn't Everyone Want to Smell Like Cher," *Forbes* (April 2, 1990), pp. 142–144.

72. "Undercover Marketing Is Gaining Ground," *Wall Street Journal* (December 18, 2000), section B.

73. Randall L. Rose, William O. Bearden, and Jesse E. Teel, "An Attributional Analysis of Resistance to Group Pressure Regarding Illicit Drug and Alcohol Consumption," *Journal of Consumer Research* 19 (June 1992), pp. 1–13.

74. Ibid.

CHAPTER 15

Household Decision Making

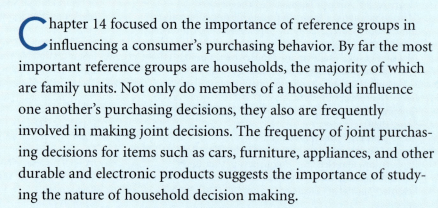

Chapter 14 focused on the importance of reference groups in influencing a consumer's purchasing behavior. By far the most important reference groups are households, the majority of which are family units. Not only do members of a household influence one another's purchasing decisions, they also are frequently involved in making joint decisions. The frequency of joint purchasing decisions for items such as cars, furniture, appliances, and other durable and electronic products suggests the importance of studying the nature of household decision making.

This chapter focuses on both joint and individual decision making within the family. We consider

▮ traditional and nontraditional households,

▮ a model of household decision making,

▮ the relative influence of the husband and wife in household decision making,

▮ the parent–child interaction in the purchasing process,

▮ the strategic implications of household influences, and

▮ the broader societal issues involved in the consumer socialization of children.

Marketers from Cars to Computers Recognize Children's Purchase Influence

Marketers today pay more attention to the influence of children on household decisions. With the great majority of mothers in the work force, three out of four American children now have no full-time parent at home. The greater proportion of single-parent households and dual-earning households means that adults are coming to rely more on children for shopping and meal preparation. The term "latchkey kids"—that is, children with no parent at home after school—reflects the increasing independence and more rapid consumer socialization of children.

Marketers now target products to kids because of their purchasing power as well as their increased purchasing roles. For example, in February 2002, Jell-O specifically targeted kids for the first time with X-treme Jell-O Gel Sticks in multiple flavors because "kid's purchasing power is higher than ever and the 'nag' factor has been a constant driver of new product success."[1] This was the first time since 1902 that the company strayed from its traditional policy of targeting moms as the purchasers for kids. Additional examples of products targeted to kids are Kellogg's PopTarts, P&G's Sunny Delight Fruit Drinks, Heinz's Funky Purple ketchup, and Heinz's Hot Bites, a line of frozen miniature pizzas and potato snacks. Heinz established a web site for these products because "they [kids] want to go on the computer and read about products they're eating."[2] Heinz also encourages kids' involvement by using the site to show them how to "build a fort using french fries as bricks and Funky Purple ketchup as mortar."[3]

Children also influence a wide array of products purchased by their parents. A poll of parents in 2000 found children influence 40 percent of parents' purchases, while 65 percent of parents explicitly solicit children's opinions about products purchased for the entire household, including cars and computers. This influence can be seen through the recent popularity of children's cable channel Nickelodeon with what were previously thought of as adult-only advertisers. For example, Ford Motor Company recently signed a three-year deal with the network that will target its cars to kids. To make the ads attractive to children, Ford is incorporating a popular Nickelodeon character, Blue, from the show "Blues Clues," into the ads (see Exhibit 15.1). Additionally, the ads will focus on safety and its importance instead of trying to hard-sell the product to children. The goal is to produce a tasteful spot that makes children think of a company that means family and safety.[4] General Motors also has entered the children's advertising game. It recently formed a partnership with Warner Brothers and introduced a Looney Tunes–themed minivan. Reinforcing Ford's and GM's decision to target children is a recent study by J. D. Power and Associates that showed that 69 percent of parents talk to their child about cars before shopping, 66 percent go as a family to the dealership, and 63 percent of parents said children influenced their decision to buy.[5]

EXHIBIT 15.1

Ford targets kids on Nickelodeon.

In addition to automobile manufacturers, a number of other industries target children because of their influence on parental decision making. Areas such as travel, telecommunications, and especially technology are now marketed to children. A study by Nickelodeon found that 40 percent of current computer owners reported their children had some influence on the decision to buy a personal computer for the home.[6] As children have become more Internet savvy, they have become more aware of high-technology products, but they do not have the funds necessary to purchase these products. Technology retailers, such as Gateway Computers who recently signed a three-year advertising deal with Nickelodeon, are now taking advantage of this increase in knowledge and influence.

The actions of car and computer manufacturers display the dynamics of parent–child influences in their advertising to children. The unresolved issue is whether such advertising to children is responsible and whether children should be encouraged to use products such as microwavable meals.

Households in the United States

Our focus in this chapter is household purchasing influences. A **household** is composed of individuals living singly or together with others in a residential unit. Since we are concerned with group influences, we focus only on multiperson households in this chapter. The majority of households, 63 percent, are in family units. A **family** is two or more people living together who are related by blood or marriage. A family is, therefore, a category of a household.

The 103 million households in the United States in 2000 were composed of the following categories:[7]

1. Married couples with children under 18: about 24 percent of all households
2. Married couples with children 18 and over: about 14 percent of households
3. Married couples without children: 15 percent
4. Single parents living with children under 18: 9 percent
5. Unmarried couples (both heterosexual and gay): 7 percent
6. Individuals living with others (either relatives such as single parents living with children over 18 or individuals living with siblings, or nonrelatives such as roommates or college students): 5 percent
7. People living alone: 26 percent

TRADITIONAL HOUSEHOLDS

Households can be divided into traditional and nontraditional. Traditional households are represented by the first two categories, married couples with children. A substantial number of U.S. households, 36 percent, are in the nontraditional category, representing married couples without children, single-parent households, unmarried couples, and individuals living with others.

The first category, households with children under 18, is also referred to as the **nuclear family.** The predominance of the nuclear family has been decreasing steadily in the last forty years, from 45 percent of all households in 1960 to the current 24 percent.[8] In the 1950s, the nuclear family was the norm as portrayed in TV programs like "Leave It to Beaver" or "Ozzie and Harriet." The husband was the breadwinner, the wife took care of the home, and the children were in grade school. The subsequent decrease in the nuclear family was explained in Chapter 9 by a number of factors—higher divorce rates, later marriages, and a decreasing birthrate. Despite this decrease, advertisers seeking a traditional context for their product occasionally portray the nuclear family.

A countertrend to the decrease in the nuclear family is the greater number of older children living with their parents. More young adults in their twenties and thirties are choosing to save money by living at home in the face of a tight job market. As a result, the Census Bureau is projecting that the number of married couples with children over 18 living at home will grow in the next five years.

A subcategory of the nuclear family is the **extended family.** Extended families are nuclear families with at least one grandparent living at home. At the turn of the century, this three-generational unit (often including aunts and uncles) was the norm. A government study found that in 1900, half of all households in Boston were extended families. Today, mobility, geographic dispersion, changing patterns of immigration, and a decrease in transgenerational ties have made the extended family almost extinct. By 1976, only 4 percent of households were extended families.[9] Today, the figure is probably lower. The virtual extinction of the extended family means that nuclear and traditional families are synonymous.

NONTRADITIONAL HOUSEHOLDS

Nontraditional households (categories 3 to 6 in the preceding list) have increased proportionately as traditional households have declined. Let us consider each of the nontraditional household categories.

▪ *Married couples without children.* Many members of the baby-boom generation decided to marry later. This trend was a function of the "me" orientation that began to develop in the midst of the Vietnam War and Watergate. Over time, it became the norm as more baby boomers focused on self and professional interests and delayed family formation. The later they got married, the more likely it was that they would be childless, for both biological and lifestyle reasons.

   Married couples without children have more discretionary income and a different set of purchasing priorities than the nuclear family. They are good targets for travel, entertainment, and higher-priced durable goods and electronic items.

▪ *Single parents with children under 18.* With one of every two marriages ending in divorce and more than 1 million divorces a year, single-parent households are likely to continue to increase. Today, 29 percent of all children live in single-parent households.[10] Over 80 percent of single-parent households are headed by a female. Many live in poverty. Adding to the financial burden is the limited time a working parent has to spend with his or her child. Single parents are likely to spend more on their children, partly out of guilt. And children in single-parent households are likely to have more influence over a wide range of purchases and more purchasing power.

   One study found negative consequences for children brought up in single-parent households from the effects of divorce and separation. Such children were found to be at higher risk of subsequent drug and alcohol abuse, smoking addiction, and other forms of compulsive behavior in their adult years.[11]

■ *Unmarried couples.* This group, representing heterosexual and homosexual couples, is often referred to as an "alternative" lifestyle. Unmarried couples are likely to increase in numbers. Many heterosexual couples today choose not to follow convention and to remain unmarried. Homosexual couples have probably been undercounted by the Census Bureau in the past due to the stigma of homosexuality. As this group becomes increasingly accepted, there is likely to be an increase in the numbers reported. Unmarried couples tend to have higher disposable incomes because they are mostly dual-earning households with higher-than-average income levels. As we saw in Chapter 12, gay couples are an affluent group and a good target for luxury goods. In general, unmarried couples are good targets for discretionary expenditures on travel, entertainment, and high-priced durable goods.

■ *Individuals living with others.* This catchall group is also likely to grow as the number of individuals who decide not to marry or remarry increases. The proportion of married couples decreased from 75 percent of all households in 1960 to 53 percent today.[12] One alternate to living alone is to live with another relative, with a sibling, or with a friend. In addition, single parents, similar to married couples, are finding that children are living with them longer to save money on housing and other necessities.

Overall, nontraditional households are likely to continue to increase in importance relative to traditional households. One indication of this trend is the Census Bureau's projection that the nuclear family will decrease from 24 percent of all households in 2000 to 20 percent by 2010.[13]

International Households

There are important differences in household structures abroad compared with those in the United States. One of the most important is the significance of the extended family in certain areas of the world. For example, in Greece, Spain, and Portugal around 20 percent of households consist of multiple generations. This is a result of the tendency of children in these countries to live in the parental home until they are ready to form another complete family unit. Multigenerational families also are very common in Asia, where offspring's care for the parents is often a priority in many cultures. In fact, Singapore recently passed a law that requires children to take care of their parents.[14]

In other respects, many of the demographic trends abroad mirror those in the United States. The percentage of traditional households in Europe has decreased since 1980, partly because of an increase in the divorce rate. Additionally, European couples are waiting longer to get married, and there has been a drop in the size of European families.

Living alone and cohabitation without marriage have also become more popular among younger generations in Europe. These two groups now account for 26 percent of European households (compared with 33 percent in the United States) and are projected to be the fastest-growing segment through 2005.[15] In addition to Europe, developing countries such as the Philippines and Malaysia have seen a decrease in the extended family as newly wealthy couples are moving out of extended families and forming Western-style nuclear ones.

Purchasing Patterns by Household Life Cycles

Spending patterns vary by type of household depending on the age of household members, their marital status, and whether children live in the household. Spending patterns also change as a household moves from one life stage to another; for example, going from a young married couple without children, to one with young children, teenagers, and children no longer living at home ("empty nesters"), or from a married couple with children to a divorced couple with the children rotating between two single-parent households.

These changes are not captured by the household categories previously described. Thus, an important dimension in understanding these *changes* in spending patterns is the **household life cycle;** that is, the progression of a household through various stages as its members get older. As noted, this progression is not only a function of age, but also reflects income and changes in family situation that affect every facet of purchasing behavior.

THE FAMILY LIFE CYCLE

In the mid-1960s, two researchers, William Wells and George Gubar, proposed eight stages to describe the **family life cycle.**[16] These stages, described in Table 15.1, reflect the progression of a traditional family from marriage to retirement. The categories in Table 15.1 affect both what is bought and the decision process by which it is purchased. This scheme was based on an analysis of demographic and spending data from the 1960 Census. Given its traditional focus, the concept was referred to as a "family" rather than a "household" life cycle. Until recently, it was a very useful framework for classifying families.

THE HOUSEHOLD LIFE CYCLE

Demographic changes since 1980 have resulted in the growth of nonfamily households, meaning that the relevant concept today is a **household life cycle.** As a result, researchers have suggested more modernized life cycle categories.

Table 15.1 presents one life cycle sequence. But there are many more life cycle sequences when one accounts for nontraditional categories. Table 15.2 lists several such examples. One is a young married couple with children that get divorced, and one of the spouses never remarries (sequence 1). Another nontraditional sequence is a couple without children that divorces and one of the spouses remarries and establishes a family with stepchildren (sequence 2). Clearly, there will be different purchasing patterns if a divorced individual does or does not have children and remarries or stays single. The life cycles in both Tables 15.1 and 15.2 can be incorporated into a concept of a household life cycle. But given that one in two marriages

TABLE 15.1
The traditional family life cycle

1. Young Singles	Single people under the age of 35. Incomes are low since they are starting a career, but they have few financial burdens and a high level of discretionary income.
2. Newly Married	Newly married couples without children. High level of discretionary income because the wife is usually working.
3. Full Nest I	Married couples with the youngest child under 6. Greater squeeze on income because of increased expenses for child care.
4. Full Nest II	Married couples with children 6 to 12. Better financial position since parents' income is rising. Most children are "latchkey kids" because both parents are working.
5. Full Nest III	Married couples with teenage children living at home. Family's financial position continues to improve. Some children work part-time. Increasing educational costs.
6. Empty Nest I	Children have left home and are not dependent on parental support. Parents are still working. Reduced expenses result in greatest level of savings and highest discretionary income.
7. Empty Nest II	Household head has retired, so couple experiences sharp drop in income. Couple relies on fixed incomes from retirement plans.
8. Solitary Survivor	Widow or widower with lower income and increasing medical needs.

Source: William D. Wells and George Gubar, "Life Cycle Concept in Marketing Research," *Journal of Marketing Research* 3 (November 1966), pp. 355–363.

TABLE 15.2
Nontraditional household life cycles

Sequence 1	• Young married couple with children • Divorced single parent with children • Older, single
Sequence 2	• Young married without children • Divorced without children • Middle-aged remarried with stepchildren • Empty nester • Older, widowed
Sequence 3	• Young married without children • Middle-aged with children • Empty nesters
Sequence 4	• Young unmarried couple without children • Middle-aged, get married without children • Older without children • Widowed

today ends in divorce,[17] the life cycle sequences in Table 15.2 are probably more realistic than those in Table 15.1.

THE NATURE OF PURCHASES

Income constraints and family responsibilities define many of the purchase decisions of families along both traditional and nontraditional life cycles. In the traditional life cycle, both young singles and newly married couples have significant discretionary income, the latter because husband and wife are likely to be employed. Whereas young singles spend more on clothing, entertainment, vacations, and other leisure pursuits, newly marrieds spend more on the required trappings of a new household such as furniture, kitchen appliances, and home entertainment systems.

When children arrive (Full Nest I), the couple is likely to move into a new home, purchase baby-related products, and buy home appliances. Discretionary income declines. As the children grow older (Full Nest II and III), the family buys more food and household items. Parents are likely to allocate money to home improvements and to replacement of old cars and appliances. They also begin to spend more on children and teen-related items such as clothing, electronic toys, and recreational products. In the later stages of the full nest, educational costs increase substantially.

In the empty nest stage, discretionary income increases; and parents can afford to spend more money on themselves. Spending for travel and luxury items increases. In the later stages of the empty nest and in the solitary survivor stage, parents generally retire from work. Their income begins to decrease, and they spend more on medical expenses.

The life cycle sequences in Table 15.2 provide other implications for purchasing patterns. Single parents are three times as likely to be females as to be males. As a result, many divorced mothers see a major decrease in financial resources. Given the limited amount of time a young single parent has to spend with his or her children, a disproportionate amount of money is likely to be spent on toys and daycare centers. As the household moves into the middle-aged single-parent category, children are likely to play an increasingly important role in shopping, meal preparation, and selection of food and household items.

Ramifications also arise from a change in living status. Going from living with a family to being a single parent may mean different needs for appliances and household furnishings. If the single parent remarries, the likelihood of stepchildren increases family size and creates a whole different set of needs. For example, larger families mean bigger washloads and buying economy-size packages in the supermarket.

LIFE CYCLES GLOBALLY

The family life cycles of other nations often differ from those in the United States. In Europe, household life cycles are similar to those in the United States. In Asian countries, there is a greater reliance on extended families for household chores and childcare. There is also a closer bond between parents and children; and many children live with parents after they are married. These relationships lessen the financial burden that many individuals feel in the early stages of the family life cycle.

Additionally, there are differences in Asian culture in the later stages of the family life cycle. Because of the close bond between parent and child, it is very common for the elderly parent to move into the child's household. At this stage, the children provide support to parents that is not often found in Western cultures.[18]

THE NATURE OF THE HOUSEHOLD DECISION PROCESS

The household life cycle operates in influencing the nature of decision making. Joint decision making is most likely early in the household's life cycle. Then, as husband and wife or unmarried couples gain experience, they are willing to delegate responsibilities for decisions to each other. If a family has children, joint decisions are even less likely as time becomes more constrained and husband and wife assume specific roles.

Regarding patterns of family influence, the husband tends to be more influential in the early stages of the life cycle. Over time, the wife becomes more assertive in decision making, particularly if she is employed and has some financial leverage over decisions. The arrival of children affects family influences for the simple reason that an additional person often must be considered in the decision process. Children not only act as influencers over a wide range of decisions, but they also serve as occasional mediators in any disagreements between husband and wife. One study of vacation decisions found that children "may have the potential to influence family decisions by forming alliances with either husband or wife to produce a 'majority' position."[19]

A Model of Household Decision Making

As mentioned, households are likely to vary in the way they make their purchasing decisions depending on their stage in the life cycle. But there are certain common denominators in household decision making. Figure 15.1 presents a model of household decision making. As the model shows, household decision making is different from individual decision making because of three factors: (1) the likelihood of joint decisions, (2) different role specifications for household members in the process of decision making, and (3) the need to resolve conflicts among household members when making purchasing decisions. These three areas are highlighted in Figure 15.1.

Consider the following example of household decision making. Larry Philips, a recently divorced father, plans to take his two children—Laurie, 14 and Michael, 12—on a one-week summer vacation. Larry could make the decision on his own, but a joint decision is likely for three reasons. First, the decision is *important* to all of them. Second, the *perceived risks* of the decision (the expense, the fact that they will be close together, and the importance of having a good time) are fairly high. Third, there is *no time pressure* as it is May and they are planning an August vacation.

Once the need for a joint decision has been established, Figure 15.1 shows that decision roles are specified for individuals in the household. Role specification may be explicitly assigned to an individual, or it may be assumed that an individual in the household will perform the role. If an individual makes a decision, all these roles would be fulfilled by one person.

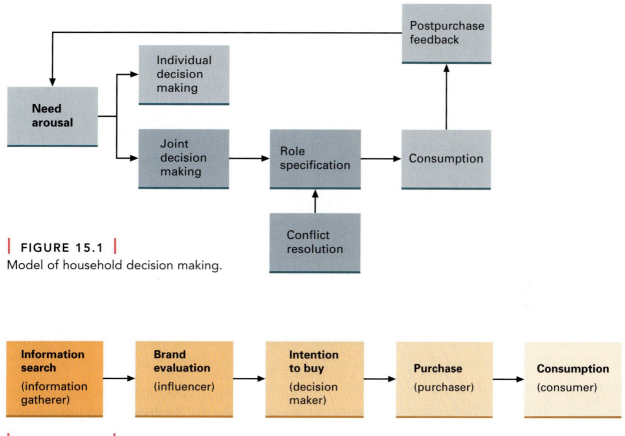

| FIGURE 15.1 |
Model of household decision making.

| FIGURE 15.2 |
Required roles in joint decisions.

Figure 15.2 shows five roles required in decision making. When Larry told his kids they would go on vacation, Laurie and Michael began collecting information on a motor trip through various regions of the United States. They were the initial *information gatherers* in the process of *information search* and made Larry aware of various options—a trip to national parks in Utah and Arizona, to the Columbia River basin in Oregon, and to Yosemite National Park and the Lake Tahoe region in California.

The prime *influencers* are the children, who specified the alternative vacations. The *decision maker* is the father, because he controls the logistics of the vacation and the budget. When Larry was married, the *purchasing agent* for any vacation was his wife, because she worked in a travel agency and easily made the arrangements. They are still friends, so Larry can rely on her to serve the same role and make the air, hotel, and car rental reservations.

In the process of collecting information and evaluating alternative vacation spots, a *conflict* arises between the two children. Michael would like to go to Oregon for white-water rafting. Laurie wants to go to the Southwest because she is interested in Native American culture. Larry settles the conflict by deciding they will go to the Southwest this year and Oregon next year.

After their vacation, they determine they all thoroughly enjoyed it *(postpurchase evaluation)* and decide they might go back to the Southwest if they can accommodate Michael and find a spot with white-water rafting.

The three components that distinguish household from individual decisions—joint decision making, role specification, and conflict resolution—are considered next.

JOINT DECISION MAKING

Under what conditions are purchasing decisions likely to be made jointly by the household, and under what conditions are they likely to be made by an individual household member? Sheth found that joint decision making is more likely in the following situations:[20]

1. *When the level of perceived risk in buying is high.* Because a wrong decision will affect the whole household, a joint decision is likely to occur, to reduce risk and uncertainty. A decision regarding the purchase of a new home is invariably a joint decision because of the financial risks, the social risks involved in neighborhood interaction, and the psychological risks.

   Some evidence suggests that joint decision making may encourage the group to make riskier decisions because all members of the group can share the blame for a wrong decision. This **risky shift phenomenon** means, for example, that a decision the husband and wife make may result in the purchase of a more expensive house than if either spouse make a decision alone.

2. *When the purchasing decision is important to the household.* Importance is closely related to risk. In some cases, however, the decision may be important and the risk low—for example, deciding whether to return to the same vacation resort the family has gone to for the past five years. Decisions to buy major appliances and automobiles are generally joint decisions because of their importance. Decisions for low-involvement products are more likely to be made individually because it may not be worth the time and effort to engage in joint decisions for such products.

3. *When there are few time pressures.* Time pressures will encourage one member of the household to make the purchase decision. The greater number of dual-earning households has created greater time pressures, a situation that encourages individual decision making for many products that ordinarily might be purchased on a joint basis.

4. *For certain demographic groups.* Several demographic factors are likely to encourage joint decision making:
   - Younger families show a higher frequency of joint decision making. As the family gets older, joint decisions tend to decrease. Family members learn to make decisions that are acceptable to each other, and there is less need for shared decisions.
   - Joint decisions are more likely if there are no children in the family. As a family adds children, roles become more clearly defined, and husband and wife are more willing to delegate authority to each other.
   - Joint decision making is more likely if only one of the parents is working, as overall time pressures are less.

ROLE SPECIFICATIONS

Household members can play one or more of the five roles shown in Figure 15.2.

1. The "information gatherer" (sometimes called the "gatekeeper") influences the household's processing of information by controlling the level and type of stimuli to which the household is exposed. The information gatherer has the greatest expertise in acquiring and evaluating information.

2. The "influencer" establishes the decision criteria by which brands are compared (cost, durability, etc.) and influences the other household members' evaluation of alternative brands.

3. The "decision maker" decides which brand to purchase, probably because he or she has budgetary power and, therefore, final approval.

4. The "purchaser" carries out the decision by purchasing the product for the household.

5. The "consumer" uses the product and evaluates it, giving some feedback to other household members regarding satisfaction with the chosen brand and desirability of purchasing the same brand again.

From the marketer's standpoint, one of the most important distinctions is that between the purchaser and consumer. Many strategic decisions are made without recognizing this important distinction. In many cases, the purchasing agent may have little importance since the consumer makes the postpurchase evaluation and decides on future brand purchases. In other cases, the purchaser may decide the brand for others in the household, particularly if the decision is made in the store; for example, a parent deciding on a brand of cereal for a child.

CONFLICT RESOLUTION

Whenever two or more people are involved in decision making, some conflict is likely in purchasing objectives, attitudes toward alternative brands, and the selection of the most desirable alternative. The household is no exception. Because households are small, closely interdependent groups, joint decisions are likely to lead to conflict. Research has shown conflicts to exist in the selection of housing, automobiles, and family planning.[21] In family planning, the differences were not whether to engage in family planning but the choice criteria. Husbands emphasized the positive effects of small family size on living costs, whereas wives viewed small families as an advantage in giving them more time.

The marketer must be aware of such conflicts and adjust marketing strategies accordingly. For example, families frequently visit automobile showrooms together. The husband may emphasize roominess and style to impress business associates, and the wife may be concerned with gas economy and service costs—or the husband may emphasize cost; the wife, style. In any case, differences are likely to occur, and the sales representative must appeal to both parties.

When are conflicts most easily resolved? In three types of situations. The first occurs when the household recognizes one person as the legitimate authority. Conflict is simply resolved by delegating decision making to this individual. The second occurs when one household member is more involved in the decision than the others. The household may agree that the highly involved individual will make the decision. The third situation is when one household member may be more empathetic to another's needs.

Burns and Granbois studied the influence of husbands and wives in automobile decisions to determine if these three factors—recognized legitimacy, involvement, and empathy—reduce conflict.[22] They found that each factor facilitated conflict resolution. Conflict was less likely if the husband and wife agreed that the decision should be made jointly or by one of them alone. Even if the couple failed to agree on authority, conflict was less likely if one of them was more involved in the purchase. Finally, conflict was less likely if one of the spouses was more empathetic. A study of husband-wife choices of investment options found that a more empathetic spouse gravitated to the other spouse's preferences as a result of empathy.[23]

Husband–Wife Influences

Given the fact that the 62 percent of households are family units,[24] we focus on husband–wife influences in this section, and parent–child influences in the next. The relative influence of the husband and the wife is likely to vary according to three things: (1) type of product considered, (2) the nature of purchase influence, and (3) family characteristics.

THE TYPE OF PRODUCT

Traditionally, husbands have been regarded as the dominant decision makers for products such as automobiles, financial services, and liquor. Wives have been viewed as the prime decision makers for foods, toiletries, and small appliances. However, as we saw in Chapter 10, many of these roles have merged and even been reversed due to the greater proportion of working wives and changes in family norms.

Davis and Rigaux undertook one of the most detailed studies of husband–wife influences by product category.[25] They studied family decision making for twenty-five products and classified them into one of four categories:

1. Products for which the husband tends to be the dominant influence
2. Products for which the wife tends to be the dominant influence
3. Products for which decisions are made by either the husband or the wife, with either person equally likely to be dominant (autonomous decisions)
4. Products for which decisions are made jointly by husband and wife

An update of the Davis and Rigaux study is shown in Figure 15.3.[26] The higher the product is on the vertical axis, the more likely it is that the wife is the dominant influence. The farther to the right it is on the horizontal axis, the more likely the decision is to be a joint one. Therefore, products in the upper left are wife-dominant, products in the middle left are based on individual decisions by either husband or wife (autonomous), and products in the lower left are husband-dominant. Products to the right are joint decisions and involve both husband and wife as equal influences. Products to the left are individual decisions.

Some of the product classifications in Figure 15.3 confirm previous studies. Husbands are more dominant in decisions for lawn mowers, sports equipment, and

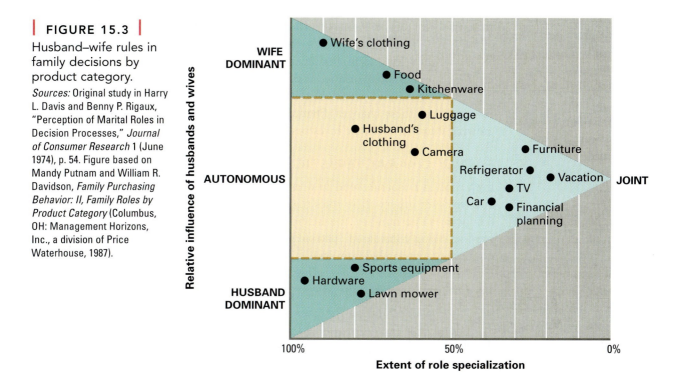

| FIGURE 15.3 |

Husband–wife rules in family decisions by product category.

Sources: Original study in Harry L. Davis and Benny P. Rigaux, "Perception of Marital Roles in Decision Processes," *Journal of Consumer Research* 1 (June 1974), p. 54. Figure based on Mandy Putnam and William R. Davidson, *Family Purchasing Behavior: II, Family Roles by Product Category* (Columbus, OH: Management Horizons, Inc., a division of Price Waterhouse, 1987).

hardware items. Wives dominate decisions for food, clothing, and kitchenware. Either the husband or the wife makes decisions for cameras and for the husband's clothing on an individual basis. They most likely make joint decisions for vacations, furniture, and financial planning.

A number of items changed positions between the original and the more recent study. In this period, cars, TV sets, and financial planning moved from a husband-dominant position to joint decision making, reflecting the greater influence of working wives.

THE NATURE OF THE PURCHASE INFLUENCE

The nature of the purchase influence may specify husband–wife roles. The most important classification by purchase influence defines instrumental versus expressive roles in family purchasing. **Instrumental roles** are related to performing tasks that help the group make the final purchasing decision. Decisions on budgets, timing, and product specifications are instrumental. **Expressive roles** facilitate expression of group norms and provide the group with social and emotional support. Decisions about color, style, and design are expressive since they reflect group norms.

Historically, the husband has been associated with the instrumental role and the wife with the expressive role. However, we saw in Chapter 10 that as more wives enter the work force, husbands are more likely to assume household roles and wives budgetary and planning roles. As a result, instrumental and expressive roles are becoming more intermingled between husband and wife. Working wives are less likely to accept traditional homemaking tasks associated with expressive roles and are as likely to fulfill certain instrumental roles as the husband. For example, the role of the wife in family finances has expanded in recent years to include involvement in the family's long-term financial planning regarding mortgages, investments, insurance, and estate planning. As of 2000, women had an equal financial say in 75 percent of all U.S. households and 28 percent managed all of the family's money.[27] As a result of these changes, financial service marketers now try to appeal to the growing number of female investors.

FAMILY CHARACTERISTICS

Even though husbands tend to dominate decisions for certain product categories and wives for others, these roles may vary in the degree of dominance within each family. In some families, the husband may be more dominant, regardless of the product being considered (patriarchal families); in others, the wife may be more dominant (matriarchal families).

Various studies show that a husband is generally more influential in the purchase decision than his wife when

1. His level of education is higher
2. His income and occupational status are higher
3. His wife is not employed
4. The couple is at an earlier stage in the family life cycle (young parents)
5. The couple has a greater than average number of children[28]

The opposite is true for a wife-dominant family; that is, the wife is employed, has a higher level of education than the husband, and so forth. One study by Skinner and Dubinsky confirmed this profile. Wives who were more involved than husbands in forming insurance decisions tended to be employed and better educated than their husbands.[29]

The profile of the husband-dominant family suggests a family with traditional values and attitudes toward marital roles. The husband's higher income provides him with financial power within the family. A nonworking wife with a lower level of education usually means that more traditional values prevail. A survey of 257 married women supported the more traditional orientation of the husband-dominant family.[30] Wives were classified as conservative, moderate, or liberal with regard to female roles. Women who had liberal views of their role were much more likely to make purchase decisions than were conservative women. They were also more than twice as likely to make decisions about family savings, vacation plans, and major appliances than were conservative women. Conversely, a study of husbands found that those with conservative perceptions of their marital role believed they had more influence on decisions for vacations, insurance, and savings than did husbands with more liberal views.[31] Both studies indicate that traditional (conservative) views of marital roles encourage greater male influence and contemporary (liberal) views encourage greater female influence.

CHANGING PATTERNS OF HUSBAND–WIFE INFLUENCE

Changes in marital roles have led to the husband's greater influence in decisions the wife has traditionally assumed (see the ad for Johnson & Johnson baby products in Exhibit 15.2) and the wife's greater influence in areas traditionally assumed to be the

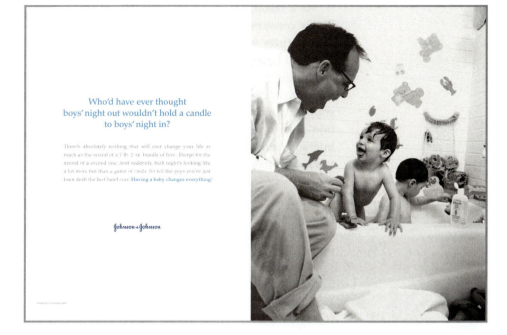

husband's domain. In a 1978 survey of shopping patterns by *Progressive Grocer,* a New York–based trade publication, men accounted for about 10 percent of the primary shoppers in U.S. households. By 1992, the number of male primary shoppers had risen to 25 percent. Further, men made more than half the household decisions for soaps, cereals, soft drinks, and snack foods.[32] It is likely these trends have continued since 1992. On the other side of the coin, we have noted that wives have an increasing role in decisions about insurance, automobiles, and financial services as a result of their greater economic power.

The implications for marketing are direct. Marketers for a wide range of products can no longer rely on traditional buying patterns. Producers of food products and household items are directing more effort toward husbands. Marketers of a wide range of "big-ticket" products and services are directing their effort toward wives. For example in 2000, the top ten automakers increased ad spending in women's magazines by 19 percent over 1999. Additionally, ad spending by automakers on Lifetime, a women's cable channel, was as much for the first three months of 2000 as it was for all of 1999.[33]

Parent–Child Influences

Children today play a more important part in family decisions in both traditional and nontraditional families than in the past. In almost 70 percent of traditional families, the husband and wife work. Dual-earning households foster greater self-reliance among children, often requiring them to shop and prepare meals. In nontraditional families, the rapid increase of single-parent households has also increased the number of children involved in shopping and meal preparation.

As a result, children are likely to influence decisions for products the whole family consumes. Children are estimated to influence over $130 billion in family expenditures across sixty-two product categories. The bulk of this influence is in food and beverage products.[34]

Studies of parent–child influences in purchasing have been divided between research on children 12 or under and on adolescents 13 to 17 years old. Research on younger children has focused on how they learn about purchasing and consumption tasks (the child's socialization in the marketplace) and on the mother–child interaction in the purchasing process. Research on adolescents has been directed toward the relative influence of parents and peer groups in teenage purchasing decisions. This focus is due to the general belief that children rely more on parents for norms and values when they are younger and more on their peer groups as they grow older. In the following sections, we first consider the consumer socialization of children, then the parent–child interaction, and finally the peer group–adolescent interaction.

CONSUMER SOCIALIZATION OF CHILDREN[35]

Consumer socialization of children is the process by which "young people acquire skills, knowledge, and attitudes relevant to their functioning in the marketplace."[36] Children learn about purchasing and consumption primarily from their parents. Although television may have a persuasive influence on what children see and how they react to certain brands, "the family is instrumental in teaching young people rational aspects of consumption, including basic consumer needs."[37] The role of parents in trying to teach their children to be more effective consumers is illustrated by the following findings:[38]

- Parents teach price-quality relations to their children, including experiences with the use of money and ways to shop for quality products.
- Parents teach their children how to be effective comparison shoppers and how to buy products on sale.
- Parents influence children's brand preferences.
- Parents have influenced children's ability to distinguish fact from exaggeration in advertising.

▌ Methods of Socialization   How do children learn these various facets of purchase and consumption behavior from their parents? Children watch and imitate parental behavior because parents serve as role models. Children also co-shop with the parent. Grossbart, Carlson, and Walsh found that mothers who co-shop have more explicit consumer socialization goals for their children than those who don't. They seek to expose children to the experiences associated with visiting stores and use these occasions to teach children consumer skills.[39]

Children also are socialized through direct experience. The increase in dual-earning and one-parent households has resulted in children often shopping on their own. As a result, the process of consumer socialization is occurring much earlier and much faster than it used to.

Television, the Internet, and the school environment are also important sources of socialization. Children learn to make associations from TV ads and programs.

According to **cultivation theory,** children learn about a culture's norms and values from the media. The greater the children's exposure to TV, the greater the likelihood that they will accept the images and associations seen. Thus, young children may learn that using a deodorant is a must in social situations, and many begin to use the product even though body odor does not occur until adolescence.

Greater time spent on the Web is also a source of socialization (see the Web Applications box). Children are becoming more and more Internet savvy at younger ages as the Internet expands. The Internet serves as a simple and easily accessible source of information as well as a way to communicate with other children. However, because of the vast reach of the Internet, parental control becomes very

WEB APPLICATIONS

Socializing Children on the Internet— Meet the Net Generation

A 2-year-old is sitting on her father's lap, takes the mouse out of his hand, and manipulates it through a colorful CD-ROM program for kids. A 7-year-old turns on the family computer to Netscape, types in an Internet address for kids' games, and spends a few hours having fun. A 12-year-old also gets on the Internet to the site for Levi jeans to check out the latest styles and costs.

Welcome to the Net generation, mostly the children of younger baby boomers. They are defined by their lack of awe for new technologies, as they have grown up with computers and treat them like any other household appliance. One study found that it takes less than five minutes to teach a 4-year-old how to use a mouse compared with several hours for adults. Two-thirds of kindergarten kids have used a computer. By the time they are 12, they are probably more adept than their parents at downloading software and accessing information on the Internet. By one estimate, more than 7 million children under 18 have their own Internet accounts.

The opportunity for socializing kids on the Internet is immense. Children are spending more and more time on the computer, and time on the computer is time taken away from television. Generation Y spends less time watching television that any other age group. As a result, tele-vision for kids as a whole has dropped from nineteen hours a week in 1998 to seventeen hours a week in 2000.

The Internet is an important vehicle for kids to get information on the latest fashions, new electronic products and games, and store availability. We can easily imagine a 10-year-old influencing her parents to buy a Volvo by downloading information on safety statistics from the Internet, or a 12-year-old who is interested in cooking downloading recipes from a Pillsbury site.

Marketers are beginning to target specific sites to the Net generation. The site for Levi jeans provides them with fashion information. Dole fruit company has integrated Bobby Banana, a popular character among school-children, into its web site in order to attract children. The site prominently displays the character and provides stuffed toys and musical CDs to children while promoting the Dole name.

It looks like the process of socialization for the Net generation is going to be a whole new ball game.

Sources: "Survey: Youth, Inc," *The Economist* (December 23, 2000), p. S9–10; "Mini Marketing," *Supermarket Business* (April 15, 2001)pp. 113–116; "Children's Computer Use Growing, But Gaps Persist, Study Says," *New York Times* (January 22, 2001); "The Rise of the Net Generation," *Advertising Age* (October 14, 1996), pp. 31, 43.

important in Internet socialization due to the variety of adult material available online. The medium's dual role as both information source and communication tool allows children to learn cultural norms from web sites and from each other.

One additional source of socialization is other children. Younger children may emulate older children's behavior and, in so doing, develop consumption skills. The child's peer group can also affect consumer socialization by influencing brand preferences and purchases.

▮ Stages in Consumer Socialization

Swiss psychologist Jean Piaget viewed socialization in the context of three phases of a child's cognitive development.[40] Children from 3 to 7 are in a "preoperational stage," when cognitive structure is poorly organized and language skills are developing. In this stage, parents may permit some limited purchase choices on an assisted basis—for example, in the flavors of ice cream or beverages.

From 8 to 11 years of age, children are in a "concrete operational stage," in which they develop more complex abilities to apply logical thought to concrete problems. In this second phase of socialization, children start developing persuasive techniques learned from their peers to influence their parents to buy them what they want (*e.g.,* "Everyone's got one except me").

In the third stage (12 to 15 years old), children enter a "formal operational stage," in which their ability to think abstractly and to associate concepts and ideas is more fully developed. During this third stage, children have greater financial resources and cognitive capabilities to make decisions on a wider range of products. Many of them influence parental purchases for adult items such as cars, computers, and electronics. This phase represents a child's ability to influence others, especially parents, and to build purchasing power for major purchases such as a computer.[41]

▮ The Role of Parents in Consumer Socialization

Carlson and Grossbart studied the role of parents in children's socialization as consumers.[42] They identified four types of parents within families:

1. *Authoritarian parents* seek a high level of control over their children and expect unquestioned obedience. They try to shield children from outside influences and are more likely to engage in socially oriented communications.

2. *Neglecting parents* are distant from their children and do not exert much control over them. They do not do much to maintain or encourage their children's capabilities.

3. *Democratic parents* foster a balance between parents' and children's rights. They encourage children's self-expression and value autonomy. They are warm and supportive, but they also expect mature behavior from children. If they regard children as "out of bounds," they use discipline.

4. *Permissive parents* seek to remove as many restraints from children as possible without endangering them. They believe children have adult rights but few responsibilities.

Although these categories are not all-encompassing, Carlson and Grossbart used them to study parent–child interactions. They found that democratic and, to a lesser extent, permissive parents had the most active role in children's socialization as consumers. These parents shop with their children and are more likely to seek their advice compared with authoritarian and neglecting parents. Democratic parents also are more likely to view TV with their children, but they express more concern about advertising to their children and try to control their TV viewing. As might be expected, authoritarian households place the most restrictions on children's consumption and media behavior.

One implication of these studies is that families most involved with children as consumers are also most concerned about their exposure to advertising and the Web. Marketers should be sensitive to these concerns. As noted in Chapter 7, children under 8 do not always distinguish program content from commercials. TV advertising in particular should be clearly delineated from program content. Web ads are even more difficult to distinguish from other web-site content. This is likely to become a more visible issue as Internet usage among children under 8 increases.

■ Intergenerational Influences   The process of consumer socialization is intergenerational; that is, influences are passed on from one generation to the next. Such influences are most apparent when researchers study brand preferences of parents and children. A comprehensive study by Moore, Wilkie, and Lutz, reported in 2002, found substantial intergenerational influences between daughters, mothers, and grandmothers. These researchers studied twenty-four product categories ranging from ketchup to facial tissues to peanut butter and found that mothers significantly influenced the daughter's choice in twenty-three categories. The daughter's preferred brand was identical to that of the mother 36 percent of the time, a figure that is significantly greater than chance considering the number of brands on the shelf in each of the categories studied.[43] The study also found that intergenerational influence produces strong emotional bonds with brands. To quote one daughter in the study: "I have salad dressing from Seven Seas—that's what my Grandma buys, and I always spend the summers with her in Michigan, so I like that kind of dressing."[44]

Intergenerational influences are not one-directional. They also pass from children to parents. We noted that companies like Ford, General Motors, and Gateway computers now target kids because of their influence over what could normally be regarded as adult purchases. The ad in Exhibit 15.3 is an example of such influence. It shows a daughter influencing her mother to get the right sources of nutrition. Children are also likely to influence parents' preferences for high-

"When I was a kid my mom was always after me to eat right...now, more than ever, I'm the one who's after her."

DRINK TO YOUR HEALTH WITH ENSURE.

The #1 Doctor Recommended Source of Nutrition.

Today more than ever, it's important to understand the benefits of good nutrition. In fact, your doctor probably has told you that good nutrition is a key to good health. Yet despite the benefits that good nutrition provides, you may experience days when it's hard for you to eat the way you know you should.

So how can you help guarantee that you get the right nutrition?

With Ensure.

Ensure is complete, balanced nutrition in a ready-to-serve drink that provides

Available in 6 Delicious Flavors.

an excellent balance of protein, carbohydrate, vitamins and minerals. It's all the nutrition you need each day to help stay healthy, be energetic and more active. Unlike vitamin supplements, Ensure is nutritionally complete.

Drink Ensure anytime. Enjoy it as a healthy meal by itself or as a healthy between-meal snack. Ensure is even recommended #1 by doctors as a complete source of nutrition.

So ask your doctor about Ensure. And make complete nutrition a regular part of your day. Drink Ensure and drink to your health.

© 1993 Ross Laboratories

EXHIBIT 15.3

An example of intergenerational influence.

Ross Products Division, Abbott Laboratories.

technology products. For example, a survey conducted in 2000 found that almost nine out of ten parents said their children's technology brand preferences carried some importance in their decisions.[45]

Intergenerational influences are likely to be stronger in those countries that have a greater proportion of extended families. Childers and Rao compared family influences in Thai and U.S. families and found that the greater number of extended families in Thailand resulted in stronger intergenerational influences.[46] Another study found that in Taiwan and the Philippines, the elderly play an important role in supporting the family economy.[47] Because of the close-knit traditional family structure, brands that parents and grandparents purchase exert a stronger influence than they do in U.S. families.

CHILDREN'S INFLUENCE IN THE PURCHASING PROCESS

Children are most likely to buy the products one would expect—candy, gum, toys, soft drinks, and snack foods. A significant proportion use their own money to buy presents, books, fast foods, and even clothing and sports equipment. Children also influence their parents' purchases of these same items, particularly clothing. And as mentioned, a significant number influence the purchase of such adult-oriented items as cars and electronic products.

Children's involvement may go beyond influencing parents. In some cases, parents and children make joint decisions, particularly when the child is highly involved in the decision. For example, many parents decide jointly with the child on the choice of a summer camp, private school, or family vacation. Exhibit 15.4 for Hyatt Resorts Hawaii shows a counselor with five children at "Camp Hyatt," which offers separate programs for kids. At Hyatt camps such as the one in Scottsdale, Arizona, kids can learn about Hopi Indian food and culture; at the Tamaya Resort in New Mexico they can take horseback riding or cooking lessons. To demonstrate the influence of children in vacation decisions, Hyatt follows up by sending kids news of contests and certificates for resort attractions. One Hyatt executive says, "There is nothing like a seven-year old asking 19 times, 'When are we going back to that hotel' to get parents to go back."[48]

Greater affluence and earlier consumer socialization of children may result in a greater likelihood that children will get their way. Children may also be more likely to get their way if their parents feel guilty for leaving them at home. As a result, marketers have begun to treat children as influentials for adult-oriented products. The ad for Belkin in Exhibit 15.5 portrays the child's influence by showing kids waiting on line to get on the Internet.

PARENT–CHILD INTERACTION

The focus in research on parent–child influences in purchasing has been on the interaction between mother and child. Several researchers have considered mothers' responses to children's requests to purchase various products.

Ward and Wackman found that the older children were, the more likely mothers were to yield to their requests. At the same time, however, older children made fewer purchase requests because they could make more purchase decisions independently. They are more likely to look to the peer group and disregard parents as

TEACH YOUR CHILDREN
CULTURE, WILDLIFE,
AND THE VALUE OF A DOLLAR.

FREE NIGHT PLUS
KIDS PLAY AND EAT FREE

Our Sunshine on Sale offer lets you indulge in
an array of authentic experiences that not only
educate but inspire. And now you can get them
at a remarkable value. You'll also get a free
night as well as a free session of Camp Hyatt.®
...icipate in "I-never-want-to-
..., kids 12 and under will eat
...ompanied by a paying adult,
... free daily buffet breakfast.
... Sunshine on Sale Family Plan
...e room for the kids at 50%
...ght ceremonies, lei-making
... culture instilled into every
...will be hard to know where
...ends and the fun begins.

[HYATT RESORTS HAWAII
SUNSHINE ON SALE®]

4th NIGHT FREE
Hyatt Regency Waikiki $265

6th NIGHT FREE
Hyatt Regency Kauai $395

7th NIGHT FREE
Hyatt Regency Maui $315

1 888 763 3902
(Ask for offer code: KIDSOS)

For air-inclusive packages, call Hyatt Vacations® at 1 800 772 0011.

HYATT
RESORTS AND SPAS
HAWAII®

Valid at properties listed, for stays between 6/1/02 and 8/31/02. Reservations are subject to availability and must be made in advance. Free night ...stay. Guest must request offer code KIDSOS at time of reservation. Children age 18 and under stay free in parents' room; existing bedding. Additional ...l hotel charges. Children age 12 and under eat free from children's menu with paying adult at hotel restaurants only. Does not include tax or ...Hyatt for children ages 3 to 12 (5 to 12 at Maui) is based on availability, up to 2 children per room per stay, at participating Hyatt resorts where ...on Sale package prices are based on double occupancy, standard guestroom accommodations. Prices do not include tax, gratuities, incidentals or ...ine on Sale includes buffet breakfast for 2 adults maximum daily and a one-level upgraded room at Hyatt Regency Waikiki. Package extras vary ...mily Plan. Family Plan includes 50% off second room for children up to age 18. No refunds for any unused portion of offer. Limited number of rooms ...not valid with groups/conventions and is not combinable with other promotional offers. Promotional blackout periods may apply, and normal ...y. Hyatt reserves the right to alter or withdraw this program at any time. Hyatt Hotels and Resorts® encompasses hotels and resorts managed, ...e groups of companies—Hyatt Corporation and its affiliates and affiliates of Hyatt International Corporation. ©2002 Hyatt Corp.

Get online without standing in one

**With Belkin Internet-sharing solutions,
you can all use one high-speed Internet
connection—at the same time.**

That means if you have two (or more) computers
and one cable or DSL line, you don't need to pay
for a second one. Belkin solutions let you set up all
your computers to share a single, always-on
Internet account, so you can all get online,
anytime. Setup is so unbelievably simple, the
reviewers* are raving about how easy it is to allow
all your computers to also share files, printers, and

other peripherals. Belkin networking products save
you the expense of additional service accounts,
modems, and devices. Now you can create a
wireless network and set everybody free to surf,
write proposals, or play online games from the
backyard, den, or kitchen. So, next time it's your
turn, check out belkin.com/networking for retail
locations, mail-in rebates on networking products,
and free product offers. We've designed great
ways to get you all online—without the line.

BELKIN
belkin.com

*Check out our reviews at www.belkin.com/reviews. Here's a sneak preview:
"Easy as pie ... up in under five minutes! ... Setting up this baby was something my mom could do." —Envynews.com

Belkin Components • 310.898.1100 • Fax 310.898.1111 • Compton, CA • United Kingdom • Holland • Australia   © 2002 Belkin Components. All rights reserved.   22AD012

STRATEGIC APPLICATIONS

Kraft's Jell-O Takes Another Look at the Mother–Child Interaction

Ever since Jell-O was first advertised in 1902 in the *Ladies Home Journal,* it targeted moms, even though kids were the primary consumers. True, kids were always in the ads with the introduction of the Jell-O girl in 1903, but the company always figured that the mother had the purchasing influence. When Bill Cosby began his twenty-seven-year tenure as a Jell-O pudding spokesperson, he was beseeching moms, not kids, to buy the product. He did the same when he also advertised the gelatin version of the product.

But a change took place in 2002 with Kraft, the brand's producer, recognizing the purchasing influence of children. As *Advertising Age* reported in November 2001:

> When kids' purchasing power is higher than ever, and the nag factor has become a critical driver of new product success for children's food products, Kraft hopes its "cool" new packaging, flavors and advertising will give kids something to beg for.

Kraft now recognizes that kids are no longer passive consumers; they are active influencers in the purchase decisions for packaged foods. The second influence cited by *Advertising Age,* the "nag factor," has always been there. But as the study cited in the previous section found, American parents are likely to listen to and negotiate with kids rather than just say no.

Given these factors, Kraft decided to introduce a new line, Jell-O Gel Sticks and Gel Cups in February 2002 under the name Jell-O X-tremes, targeted directly to kids. The product was launched with TV ads on kid-oriented cable channels like Nickelodeon. Kraft now sees the children's segment as the market of opportunity in an industry with only a 5 percent growth rate and the mother–child interaction as a two-way street.

Source: Adapted from "Kraft's Jello Takes Another Look at the Mother-Child Interaction," *Advertising Age* (November 19, 2001), p. 4.

sources of information, and parents view them as more competent in making purchasing judgments.[49]

An interesting cross-cultural study of younger children's influence found that American children made the most requests (nineteen over a two-week period), and Japanese children made the fewest requests (nine in two weeks). However, Japanese parents were more likely to accede to children's requests when made. The authors observed that "Japanese children are encouraged to be respectful and harmonious in the family and purchase requests may be viewed as 'pushy'; however, since Japanese parents are highly indulgent of their children, they most often agree to buy requested items."[50] When it came to American parents, they were more likely to negotiate and discuss purchase requests with the child or to just say "no." An ad for Betty Crocker Fruit Snacks pictured a mother giving in to a child's request for the product with the tag line: "After 27 'No's' and 13 'Put it back's,' it's nice to say 'Yes.'" The ad reflected the American mother's willingness to say "no" by associating the product with a rare "yes" on the mother's part.

PARENT VERSUS PEER-GROUP INFLUENCE AMONG ADOLESCENTS

As we saw in Chapter 12, the purchasing influence of teenagers has increased as working parents have shifted more responsibilities to them for shopping and other chores. One survey found that, on average, teenage girls spend over an hour a week shopping for the family and that over 80 percent do some cooking at home. One marketing expert concluded that the influence of teens in food shopping is almost on a par with their mothers.

When do adolescents exert the most influence on purchases? In a survey of 429 college freshmen in which their influence on family decisions for durable goods was examined, Beatty and Talpade found that the students saw themselves as exerting the most influence when they[51]

■ *have more purchasing power.* The greater the teenager's purchasing power, the more likely the parent will respect his or her purchasing opinions.

■ *have more perceived knowledge of the product.* Teenagers often have more knowledge than parents for such products as computers, sound systems, camcorders, cellular phones, and even automobiles. In such cases, parents are more likely to accept the teenager's opinions.

■ *regard the product as important.* The more important the product to the teenager, the more likely it is that he or she will exert purchasing influence on the family decision.

The nature of adolescent influence on parents can be fairly sophisticated. One study found that adolescents often anticipate the nature of parental responses to their attempts at influence. They attempt to reason with their parents and to bargain to get their way. They also learn which strategy works best, and employ it again.[52]

Such teenage influence is often ascribed to the greater independence of adolescents. The traditional view is that as children enter adolescence, they shift their allegiance from parents to the peer group, and parental purchase influence declines. However, various studies suggest that children continue to rely on parents for information and influence into adolescence. One study found that high school students were just as concerned with parents' approval as were elementary school students. Another found that 16- to 19-year-olds were more likely to be influenced by parents than by friends in the purchase of sports equipment and small appliances.[53]

A study by Moschis and Moore found that the fact a parent liked the product was a more important criterion than the fact a friend liked the product.[54] This means that joint decision making is not a one-way street: Adolescents and parents influence each other. The same study found that the importance of parents in purchasing decisions does not diminish the importance of the peer group. As teenagers get older, they rely on more information sources, and peer groups become increasingly influential in purchase decisions.

Household Decision Making and Marketing Strategies

Household decision making influences every phase of marketing strategy—the advertising message, the media selected, product development, pricing strategies, and distribution. In this section, we consider the marketing implications of (1) children's socialization, (2) decision making in traditional households, and (3) decision making in nontraditional households.

CHILDREN'S SOCIALIZATION

Marketers have attempted to influence children's consumer socialization by getting kids to recognize company and brand names early even if these companies do not sell children's products. Yogurt, a decidedly adult, health-oriented category, is an example. Children generally tell their moms that they hate the taste. However, as baby-boomer parents began to extend their nutritional orientation to their children, yogurt marketers saw an opening. In 1993, Dannon introduced Sprinkl'ins, with a thicker consistency that children like, and Yoplait introduced Trix fruit flavor layered into the cup. Advertising targets children with fun themes, while targeting moms with nutritionally oriented benefits. The president of Yoplait explains the consumer socialization strategy for children, saying, "If you can get kids hooked on yogurt, you can develop a habit that hopefully will continue through their entire life."[55]

Another producer of adult products, Black & Decker, has engaged in a similar strategy. The company manufactures power tools and appliances. It licensed its name to a line of toys that are miniature versions of its small appliance line. One company executive reasoned, "Youngsters don't buy Black & Decker drills. But they might someday if they start out on toy Dustbusters."[56] Socialization strategies also have been educationally motivated. For example, First National Bank of Tennessee introduced a savings club for children under 12 to teach them fiscal responsibility with a marketing campaign featuring Moola-Moola, a fuzzy monster who visits schools.

Marketers also influence children's consumer socialization by introducing children's versions of adult brands. These children's products are often offshoots of adult products in very competitive markets with little room for growth. Children present a new growth opportunity. For example, Unilever recently introduced Suave for Kids. The product appeals to children from 6 to 12 who are too old for baby shampoos and not ready for adult shampoos. The products rely on unique scents and clever names such as "Awesome Apple" to appeal to their age group. Similarly, Trident gum has introduced a sugarless gum targeted to children. By using fun names and bright packaging, Trident is looking to expand its otherwise stagnant gum business. By targeting children, marketers can achieve the dual goal of attracting lifelong users and growing slow-moving categories.[57]

TRADITIONAL HOUSEHOLDS

Different strategic implications arise in targeting traditional and nontraditional households. Implications for marketing to traditional households center on the husband–wife and parent–child relationship. The key question is who has the dominant influence.

■ **Husband–Wife Influences**   If the husband or wife is dominant in decision making, the marketer typically directs the advertising message to the needs of the dominant party and selects media to reach either the husband or the wife. A more difficult strategic issue arises when spouses make decisions jointly or autonomously. If the decision is joint, should marketers direct separate messages to husband and wife, or should they design one campaign to appeal to both? In car advertising, some manufacturers have used separate campaigns on the assumption that husband and wife emphasize different benefits. Chevrolet, for example, began targeting 30 percent of its ad budget to women, gearing its themes to fashion and style. However,

| EXHIBIT 15.6 |

An auto campaign that targets both husband and wife.

Courtesy Nissan North America.

The car you've always dreamed of. (At least since you married, had kids and enrolled them in swim class.)

Enjoy the ride.

one study found that 65 percent of women felt misrepresented by such advertising because it implied they were not very interested in performance.[58] Increasingly, automakers now target their campaigns to both husband and wife, with style and comfort on a par with performance (see the Nissan ad in Exhibit 15.6).

If the decision is autonomous—that is, made by husband or wife and either one is equally likely to make it—the marketer is faced with a difficult choice. Should the advertising budget be split equally between male- and female-oriented media, or should the marketer appeal to one or the other? Men's clothing is a good example. The marketer could advertise men's clothing in women's magazines, in men's magazines, or in both. If both are used, marketers need two separate campaigns. The danger of this approach is that the media budget may be spread too thin.

As patterns of husband–wife influence have changed, marketing strategies have adapted. For example, until recently, life insurance was designed primarily to the husband's specifications, but companies now are developing policies geared specifically to the working wife. Similarly, marketers can no longer assume that the coupon redeemer is necessarily the wife. Husbands' increasing involvement in food shopping means they are more likely to redeem coupons.

| Parent–Child Influences   A similar strategic issue is whether to target the child alone or to target both child and parent when both have influence on the purchase decision. Marketers generally reach the parent and child separately to emphasize different benefits. Banquet's Kid Cuisine follows a strategy of advertising to both parents and children. Thus, it advertises its microwavable product to children on the Nickelodeon cable channel and on TV shows such as "The Simpsons," whereas it targets nutritionally oriented print ads to mothers in magazines such as *Good Housekeeping* and *Parents.*[59]

In contrast, Hawaiian Punch targets kids rather than parents with themes like "The only 'Punch' that won't get you sent to the principal's office," and "If you tried blending 7 Natural Fruits, you'd make a mess and Mom would have a cow." In 2001 it introduced Hawaiian Punch Soft and Chewy candy for the children's market.[60] The company may feel that kids often make the purchase decision without parental influence.

Marketers are also increasingly willing to change the characteristics of adult products to suit the needs of children. Procter & Gamble launched Pert Plus for Kids in a tear-free formulation. The company also introduced a sparkle-filled version of Crest toothpaste to get children to brush.[61]

NONTRADITIONAL HOUSEHOLDS

A different set of strategic issues arise when dealing with nontraditional households. Nontraditional households represent diverse groupings that require specific targeting—for example, single-parent households, gay households, college roommates, friends living together, and so forth. The following strategic questions arise in targeting these groups:

▮ *Is the nontraditional household grouping large enough to target?* A grouping such as single-parent households represented over 9 million households in 2000, certainly a grouping large enough to target for most products. But the key question is whether a separate effort is required to target such a group or whether a general campaign is sufficient. If a company like Tyson wants to target parents of latchkey kids, advertising depicting single-parent households might be warranted. Similarly, marketers such as Ikea stores are targeting the gay market even though it represents only 3 percent of households, because gays are an affluent group with significant purchasing potential.

▮ *Can appeals be geared to the particular needs of these groups?* Tyson appealed to single-parent households in the early 1990s with Looney Tunes microwavable meals because almost all single parents work and have latchkey kids. In contrast, Campbell would probably not advertise its condensed soups specifically to single parents because the same appeals would be used for all families with children. If the needs of nontraditional households do not differ from the general population, then a separate marketing campaign is not warranted.

▮ *Are media vehicles available to reach nontraditional households?* The absence of specific media vehicles inhibits reaching nontraditional households. For example, to reach single parents, magazines, web sites, or cable channels must be available that are targeted to this group. In the absence of such media, prime-time TV would have to be used to reach the working single parent, an expensive alternative given the size of the segment.

Societal Implications of Household Influence

The primary societal issue in household decision making is the effect of advertising on children. Armstrong and Brucks cite two issues regarding the effects of children's advertising in the context of household influence: (1) does children's advertising increase parent–child conflict? and (2) does such advertising create undesirable consumer socialization by teaching children poor consumption and social values?[62]

INCREASED PARENT–CHILD CONFLICT

Critics of children's advertising suggest that advertising may undermine parental control. Seeing ads makes children badger their parents for products they cannot afford or do not want to give to their children. As one Federal Trade Commission critique says, the effect is to turn the child unwittingly into an "assistant salesperson."[63]

Advertisers retort by saying that children's requests of parents are a natural part of the parent–child relationship. They also cite polls showing little support from parents for increased advertising regulation.

UNDESIRABLE CONSUMER SOCIALIZATION

Critics claim that children's advertising teaches children materialism, impulsiveness, and immediate gratification. As a result, it creates poor consumption values. Further, in fostering impulsive choices, advertising encourages children to buy inappropriate products such as expensive or unneeded toys, sugared cereals, and junk food. For example, status-conscious 15-year-olds in Southern California bought Bausch & Lomb's Killer Loop sunglasses for up to $120 because they were "in."[64] Advertising may also create favorable attitudes toward harmful products such as cigarettes. When R. J. Reynolds ran its Joe Camel campaign, it was faulted on this score.

Consumers Union, which publishes a version of its *Consumer Reports* for kids, summarized the criticisms of marketers for negative influences in socializing children: "At a time when kids need to learn how to consume thoughtfully, numerous promotional messages are teaching the opposite."[65]

Defenders claim that advertising provides information that helps children make more informed decisions, and they cite consumer socialization as a parental, rather than an advertising, responsibility. Further, they note that advertisers have been instrumental in promoting positive socialization by funding such high-quality children's programs as CBS's Schoolbreak Specials and ABC's Afterschool Breaks.

ALTERNATIVE SOLUTIONS

Government regulations have limited the amount of commercial time on children's programs. Further, an industry-sponsored organization, the Children's Advertising Review Unit, monitors TV ads on children's programs to determine their suitability and issues complaints against advertisers who violate their guidelines.

These efforts, however, do not address how to prepare children to better process and evaluate advertising. Advertisers might try to develop commercials that children can process more easily, assuming such commercials are responsible. For example, Peracchio found that when ideas and events were repeated visually and were put in a relevant context, younger children were as effective as older children in processing information.[66] Advertisers using repetitive themes in a salient context might improve children's processing of the message, but the question remains whether the message is responsible and improves children's consumer socialization skills.

Ultimately, the primary role for improving children's skills in evaluating advertising rests with the parents. As Armstrong and Brucks note, "Parents can [best] monitor their children's television viewing, get children to think about advertising claims, evaluate children's purchase requests, and help children compare advertising claims against product performance."[67] However, such consumer socialization requires active and involved parents. In this respect, little can be done in protecting children from undue advertising influence if parents simply do not care.

SUMMARY

This chapter focused on the most important reference group—the household. Both traditional households (married couples with children) and nontraditional households (single parents, unmarried couples, gay households, friends living together) were described. The proportion of nontraditional households has increased as a result of couples marrying later or not marrying at all and a higher divorce rate.

The chapter also considered the purchasing implications of changes in household composition over time. Originally, such changes were considered in the context of a family life cycle that described a progression from single to married to married with children to empty nesters. As a family moves from one stage to another, their discretionary income, need for household appliances, and expenditures on food, clothing, and education change. Given the increase in nontraditional households, a more appropriate context is the household life cycle to incorporate a series of changes such as married, divorced single parent, and remarried with stepchildren. The focus on purchasing implications changes when one considers the needs of a single parent as opposed to a married couple, and the formation of a family with stepchildren.

The chapter then considered a model of household decision making and identified three distinguishing characteristics of household decisions. First, decisions within households are likely to be made jointly. The likelihood of joint decisions increases when perceived risk is high, the purchase decision is important to the household, and time pressures are minimal.

Second, household members have prescribed roles in the decision process. They can perform the roles of information gatherer, influencer, decision maker, purchasing agent, and consumer. Third, joint decisions invariably produce some conflict in purchase objectives.

Husband–wife influences dominate the family purchasing process. Four types of decision processes were defined: (1) husband-dominant, (2) wife-dominant, (3) autonomous (either husband or wife is equally likely to make an individual decision), and (4) joint decision making. Traditionally, husbands dominate decisions for cars and insurance; wives, for food and toiletries. However, these traditional domains have become blurred as working wives have gained more influence in household decisions for products such as automobiles and financial services.

Parent–child influences were also considered. Children have exerted more influence over family purchase decisions, especially in single-parent and dual-earning households. An important aspect of parent–child interaction is children's consumer socialization. Parents teach children how to be effective consumers and influence their brand preferences. Purchase influences and consumer learning are intergenerational in that they are passed from one generation to another. Another source of socialization is the media. Cultivation theory says that children learn a culture's norms and values from the media. Increasingly, the Web is becoming a source of such socialization, particularly among what has been referred to as the "Net generation."

The chapter also considered the strategic implications of household decision making. Specifically, the strategic implications of the socialization of children and of husband–wife and parent–child influences were considered.

In the last section, we considered the societal implications of advertising to children in the context of household influences. Advertising may have two negative consequences in regard to parent–child relations: first, it may create parent–child conflict by encouraging children's purchase requests; second, it may instill poor consumption values. Both government and industry have a role in regulating children's advertising, but it is ultimately the parents' responsibility to try to counter any negative effects of advertising by improving their children's capacity to process and evaluate advertising messages.

In Chapter 16, we consider another essential component in understanding groups, the nature of group communications.

QUESTIONS FOR DISCUSSION

1. What are the strategic implications of the increase in nontraditional households?

2. What are the strategic implications in referring to a household rather than a family life cycle?

3. Are families likely to make the following product decisions on a joint basis or on an individual basis? Why?
   - Life insurance
   - Toothpaste
   - Personal computers

4. Advertising campaigns for products in which spouses make decisions on an autonomous basis are difficult to formulate because either spouse can make an individual decision. The advertiser could try to develop (a) separate campaigns for each spouse, (b) a joint campaign for both, or (c) a campaign aimed at one or the other. Under what conditions will each of the these strategies be most effective?

5. What may be the effect of a contemporary versus a traditional view of the woman's role in the family on (a) the purchase of convenience foods, (b) family shopping behavior, and (c) the management of family finances?

6. Instrumental roles traditionally have been associated with the husband; expressive roles, with the wife. What changes have taken place in American society that have caused a blurring of these traditional roles?

7. There has been a shift toward joint decision making for many product categories that have been within the husband's traditional domain (autos, financial planning) and the wife's (appliances, furniture). What are the implications of this shift for (a) new product development, (b) product-line strategies, and (c) advertising?

8. What are the implications for children's consumer socialization in each of Piaget's three phases of child development?

9. Why is the Web likely to be an increasingly important source of the consumer socialization of children?

10. What are the marketing implications of the "Net generation's" facility with new technologies?

11. What are the pros and cons of marketers attempting to influence children's socialization as consumers?

12. Research has found that mothers are more likely to yield to children's requests that are made in the store rather than in the home. Why do you suppose this is true? What are the strategic implications of this finding for (a) advertising and (b) in-store promotional policy?

13. What may be the potential negative effects of advertising on the consumer socialization of children? How can children's consumer socialization skills be improved?

RESEARCH ASSIGNMENTS

1 Visit the following Web sites: *www.hifi.com* and *www.herhifi.com.*
- Does the site suggest that stereo products are individual, autonomous, or joint purchases?
- On this basis, should there be a separate site for women in shopping for stereo and audio products?

2 Trace a family decision for two families: one a couple with two or more children, the other a single-parent household with one child or more. Be sure the product or service involves joint decisions by parent(s) and children (*e.g.,* a family vacation, selection of a college, purchase of an automobile). Identify each family member's (a) specific roles, (b) perceptions and attitudes of the alternatives being considered, (c) conflicts in decision making, (d) modes of conflict resolution, and (e) postpurchase evaluation.
- What are the differences in the decision processes between the two families?
- What are the implications of decision making for (a) advertising, (b) product-line development, (c) product positioning, and (d) pricing?

3 Conduct separate interviews with third- or fourth-grade children and their mothers to determine perceptions of each child's influence. A good way to do this is to make contact with an elementary school and gain permission to conduct such interviews. Interviews with children should be conducted in class with the teacher's cooperation. Mothers can be interviewed at home.

- Ask mothers about the influence of their children and ask children about their influence relative to their mothers' for products such as cereal, toothpaste, candy, fast-food restaurants, and household electronics. Use a simple scale that children can understand, such as "I make the decision," "My mother makes the decision," and "We both make the decision." Ask both mothers and children what brand they last purchased and to rate the brand from excellent to poor.

- Is there agreement between mother and child on (a) degree of influence, (b) brand purchased, and (c) brand ratings? If there are differences, why?

4 Replicate assignment 3 for 12- to 13-year-old girls buying clothes. In this case, ask children and mothers to divide up ten points based on purchase influence. Determine degree of agreement on (a) purchase influence, (b) evaluation of the store in which clothing was purchased, and (c) evaluation of the clothing purchased.

NOTES

1. "Jell-O Taken to 'X-Tremes'," *Advertising Age* (November 19, 2001), p. 4.
2. "Advertising: Heinz Is Putting Its Money Where the Young Mouths Are," *New York Times* (July 26, 2001), p. C6.
3. "Edible Entertainment," *New York Times* (October 24, 2001), p. B1.
4. "Ford to Sell Safety to Kids on Nickelodeon," *Wall Street Journal* (April 18, 2000), p. 1.
5. "Marketing Is Kid Stuff," *Automotive News* (May 15, 2000), p. 26.
6. Jim Cooper, "Parents: Kids Know Best," *Mediaweek* (December 12, 1999), p. 14.
7. U.S. Bureau of the Census, *Statistical Abstract of the United States, 2000,* Tables 60–70.
8. "For First Time Nuclear Families Drop Below 25% of Households," *New York Times* (May 16, 2001), p. A1.
9. U. S. Bureau of the Census, *Statistical Abstract of the United States, 1996,* Table 67, p. 58.
10. *Statistical Abstract, 2000,* Table 70.
11. Aric Rindfleisch, James E. Burroughs, and Frank Denton, "Family Structure, Materialism, and Compulsive Consumption," *Journal of Consumer Research* 23 (March 1997), pp. 312–325.
12. *Statistical Abstract, 2000,* Table 60.
13. Ibid.
14. "A Tribunal to Get Neglected Parents Smiling Again," *New York Times* (December 1996), p. A4.
15. Ibid.
16. William D. Wells and George Gubar, "Life Cycle Concept in Marketing Research," *Journal of Marketing Research* 3 (November 1966), pp. 355–363.
17. *Statistical Abstract, 2000,* Table 90.
18. Takeshi Tamura and Annie Lau, *Connectedness vs. Separateness: Applicability of Family Therapy to Japanese Families* (Ilford, England: Redbridge Child and Family Consultation Centre and King George Hospital), 2000.
19. Pierre Filiatrault and J. R. Brent Richie, "Joint Purchasing Decisions: A Comparison of Influence Structure in Family and Couple Decision-Making Units," *Journal of Consumer Research* 7 (September 1980), p. 139.
20. Jagdish N. Sheth, "A Theory of Family Buying Decisions," in Jagdish N. Sheth, ed., *Models of Buyer Behavior* (New York: Harper & Row, 1974), pp. 17–33.
21. Raymond Loewy/William Snaith, Inc., *Project Home: The Motivations Towards Homes and Housing,* report prepared for the Project Home Committee, 1967; P. Doyle and P. Hutchinson, "Individual Differences in Family Decision Making," *Journal of the Market Research Society* 15 (October 1973), pp. 193–206; T. Poffenberger, *Husband-Wife Communication and Motivational Aspects of Population Control in an Indian Village* (Green Park, New Delhi: Central Family Planning Institute, 1969).
22. Alvin C. Burns and Donald H. Granbois, "Factors Moderating the Resolution of Preference Conflict in Family Automobile Purchasing," *Journal of Marketing Research,* 14 (February, 1977), pp. 77–86.
23. Michael B. Menasco and David J. Curry, "Utility and Choice: An Empirical Study of Wife/Husband Decision Making," *Journal of Consumer Research,* 16 (June, 1989), p. 95.
24. *Statistical Abstract, 2000,* Table 60.
25. Harry L. Davis and Benny P. Rigaux, "Perceptions of Marital Roles in Decision Processes," *Journal of Consumer Research* 1 (June 1974), pp. 51–62.
26. Mandy Putnam and William R. Davidson, *Family Purchasing Behavior: II, Family Roles by Product Category* (Columbus, Ohio: Management Horizons, Inc., a division of Price Waterhouse, 1987).
27. "For Richer, for Poorer," *American Demographics* (July 2000), pp. 58–64.
28. Benny Rigaux-Bricmont, "Explaining the Marital Influences in Family Economic Decision-Making," in Subhash C. Jain, ed., *Proceedings of the American Marketing Association Educators' Conference,* Series No. 43 (Chicago: American Marketing Association, 1978), pp. 126–129.
29. Steven J. Skinner and Alan J. Dubinsky, "Purchase Insurance: Predictors of Family Decision-Making Responsibility," *Journal of Risk and Insurance* 51 (September 1984), p. 521.
30. Robert T. Green and Isabella C. M. Cunningham, "Feminine Role Perception and Family Purchasing Decisions," *Journal of Marketing Research* 12 (August 1975), pp. 325–332.
31. William J. Qualls, "Changing Sex Roles: Its Impact upon Family Decision Making," in Andrew Mitchell, ed.,

Advances in Consumer Research, Vol. 9 (Ann Arbor, Mich.: Association for Consumer Research, 1982), p. 269.

32. "Real Men Buy Paper Towels Too," *Business Week* (November 9, 1992), p. 75; and "Study Boosts Men's Buying Role," *Advertising Age* (December 4, 1989), p. 75.

33. "Spending Soars for Women's Attention," *Automotive News* (June 19, 2000), p. 20.

34. "Born to Shop," *American Demographics* (June 1993), pp. 34–39 and "The Littlest Shoppers," *American Demographics* (February 1992), pp. 48, 50.

35. Deborah Roedder John, "Consumer Socialization of Children," *Journal of Consumer Research* 26 (December 1999), pp. 183–213.

36. Scott Ward, "Consumer Socialization," in Harold H. Kassarjian and Thomas S. Robertson, eds., *Perspectives in Consumer Behavior* (Glencoe, Ill.: Scott, Foresman, 1980).

37. George P. Moschis, "The Role of Family Communication in Consumer Socialization of Children and Adolescents," *Journal of Consumer Research* 11 (March 1985), pp. 898–913, at p. 902.

38. Scott Ward, Daniel B. Wackman, and Ellen Wartella, *How Children Learn to Buy: The Development of Consumer Information Processing Skills* (Beverly Hills, Calif.: Sage, 1977); "Born to Shop," pp. 34–39; George P. Moschis, "A Longitudinal Study of Consumer Socialization," in Michael Ryan, ed., *Proceedings of the American Marketing Association Theory Conference* (Chicago: American Marketing Association, 1984).

39. Sanford Grossbart, Les Carlson and Anna Walsh, "Consumer Socialization and Frequency of Shopping with Children," *Journal of the Academy of Marketing Science,* 19 (Summer 1991), pp. 155–162.

40. B. J. Wadsworth, *Piaget's Theory of Cognitive Development* (New York: David McKay, 1971).

41. "Born to Shop," pp. 34–39.

42. Les Carlson and Sanford Grossbart, "Parental Style and Consumer Socialization of Children," *Journal of Consumer Research* 15 (June 1988), pp. 77–94.

43. Elizabeth S. Moore, William L. Wilkie, and Richard J. Lutz, "Passing the Torch: Intergenerational Influences as a Source of Brand Equity," *Journal of Marketing* 66 (April 2002), pp.17–37. See also Elizabeth S. Moore, William L. Wilkie, and Julie A. Alder, "Lighting the Torch: How Do Intergenerational Influences Develop," in Mary C. Gilly and Joan Myers-Levy, eds., *Advances in Consumer Research,* Vol. 28 (Valdesta, Ga.: Association of Consumer Research, 2001), pp. 287–293.

44. "Passing the Torch," pp. 287–293.

45. "Parents Kids Know Best," *Mediaweek* February 8 1999), p. 14.

46. Terry L. Childers and Aksay R. Rao, "The Influence of Familial and Peer-Based Referenced Groups on Consumer Decisions," *Journal of Consumer Research* 19 (September 1992), pp. 198–211.

47. Emily Agree, Ann E. Biddlecom, Ming-Cheng Chang, and Aurora E. Perez, *Generalized Exchange and Intergenerational Transfers in Taiwanese and Filipino Families* (Baltimore, Md.: Johns Hopkins University, 2000).

48. "Hotels Develop More Learning Programs for Kids Travelers," *USA Today* (May 18, 1999), p. 11E; and "Getting 'Em While They're Young," *Business Week* (September 9, 1991), p. 94.

49. Scott Ward and Daniel B. Wackman, "Children's Influence Attempts and Parental Yielding," *Journal of Marketing Research* 9 (August 1972), pp. 316–319.

50. "Children's Requests: When Do Parents Yield," *Wharton Alumni Magazine* (Fall 1987), p. 19.

51. Sharon E. Beatty and Salil Talpade, "Adolescent Influence in Family Decision Making: A Replication with Extension," *Journal of Consumer Research* 21 (September 1994), pp. 332–340.

52. Kay M. Palan and Robert E. Wilkes, "Adolescent-Parent Interaction in Family Decision Making," *Journal of Consumer Research* 24 (September 1997), pp. 159–169.

53. David C. Epperson, "Reassessment of Indices of Parents Influence in American Society," *American Sociological Review* 29 (February 1964); Paul Gilikson, "What Influences the Buying Decisions of Teenagers," *Journal of Retailing* 4 (Fall 1965), pp. 36–41.

54. George P. Moschis and Roy L. Moore, "Decision Making Among the Young: A Socialization Perspective," *Journal of Consumer Research* 6 (September 1979), pp. 101–112; George P. Moschis and Roy L. Moore, "Purchasing Behavior of Adolescent Consumers," in Richard P. Bagozzi et al., eds., *Proceedings of the American Marketing Association Educators' Conference,* Series No. 46 (Chicago: American Marketing Association, 1980), p. 93.

55. "Dannon Stirs Up Two Kiddie Yogurt Lines," *Brandweek* (June 18, 2001), p. 4; "When Two Brands Are Better Than One," *Consumer Digest* (July 1995), p. 10; "Yogurts Sprinkle in Fun to Stir Kids," *Advertising Age* (February 8, 1993), p. S22.

56. "Growing Up in the Market," *American Demographics* (October 1992), pp. 47–48.

57. "Products for the Sophisticated Nipper," *Brandweek* (February 22, 1999), pp. 1–2.

58. "Auto Makers Set New Ad Strategy to Reach Women," *Advertising Age,* (September 23, 1985), p. 80.

59. "Kids 'Question Mark' Is Now Con/Agra Exclamation Point," *Advertising Age* (September 2, 1996), p. 12.

60. "Cadbury's Candy Push," *Advertising Age* (December 3, 2001), p. 8.

61. "Makers of Personal Care Products Hope to Clean Up with Brands for Children," *Wall Street Journal* (January 28, 1993), p. 8.

62. Garrie R. Armstrong and Merrie Brucks, "Dealing with Children's Public Policy Issues and Alternatives," *Journal of Public Policy and Marketing* 7 (1988), pp. 93–113.

63. Ibid, p. 102.

64. Ibid, p. 101.

65. "Getting 'Em While They're Young," p. 94.

66. Laura A. Peracchio, "How Do Young Children Learn to Be Consumers? A Script Processing Approach," *Journal of Consumer Research* 18 (March 1992), pp. 425–440.

67. Armstrong and Brucks, "Dealing with Children's Public Policy Issues," p. 104.

Group Communications: Word-of-Mouth and Diffusion Processes

Group communications are central to consumer decision making because groups are the primary source of information and influence. Group communications occur within and across groups. Communication within groups occurs through **word of mouth**—that is, interpersonal communication between two or more individuals, such as a customer and a salesperson, or members of a reference group. Word of mouth is the most influential type of communication because it comes from family, friends, and neighbors—all highly credible sources of information. Communications across groups occurs through a process of diffusion of information and influence. Such a process of **diffusion** is likely to occur for new products, as information and adoption of new products spreads across groups. Marketers must trace such diffusion processes, because new products are a primary source of profits to the firm.

In this chapter, we first consider word-of-mouth communications by describing

▌ the process by which word of mouth occurs,

▌ the nature of "opinion leadership"; that is, the influence that individuals who are interested in the product exert over others, and

▌ how marketers attempt to influence word-of-mouth communications.

We then consider the process of diffusion by describing how information and influence are communicated to other groups. Consumers are categorized by the time they take to adopt new products—innovators, early adopters, the majority, and laggards. Particular emphasis is given to those who are among the first to adopt; namely, innovators and early adopters. The chapter concludes with an examination of the strategic implications of the diffusion process.

Viral Marketing: Stimulating Word of Mouth and Diffusion on the Web

Marketers have attempted to stimulate word-of-mouth communications about their products on the Web through a strategy known as "viral marketing." As the name implies, **viral marketing** encourages the spread of information about a product or service from one person to the next, much like a virus. And like a virus, the network of communications spreads wider and wider as information is diffused. As a result, viral marketing stimulates both word-of-mouth communications and the process of diffusion: word of mouth in encouraging communications between people who generally trust each other and find one another's messages credible, and diffusion in encouraging a spread of information from one person to the next and ultimately from one group to other groups.

Digitas Inc., a Boston-based marketing company, has specialized in developing viral marketing programs for many Fortune 500 firms. When Johnson & Johnson approached Digitas to seek ways to get teenage girls to try its Clean & Clear skin care products, Digitas developed a viral marketing campaign for the firm. It created pop-up web ads that allowed teens to send a talking postcard to friends. The ads appeared on teen-oriented sites such as *www.bolt.com*. When teens clicked on the ad, they were connected to a web

site that allowed them to design an e-greeting card. Recipients of the greeting card were invited to click on a button called "What Products are Right for Your Skin" that provided information on the product and how to care for their skin (see Exhibit 16.1). The viral aspect was also reinforced by allowing recipients to, in turn, send an e-greeting card to other friends.[1]

The creative director of Digitas says that viral marketing is highly effective because friends can target messages much more effectively than marketers. "The idea is to get your constituency to do your marketing for you."[2] That is truly the power of word-of-mouth influence.

EXHIBIT 16.1

Johnson & Johnson's Clean & Clear web site.
Reprinted with permission.

The adage "a satisfied customer is your best salesperson" illustrates the importance of word of mouth to the marketer: Satisfied customers influence friends and relatives to buy; dissatisfied customers inhibit sales.

Word-of-Mouth Communication within Groups

As noted, personal influence is powerful because consumers generally regard friends and relatives as more credible and trustworthy than commercial sources of information. Moreover, information from reference and family groups is a means of reducing the risk in a purchase decision. Consumers who consider purchasing an expensive item such as a car or socially visible items such as clothing or furniture are likely to obtain the opinion of "relevant others." Such opinions not only provide information to reduce financial and performance risk, but they also serve as a means of group sanction to reduce social risk.

The importance of word of mouth is related to cultural values. In cultures dominated by group cohesion and adherence to group norms, communications from group members have more influence. In Chinese and Japanese cultures, adherence to group norms is ingrained from childhood. As a result, word of mouth is an even more important influence in these countries than it is in the United States.

THE NATURE OF WORD OF MOUTH

If marketers are to encourage positive word-of-mouth communication about their products, they must understand the

- types of word-of-mouth communication that occur.
- process by which word-of-mouth communication occurs.
- conditions for word-of-mouth communication.

▮ Types of Word-of-Mouth Communication   In a study investigating personal influence in buying autos, Richins and Root-Shaffer identified three types of word-of-mouth communications: product news, advice giving, and personal experience.[3] Using the example of cars, *product news* is information about the product, such as features of models, new advances in car technology, or performance attributes. *Advice giving* involves expressions of opinions about the car or advice about which model to buy. *Personal experience* relates to comments about the performance of the consumer's car or why the consumer bought it. Product news is fairly straightforward, but the advice and personal experience dimensions of word-of-mouth communication can be either positive or negative.

These categories suggest that word of mouth serves two functions: to inform and to influence. Product news informs consumers; advice and personal experience are likely to influence consumer decisions. As a result, each type of communication is probably most important at different stages in the purchasing decision. Product news is important as a means of developing awareness about product features or about a new product. Once awareness is established, hearing about product experiences from a friend or relative gives consumers the ability to judge the relative merits of one brand or another. Finally, advice is most important in making the final decision, because the opinion of a "relevant other" regarding a purchase is likely to be influential.

■ **The Process of Word-of-Mouth Communication**   The process of word-of-mouth communication has been described as a communication flow from those who are likely to influence others (**opinion leaders**) to those who are likely to be influenced (**followers**).

Two-Step Flow of Communication.   Katz and Lazarsfeld conducted one of the first studies establishing the importance of word-of-mouth communication in a small midwestern community shortly after World War II. They described it as a *two-step flow* from the mass media to opinion leaders and from opinion leaders to followers[4] (see the top of Figure 16.1). They believed that opinion leaders are more exposed to the mass media than are those whom they influence. As a result, opinion leaders are viewed as intermediaries between the mass media and other consumers. The majority of consumers—the followers—are viewed as passive recipients of information.

The principal contribution of the two-step flow theory is that it encouraged the view that personal influence, not advertising, was the principal means of communication and influence.

Multistep Flow of Communication.   Although the two-step flow model was important in understanding the process of personal influence, it was not an accurate representation of the flow of information and influence for three reasons:

1. *Followers are not passive.* They may initiate requests for information as well as listen to the unsolicited opinions of others.
2. *Those who transmit information are also likely to receive it;* that is, opinion leaders are also influenced by followers. Conversely, those who seek information are likely to give it. Word-of-mouth influence is frequently a two-directional flow between transmitter and receiver.

| **FIGURE 16.1** |

Two models of word-of-mouth communication.

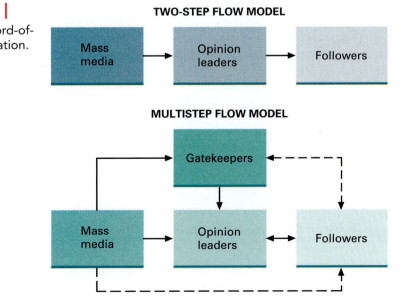

3. *Opinion leaders are not the only ones to receive information from the mass media.* Followers are also influenced by advertising. Moreover, opinion leaders may not control the flow of information from the mass media to the group. Katz and Lazarsfeld realized that there may be "gatekeepers" who serve this function.[5] **Gatekeepers** may be distinct from opinion leaders in that they introduce ideas and information to the group, but they may not influence it.

Researchers have also described **market mavens;** that is, individuals who are gatekeepers across many product categories because of their general expertise about places to shop, product characteristics, prices, and other marketing information.[6] Market mavens like helping others by providing information about the marketplace; but like gatekeepers, they may not necessarily be opinion leaders.

Because of the limitations in the concept of a two-step flow, a more realistic model of word-of-mouth communication is a *multistep flow,* represented at the bottom of Figure 16.1. In this model, the mass media can reach gatekeepers, opinion leaders, or followers directly, but they are less likely to reach the followers (as indicated by the dotted line). Gatekeepers, although represented as a source of information to both opinion leaders and followers, are more likely to disseminate information to opinion leaders. Furthermore, word-of-mouth communication between opinion leaders and followers is represented as a two-directional flow: Opinion leaders may seek information from followers, and followers may solicit information from opinion leaders.

▌ Negative Word-of-Mouth Communication

Word-of-mouth communication can be negative as well as positive. Negative word of mouth is more influential than positive word of mouth. If consumers are dissatisfied, they are three times more likely to communicate their experiences than if they are satisfied. If negative word of mouth is widespread, it can lead to negative diffusion of information—diffusion of information across groups that becomes widespread. Due to the multiplier effect, one person tells two or three others, who in turn tell two or three others, and so on. Negative word of mouth cuts across groups and often has a nationwide or worldwide effect.

Negative word of mouth can result in two ways: (1) by the communication of *direct experiences* such as poor product performance, lack of service, high prices, or rude sales personnel, and (2) by *rumors* about a product or company.

Direct Experience. Negative word-of-mouth information tends to be more powerful than positive information. As mentioned, when consumers are dissatisfied, they complain to approximately three times as many friends and relatives as when they are satisfied. Richins studied dissatisfied purchasers of clothing and appliances and found that over half engaged in negative word-of-mouth communication about their experiences.[7] Such negative communication was most likely when consumers

▌ viewed the problem as serious.
▌ placed the blame for dissatisfaction directly on the manufacturer or retailer.
▌ believed that complaining directly to the source would not do any good.

Most dissatisfied consumers do not complain about products to manufacturers or seek satisfaction by returning them. As a result, many companies conclude that their consumers are generally satisfied and that negative word of mouth is unlikely. This reaction effectively ignores the damaging effects of negative word-of-mouth communications. Other companies recognize that silence does not necessarily mean satisfaction. Companies such as Procter & Gamble, General Electric, and Whirlpool have encouraged consumers to provide product feedback through toll-free telephone numbers.

Rumors. A second type of negative word-of-mouth communication is false rumors about a company or product. Occasionally, false rumors have proved harmful to sales. One pervasive rumor held that Procter & Gamble was "in league with Satan," based on the company's 108-year-old logo—a man in the moon with thirteen stars. The problem was that the man in the moon's curly hair looked like an inverted 666, a number that has long been associated with Satan. The company withdrew the logo after a five-year effort, numerous court cases against rumor generators, and hundreds of thousands of dollars spent to dispel the rumor. In the late 1980s, P&G brought the logo back on four products only to have the rumors start afresh. By 1990, the company was reporting an average of 150 calls a day from consumers who wanted to know if the company had pledged its profits to the devil. In 1991, the company revised the logo by giving the man in the moon straighter hair. But that did not dispel the rumors. In 1995, P&G sued an independent Amway distributor for linking the company to a rumor that a large part of its profits go to support satanic churches and forwarding the rumor to other Amway distributors. In 2001, a federal appeals court revived the suit on the grounds that Amway communicated the rumors to help it take business away from P&G.[8]

Sometimes, advertisers try to combat rumors with advertising campaigns that attempt to set the record straight. Consumers may have misconceptions about a product or company, and marketers use advertising to combat this negative information. A good example was an ad by Norton Simon that countered the misperception among consumers that one of its companies, Hunt-Wesson, was owned by a rich Texas magnate called Hunt. The ad portrayed one consumer talking to another, who then talked to another, in a chain that conveyed the false rumor. The ad then dispelled the false rumor by identifying the true owner, the Norton Simon company, and the true company location, California.

In most cases, rumors eventually die. However, as we saw in the case of the P&G logo, they can be persistent. Entenmann's (actually owned by Warner-Lambert at the time) fought rumors that it was owned by the Reverend Sun Myung Moon's Unification Church with advertising, press conferences, and letters of denial.[9] A rumor that Tropical Fantasy, a low-priced soft drink, was owned by the Ku Klux Klan prompted an investigation by a state district attorney's office to determine if competitors were behind the rumors.[10]

▌ Conditions for Word-of-Mouth Communication Word-of-mouth communication is not the dominant factor in every situation. For instance, Herr, Kardes, and Kim found that word of mouth is not as important in the evaluation of an automobile if (1) consumers already have a strong impression of the product or (2) negative information regarding the product is available.[11] This means that word-of-mouth communication is unlikely to change consumers with strong positive or negative brand attitudes.

Word of mouth is also not dominant for every product category. It is most important when reference groups are likely to be sources of information and influence. Thus, word of mouth is most important when

- the product is visible, and therefore behavior is apparent.

- the product is distinctive and can easily be identified with style, taste, and other personal norms.

- the product has just been introduced, and consumers have not formed impressions and attitudes about it.

- the product is important to the reference group's norms and belief system (*e.g.,* teenagers' reactions to a new rock album or older consumers' reactions to a new salt-free breakfast product).

- consumers are involved in the purchase decision, and as a result are more likely to communicate about it and influence others.

- consumers see the purchase of the product as risky, and thus are more likely to initiate product-related conversations and to request information from friends and relatives.

STRATEGIC APPLICATIONS

Corona Succeeds Based on Word of Mouth

The importance of communications within and across groups is illustrated by Corona beer. Before the beer was imported to the United States, many residents of the Southwest brought it back from vacation in Mexico. This led Corona to import the beer—first to Austin, Texas, where it began to appear in bars, chili parlors, and Mexican restaurants. The beer's popularity quickly spread by *word of mouth.* The next market was San Diego, where surfers and beach people adopted the brand. From there, word spread up and down the California coast. That is, communications traveled across groups, illustrating a process of *diffusion.* The brand began moving east and won acceptance in Chicago, where it was most popular among yuppies. By 1984, sales had grown from three hundred thousand to 1.7 million cases on the strength of word of mouth within and across groups. All of this growth occurred on the basis of on-premises sales in bars and restaurants.

In 1987, as the brand began appearing in supermarkets, sales hit 13.7 million cases, making Corona the second largest-selling imported beer after Heineken. Limited advertising in select magazines began, but Corona planned no television advertising. By that time, Corona was being distributed on the eastern seaboard, where it once again relied on word of mouth, rather than advertising, for sales.

By the mid-1990s, Corona had surpassed Heineken as the leading import and began TV advertising. It even felt strong enough to buy advertising space during the Superbowl in 2000. The ultimate sign of success was Anheuser Busch's decision to roll out a brand, Tequiza, designed to compete directly with Corona.

Although Corona is now undertaking a traditional advertising strategy to maintain its market, company executives do not forget the genesis of success, word-of-mouth communications.

Sources: "Corona Beer Emerges as Key Model for U.S. Importers," *Wall Street Journal* (March 8, 2000), p. B4; "Gambrinus Sets Goal-Lime Stand in First Super Bowl Ads for Corona Beer," *Brandweek* (November 15, 1999), p. 9; "Olé," *Marketing & Media Decisions* (June 1987), pp. 95–98.

OF CONSUMER BEHAVIOR

WORD OF MOUTH ON THE WEB

Word-of-mouth communication on the Web is likely to be more influential in advertising than face-to-face interaction. For example, a study by Young & Rubicam, a large advertising agency, found that one person may influence the purchase behavior of two others through face-to-face communication, but online, one person influences eight others.

One reason for greater influence on the Web is that it is easier to communicate. It takes very little effort to send an email to family and friends or to post comments on a bulletin board or in a chatroom. Also, the Internet has immediacy because opinions can be expressed to a large circle of friends and acquaintances at the time they are formed. In addition, as we saw in Chapter 14, people are more likely to influence others on the Web because it provides anonymity. People may find it easier to express their concerns and opinions to strangers because they perceive less risk than in face-to-face interactions.

▮ The Multiplier Effect of the Web

As a result of the ease of communication and anonymity the Internet provides users, the Web has a major multiplier effect. One study found that 67 percent of online users are comfortable enough with the Internet to discuss their likes and dislikes with others. About 33 percent enjoy changing people's minds about issues and look for ways to influence others. And 71 percent say they listen carefully to the opinions of others. Only 19 percent worry that sharing opinions and advice online can cause trouble.[12]

The power of word of mouth on the Web can be evidenced in the success of Hotmail (the free email service provider), now owned by Microsoft. According to *Business 2.0,* the company spent less that $500,000 on a web-based marketing campaign that resulted in 12 million subscribers within eighteen months. Hotmail now signs up more than a hundred fifty thousand subscribers every day, making it the world's largest web-based email provider. Hotmail credits much of its success to the multiplier effect of subscriber word of mouth.[13]

▮ Viral Marketing

Recognition of the power of the multiplier effect on the Web has encouraged marketers to initiate viral marketing strategies. As a result, viral marketing is becoming more widely used. According to a 2000 Jupiter Research survey, 80 percent of web marketers surveyed said they incorporate some form of viral marketing strategies. The reason is its effectiveness. Eight out of ten people receiving viral marketing messages pass them on to at least one other person, and almost half are likely to pass them on to more than one person.[14]

Viral marketing is being implemented in a variety of ways.[15] First, firms are making it easier for users to tell others about their web sites. As we saw, Digitas creates pop-up ads that allow customers to send talking postcards about products to friends. Another tactic involves using "Tell a Friend" buttons to allow customers to recommend products or web pages via email to friends. Many companies get blind carbon copies of the Tell a Friend emails and can track how long it takes for the friends to visit the site and become customers. Blind carbon copies can create privacy concerns, however.[16] Another tactic is the use of web-based bookmarks. Backflip (*www.backflip.com*) gives visitors the ability to save files and set up folders where they can share the information obtained with friends.[17]

WEB APPLICATIONS

Negative Word of Mouth Can Get Nasty When Consumers Set Up Web Sites to Complain

Cybersurfers with a gripe are getting back at corporate America. Unlike registering a complaint on an existing web site like eComplaints for this purpose, they are creating their own sites with names like "Still looking for the softer side of Sears," and "US Worst," which lampoons US West. Hundreds of these sites have sprung up. They are an effective means of word of mouth because, as the *Wall Street Journal* reports, "Circulation of complaints on the Internet is global, instantaneous and cheap." But the paper goes on to say that "People with a gripe can be unfair, nasty, and even libelous."

As an example of the power of the Web, one disgruntled Allstate customer set up a site called "You're in Bad Hands With Allstate," which drew seventeen hundred visitors in three weeks and five thousand visitors in all. But Allstate continues to deny her claim for losses from a burglary. The company is aware of the web site but

explains that state regulators reviewed the case twice and declined to intervene. The web site, sporting a sign "Cyber Vigilante," has other Allstate horror stories and was set up through Yahoo's Geo Cities facility that allows its customers to establish sites.

In another case, a customer unhappy with Comcast's Internet service set up a site called "Comcast@Home Sucks." In this case, the consumer got results. Comcast made a number of service calls to correct the problem, and the user even had a breakfast meeting with the general manager. But if problems resurface, the consumer will have no problems reinstituting the site.

Corporate America, beware. Angry consumers can exert a fair amount of clout on the Web.

Source: "Cranky Consumers Devise Web Sites to Air Complaints," *Wall Street Journal* (January 2002), pp. B1, B11.

OF CONSUMER BEHAVIOR

■ **Negative Word of Mouth on the Web**   Some web sites are designed to spread negative word-of-mouth communications. For instance, Yahoo has a category called "Consumer Opinion" that links to sites blasting more than eighty companies. There is also a host of web sites that allow consumers to air their complaints against companies. For instance, eComplaints.com has billed itself as "Your chance to fight back." According to Jennifer Biscoe, the founder of eComplaints, for every person who writes a complaint on a web site, at least ten others read it. At *www.fightback.com,* set up by a consumer advocate, users pay $50 for the site personnel to write to companies on their behalf and to follow up if necessary.[18]

OPINION LEADERSHIP

The influence of word-of-mouth communication in consumer behavior is tied closely to the concept of opinion leadership. As we saw earlier, individuals most likely to influence others through word of mouth are opinion leaders; and individuals most likely to be influenced are followers.

■ **The Nature of Opinion Leadership**   The marketer must answer two questions before directing appeals to opinion leaders or attempting to stimulate positive word-of-mouth communication:

1. Is there a general opinion leader, or is opinion leadership specific to particular product categories?
2. Is opinion leadership really leadership?

Is There a General Opinion Leader? Most studies have found that there is no general opinion leader. Instead, *opinion leadership is product-specific.* That is, an opinion leader for one category is not likely to be influential across unrelated categories.

Although most studies suggest that a general opinion leader does not exist, three categories of consumers do suggest generalized influence across product categories: influentials, market mavens, and surrogate consumers.

■ *Influentials.* The Roper Organization, a well-known market research firm, has conducted yearly surveys since World War II to identify influentials.[19] **Influentials** are defined as those individuals who are active in community and public affairs. For example, three-fourths have attended town meetings, compared with less than 20 percent of the general population; one-half have attended a political rally and one-third have made a speech, compared with less than 10 percent of the general population.

Influentials tend to be upscale, well educated, and well read. They are much more likely to be asked their opinions about products and services that depend on word-of-mouth recommendations, such as restaurants, books, movies, and financial services. Influentials also tend to buy new products when they are first marketed. They were among the first to buy cell phones and to have Internet access. Overall, it is clear that influentials come close to being general opinion leaders. However, they are not influential in every product category.

■ *Market Mavens.* **Market mavens** come closer to being general gatekeepers than opinion leaders. Feick and Price found that a market maven has "information on many kinds of products, places to shop, and other facets of markets, and initiates discussions with consumers and responds to requests from consumers for market information."[20]

Although market mavens are not necessarily opinion leaders, they are likely to influence as well as to inform. They are good targets for product information—messages about product changes, prices, and new products—because they are likely to pass on this information.

■ *Surrogate Consumers.* A **surrogate consumer** is "an agent retained by a consumer to guide, direct, and/or transact marketplace activities."[21] Surrogates can play a wide range of roles, such as tax consultants, wine stewards, interior decorators, or financial managers. Their degree of influence varies; but in many cases, they are asked to assume the decision role for consumers. As such, they are not general opinion leaders but are clearly opinion leaders in their surrogate role.

Consumers use surrogates because they may not have the time, inclination, or expertise to go through information search and decision making. Also, consumers can use surrogates to narrow their choices, to collect information, or to make the actual purchase decision.

Is Opinion Leadership Really Leadership? A number of studies have consistently found that individuals who transmit information to others are also more likely to receive information from others. That is, a consumer who frequently expresses opinions about sports equipment is also more likely to listen to others' opinions about such equipment. A study of the adopters of stainless steel razor blades when they were first introduced found that 75 percent of opinion leaders were also influenced by others.[22] A study of women's influence in four product categories found that 80 percent of the influencers also received information from others.[23]

These findings suggest that the key element in face-to-face influence is not leadership but social communication. Those who are most likely to do the influencing are also most likely to be influenced. Therefore, individuals who transmit information and influence about a product do not have to be group leaders. Opinion leaders do not dominate others or communicate in a one-sided way. Communication occurs both ways between transmitter and receiver. As a result, an alternative way to view the two-way exchange in word-of-mouth communications is as communication between an "opinion giver" and an "opinion receiver."

▊ Characteristics of the Opinion Leader

Some general traits have been associated with opinion leaders. Opinion leaders are likely to[24]

- ▊ be knowledgeable about the product category.
- ▊ be involved in the product category.
- ▊ be active in receiving communications about the product from personal sources.
- ▊ be interested in new products.
- ▊ read magazines and other print media relevant to their area of product interest.
- ▊ be self-confident in their appraisal of the product category.
- ▊ be socially active, reflecting their willingness to communicate with others.

Few demographic and lifestyle characteristics have been found to identify opinion leaders. As a result, a strategy of trying to pinpoint opinion leaders and reach them through specific media is likely to fail. These findings do not mean that the study of word-of-mouth communication provides the marketer with few strategic applications. Rather, they suggest that strategic applications are best directed to stimulating word-of-mouth communication through advertising or through some direct identification of opinion leaders.

▊ Opinion Leaders Online: The E-fluentials

Studies have identified a group of opinion leaders online who have "exponential influence shaping and driving public opinion through the Internet."[25] Designated as "e-fluentials," this group is much more active than other Internet users in using email, bulletin boards, chatrooms, and other online vehicles to convey their messages.

Representing 8 percent of the Internet population, about 9 million users, this group influences more people on more topics than other online users.[26] E-fluentials make waves, projecting their opinions far beyond the scope of their individual contacts. They are three times as likely as the typical online user to be asked for advice online.[27] Further, they communicate with more people online, regularly emailing twice as many people as the general online population. They also absorb more information than general Internet users and glean it from a more diverse array of sources. Seventy-two percent have visited company web sites versus only 41 percent of the general online population.

Strategic Applications of Word-of-Mouth Communication

Marketers try to influence word-of-mouth communication among consumers in various ways. They can try to

▮ stimulate word of mouth through free product trials.

▮ stimulate word of mouth in advertising by suggesting that consumers tell friends about the product or service.

▮ simulate word of mouth through advertising showing typical consumers saying positive things about the product.

▮ portray communications from opinion leaders.

In this section, we consider each of these strategies.

STIMULATING WORD OF MOUTH THROUGH PRODUCT TRIAL

Companies can try to stimulate word-of-mouth communication by offering products for trial. Such strategies are generally targeted to opinion leaders. If successful, product trial should stimulate a social multiplier effect, because these individuals would disseminate information and exert a disproportionate amount of influence on friends and relatives.

When Ford introduced its subcompact Focus model in 2001, it recruited 120 young trendsetters in five key markets and gave them a Focus to drive around for six months. The purpose was to be seen with the car and to hand out Focus-themed trinkets to those who expressed interest. As one Ford executive said, "We were looking for the assistants to celebrities—party planners, disk jockeys—the people who really seemed to influence what was cool."[28] Ford was counting on a multiplier effect from these 120 individuals as word of mouth was generated.

How can marketers identify such opinion leaders? Three approaches have frequently been used. First, because of the close relationship between opinion leadership and new product adoption, it is possible to identify consumers who are among the first to adopt a new appliance or other product with a purchase record and assume that these individuals are opinion leaders. A second approach is to identify influentials based on their community activities. Third, opinion leaders can be identified by social status, as in the Ford example.

STIMULATING WORD OF MOUTH THROUGH ADVERTISING AND PROMOTION

Advertisers can try to encourage consumers to talk about the product. One approach is to encourage consumers to "tell your friends" or to "ask your friends." The Acme Supermarket Chain advertised, "Tell a friend. Save at Acme." Commercials for Fabergé Organics shampoo urged users to tell two friends so they would tell two friends and so on as the faces on the screen multiplied to show the spread of word of mouth. For such strategies to work, the product must be in a strong position and word-of-mouth communication must be positive.

Another approach is to organize events to stimulate word of mouth. Harley-Davidson holds family-oriented events to get Harley owners together. Similarly, off-road-vehicle manufacturers like Jeep, Isuzu, and Land Rover hold jamborees to stimulate word of mouth. Jeep has been sponsoring these events for more than forty years. One Jeep executive says, "Our best endorsement is word of mouth. A Jamboree makes for good cocktail talk. That just reinforces the Jeep name."[29]

SIMULATING WORD-OF-MOUTH COMMUNICATION

By portraying recommendations from typical consumers, advertising can simulate word-of-mouth communication. In portraying personal influence, these ads seek to simulate direct contact by consumers with friends and relatives. The assumption is that the typical person in the ad is credible enough to convince consumers to believe the information this individual provides.

General Motors built its first advertising campaign for Saturn cars around word-of-mouth communication. When it introduced Saturn in 1991, GM received unsolicited letters from satisfied customers. These letters were then routed to the company's advertising agency and used in print ads. Saturn's president provided the rationale for simulating word of mouth as follows: "We want the actual owners to tell their stories. . . . The ads are just like listening to other people, like your neighbors, tell you about their new car."[30] Another example is the ad in Exhibit 16.2. This ad encourages women to engage in word-of-mouth communication to "tell your friends about breast cancer." The ad suggests that women remind their loved ones that they can prevent breast cancer by getting regular mammograms and medical exams. The ad not only serves to remind women that there are ways to prevent breast cancer, but it also suggests that they should spread the word to the people they care about.

EXHIBIT 16.2

Simulating word-of-mouth influence.

Reprinted with permission of The American Cancer Society.

PORTRAYING COMMUNICATIONS FROM OPINION LEADERS

Another strategy related to simulating word of mouth is to portray communications from opinion leaders that influence followers. For example, at one time an ad for Vaniqa showed an opinion leader for pharmaceuticals, a laser surgeon, discussing with three typical consumers the benefits of Vaniqa for removing unwanted facial hair.

Companies occasionally attempt to discourage and discredit certain types of word-of-mouth communication. Schering has used advertising to encourage consumers to rely on pharmacists, rather than on friends or neighbors, for information about medication. By depicting inaccurate sources of information, Schering's ad in Exhibit 16.3 attempts to discredit nonexpert medical advice.

EXHIBIT 16.3

An ad portraying credible and noncredible opinion leaders.

Courtesy of Schering Corporation.

The Diffusion Process

In this section, emphasis is shifted from communications within groups to communications across groups that occur through the diffusion of information and influence over a wider segment of society. Research on word of mouth and opinion leadership views communications on a *micro* level because they take place among a small number of individuals. In contrast, research on the process of diffusion views communications on a *macro* level because communications and product ownership are traced across a large number of individuals over time.

The process of diffusion is shown in American consumers' rapid acceptance of VCRs and their rejection of videodiscs in the early 1980s. Videocassette recorders won quick acceptance because they provided an important benefit, recording capability. Furthermore, consumers could observe VCRs in use, and VCRs were compatible with frequent TV viewing. Diffusion theory predicts that innovations with these characteristics—obvious benefits, observability, compatibility with past

| FIGURE 16.2 |

Distribution of adopter categories.

Source: Reprinted with the permission of The Free Press, an imprint of Simon & Shuster Adult Publishing group, from *Diffusion of Innovations,* Fourth Edition by Everett M. Rogers. Copyright © 1962, 1971, 1983 by The Free Press.

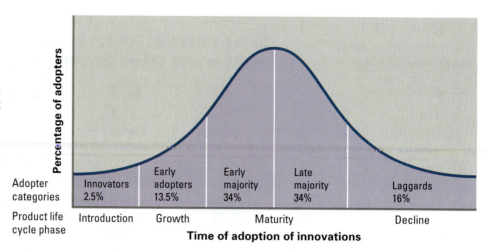

DIFFUSION RESEARCH AND MARKETING STRATEGY

usage—would be successful. Videodiscs, however, although they were observable and compatible with current TV usage, did not produce any obvious benefit compared with VCRs because of their lack of recording capabilities. As a result, RCA lost hundreds of millions of dollars when its videodisc entry, SelectaVision, failed.

Diffusion research traces the spread of product acceptance across its life cycle. Figure 16.2 shows the phases of the product life cycle from introduction to decline and the associated categories of product adopters by time of adoption. The diffusion process identifies innovators in the introductory period of the life cycle, early adopters during growth, the majority of adopters during the mature phase, and laggards (late adopters) during decline. These phases of adoption are important because they are linked to different marketing strategies during the product life cycle. In the introductory phase, the firm tries to establish distribution, build brand awareness, and encourage trial to begin the diffusion process. As the product takes hold and enters the growth phase, the firm can define its primary target, the early adopters. It tries to reinforce the toehold it has in the market by moving from an objective of creating awareness to one of broadening product appeals and product availability.

As the brand matures, competition intensifies and sales begin to level off. The firm starts to emphasize price appeals and sales promotions and begins to consider some product modifications to gain a competitive advantage. At this stage, the majority of adopters enter the market, based largely on the influence of the early adopters. Since others have already gone through an adoption process, the majority do not need to rely as much on the mass media for information. When the brand is in the decline phase, lower prices become more prevalent. The firm begins to consider either revitalizing the brand or deleting it. At this point, late adopters enter the market.

Because diffusion research traces the rate of acceptance of new products and identifies adopter categories by stages in the product's life cycle, it is directly tied to these strategic shifts.

STEPS IN THE DIFFUSION PROCESS

As we have seen, the diffusion process encourages communication regarding a product to the community as a whole. **Diffusion** is the process by which the *adoption* of an innovation or idea spreads *over time* to other consumer groups through *communications.* Suppose a consumer bought a DVD player soon after it was introduced. Through word of mouth, the consumer tells friends and relatives that the DVD provides finer visuals and sound and is easy to use. Others in the consumer's reference group buy. These individuals are regarded as early adopters. Over time, they begin to communicate positive experiences with DVDs, not only to members of their reference group, but also to other groups as well—casual acquaintances, members of sports clubs, and business associates with whom they have infrequent contact. At this point, diffusion begins to spread rapidly. The characteristics of these adopters differ from those of earlier adopters, which means that the target for DVDs differed in the earlier stages of adoption than it does now.

Based on this description, an understanding of the diffusion process in marketing requires an understanding of (1) the nature of *adoption,* (2) the *time* of adoption (earlier or later,) and (3) *communication* across groups. Most of the rest of this chapter is devoted to these three elements of diffusion.

▌ The Adoption Decision   The adoption of an innovation requires an individual or a group of consumers to make a decision regarding a new product. If adopters influence others to buy, both within their reference group and across groups, a diffusion process starts. Therefore, it is logical to think of adoption as the first step in the diffusion process.

The adoption of an innovation is likely to be an involving decision to those who are among the first to adopt. The steps of the adoption process are shown on the left in Figure 16.3 and reflect the high-involvement hierarchy of effects described in Chapter 4. These steps parallel those in the process of complex decision making, which are shown on the right in Figure 16.3. The consumer

- becomes *aware* of and recognizes a need for the product,
- searches for information (*knowledge* acquisition),
- *evaluates* the alternatives,
- decides whether to try it before making a decision (*trial*),
- makes a decision whether to *adopt* or not, and
- *evaluates* the product after the purchase.

Three components of this process should be emphasized in understanding diffusion. First, product trial is more important than in most other decisions because the product is new and risk is likely to be higher.

Second, postpurchase evaluation is likely to be more important for innovations because of their expense and complexity and the rapid pace of technological change. Many personal

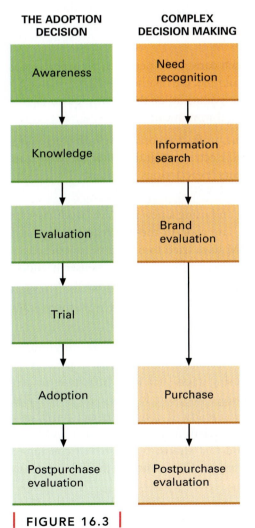

THE ADOPTION DECISION

Awareness → Knowledge → Evaluation → Trial → Adoption → Postpurchase evaluation

COMPLEX DECISION MAKING

Need recognition → Information search → Brand evaluation → Purchase → Postpurchase evaluation

▌ FIGURE 16.3 ▌

Steps in the adoption process.

computer owners have already purchased their third or fourth machines to keep up with improved speed, capacity, and software. If many of these consumers had discontinued the use of PCs because of the complexity of use or dissatisfaction with their first purchase, the PC market would never have expanded to the degree it has.

Third, the outcome of the decision process can be rejection as well as adoption. A high rate of rejection could mean failure, as was the case with consumer rejection of RCA's videodiscs. Or rejection could mean a slow rate of adoption, as is the case with the use of solar energy panels to heat homes.

The stages in adoption in Figure 16.3 are important to the marketer because they indicate the acceptance of the product and the effect of a promotional campaign based on answers to the following questions: To what degree is the public aware of the new innovation? Is the public's information accurate? What are consumers' attitudes toward the innovation? What is the likelihood of trial and subsequent adoption? Are consumers satisfied after adopting the innovation?

Characteristics That Encourage Adoption. The likelihood of adoption and subsequent diffusion of a new product depend on the nature of the product. Rogers and Shoemaker identified the following five characteristics that increase the rate of acceptance and diffusion of a new product.[31]

1. *Relative advantage* is the degree to which consumers perceive a new product as superior to existing substitutes—for example, the relative advantage of an electric car in saving money and reducing pollution, or the relative advantage of cellular telephones in providing mobile communications.

2. *Compatibility* is the degree to which the product is consistent with consumers' needs, attitudes, and past experiences. If electric cars and cellular telephones are not markedly different from consumers' expectations regarding driving and phone usage, they are compatible.

3. *Simplicity* is the ease in understanding and using a new product. Products such as electric toothbrushes, instant foods, and cook-in-the-bag vegetables are easy to understand and use. Apple and IBM have tried to overcome any perceived complexity of using computers by advertising their machines as user-friendly.

4. *Observability* is the ease with which the product can be observed and communicated to potential consumers. Products that are highly visible are more easily diffused. Fashion items and cars are good examples.

5. *Trialability* is the degree to which a product can be tried before adoption. As noted, many innovations have little trialability. Limited trial is possible by demonstrations in showrooms or by using items such as fax machines or personal computers at work and determining if adoption for home use is desirable. An element related to trialability is *divisibility.* If consumers can purchase a product in small quantities, then trial is relatively easy. Shoemaker and Shoaf studied five packaged goods and found that almost two-thirds of consumers made trial purchases of new brands in smaller quantities than they usually purchased.[32]

Characteristics That Encourage Rejection. The negative side of each of the five factors cited in the previous section could cause consumers to reject an innovation. Ram and Sheth considered these factors in citing three major barriers to adopting an innovation: value barrier, usage barrier, and risk barrier.[33]

■ *Value barrier.* The **value barrier** is a product's lack of relative advantage compared with substitute products. When first introduced, cellular telephones cost about $2,000 per unit. They were accepted in business markets because the advantage of mobile communications was worth the cost. However, the cost was too high for most consumers relative to the value they could get from regular telephones.

Manufacturers can overcome the value barrier in two ways. First, they can reduce the price through technological advances. Costs of cellular phones have decreased to bring the value of mobile communications into line with price for most consumers. The primary issue now is not the cost of the phone but the cost of monthly cellular service charges. Second, manufacturers can convey information to consumers through advertising to convince them of the product's value. One of IBM's initial advantages in the PC market was its ability to convey the value of PCs to small business owners who doubted the worth of PCs relative to their cost.

■ *Usage barrier.* A **usage barrier** occurs when an item is not compatible with consumers' existing practices or habits. Systems that offer interactive in-home shopping and banking services by computer have encountered stiff resistance from consumers. For example, Sears poured millions of dollars into its Prodigy system, a precursor of the Internet in an effort to convince a doubting public to accept the innovation. The problem was that consumers like to interact with store personnel and to see the merchandise when they shop. The exact same problem occurred when department stores such as Nordstrom and Bloomingdale's established web sites. Purchasing on the Web never met expectations because shopping is often a social occasion for many consumers who shop with friends. For these consumers, shopping on the Web is not compatible with their desire for the visual and social stimuli of shopping.

■ *Risk barrier.* A **risk barrier** represents consumers' physical, economic, performance, or social risk of adopting an innovation. Adopters of home computers had fears of economic and performance risks, which were largely overcome by decreasing prices and improved software.

One of the most effective ways to reduce consumer risk in adopting an innovation is through trial. Free samples are an effective tool for continuous innovations such as tartar control toothpaste. Car manufacturers offer a form of trial with test rides for new models. Software companies sometimes promote free trial to opinion leaders in organizations and universities in the hope that adoption will lead to more widespread acceptance.

■ **Time** Time is a key component of diffusion theory, based on two measures: (1) the time of adoption by consumers (whether consumers are earlier or later adopters of the innovation) and (2) the rate of diffusion (the speed and extent with which adoption takes place across groups).

Time of Adoption. Rogers developed a classification of adopters by time of adoption. Examining more than five hundred studies of diffusion, he concluded that there are five categories of adopters, as shown earlier in Figure 16.2: (1) innovators, (2) early adopters, (3) the early majority, (4) the late majority, and (5) laggards.[34] Using past research, Rogers determined that these categories follow a normal distribution. Rogers described each adopter category as follows:[35]

1. **Innovators** represent on average the first 2.5 percent of all those who adopt. They are almost obsessed in their eagerness to try new ideas and products. They have higher incomes, are better educated, are more cosmopolitan, and are more active outside of their community than noninnovators. In addition, they are less reliant on group norms, more self-confident, and more likely to obtain their information from scientific sources and experts.

2. **Early adopters** represent on average the next 13.5 percent to adopt the product. Although they are not the very first, they adopt early in the product's life cycle. More reliant on group norms and values than innovators, they are also more oriented to the local community, in contrast to the innovators' cosmopolitan outlook. Early adopters are most likely to be opinion leaders because of their closer affiliation to groups. Because they are more likely to transmit word-of-mouth influence, early adopters are probably the most important group in determining whether the new product is successful.

3. The **early majority** (next 34 percent to adopt) deliberates carefully before adopting a new product. People in the early majority are likely to collect more information and evaluate more brands than early adopters do; therefore, the process of adoption takes longer. The early majority is an important link in the process of diffusing new ideas, as it is positioned between earlier and later adopters.

4. Rogers describes the **late majority** (next 34 percent to adopt) as skeptical. They adopt because most of their friends have already done so. Since they also rely on group norms, adoption is the result of pressure to conform. This group tends to be older and below average in income and education.

5. **Laggards** are the final 16 percent to adopt. They are similar to innovators in not relying on the group's norms. Independent because they are tradition bound, laggards make decisions in terms of the past. By the time laggards adopt an innovation, it has probably been superseded by something else. They purchased their first television set when color television was already widely owned, and many do not own a computer. Laggards have the lowest socioeconomic status. They tend to be suspicious of new products and alienated from a technologically advancing society.

The Adoption Curve.   Figure 16.4 shows the adoption curve for black-and-white and color TV sets and for Internet usage. Both black-and-white and color TVs went from 0 to 50 percent adoption by U.S. households in their first seven and ten years, respectively. Although the curve for Internet adoption is flatter because of a shorter time period, the adoption rate is actually faster—over 50 percent adoption in the first six years.[36] If Internet usage follows the same adoption curve as color TV, we can expect close to 100 percent adoption by 2025. If a new technology begins to replace the Internet, the adoption curve may look more like black-and-white TVs, and usage may begin to decline well before 2025.

| FIGURE 16.4 |

Product life cycles for TV and Internet usage.

Source: Reprinted with permission of the *Wall Street Journal.*

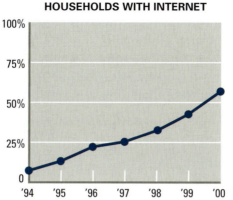

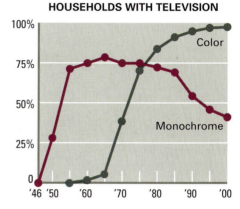

| FIGURE 16.5 |

Variations from the normal adoption curve.

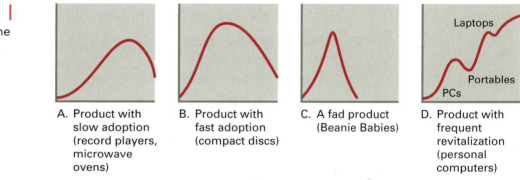

A. Product with slow adoption (record players, microwave ovens)

B. Product with fast adoption (compact discs)

C. A fad product (Beanie Babies)

D. Product with frequent revitalization (personal computers)

Figure 16.2 shows adoption based on Rogers's scheme as a normal bell-shaped curve. But as the curve for black-and-white TV shows in Figure 16.4, adoption curves can take different shapes. The nature of the adoption curve may vary depending on the type of product. Figure 16.5 illustrates some of the more common variations from the normal curve.

The first curve shows a product that has a long introduction stage because consumers adopt it slowly. This is typical of a major innovation. In this case, fewer individuals adopt early but more do in the late majority and laggard categories. The life cycle for record albums, for example, was gradual because their adoption was tied to ownership of a record player; and it took at least twenty years for record players to achieve widespread adoption. The second curve is an innovation with a fast adoption rate and a short introductory stage. Adoption of compact discs was more rapid in a more technologically sophisticated and affluent society.

The third curve in Figure 16.5 is a fad product with a rapid rise and a rapid decline. The adoption of Beanie Babies, beanbag creatures with names like Bones the Dog, caught on rapidly in 1996. The strategy for the frequently out-of-stock fad product was to create deliberate scarcity "which pumps up word-of-mouth demand to a frenzied level."[37] But the creators also knew that demand was likely to be short-lived.

The fourth curve shows a product that has been frequently revitalized, going through periods of decline and subsequent growth. Such products go through phases of technological improvements, requiring adoption of new technology at each phase. Personal computers are an example. The curve shows adoption in three phases, the first when PCs were introduced, then the introduction of portable computers, and then laptops.

Rate of Diffusion. The speed of adoption of innovations seems to be increasing, as reflected by Internet usage. Why are innovations being adopted more rapidly?

■ Disposable income among U.S. households is increasing, making new products more affordable.

■ Technological advances are more rapid, requiring quicker adoption cycles.

■ Technology is becoming more standardized, reducing consumers' risk of adopting a new product. The rate of diffusion for PCs was fairly rapid because of acceptance of DOS and then Windows as the industrywide standard operating system.

■ Information is being communicated quickly. The more rapidly people learn about a new product through the mass media and the Internet, the more rapid communication is within and across groups.

■ Communication in the Diffusion Process Communication is the last key element in the definition of diffusion. Diffusion requires the spread of information *across* groups. But how is this to occur if personal influence takes place primarily within a consumer's own peer group? It happens because consumers spread the word by interacting with individuals outside their personal networks.

Groups outside an individual's personal network are known as **heterophilous;** peer and family groups are **homophilous.**[38] Individuals within heterophilous groups are dissimilar, and ties holding them together are weak; individuals within homophilous groups tend to be similar and are bonded by stronger reference-group ties. Associates at higher or lower levels in an organization or individuals with whom the consumer has occasional contact, such as tennis partners or carpool riders, are examples of members of heterophilous groups.

Consumers often spread the word about new products and ideas to passing acquaintances in heterophilous groups. This process has come to be known as *the strength of weak ties* because the weak ties of heterophilous groups are strong enough to fuel the process of diffusion.

Brown and Reingen showed the importance of communication to weaker groups in a study of the adoption of a personal service. They found that most word of mouth occurred among friends and relatives in homophilous groups. Word of mouth in heterophilous groups (weak ties) occurred in only 18 percent of communications among people.[39] When these weak ties did occur, however, they were very likely to be bridges across groups in communicating about the service.

Trickle Up and Trickle Down. One of the basic questions in analyzing communications across groups is how information and influence travel from one socioeconomic group to another.

The transmission of influence between socioeconomic groups can be described as a **trickle-down process** from higher to lower groups (as with the diffusion of fashion items such as Izod alligator shirts) and a **trickle-up process** from lower to higher groups (as with the diffusion of jeans and rock music). Traditionally, the view has been that diffusion occurs in a trickle-down manner. Two famous sociologists, Thorstein Veblen[40] and George Simmel,[41] stated this view. Both believed that the upper classes bought primarily for status and ostentation ("conspicuous consumption") and that lower-quality duplicates of these products were then made for the lower classes (*e.g.,* knockoffs of Rolex watches or Gucci handbags and scarves). Communication and influence moved from one class down to the next in the social hierarchy.

The transmission of influence occurs occasionally in a trickle-up direction, however. For example, innovators and early adopters of jeans and of bluegrass and rock music were those in lower socioeconomic classes who did not feel the need to conform to the norms of the dominant culture. They were free to innovate in the areas of clothing and music. Known as **grassroots innovators,** these individuals then disseminated their tastes to higher social classes. For example, African-American mule drivers working the coal mines of Appalachia created bluegrass music by fusing their instrumentation with white Appalachian music.[42] As the lower socioeconomic groups adopted bluegrass, it also began to be disseminated to a wider public through concerts, radio, and finally TV. The innovators and early adopters clearly were not the cosmopolitan, upscale consumers associated with early adopters. Studies that describe early adopters of many innovations as upscale are reported in the next section. However, it is important to recognize that early adopters can emerge in any segment of society, depending on the innovation.

Trickle Across.   The trickle-down and trickle-up processes show that early adoption of an innovation can go in either direction on the social scale. Marketers have come to question whether social status is as relevant as it used to be in defining the transmission of influence, up or down. The views of Veblen and Simmel espousing a trickle-down effect were expressed at the turn of the century, a time when class distinctions were much sharper than they are today. The post–World War II period produced a leveling effect in socioeconomic status, making trickle-down and trickle-up effects less relevant. Moreover, the mass media has come to communicate rapidly information on innovations to all classes. A more likely process of diffusion is one that occurs across groups, regardless of socioeconomic status, known as a **trickle-across effect.**

King's study of fashion adoption in the Boston area over thirty years ago illustrates this leveling effect. King found that early buyers of new fashions were not the upper-crust elite. Almost two-thirds were middle class or lower. Moreover, there was no evidence that communications went from individuals of a higher social class to those of a lower class. Four-fifths of respondents were influenced by members of their own social class. Explaining these results, King stated, "The traditional upper-class fashion leader directing the lower levels is largely short-circuited in the communication process. Within hours after the exclusive Paris and American designers' showings, the season's styles have been passed to the mass audiences via newspaper and television."[43]

King's study tends to confirm a trickle-across, rather than a trickle-down, effect in the diffusion of fashion styles. King's ideas closely conform to the social multiplier effect. That is, individuals are more likely to come into contact with new products and ideas because of the leveling of social status in American society; as a result, influence travels in a lateral fashion across markets. A trickle-down effect is much more marked in countries with sharp social class distinctions. In the United States, it is more likely that a trickle of information and influence across groups will result in the diffusion of new products.

THE DIFFUSION OF INTERNET USAGE

In January 1993, most Americans outside of government and academic circles were completely unaware of the Internet. Fewer than ninety thousand people worldwide used the Internet at that time. By 2000, there were more than 300 million users. Current predictions estimate that Internet users could exceed the 1 billion mark by 2005.[44]

Internet usage varies significantly by country. In the United States, over 60 percent of households have Internet access, representing over 150 million users.[45] Europe has more than 83 million users, with penetration rates varying from a high of over 60 percent in Finland and Sweden to a low of 6 percent in Portugal.

The Asian-Pacific region is third in Internet growth, currently boasting approximately 70 million Internet users. Japan leads the region in most aspects of Internet growth, including user growth and e-commerce. Although Internet usage is low in the developing world, it is growing at a much faster rate than expected. Despite problems with telecommunications infrastructure and poverty, officials and business owners in these countries understand the advantages of Internet access and e-commerce. As the cost of computers and Internet access continues to drop, penetration rates and e-commerce ventures will significantly rise.[46]

■ Characteristics Encouraging Diffusion of the Internet   The Web has characteristics that encourage Internet diffusion. We next consider how each of Rogers and Shoemaker's five characteristics, described earlier, influence the rate of diffusion.

The most important driver of diffusion of the Web is *relative advantage*. The Web has provided more widespread access to information than ever before and a more effective means to communicate information, opinions, and preferences. In so doing, the Web has provided consumers with time utility in being able to obtain and deliver information and communications from home or office. It has also delivered place utility. Prior to the Internet, people had to go to the library to do research, write letters or memos to friends and business associates to communicate, go to the mall or store to shop, drive from location to location to get product information, and so on. The Internet saves people time and energy by providing a faster means with which to obtain and share information.

The level of *compatibility* might have initially slowed the diffusion rate of the Web, because at first, it was regarded by many as unique and intimidating. Over time, people have adapted to the means to gain Web access, surf various web sites, and use search engines. Today, the Internet is becoming an essential part of every classroom; students at all levels of education utilize it to do research and participate in a variety of online educational activities. This means that children are being raised to view the Web as an everyday tool that is as simple to use as opening a book.

Simplicity in using the Internet has increased as it has become more user-friendly. Companies like Netscape and AOL have simplified Internet access, and search engines like *www.google.com* have simplified the process of information search. This has also helped speed diffusion of the Web.

Web usage is easily *observable* because it is so highly visible in the classroom or office. This visibility has accelerated the multiplier effect. Nonusers become users by observing friends and associates gaining the advantages of the Web. The network of usage spreads more easily as a result. The Web also facilitates *trialability.* One can easily access the Web in most organizations or can try it in friends' homes. Web access companies such as AOL provide trial by offering free hours of access.

Greater access to and ease of using the Web have reduced *value, usage,* and *risk barriers* that existed initially. Value barriers have declined as the costs of computers and of Internet access have decreased. Usage barriers have declined as web connections have become faster and surfing has become simpler. Risk barriers have declined as consumers have become more knowledgeable in the use of the Web, reducing psychological risk, and as web features have become more standardized and reliable, reducing performance risk.

■ **The Diffusion of Products and Ideas on the Internet**   Not only is Internet usage being diffused rapidly, but the Internet also serves as a vehicle for diffusing influence and information about other products and innovations. Information on the Web is most likely to speed across groups, whereas face-to-face information is more likely to be confined within groups. This is because group ties on the Web are likely to be weaker than in face-to-face groups. As noted, the weaker the ties in the group, the more likely that information will diffuse across different groups. Because ties are weaker on the Internet, people are more likely to communicate across social-class lines. In addition, the Web produces more linkages compared with face-to-face communication. As a result, the Web promotes both positive and negative diffusion.

THE CULTURAL CONTEXT OF DIFFUSION

Cultural norms often determine the acceptance of new products and the rate of diffusion. Consumers reject many new product innovations because they contradict cultural norms. This was the reason that prepared baby foods were rejected in Brazil and that condensed soups had a hard time winning acceptance in England. Brazilian mothers insisted on giving their babies homemade, rather than prepared, foods; English consumers equated quality in canned soups with hefty soups in larger cans.

Two concepts that help us understand the diffusion of innovations in different cultures are **cultural context** and **cultural homogeneity.** Hall introduced the concept of cultural context by dividing cultures into two groups: those that rely primarily on verbal and written communication to transmit meaning (*low-context cultures*) and those that rely primarily on nonverbal communication such as signs, expressions, and implicit understandings (*high-context cultures*).[47] The concept of homophilous and heterophilous groups can also be extended to cultures by identifying uniform cultures with little difference in norms, values, and socioeconomic status among groups (homophilous), versus more disparate cultures with wider differences among groups (heterophilous).[48]

High-context cultures, those that place more emphasis on nonwritten communications, tend to be more homophilous. Such cultures place more value on interpersonal contacts and associations. They put more value on the group than on the individual, and they emphasize subscribing to the norms and long-standing rituals of society. Low-context cultures, those that depend more on verbal and written communications, place more value on individual initiative and rely more on the mass media for communication. Most Far Eastern countries can be described as high context/homophilous, whereas the United States and Western Europe can be described as low context/heterophilous.

The rate of diffusion is expected to be faster in high-context/homophilous cultures because of their uniformity. The barrier in transmitting information from one dissimilar group to another is much lower. Further, the credibility of information on innovations is higher because the source is more likely to be friends and relatives rather than the mass media.

Takada and Jain compared the rate of adoption for three products—air conditioners, washing machines, and calculators—in high-context cultures (Japan, Taiwan, South Korea) versus a low-context culture (United States).[49] In most cases, the rate of diffusion was more rapid in the three high-context cultures than it was in the United States for all three categories.

INNOVATIVENESS AND THE DIFFUSION PROCESS

Innovativeness refers to the predisposition of a consumer to adopt a product earlier than most other people. We next look at the characteristics of those who adopt earlier and refer to them as innovators, recognizing that they represent Rogers's classification of both the true innovator group (the first 2.5 percent to adopt) and the early adopter group (the next 13.5 percent to adopt). The combination of innovators and early adopters into one group is necessary from a marketing standpoint, because the 2.5 percent of the market that is the first to adopt is too small a group to target. Therefore, in this discussion, the general designation of "innovator" refers to both true innovators and early adopters.

▌ **The Nature of Innovativeness**   Two key questions can be asked about innovators. First, can generalized innovators be identified, and if so, what are their characteristics? The answer will help marketers determine whether marketing strategy can be directed to a general group of innovators or whether specific target segments of early buyers have to be defined on a product-by-product basis. Second, is there a negative as well as a positive innovator? That is, can one trace a negative diffusion process leading to rejection of an innovation?

Characteristics of Innovators.   It is likely that a general innovator exists for true (*discontinuous*) innovations. That is, the innovator who was among the first to consider getting a high-speed Internet connection will also be among the first to consider buying a DVD player. One study found that when personal computers were first introduced, early adopters were also more likely to use automatic bill paying and cable TV services, programmable pocket calculators, and video TV games, all innovations at the time.[50]

Various studies have shown that across product categories, innovators tend to be[51]

■ opinion leaders.

■ risk takers.

■ inner directed, self-confident, and independent of group norms.

■ more likely to obtain information from mass media than through word of mouth.

■ more likely to read newspapers and magazines, and less likely to watch TV.

■ open to new ideas and change.

■ relatively young and mobile.

Also, most studies have identified innovators as cosmopolitan and in higher socioeconomic groups (although as we noted, grassroots innovators are in lower socioeconomic groups and often from rural areas).

Most findings suggest that for less innovative products, a general innovator does not exist. That is, the individual who is one of the first to have owned a color printer will not necessarily be one of the first to adopt a DVD player. As with opinion leadership, innovativeness is likely to extend across related product categories, but an innovator in one category is not likely to be an innovator in an unrelated category. Thus, for most new products, marketers must define the target market on a product-by-product basis.

Some companies have portrayed innovators for new products such as Samsung's DigitAll, its latest version of high-definition television (see Exhibit 16.4). The implication is that an innovator for such a product is likely to be an innovator for other related technology products.

Segmenting Innovators.   According to Forrester, a leading web-based research firm, marketers need a new typology that captures consumers' attitudes toward high-technology innovations. To that end, Forrester proposes a new way of looking at innovators based on what they call "technographics."[52] **Technographics** is an approach to segmenting consumers according to their motivation, desire, and ability to invest in technology products. On this basis, Forrester defined twelve segments on two dimensions: (1) consumer knowledge of and attitudes towards technology and (2) whether the consumer uses technology for family, career, or entertainment purposes.

Forrester used technographic segmentation to analyze why Kodak's Photo CD, designed to attach a photo CD player to a TV, failed.[53] Kodak thought that the product's low cost and ease of use required targeting "traditionalists" (those who are indifferent to technology) and "media junkies" (those who have little patience with new technologies and prefer watching TV). But these groups were technology resistant and viewing photos on TV was not compelling enough to get them to invest in the technology. Kodak's real target should have been "gadget grabbers" (technology-friendly consumers who used technology primarily for entertainment).

EXHIBIT 16.4

An ad portraying an innovator of a technology product.

Courtesy of Samsung DigitAll.

Are There Positive and Negative Innovators? We are assuming that the general innovator reacts positively to most discontinuous innovations. The same individual might reject an innovation, however. The consumer who was one of the first to accept DVD players might have been one of the first to reject videodiscs. Midgley proposed three categories of adopters:[54]

1. **Active adopters** are those who have adopted the product and give favorable information about it.

2. **Active rejectors** are those who have tried the product, found it deficient, and give unfavorable information about it.

3. **Passives** are those who have adopted the product but do not give information or exert influence.

Leonard-Barton has conducted one of the few marketing studies that has distinguished between active adopters and rejectors. She found that rejectors frequently sought experts who evaluated the innovation negatively, possibly to justify discontinuing the use of the innovation.[55] In general, little documentation of a negative diffusion process is available. It may be that marketers are reluctant to provide evidence of failures, even though studies of negative diffusion could provide insights on ways to avoid future market failures.

Strategic Applications of Diffusion Theory

Companies attempt to influence both the likelihood of adoption and the rate of diffusion of innovations through marketing strategies.

ADOPTION

Companies use various strategies to influence consumers to adopt innovations. As mentioned, they try to encourage trial through free samples and price promotions. If trial is not reasonable, companies use advertising to create product awareness and to communicate product features. The ad for Johnson & Johnson Acuvue contact lenses in Exhibit 16.5 is an example. The ad informs consumers that there is now a contact lens specifically for people with astigmatism. In addition, it encourages consumers with astigmatism to visit the company's web site, which will help them find an eye care professional nearby. It also provides a coupon to motivate consumers to try the product. Companies also have tried to portray innovative behavior in advertising by showing astute users of the most advanced products. The ad for Panasonic's e-wear in Exhibit 16.6 portrays innovative behavior by showing a young, hip consumer using the product—a midget-sized audio player that can load music files from the Web or CDs and be worn as an armband.

| **EXHIBIT 16.5** |

Creating awareness for a new product.

Courtesy of Johnson & Johnson.

In addition, marketers can attempt to overcome resistance to adoption by employing change agents. Pharmaceutical companies seek early adoption of medical innovations by respected hospitals, clinics, and physicians who have reputations as opinion leaders in the hope that these individuals and institutions will encourage others to adopt.

RATE OF DIFFUSION

Diffusion theory can provide marketers with guidelines for adjusting strategies according to the projected rate of diffusion. Marketers have two strategic options in influencing the rate of diffusion, as shown in Table 16.1. In a **skimming strategy,** marketers project a slow rate of diffusion. As a result, prices have to be set higher initially to sustain the costs of introduction. The policy aims at "skimming the cream off the market" by strategically aiming at the small, price-insensitive segment.

Such a segment is likely to be well defined by demographic and lifestyle characteristics. Advertising will probably be informationally oriented to create awareness and to supply necessary technical information. Distribution of the product will be selective. A skimming policy is most likely for major innovations such as

TABLE 16.1
Strategic alternatives based on the diffusion curve

Marketing strategy	Skimming	Penetration
Initial price	High	Low
Market segmentation	Target market is • Small • Well specified by demographics and lifestyle	Target market is • Larger • Harder to specify by demographics and lifestyle
Advertising	Informational approach	Use of symbols and imagery
Distribution	Selective	Intensive
Product characteristics	Discontinuous innovation	Continuous innovation

Note: The rate of diffusion for skimming is slow; the rate of diffusion for penetration is fast.

electric cars or DVD players. There may be barriers to widespread acceptance because the product is not likely to be simple and may not be compatible with existing products or systems. Therefore, it is logical to establish a small and specific target for adoption.

The alternative to a skimming policy is a **penetration strategy.** In this case, marketers encourage rapid and widespread diffusion by introducing the product at a low price. The intention is to try to sell to a general market through an intensive campaign that uses imagery and symbolism. Distribution is widespread. Because the market is so general, however, identifying the characteristics of early adopters may be difficult. A penetration strategy is likely for new products that are not major innovations, such as diet soda or freeze-dried coffee, since closely competitive product substitutes exist. Both diet soda and freeze-dried coffee were introduced at competitive prices on a widespread basis with intensive advertising campaigns using symbolism and imagery.

Once an initial strategy is established, diffusion theory can give marketers guidelines for changing marketing strategy, depending on where the product is on the diffusion curve. A product introduced by a skimming strategy eventually moves toward a penetration strategy. For example, personal computers, CD players, and cell phones were first introduced into the market at very high prices with little advertising and limited distribution. With technological improvements and competitive entry, prices came down quickly and diffusion became more rapid. As adoption increased, distribution became more intense. Knowledge of the diffusion curve could help marketers of these types of products define the proper time to begin to shift from a skimming to a penetration strategy.

Similarly, marketers introducing a penetration strategy may find that a slow increase in prices is warranted when there is widespread acceptance of the product. Advertising and distribution remain intensive, but the proper time for a change in pricing policy may be defined by the diffusion curve.

SUMMARY

Word-of-mouth communication among consumers is the most important source of information and influence in consumer behavior. Individuals who influence the purchasing behavior of other consumers are the opinion leaders; the consumers being influenced are the followers.

Several studies have documented the greater importance of word-of-mouth communication compared with commercial information sources. Word-of-mouth influence is more likely to be important when the product is visible, distinctive, and important to the group's belief system and when consumers are involved with the purchase decision and see it as risky.

The process of word-of-mouth communication can best be described as a transmission of information between opinion leaders and followers. The mass media often serve as the source of information, with gatekeepers (those most sensitive to product information) serving as intermediaries in the information flow. Marketers try to encourage positive word-of-mouth communications, but negative word of mouth may occur as well; the latter tends to be a more powerful influence on consumers than positive word of mouth.

Word-of-mouth communications increase exponentially on the Internet because of the multiplier effect. Due to the impact of word of mouth on the Web, marketers have started using viral marketing to get their messages to consumers. Viral marketing is the process of encouraging the dissemination of word of mouth to others, who in turn are encouraged to further disseminate information, creating a multiplier effect.

The influence of word-of-mouth communication is tied closely to the concept of opinion leadership. Opinion leaders are likely to both transmit and receive information to and from others for specific product categories. The transmission of influence through word of mouth is most likely to occur in specific situational and social settings. Opinion leaders on the Web were identified as e-fluentials; that is, those who are most active in communicating and influencing others on the Web.

Marketers have several strategic options in trying to encourage positive word-of-mouth communications about their product. They can (1) stimulate word of mouth through product trial, generally targeting opinion leaders, (2) stimulate word of mouth through advertising by encouraging consumers to transmit positive experiences with the product, (3) simulate word of mouth by portraying communications from typical consumers, and (4) portray communications from opinion leaders to followers.

The second major section in the chapter dealt with the diffusion of communications across groups. The diffusion process involves the consumers' adoption of an innovation and communication to other groups over time. Adoption of a new product requires awareness, knowledge, evaluation, and trial. Consumers are more likely to adopt a product if it has a relative advantage, is compatible with their needs and past experiences, is visible, is simple to understand, and is easily tried. Consumers' rejection of an innovation can occur because of lack of perceived value, lack of compatibility with current habits and usage, and perceived risk in buying the innovation.

Time is a crucial part of the diffusion process because it determines the rate of diffusion. Time is also important in defining adoption. Adopter categories—innovators, early adopters, the majority, and laggards—are defined according to time of adoption. In communication among groups, information is likely to trickle up or down from one socioeconomic group to another or to trickle across similar groups, regardless of economic status. Because of the great mobility and lack of sharp socioeconomic distinctions in the United States, diffusion is likely to be based on a trickle-across effect.

This chapter discussed the diffusion of Internet usage both in the United States and abroad and how the characteristics of acceptance and rejection of an innovation apply to the Internet. The factors that affect diffusion of communications across groups have increased the rate of diffusion of the Internet. The Internet also is a vehicle for diffusing other new products and ideas.

Innovativeness was defined as a consumer's predisposition to buy a new product early. Innovators (*i.e.*, the true innovator group plus early adopters) may be generally predisposed to adopt innovations. General innovators tend to be better educated, more self-confident, more willing to take risks and accept change, and more socially active than other adopters. In addition, innovators are more likely to be opinion leaders. Technographic segmentation was described as a means of profiling innovator segments for high-technology products.

In the next chapter, we consider how markets can be segmented by consumer needs and characteristics, and how individual consumers can be targeted with marketing efforts.

QUESTIONS FOR DISCUSSION

1. What kinds of product categories are good candidates for a viral marketing strategy? Why?

2. It was stated that word-of-mouth communication is the most important influence on consumer behavior. Why? Under what circumstances are other types of communication (advertising, personal selling, information from government sources) likely to be more influential than word of mouth?

3. What were the conditions that made it possible for Corona beer to be successful based on word of mouth alone? What are the limitations of relying solely on word-of-mouth communications to market a product on a national basis?

4. A major study documenting the importance of word-of-mouth communication—Katz and Lazarsfeld's study of influence in a midwestern town—was conducted before the advent of television. Some have argued that TV provides a basis for simulating word-of-mouth communication and, thereby, reduces the importance of word-of-mouth influence.
   - Do you agree?
   - Is it possible that TV is a more important force than word-of-mouth influence for certain groups (for example, children)?

5. What are the likely roles of the three types of word-of-mouth communication—product news, product experiences, and advice—in the consumer's decision process?

6. What are the limitations of the two-step flow model of word-of-mouth communications? What evidence supports the multistep model of communications in Figure 16.1?

7. Why is negative word-of-mouth communication likely to be a more potent influence on consumer behavior than positive word of mouth?

8. How has the Web influenced word-of-mouth communications (both positive and negative)? Why is the multiplier effect strong on the Internet?

9. How have marketers used viral marketing to spread their advertising messages?

10. What are the limitations of the concept of opinion leadership?

11. Marketing studies have not identified any distinctive characteristics of opinion leaders. Because it is so difficult to identify opinion leaders, can the concept of opinion leadership be used in developing marketing strategies? If so, in what ways?

12. What types of appeals should marketers direct to e-fluentials? For what types of products?

13. Cite an example of a value barrier, a usage barrier, and a risk barrier to adoption of an innovation. How can marketers overcome each barrier?

14. What do we mean by the "strength of weak ties"? Provide an example. Why is this concept important in the diffusion process?

15. The chapter cites three types of communication between groups: a trickle-up, a trickle-down, and a trickle-across effect.
    - In what types of societies is a trickle-down flow of communication more likely than a trickle-up?
    - Are there any groups or regions in the United States where a trickle-down flow is more likely to occur?
    - Under what conditions is a trickle-up flow likely? Cite examples.

16. What factors have encouraged the diffusion of the Internet? What factors have discouraged diffusion?

17. What are the strategic implications of introducing a new product to a high-context/

homophilous culture versus a low-context/heterophilous culture?

18. The chapter cites an important gap in diffusion research—the lack of any study of a negative diffusion process. The fact that marketing managers do not like to advertise failures may explain the lack of research on negative diffusion. Such studies, however, could provide insights on how to avoid product failures.

- Cite an example of negative diffusion for a product.
- What insights might a marketing manager gain from studying negative diffusion to better understand (a) word-of-mouth communication and (b) product positioning?

RESEARCH ASSIGNMENTS

1 Visit *www.epinions.com*. Does the site reflect word-of-mouth influence? Would you use the opinions expressed on the site in your purchasing decisions for any of the products listed? What other sites might you use for product opinions? Why?

2 Use the following questions to identify innovators for men's cosmetics. "How do you see yourself with regard to buying a new facial care preparation for men? As one of the first to buy? As one who purchases after a few others have tried it? As one who purchases after many people have bought it? As a nonpurchaser?" Identify the innovators as those who say they would be one of the first to buy. In addition to the innovativeness question, ask the sample of males: (a) lifestyle questions based on the statements listed in Table 10.1, (b) an opinion leadership question, (c) self-confidence questions in selecting cosmetics and toiletry items, and (d) questions about demographic characteristics.

- What are the differences between the innovators and noninnovators on each of the items listed? (If your sample is large enough, split it into three groups—innovators, those tending to be innovators, and noninnovators—and determine differences among these groups.)
- What are the implications of these differences for a marketing strategy for men's cosmetics in regard to (a) market segmentation, (b) advertising and product positioning, (c) pricing, (d) product development, and (e) distribution?

NOTES

1. "Pass It On," *Wall Street Journal* (January 14, 2002), pp. R6, R7.
2. Ibid.
3. Marsha L. Richins and Teri Root-Shaffer, "The Role of Involvement and Opinion Leadership in Consumer Word-of-Mouth: An Implicit Model Made Explicit," in Michael J. Houston, ed., *Advances in Consumer Research*, Vol. 15 (Provo, Utah: Association for Consumer Research, 1987), pp. 32–36.
4. Elihu Katz and Paul F. Lazarsfeld, *Personal Influence* (Glencoe, IL: The Free Press, 1955).
5. Katz and Lazarsfeld, *Personal Influence*, pp. 118–119.
6. Lawrence Feick and Linda Price, "The Market Maven: A Diffuser of Marketplace Information," *Journal of Marketing* 51 (January 1987), pp. 83–87.
7. Marsha L. Richins, "Negative Word-of-Mouth by Dissatisfied Consumers: A Pilot Study," *Journal of Marketing* 47 (Winter 1983), pp. 68–78.
8. "P&G Suit Against Amway Is Revived," *New York Times* (March 27, 2001), section C.
9. "Entenmann's Fights Moonie Link," *Advertising Age* (November 23, 1981), p. 33.
10. "Rumor Turns Fantasy into Bad Dream," *Wall Street Journal* (May 19, 1991), pp. B1, B5.
11. Paul M. Herr, Frank R. Kardes, and John Kim, "Effects of Word-of-Mouth and Product-Attribute Information on Persuasion: An Accessibility Diagnosticity Perspective," *Journal of Consumer Research* 17 (March 1991), pp. 454–462.
12. "The e-Fluentials," Burson-Marstellar 2000, www.efluentials.com.
13. Michel Fortin, "Why Word-of-Mouth Works Wonders," http://hostidea.subportal.com/ebiz/promote/marketi. . ./0097.html, as of May 14, 2000; and "The Value of Word-of-Mouth," as of May 14, 2000.
14. "Marketers: About Viral Marketing," www.recommend-it.com/rec/marketers/viral_about.jsp, May 14, 2001.
15. "This Is One Virus You Want to Spread," *Fortune* (November 27, 2000), pp. 297–300.
16. Zimmerman, "Marketing on the Cheap," as of May 14, 2000.
17. "Viral Marketing Works, But It's Not for Everyone," *The Industry Standard* (September 25, 2000).
18. "I Scream, You Scream: Consumers Vent Over the Net," *New York Times* (March 4, 2001), p. 3, 13.

19. "The Influentials," *American Demographics* (October 1992), pp. 30–38.

20. Feick and Price, "The Market Maven," pp. 83–87.

21. Michael R. Solomon, "The Missing Link: Surrogate Consumers in the Marketing Chain," *Journal of Marketing* 50 (October 1986), pp. 208–218.

22. Jagdish N. Sheth, "Word-of-Mouth in Low-Risk Innovations," *Journal of Advertising Research* 11 (June 1971), pp. 15–18.

23. John O. Summers and Charles W. King, "Interpersonal Communication and New Product Attitudes," in Philip R. McDonald (ed.), *Proceedings of the American Marketing Association's Educator's Conference* (Chicago: American Marketing Association, 1969), pp. 292–299.

24. Proprietary study by a large appliance manufacturer; "The Influentials," *Research Alert* (December 2, 1988), p. 1; and Rogin A. Higie, Lawrence F. Feick, and Linda L. Price, "Types and Amount of Word-of-Mouth Communications About Retailers," *Journal of Retailing* 63 (Fall 1987), pp. 260–277.

25. "The e-fluentials," Burson-Marstellar 2000, www.efluentials.com.

26. Pastore, "The Value of Word of Mouth," as of May 14, 2000.

27. "The e-fluentials."

28. "Buzz-z-z Marketing," *Business Week* (July 30, 2001), pp. 50–56.

29. "Marketer of the Year: Donald Hudler," *Brandweek* (November 16, 1992), p. 21.

30. Ibid.

31. Everett M. Rogers and F. Floyd Shoemaker, *Communication of Innovations,* 2nd ed. (New York: The Free Press, 1971).

32. Robert W. Shoemaker and F. Robert Shoaf, "Behavioral Changes in the Trial of New Products," *Journal of Consumer Research* 2 (September 1975), pp. 104–109.

33. S. Ram and Jagdish Sheth, "Consumer Resistance to Innovations: The Marketing Problem and Its Solutions," *Journal of Consumer Marketing* 6 (Spring 1989), pp. 5–14. See also Hubert Gatignon and Thomas S. Robertson, "A Propositional Inventory for New Diffusion Research," *Journal of Consumer Research* 11 (March 1985), pp. 849–867.

34. Everett M. Rogers, *Diffusion of Innovations* (New York: The Free Press, 1962).

35. Ibid., pp. 168–171.

36. "Has Growth of the Net Flattened?" *Wall Street Journal* (July 16, 2001), pp.B1, B8.

37. "Mystique Marketing," *Forbes* (October 21, 1996), pp. 276–277.

38. Gatignon and Robertson, "A Propositional Inventory," p. 857.

39. Jacqueline Johnson Brown and Peter H. Reingen, "Social Ties and Word-of-Mouth Referral Behavior," *Journal of Consumer Research* 14 (December 1987), pp. 350–362.

40. Thorstein Veblen, *The Theory of the Leisure Class* (New York: Macmillan, 1912).

41. George Simmel, "Fashion," *International Quarterly* 10 (October 1904), pp. 130–155.

42. "Grassroots Innovation," *Marketing Insights* (Summer 1991), pp. 44–50.

43. Charles W. King, "Fashion Adoption: A Rebuttal to the 'Trickle Down' Theory," in James U. McNeal, ed., *Dimensions of Consumer Behavior* (New York: Appleton-Century-Crofts, 1969), p. 172.

44. State of the Internet 2000, United States Internet Council & ITTA Inc, 2000.

45. "Has Growth of the Net Flattened?" pp. B1, B8.

46. State of the Internet 2000.

47. Edward T. Hall, *Hidden Differences* (New York: Doubleday, 1987).

48. Rogers, *Diffusion of Innovations.*

49. Hirokazu Takada and Dipak Jain, "Cross-National Analysis of Diffusion of Consumer Durable Goods in Pacific Rim Countries," *Journal of Marketing* 55 (April 1991), pp. 48–54.

50. Mary Dee Dickenson and James W. Gentry, "Characteristics of Adopters and Non-Adopters of Home Computers," *Journal of Consumer Research* 10 (September 1983), pp. 225–235.

51. Zarrel V. Lambert, "Perceptual Patterns, Information Handling, and Innovativeness," *Journal of Marketing Research* 9 (November 1972), pp. 427–431; Robert L. Brittingham, Brent G. Goff, and Robert C. Haring, "Refinancers and Non-Refinancers: A Comparative Analysis," *Journal of Retail Banking* 11 (Spring 1989), pp. 27–34; and John O. Summers, "Media Exposure Patterns of Consumer Innovators," *Journal of Marketing* 36 (January 1972), pp. 43–49.

52. Forrester Research web site, www.forrester.com/ER/Research/Report/, as of September 2000.

53. Ibid.

54. David F. Midgley, "A Simple Mathematical Theory of Innovative Behavior," *Journal of Consumer Research* 3 (June 1976), pp. 31–41.

55. Dorothy Leonard-Barton, "Experts as Negative Opinion Leaders in the Diffusion of a Technological Innovation," *Journal of Consumer Research* 11 (March 1985), pp. 914–926.

Marketing Action

CHAPTER 17

The Marketing Communications Process

Once a product or service is developed, the next important strategic requirement is to communicate its benefits to a target market. In this chapter, we consider the process of marketing communications from a consumer perspective. In particular, we

▮ describe a marketing communications model;

▮ discuss the key components of this model; namely, the (1) source of the message, (2) the nature of the message, and (3) the media used to communicate it;

▮ describe the process by which the consumer evaluates marketing communications; and

▮ consider social and ethical implications of marketing communications strategies.

Marketing communications have two primary purposes, to inform and to persuade—to inform consumers of product attributes and benefits, and of new product introductions; to persuade them to buy. Without information, consumers cannot act. Through marketing communications, consumers learn about new products, the prices and availability of existing products, and the characteristics of alternative brands. But marketing communications are clearly biased in favoring the advertised brand. So influencing consumers is a consistent objective. As a result, the process marketers use to *communicate* information and influence and the way consumers *interpret* this information are key elements in the study of consumer behavior.

McDonald's Emotional Themes Appeal to Consumer Needs

A good example of the effects of marketing communications is McDonald's promotional strategy. Consumers have associated McDonald's symbols such as the golden arches and the Ronald McDonald character with food, fun, and family values for years (see Exhibit 17.1). Past campaigns such as "You deserve a break today," showing a family enjoying a Big Mac, have reinforced this image. McDonald's communication prowess is partly a function of a promotional budget that eclipses that of its competitors. However, it is also a function of McDonald's ability to change its message to avoid it becoming stale.

In the mid-1980s, the company quickly shifted from a lackluster "McDonald's and You" advertising campaign to a more effective and upbeat "It's a good time for the great taste of McDonald's." The theme associated McDonald's with fun and pleasure. Then with the advent of a recession in 1990, the company switched to a more utilitarian emphasis on economy with the theme "Good Food, Good Value." In 1995, it returned to a hedonic theme with a takeoff on its classic "You deserve a break today." The new slogan, "Have you had your break today," implied that a break no longer needs to be deserved; it is a given. Going to McDonald's should now be guilt-free. As one advertising expert put it, the campaign gives consumers "a waiver of dietary correctness."[1] McDonald's continued this trend in 2000 with its new campaign, "We love to see you smile." The ad campaign is emotionally based and focuses on happy families and dedicated workers.[2] The campaign's objective is to show customers that they are McDonald's top priority and that the firm wants to make customers smile during every visit.

McDonald's communications strategy does not rely solely on advertising. Sales promotions such as sweepstakes, contests, and coupons support the benefits that advertising conveys. For example, McDonald's used a Monopoly game promotion that gave away $40 million in prizes based on "deeds" to Monopoly board locations. And in 1995, McDonald's launched its first interactive site on America Online called McFamily. The site is designed to give parenting advice and to obtain data from participants so they can be reached for future promotions.[3]

McDonald's has continually expanded its online presence, even after the Internet bubble burst in April 2000. For example, the Monopoly promotion has gone online to allow consumers to choose prize options, download the game board, and track their game pieces.[4]

In contrast to McDonald's, Burger King has had trouble staying on track and communicating product benefits. The company floundered in the mid-1980s with the $40 million "Search for Herb"

| **EXHIBIT 17.1** |
McDonald's keeps consumers smiling.
Peter Hvizdak/The Image Works.

campaign, based on a search for a mythical figure called Herb who had never tasted a Whopper. The focus on Herb as a balding eccentric in glasses, white socks, and gaudy plaids did not get any particular message across regarding the benefits of visiting a Burger King rather than a McDonald's. Burger King then changed its slogan to "Sometimes you've got to break the rules." Again, customers could not understand what benefits the slogan was trying to convey. One Burger King franchisee asked, "Are we telling kids to go out and buy drugs?"[5]

Having gone through ten campaigns since 1976, Burger King finally hit on a campaign in 1991 that communicated a consistent benefits-oriented message, "Your way. Right away." The slogan communicated satisfaction and quick service at Burger King outlets. But in 1995, the company again seemed to lose its way, changing its campaign three times in the next five years.

Whereas Burger King's campaign focused on people's minds, McDonald's, with a market share over twice that of Burger King's, seems to be the winner in the contest over people's hearts. The key to McDonald's success is consistently focusing on family themes and thereby meeting consumer needs. When it comes to family, hearts win out over minds.

A Model of Marketing Communications

A detailed model of marketing communications is presented in Figure 17.1. There are five components in any communications process:

1. A *source* of the message that develops communications objectives and identifies a target for its communications. Marketing organizations develop objectives for their advertising and promotional campaigns and target these campaigns to defined target segments.

2. A process of **encoding,** which requires translating these objectives into a message. Advertising agencies develop messages that are encoded into ads. Salespeople encode messages in developing a sales presentation for customers.

3. *Transmission* of the message through media designed to reach the intended audience. Transmission of marketing communications might involve mass media, word-of-mouth communications from salespeople, or direct mail literature sent to targeted households.

4. **Decoding** the message by the recipient so as to understand it and possibly retain it in memory. The two key questions here are whether consumers interpret the message in the manner the advertiser intends, and whether the message positively influences consumer attitudes and behavior.

5. *Feedback* to the source on the effectiveness of the communications process.

Figure 17.2 cites the first four components above in the context of the results of the marketing communications process, including possible barriers to effective communication from advertiser to consumer.

In the first step, the source (the marketer) *defines communications objectives.* For example, when Ralston Purina bought Eveready in 1986, it found Duracell closing in on Eveready's 52 percent share of the $2.5 billion U.S. battery market.[6] Duracell's

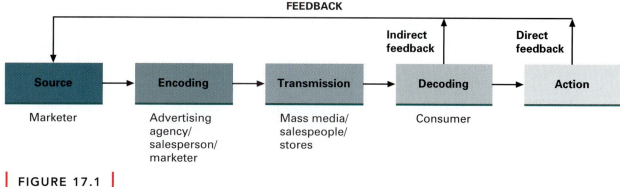

| FIGURE 17.1 |

The marketing communications process.

campaign showing battery-powered toys outlasting competitors in endurance contests was effective in conveying product benefits, while Eveready's spokesperson, Robert Conrad, was lackluster in comparison. Eveready's management realized it would have to do a more effective job in communicating key benefits—durability and a steady power source.

Next, the advertising agency encodes messages to *communicate product benefits.* Eveready communicated product benefits through its long-running Energizer Bunny campaign. By parodying Duracell's endurance toys, the ads were meant to convey the same benefits that Duracell was communicating—durability and reliability in a power source—but in a humorous way that was also meant to undercut Duracell.

The third step in the communications model, *transmitting the message to a target* segment, requires a media plan that is cost-effective. An effective media plan achieves a delicate balance between several potentially conflicting objectives. One possible conflict occurs between trying to reach as many people as possible versus reaching them as frequently as possible. Given a limited budget, advertisers cannot maximize both **reach** (the number of people exposed to the message) and **frequency** (the number of times an individual consumer or household is exposed). Reaching as many people as possible is more important for broadly targeted products such as Crest toothpaste or Coca-Cola. Frequency is more important when trying to influence a particular target group such as young, upscale car buyers. In this case, the objective is to reach a limited market segment as often as possible within budgetary constraints.

In the Energizer Bunny campaign, the media plan involved a balance between reach and frequency. Initially, Ralston Purina used network television to reach as broad an audience as possible. By 1990, print ads began appearing in magazines such as *Newsweek, People,* and *Sports Illustrated* to ensure greater frequency of exposure among battery purchasers.

The next steps involve consumers—*exposure to the message, decoding it (perception and interpretation), and possible action* based on the message. When the Energizer Bunny campaign was first introduced, many consumers remembered a Duracell, rather than an Eveready, campaign. Why? Because the Bunny's theme,

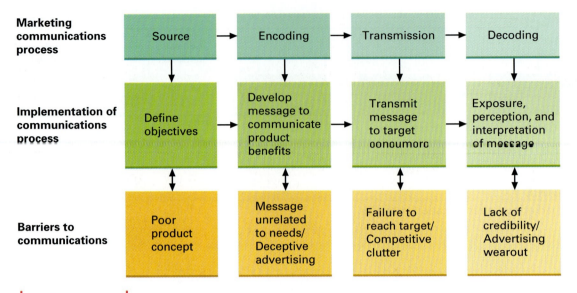

| **FIGURE 17.2** |

Results of and barriers to the marketing communications process.

"Still going," was a spinoff of Duracell's earlier endurance theme, and consumers simply did not decode the message correctly. There was evidence that the campaign was boosting Duracell's sales. However, Ralston Purina's management was not deterred. They had faith in the campaign; and eventually, most consumers associated the Bunny correctly with Eveready.

The last step in Figure 17.1, *feedback,* is designed to determine whether consumers have decoded the message as intended and whether they are likely to translate perceptions of the message into purchasing actions. Such feedback should help advertisers determine whether to continue, change, or cancel the campaign. By 1991, Eveready claimed that brand awareness rose 33 percent from the year before, and recall of the advertising message was up 50 percent. The most difficult question to answer is whether such improvements in brand awareness and recall are translated into brand purchases. For Eveready, apparently they were, because by 1991, Eveready stopped the hemorrhaging of its market and maintained its market position relative to Duracell. By 1995, Eveready was ready to invest another $20 million in the campaign.

Eveready put the Bunny in cyberspace in 2000 by creating fake ads with the Bunny interrupting unexpectedly[7] (see Exhibit 17.2). And in 2001, Eveready put the Bunny on its packaging and in-store displays.[8] The Energizer Bunny campaign seems to be going and going and going.

BARRIERS TO COMMUNICATIONS

In evaluating the advertising communications process, marketers must ask four questions:

1. Have communications objectives been defined by the source to reflect consumer needs?

2. Have marketers adequately encoded product benefits?

3. Has the message been transmitted to the target segment using the right media?

4. Have consumers decoded the message in the manner the advertiser intended?

Figure 17.2 shows that a negative answer to any of these questions can lead to barriers in the communications process at the source, in encoding, in transmission, or with the receiver in decoding the message. A fifth question, whether the communication leads to a purchase, bears on the results of the communications process and is considered later in this chapter.

▌ Barriers at the Source The barrier to communication at the source is an inadequate definition of objectives. In many cases, this means a poor focus on product benefits. Such a failure is most likely to lead to an advertising message that is unrelated to consumer needs. A number of years ago, a popularly priced beer wanted to create a prestige image by advertising its beer in status-oriented surroundings such as a country club or a fox hunt. The campaign only succeeded in alienating loyal users who could not relate to the settings. Clearly, the objectives of the campaign in creating a more upscale image did not relate to consumer needs.

The failure of Internet toy retailer, eToys, shows that Internet companies also must deliver on promised product benefits. Consumers use the Internet as a quick and convenient way to access goods. However, eToys failed to deliver on these benefits as a combination of out-of-stock items, late deliveries, and poor customer service plagued the site.[9] Consumers expected a convenient shopping experience and the web site did not deliver on that objective. eToys exemplifies the harsh consequences of not delivering on consumer needs; it declared bankruptcy in the spring of 2001.

▌ Barriers in Encoding   Failures in marketing communications can also be attributable to the process of encoding. At times, copywriters and artists may be more interested in developing creative, original advertising than in conveying product benefits. The result may be a message that gains attention but does not communicate benefits to the consumer. For example, during the boom in dot-com advertising in 1999 and 2000, many firms concentrated solely on developing brand recognition instead of relating the message to the consumer. For example, Outpost.com gained media recognition with a 1999 Super Bowl commercial that showed gerbils being shot out of a cannon. The campaign did nothing to convey the site's actual focus on selling technology equipment.[10] It created barriers in communicating by poorly encoding product benefits.

Figure 17.2 shows that deceptive advertising is also a barrier to encoding in misleading the consumer as to the nature of product benefits. The Federal Trade Commission can force companies to undertake corrective advertising if they make fraudulent claims. But most misleading advertising is not an outright fraudulent claim. Many claims are likely to be inflated, leaving it to the consumer to sort out what is accurate and what is not.

▌ Barriers in Transmission   Barriers to communication can occur in the process of transmission. Anything that interferes with the consumer's ability to pay attention to the message is defined as "noise." Perhaps the greatest source of noise in marketing communications is "competitive clutter." The number of commercials and print advertisements has been increasing for several reasons. First, the proliferation of new products demands more commercial time. Second, competitive intensity has caused advertising budgets to rise proportionately faster than sales. Third, TV commercials are getting shorter with a shift from thirty- to fifteen-second spot commercials. *Business Week* has estimated that U.S. adults are "bombarded with 3,000 marketing messages a day."[11] Because of such clutter, it is estimated that consumers are half as likely to remember the last commercial seen on TV as they were thirty years ago. Clearly, the increase in the number of commercials has inhibited consumers' decoding processes. (An illustration of the problem of competitive clutter is shown in Exhibit 17.3.)

Clutter on the Web is also becoming more of a problem, given the medium's rapid expansion. As of 1999, there were 3.6 million sites with about 1.5 billion web pages, according to one prominent research firm. By 2002, there were an estimated 8 billion web pages.[12] The ease with which individuals can register domains and create web pages has been the major contributor to this increased clutter.

Several studies have documented the fact that more frequent advertising has resulted in less consumer attention to messages. Webb found that attention and recall dropped off as the number of ads increased.[13] Burke and Srull found that more exposure to competing ads

"We'll return to our commercials in a moment, but first this program . . ."

▌ EXHIBIT 17.3 ▌

An example of competitive clutter.

Permission granted by Cartoon Feature Syndicate.

inhibits consumers' ability to remember the advertised brand.[14] They concluded that greater similarity between brands and between advertising themes creates confusion and makes retrieval of specific brand information from memory more difficult. As a result, consumers are more likely to confuse ad themes for Pepsi and Coke, for Crest and Colgate, and as we saw, for Eveready and Duracell.

What can marketers do to combat the confusion competitive clutter creates? An easy answer is to increase the frequency of advertising to make a more lasting impression on consumers. This can be a solution, however, only if the message is closely tied to consumer needs (*i.e.,* the message has no source or encoding barriers). Increased frequency rescued the Eveready Bunny campaign because greater exposure caused consumers to correctly identify the source as Eveready rather than Duracell. However, success depended on the Bunny commercials' ability to convey the key benefits of durability and dependability. Without communicating benefits, increasing frequency is likely to decrease, not increase consumer attention.

▌Barriers in Decoding   Barriers can also occur in the decoding process. A failure to develop a product concept or to create an advertising message related to consumer needs is likely to lead to such barriers. Consumers selectively ignore messages of no interest to them, as they did with Burger King's "Where's Herb?" because of their failure to communicate benefits. Furthermore, if consumers find that the source of the message is not credible, they reject it. For example, consumers may reject an advertisement from a large utility company justifying higher prices to finance nuclear energy for lack of credibility. However, consumers are more likely to accept a similar message from the Environmental Protection Agency.

Barriers to decoding may occur if consumers are confused or misinterpret a message. As we saw in Chapter 8, many consumers did not understand how Benetton's socially conscious ads featuring death row inmates and AIDS victims related to clothing. Some became offended by the graphic content of these messages, causing Benetton to revert to more traditional themes.

Barriers to decoding may also occur because of lack of attention to the message. Thus, competitive clutter is a barrier not only in transmission, but also in the decoding process because it encourages inattention. The continued use of an ad for a long period of time is another cause of inattention. *Advertising wearout* may occur because of consumer boredom and familiarity with the campaign.

Banner ads on the Web are a prime example of advertising wearout. When banner ads were first introduced, viewers would click on ads to visit the advertisers site about 7 percent of the time. However, a lot of these clicks came from new web users who were attracted to the novelty of the banner ads. By 1997 click-through rates had dropped to 2.0 percent, and four years later, in 2001, to just 0.1 percent.[15] As marketing information on the Web has begun to overwhelm consumers, email marketing response rates have fallen, from 10 percent in 2000 to 5 percent in 2001.[16]

RESULTS OF COMMUNICATIONS

Consumers may avoid exposure to a message or, if exposed, may accept or reject it. *Message acceptance* is due to an effective process of communicating product benefits that are important to a target segment. *Message rejection* may be due to lack of message credibility or believability, or it may be independent of message content and reflect consumers' attitudes, past experiences, and beliefs. For example, a consumer who has had consistently poor performance from a certain automobile make is unlikely to accept the validity of a claim that the car is well engineered and durable and provides maximum performance on the road.

From the advertiser's standpoint, the most desirable result of the communication process is a purchase as a result of message acceptance. Message acceptance may lead to a purchase, or consumers may decide not to purchase for reasons other than the information in the communication. Price and availability are obvious restrictions to purchase. Another is lack of an immediate need; that is, consumers may be attracted to a car because of the advertising but may not be in the market for one.

Regardless of the outcome, marketers like to assess the effect of the marketing communication on the purchase. Evaluation of the communication by marketing and advertising research provides marketers with *feedback.* Figure 17.1 shows that **direct feedback** is provided when a marketing communication can be directly linked to consumer actions, that is, sales. Marketers can judge retail advertising announcing a sale on a given day by the number of shoppers, and they can evaluate the effects of in-store displays by comparing sales with and without displays. Also, marketers can relate coupon returns to the advertising source. However, the sales effectiveness of an advertising message in the mass media is harder to judge. Marketers have difficulty determining the degree to which an advertising campaign is instrumental in brand choice because so many other factors enter into the purchase decision.

As a result, indirect feedback assumes more importance in evaluating ad campaigns. **Indirect feedback** is provided when the marketing communication is evaluated on the basis of the consumers' process of decoding the message. Indirect criteria of effectiveness relate to the advertisement's ability to produce exposure, awareness, comprehension, and retention of the advertising message.

In the rest of this chapter, the primary components of the marketing communications process are considered in detail: (1) source, (2) message (encoding), (3) media (transmission), (4) consumer (decoding), and (5) feedback.

Source Effects in Marketing Communications

The source of information (*e.g.,* advertisers, salespersons, friends) directly influences consumers' acceptance and interpretation of a message. It is important to consider the *credibility* and *attractiveness* of the source to consumers to understand the effects the source has on consumer behavior.

SOURCE CREDIBILITY

Source credibility is the level of expertise and trustworthiness consumers attribute to the source of the message.[17] *Expertise* is the ability of the source to make valid statements about the product's characteristics and performance. Since signing Tiger Woods, Nike's share of the golf ball market jumped from 1 percent to 6 percent. Woods has made suggestions regarding the range and velocity of Nike's golf balls and uses them. Few would question his expertise in the area.[18] *Trustworthiness* is the perception that a source has made a valid statement about the product. Some spokespersons may be regarded as experts in their field, but consumers may question the trustworthiness of their product endorsements because the advertiser is paying them.

Consumers frequently question the trustworthiness of ad claims because advertisers have a vested interest in selling the brand. The use of puffery reinforces this view. Some researchers have used **attribution theory** to explain why consumers view advertising as less credible than personal and neutral sources. Attribution theory states that receivers attribute certain motives to a communication source. When all ads consumers see are making uniformly positive claims (the best-tasting coffee, the most reliable airline, the best-performing car, etc.), consumers begin to doubt the advertiser's motives. Uniformly positive claims lead consumers to attribute the message to the advertiser's desire to sell the product rather than to a desire to transmit valid information about product performance.

On the other hand, if a message provides some variation in the claim (*e.g.,* headache remedy A is stronger and provides quick relief, but it is more likely to upset the stomach), consumers are more likely to accept the source as credible. As we will see, consumers are more likely to attribute such two-sided advertising appeals to the product's actual characteristics than to the advertiser's desire to sell.

Consumers regard neutral sources such as *Consumer Reports* magazine or the J. D. Power product ratings as trustworthy because these sources have no vested interest in any brand and make no attempt to change attitudes or influence behavior. Newscasters and editorial sources also have a high degree of credibility. Walter Cronkite, the former CBS newscaster, has been cited in polls as the most credible individual in the eyes of the American public. In addition, consumers are likely to accept the brand judgments of family and friends, particularly those viewed as opinion leaders for the product category.

The Internet has become a widely used medium for neutral sources of information. *Consumer Reports* and J. D. Power have web sites that provide product information. Many sites have developed into what is known as **infomediaries;** that is, sites that bring together diverse sources of information in one place to help the consumer. Autobytel.com was originally designed to allow consumers to buy cars based on their specifications. But the site is serving a more important function—being an infomediary for auto information by providing links to other sites such as Edmunds.com and J. D. Power so consumers can get ratings and specifications on car markets.

▌ Credibility and Message Acceptance   Studies have concluded that the greater the perceived credibility of the source, the greater the likelihood receivers will accept the message.[19] Marketers' credibility suffers if they are not up front with consumers concerning neutral versus advertising-sponsored information. Amazon.com offers users suggestions for purchases based on a *collaborative filtering system;* that is, a system that makes recommendations to consumers based on the choices of other similar consumers. But the company began to accept fees both to increase publishers' chances of receiving a featured slot on the site, and for a better opportunity at having books recommended in email promotions. These fees run as high as $10,000 per title for an Amazon editor's recommendation.[20] When these practices became known, Amazon came under fire from consumers. Consumers were naturally concerned about the credibility of the source once Amazon began accepting payments. By 2001, pressure from consumers led Amazon to disclose for which books it was receiving a promotional fee. Not distinguishing between editorial content and advertising can severely hurt a firm's credibility.[21]

Source credibility in itself does not ensure message acceptance. Source credibility is not likely to increase message acceptance if [22]

- consumers rely on their past experiences rather than on the ad in evaluating a brand.

- the message conflicts with consumers' best interests.

- the message is threatening. An ad on the risks of smoking from a credible source like the American Cancer Society will not increase message acceptance by many confirmed smokers because they see the message as a threat and want to avoid it.

▐ Increasing the Credibility of the Source   Because lack of credibility is a major limitation to consumers' acceptance of advertising messages, advertisers should consider how they can increase their credibility. The implication from attribution theory is to vary the claim so that it is not uniformly positive. If advertisers present both positive and negative information about the product (a two-sided message), consumers are more likely to attribute the claim to the product's actual characteristics rather than to the advertiser's desire to sell. However, marketers have rarely used such two-sided advertising because they are reluctant to present negative information about their product, even on relatively unimportant attributes. Research has demonstrated, however, that consumers have more confidence in claims that cite the pros and cons of a brand.[23]

Two other strategies enhance advertisers' credibility. First, they can utilize expertise. Advertising that uses spokespersons whom consumers accept as experts increases credibility (*e.g.,* Nolan Ryan for Advil based on a sore arm when he was a pitcher in his 40s). A second strategy to enhance credibility is to increase trustworthiness. Marketers often utilize neutral sources to encourage trustworthiness. Ads that cite neutral sources such as ratings from *Consumer Reports* or *Good Housekeeping* Seal of Approval are more likely to gain trustworthiness.

SOURCE ATTRACTIVENESS

Another basis by which consumers evaluate the source is its attractiveness, which is determined by its likability and its similarity to consumers. Research has shown that when consumers see salespeople as similar to themselves, they are more likely to accept and be influenced by the sales messages.[24] Such similarity creates a common bond between consumer and salesperson.

Because source attractiveness increases message acceptance, marketers try to emphasize similarity and enhance likability to increase attractiveness. Advertisers have emphasized the similarity between the source and the consumer by portraying "typical consumers" using and endorsing products. Brands as diverse as Subaru and Tylenol have used this approach. The success of Dave Thomas, Wendy's late spokesperson and CEO, was largely due to his "regular Joe" image.[25] Salespeople

EXHIBIT 17.4

Tiger Woods: An effective spokesperson for Nike.

AP Photo/Don Ryan.

often emphasize similarity with consumers because a salesperson who is seen as a peer becomes more attractive as a source of information.

Marketers can use spokespersons in advertising to increase credibility and/or attractiveness. Two types of spokespersons are used in advertising, **expert spokespersons** to increase credibility and **referent spokespersons** (those to whom consumers can easily relate), as a means of increasing source attractiveness. For example, Wayne Gretzky, the hockey star, was successful as a referent spokesperson for Sharp camcorders. He was likable but had no particular credibility as an expert in electronics. Conversely, the late John Houseman was effective in conveying expertise as a spokesman for the brokerage house Smith Barney, based on his role as a law professor in the TV series *The Paper Chase.* However, he was not particularly likable as he intoned "Smith Barney makes money the old-fashioned way. They earn it!"

When should advertisers emphasize attractiveness or expertise? Mazursky and Schul found that if consumers are involved in the purchase, expertise should be emphasized; if consumers are not involved, attractiveness should be emphasized.[26] In the high-involvement case, consumers focus on the message, and an expert best presents credible information. In the low-involvement case, consumers are not that focused on the message, and the source has more of an impact. As a result, the attractiveness of the spokesperson may be effective in gaining attention. Thus, Tiger Woods is an effective *expert* spokesperson for Nike, given his stature as a prominent athlete (see Exhibit 17.4). In contrast, Bill Cosby could be an effective *referent* spokesperson, given his likability, for an uninvolving product like Jell-O.

SOURCE VERSUS MESSAGE EFFECTS

Source credibility and attractiveness do not always operate to increase message acceptance. As the research by Mazursky and Schul showed, involved consumers are likely to focus primarily on the message's content rather than its source. This finding conforms to the Elaboration Likelihood Model (ELM) discussed in Chapter 4. According to ELM, involved consumers process messages through a central route that focuses on message content, whereas less involved consumers process messages through a peripheral route that focuses on factors extraneous to the message (peripheral cues). The source of the message is a peripheral cue. Therefore, according to ELM, source credibility and attractiveness are most important in influencing message acceptance in low-involvement conditions. Message effects are most important in high-involvement conditions.

Effects of the Message

The advertising message is meant to inform and persuade. Informational objectives may be directed toward announcing new products or changes in existing products, informing consumers of product characteristics, or providing information on price and availability. Persuasive objectives may be directed toward convincing consumers of product benefits, trying to induce trial, or reducing uncertainty about buying the product. The methods of developing and presenting advertising messages are beyond the scope of this text, but certain aspects of message content bear directly on the likelihood that consumers will accept and act on the message. Consumer researchers have considered five questions:

1. Should the message take a more *hedonic* (emotional and fantasy-oriented) or a more *utilitarian* approach?
2. Should the message be *one-sided* or *two-sided*?
3. Is *comparative advertising* (naming a competitor in the ad) an effective means of communicating product benefits?
4. What are the advantages of using *fear appeals*?
5. What is the appropriate role of *humor* in advertising?

HEDONIC VERSUS UTILITARIAN APPEALS

An important issue for advertisers is whether the message should appeal to the emotions of consumers or be directed to transmitting information about product features. We have seen in past chapters that advertisers frequently use appeals directed to pleasure-seeking, sentiment, and fantasy; that is, "hedonic" themes. Such appeals are most likely to be chosen for

▮ involving products that are more likely to arouse emotions.

▮ products that consumers often view as part of their self-image (clothing, cars, athletic shoes).

▮ nontechnical products that do not require information about features.

An example of an appeal to pleasure, excitement, and fantasy was an ad for Champion bras. It portrayed a woman soccer player being able to defy the forces of gravity by jumping 30 feet into the air.

Emotionally based advertising has been used in an attempt to increase involvement for less involving products. A Michelin ad depicting a baby in a tire was an example. Tires are a product that consumers view as a necessity and as having little emotional context. Michelin tried to increase involvement by equating tires with the safety of loved ones. The ad made the point that anyone worried about their child's safety should be willing to pay a premium price to buy a Michelin tire.

The attempt to portray uninvolving products in a more hedonic context has increased in the last ten years. Why has this trend toward emotional themes for uninvolving products occurred? First, many products have become more standardized. When a tire advertiser has no unique product claim, what better approach than to develop an emotionally based positioning strategy? Second, the intensity of competition has increased in many categories. More product alternatives make it harder for any one product to be noticed. What better way to stand out from the crowd than to take an emotional approach? Taster's Choice brand instant coffee—certainly

STRATEGIC APPLICATIONS

Can Computers Be Sold Based on Hedonic Appeals?

For the first fifteen years that personal computers were readily available, computer ads tended to be aimed at high-tech users, people who can truly get excited about the size of a hard drive or the amount of a machine's random access memory. That was fine when the market was relatively open and computer companies advertised almost exclusively in computer magazines.

But since the late 1990s personal computers have reached the mature stage of their life cycle and the market has become highly competitive. High-tech companies have found themselves in a pitched battle not for the brains of consumers, but for their hearts and souls. The new reality has computing companies scrambling to create emotional bonds with their customers. Computer advertising has now taken a turn toward the hedonic.

One IBM executive says that advertising misses the mark in emphasizing technical specifications. IBM is now using its advertising to try to build a strong, positive bond with consumers. And so are IBM's main competitors. In 1998, Apple introduced its new iMac computer with a $100 million dollar ad campaign. The ads focused primarily on the fact that the new computers came in a variety of colors instead of promoting the product's benefits. Apple's 2001 ads incorporated star musicians such as Lil' Kim and Smash Mouth to promote the computer's innovative music software.

In 1999, Dell unleashed its largest mass consumer marketing campaign to date, focusing on a style-driven PC. The campaign, "Born to Web," appealed to a broad consumer audience and is geared toward people celebrating what they can do online.

Compaq took an even more creative approach to appeal to consumers. In 1999, the company sponsored Sting's eighty-city "Brand New Day" tour. The company saw the sponsorship as an opportunity to create an image as "a pacesetter, not afraid to try new things." The group also appeared in Compaq's television and print ads to complement the tour sponsorship. And, in the fourth quarter of 2000, Compaq unveiled a $350 million ad campaign that focused on image instead of performance. The campaign is anchored by a television ad that asks simply "Where do you find inspiration?" "It's critical that we not distract consumers with a lot of information about bits and bytes," says Mark Rosen, Compaq's ad director. "We've got to show how and why computers will help them do things better and smarter" ("Compaq's Ads Leave Viewers to Imagine Product Benefits," p. 83).

The goal, it seems, is no longer to get Americans to buy computers because they are highly efficient technical marvels. Now the idea is to get people to feel warm and fuzzy about their computers and the companies that make them.

Sources: "Apple's Latest Spots Turn on Tunes," *Advertising Age* (March 19, 2001), p. 46; "Goofy Dell Guy Exudes Star Power," *USA Today* (January 14, 2002), p. 5B; "Compaq's Ads Leave Viewers to Imagine Product Benefits," *Advertising Age* (October 16, 2000), p. 83. "Dell Ads Aim at Broad Market," *Advertising Age* (December 6, 1999), p 12; "Compaq's Brand New Day," *Brandweek* (August 6, 1999), pp. 1–2; "Computer Selling Moves into "Warm, Fuzzy" Phase," *Advertising Age* (November 14, 1994), p. S4; "Computer Companies Try TV Ads' Mass Appeal," *Wall Street Journal* (September 20, 1994), p. B1; "IBM's Flawed Advertising Strategy to Get an Overhaul," *Wall Street Journal* (October 22, 1993), p. B1.

OF CONSUMER BEHAVIOR

a product that's hard to get steamed up about—leapfrogged Folgers and Maxwell House to become the nation's number one soluble brew with an emotional ad campaign centered around a budding romance between a couple who meet as new neighbors.

Web sites have taken the same approach as print advertisers to appeal to their core consumers. Soft drink companies, such as Dr Pepper, have developed web sites that appeal to the user's self-image, rather than focusing on product attributes. Drpepper.com has a trendy, urban look that is complemented by various links like "What's Your Passion," or "Join the Party." The site appeals to the "cool," modern consumer. On the other hand, Ford takes a utilitarian approach to its web site. Ford.com is a simple, well-organized site that quickly leads consumers to Ford's main product areas: new cars, dealers, service, and company history. The site's objective is to make it as easy as possible for Ford's diverse consumer population to find the information it needs.

ONE-SIDED VERSUS TWO-SIDED APPEALS

Two-sided messages are those that provide both positive and negative information about a product. The negative information is usually relatively unimportant compared with the positive information. Such messages are effective because they increase source credibility and reduce resistance to the message among skeptics.

▌ **Refuting Negative Information**   Two-sided ads can be refutational (the negative information is presented and then refuted) or nonrefutational. A two-sided refutational ad might say that a car is relatively small; but for the young professional just starting out, economy is more important than comfort, and this car is the most economical on the market. A nonrefutational ad would simply present the pros and cons of the car in a straightforward fashion.

Presenting negative information about the company's product is an infrequent strategy in advertising. Advertisers are fearful that it could point out product deficiencies and discourage consumers from buying, even if the negative information is refuted. However, such a strategy can be quite effective if refuting a negative factor actually reinforces the benefits of the product. For example, for years Avis used a two-sided refutational strategy by first stating that it was not the largest company and then discounting that by saying they provide superior cars and service (see Exhibit 17.5). The Avis campaign actually turned an unimportant negative into a positive benefit by convincing many consumers that being number two prompted the company to pay more attention to its customers.

▌ **Defusing Objections to the Product**   Another reason for favoring two-sided appeals is that they may defuse nonusers' objections to a product. Szybillo and Heslin found that when messages were presented to consumers supporting the use of air bags (one-sided) and both supporting and rejecting their use (two-sided), the two-sided ads were more effective in convincing consumers of the air bags' merits.[27] They used **inoculation theory** to posit that the two-sided ad "inoculated" consumers by preempting any of their negative thoughts. The conclusion is that two-sided ads are more effective than one-sided ads in introducing a new product that must overcome some consumer objections.

Two-sided ads are less effective when consumers are not involved with the product, because less involved consumers are not as attentive to the pros and cons stated in two-sided advertising.[28] Evidence also suggests that one-sided ads produce greater message acceptance when[29]

▐ consumers are less educated,

▐ there is agreement with the advertiser's position, and

▐ consumers are loyal to the advertiser's brand.

In today's environment, advertisers should consider increasing their use of two-sided advertising to enhance their credibility in the eyes of a doubting public.

COMPARATIVE ADVERTISING

Another type of advertising that has experienced increased usage is comparative advertising; that is, naming a competitor in the ad. The use of comparative advertising has increased since the networks removed a ban on its use in 1976. Most comparative advertising is one-sided; that is, it presents the strengths of the advertised product and the weaknesses of the competitive product. For example, MCI names AT&T in its ads and claims it provides better service, Nissan compares its price to that of a Toyota, and Almay claims that Clinique's moisturizer can cost twice as much.

At times, the use of comparative ads can get heated. In 1998, Papa John's pizza claimed that its dough was made from clear filtered water and its "yeast was given several days to work its magic."[30] The dough was compared with Pizza Hut's, which Papa John's said uses whatever water comes out of the tap to make frozen dough. The statement was accompanied by the image of a backyard cleanup area showing a grungy youth washing a dirty pile of dishes. Not surprisingly, Pizza Hut sued. The issue went all the way to the Supreme Court, which in March 2001 sided with a lower court's ruling that Pizza Hut failed to provide ample evidence that consumers were actually misled in their purchasing decisions.[31]

Despite this potential for undermining other brands and being undermined in turn, evidence suggests that comparative ads can be highly effective in influencing consumers. The arguments in favor of comparative advertising are that (1) users of competing brands are more likely to notice the ad and are, therefore, more likely to consider the advertiser's brand, and (2) claims made in comparative ads provide consumers with more information and a more rational basis for choice (an advantage cited by the Federal Trade Commission).

Some studies have questioned the effectiveness of comparative advertising. Swinyard found that when it is one-sided, comparative advertising loses credibility and generates sympathy for the brand being attacked.[32] A study by Ogilvy-Mather, a large ad agency, found that consumers frequently confuse the sponsor for the competitor in many comparative ads. Furthermore, there was no difference in the persuasiveness of comparative and noncomparative ads.[33]

On the other hand, other studies have found that if the source is credible, comparative advertising is effective. For example, Gotlieb and Sarel found that credible comparative ads were more likely to be noticed and were more likely to influence intentions to buy the advertised brand compared with noncomparative ads. They also found that credible comparative ads were particularly effective for new products.[34] Swinyard found that credibility can best be achieved by making a comparative ad two-sided—that is, a comparative ad that names a competitor, cites some of the advantages of the competitive brand, and then points out the arguments for the advertised brand.[35]

A study by Pechmann and Stewart showed that comparative advertising is best used for brands with lower market share.[36] Consumers like underdogs and are more likely to accept comparative ads from smaller challengers. Also, a comparison with the market leader may elevate the low-share brand to the same level of quality and popularity in the consumers' eyes. That is probably why MCI compares itself with AT&T. Conversely, if a market leader compares itself with a lower-share brand, it may enhance the underdog status of the competitor. When AT&T retaliated by naming MCI in its ads, one MCI executive said, "AT&T made this a two-horse race. They are Goliath taking on David."[37]

FEAR APPEALS

Most marketing communications attempt to inform consumers of the benefits of using a product. Fear appeals do the opposite: They inform consumers of the risks of using a product (such as cigarettes) or of not using one (such as deodorants).

Fear appeals are likely to be ineffective if they are too threatening. Carmakers have begun to use fear appeals, depicting crashes in ads using test dummies to emphasize safety. By 2001, Mercedes, Saturn, Toyota, and Volkswagen used ads depicting crash test results. But automakers are rethinking the strategy because the ads are turning consumers off. As one BMW executive noted in explaining why his company had not used such ads, "Americans really don't want to see negative themes such as crashes."[38]

At the other extreme, fear appeals are likely to be ineffective when consumers associate little or no anxiety with the message. A fear appeal for floor cleaners picturing neighbors commenting on a dirty floor is not likely to work these days because homemakers are just not very concerned. Fear appeals, therefore, are most likely to influence consumers when anxiety is moderate. Research has confirmed the effectiveness of moderate fear appeals. One study tested the effects of high-, moderate-, and low-level fear appeals on attitudes toward drinking. Moderate-level warnings, which consumers considered more truthful, were most effective in changing attitudes toward drinking.[39]

When are fear appeals most likely to succeed? Tanner, Hunt, and Eppright investigated the effectiveness of fear appeals in changing behavior related to socially transmitted diseases (*e.g.*, the effectiveness of fear appeals in getting individuals to practice safe sex to prevent AIDS).[40] They found that fear appeals were most effective when

▮ consumers recognize the severity of the threat. (AIDS can kill.)

▮ consumers recognize they can be affected by the threat. (I could be exposed to AIDS.)

▮ the ad shows how to deal with the problem. (The threat of AIDS can be reduced by using condoms.)

▮ the proposed course of action is easily implemented. (One can just walk into a drugstore to buy condoms.)

Raghubir and Menon found that when people were made aware of the behaviors that cause AIDS (*e.g.*, a theme such as "The HIV virus can be transmitted through unprotected sex. Have you had unprotected sex?"), they increase their estimate of being at risk and are more likely to accept messages encouraging safe sex.[41]

The most important finding is that fear appeals must show consumers how to deal with the problem. Beer companies have run ads targeted to teenagers and young adults urging them not to drink and drive. These ads demonstrate how to prevent death from alcohol consumption. The ad in Exhibit 17.6, a takeoff on the Marlboro Cowboy ads, shows the potentially devastating effects of smoking. The first approach, reflected in the beer ads, is more effective because it suggests a positive action. The second approach, the pseudo Marlboro ad, is less likely to be effective because it suggests a potentially negative outcome.

HUMOR IN ADVERTISING

Marketers use humorous messages because they attract attention and because advertisers believe that humor can be persuasive. The use of humor in advertising has been increasing to the point where the majority of ads use humor. One reason is that a 2002 survey by Roper, a large marketing research firm, found that 85

percent of respondents said they like ads with humorous themes.[42] After the September 11, 2001, terrorist attacks, much of the humor in advertising was thought to be in bad taste. But it took only about four months for the use of humor to be back to where it was before September 11.[43]

There are pros and cons for the use of humor in advertising. On the positive side, humor is likely to increase attention and memorability. It is also likely to enhance the advertiser's credibility. Humor may create a positive feeling toward the advertiser and increase the persuasiveness of the message.[44] It also may distract consumers who use competitive products from developing arguments against the advertiser's brand and may lead them to accept the message.[45]

There is a risk in using humor, however. If it does not communicate product benefits, it may have a negative effect on message comprehension.[46] The use of a Chihuahua in Taco Bell commercials flopped because, as one marketing analyst noted, "What does a dog have to do with tacos?"[47]

Humor may also be considered inappropriate based on the economic or political climate. Hartford Insurance switched from a campaign based on humor to one emphasizing honesty and reliability in the aftermath of September 11 because the campaign seemed more appropriate in the climate of that time.[48]

When is the use of humor most effective? Researchers have found that humor is most effective in gaining message acceptance

- *when consumers are not involved.*[49] Because humor is peripheral to the message, it is more likely to influence consumers who are not involved with the product than those who are.

- *for existing products.*[50] Advertising new products requires conveying information. Humor is a more effective means of establishing a mood than of conveying information.

- *when consumers have a positive attitude toward the brand.*[51] Humor can reinforce positive feelings toward a brand, but it is unlikely to reverse negative feelings.

STRATEGIC APPLICATIONS

Airline Advertising After September 11: Message Effects Become More Emotionally Focused

The September 11 terrorist attacks affected every facet of American society, including advertising. In particular, the airlines industry faced a difficult problem in advertising to try to increase confidence in flying with sufficient sensitivity to consumer anxieties and concerns.

Southwest Airlines was the first to change its themes from fun and entertainment to raw emotion. Initially, Southwest took a straightforward patriotic approach in its ads. It then switched to messages extolling personal relationships, such as "You can't tickle a voice mail, you can't e-mail a kiss. Some things are just better in person." As one executive explains the rationale for the campaign: "It elevates it to a smart, emotional level of 'Oh, that's why we used to do this [that is, fly]'" ("Airlines' New Pitch," p. B8).

United used an emotional campaign more closely tied to the events of September 11. Employees gave personal accounts of events in sixty-second spot commercials. In one, a customer-service agent talked about the outpouring that occurred on a flight when the captain announced that a New York fireman was on board with his wife headed for their honeymoon. One United executive said that the company wanted to send a message of moving beyond the event while giving consumers a sense of comfort in flying.

But there is a downside to reminding consumers of September 11. Too blatant a reference may be regarded as an attempt to commercialize the event and may drag consumers back when they want to forget. After September 11, Siebel Systems sold security software systems dubbed "homeland security" with the question, "Who are the Mohamed Attas of tomorrow?"

Nothing has been the same since September 11, yet the airlines are trying to take a softer approach in convincing consumers that they should consider resuming traveling. And they are doing it with sensitivity.

Sources: "Airlines' New Pitches Embrace Emotion," *Wall Street Journal* (October 24, 2001), p. B8; "Marketers Tread Precarious Terrain," *Wall Street Journal* (February 5, 2002), pp. B1, B4.

Media Effects

The third component in the communications model is message transmission. Marshall McLuhan's statement "The medium is the message" implies that the medium communicates an image independent of any single message that is being transmitted.[52] The media environment influences consumers' reaction to a communication in two ways. First, particular types of media such as magazines may influence message evaluation. Magazines like the *New Yorker, Reader's Digest,* and *Playboy* have different images based on different editorial content, reputation, and subscribers. Second, different types of media (*e.g.,* magazines versus television) influence consumers' reaction to the message.

DIFFERENCES WITHIN MEDIA

The role of a particular medium in communications is illustrated by the fact that the same advertisement results in different communications effects when run in different magazines or when aired on different TV shows. For example, Aaker and

Brown placed identical ads in two contrasting magazines, the *New Yorker* (a prestige magazine) and *Tennis World* (a specialty magazine).[53] The *New Yorker* was more effective in persuading nonusers to consider a product when the ad stressed product quality. *Tennis World* was more effective when the ad stressed reasons for usage. The findings suggest that the medium's environment conveys a message. Specialty media were more effective as vehicles for conveying information, and prestige media were more effective as vehicles for conveying image. Similarly, an ad for Levi's jeans on Alloy.com, a teen-oriented site, is likely to elicit different reactions from those to the same ad appearing on AOL. Teens are more likely to relate to the ad on a lifestyle basis, whereas visitors to AOL, a more generalized audience, are more likely to view the ad in the context of features and styles.

DIFFERENCES BETWEEN MEDIA

Different types of media also influence reaction to a communication. The most important distinction between media types is broadcast (TV and radio) and print (newspapers and magazines). Broadcast media are better at communicating imagery and symbolism, but they are not as effective as print in communicating detailed information. As a result, TV is more suitable for developing a mood or establishing a good feeling about the product, whereas print is more effective in communicating information.

Broadcast media, particularly television, have been described as low-involvement media because the rate of viewing and understanding is out of the viewer's control. That is, the viewer has little opportunity to dwell on a point in television advertising. In contrast, magazines allow the reader to set the pace.[54] Thus, the reader has more opportunity for making connections and dwelling on points of interest. The result is that the print media allow for a more traditional learning environment in which information can be absorbed and integrated. In this respect, the Web is much closer to print than to broadcast media. It provides even more control than traditional print media because information search and content are within the consumer's control. Personalization gives consumers the capability to design their own web page for news, entertainment, and communications. Customization allows consumers to control product specifications so products are designed to their needs.

Other environmental factors also distinguish media categories. Television is a good medium for products that require a demonstration of usage or action (such as automobiles or children's toys). Radio is an effective medium for products requiring sounds: records, theater productions, and political candidates. Magazines are important as sources of information on product performance because of the ability to present messages in print. Newspapers are a particularly effective source of information on local sales and merchandise as sources of shopping information. Product samples are another type of medium that marketers can use to communicate. In this case, the message is direct product experience rather than the symbolism and imagery provided in advertising. Product samples are particularly useful in introducing a new product because they provide immediate experience in an attempt to encourage further trial.

The Web's primary advantage is in transmitting information, whether it is from marketer to consumer, consumer to marketer, or consumer to consumer. Marketers can provide large volumes of information, and search engines help consumers find the information they need. The Web can also provide feedback to the marketer by tracking consumers' preferences and actions. As we saw in Chapter 16, the Web makes it easy for consumers to spread opinions and ideas to others through chatrooms and email, and to communicate to marketers through sites such as e-pinions and Yahoo!'s Consumer Opinions.

Consumer Decoding of Marketing Communications

The fourth step in the communications model in Figure 17.1 is consumer decoding of marketing communications. Decoding requires that consumers acquire and process marketing information. The acquisition and processing of information were described in Chapter 7. Here we are concerned with the process of decoding in the context of marketing communications.

When consumers process marketing communications, they must (1) identify and evaluate the *source* of the message, (2) evaluate the *message* itself, and (3) evaluate the *media* by which information is transmitted. In this section, we consider consumers' evaluation of each of these three components of marketing communications.

SOURCE IDENTIFICATION AND EVALUATION

When consumers receive a marketing communication, they first identify and then evaluate the source of information.

▮ **Source Identification**   Consumers must be able to identify the source of the message if it is to be effective. Yet they sometimes identify the wrong company with the message. As noted earlier, competitive clutter can cause confusion as to the identity of the source of the message. One study in Holland found that 39 percent of consumers mistakenly attributed Amstel beer's slogan to other brands. Similarly, Coca-Cola was the official sponsor of the Olympic games in 1996 and in previous games, yet on average, only 12 percent of consumers correctly identified Coke as the sponsor, and 5 percent incorrectly identified Pepsi.[55]

What can marketers do to ensure source identification? Two things. First, they can link the brand or company more closely to the message. Second, they can repeat the message to ensure the linkage is remembered.

▮ **Source Evaluation**   When consumers evaluate a source of information, they develop **cognitive responses** (thoughts consumers develop in response to a communication) regarding the source. For example, a consumer viewing an ad for TD Waterhouse featuring Steven Hill (the former DA on "Law & Order") as a spokesperson might think, "Why should I accept an actor's advice on investments?" (**source derogation**). Or the consumer might think, "If Steven Hill is willing to sponsor Price Waterhouse, the company must be reliable" (**source bolstering**). These source-oriented responses are important to marketers because they indicate the acceptability of the source.

Advertisers try to avoid source derogation by enhancing trustworthiness and credibility. As mentioned, one strategy is to link the product to a spokesperson with expertise regarding product performance. A second strategy is to use two-sided, nonrefutational advertising as evidence that the advertiser is presenting a balanced view of the product. A third strategy is to cite an impartial source; for example, findings from *Consumer Reports* magazine or an established medical organization. Crest became the leading toothpaste because the American Dental Association endorsed its claim that fluoride in the brand helps fight cavities. A fourth strategy to reduce source derogation is to moderate claims to avoid any attribution that the advertiser is biased. Claims such as "gets clothes whiter than new" or "best gas mileage of any car on the road" encourage source derogation because consumers have doubts about the veracity of the claim.

MESSAGE EVALUATION

In evaluating the message, consumers arrive at a judgment regarding the relevance, believability, and likability of the message. These responses can be divided into two types of general reactions: cognitive and affective. Cognitive responses evaluate acceptability of the claims (supportive of or counter to prior beliefs). Affective responses reflect consumers' positive or negative attitudes toward the message.

▌ Cognitive Response

Consumers develop cognitive responses to the message as well as to the source. They develop thoughts that support or counter the claims made in ads or other communications. These cognitive responses are formed based on consumers' prior beliefs.[56] For example, a consumer viewing an ad making a claim for gas economy and low service costs might think, "This claim is consistent with what some of my friends have told me. The car is one of the most economical on the market" (a **support argument**). Or the consumer might think, "In the long run, the car is not going to be very economical because I hear it has a lot of mechanical problems" (a **counterargument**). Cognitive responses are important to marketers because support arguments and counterarguments indicate consumers' acceptance or rejection of the advertised claim.

On this basis, support arguments are most likely when the information is consistent with consumer beliefs, and counterarguments are most likely when the information is inconsistent. Further, counterarguments are likely to be based on more detailed information.[57] For example, a consumer will be more attentive to an ad citing a car's sterling performance if the consumer has heard otherwise from friends and family.

Message-oriented cognitive responses (support arguments and counterarguments) are more likely to occur for high-involvement products, and source-oriented responses (source bolstering and source derogation) are more prevalent for low-involvement products.[58] Involved consumers are more likely to process messages related to product performance. Less involved consumers are more likely to focus on cues that are peripheral to the message, such as the source or background scenery. The strategic implication for high-involvement products is that advertisers should focus on gaining acceptance of the message by generating support arguments. For low-involvement products, communication strategies should increase credibility and acceptance of the source.

▌ Affective Response: Attitude toward the Ad

Cognitive responses arise from the way consumers *think* about an advertisement; attitudes toward the ad (*i.e.,* affect) are the way consumers *feel* about it. **Attitude toward the ad** is the consumer's predisposition to respond favorably or unfavorably to a particular ad.[59] Positive cognitive responses (support arguments and source bolstering) are likely to produce positive consumer attitudes toward an ad; negative cognitive responses (counterarguments and source derogation) are likely to produce negative attitudes.

Cognitive and affective responses to an ad have different strategic implications. Cognitive responses are reactions to message content. Consumers' attitudes toward an ad are influenced by a wider range of peripheral factors, such as color, music, symbols, and imagery. The key question is how consumers' attitudes toward an ad affect their evaluation of the advertised brand.

Effects of Positive Attitudes.

Studies have found that positive attitudes toward an ad create two desirable effects. First, positive attitudes are likely to increase attention and persuasion. Mehta found that consumers who were more positive toward advertising in general were more likely to recall ads and be persuaded by them.[60] Second, most studies have found that when consumers have a positive attitude toward an ad, they are more likely to have a positive attitude toward the advertised brand.[61] These findings suggest the desirability of creating a positive mood or feeling so that a positive attitude toward the ad will carry over to the brand.

If the attitude toward the ad carries over to the brand, it can create a **transformational effect** in which the experience of using the brand becomes even more positive due to the positive feelings the ad evokes.[62] The transformational effect explains in part why consumers who cannot tell the difference between soft drinks when the cans are unlabeled nevertheless still have strong brand preferences. Consumers link the advertising to the usage experience so that even though they cannot tell the difference in taste between brands, they remain loyal to a particular brand once they can identify it.

Effects of Negative Attitudes.

The studies cited in this section suggest that advertisers should try to create positive consumer attitudes toward the advertising. Some of the most successful ad campaigns, however, have been the most disliked— for example, Wisk's "Ring around the collar," Ajax's "White Tornado," and "Don't squeeze the Charmin." As a result, several researchers have suggested a more complicated relationship between consumers' attitudes toward the ad and the brand; namely, that the most successful ads are those that produce either very positive or very negative attitudes.[63] Thus, a disliked ad can produce a positive consumer response because it creates attention and retention. Even though consumers disliked the Wisk ad, it created greater brand awareness. Therefore, the key to influencing consumers is to create "arousal" (a direct positive *or* negative response to the ad), which results in brand familiarity and recognition once consumers are in the store.[64]

The problem with this conclusion is that it could lead advertisers to create purposefully irritating ads and negative attitudes toward the ad to gain attention and brand recognition. Irritating ads may be effective in creating arousal for certain products, but advertisers run the risk of creating negative brand evaluations. Furthermore, the American public does not particularly like advertising. A study by a large advertising agency conducted in the mid-1980s found that 73 percent of consumers considered advertising to be exaggerated, 64 percent thought it was misleading at times, and 51 percent viewed it as not believable.[65] Attitudes toward advertising today are probably as negative as they were then. Given a generally poor view of advertising, it would be dangerous to encourage a negative attitude toward a specific campaign as a means of gaining attention and recognition.

▌ Consumer Mood States

An important determination of consumers' attitudes toward an ad is their mood state at the time of exposure.[66] **Moods** refer to passing feelings that occur at a point in time (feeling happy, sad, silly, anxious, sexy, etc.). Studies have shown that positive moods can create positive reactions to the ad, and negative moods can create negative reactions.[67]

Studies also have shown that program and advertising content can influence consumers' moods. Howard and Gengler identify the transference of feelings from TV programs as "emotional contagion." In two experiments, they found that when a communicator smiled and portrayed happy feelings, recipients of the communication were more likely to be in a happy mood and react positively toward a product.[68] The implication is that advertisers can influence a desired mood state through program or readership content. This requires placing advertising with happy themes on "happy" TV shows. However, the converse does not necessarily apply. Burnkrant, Unnava, and Lord found that if the advertising has a sad theme, program content does not affect reactions to the ad.[69] The conclusion is that ads with sad themes (*e.g.,* an insurance ad showing a family that lost its home) can be equally effective on happy or sad programming.

MEDIA EVALUATION

Consumers evaluate an advertising message in the context of the medium in which it is transmitted. They develop images of media that influence message acceptance.

Programs or editorial content may vary in a given medium; therefore, advertisers must consider whether the specific environment in which a print ad or commercial is placed may influence message acceptance. One study by Kennedy found that the effectiveness of TV commercials varied, depending on the type of show (*e.g.,* situation comedies versus suspense thrillers).[70] Another by Soldow and Principe found that when consumers were involved in a TV program, commercial effectiveness was likely to be lower because consumers focused on the program rather than the commercial. Frequently, consumers see the commercial as an irritant. When consumers are not involved in the program, they are likely to see the commercial as part of the programmatic material and are more likely to accept the message.[71]

The effects of the program environment can be applied to print ads as well as to TV commercials. The nature of the story in which a print ad is placed may influence message acceptance. One study found that for most products, placing an ad next to an upbeat story has a positive effect on message acceptance. An exception was advertising for cookies, candy, or other products that may be used to cope with anxieties. Placing ads for these types of products next to anxiety-producing stories may be more likely to promote message acceptance.[72]

Communications Feedback

The final step in the communication process is feedback to the marketer to evaluate the effectiveness of the marketing communication. Figure 17.1 shows that marketers can obtain direct feedback by establishing a link between message effectiveness and purchase behavior or indirect feedback by evaluating the way consumers decode the message. As we saw, it is difficult to determine the effect of advertising on consumers' purchasing behavior, so advertisers have relied on indirect feedback in evaluating advertising. That is, they determine whether the ad results in consumer exposure, attention, comprehension, and retention.

McGuire summarized the types of feedback provided in each of these steps[73] (see Figure 17.3). These steps reflect a hierarchy of effects leading to a purchase. The assumption is that as consumers move from exposure to attention, comprehension, message acceptance, and retention, the probability consumers will buy the advertised brand increases with each step. We consider the measurement of each of these steps in the decoding process that follows.

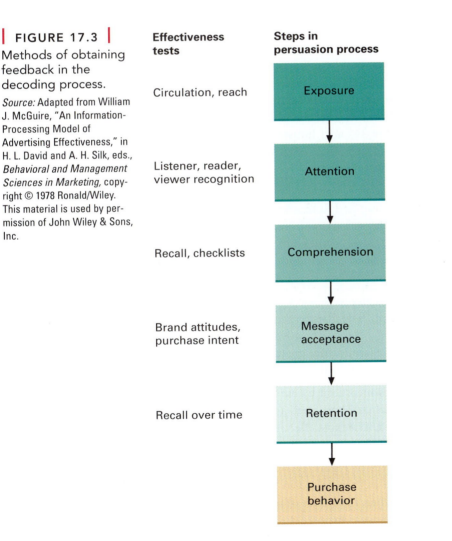

| **FIGURE 17.3** |

Methods of obtaining feedback in the decoding process.

Source: Adapted from William J. McGuire, "An Information-Processing Model of Advertising Effectiveness," in H. L. David and A. H. Silk, eds., *Behavioral and Management Sciences in Marketing,* copyright © 1978 Ronald/Wiley. This material is used by permission of John Wiley & Sons, Inc.

Effectiveness tests

Circulation, reach

Listener, reader, viewer recognition

Recall, checklists

Brand attitudes, purchase intent

Recall over time

Steps in persuasion process

Exposure

Attention

Comprehension

Message acceptance

Retention

Purchase behavior

1. *Exposure* can be measured for print media by circulation and for broadcast media by reach. Circulation figures are generally available for magazines and newspapers and are usually broken out by demographic characteristics to allow advertisers to determine the best media to reach their target audience. Determining consumers' exposure to TV is more difficult. In the past, research companies such as A. C. Nielsen determined TV exposure through electronic meters attached to a sample of TV sets to record the programs consumers watch. These devices, however, could not determine who was watching the set. Recently, "People Meters" have been installed in TV sets in a sample of households. These devices, which require viewers to "punch in" when they are watching TV, record who is watching as well as what is being watched.

   Exposure on the Web is usually measured by the number of visitors. Another measure of exposure is the cumulative number of pages viewed on the site. In both cases, exposure can be determined by a "cookie" on an individual's computer that allows a marketer to record the site consumers are viewing, but not their identity. Another factor in web exposure is how long an individual stays on the site, or the site's "stickiness." The assumption is that the longer each visitor stays on a site, the more effective online advertising will be. Companies such as Media Metrix track this information to determine the most popular web sites.

2. *Attention* can best be measured by recognition of an advertisement. The Starch service computes a "seen-associated" measure for print ads, in which consumers are asked whether they have seen the ad and whether they can associate it with a brand or manufacturer. Advertising agencies have developed a similar measure for TV ads; households are called the day after a TV commercial appears and are asked what commercials they remember seeing ("day-after recall" measures).

3. *Comprehension* is measured primarily by tests of recall of specific points in the ad. The Gallup and Robinson readership service asks respondents to recall and describe sales messages of specific print ads. Similarly, advertisers can use "day-after recall" tests to measure comprehension of TV commercials by probing consumers who recalled the ad to play back specific points in the commercial. In this manner, advertisers can evaluate comprehension of the ad's theme.

4. *Message acceptance* is best measured by its impact on brand attitudes or purchase intent. The Partnership for a Drug-Free America measured message acceptance by comparing attitudes in areas with heavy and light exposure to the campaign. Significantly greater shifts in attitudes against drug use in high-exposure areas indicated acceptance of the campaign's message.

5. *Retention* is measured by consumers' recall of the advertising message after a period of time. Consumers are likely to forget messages over time unless they are repeated. The most effective messages are those that are likely to be retained longest.

The measures in Figure 17.3 assume indirect feedback; that is, no direct link among the five steps involved in the decoding process and purchase behavior. In other words, when marketers obtain sales results, they do not know if consumers who purchased were exposed to the advertising campaign, comprehended it, or retained its messages. Recently, technology has created the possibility of establishing a link between consumers' exposure to advertising and subsequent behavior. The link is **scanner data;** that is, recording sales at checkout counters through electronic scanners. Research companies have identified households who shop in scanner stores and have installed TV meters in these households to record television exposure. In this way, researchers know if consumers who bought Diet Coke, for example, watched a Diet Coke commercial during the previous week.

Despite these advances, advertisers are a long way from determining with any precision the effects of marketing communications on purchasing behavior. Advertisers still have difficulty separating their communications strategies from the many other variables that influence consumers' purchasing behavior. The problem remains much as John Wanamaker, the famous Philadelphia retailer, described it over a century ago: "I know half my advertising is working, but I don't know which half."

Societal Implications of Marketing Communications

Most marketing communication is socially responsible. Unfortunately, however, some strategies violate the public trust. Two types of communication are of concern: deceptive advertising and irresponsible advertising.

DECEPTIVE ADVERTISING

Deceptive advertising is advertising that gives false information or that willfully misleads consumers about the brand's benefits. Deception occurs when consumers acquire false beliefs because of exposure to advertising. In 2001, a federal judge ordered H&R Block, the nation's largest income tax preparer, to stop advertising assurances of "rapid refunds" on overpaid taxes. Rather than receiving refunds from the government, clients were taking out expensive loans to get their money a few days sooner than the actual refund check. Some loans were at a rate of more than 500 percent per annum. The judge cited Block for "false and misleading advertising," leading consumers to believe they were getting a refund rather than a costly loan.[74]

The Federal Trade Commission monitors deceptive advertising either by ordering a company to cease its campaign or by ordering the advertiser to correct deceptive claims through new advertising. The Food and Drug Administration also has a role in controlling deceptive advertising. It can order manufacturers of foods and drugs to change claims in advertising or on packages. For example, the FDA ordered several marketers of fiber cereals to stop claiming that they reduce the risk of heart disease.

IRRESPONSIBLE ADVERTISING

An advertising claim does not have to be deceptive to violate the public trust; it can be irresponsible. **Irresponsible advertising** depicts or encourages irresponsible behavior or portrays groups in an irresponsible manner.

An example of encouraging irresponsible behavior was an ad for Reebok sneakers in which two bungee-cord jumpers are shown diving from a bridge. The final

Good beer is properly aged.
You should be too.

If you're under 21, don't even think about it. *Miller.*

shot shows only the Reebok jumper connected to his bungee cord; the other cord has a pair of empty Nikes attached to it. The campaign was meant to combine comparative advertising and humor, but it gave the unfortunate impression that the Nike wearer plunged to his death. *Adweek* magazine editorialized that "This is the sort of [advertising] that gives bad taste a bad name."[75]

Advertisers are also more conscious in dealing with female target audiences to portray women in more realistic purchasing roles. Saturn, for example, has changed the traditional image of women as being interested only in the styling and interior of a car. The company's ads feature actual women who have bought Saturns and situations where the car proves indispensable (see Exhibit 17.7).

Deceptive and irresponsible advertising is unlikely to disappear. The Federal Trade Commission and Food and Drug Administration will continue an important monitoring role. However, ultimately, marketers must regulate themselves. A positive sign is the greater awareness that marketers have of their responsibility to society. An example is advertising by some beer companies to discourage underage persons from drinking (see Exhibit 17.8 for an example).

SUMMARY

The chapter first presented a model of the marketing communications process in five steps: (1) development of an idea to be communicated by the marketer, (2) encoding the idea by the advertiser, (3) transmission by the mass media, (4) decoding of the message by the consumer, and (5) action by the consumer providing feedback to the advertiser to evaluate the effectiveness of the campaign. Marketers must consider the following questions in evaluating the effectiveness of advertising and other marketing communications:

- Have communications objectives been formulated to reflect consumer needs?

- Have marketers adequately encoded product benefits?

- Has the message been transmitted to the target segment utilizing the right media?

- Did consumers decode the message in the manner the advertiser intended?

- Does exposure to and acceptance of the message lead to a purchase?

The remainder of the chapter discussed the primary components of communications: source, message, media, receiver (consumer), and feedback.

Source effects focus on the credibility and acceptance of the source of the message. The greater the credibility of the source, the greater the likelihood consumers will accept the message. Source credibility is most important when consumers are not involved with the purchase. Involved consumers are more likely to focus on the message than on the source. Consumers regard reference groups, family, and impartial sources such as *Consumer Reports* and government agencies as more credible than commercial sources of information. Methods by which marketers could increase the level of their credibility were considered.

The main issues considered in evaluating message effects were the merits of (1) hedonic versus utilitarian appeals, (2) one-sided versus two-sided appeals, (3) comparative advertising, (4) fear appeals, and (5) humor in advertising.

Studies of media effects demonstrate the importance of the media environment in affecting consumers' perception of an ad and acceptance of the message.

The consumers' role in the communication process was also considered. Consumers evaluate the source of a communication, the message, and the media in which the message is transmitted. In evaluating the message, consumers develop cognitive responses that determine message acceptance. They also develop attitudes toward ads that might influence their attitudes toward the advertised brand.

In the last step of the communications process, we considered certain key issues in feedback: the measurement of indirect feedback through consumer thought variables, and the desirability yet difficulty of evaluating advertising based on direct consumer purchase response.

The chapter concluded by considering societal issues in marketing communications; namely, the need to monitor and control deceptive and irresponsible advertising.

QUESTIONS FOR DISCUSSION

1. Cite an example of an advertising campaign by describing the following:
   a. Advertising objectives and product concept established by the source
   b. How these objectives were encoded into an advertising campaign
   c. The media plan used to transmit the message to the target group
   d. Criteria the company will use in evaluating consumers' process of decoding the message

2. What are the barriers to communication (as illustrated in Figure 17.2) that might occur in the campaign you cited in Question 1?

3. What are some of the barriers to communication that marketers face on the Web?

4. Provide some examples of advertising wearout. How does advertising wearout apply to web advertising?

5. What criteria could Eveready use in evaluating the effectiveness of the Eveready Bunny campaign?

6. Use attribution theory to explain why consumers are more likely to consider advertising less credible than personal or neutral sources of information.

7. What are the pros and cons in stating that the Web is a highly credible source of information?

8. Why are source effects more important in gaining message acceptance for low-involvement compared with high-involvement consumers?

9. Assume Exxon initiates a campaign to convince the public that high gas prices are justified as a means of encouraging domestic exploration for oil. What principles could Exxon use to increase its credibility?

10. What strategies can companies use to increase their attractiveness as sources of marketing communications? Provide examples.

11. One use of emotional advertising is to try to increase the consumer's involvement with a product. Why has use of this type of advertising increased since the mid-1980s?

12. Why has computer advertising moved increasingly from utilitarian to more hedonic themes?

13. Two-sided advertisements were described as means of increasing both credibility and message acceptance. If so, why are so few advertisements two-sided?

14. Assume state and local agencies in California wish to undertake an educational campaign to alert the public to the dangers of earthquakes. They use several ads to show the severe devastation that earthquakes can produce to convince the public of the importance of the educational campaign. What factors are likely to encourage and discourage the acceptance of the message?

15. What are the risks of relying on an advertising campaign based on (a) comparative advertising and (b) humor?

16. In what ways is the Web a more involving medium than traditional broadcast and print media?

17. Under what conditions is source derogation most likely take place? Counterarguing?

18. How can advertisers discourage counterarguments when consumers are viewing an ad?

19. Given the difficulties in evaluating the effects of an advertising message on consumers' purchase decision, advertisers have used measures of con-

sumer attention, comprehension, and retention of advertising as criteria of effectiveness.

- What are some of the limitations of using these measures as criteria of advertising effectiveness?
- What approaches to advertising evaluation hold promise for providing direct feedback to establish the link between the advertising message and consumer behavior?
- How do advertisers measure advertising effectiveness on the Web?

20. Provide examples of deceptive and irresponsible advertising. Who should be responsible for monitoring and controlling such advertising?

RESEARCH ASSIGNMENTS

1 Visit *www.roche-bobois.com* and *www.ikea.com.* Does one site reflect hedonic themes and the other utilitarian? In what ways? Why?

2 Show consumers an ad for a high-involvement product (a car or an investment service) and a low-involvement product (toothpaste, paper towels). As consumers are looking at each ad, ask them to express their thoughts. Classify their comments into those that are related to message content versus those that are related to nonmessage (peripheral) elements in the ad (the use of a spokesperson, scenery, etc.).

Based on research cited in the text (see the subsection entitled "Cognitive Response"), we would expect consumers to express more message-related thoughts when viewing high-involvement ads and more nonmessage thoughts when viewing low-involvement ads. Did your study confirm this hypothesis?

3 Develop three advertising messages:
  a. One-sided ad (*e.g.,* "Avis is great")
  b. Two-sided refutational ad (*e.g.,* "Avis is number 2, but we try harder [than Hertz]")
  c. Two-sided nonrefutational ad (*e.g.,* "Avis may be smaller and may not have as many locations, but Avis is best in terms of price, the reliability of their cars, and service")

Ask fifty consumers to rate all three ads on (a) believability, (b) trustworthiness, and (c) expertise of the source. Ask consumers how likely they would be to buy the product or service after seeing each ad.

- Do the results conform to the findings on credibility and the effects of two-sided and comparative advertising cited in the text?
- What are the strategic implications of the findings?

4 Internet advertising is often criticized for not being as effective as offline advertising, due to decreasing click-through rates. Locate two ads—one online and one offline—that appeal to consumers through fear appeals. Also locate one online and one offline ad that is humorous, and one of each that appeals to fantasy. Ask fifty consumers to compare the ads from each medium.

- Do consumers find the on- or offline ads more effective?
- Are the online ads effective in conveying emotion? How can advertisers make online advertisements more effective?

NOTES

1. "Big Mac Takes a New Break with a Familiar McD's Twist," *Advertising Age* (March 13, 1995), p. 3.
2. "McDonald's New Ads Aiming for Smiles," *USA Today,* Ad Track (October 9, 2000), p. B7.
3. "Mickey, McD Hop Online," *Advertising Age* (August 28, 1995), p. 34.
4. "McDonald's," *Advertising Age* (August 6, 2001), p. S4.
5. "Burger King Hypes Herb Ads, But Many People Are Fed Up," *Wall Street Journal* (January 23, 1986), p. 33.
6. "How the Bunny Charged Eveready," *Advertising Age* (April 9, 1991), p. 20; and "Eveready Loses Power in Market," *Advertising Age* (July 11, 1988), p. 4.
7. "Energizer 'Fraud' Keeps Going and Going, Right to Cyberspace," *Advertising Age* (October 9, 2000), p. 103.
8. "Energizer Brands Set for Upgrades," *Twice* (May 21, 2000), p. 31.
9. David Streitfeld, "At eToys Site, It's Service with a Nervous Smile; Dot-com Pins Future on Customer Hand-Holding," *Washington Post* (December 3, 2000), p. A.1.
10. "Where Have All the Gerbils Gone?" *Wall Street Journal* (March 30, 2000), p. B1.
11. "What Happened to Advertising?" *Business Week* (September 23, 1991), p. 68.

12. http://www.thestandard.com/article/display/ 0,1151,22663,00.html, as of 2001.

13. Peter H. Webb, "Consumer Initial Processing in a Difficult Media Environment," *Journal of Consumer Research* 6 (December 1979), pp. 225–236.

14. Raymond R. Burke and Thomas K. Srull, "Competitive Interference and Consumer Memory for Advertising," *Journal of Consumer Research* 15 (June 1988), pp. 55–68.

15. "The Future of Advertising," *Business Week* (March 26, 2001), p. 138; and http://www.thestandard.com/article/ display/0,1151,22663,00.html, as of 2001.

16. Ibid.

17. Carl I. Hovland, Irving L. Janis, and Harold H. Kelley, *Communication and Persuasion* (New Haven, Conn.: Yale University Press, 1953). See also Grant McCracken, "Who Is the Celebrity Endorser? Cultural Foundations of the Endorsement Process," *Journal of Consumer Research* 16 (December 1989), pp. 310–321.

18. "Star Power," *Sales and Marketing Management* (April 2001), pp. 52–59.

19. C. Samuel Craig and John M. McCann, "Assessing Communication Effects on Energy Conservation," *Journal of Consumer Research* 5 (September 1978), pp. 82–88.

20. http://www.thestandard.com/article/display/ 0,1151,22663,00.html, as of 2001.

21. "Amazon Plans to Charge Publishers Fee for Online Recommendations," *Wall Street Journal* (February 7, 2001), p. B1.

22. Ruby Roy Dholakia and Brian Sternthal, "Highly Credible Sources: Persuasive Facilitators or Persuasive Liabilities?" *Journal of Consumer Research* 3 (March 1977), pp. 223–232; Alice Eagly and Shelly Chaiken, "An Attribution Analysis of the Effect of Communicator Characteristics on Opinion Change: The Case of Communicator Attractiveness," *Journal of Personality and Social Psychology* 32 (1975), pp. 136–144; H. Sigall and R. Helmreigh, "Opinion Change as a Function of Stress and Communicator Credibility," *Journal of Experimental Social Psychology* 5 (1969), pp. 70–78.

23. Michael A. Kamins and Henry Assael, "Two-Sided Versus One-Sided Appeals: A Cognitive Perspective on Argumentation, Source Derogation, and the Effect of Disconfirming Trial on Belief Change," *Journal of Marketing Research* 24 (February 1987), pp. 29–39; and Robert B. Settle and Linda L. Golden, "Attribution Theory and Advertiser Credibility," *Journal of Marketing Research* 11 (May 1974), pp. 181–185.

24. William J. McGuire, "Attitudes and Attitude Change," in Gardner Lindzey and Elliot Aronson, eds., *Handbook of Social Psychology* (New York: Random House, 1985), pp. 233–346; Timothy C. Brock, "Communication-Recipient Similarity and Decision Change," *Journal of Personality and Social Psychology* 1 (June 1965), pp. 650–654; and Arch J. Woodside and J. William Davenport, "The Effect of Salesman Similarity and Expertise on Consumer Purchasing Behavior," *Journal of Marketing Research* 11 (May 1974), pp. 198–202.

25. "Goofy Dell Guy Exudes Star Power," *USA Today* (January 14, 2002), p. 5B.

26. David Mazursky and Yaacov Schul, "Learning from the Ad or Relying on Related Attitudes: The Moderating Role of Involvement," *Journal of Business Research* 25 (1992), pp. 81–93.

27. George J. Szybillo and Richard Heslin, "Resistance to Persuasion: Inoculation Theory in a Marketing Context," *Journal of Marketing Research* 10 (November 1973), pp. 396–403; and Kamins and Assael, "Two-Sided Versus One-Sided Appeals," pp. 29–39.

28. Smith and Hunt, "Attribution Processes and Effects," pp. 149–158; Toy, "Monitoring Communication Effects," pp. 66–76; and Swanson, "The Persuasive Effect of Volunteering Negative Information," pp. 237–248.

29. Mark I. Alpert and Linda L. Golden, "The Impact of Education on the Relative Effectiveness of One-Sided Communications," in Bruce J. Walker et al., *Proceedings of the American Marketing Association Educators' Conference,* Series No. 48 (Chicago: American Marketing Association, 1982), pp. 30–33; and Edmund W. J. Faison, "Effectiveness of One-Sided and Two-Sided Mass Communications in Advertising," *Public Opinion Quarterly* 25 (1961), pp. 468–469.

30. "Sour Dough: Pizza Hut vs. Papa John's," *Brandweek* (May 21, 2001), pp. 26–30.

31. Ibid.

32. William R. Swinyard, "The Interaction Between Comparative Advertising and Copy Claim Variation," *Journal of Marketing Research* 18 (May 1981), pp. 175–186.

33. "The Effects of Comparative Television Advertising that Names Competing Brands," Private report by Ogilvy and Mather Research, New York.

34. Jerry B. Gotlieb and Dan Sarel, "Comparative Advertising Effectiveness: The Role of Involvement and Source Credibility," *Journal of Advertising* 20 (1991), pp. 38–45; and Jerry B. Gotlieb and Dan Sarel, "The Influence of Type of Advertisement, Price, and Source Credibility on Perceived Quality," *Journal of the Academy of Marketing Science* 20 (1992), pp. 253–260.

35. Swinyard, "The Interaction Between Comparative Advertising and Copy Claim Variation," pp. 175–186.

36. Cornelia Pechmann and David W. Stewart, "The Effects of Comparative Advertising on Attention, Memory, and Purchase Intentions," *Journal of Consumer Research* 17 (September 1990), pp. 180–191. See also Cornelia Pechmann and S. Ratneshwar, "The Use of Comparative Advertising for Brand Positioning: Association Versus Differentiation," *Journal of Consumer Research* 18 (September 1991), pp. 145–160.

37. "Theories of Negativity," *Brandweek* (February 20, 1995), pp. 20–22.

38. "Smash, Bang, Crunch, Screech—Wow, What a Car," *Wall Street Journal* (April 13, 2001), p. B1.

39. Mark A. deTuck, Gerald M. Goldhaber, Gary M. Richetto, and Melissa J. Young, "Effects of Fear-Arousing Warning Messages," *Journal of Products Liability* 14 (1992), pp. 217–223.

40. John F. Tanner, Jr., James B. Hunt, and David R. Eppright, "The Protection Motivation Model: A Normative Model of Fear Appeals," *Journal of Marketing* 55 (July 1991), pp. 36–45.

41. Priya Raghubir and Geeta Menon, "AIDS and Me, Never the Twain Shall Meet: The Effects of Information Accessibility on Judgments of Risk and Advertising Effectiveness," *Journal of Consumer Research* 25 (June 1998), pp. 52–63.

42. "Humorous, Feel-Good Advertising Hits Home with Consumers," *DSN Retailing Today* (April 22, 2002), p. 14.

43. "Funny Ads Make Comeback," *Los Angeles Times* (January 10, 2002), p. C1.

44. Calvin P. Duncan, James E. Nelson, and Nancy T. Frontczak, "The Effect of Humor on Advertising Comprehension," in Thomas C. Kinnear, ed., *Advances in Consumer Research,* Vol. 11 (Provo, Utah: Association for Consumer Research, 1984), pp. 432–437; and Calvin P. Duncan and James E. Nelson, "Effects of Humor in a Radio Advertising Experiment," *Journal of Advertising* 14 (1985), pp. 33–40; "After Serious 70s, Advertisers Are Going for Laughs Again," *Wall Street Journal* (February 23, 1984), p. 31; and Brian Sternthal and C. Samuel Craig, "Humor in Advertising," *Journal of Marketing* 37 (October 1973), pp. 12–18.

45. Duncan, Nelson, and Frontczak, "The Effect of Humor," pp. 432–437.

46. Sternthal and Craig, "Humor in Advertising," pp. 12–18.

47. "Speed Bumps," *Forbes* (April 30, 2001), pp. 113–115.

48. "Hartford Life Turns from Humor to Family Concerns," *New York Times* (March 4, 2002), p. C11.

49. Marc G. Weinberger and Leland Campbell, "The Use and Impact of Humor in Radio Advertising," *Journal of Advertising Research* 31 (December/January 1991), pp. 44–52.

50. David M. Stewart and David H. Furse, *Effective Television Advertising* (Lexington, Mass.: D.C. Heath, 1986).

51. Amitava Chattopadhyay and Kunal Basu, "Humor in Advertising: The Moderating Role of Prior Brand Evaluation," *Journal of Marketing Research* 27 (November 1990), pp. 466–476.

52. Marshall McLuhan, *The Medium Is the Message* (New York: Random House, 1967).

53. David A. Aaker and Phillip K. Brown, "Evaluating Vehicle Source Effects," Journal of *Advertising Research* 12 (August 1972), pp. 11–16.

54. Herbert E. Krugman, "The Impact of Television Advertising: Learning Without Involvement," *Public Opinion Quarterly* 29 (Fall 1965), pp. 349–356; and Herbert E. Krugman, "The Measurement of Advertising Involvement," *Public Opinion Quarterly* 30 (Winter 1966–1967), pp. 583–596.

55. Michael Tuan Pham and Gita Venkataramani Johar, "Contingent Processes of Source Identification," *Journal of Consumer Research* 24 (December 1997), pp. 249–265.

56. Peter L. Wright, "The Cognitive Processes Mediating Acceptance of Advertising," *Journal of Marketing Research* 10 (February 1973), pp. 53–62.

57. Shailendra Pratap Jain and Durairaj Maheswaran, "Motivated Reasoning: A Depth-of-Processing Perspective," *Journal of Consumer Research* (March 2000), pp. 358–371.

58. Martin R. Lautman and Larry Percy, "Cognitive and Affective Responses in Attribute-Based Versus End-Benefit Oriented Advertising," in Thomas C. Kinnear, ed., *Advances in Consumer Research,* Vol. 11 (Provo, Utah: Association for Consumer Research, 1984), pp. 11–17.

59. Scott B. MacKenzie and Richard J. Lutz, "An Empirical Examination of the Structural Antecedents of Attitude Toward the Ad in an Advertising Pretesting Context," *Journal of Marketing* 53 (April 1989), pp. 48–61.

60. Abhilasha Mehta, "Advertising Attitudes and Advertising Effectiveness," *Journal of Advertising Research* 40 (May/June 2000), pp. 67–72.

61. Thomas J. Olney, Morris B. Holbrook, and Rajeev Batra, "Consumer Responses to Advertising: The Effects of Ad Content, Emotions, and Attitude Toward the Ad on Viewing Time," *Journal of Consumer Research* 17 (March 1991), pp. 440–453; and Meryl Paula Gardner, "Does Attitude Toward the Ad Affect Brand Attitude Under a Brand Evaluation Set?" *Journal of Marketing Research* 22 (May 1985), pp. 192–198. See also Paul W. Miniard, Sunil Bhatla, and Randall L. Rose, "On the Formation and Relationship of Ad and Brand Attitudes: An Experimental and Causal Analysis," *Journal of Marketing Research* 27 (August 1990), pp. 290–303.

62. Christopher P. Puto and William D. Wells, "Informational and Transformational Advertising: The Differential Effects of Time," in Thomas C. Kinnear, ed., *Advances in Consumer Research,* Vol. 11 (Provo, Utah: Association for Consumer Research, 1984), pp. 572–576. See also Julie A. Edell and Marian Chapman Burke, "The Power of Feelings in Understanding Advertising Effects," *Journal of Consumer Research* 14 (December 1987), pp. 421–433.

63. See Alvin J. Silk and T. G. Vavra, "The Influence of Advertising's Affective Qualities On Consumer Responses," in G. R. Hughes, ed., *Buyer/Consumer Information Processing* (Chapel Hill: University of North Carolina Press, 1974), pp. 157–186; and Danny L. Moore and J. Wesley Hutchinson, "The Effects of Ad Affect on Advertising Effectiveness," in Richard P. Bagozzi and Alice M. Tybout, eds., *Advances in Consumer Research,* Vol. 10 (Ann Arbor, Mich.: Association for Consumer Research, 1983), pp. 526–531.

64. Silk and Vavra, "The Influence of Advertising's Affective Qualities," pp. 157–186.

65. "Naming the Competition in Advertising," *Listening Post* (New York: Ogilvy and Mather, 1984).

66. See Meryl Paula Gardner, "Mood States and Consumer Research: A Critical Review," *Journal of Consumer Research* 12 (December 1985), pp. 281–300.

67. Thomas R. Srull, "Memory, Mood, and Consumer Judgment," in Melanie Wallendorf and Paul Anderson, eds., *Advances in Consumer Research,* Vol. 14 (Provo, Utah: Association for Consumer Research, 1987), pp. 404–407.

68. Daniel J. Howard and Charles Gengler, "Emotional Contagion Effects on Product Attitudes," *Journal of Consumer Research* 28 (September 2001), pp. 189–201.

69. Robert E. Burnkrant, H. Rao Unnava, and Kenneth R. Lord, "The Effects of Programming Induced Mood States on Memory for Commercial Information," working paper series, The Ohio State University, October, 1987.

70. John R. Kennedy, "How Program Environment Affects TV Commercials," *Journal of Advertising Research* 11 (February 1971), pp. 33–38.

71. Gary F. Soldow and Victor Principe, "Response to Commercials as a Function of Program Context," *Journal of Advertising Research* 21 (April 1981), pp. 59–65.

72. "For Some Ads, Glum People Make the Best Sales Prospects," *Wall Street Journal* (July 25, 1985), p. 23.

73. William J. McGuire, "An Information-Processing Model of Advertising Effectiveness," in Harry L. Davis and Alvin J. Silk, eds., *Behavioral and Management Sciences in Marketing* (New York: Ronald/Wiley, 1978), pp. 156–180.

74. "Block Is Ordered to Stop Advertising 'Rapid Refunds' of Taxes," *New York Times* (January 28, 2001), pp. C1, C2.

75. "Reebok: If the Shoe Fits," *Adweek* (January 7, 1991), p. 23.

18

Market Segmentation and Micromarketing

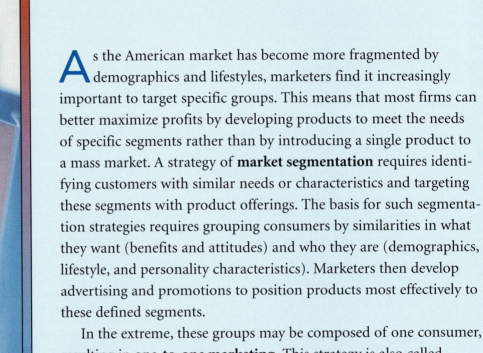

As the American market has become more fragmented by demographics and lifestyles, marketers find it increasingly important to target specific groups. This means that most firms can better maximize profits by developing products to meet the needs of specific segments rather than by introducing a single product to a mass market. A strategy of **market segmentation** requires identifying customers with similar needs or characteristics and targeting these segments with product offerings. The basis for such segmentation strategies requires grouping consumers by similarities in what they want (benefits and attitudes) and who they are (demographics, lifestyle, and personality characteristics). Marketers then develop advertising and promotions to position products most effectively to these defined segments.

In the extreme, these groups may be composed of one consumer, resulting in **one-to-one marketing.** This strategy is also called **micromarketing** and is a logical extension of market segmentation strategies. In micromarketing, producers often allow many consumers to customize products to their individual needs, a process known as **mass customization.**

Volvo Reinvents Itself through a Strategy of Market Segmentation

The importance of defining consumer segments is reflected in Volvo's past strategy of identifying its cars with safety. The company recognized that a segment of consumers emphasized car safety above all and, within reasonable limits, was willing to trade off style or comfort for safety. A majority of the individuals willing to make this tradeoff were safety-oriented baby boomers who embraced family security, and soccer moms, middle-aged suburban mothers. As of 1999, 90 percent of Volvo buyers were defined as being in these two segments. The typical demographic profile was a consumer who was married with two kids, made over $125,000 annually, and was in his or her mid to late 40s.[1]

The brand's demographic was largely a result of Volvo's traditional, safety-based advertising campaigns. Throughout its history, the company focused on safety as its sole defining feature, using tag lines such as "A car you can believe in" and "Drive safely."[2] Television and print ads focused on the car's safety features and reliability, reinforcing the boxy, boring mindset consumers developed about Volvo.

But Volvo began to see its share shrinking among older baby boomers as other brands began to zone in successfully on the same safety message. As a result, in the early 1990s, Volvo started to see its sales dip. Volvo needed to increase car sales by increasing its appeal to a broader group of consumers; namely, empty nesters and young couples who were under 35, made more than $75,000 annually, and had no children.[3] This group, composed primarily of Generation Xers, valued performance and style above safety in car purchase decisions.

To appeal to this group, Volvo decided to reposition itself with a sportier, fun image without eroding its traditional safety message. It was a delicate balancing act, especially for a niche player like Volvo, because it needed to expand its appeal without alienating its safety-conscious, family-oriented core customers. Volvo's challenge was to develop a repositioning strategy to appeal to both Generation Xers and baby boomers.

Another challenge for Volvo was reconciling the different consumer perceptions in different countries in order to reposition its brand effectively worldwide. In the United States, Volvo was perceived as a safe, but upscale automobile. In the United Kingdom, Volvo's image was much more lackluster and required a more dramatic message to change consumer perceptions. In other areas of the world, like the Far East, Volvo was typically seen as an upscale, prestige brand.[4]

The repositioning effort began by changing the actual product line to appeal to the new target.[5] The photo in Exhibit 18.1 shows the C70 convertible.

EXHIBIT 18.1

Volvo expands its model line to appeal to new market segments.
Visuals Unlimited.

The campaign for the car was part of a $30 million effort in 2000 to position the model with a tongue-in-cheek reference to Volvo's past stodgy image, using the tag line "Yet another safe and practical family car from Volvo."[6] The basic theme is "fun." But Volvo continues to focus on safety as well, to maintain a link to its core customers.

Volvo also took a step toward micromarketing in 2000 by initiating the first exclusive, digital-media-only campaign to reach the 30-something crowd and further distance the brand from its past perceptions. The car company partnered with America Online (AOL) to develop a campaign using banner ads and promotions on the Internet to attract technology-oriented customers. Volvo sent out five hundred thousand CD-ROMs to current and potential owners to entrench itself further in its new market.[7] The company expects to channel a larger and larger portion of its media spending to Internet marketing. Volvo also developed a customization capability on its web site *(www.volvocars.com)* to allow customers to develop models to individual specifications, a prime example of mass customization.

Even with all of Volvo's careful efforts to expand its target segments and shift consumers' perceptions of the brand, Volvo is still mostly associated with safety and upper-middle-class suburban families in consumers' minds. This demonstrates the difficulty of repositioning brands, especially for established and well-known brands and high-involvement products like automobiles. Volvo runs the risk of creating a fuzzy brand image by trying to appeal to two segments with a strong safety and performance image at the same time. Volvo's own research has shown that many consumers "are unclear whether the cars are luxury vehicles, what their average prices are and who the brand's target is."[8]

Volvo's strategy illustrates the potential and the risks of segmenting markets: the potential of targeting specific products to defined segments to better meet their needs; the risk that unless there is consistency and uniformity in these strategies, the brand's image might be diluted.

Mass Marketing, Market Segmentation, and Micromarketing

Consumers today face a growing range of choices across all categories of products. Since the early 1970s, for example, the variety of new vehicle models has grown from 140 to over 260, soft drinks from 20 to nearly 90, television channels from 5 to 185 (and ever increasing), and over-the-counter pain relievers from 17 to 141.[9] Even more mundane products like bottled water appeal to every consumer taste—still or carbonated, flavored or nonflavored, spring or mineral, all-natural or mineral-enhanced, with or without vitamins. The proliferation of consumer products results from marketers' responses to the changes occurring in the marketplace—the fragmentation of the American marketplace, new technologies, and more intense competition.

In this chapter, we consider the movement of the marketplace from an environment of limited choice characterized by mass marketing to one of greater choice through market segmentation and, the ultimate in consumer choice, micromarketing and mass customization.

Mass Marketing

Mass marketing resulted from scale-driven mass production and distribution technologies that allowed marketers to follow a product- and sales-oriented approach rather than a customer-driven approach.[10] Consumers in the post–World War II period had many unmet needs and were satisfied with reasonably priced, standardized products. An understanding of consumer behavior was less important in this environment. Marketing efforts instead focused on the "4Ps" (price, promotion, place, and product) for the mass market. This marketing strategy is known as a "product-centric approach"; that is, a "sell what we make" marketing philosophy. Mass marketing reflected a "one-to-many" model with producers offering a single standardized brand for everyone and leveraging economies of scale to control costs.

Mass marketing strategies relied on nationally focused media such as major television networks and national magazines. Advertising primarily served up repetitive themes and jingles to create brand awareness. Consumers did not have many choices. Coca-Cola was a one-brand company; Chevrolet, a one-model division. The mass marketing approach was an effective strategy during this period given the relative homogeneity of the U.S. mass market—broadly defined as a "middle-class family with one wage earner and a homemaker with two or three children."[11]

Market Segmentation

Starting in the mid-1960s, mass marketing became increasingly ineffective as a result of two macro trends. The first was an increase in competitive forces. With more firms entering the market, product variety increased, and consequently consumers could make choices, rendering the one-to-many model less effective.[12] Firms began to shift from product-centric marketing to a more consumer-oriented approach. This trend could be witnessed in firms like AT&T, which reorganized in this period along household and business markets with subdivisions within each of these major groupings.[13]

The second trend was the demographic and lifestyle fragmentation of the American marketplace. The major shifts, which included more single-person and single-parent households, more varied lifestyle choices, greater ethnic diversity, and more specific and well-defined age cohorts, were covered in Chapters 9 and 10.

Given this fragmentation, achieving economies of scale no longer justified ignoring segmentation and targeting. The disaggregation of markets meant that the increase in marginal revenues from targeting to smaller consumer segments became greater than the consequent increase in marginal costs from losses of economies of scale. In the 1960s and 1970s, segments such as minority groups and working women increasingly gained importance as viable markets for refined marketing efforts. In the 1980s and 1990s, these groups were further defined. Today, rather than defining a Hispanic market, many companies segment it into Mexican, Puerto Rican, Cuban, and South American segments. Rather than targeting working women, marketers are dividing them into professional, white-collar, blue-collar, and part-time segments.

Although mass market advertising channels such as television and national magazines are still a necessary component of a company's promotional mix, marketers are directing more dollars to more focused alternatives like specialized magazines, direct mail, catalogs, and the Internet to reach specific segments. For example, Cable TV channels now reach defined demographics, such as Univision for the Spanish-speaking community, Oxygen and We for women, and BET for African Americans. In magazines, new titles appeal to specific consumer segments, such as *Latina* for young Hispanic women. Although the cost of advertising in these targeted channels is higher than in mass market media, the ad itself is arguably more powerful because it reaches its intended audience more effectively.

STRATEGIC RESULTS OF A TARGETED APPROACH

We can assess the strategic results of disaggregation in the last thirty to forty years based on marketing's classical 4Ps framework.

■ **Product**   Consumers now enjoy a broader product mix. Coca-Cola offers Coke Classic, Diet Coke, Caffeine-free Diet Coke, and Cherry Coke; PepsiCo offers a similar product mix. These companies have also targeted Generations X and Y with a series of New Age beverages. Altogether, these product extensions coupled with a multitude of bottle size and shape options have resulted in more SKUs (stock keeping units) than ever before in supermarkets and mass merchandisers. Moreover, companies have leveraged their brands in marketing new products such as Coca-Cola's Vanilla Coke and Pepsi-Co's Mountain Dew Code Red.

■ **Promotion**   In advertising, marketers have shifted emphasis from a behavioral to a cognitive approach; that is, message content over form (see Chapter 3). Jingles and memorable tag lines still exist, as evidenced in Mountain Dew's "Do the Dew" campaign, but ads now are more focused on delivering product and service information to an increasingly knowledgeable consumer public. Volvo's web site not only displays the logo, most recent tag line, and newest car models, but it also offers performance and other details regarding its models. As the ad content becomes more information-driven, the media mix is also shifting from mass marketing delivery channels such as network television to cable, specialized magazines, and increasingly, the Internet. As a result, today media buys are more targeted.

■ **Place**   In addition to specialty stores such as ethnic supermarkets, marketers increasingly rely on scanner data to assist in more targeted distribution of merchandise across various regions. For example, supermarkets in Miami's Little Havana may carry corn tortillas to serve the large Hispanic population. Although the Web has not met expectations as a vehicle for purchasing goods, web sales are still increasing exponentially, providing consumers with greater time and place utility.

Price Companies are shifting from a cost-plus pricing structure to a demand-oriented pricing structure. The most apparent manifestation of demand-oriented pricing is "value pricing" on the Web; that is, setting a price based on the perceived consumer value of a product or service. On Priceline.com, for example, consumers offer the price they are willing to pay for an airline ticket and airline companies bid for the consumer's business based on that price (see Exhibit 18.2).

APPROACHES TO MARKET SEGMENTATION

Market segments must be identified before they can be targeted for marketing effort. That is, the needs, brand attitudes, and demographic and lifestyle characteristics of a target segment must be determined to permit marketers to develop products and marketing strategies to appeal to it. Table 18.1 lists three bases for identifying market segments: by *benefits, behavior,* and *consumer response elasticity.*

TABLE 18.1
Three bases for market segmentation analysis

Basis for segmentation	Strategic objective	Criteria
Benefits (needs)	Develop new products and position existing products	• Nutrition • Health • Economy • Good taste • Performance • Prestige
Behavior	Develop marketing strategies	• Brand usage • Product category usage • Level of use (heavy or light)
Response elasticity	Target the marketing effort	• Price elasticity • Deal elasticity • Advertising elasticity

■ **Benefit Segmentation** A consumer-oriented approach to marketing requires defining segments by the benefits they desire in a product, an approach known as **benefit segmentation.** Marketers use benefit (need) criteria to determine the potential for new products. A beverage company might identify a common need among many women over 50 for calcium-enriched products to strengthen bones. Women within this group would be a benefit segment because they have a common need. The company might consider introducing a calcium-fortified fruit drink to appeal to this group based on the similarity of their needs.

An example of benefit segmentation for a total product line is provided by Coca-Cola (see Figure 18.1). It was one of the first companies to recognize the importance of diet products when it introduced Tab in 1963 as a diet cola positioned to women. Twenty years later, it used the magic name Coke on a product other than its flagship brand for the first time by introducing Diet Coke, positioned to men. In the 1980s, it also introduced caffeine-free versions of Coca-Cola, Diet Coke, and Tab, positioned to a health-oriented segment. Cherry Coke and later, Vanilla Coke, were further extensions of the Coke name to appeal to teenagers who wanted a sweeter cola drink. The company also positioned Sprite to those who like lemon-lime and introduced Minute Maid soda as a fruit-based drink that was leveraged from Coca-Cola–owned Minute Maid fruit juice.

| **FIGURE 18.1** |

Benefit segmentation of Coca Cola's product line.

Benefit segments / **Products**

Benefit segments	Cola	Diet cola	Caffeine-free	Fruit-based	Lemon-lime
Taste-oriented: Like sweet-tasting colas	Vanilla Coke, Cherry Coke				
Taste-oriented: Like unsweetened colas	Coca-Cola Classic				
Taste-oriented: Like fruit juice				Minute Maid	
Taste-oriented: Like lemon-lime					Sprite
Health/nutrition-conscious			Caffeine-Free Tab, Coke, and Diet Coke	Minute Maid	
Weight watchers		Diet Coke, Tab, and Diet Cherry Coke			

Overall, Figure 18.1 represents a consistent benefit segmentation strategy, particularly since 1983, when Coca-Cola started expanding its product line in earnest.

▌Behavioral Segmentation Once a product is in the marketplace, companies must define segments by who is buying, an approach known as **behavioral segmentation.** Table 18.1 lists three criteria for defining segments by consumer behavior: (1) brand usage, (2) product category usage, and (3) level of product use (heavy to light). In each case, the demographics, lifestyles, and brand attitudes of these user groups must be identified.

Brand Usage. The most frequently used form of behavioral segmentation is distinguishing those who purchase the company's brand from those who purchase competitive brands.

Once brand users are defined, two approaches can be taken. The first directs resources to those segments with the highest probability of purchasing the brand. Yamaha uses this approach in choosing sites for new dealerships.[14] Yamaha assumes that prospective purchasers of its motorcycles will be similar to existing owners. It then determines the demographic characteristics of areas where it is considering new dealerships by using Census Bureau data. It locates dealerships in those areas whose demographic profiles most closely match the demographic profile of the Yamaha owner. The basic assumption is that nonowners with similar characteristics to owners are most likely to buy the brand.

The second approach in segmenting by brand usage is to direct new products to segments that are unlikely to buy the existing brand. Volvo followed this approach by targeting a new line of cars to single Generation Xers and empty nesters, groups that were unlikely to buy its traditional models.

Product Category Usage. Product category usage is a common basis for behavioral segmentation. Marketers may wish to identify consumers who buy a product category rather than a brand. Purchasers of salt-free snacks may tend to be older, health-conscious consumers, regardless of what brand of snack food they buy. Their demographic characteristics reflect the need for the product. In such cases, marketers are more likely to use product rather than brand purchase as a guide in selecting media or determining advertising appeals.

Segmenting by product usage is particularly useful when companies band together to advertise a product—for example, the California Milk Advisory Board, America's Dairy Farmers and Milk Processors, or the Beef Council. In such cases, the cooperative wants to determine the characteristics of nonusers to target them more effectively with advertising and other promotions. Exhibit 18.3 is an example of the widely acclaimed "milk mustache" print ad campaign from America's Dairy Farmers and Milk Processors cooperative. The campaign is targeted to consumers interested in health and fitness.

Level of Usage. A common practice among marketers is to segment markets by level of product usage (heavy versus light users). A company then has two options: (1) to position a product to the heavy users, who generate more product volume and revenues, or (2) to position a product to light users, who may represent an ignored niche in the marketplace.

Father knows best.
Want to win? Milk has 9 essential nutrients active bodies need.
In other words, it's the greatest.

got milk?

For example, Nestlé chose to position its iced tea to heavy users. It segmented consumers of tea by their level of usage and identified the benefits heavy and light users associated with iced tea. The company found that the heaviest usage group drank twice as much tea as the average consumer and represented over one-third of total iced tea volume. This group saw iced tea as a year-round drink that restores energy. Nestle used this information to target heavy users with a year-round energy theme.

▌ **Segmenting by Response Elasticity**   The third basis for segmenting markets is by consumer sensitivity to marketers' strategies, known as **response elasticity.** Some customers are more sensitive to a price increase, a change in advertising expenditures, or an increase in the effort to provide deals than are others. Response elasticity measures a consumer's sensitivity to a particular marketing stimulus by associating a percentage change in the stimulus with a percentage change in quantity purchased. Underlying segmentation by response elasticities is the basic principle that marketers should increase or decrease allocations to a segment according to the response of that segment. If all segments responded equally to marketing effort, there would be no basis for differentially allocating resources.

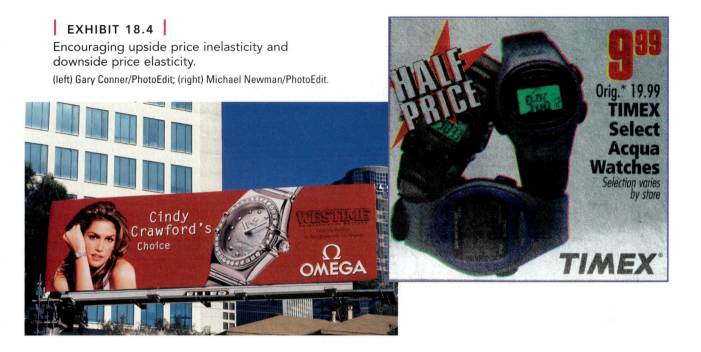

Segmenting by Price Elasticity. The most common basis for segmenting by
response elasticity is based on sensitivity to changes in price, as measured by a consumer's price elasticity. Price elasticity is measured by the percentage change in
quantity purchased divided by the percentage change in price.

If the percentage change in quantity is more than the percentage change in price,
demand is elastic. In such a case, a decrease in price will produce a more than pro-
portionate increase in quantity, resulting in an increase in the company's revenues.
If the percentage change in quantity is less than the percentage change in price,
demand is inelastic. In this case, an increase in price will produce a less than pro-
portionate decrease in quantity, resulting in an increase in revenue. Therefore, price
decreases in an elastic market and price increases in an inelastic market generally
increase a company's revenues.

When consumers are price elastic, they switch brands based on price. When they
are inelastic, they tend to remain loyal to a brand. Price is fairly elastic for items
ordinarily purchased in supermarkets or drugstores and inelastic for prestige products such as designer clothes or gourmet foods. Demand can be inelastic for everyday products, however. For example, a consumer loyal to Pampers disposable
diapers or to Bounty paper towels may continue to buy even if prices increase by 10
percent or 20 percent.

There is a distinction between **upside price elasticity** (sensitivity to price
increases) and **downside price elasticity** (sensitivity to price decreases). Marketers
try to encourage upside price inelasticity by advertising products on a prestige basis
and downside price elasticity by advertising low prices or price promotions. For
example, the Omega ad in Exhibit 18.4 is an attempt to create upside price inelasticity by conveying luxury and using Cindy Crawford as a spokeswoman. Timex is
appealing to downside elasticity by advertising a reliable watch with a well-known
name for less than $10.

A good example of segmenting by price elasticity is shown in a study AT&T conducted after an increase in long-distance rates.[15] The company identified consumers who either increased or maintained their rate of calling in the face of a price increase (the price inelastic segment) and those who decreased their usage (the price elastic segment). The study found that the price inelastic segment tended to be higher-income consumers who were either young married couples or families with teenagers. These two groups are less sensitive to a price increase because of their greater dependence on the phone. Because of the price sensitivity of lower-income consumers, one implication of the study was to better inform these segments of lower rates for off-peak and direct-dial calls.

Segmenting by Responses to Other Marketing Stimuli. Consumers can be segmented by their responses to marketing stimuli other than price; for example, deal, coupon, advertising, and even package-size elasticity. The value of segmenting by such response elasticities is that it provides management with a basis to

- direct price promotions, deals, and coupons to the most responsive consumers (an important consideration in a recessionary period).
- identify groups most likely to respond positively to increases in advertising expenditures.

Studies of response elasticity depend on scanner data; that is, sales data from stores with laser scanners. Research has utilized scanner panels where consumers buy groceries using magnetically coded cards, allowing manufacturers to determine what an individual consumer has purchased and at what price. Companies can then identify consumers who tend to switch brands frequently because of changes in price and promotions (the price-elastic segment), and consumers who stay loyal to a given brand (the price-inelastic segment). In addition, some of these households have monitors in their homes to determine their television viewing. This allows marketers to relate what consumers have viewed to what they are buying, providing a measure of advertising elasticity for individual households.

LIMITS TO MARKET SEGMENTATION

The segmentation strategies cited in the last section have several limits. One is that companies may go too far in dividing the market and targeting products to smaller and smaller segments. Such "oversegmentation" means that the costs of appealing to these segments are greater than the revenues derived. Soft drink companies like Coca-Cola have been criticized for oversegmenting their markets. For example, is it necessary to have a caffeine-free version of both Diet Coke and Tab, especially given the latter's low market share? A tongue-in-cheek representation of such oversegmentation is presented in Figure 18.2.

Another problem with segmentation strategies is that they run counter to the greater price sensitivity of many consumers. Developing specific products to target segments comes at a price, and consumers are often willing to accept more standardized, lower-priced generic and no-frill products rather than higher-priced branded goods. Despite these limitations, segmentation strategies have become the rule in an attempt to meet the needs of a more fragmented American marketplace.

New Coke

Coke Classic

Cherry New Coke

Cherry Coke Classic

Diet New Coke

Diet Coke Classic

Diet Cherry New Coke

Diet Cherry Coke Classic

Low-Caffeine New Coke

Low-Caffeine Coke Classic

Low-Caffeine Cherry New Coke

Low-Caffeine Cherry Coke Classic

Low-Caffeine Diet New Coke

Low-Caffeine Diet Coke Classic

Low-Caffeine Diet Cherry New Coke

Low-Caffeine Diet Cherry Coke Classic

Caffeine-Free New Coke

Caffeine-Free Coke Classic

Caffeine-Free Cherry New Coke

Caffeine-Free Cherry Coke Classic

Caffeine-Free Diet New Coke

Caffeine-Free Diet Coke Classic

Caffeine-Free Diet Cherry New Coke

Caffeine-Free Diet Cherry Coke Classic

Micromarketing

Micromarketing is not a new concept. Direct mail and telemarketing have been long-standing tools marketers use to appeal to individual consumers. What has changed, however, is the emphasis product managers place on the needs of individual consumers, and their ability to meet individual needs with new technologies. As a result, marketers have focused increasingly on one-to-one marketing strategies.

The driving force behind the shift toward micromarketing is disaggregation of the U.S. consumer market due to demographic and lifestyle changes. As a result, increased competition has spurred companies to refine the definition of their target groups. Technology has enabled targeting to occur on a one-to-one basis. The Internet has made possible (1) access to a greater range of information, (2) access to broader choices, and (3) interactivity with marketers that allows consumers to express their individual wants. As a result, consumers have become more empowered. Armed with information and knowledge of alternatives, consumers can be more efficient decision makers. Moreover, the interactivity of the Internet means that consumers can shape information and products to their needs, creating a higher level of involvement in product purchase decisions.

Fragmentation and consumer empowerment have led many companies to embrace mass customization; that is, delivering a product or service to many customers at their specifications.[16] With mass customization, consumers gain from products designed to meet their unique needs, while marketers gain from the ability to differentiate their products from the competition.[17] Moreover, marketers hope to win customer loyalty, creating greater price inelasticity to allow premium pricing and higher margins.

Mass customization reflects an evolution from a one-to-many approach to a one-to-one focus, from the mass marketing strategy of Henry Ford's Model T era to the purchase of customized products ranging from Levi's jeans to Dell's desktop computers to Volvo's newest car models. The differences are reflected in a shift from

∎ standardized to customized brands.

∎ low- to high-involvement purchases as a result of the ability to customize.

∎ economies of scale to targeted efficiency.

Customized products are no longer an option reserved for the wealthy few who could afford premium prices. Technologies such as the Web and just-in-time manufacturing and distribution systems allow companies to offer customization to the masses at reasonable prices.

An important aspect of micromarketing is establishing relationships with customers on a one-to-one basis, even after the purchase, based on the objective of retaining the customer for the long term. Such **relationship marketing** strategies frequently utilize the Web because of its facility for interactivity in directing messages to the specific needs of customers. Micromarketing and relationship marketing require that marketers understand consumers' needs and wants. Consumers must be willing to provide this information. In return they are likely to experience greater satisfaction with the marketer's products.

The rest of this section discusses micromarketing in the context of consumer empowerment. It also assesses the requirements and strategic implications for such an approach.

CONSUMER EMPOWERMENT

Consumer empowerment is the driver behind one-to-one marketing. A greater focus on direct marketing, particularly through the Internet, has helped shift bargaining power from manufacturers to consumers, turning consumers into business collaborators.[18]

❚ How the Internet Empowers Consumers The Internet empowers consumers in five ways:

1. *Access to more product information.* Consumers can efficiently and easily retrieve information on nearly any product or service via the Internet, thanks to search engines such as google.com and askjeeves.com. and portals like yahoo.com and aol.com. More than ever, consumers possess heightened awareness of brand and price alternatives with infomediaries and BOTS devoted to providing comparison shopping information and brand recommendations. Product or service sites such as Autobytel.com are finding that consumers use them more for research than for the actual purchase.

2. *Potential for influencing other consumers.* As we saw in Chapter 16, word of mouth gains much greater power and speed with the Internet as a communication medium. Consumers can log onto or establish chatrooms, message boards, and entire web sites devoted to disseminating opinions on products.

3. *Interactivity.* The Internet allows customers to "talk back" to marketers and producers. Consumers no longer have to receive information passively. Many producers' web sites now provide options for directly emailing opinions. Moreover, customers can participate in live chat sessions with marketers, offering their perspectives and input for existing and new products. On Procter & Gamble's product web site, tide.com, visitors can offer suggestions for product improvements and new product ideas by clicking on that option.

4. *Customization.* Customization enables consumers to design their own products based on a set of specifications offered by the marketer.

5. *Personalization.* Almost every web site now offers the option for some form of personalization to the consumer, ranging from the arrangement of the web page to the content exhibited. Sites such as yahoo.com even allow users to select the types of news stories and other information to be emailed daily. Whereas customization enables consumers to specify product characteristics, personalization enables them to personalize the product's information or marketing message to meet their individual preferences.

❚ Limits to Consumer Empowerment The most basic limitation to consumer empowerment through the Web is lack of access by a significant proportion of households. About 40 percent of American consumers lack access to the Web. Who are these consumers? Primarily, they are older consumers. Consumers over 60 are half as likely to have web access as the rest of the population.[19] Although the racial gap on the Web has narrowed significantly, African Americans and Hispanic Americans are still from 10 percent to 20 percent less likely to have Internet access compared with whites.[20]

Even those consumers with access to the Web are not necessarily taking full advantage of their power. As noted in Chapter 7, consumers may suffer from information overload on the Web given the number of web sites and the wealth of information. Such information overload may decrease interest in surfing the Web for new discoveries. Although the number of hours people spend online is increasing, they are visiting fewer sites. According to one well-known research firm tracking online traffic, the average U.S. user spent 20.7 hours online per week in July 2001, an increase of two hours from the previous year.[21] The same firm also cited that in 2000 approximately 60 percent of Internet users went to more than twenty web sites in an average month, whereas in 2001 only 50 percent of users visited more than twenty sites. Although additional information may be available in the area of interest, web users are relying on fewer and better-known sources.

DEVELOPING WEB SITE LOYALTY

Given these results, web retailers and marketers face great opportunities for creating and nurturing consumer loyalty to their sites. They can develop web site loyalty in the following ways:

- *Know more about consumers.* Producers and marketers can strive to better understand consumers' experiences with their products and solicit customer feedback on the Web to get opinions regarding current and future products. For example, online hotel reservation site *www.quikbook.com* emails customers a brief follow-up survey asking them to rate their hotel stays. These results are then utilized to ensure customer satisfaction at those hotels and to update hotel ratings.

- *Encourage more active dialogue with consumers.* Amazon.com's book recommendations function allows consumers to post their reviews of books online for others to read. The online city guide service Citysearch.com encourages users to provide reviews of restaurants, nightclubs, and other sites of interest to visitors. These reviews are posted for others to browse.

- *Encourage consumer communities to form around the product.* By engendering more of an emotional attachment to the product, producers can build brand loyalty. Cisco Systems maintains a customer support web site called Cisco Connection Online, which provides a forum for customers to help each other solve technical problems.[22] Not only is Cisco building brand equity, but the company is also giving customers what they want by getting them to become each other's customer help representatives.

- *Personalize consumer experience.* Yahoo.com is a pioneer in this area; it allows each member to create a personalized web view and content through MyYahoo! In doing so, the web portal creates a loyalty to the site whereby the user comes to rely on the site as the primary interface for further web interaction.

REQUIREMENTS FOR EFFECTIVE MICROMARKETING

To be effective, micromarketing requires (1) information at the individual level, (2) interactivity, (3) a mass customization capability, and (4) the right corporate culture. Each of these is described next.

▌ Information at the Individual Level   The marketers' goal is to link information search and advertising exposure to the customer's behavior. Marketers can then develop messages and marketing stimuli based on the individual customer's explicit and implicit preferences and behavior. For example, Amazon.com customers receive recommendations on titles of potential interest based on the selections of other customers with similar interests. This type of personalization tool, called "collaborative filtering," is discussed in greater detail later in this chapter.

Customer data remain at the core of effective micromarketing. The customer database functions as the starting point for building relationships with customers and for executing micromarketing strategies. This database houses information such as customers' demographics, lifestyles, attitudes, interests, preferences, behavior, ownership patterns, and other details that allow companies to provide highly targeted products, services, and communications. The database is the equivalent of a company's "one-to-one memory."[23] At Rosewood Hotels & Resorts, for example, the hotel chain is renowned for its customer service thanks in large part to its database of detailed accounts on each guest. Prior to a guest's arrival, the hotel sends a questionnaire requesting information on preferences such as feather or hypoallergenic pillow, beverages in the minibar, dietary requests, and even preferences for a backboard on the guest's bed. The information is entered into the hotel's database system and updated by employees as they become more familiar with guests' habits. The result has been a high repeat visit rate with returning guests comprising 60 percent of Rosewood's clientele.[24]

▌ Interactivity   Micromarketing requires a two-way relationship with the customer to enable accurate targeting, communications, and customization. In this way, customers must actively participate in a learning relationship. In return, companies must adapt their own behavior and products to meet individual customer's expressed needs and desires. Each interaction with a customer then must occur in the context of all prior interactions with that customer.[25] The result is similar to the relationship people used to maintain with their neighborhood pharmacist or restaurant owner, who knew each customer's name and history by heart through years of interaction.

Interactivity can be manifested in several ways. For example, customers can state preferences and receive suggestions. American Express's web site recommends products and services based on visitor responses to questions regarding credit card usage, benefits desired, payment preference, and basic demographic data.

Maintaining postpurchase contact with the customer is another example of interactivity. Web-based postpurchase contacts allow the company to identify both satisfied and dissatisfied customers with the opportunity to reduce postpurchase dissonance. Saturn, for example, emails customers to ask them about auto service and elicits suggestions regarding improvements.

A relatively new tool for interactivity was pioneered by *www.landsend.com*, the online version of the catalog retailer.[26] The company introduced live customer service to its online store, enabling shoppers to send messages to customer support representatives and receive replies in real time. The service also allows company representatives to synchronize screens with the shopper so that they can see exactly what the customer is viewing from home.

▌ **Mass Customization**   Micromarketing often requires mass customization of both products and promotions. Products are customized through computer-assisted manufacturing (CAM) techniques that allow individual units to be produced to specification. CAM relies on a customer database that provides inputs regarding individual consumer needs. Levi Strauss's database of its customers and its flexible manufacturing system allow customization of its pants.

Customization of promotions requires databases that allow a company to direct tailor-made messages. American Express offers its customers promotions and

---

GLOBAL APPLICATIONS

OF CONSUMER BEHAVIOR

Micromarketing in Russia? Maybe on a Limited Basis

Russia embraced a free market economy after the fall of Communism. Today, it has a stock exchange, venture capitalists, American fast-food chains galore, and crowded department stores. One thing it does not have is the infrastructure to establish strategies based on micromarketing and mass customization.

Micromarketing is driven by two things: (1) recognition by marketers that a fragmented market place affords an opportunity to target individual consumers and (2) technology enabling such individual targeting. Russia has neither. Although capitalism is developing rapidly, the economy is driven by a mass marketing mentality that is a residue of the centralization of the Soviet system. Marketers have not established the prime requisite for micromarketing—information at the individual level. They have not even developed the informational capabilities to segment markets by demographic and lifestyle characteristics.

Part of the reason that micromarketing is lagging in Russia is the lack of Internet penetration among Russian consumers. With an installed base of only 5 million computers and with only 21 percent of residents having phone lines, it is not surprising that Internet penetration was

only 5 percent in 2001. Given that the average Russian earns $60 per month, the prospects for future Internet growth are dim.

Despite the prospects for limited growth, some firms view the Web as an opportunity to attract the small proportion of Russian consumers that are online. One, DKM, has established a web market shopping mall, allowing Russian consumers linked to the Internet to buy on the Web. Another, *www.bazar.com,* launched a news and shopping portal. A third, *www.24x7.com/ru,* offers books, CDs, and a toy shop. As one Russian executive who builds retail web systems online said, "Five hundred thousand to a million people who are willing to buy online now is a very good audience for any retail business."

Russia may not have the infrastructure to implement micromarketing strategies to nearly the same extent as the United States or Western Europe, but for those entrepreneurs willing to pursue small niche markets, the opportunities may be there.

Sources: "Russia's Fledgling E-Commerce Sector Is Seeking Its Missing Link: Consumers," *Wall Street Journal* (June 21, 2000), p. B11C; "Russian Internet Usage Doubled in 2001," *BBC Monitoring Former Soviet Union—Interfax* (May 3, 2002).

coupons based on past behavior. For example, a customer who uses the Amex card frequently at Italian restaurants might get promotions for Italian restaurants in the neighborhood. A customer who frequently charges merchandise at Gap stores might get discount coupons for the Gap.

▌ Corporate Culture

An important requirement for success in micromarketing is a corporate culture oriented toward customers. As one author comments, "It's one thing to train a sales staff to be warm and attentive; it's quite another to identify, track and interact with an individual customer and then reconfigure your product or service to meet that customer's needs."[27] Micromarketing, therefore, goes far beyond the traditional concept of customer service. It requires the entire company to participate actively in marketing to the individual, so that every contact a customer has with an organization is specific to that customer.

STRATEGIC APPLICATIONS

The requirements for micromarketing have strategic applications for marketers. These are discussed next, using the same 4Ps framework we used previously for market segmentation.

▌ Product

To deliver mass customized products, companies must build an interface with the customer. Holiday Inn maintains a web-based worldwide reservation system, which allows customers to locate the hotel in the desired city, check availability, take a virtual tour, and book a room—all online. Computer makers Dell and Gateway have long used the Web to allow customers to configure, order, and pay for products.

One of the key requirements for effective online micromarketing is to build brand equity for a web site. Brands like Coke, Pepsi, or McDonald's have achieved phenomenal success offline by establishing strong brand name associations and credibility in the consumer's mind, as well as loyalty to the brand—all hallmarks of strong brand equity. The same criteria apply to establishing brand equity online. Without powerful brand recognition and the assurance it offers to consumers, a company's web presence may translate into its products becoming a commodity competing solely on price. If brand equity is not achieved, mass customization loses its significance as a competitive tool to build customer loyalty.[28] A brand such as Dell cannot attain online legitimacy in customizing products without the reputation it achieved in its offline operations. Pure dot-coms such as Amazon provide tailor-made recommendations for books and music that customers accept because of the brand equity Amazon has established online.

▌ Place

Micromarketing also has implications for distribution. Offline delivery of customized products requires that companies create a direct manufacturer-to-customer distribution system. For example, Amazon built a physical infrastructure from scratch to carry out its promise of fast, easy online purchasing and delivery direct to the customer. Costs increased as the infrastructure required additional warehouses, inventory tracking systems, and delivery vehicles. Toys "R" Us faced a different set of issues as it entered e-commerce. Its success with a conventional distribution system in which toys were distributed and then purchased in stores failed to prepare it for the requirements of individual home delivery. The debacle created by missed deliveries and general service failures in the 1999 Christmas season underscored the difficulty of a traditional company transitioning to electronic commerce.

▌ Promotion and Advertising

Micromarketing requires targeted promotional activities to attract customers. Technology is playing a crucial role in facilitating interactive advertising. Several types of customized communications exist, as follows:[29]

- ▌ *Banner advertisements.* These rectangular ad strips usually appear at the top or bottom of web pages delivered by commercial sites. They offer click-through capability to the advertiser's web site or other host site so that interested viewers can interact directly with the advertiser. Various offshoots of banner ads have surfaced, including pop-up windows that appear on the screen as the viewer is surfing on the Internet. The most effective online ads are those that appear when the user is viewing related topics on the Web. For example, an individual researching information on dieting may see banner ads for weight loss programs or low-fat foods.

- ▌ *Email.* Emails are similar to direct mail marketing, as firms use a database of contact information to send messages directly to people in the database.

- ▌ *Viral marketing.* As we saw in Chapter 16, viral marketing refers to using the Internet to accelerate word of mouth to encourage adoption or trial of a product or service. Many online companies employ some form of viral marketing to get customers to promote their products to friends and family. Although the use of viral marketing is not new (MCI's Friends and Family program is an example of offline viral marketing), it can leverage the speed and breadth by which communications travel on the Internet at very little cost to the company.

- ▌ *Interactive television.* Interactive television may soon offer another medium by which companies can personalize and target ads to consumers. Interactive television allows advertisers to gather information about individuals, including gender, age, response to an ad, and length of time on a site.[30] All this data can be used to personalize ads and send them to individuals likely to be interested. Domino's Pizza, for example, will have interactive ads offering viewers the chance to order a pizza with a reduced rate satellite movie or pay-per-view sporting event. Ultimately, the technology may allow viewers to select their own endings to ads and to provide comment on the ads via email.[31]

▌ Price

Micromarketing allows companies to charge different prices to individual consumers for the same product, depending on the value consumers place on the product or service. Such differential pricing (known as *price discrimination*) is not new. Airlines, telecommunications companies, and restaurants charge different prices for the same product or service depending on the type of customer and time of service. Interactive technology has made such differential pricing easier and more accurate due to the ability to track customers' behavior in real time. There are two types of differential pricing:[32]

1. *Personalized pricing* allows the firm to sell to users at different prices, depending on their past purchases. For example, *www.wine.com* tracks the behavior of

its customers online, making them instant special offers based on their frequency of purchase and choice of wines.

2. *Bundled pricing* occurs when customers are charged different prices based on the customization options selected. It is best suited for those products where customized options can be offered, such as automobiles and computers. On Volvo's web site, the price quoted for a customized vehicle depends on the options selected.

▌ Relationship Marketing

In addition to the 4Ps described in this section, a fifth strategic application of micromarketing is relationship marketing; that is, the attempt to build long-term customer loyalty through the development of relationships centered on ongoing two-way learning between a company and its customers. As more data are collected about each customer, the company increases its ability to target messages and services to consumers and to predict how they will respond. Over time, each interaction becomes more concise and effective because the company knows "what to say and how to say it."[33]

Relationship marketing provides several competitive advantages.[34] It increases customer loyalty and retention over time. Relationship marketing strategies also may increase the costs of switching to other brands or services as the consumer learns to deal effectively with the company. In so doing, relationship marketing reduces transaction costs by making future purchases more convenient and easy. For example, Amazon's repeat customers can make new purchases with a single click, thanks to the company's storage of customer data such as names, addresses, and credit card information. The goal is to create ongoing customer value, resulting in customers revisiting sites for a wider range of products and services over a longer period of time, and exhibiting a willingness to pay more for specialized treatment and convenience.

Chase Manhattan Bank implemented a relationship marketing strategy. The company developed a detailed customer database from the Web and used it to create targeted pitches for products such as college and retirement funds. Sales calls can now be timed to events occurring in the customer's life. For example, a customer may mention the purchase of a house in the near future, which is noted in the system so that information on home mortgage products can be provided to that customer. According to bank officials, the initiative is paying off with increased retention of high-net-worth customers and a higher amount of assets under the bank's management.[35]

Beyond the costs and difficulties associated with implementation, successful relationship marketing strategies are difficult to achieve. One study found that only a few brands had earned true "relationship" status in consumers' minds, with only 35 percent of consumers stating that they had a solid, growing relationship with any of the more than forty brands listed across seven major categories.[36] The same study found a few noteworthy "relationship brands"—Dell Computer. American Express, Palm, and Wal-Mart. These companies met consumers' expectations and needs better than the competition, and they treated customers in a way that showed they understood them. Additionally, these "relationship winning" brands did not necessarily have more contact with customers. Rather, the quality of each contact was rated higher.

Companies attempting to use relationship marketing must also keep in mind the applicability of their strategies for different types of businesses. Relationship marketing is most appropriate when consumers seek personal sales or service.[37] It may not be as effective for consumer packaged goods because consumers do not ordinarily seek assistance in making decisions about low-involvement products.

MICROMARKETING AND LOW-INVOLVEMENT PRODUCTS

Web-based micromarketing strategies tend to be associated with products consumers are highly involved with, such as cars and electronics. But they may also apply to products consumers are less involved with. Web marketers have implemented mass customization strategies for high-involvement products. In contrast, web-based applications for low-involvement products tend to be in the form of customizing information and providing product-related services to build stronger relationships with consumers.

Procter & Gamble, the leading marketer of low-involvement packaged goods with household names like Tide, Pampers, and Charmin, has implemented such web-based strategies. The company believes the Internet's information orientation and two-way communication capability can be leveraged effectively for low-involvement products.[38] The goal of its online strategy is to increase customer loyalty and brand equity by building relationships with customers and, hence, greater customer ties to the brands. In so doing, P&G also hopes to increase consumer involvement with its products. It plans to achieve these objectives by the following strategies:

▪ *Providing consumers with product information.* P&G hopes to expand a product's value proposition beyond the product itself. For example, *www.pampers.com* offers information to new parents through the Pampers Parenting Institute with discussions such as "Toilet Training 101" and "Healthy Baby Skin." The Stain Detective on *www.tide.com* offers tips on cleaning clothes and ridding them of stains (see Exhibit 18.5). The Crest site offers information on dental hygiene.

▪ *Personalizing such information to increase product involvement.* When visiting *www.scope-mouthwash.com,* users can send animated kiss messages to family and friends via email, while tide.com allows consumers to share product experiences with other consumers through its "Neighbor to Neighbor" web section.

Aside from increasing brand equity and relationship building, P&G's web presence allows it to reinforce its relationship with consumer segments that may already be more involved. P&G can also gather data on customers through its web sites. Tide.com recently conducted online surveys to find out why visitors came to the site, what they wanted from it, and how they felt about the product and brand.

Despite the possible advantages, there may also be limitations to the effectiveness of a web presence for companies marketing low-involvement products. Consumers may have little motivation to go to a low-involvement, product-specific web site regardless of the level of interactivity and information provided. Consumers may be more likely to search for answers to oral care questions on medical sites than on scope.com. Moreover, consumers may not view time on these sites as well spent. Studies show that, with increasingly less time to spare for nonessential activities, consumers are looking for convenience and time to spend with family and friends rather than surfing the Internet.

WHY TODAY'S CONSUMERS ARE MORE RECEPTIVE TO MICROMARKETING

Consumers increasingly prefer to make decisions for themselves to ensure that they get exactly what they want, contributing to the desire to be the "architect of [their own products and services]."[39] Some observers contend that this desire is a backlash against the "massification" of America, a reaction to the mass marketing strategies and standardization of the past.[40] Increasing diversity in family, work, and social structures further creates a demand and need for customization. Consumers require products that are multipurpose and multisituational to fit their more complex lifestyles.

The demand for and consumer acceptance of micromarketing will likely continue. Empowered by parents at a young age to make decisions, Generation X and Y consumers may be the most receptive to mass customization. These age cohorts became independent at an early age as a result of dual-income households, rising divorce rates, and single-parent families. They grew up with more purchasing responsibilities and power than past generations. They are comfortable with choice and have come to expect it. Further, they are more consumer savvy, and are the age group that has made the Internet an effective vehicle for delivering customization and personalization.

Positioning Products to Customer Targets

Products are positioned to market segments through advertising and promotional strategies. Market segmentation and product positioning strategies must be developed together. Market segments must be identified by their common needs, and products must be positioned to meet those needs.

In micromarketing, products are positioned to individual consumers. This requires targeting products to individuals based on their past behavior and current preferences. In this section, we consider positioning both to market segments and to individual consumers.

WEB APPLICATIONS

Should Low-Involvement Products Be Sold on the Web?

Procter & Gamble's web sites are designed to provide information, not to sell their branded products. But some marketers suggest that the Web may be the ideal vehicle for selling low-involvement products for several reasons. First, consumers are reluctant to spend time and energy buying these products. By providing timesaving convenience, consumers may see the Web as an efficient vehicle for purchasing such items. Second, the risk of purchasing on the Web is minimal since most low-involvement items are standardized and consumers know exactly what they will be getting. Third, many low-involvement products possess strong brand equity that can be easily transferred to the Web. Brands like Charmin, Tide, and Crest are known commodities on the Web as well as on store shelves. Fourth, if companies like P&G and Unilever have a constellation of products that consumers typically buy together and often, selling on the Web makes more sense. Along with Charmin toilet paper, consumers could also purchase laundry and cleaning products, beauty and health care items, and even certain foods and beverages—all direct from P&G online.

But the drawbacks of selling low-involvement products on the Web may outweigh the advantages. Companies such as WebVan, Pets.com, and eToys went bankrupt in their attempt at selling online. These companies underestimated the costs of attracting and retaining consumers to their sites. Less than 1 percent of supermarket items are purchased on the Web. Consumers simply have not accepted the advantages of Web-based relative to in-store purchasing for such products.

Another problem is that even though these companies were selling online, this did not eliminate the need for a distribution infrastructure to store and deliver products, with all its attendant costs. A third limiting factor is the problem of antagonizing retailers. Establishing Internet sales facilities bypasses a company's retailers and wholesalers, a process known as *disintermediation.* Levi Strauss stopped selling on the Web because large customers like Macy's threatened to stop carrying the company's product if it continued to bypass its retailers. P&G's policy is to avoid such channel conflict by restricting itself to information and services on the Web. Many companies avoid channel conflict by establishing tie-ins and links to retailers on their web sites to allow customers to purchase from established intermediaries.

It is probably going to be a long time (if ever) before consumers see low-involvement products sold on the Web.

POSITIONING PRODUCTS TO TARGET SEGMENTS

Products must be positioned to meet the needs of target segments. Marketers must determine these needs and target their products accordingly.

A key consideration is whether the brand is seen as meeting the needs of the target segment. A number of years ago, General Foods introduced an artificial bacon product called Lean Strips, positioned as a leaner and more nutritious alternative to bacon to meet the needs of nutritionally minded consumers. The problem was that consumers considered the product as greasy and fatty as regular bacon. A reformulation of the product was required to ensure that consumers' perceptions would conform to the company's positioning strategy.

Existing products might also be seen in a manner that is inconsistent with the company's intended positioning. We saw that Oldsmobile could not change perceptions from an old and stodgy car to the intended positioning of an innovative one, and Kmart is facing a difficult road in repositioning itself from the polyester palace to a more fashion-oriented retailer. Although difficult to implement, such repositioning strategies are often necessary to maintain a company's ability to meet consumer needs, as detailed in the Volvo illustration.

Perceptual maps have been used to evaluate the effectiveness of a product's position to target segments. An example is a study Nabisco Brands conducted a number of years ago. The company's objective was to develop a more nutritional snack. Research showed that a chip-nut-and-fruit-type snack might appeal to nutritionally oriented snackers. The map in Figure 18.3 summarizes the results of Nabisco's study of the snack food market. Consumers were segmented by the snacking benefits they emphasized most, resulting in the six "benefit segments" in Figure 18.3. They were then asked to rate a number of snacking products including the new snack. As expected, the new product appealed most to nutritional snackers.

Three questions were used to evaluate the positioning of the new concept. First, is it in a distinctive position relative to competition? In this case, the answer is no because there is a danger that the new chip-nut-and-fruit snack will compete head on with Brands A and B. Second, is the positioning in line with managerial objectives? Yes, because the concept is perceived as having nutritional benefits and thus is positioned to the intended target. Third, does it appeal to a sufficiently large segment to warrant further testing? Yes, because nutritional snackers comprise the largest segment, shown by the size of the circle.

Further testing is required to answer the following questions before a decision is made to introduce the product: Can the concept be distinguished from Brands A and B on key nutritional benefits? Will enough consumers select the new product over Brands A and B? What are the needs and characteristics of consumers who

| **FIGURE 18.3** |

Perceptual mapping to evaluate a new product concept.

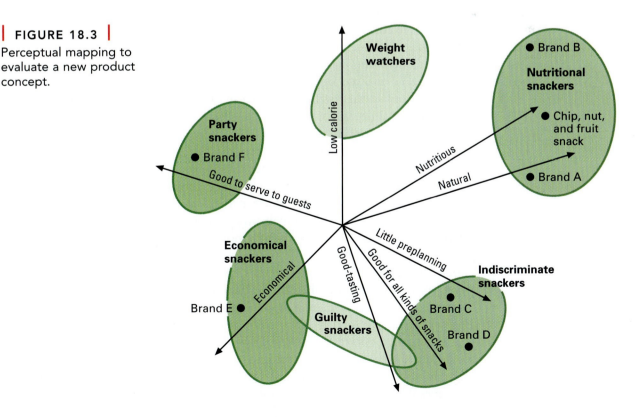

would buy the chip-nut-and-fruit snack? Once the concept is translated into a product and tested, will the same positioning be maintained, or will consumers change their perceptions?

The analysis in Figure 18.3 also provides implications for additional new product possibilities by defining "gaps" in the perceptual space. The most obvious is the failure of any product to be perceived as a low-calorie snack. A snack product positioned to weight watchers might represent a prime marketing opportunity. In addition, there may be an opportunity to position a snack to guilty snackers since they have no strong preference for any existing snack products. If these concepts are considered by the company, additional concept tests would have to be run and perceptual maps developed to position the new concepts against existing brands.

POSITIONING PRODUCTS TO INDIVIDUAL CONSUMERS

Micromarketing strategies require positioning products to individual consumers. Such a positioning relies on knowledge of individual consumers' needs as reflected in their past behavior and current preferences.

Two approaches have been developed to position products on the Web. One, known as a **rules-based system,** relies on developing statistical relationships between a consumer's characteristics and behavior, and his or her likelihood to purchase. The other, known as **collaborative filtering,** relies on a knowledge of the actions of consumers who have similar preferences as the target consumer. The assumption is that the target consumer will prefer the same products as other similar consumers. Rules-based systems are a form of *customization,* whereas collaborative filtering is a form of *personalization.*

▌ Rules-Based Systems (Customization)   **Rules-based systems** allow marketers to customize ad messages, coupons, and email communications based on individual consumer characteristics and past behavior. One company that has helped pioneer rules-based systems is BroadVision. Founded in 1993, BroadVision develops and markets one-to-one software applications that allow companies to profile visitors to their web sites so that marketing messages can be customized to their individual needs.

The primary advantage of this approach is that marketers maintain control, ensuring accurate implementation of marketing strategies. Other advantages include the opportunity for consumers to receive recommendations from experts, an important advantage for products where consumers seek more information from credible sources. These products include automobiles, electronics, appliances, and financial services—largely high-involvement, high-risk purchases. Since rules-based systems collect customer information on an ongoing basis, they can serve as a real-time market research tool. The State of California's government web site uses BroadVision's rules-based software to dynamically configure pages according to a user's profile. The site can then deliver customized content based on stated interests and needs. The user's customized home page can show news-related items, links to other relevant sites, and specific government information.

Rules-based systems have their drawbacks. In a rules-based approach, the marketer sets the parameters for customization. The State of California's web page is determined by the marketer (the state government), not the consumer. This assumes that the marketer knows more about what consumers want than the consumers themselves. This assumption could be highly flawed, particularly when consumers have a clear sense of what they want or are influenced by others. Further, rules-based systems are based on past consumer preferences and actions. They may not reflect the consumer's current status. As a result, rules-based systems may not reflect in real time the ongoing changes in the consumer's behavior or preferences.

▮ Collaborative Filtering (Personalization)

Collaborative filtering addresses several of the drawbacks of rules-based systems by relying solely on consumer preferences rather than on marketers' rules to make product recommendations. Such recommendations are based on the opinions of customers with tastes similar to those of the target consumer.

The pioneer of collaborative filtering systems was Firefly, now owned by Microsoft. Firefly's technology was designed to give customers recommendations of others by matching their personal profiles to those of other customers.

Because collaborative filtering and rules-based systems are used for different purposes in targeting individual consumers, they are best suited for different types of product categories. Collaborative filtering relies on surrogates for personal influence, the preferences of "relevant others." As a result, collaborative filtering is ideally suited for those companies selling taste-based products such as clothes, books, music, and even restaurants, where the opinions of others might be more important than company-directed messages. This means that collaborative filtering may be most relevant for online travel agencies, financial service sites, or online retailers such as Amazon.com. Rules-based systems are most relevant for marketers selling products for which information on product attributes and performance is important. Marketing efforts require guidelines for the types of advertising and promotional messages to deliver to consumers, requirements that are well suited for rules-based systems.

SUMMARY

In this chapter, we reviewed market segmentation and micromarketing. Market segmentation seeks to identify groups of consumers with similar needs for purposes of targeting. Micromarketing is a logical extension of market segmentation, targeting consumers at the individual level.

In the first part of the chapter, we considered the reasons behind market segmentation and micromarketing. The American marketplace has become more fragmented, leading to marketing strategies targeted to smaller segments. New technologies have enabled strategies targeted to individual consumers. Mass customization has emerged as one way of serving the varying needs of a disaggregated market. Consumers today are more educated, have greater access to information, and are ready to use their knowledge to demand choices that better meet their individual needs. Moreover, companies cannot ignore this diversity, for the buying power of minority and niche markets continues to grow.

To target consumers, companies must first segment their markets. Three approaches were described for identifying market segments. In benefit segmentation, consumers are defined by similarity in needs (*e.g.*, consumers emphasizing cavity prevention versus white teeth in the toothpaste market). New products are positioned and existing products are repositioned to meet these needs. In behavioral segmentation, marketers identify users based on several behavioral criteria, such as brand usage, product usage, and level of usage (heavy versus light users). Markets also can be segmented by consumer response elasticities; that is, consumer sensitivity to changes in price, advertising, or other marketing stimuli. The purpose is to identify the characteristics of consumers who may be induced to buy based on a price deal or who may be influenced by an increase in advertising expenditures.

Micromarketing seeks to target consumers on a one-to-one basis. The key to micromarketing is (1) mass customization; that is, the ability to customize products and information to meet consumer needs and (2) personalization; that is, the ability on the part of the consumer to develop tailor-made information resources and personal contacts like chatrooms. Requirements for implementing micromarketing strategies include information gathering at the individual consumer level and product and distribution technologies designed to reach individual consumers. These requirements have strategic implications, which were discussed using the 4 Ps (product, place, promotion, and pricing).

We next considered the importance of relationship marketing and its connection to micromarketing. At the core of relationship marketing is gathering and using consumer data to communicate with consumers interactively so as to retain them over the long term. Without this information, companies can neither execute successful micromarketing strategies nor build ongoing relationships with customers.

The chapter concluded by considering positioning strategies to target segments and individual consumers. Two approaches were considered in targeting individual consumers—rules-based systems and collaborative filtering.

In the concluding chapter, we consider a broader strategic issue, the rights of consumers, and the responsibilities of marketers in ensuring these rights.

QUESTIONS FOR DISCUSSION

1. Do you agree with the following statement: "The driving force behind micromarketing and mass customization is new technologies"? Why or why not?

2. Why is mass marketing a less effective strategy today than it was in the post–World War II period?

3. Is mass customization a contradiction in terms? Why or why not?

4. What benefit segments may be identified for the following markets: (a) soft drinks, (b) household cleaners, (c) personal care appliances, and (d) credit cards?

5. Under what circumstances would a marketer wish to segment by the following behavioral criteria: (a) brand users versus nonusers, (b) product users versus nonusers, (c) heavy versus light users of the product category?

6. Cite an example (other than those in the text) of segmenting by response elasticity.

7. What is the relevance of upside and downside price elasticity to marketers? Cite an example of each.

8. Are the limits of consumer empowerment through the Web likely to restrain its future growth? Why or why not?

9. What are some downsides of a micromarketing strategy? Cite examples.

10. Why are younger consumers more receptive to micromarketing and mass customization?

11. What is the strategic relevance of the distinction between customization and personalization?

12. What are the advantages and disadvantages of low-involvement products having an online presence? Should they be sold on the Web?

13. How can perceptual maps be used to evaluate the effectiveness of a product's positioning? Provide an example.

14. When should a company use rules-based systems and collaborative filtering? Are they complementary?

RESEARCH ASSIGNMENTS

1 Visit *www.customatix.com* and *www.nikeid.com* and explore the customization options available on each site.

- Is each site effective in customizing shoes?
- What types of consumers are likely to visit each site?

2 Select a product category and identify three or four key benefits. Select a sample of product users and ask them to identify the most important benefit desired. On this basis, form three or four benefit segments (*e.g.,* consumers who emphasize "lets me sleep," "freshly brewed," or "economy" for coffee). Try to ensure that there are at least ten consumers in each benefit segment. Ask the sample for information on the following: (a) demographic characteristics, (b) brand regularly used, (c) frequency of use, and (d) a select number of lifestyle characteristics.

- What are the differences between benefit segments based on this information?

- What are the implications for (a) new product positioning, (b) repositioning of existing products, (c) advertising, (d) media selection, and (e) pricing strategies?

3 Select a web site that uses a rules-based system to provide recommendations to consumers. Select another Web site that uses collaborative filtering to provide recommendations to consumers.

- How does the design and purpose of each web site differ?

- What are the strategic implications of the differences you have identified?

NOTES

1. "Driving Through the Clutter," *Mediaweek* (November 27, 2000), pp. IQ34–IQ36; and "Volvo, Seeking Younger Buyers, Tries to Create a Sexier Image," *Wall Street Journal* (August 26, 1999), p. B1.
2. "Volvo's New Agency Sticking to Safety Theme," *New York Times Current Events Edition* (October 7, 1991).
3. "Volvo, Seeking Younger Buyers," p. B1.
4. "Danger in the Safety Zone," *Financial Times* (July 20, 1995), p. 15.
5. "Pontiac, Volvo Alter Images in New Cars," *Advertising Age* (September 20, 1993), p. 52.
6. "Volvo to Drop Boxy Image in $30 Million Push," *Brandweek* (October 9, 2000), p. 12.
7. "Safe Bet to Help Ford," *Professional Engineering* (August 11, 1999), p. 28.
8. "Driving Through the Clutter," pp. IQ34–IQ36.
9. "Volvo Plans Ad Campaign to Clarify Automaker's Image," *Advertising Age* (October 9, 2000), p. 4.
10. W. Michael Cox and Richard Alm, "America's Move to Mass Customization," *Consumer's Research Magazine* (June 1999), pp. 15–19.
11. Jagdish N. Sheth, Rajendra S. Sisodia, and Arun Sharma, "The Antecedents and Consequences of Customer-Centric Marketing," *Academy of Marketing Science Journal* 28 (Winter 2000), pp. 55–66.
12. Ibid.
13. Ibid.
14. "Computer Mapping of Demographic Lifestyle Data Locates 'Pockets' of Potential Customers at Micrographic Level," *Marketing News* (November 27, 1981), p. 162.
15. Henry Assael and A. Marvin Roscoe Jr., "Approaches to Market Segmentation Analysis," *Journal of Marketing* 40 (October 1976), p. 74.
16. Carol L. Karnes and Larry P. Karnes, "Ross Controls: A Case Study in Mass Customization," *Production and Inventory Management Journal* 41 (3rd Quarter 2000), pp. 1–4.
17. "Mass Customization Could Be the Key to Getting Our Industry Back on Track," *Apparel Industry Magazine* (July 2000), p. 104.
18. Don Peppers, Martha Rogers, and Bob Dorf, "Is Your Company Ready for One to One Marketing?" *Harvard Business Review* 77 (January/February 1999), pp. 151–160.

19. Cyber Atlas, *Insight Express,* 2001.
20. Department of Commerce, U.S. Bureau of the Census Current Population Survey Supplements, *Falling Through the Net: Toward Digital Inclusion,* 2000.
21. "Exploration of World Wide Web Tilts from Eclectic to Mundane," *New York Times* (August 26, 2001), pp. 1, 22.
22. "Interactive Technologies and Relationship Marketing Strategies," Harvard Business School, Case # 599-101 (January 19, 2000), pp. 1–12.
23. "The Evolution of Relationship Marketing: Reaching an Audience of One," *Direct Marketing* (April 1999), pp. 54–59.
24. "From Data to Dollars," *Hotels* (March 2000), pp. 91–94.
25. Peppers, Rogers, and Dorf, "Is Your Company Ready?," pp. 151–160.
26. "Make the Sale," *Wall Street Journal* (September 24, 2001), p. R6.
27. Peppers, Rogers, and Dorf, "Is Your Company Ready?," pp. 151–160.
28. "Marketers Find Internet Opens New Avenues to Customers," *New York Times* (March 26, 2001), p. C1.
29. "Interactive Technologies," pp. 1–12.
30. "Will Viewers Interact with TV Advertising?" *Marketing* (March 16, 2000), p. 9.
31. Ibid.
32. "Interactive Technologies," pp. 1–12.
33. "The Evolution of Relationship Marketing," pp. 54–59.
34. Peppers, Rogers, and Dorf, "Is Your Company Ready?," pp. 151–160.
35. Ibid.
36. "Consumers Say 'No Thanks' to Relationships with Brands," *Direct Marketing* (May 2001), pp. 48–51.
37. Sally Dibb and Maureen Meadows, "The Application of a Relationship Marketing Perspective in Retail Banking," *The Service Industries Journal* (January 2001), pp. 169–194.
38. "Proctor & Gamble Online: Tide and Pampers Hit the Web," University of Michigan Business School.
39. Paul Zipkin, "The Limits of Mass Customization," *MIT Sloan Management Review* 42 (March 16, 2001), pp. 81–87.
40. Ibid.

CHAPTER 19

Consumer Rights and Social Responsibility

Previous chapters focused on the strategic implications of consumer behavior. Equally important are considerations of consumer rights in the marketplace. Consumers have a right to accurate and full information, to safe products, to adequate product choices, and to products that do not harm the environment. In this respect, it is important to view purchasing decisions from the standpoint of consumer rights and management's responsibilities to consumers. Without a focus on consumer rights, businesses could easily engage in abuses such as deceptive advertising, failing to provide consumers with full information on product contents, developing unsafe products, or charging unreasonably high prices.

This chapter deals with the following topics:

▮ basic consumer rights,

▮ the historical development of these rights both in the United States and abroad, and

▮ four issues that have been a battleground for consumer rights in the 1990s and early 2000s: (1) environmental protection; (2) accurate health and nutritional claims; (3) regulation of advertising to children; and (4) consumer privacy.

To some extent, competitive forces and government regulation act to ensure consumer rights—but not fully. The socially responsible firm recognizes its responsibility to provide consumers with full and accurate information and safe products. Beyond such recognition, the socially responsible firm also realizes it has a responsibility to address social issues—ensuring a clean environment, discouraging drug use and teenage drinking, avoiding indirect appeals to youth to smoke (*e.g.,* by the use of cartoon characters such as Joe Camel), and accounting for the inability of young children to evaluate ads and promotional appeals.

The Body Shop: A Company That Supports Social Causes and Consumer Rights

Some businesses have begun to recognize that social responsibility should be part of their strategic focus. A good example is The Body Shop and its iconoclastic founder, Anita Roddick. For years, Roddick has tapped into a vein of environmentalism and corporate mistrust that runs deep among many of today's consumers.[1] In her native Britain, for instance, one study found that the majority of shoppers are suspicious of environmental claims. Roddick clings to a simple credo: Companies must be socially responsible. As a result, "the company promotes recycling, buys from indigenous people in developing countries, sticks to natural ingredients . . . and avoids selling products tested on animals."[2] The photo in Exhibit 19.1 shows the Body's Shop's community and social focus.

Roddick has followed a policy centered on social issues since 1976, when she opened her first London store filled with bottles of her handmade lotions and shampoos. Roddick drew a solid following among a new generation of consumers who were carefully scouring labels for proof that products they bought were all natural.

The Body Shop's popularity took off in the mid-1980s, when a wave of consumer protests was launched against companies accused of abusing animals for commercial profit. Widely publicized boycotts were organized against fur makers for inhumanely trapping minks and against cosmetics companies for testing their products on animals. Roddick became one of the movement's most fiery supporters, going so far as to sell bath soaps in the shape of endangered animals and to label her products with the explicit promise that she did not engage in animal testing.[3] In 2001, Roddick and a colleague spun off a web site, *www.ResponsibleTravel.com,* to encourage travelers to avoid buying products threatening endangered species.[4]

These actions would have been of little impact had her products not caught the imagination of shoppers. Blue corn oil made by indigenous Indian tribes from the American Southwest became a best-selling face lotion; mixtures from obscure African villages began appearing in bathrooms from Dallas to Dakar. In 2002, she had 1,965 stores across nearly

| **EXHIBIT 19.1** |

An example of The Body Shop's socially conscious strategy.

Monika Graff/The Image Works.

fifty countries in Asia, Europe, the Middle East, and the Americas with just under $1 billion in sales.[5]

But consumer distrust of such corporate actions as self-serving caught up with Roddick. Critics began accusing her of latching onto every cause to build her media celebrity status, thereby getting free advertising. They cited Body Shop claims as using only organic ingredients as false and the fight against animal testing as a straw man because testing had decreased by the time Roddick got on the bandwagon.[6] Others considered the charges unfair, pointing to Roddick's willingness to spend corporate profits on social causes. Roddick waves off such criticism, saying that she is trying to create a new definition of corporate responsibility by setting an example through her own business practices.[7]

As a recent testament to this belief, Roddick launched The Body Shop Human Rights Award in 2000. The award is a biennial event with a cash prize to recognize achievements in all areas of human rights.

Clearly, Roddick's business ethics are perfectly timed for the desires of a public that has begun to rebel against businesses that purposefully mislead, offer a restricted choice of alternatives, or sell unsafe products. The manifestation of this trend has come to be known as **the consumer movement.** Broadly defined, the consumer movement represents activities by consumer groups, government agencies, and at times, business organizations that are designed to protect the consumer. The term "consumer movement" is somewhat misleading, because there is no actual organization of consumers but, instead, a conglomeration of groups with separate concerns. As a result, the activities of these groups in the consumer interest have also been referred to as **consumerism.**

The Consumer Movement

The primary concern of the consumer movement is to ensure consumer's rights in the process of exchange. These rights include the right to be informed, to be told the truth, to be given adequate alternatives, and to be assured of safety in the process of consumption.[8]

Three types of organizations make up the consumer movement: (1) consumer-oriented groups concerned primarily with increasing consumer consciousness and providing consumers with information to improve their basis for choice, (2) government agencies responsible for legislation and regulation, and at times, (3) businesses that focus on competition and self-regulation. These forces are summarized in Figure 19.1.

THE ROLE OF CONSUMER ACTIVISTS AND ORGANIZATIONS

Consumers have made their voices felt through *activists, organizations,* and *boycotts.*

FIGURE 19.1

Agencies involved in consumerism.

Source: Adapted from Jagdish N. Sheth and Nicholas Mammana, "Why Consumer Protection Efforts Are Likely to Fail," Faculty Working Paper No. 104, College of Commerce and Business Administration, University of Illinois at Urbana-Champaign, April 11, 1973.

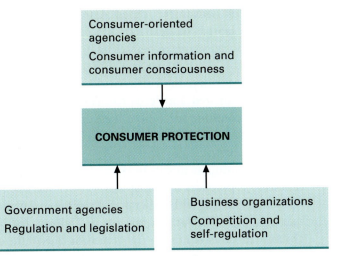

Consumer Activists   The most visible forces in the consumer movement have been consumer activists. John Muir was probably the first well-known consumer activist, being a champion of nature conservation in the United States during the late nineteenth century and having founded the Sierra Club, an organization devoted to the causes of conservancy. In the early 1900s, Upton Sinclair exposed the unsanitary conditions in Chicago's meatpacking houses. During the Depression in the 1930s, several authors exposed unsafe food and drug products. In the 1960s, Ralph Nader, probably the most famous consumer activist, started his career by exposing safety failures in cars. In the 1980s, Dennis Hayes founded an environmental group, called Green Seal, to monitor environmental claims and expose companies that use such claims to sell products without protecting the environment.

Consumer Organizations   Consumers Union, established in 1936 as a product-testing and consumer education agency, now has a membership of 2 million and publishes *Consumer Reports* magazine. It has undertaken broad consumer education programs regarding interest rates, life insurance, product safety, doctor selection, and the problems of low-income consumers. Consumers regard Consumers Union as an objective, impartial third party that can assess product quality and consumer complaints through its product-testing facilities. Similar magazine-based consumer organizations exist in Europe, including *Which?* in the United Kingdom and *Consumentengids* in Holland. These organizations' publications have helped educate the public and influence public-interest legislation in these countries.

Other groups such as the Sierra Club, the National Audubon Society, and Greenpeace have been active on environmental issues. In another area of concern, the Citizen Health Research Group and the Center for Science in the Public Interest monitor health claims. The latter is also active in monitoring cigarette and alcohol advertising to minorities and teens.

Consumer Boycotts   Boycotts have been a primary means employed by consumer activists and organizations to pressure business organizations. In 1988, thousands of consumers joined Action for Corporate Accountability when it resumed a lapsed six-year boycott of Nestlé S.A. for violating World Health Organization standards in marketing infant formula to developing nations.[9] Nestlé, which controls about 40 percent of the world baby food market, promotes its powdered baby milk in many Third-World countries where water used in the formula is often contaminated and leads to disease. In 1997, a new action committee was formed to continue to combat the company's role in promoting artificial infant feeding.[10] By 2000, the boycott was still in effect in nineteen countries, including the United States.[11]

Other consumer threats to boycott products of companies with alleged unethical business practices have met with greater success. In 1998, a boycott of PepsiCo for doing business with a dictatorial regime in Burma caused Pepsi to pull out of that country.[12] Similarly, a boycott of DeBeers for buying diamonds from rebel groups with abusive human rights records caused the company to stop the practice.

Overall, consumers' group action has been sporadic and uncoordinated. For instance, Jesse Jackson's PUSH organization tried convincing the major sneaker companies to put their money in black-owned banks and to hire African-American executives, but the effort had few tangible results. The feminist organization Media Watch tried to boycott Guess? jeans for sexist advertising and had mixed results. On average, there are more than a hundred national boycotts each year, and most fail.[13] One reason is that consumers are difficult to organize and to represent because of their diverse interests. Another is the frequent lack of commitment of consumers to boycotts. A study by Sen, Gurhan-Canli, and Morwitz found that consumers are unlikely to join a boycott if they prefer the boycotted product and have no obvious substitutes available.[14]

THE ROLE OF GOVERNMENT

Government has a responsibility to protect consumer interests and does so through legislation and the actions of regulatory agencies.

▌ **Legislation**   In the area of legislation, Congress has outlawed deceptive packaging, required warning labels on cigarettes, mandated full disclosure of all finance charges in consumer credit agreements, prohibited the sale of unsafe products to children, and required full disclosure of health claims and ingredients for food products. The most important consumer protection laws passed since 1966 are listed in Table 19.1. States also have a legislative role in protecting consumer rights. State laws have required unit pricing on food products and open dating of perishable foods and drugs. States and local communities have also enforced laws regarding recycling and waste disposal.

▌ **Regulation**   Federal regulatory agencies play a critical role in ensuring consumer rights. The two most important are the **Federal Trade Commission (FTC)** and **Food and Drug Administration (FDA).** The FTC, established in 1914 to curb the monopoly powers of big business and unfair trade practices, is also a watchdog over deceptive advertising. The FDA, created in 1906 as a result of the outcry over Sinclair's *The Jungle,* sets product standards and requires disclosure of product contents. The **Federal Communications Commission (FCC)** oversees advertising directed to children.

TABLE 19.1

Key consumer rights legislation in the United States since 1966

1966	**Fair Packaging and Labeling Act**
	requires manufacturers to disclose ingredients and volume on the package.
1967	**Federal Cigarette Labeling Act**
	requires warning label on cigarette packages and advertising.
1968	**Truth-In-Lending Act**
	requires full disclosure of all finance charges in consumer credit agreements.
1969	**Child Protection Act**
	allows the Food and Drug Administration to remove dangerous children's products from the market.
1972	**Consumer Product Safety Commission Act**
	establishes the Consumer Product Safety Commission to recall and ban unsafe products.
1975	**Magnuson-Moss Warranty Act**
	sets disclosure standards for product warranties.
1990	**Nutritional Labeling Act**
	regulates health claims and requires disclosure of nutritional content.
1990	**Clean Air Act**
	establishes strict controls on companies to avoid air pollution and acid rain emissions.
1990	**Children's Television Act**
	reduces amount of commercials on children's TV programs and requires more educational programs for children.
1994	**Telemarketing and Consumer Fraud and Abuse Prevention Act**
	establishes rules prohibiting deceptive and abusive telemarketing acts or practices.
1998	**Children's Online Privacy Protection Act**
	sets standards for collection and use of personal information from and about children on the Internet.

The FDA has been particularly active in controlling health claims and ensuring accurate labeling as a result of passage of the Nutritional Labeling Act in 1990. In 2001, the FDA ordered a review of the accuracy of cholesterol claims.[15] Earlier, Citrus Hill was made to take the word "fresh" off its orange juice label because it is made from concentrate; and restaurants were ordered to begin backing up nutrition claims with hard data on their menus.[16] On the other hand, the FDA did authorize a health claim that soy protein lowered the incidence of heart disease based on the accumulated evidence of thirty-eight studies.[17]

Two other agencies, established in the 1970s, are important. The **Consumer Product Safety Commission (CPSC)** is empowered to set product safety standards to protect consumers from risk or injury. The **Environmental Protection Agency (EPA)** sets controls on industry emissions, toxic wastes, and automobile pollution.

THE ROLE OF BUSINESS ORGANIZATIONS

Business has been both reactive and proactive in protecting consumer rights. It has been reactive in responding to government regulation. Businesses must conform to a variety of laws dealing with areas such as pollution controls, product safety, product labeling, truth in advertising, and controls over price fixing and antimonopoly activities. They must also conform to guidelines established by regulatory agencies such as the FTC's restrictions on deceptive advertising and health and the FDA's nutritional labeling requirements. At times, the business community has strongly resisted such regulation. For example, when the Carter administration put more teeth into the EPA and sought greater powers for the FTC and the FDA, the response from business was intensely negative.

A more proactive response from business is self-regulation. Many companies are adopting sophisticated antipollution policies, forthright labeling practices, and new channels for customers to exercise their rights. For example, Lever Brothers commits itself to using recycled plastics in packages for its household products; General Electric spends millions on reducing pollutants that deplete the ozone barrier; Procter & Gamble is advertising refills for its products to reduce waste by 25 to 35 percent; and Wal-Mart is experimenting with an eco-store that features recycling as its wall-to-wall theme.[18] But as we saw in the case of The Body Shop, the public is often skeptical of such efforts, regarding them as self-serving rather than motivated by a true interest in environmental protection or consumer rights.

The History of the Consumer Movement in the United States

The consumer movement in the United States has consistently sought to protect consumer rights. Whereas consumerism abroad has tended to encourage governmental action, the consumer movement in the United States has tended to encourage self-regulation in trying to get corporate America to accept a concept of social responsibility.

FOUR PERIODS OF CONSUMERISM

The first recorded consumer protest in this country occurred in 1775 in Massachusetts, where people who sold tainted food were sentenced to the pillory.[19] The first consistent consumer movement started around 1890 and was followed by three distinct periods prior to 1980, when consumer protection became a national issue. Each of these periods was marked by rising consumer prices coupled with muckraking exposés, which resulted in consumer protection legislation.

▌ First Period of Consumerism   The first period came at the start of the twentieth century, a time when huge corporations such as Standard Oil were amassing power. As a result, the Sherman Antitrust Act was passed in 1890 to limit big business from restraining competition. Also, national brands gained prominence for the first time, and consumers began to focus on their performance. In 1906, Upton Sinclair's *The Jungle* not only helped establish the FDA, but also prompted Congress to pass the Meat Inspection Act. Another development in this period was the passage in 1914 of the Federal Trade Commission Act, which established the FTC to curb monopoly and unfair trade practices.

▌ Second Period of Consumerism   The Great Depression and the 1933 book *100,000,000 Guinea Pigs,* which exposed unsafe medicines, cosmetics, and foods, sparked the second period of consumerism. These revelations led to other exposés of advertising through two books, *Our Master's Voice* and *The Popular Practice of Fraud,* and exposés regarding the preparation of foodstuffs through two other books, *Eat, Drink and Be Wary* and *American Chamber of Horrors: The Truth About Food and Drugs.* Thanks to such books, the Consumers Union was formed in 1936 and the Wheeler-Lea Amendment to the Federal Trade Commission Act was passed in 1938. The amendment enlarged the powers of the FTC to prosecute unfair and deceptive trade practices, particularly advertising.

▌ Third Period of Consumerism

The third period of consumerism began in the 1960s, when another series of exposés followed the relative quiet of the post–World War II years. In 1962, Rachel Carson's *Silent Spring* made consumers aware of the dangers of pesticides and other chemicals in foods and other products. In 1965, Ralph Nader's *Unsafe at Any Speed* exposed the automobile industry's disregard for even rudimentary safety precautions. Nader's study was instrumental in the passage of laws to set safety standards for cars.

From 1974 to 1978, federal expenditures on consumer safety, job safety, and other industry-specific regulation increased by 85 percent.[20] President Carter created a cabinet post to deal with energy conservation and the environment. Further, new agencies such as the EPA were formed, and older regulatory agencies were rejuvenated. The FDA became more activist, requiring additional information on food labels. The FTC established clear rules to define deceptive advertising, made cigarette companies disclose harmful tar content on their packages, and energetically investigated TV advertising's effect on children.[21] By decade's end, the FTC's budget had increased by 500 percent.[22]

▌ Decline of Consumerism in the 1980s

The Reagan administration reversed the drive to regulation and de-emphasized consumer issues. The basic philosophy was stated in Reagan's 1982 economic report: "While regulation is necessary to protect such vital areas as food, health and safety, too much unnecessary regulation simply adds to the costs to businesses and consumers alike without commensurate benefits."[23]

To the Reagan administration, self-regulation was preferable to government regulation in protecting consumer interests. Regulatory agencies were required to justify their actions with a cost-benefit analysis demonstrating the value of their proposals.[24] Unlike the 1970s, where the burden of proof was on industry to ensure consumer protection, the burden was now on the regulatory agencies.[25] Environmental control was also de-emphasized, and the EPA was weakened by a 50 percent staff cut.[26]

▌ Fourth Period of Consumerism: Rebirth in the 1990s and 2000s

A rebirth of consumerism occurred in the 1990s and early 2000s, primarily as a reaction to the deregulation of the Reagan years. The first Bush administration initiated this rebirth, putting more teeth into some of the regulatory agencies that were all but ignored during the Reagan years.[27] The Clinton administration carried this focus forward. If there was a single reason for this change, it was that most surveys showed American consumers thought deregulation hurt them.

The second Bush administration is slowing the focus on environmental issues with its refusal to sign the Kyoto Protocols that place restrictions on industrial emissions,[28] and its decision in 2001 to abandon a treaty on global warming.[29] But the focus on consumer rights is likely to remain active through the decade of 2000.

The rebirth of consumerism since 1990 will be discussed in later sections, largely in the context of the issue of consumer rights. Before we do, however, it is important to recognize that the consumer movement is a global phenomenon.

History of the Consumer Movement Abroad

Since 1970 the consumer movement has been an important force in Western Europe, and to a lesser extent in Asia. After years of economic prosperity and increased consumption, European consumers shifted their focus to quality-of-life issues such as the environment, personal health and nutrition, and safety.[30] Early consumer groups focused primarily on nutrition and product testing. After the European Union (EU) was created in the late 1950s, consumer organizations realized that they must get involved in creating and implementing legislation to improve consumer rights, environmental protection, and consumer information.

BEFORE 1990

In Western Europe, the ecological focus of consumerism began in response to growing concerns about pollution. Consumer organizations, such as Friends of the Earth and Greenpeace, developed in the late 1960s as vehicles for environmental action and consumer participation. Many other organizations and local groups also organized around consumer-related causes at this time. For example, the German *Stiftung Warentest* was formed as an independent product-testing organization. It tests nearly two thousand products a year and publishes the results in its monthly "test" magazine and other specialty publications.[31]

In the 1970s there was a shift from creating national policies to creating European Community–wide policies.[32] The Stockholm Conference in 1972 brought attention to environmental issues in industrialized countries.[33] Soon after, the European Community (now the European Union) approved the First Action Program on consumer policy. It focused on five consumer rights: the right to protection of health and safety, the right to protection of economic interests, the right to damages, the right to information and education, and the right to representation.[34]

The Green movement took root as a political force in the early 1980s to protest acid rain's detrimental impact on Europe's forests. It gained momentum in the mid 1980s after widespread publicity about the Chernobyl nuclear power plant accident. Green parties were established in the United Kingdom and in Germany by 1985. By decade's end, Greens had become establishment politicians, accounting for 14 percent of the parliamentary vote in Belgium, 8.4 percent in West Germany, and 10.5 percent in France. The Greens were responsible for many of the environmental protection laws and other consumer protection measures in the 1980s and 1990s, such as cosmetics safety regulations, labeling of food products, noise pollution, misleading advertising, waste disposal, provision of consumer credit, and water-quality regulations. Each country mandated its own consumer protection laws, and many of the most important measures became EU standards.

AFTER 1990

Throughout the 1990s, the EU and individual countries passed many consumer-oriented laws, as a result of the continued influence of the Green parties and consumer groups. The public mood can best be summed up by a 1995 survey that showed that 82 percent of German consumers; 67 percent, Dutch; 50 percent, French; and 50 percent, British said they "incorporate environmental concerns in their shopping behavior."[35] The 1992 Maastricht Treaty promoted consumer protection to a full-scope EU policy by giving the European Parliament of the EU enforcement powers regarding environmental protection. The Environmental Action Program (EAP), in effect from 1993 to 2000, broadened the environmental protection standards for EU countries and focused on sustainable environmental development, rather than narrowly focused environmental standards.[36]

Another consumer policy area that has gained momentum recently is consumer health and food safety. Numerous laws have been passed to regulate food products. For example, restrictions on the use of genetically modified (GM) microorganisms in food products were established in the early 1990s and have been frequently expanded. Europe's recent decision not to import hormone-injected beef from the United States and Canada is part of a precautionary measure to help protect consumers, even in the absence of proven negative effects.[37] Genetically modified foods, which have only recently become an issue among American consumers, are extremely unpopular with European consumers. European consumers' objections appear to rest on three main claims: (1) GM foods are unnatural, (2) genetic modification produces dangerous food, and (3) GM foods are bad for the environment.[38] After such largely publicized food-related diseases as mad cow disease, many Europeans are skeptical about the safety of any unnatural additive and about the ability of government to regulate its safety.[39]

One area in which Western Europe has lagged behind the United States is in regulating the promotion of cigarettes. But that has changed. The EU banned cigarette ads on TV in 1989, nineteen years after the U.S. ban. And in 1998, the EU banned all forms of advertising of tobacco products. In 2003, the World Health Assembly adopted a treaty to encourage member nations worldwide to ban cigarette ads.[40] There is also a more concerted effort to prevent teenage smoking. In addition, consumer activists are emerging in Asia to attack cigarette marketing methods, bolstered by a World Health Organization report that found aggressive cigarette promotions by U.S. companies caused increases in consumption primarily among women and teens, traditionally groups less likely to smoke in underdeveloped countries.

Consumerism has received less emphasis in Asia and in Eastern Europe (see the Global Applications box), than in Western Europe. In Japan, for example, a closer relationship between industry and government has resulted in more emphasis on forming protective trade barriers than in protecting consumer rights. Although cooperation between government and industry may be suited to Japanese preferences for harmony and consensus, it leaves consumers with fewer brand alternatives. However, because of an increase of political parties more sympathetic to

GLOBAL APPLICATIONS

Environmentalism Has a Long Way to Go in Eastern Europe

Through much of this century, the chokehold of centralized planning and massive spending on arms led to one environmental crisis after another in the nations of Eastern Europe and the former Soviet Union. The most famous was the nuclear meltdown at Chernobyl in 1985. As William Reilly, former head of the Environmental Protection Agency, wrote in 1992:

> To those who doubt the wisdom of pollution control . . . let them travel to Eastern Europe. Let them see the Vistula River in Poland, over 80 percent of it so corrosive that it is useless for even cooling machinery. Let them confront Eastern Europe's high rate of infant mortality, lung disorders, worker absenteeism, and premature death. Poland, Hungary, Bulgaria, Romania and Czechoslovakia, not to mention Russia itself—these are entire nations living in the dark shadow of an environmental catastrophe. ("Environment Inc.," March/April 1992, p. 9.)

With the possible exception of the Czech Republic, not much has improved in these countries since Reilly's pessimistic statement. Toxic dumps still contaminate ground water, and raw sewage from cities still spews into rivers and coastal waters. Even more discouraging, countries that have instituted new regulations have no efficient means of enforcement.

In 1996, the EU sent a stern message that unless the countries of Eastern Europe attempt to tackle these environmental problems, they would not be considered for future membership. "The message here was: Environment is not something you can forget about," according to one official. "We're saying you have to take this seriously, and now is the time." ("Clean up Your Land, European Union Tells Ex-Eastern Bloc," September 25, 1996, p. A11.)

There are a couple rays of light: the growing awareness among these countries that economic growth might be hindered without more awareness of consumer interests, and a fledgling Green movement that is starting to exert some pressure on public officials. In every Eastern European country today, some kind of agency is responsible for environmental protection. Improvements are visible in controlled use of brown coal (a poor-quality fuel high in sulfur and nitrogen), growing use of clean natural gas by power plants, and installation of "scrubbers" in coal-burning stations to reduce pollutant levels. Still, Eastern Europe has a long way to go to establish a consumer-friendly environment.

As many Eastern European countries try to gain full membership in the EU, they are expected to implement significant environmental efforts to begin repairing the environmental damage from years of centralized planning, rapid population growth, and exploitation of natural resources. On the other hand, inclusion in the EU will help fuel rapid growth in the new member countries and is likely to contribute to high industrialism, energy consumption, and pollution.

Evidence of the negative consequences of rapid industrialization is increasingly prevalent in growing cities like Bucharest and Warsaw, where rapid economic development has increased plastic packaging, highlighted new waste management issues, and brought a booming number of toxin-emitting cars. Significant environmental improvement in Central and Eastern Europe is needed. As consumer awareness increases and mobilizes, and the EU continues to provide a clear direction for improvement, Eastern and Central Europe should make progress toward a consumer-friendly environment. And, in some respects, Eastern Europeans are faring better than their EU counterparts. Household waste per capita in Eastern Europe is about half the EU average, and more Eastern European farms are organic.

Sources: "Europe: Clean Up or Clear Out," *The Economist* (December 11, 1999), p. 47; "Fit for Europe," *Chemical Market Reporter* (September 20, 1999), p. S27. "Clean Up Your Land, European Union Tells Ex-Eastern Bloc," *New York Times* (September 25, 1996), p. A11; "Environment Inc.," *Business Horizons* (March/April 1992), p. 9.

OF CONSUMER BEHAVIOR

consumer rights and consumer awareness of the need for environmental protection, the pendulum may soon start swinging toward consumerism. One step in this direction is the government's support of the 1997 Kyoto Protocols to promote voluntary reduction of carbon emissions.[41] The Kyoto Protocols have also been endorsed by many of the nations of Eastern and Central Europe and the former Soviet Union.

Consumer Rights in the United States

Four issues have dominated the attention of consumer activists, government, and business in the United States in the 1990s and early 2000s: (1) the environment, (2) health claims, (3) advertising to children, and (4) the right to privacy and nondisclosure of personal information. As we will see, these issues are not unique to the United States and have received global attention.

THE NEW ENVIRONMENTALISM

The 1990s saw greater enforcement of environmental controls and new initiatives to promote a clean environment. The impetus for these moves did not come from government but from an increased awareness among consumers for protecting the environment. Highly publicized environmental disasters such as the Exxon Valdez oil spill, the issue of global warming, and the deterioration of the ozone barrier have reinforced the notion among consumers that the environment is deteriorating.

A 2001 survey found that when consumers were asked which was more important, the economy or the environment, 63 percent said the environment. And 57 percent said protection of the environment should be given precedence, even at the expense of economic growth.[42] Some consumers act on these concerns. For example, 14 percent of consumers stopped buying Exxon products because of the Exxon Valdez oil spill.[43] Moreover, these numbers may increase as Generation Y begins to have a greater impact on society. Many Generation Y children first learned about environmental issues in their preschool years, suggesting a greater awareness and concern about environmental issues as part of their everyday lives.[44]

On the other side of the coin, consumers do not necessarily buy "green" products. As one report stated, "A lot of misperceptions that green products are inferior still linger, even though most reviews suggest otherwise."[45] Unless they consider environmentally sound products to be the equal of regular brands based on quality and purpose, most consumers are unlikely to pay the higher prices such products often require. When green goods were a novelty, shoppers were willing to spend more to test them; but as time passed, they began to apply the same value and quality standards to green products as to any other product.

The new environmentalism of the 1990s and early 2000s has found a voice in each of the three parties to consumerism in Figure 19.1: the consumer, government, and business organizations.

▌ Reaction of Consumer Activists and Agencies   Increased environmental concerns have led consumer groups and politicians to target marketers they believe produce needless pollutants and clog precious landfill space. Such actions

often center on consumer organizations that have played a public role in opposing business activities that harm the environment. The most prominent is the Sierra Club, an organization that seeks to protect land areas from development and publicizes negative environmental activities. Another, the Environmental Defense Fund (EDF), attempts to increase public awareness regarding issues such as waste disposal and encourages consumers to recycle trash[46] (see Exhibit 19.2). The EDF was instrumental in influencing McDonald's to change its packaging from plastics to paper.

▌ **Government Controls** The new environmentalism also has resulted in renewed activism by government. In 1990, the Clean Air Act was revised to combat interstate pollution and enforced controls to avoid air pollution and acid-rain emissions.[47] The Clinton administration strengthened the commitment to conservation. In 1993, it established a new White House Office of Environmental Policy and signed a biodiversity treaty to protect plant and animal life worldwide. Clinton also signed a law in 1996 to protect millions of acres of forests and grasslands in the Southwest from mining and lumbering. In the same year, the Clinton administration directed the EPA to focus all environmental protection standards on the risks that pollution poses to the health of children, leading to tougher rules on pollution emissions.[48] And in 2000, it endorsed the Kyoto Protocols.

▌ **EXHIBIT 19.2** ▌

Environmental ads from a consumerist organization.

Reprinted with permission of the Environmental Defense Fund.

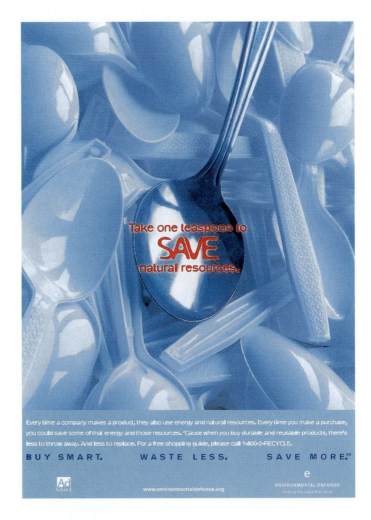

The current Bush administration is taking a much less activist stance regarding environmental issues. For example, it is on record in stating that the guidelines in the Kyoto Protocols for restricting carbon emissions are too strict for the major capitalist countries and plans to issue less restrictive standards.[49] In addition, the Energy Department has undertaken a review of the nation's clean air policy with the intent of relaxing air pollution regulations that the energy industry argues impose billions in extra costs.[50] At present, the states are taking a more activist stance on the environment than the federal government. From coast to coast, local governments are recognizing that shrinking landfill space and finite resources make environmentalism good policy. States are also trying to lessen gasoline consumption by encouraging carpooling, mass transit, and even walking.[51]

■ **Reaction of Business**   The reaction of the third leg in the consumer movement, business organizations, has been mixed. On the positive side, some companies have taken steps to ensure environmentally responsible actions. In 1990, McDonald's switched from plastic to paper wrapping, and it uses recyclable products to build its restaurants. By 2000, it had reduced its waste by more than 30 percent, becoming one of the country's leading buyers of recycled materials.[52] Following McDonald's lead, six major paper users, among them Time Warner and Johnson & Johnson, agreed to help the EDF build a market for recycled paper by using secondhand pulp. Similarly, in 1999 Honda and Toyota started selling hybrid cars combining internal combustion and electric propulsion in an attempt to reduce pollution by minimizing damaging emissions.

Marketers have unleashed a torrent of new products with environmental claims. Companies such as Ben & Jerry's, The Body Shop, and Patagonia (see Exhibit 19.3) have made environmentalism a fundamental component of their companies' overall corporate strategies and values. According to one new product-tracking service company, in 2000 approximately 5 percent of new consumer products made claims about recyclability or recycled contents.[53]

| **EXHIBIT 19.3** |
A web site that promotes environmental issues.

Reproduced by permission.

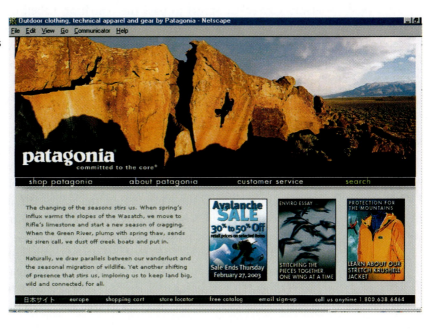

On the negative side, many of these green claims are dubious at best. For example, when Hefty, Glad, and Handi-Wrap trash bags added chemicals to promote the decomposition of their products, they advertised them as degradable. The problem is that biodegradability requires the action of sunlight, and most of these products wind up in landfills where they do not actually decompose.

Such claims have led to a series of actions on the federal and state levels. In 1992, the FTC and eight states investigated whether recycling claims violate truth-in-advertising laws. In addition, the FTC issued a set of guidelines on environmental labeling. For example, calling a trash bag recyclable is considered misleading because bags are not generally separated from other trash at landfills.[54]

HEALTH CLAIMS

A second issue that has generated consumer activism in the 1990s and early 2000s is concern with health claims related to foods. Changing lifestyles have led to an increased focus on health and nutrition. Now, consumers are more aware of nutritional information in ads and on packages.

One survey found that over half of consumers interviewed said that health claims are an important factor in influencing their purchasing decision, and 44 percent said they read most health and nutritional information on the package.[55] The focus on health claims has been heightened by greater awareness of the potential harm cigarettes, liquor, drugs, and even coffee can cause. This concern was shown in another poll that found three of four consumers support warnings on beer, wine, and liquor advertising and packaging.[56]

Protection of consumer rights in advertising health claims has been the primary responsibility of only one of the three legs of the consumer movement: government agencies (see Figure 19.1). Although they have begun to raise their voices, consumer activists and organizations have played a minor role in this area.[57]

■ **Government Controls**   By 1990, studies casting doubt on many health claims caused Congress to pass the Nutrition Labeling and Education Act, which requires fuller disclosure of the nutritional content of foods in packaging.[58] In conjunction with the Nutritional Labeling Act, the FDA developed new rules requiring that advertisers must substantiate their claims for foods such as oat bran and high-fiber cereals with scientific evidence.[59] In 1991, the FDA forced Kellogg to withdraw its claim that Heartwise cereal helped reduce cholesterol. The company then changed the cereal's name to Fiberwise to avoid any connotation that the cereal fights heart disease.

The FDA has also forced several food makers to eliminate no-cholesterol claims on vegetable oils. The agency said that such claims were misleading since they implied that no-cholesterol products are fat-free, which is not the case. Procter & Gamble immediately took no-cholesterol claims off its Crisco and Puritan oils. More recently, the FDA softened its stand, allowing companies like Quaker Oats to advertise the health benefits of oatmeal.

Another area of growing FDA interest and regulation is the Internet, where most major consumer products companies now have home pages. For example, in 2001 the FDA gave a warning to Ocean Spray Cranberries to stop making unapproved health claims regarding its juices on its web site.[60] On the site, the company claimed that Ocean Spray juices "may help the body fight cancer" or "may help lower cholesterol." The company complied by eliminating these claims.

▌ Reaction of Business   Food and drug companies have attempted to get on the nutritional bandwagon with a proliferation of products that have advertised fewer calories, less salt, lower fat, less cholesterol, more calcium, and higher vitamin content. Some companies have specialized in all-natural products. For instance, Tom's of Maine started with an all-natural toothpaste and is now branching out into other all-natural drug products. In 1995, Frito-Lay sank $225 million into developing low- or no-fat versions of its entire snack food line. However, with about 60 percent of foods sold in U.S. grocery stores having nutritional labels and one-third of all food advertising containing some kind of health message, it is no wonder that consumers are confused. For example, in 2001 Benecol spread claimed it was a cholesterol-reducing dietary supplement. The FDA forced the company to withdraw the dietary association and to limit its advertising to focus on the product as a food spread.[61]

Companies are becoming more conscious of health and nutritional claims as a result of the FDA's more activist stance and new laws requiring fuller disclosure of nutritional contents. Benecol's withdrawal of its claim to be a dietary supplement is an example.

ADVERTISING TO CHILDREN

A third consumer rights issue that is receiving increasing attention of consumer activists is advertising to children.

A number of studies support the position that excessive advertising to children is not in their best interest. Stephens and Stutts found that children between ages 3 and 5 had difficulty distinguishing between TV programming and commercials.[62] Roedder, Sternthal, and Calder found that preteens are likely to respond to the immediate influence of a commercial in buying decisions. They tend to ignore their own past experiences with products.[63] Moore and Lutz found that younger children did not engage in much interpretation or evaluation of ads, but formed simple likes and dislikes.[64] All of these studies support the notion that children may be unduly influenced by advertising because they have not developed abilities for perceptual discrimination and information processing.[65]

Others have argued that exposing children to advertising permits them to become more informed consumers at an early age. They learn to discriminate claims and to process marketing information. Eliminating advertising would deprive them of such consumer socialization, and they would then become more vulnerable consumers later in life. Both consumer organizations and government agencies have been active in controlling advertising to children. The response of business has been mixed.

▌ Reaction of Consumer Activists and Organizations   Whereas government agencies have taken the lead in protecting consumer rights regarding nutritional claims, consumer organizations have taken a more active part regarding advertising to children. Advocacy groups such as Action for Children's Television (ACT) have attacked advertising to children as unfair and deceptive based on the findings cited in the last section. These organizations have focused primarily on tobacco and liquor advertising.

A coalition of groups, including ACT and the American Cancer Society, successfully lobbied the FTC in 1999 to ban all cartoon characters that sell cigarettes, because of their appeal to minors.[66] Precipitating this campaign was R. J. Reynolds's (RJR) use of the Joe Camel cartoon character that particularly appealed to kids.[67] One survey found that when asked to name a familiar cigarette, 90 percent of children 8 to 13 years old named Camel.[68] Another study of teens found that they were particularly influenced by symbols like Joe Camel because adolescence is a time of identity formation that makes teens particularly subject to advertising symbols connoting that it is "cool" or "with it" to smoke.[69]

A group called the Smoking Control Advocacy Resource Center has publicized the past role of cigarette companies in consciously promoting cigarettes to the youth market. One RJR memo dated 1976 made public by the group states:

> Evidence is now available to indicate that the 14- to 18-year-old group is an increasing segment of the smoking population. RJR-T[obacco] must soon establish a successful new brand in this market if our position in the industry is to be maintained over the long term.[70]

There is also increasing concern about teenage drinking. In 1996 small, local breweries began introducing lemonade-flavor drinks that contain the same level of alcohol as beer. Brands with names like Two Dogs Lemon Brew and Hooper's Hooch are targeting younger people more used to orange soda than beer. Anheuser-Busch and Miller tested their own versions but decided against targeting a younger market for fear of a public backlash.[71] Of equal concern is a 2001 study that found that the favorite ad cited by children was one for Budweiser.[72]

▌ **Government Controls**   Concern about advertising and marketing practices to children resulted in greater government controls in the 1990s. In 1990, Congress passed the Children's Television Act, which reduced the amount of commercials on children's television programming from as many as fourteen minutes of ads per hour to no more than ten minutes per hour on weekends and twelve minutes on weekdays.[73] Broadcasters must also offer more educational programs for children.

Although guidelines limiting commercial time have been effective, government regulation has had less success in controlling commercial content. The Joe Camel experience demonstrates this difficulty. In 1992, Surgeon General Antonia Novello demanded that Reynolds stop using the Joe Camel promotion, only to be rebuffed by the company. Later, when she asked magazines to stop accepting the ads, Novello did not fare much better.[74] In 1994, the FTC also refused to recommend an outright ban of the campaign, although the Commission was badly divided on the issue.[75] It was not until 1999 that action was finally taken that resulted in the elimination of the campaign.[76]

▌ **Reaction of Business**   The reaction of business to the issue of children's advertising has been mixed. Marketers have argued that banning children's ads would have the effect of worsening children's programming because of reduced funding sources.[77] The business community has promoted self-regulation in lieu of government regulation, fearing that the strict advertising standards imposed for tobacco ads would be applied to other industries.[78] Most advertisers avoid manipulating advertising claims to influence children unduly, and the Joe Camel experience seems to have been the exception rather than the rule. Companies are particularly sensitive to the charge that they may be endangering the welfare of children or are acting in bad taste. Whereas R. J. Reynolds had been stubbornly insistent that its Joe Camel character was not affecting children and seemed to fuel the fires by including the character in catalogs featuring sportswear and other products, Kenner Products reacted differently to parents' concerns about a line of its toys. When parent groups railed at Kenner Products for introducing a line of wheeled action toys called Savage Mondo Blitzers that had names such as Chunk Blowers, Puke Shooters, and Butt Kickers, the company did an about-face and discontinued the line.[79]

THE RIGHT TO PRIVACY

Another issue that has received attention from consumer advocates in the 1990s and early 2000s is the right to privacy. The availability of increasingly powerful computers has allowed companies to merge and analyze vast amounts of consumer data from sources such as credit card bills, telephone records, and coupon redemptions. The problem is that such information can be used without the consumer's consent. For example, a customer renting a car from Hertz might get a letter from Ford saying it is "collecting information" on people who rent their products. One report even accused MCI of using phone records to identify people customers frequently call so it could ask them to join MCI's discount calling circle.

Some databases are sometimes welcome by consumers. For example, frequent purchaser programs at department stores such as Bloomingdale's identify heavy purchasers and provide services such as sending reminders to spouses to buy birthday presents or offering free delivery. But the potential for using personal information is of increasing concern to consumers as an invasion of privacy. Surveys show that 76 percent of consumers in the United States are "very concerned" about the amount of personal data accumulated by business, and 93 percent feel that companies should be legally required to ask permission before using it.

The New York Attorney General's Office reflected this concern when it took action against American Express for making its 20-million-cardholder database available to The Sharper Image to enable it to better target its customers. New York State argued that customers should not have their spending patterns and lifestyles analyzed for the use of merchants without their permission. As a result, American Express has been giving customers a choice as to whether they want to be contacted.

Concerns regarding privacy have grown markedly with the increase in Internet usage. Recent surveys taken by various organizations indicate that consumers are most concerned about privacy issues on the Internet and the use of personal data by web sites.[80] One survey by *Advertising Age* conducted in 2001 found that three of the four greatest concerns in Internet usage were security, trustworthiness, and privacy; the other concern was convenience.

The main concern among consumers is the ability of Internet sites to implant files or "cookies" on an individual's computer when a consumer visits a site, allowing sites to identify you on all subsequent visits. The problem is that these sites are often linked to other sites and if the consumer provides personal information on one site, it could be linked to others as well. Compounding the problem is the possibility that online behavior can be linked to offline records. When the web-based advertising agency Double Click bought Abacus, an offline direct mail company with records on millions of consumers, it gave the company the ability to link online to offline behavior.[81] This potential greatly concerned consumers who were aware of it. To allay consumer concerns, Double Click developed a rigorous privacy policy assuring customers it would use personal information only with their knowledge and consent. But the question is: How many consumers are aware of such guarantees and their rights to online privacy?

Current federal and state laws do not provide consumers with comprehensive protection against violations of privacy in online information collection. In response and for the present, the U.S. government has opted for a "wait-and-see" position to determine if self-regulation by businesses will be sufficient.[82] European regulations and privacy laws are much more stringent, preventing foreign companies from doing online commerce in EU countries if they fail to comply.

In an effort to prevent government intervention into online commerce, industry leaders have begun to promote self-regulation. Double Click's privacy policy is one example. Pace-setting companies such as IBM and Microsoft Corporation have named chief privacy officers, while other companies such as Expedia have hired consulting firms for "privacy audits." Microsoft has developed a "passport" that gives individuals control over what personal information they provide to any given web site.[83] Passport is a mobile identity card that allows the consumer to negotiate with the web site the information to be revealed.

Some legislators, however, remain skeptical of private industry's ability to self-regulate. Hundreds of bills are pending in state legislatures to regulate access of personal information. At the federal level, several bills have been enacted, including:

- Consumer Privacy Protection Act of 2000, requiring web sites to provide notice, choice, access, and security to users and give the Federal Trade Commission (FTC) power to enforce compliance
- Secure Online Communication Enforcement Act of 2000, requiring commercial web sites to obtain consumers' permission prior to collecting their personal data
- Privacy Commission Act, creating a seventeen-member panel to study online privacy
- Online Privacy Protection Act of 1999, requiring the FTC to develop regulations to protect adult privacy on the Internet[84]

As one legislator said, consumers should be given the right to be given notice and to say no to the disclosure of private information.

Consumer Rights Abroad

The same consumerist issues that have dominated the U.S. economy in the 1990s and early 2000s have been evident abroad, particularly in Western Europe. In some cases, the EU has taken a more activist stand than the United States has in protecting consumer rights through regulation and legislation.

THE NEW ENVIRONMENTALISM

The continued promotion of "green laws" in the EU has been led primarily by the "Green Trio"—Germany, Denmark, and the Netherlands. The 1995 admission to the EU of environmentally friendly Finland and Sweden helped bolster these countries' efforts to pass more environmentally favorable legislation and strengthen enforcement in the EU. As noted, the European Parliament of the EU has broad enforcement powers regarding pollution controls.

Companies such as the Netherlands' Philips Electronics are proving that green marketing can pay off with consumers if implemented wisely. Philips represents one of Europe's leading companies in "eco-friendly" product design in large part due to its corporate-wide Eco-Vision program established in 1998. The program requires that each Business Group design or redesign at least one "Green Flagship" product each year.[85]

There are signs of increasing awareness of the importance of pollution controls in Asia. One demonstration is the acceptance of the Kyoto Protocols by most Asian countries. In Japan, a group known as the Responsible Care Council has their 109 member companies committed to reducing industrial emissions, the biggest such initiative in Asia.[86] In 2000 Japan also adopted a new recycling law that requires appliance manufacturers to be responsible for the collection and recycling of used products.[87] Exhibit 19.4, which promotes pollution control, illustrates environmental awareness on the part of Komatsu, a Japanese electronics producer.

HEALTH CLAIMS

There has been greater concern over genetically modified (GM) foods in Europe than in the United States. Asia has also seen concern with regard to GM foods. Consumer movements to restrict GM foods have sprung up in India, Japan, Thailand, and the Philippines.[88] In Japan, one food maker recalled potato snacks

| **EXHIBIT 19.4**
Promoting pollution controls in Japan.
Courtesy of Komatsu.

nationwide because of traces of an unapproved GM potato.[89] In the Philippines, the government is considering setting up a labeling system to inform consumers of any GM ingredients in products.[90] "Functional foods" represent another area gaining attention in the food industry and on the labeling front by regulatory bodies and consumers. Also known as "nutriceuticals," these are foods that promise health benefits beyond what the foods' normal contents would typically provide.[91] Currently, the functional foods segment is valued at $14 billion in Europe and $10 billion in Japan.[92] Companies marketing functional foods face a minefield of complicated regulations, as health claims must be supported by scientific data and test results similar to pharmaceutical products. The United Kingdom's Advertising Standards Authority, for instance, forced the Danish firm MD Foods to withdraw its advertisements for its Pact range of products from the United Kingdom because of exaggerated health claims based on the calcium and folic acid content of its products.[93]

ADVERTISING TO CHILDREN

The issue of advertising to children has received increasing attention in Europe because the number and frequency of television ads targeted to children has grown by 15 to 20 percent since the mid-1990s.[94] Greater availability of television programming on a Pan-European basis has resulted in broader exposure in Europe to advertising targeted at children.

Most European countries already have at least some restrictions on marketing targeted to children. These restrictions range widely in level of strictness. In Sweden, no television advertising targeted to children under 12 is permitted.[95] Belgium prohibits state broadcasters from running advertisements directed to children five minutes before and after children's programs. Greece banned all toy advertising on television during children's viewing hours.[96] Restrictions on children's advertising are much more lenient in other countries. In the United Kingdom, for example, marketers are advised to follow a code of reasonable ethics and self-regulation when advertising to children. The EU considered a ban on children's advertising similar to Sweden's but concluded there was no need for further restrictions. As a result, no EU-wide broadcasting restrictions for advertising to children exists currently.[97]

Due to the increasing concern regarding children's advertising in Europe, several savvy companies have attempted to incorporate constructive activities in their strategies in targeting children. For example, Unilever developed a "Make it, Bake it" program for its Stork margarine to promote baking in home economics classes.[98]

RIGHT TO PRIVACY

Europeans tend to be culturally even more sensitive to issues of data privacy than Americans. They tend to be more trusting of governments to protect consumers through legislation and regulations.[99] Europe has taken the lead in legislating for the protection of data privacy. Each country in Western Europe possesses extensive data protection and privacy laws, which are being updated to include the effects of the Internet and e-commerce on these areas. The EU in 1995 passed the EU Data Privacy Directive, which requires unambiguous consent from individuals for the use of their personal data and permits these individuals to access and check the accuracy and extent of data held in a company's database.[100] Business's response to these privacy regulations has remained fragmented, and only recently have some organized forces taken shape to represent private-sector interests amid all the legislative activity. One such organization is the Internet Users Privacy Forum based in the United Kingdom. This forum is composed of Internet service providers and user organizations. Its first task was to devise a code of best practices to insure privacy.

Additional Consumer Rights

Four additional consumer rights are long-standing issues that predate the rebirth of consumerism in the 1990s and early 2000s:

1. *The right to safety.* To be protected against the marketing of goods that are hazardous to health or life.

2. *The right to be informed.* To be protected against fraudulent or misleading information, advertising, labeling, or other practices and to be given the facts needed to make an informed choice.

3. *The right to be heard.* To be assured that consumer interests will receive full and sympathetic consideration in the formulation of government policy.[101]

4. *The right to be a minority consumer without disadvantage.* To ensure that minority groups or low-income consumers will not be at a disadvantage in relation to any of the preceding rights compared with other groups.

In the United States, these rights were first formulated in 1962 by President John F. Kennedy in a message to Congress titled *Special Message on Protecting the Consumer Interest.* This was the first message a U.S. president ever delivered on this topic. For the federal government to meet its responsibilities to consumers in the exercise of their rights, Kennedy stated that legislative and administrative action was required. Although the United States has led in protecting these consumer rights, they have received global attention.

THE RIGHT TO SAFETY

Government agencies, businesspeople, and consumerists generally agree that abuses related to product safety must be eliminated. Most companies try to ensure product safety and reliability, but abuses occasionally exist.

The primary government agency responsible for eliminating these abuses is the Consumer Product Safety Commission (CPSC.) The Commission can ban the sale of products, require manufacturers to perform safety tests, and require repair or recall of unsafe products. It operates a hotline to report hazardous products and also runs the National Electronic Injury Surveillance System, a computer-based system that monitors 119 hospital emergency rooms across the country. On the basis of this system, the Commission computes a product Hazard Index. Among products with the highest hazard index are cleaning agents, swings and slides, liquid fuels, snowmobiles, all-terrain vehicles (ATVs), and more recently, in-line skates. The CPSC also has been active in recalling products at an average of two hundred recalls issued per year.

Since July 2001 the CPSC has recalled the following products:

- Daisy-made BB guns[102]
- Whirlpool dehumidifiers, because components were overheating and causing fires[103]
- Gas-fired water heaters that created the risk of carbon monoxide poisoning[104]
- Sunbeam sprinkler systems that were faulty[105]
- 115,000 strollers in which the lock mechanism could break, causing the stroller to collapse[106]

The trend toward strengthening consumers' safety rights is spreading around the globe. In Japan, the nascent consumer movement may finally be increasing awareness of product safety as a consumer issue partly due to heightened media reports about the growing number of product defect cases that have resulted in human injury or property damage. The parliamentary victory of parties less committed to government protection of business may hasten change.

Europe has adopted more stringent laws regarding product safety. The EU passed two directives related to the issue—the Product Liability Directive, to protect consumers from defective products; and the General Product Safety Directive, which gives members authority to enforce Product Liability suits. The EU also requires all products to contain a European Conformity marking, to show that the products conform to all relevant directives and standards, many of which refer to product safety standards. The marking is also required for imported goods.[107]

THE RIGHT TO BE INFORMED

The consumer's right to be informed covers two components: (1) the right to be protected against misleading and deceptive information and (2) the right to be given sufficient information to make an informed choice. The explosion of media outlets and web sites makes these rights even more important today.

Deceptive Advertising   Over the years, the FTC has established a set of clearly defined guidelines for determining what is deceptive advertising. Advertising need only have the capacity to deceive to be considered deceptive; that is, the FTC does not need to prove deception actually occurred. Furthermore, the advertiser can be ignorant of any false claim and still be liable. Consumer researchers have tried to grapple with the question, Where does puffery end and deception begin?

Gardner identified three types of deceptive advertising.[108] The first is **fraudulent advertising;** that is, a straightforward lie. The second is **false advertising,** which involves a claim-fact discrepancy. That is, the product's claimed benefits are fulfilled only under certain conditions that may not be clear in the advertising. Or, the product must be used in a certain manner or with certain precautions. For example, Superior Rent A Car advertised a $69-a-week rate in Miami's Yellow Pages, but it did not disclose that the rate applies only to cars with manual transmissions.[109]

A third type of deception is **misleading advertising.** It involves a claim-belief interaction. In this case, an advertisement interacts with certain consumer beliefs and results in a misleading claim. In 2001, the FDA warned drug makers about potentially misleading ads for treatment of HIV, the virus that causes AIDS. Ads showed "robust individuals engaged in strenuous physical activity."[110] The ads were misleading in suggesting the drugs could totally restore AIDS victims' health. There was also concern that the ads might discourage individuals who could be exposed to the HIV virus from practicing safe sex.

In some cases, the FTC has asked certain companies not only to stop making deceptive claims, but also to correct these claims publicly. The rationale for requiring such **corrective advertising** is that deceptive claims have a residual effect and, if uncorrected, could remain in consumer memory for a period of time. Without corrective advertising, companies continue to benefit from such past claims. For example, in the past, the FTC required

- Doan's analgesics to correct its claim that it was superior for back pain relief.[111]
- ITT-Continental to correct past advertising that its Profile Bread was effective in weight reduction.
- Warner-Lambert to correct the claim that Listerine helps prevent colds.
- Hawaiian Punch to correct its claim that its drink was composed of natural fruit juices, when actually it contained only 11 to 15 percent fruit juice.[112]

Do such corrected claims have an impact on consumer beliefs? One study found that the proportion of consumers who believed that Hawaiian Punch had little fruit juice went from 20 percent to 70 percent during the period of corrective advertising.[113]

Deceptive advertising is not just an American phenomenon. In China, inadequate regulation of ads has led some businesses to use deceptive advertising to boost profits. In one case, a skin care product promising more delicate skin succeeded in producing rashes. In another case, a soft drink claiming 100 percent natural ingredients was made of preservatives and artificial coloring. China has had laws against misleading advertising since 1987, but in a country more concerned with industrial production than consumer rights, they are rarely carried out.[114]

In Europe, regulations and enforcement practices vary across countries with regard to misleading advertising. The United Kingdom regulates advertising extensively, led by the Advertising Standards Authority (ASA), arguably the largest, most involved and well-financed regulatory system in the region. In one recent case, the authority forced a security company to rescind an ad condoning the use of a shotgun to protect private property.[115] The Scandinavian countries have established the Office of Consumer Ombudsman, which mirrors the FTC in handling advertising complaints. Germany and Austria, on the other hand, rely heavily on private lawsuits and consumer organizations to uphold regulations and laws against misleading advertising.

▌ Control of Other Deceptive Marketing Practices

Deception can occur in other areas of marketing strategy besides advertising. Packaging can be deceptive when a company reduces the contents or size of the package while maintaining price. Such a practice would represent a deceptive price increase because consumers are getting less quantity for the same price. In the 1991–1992 recession, Star-Kist tuna decreased the contents of its cans by about 6 percent, Procter & Gamble and Kimberly Clark decreased the number of disposable diapers in a standard package by about 10 percent, and Lipton cut the weight of a jar of instant

WEB APPLICATIONS

Are Search Engines on the Web Engaging in Deceptive Advertising?

When a search engine gives a company a higher rating for its products because the company is advertising on its site, is it engaging in deceptive advertising? Yes, says Commercial Alert, a consumer watchdog group formed by consumer activist Ralph Nader. The group filed a complaint in July 2001 with the FTC asserting that eight of the largest online search engines are concealing the effects of special fees from consumers. According to the group, search engines like Netscape owned by AOL, MSN owned by Microsoft, and Directhit owned by Ask Jeeves are abandoning their objective formulas for determining the order of their best buys or top product ratings by giving preference to the highest bidder.

The problem is that these firms are not making the practice known to consumers. According to Gary Ruskin, Commercial Alert's executive director, "Search engines have become central in the quest for learning and knowledge in our society. The ability to skew the results in favor of hucksters without telling consumers is a serious problem" ("Complaint Says Search Engines Break Law with 'Pay for Placement,'" July 17, 2001, p. 4). It is a particularly serious problem because with more than 2 billion pages on the Web, search requests rank second to email in popularity.

Why have some of the most renowned names on the Web threatened their own credibility by taking payments? They've done so because since the Internet meltdown in 2000, search engines are looking for alternative sources of revenue. The most onerous practice according to Commercial Alert is when a search engine ranks a business based on the amount of money it pays, a practice known as "pay for placement."

As of March 2002, the FTC has not made a decision as to whether it will pursue the complaint. In the past, the agency ordered TV stations to identify infomercials as advertisements, so it is likely that the FTC may ask search engines to inform consumers anytime a company that is being ranked has paid a fee to the search engine. One search engine, *www.goto.com,* does disclose this practice, even listing how much the advertiser paid for the link.

If the credibility of search engines is undermined by deceptive practices, it could spell the beginning of the end for the Internet as an objective source of information.

Sources: "Complaint Says Search Engines Break Law with 'Pay for Placement,'" *Houston Chronicle* (July 17, 2001), p. 4; "Group Files Complaint with FTC on Web Search," *San Francisco Chronicle* (July 17, 2001), p. B3; "Key Internet Search Engines Accused of Misleading Users," *Los Angeles Times* (July 17, 2001), p. C1; "Search Engines: Leading Us Astray?" *Business Week* (August 6, 2001), p. 8.

---

tea by about 7 percent. In each case, the company maintained the price of the product.[116] Marketers often reduce a product's content incrementally so it is below the consumer's "just-noticeable difference" (see Chapter 6).

Deception can also occur in pricing practices. One such practice, **bait-and-switch pricing,** involves a low-price offer intended to lure customers into a store where a salesperson tries to influence them to buy higher-priced items. Such practices are illegal, and the FTC and states' attorneys general police them. An example of this is the case of Craftmatic, which advertised low-priced therapeutic chairs on television. It then sent salespeople into the field to sell more expensive ones to the elderly. A Massachusetts judge barred the practice after the state's attorney general's office revealed the scam.[117]

Selling practices can also be deceptive, as when a realtor glosses over defects in a home, for example. However, government can do little to legislate fair sales practices. If the sales transaction is fraudulent, the consumer can take the seller to court; but few consumers do. In most cases, companies have become more sensitive to the need to maintain high standards in selling.

▌ Provision of Adequate Information

Does the right to be informed include the right to adequate information to ensure a wise purchase? There are two positions on this issue. The view of most businesses is that the buyer should be guided by his or her judgment of the brand's quality. Consumer activists believe that business and impartial sources should provide full information and should reveal performance characteristics.

Regardless of the position one takes, the trend is toward more disclosure of information. An increasing number of states are requiring unit pricing of grocery products and open dating of perishables. The Nutritional Labeling Act requires disclosure of health and nutritional information on packages. Recent rules the FDA formulated require even more information on content on food labels.

Will consumers use the additional information provided by marketers? Not always. As noted in Chapter 7, consumers often experience information overload and therefore visit only one or two web sites in making a product choice, or one dealership in buying a car. In particular, if product involvement is low, informational requirements may be minimal. Adequate information is not as important a consumer rights issue for low-involvement products such as toothpaste or paper towels.

THE RIGHT TO BE HEARD

The consumer has the right to express dissatisfaction with a product and to have complaints resolved (redressed). Most surveys agree that the overall level of product dissatisfaction among consumers is low, but dissatisfaction is increasing. Recessions in the early 1990s and 2000s resulted in a greater value orientation on the part of consumers. Consumers now take a more critical look at products and demand product quality at fair prices. Consumers are increasingly dissatisfied with the higher prices of national brands relative to their quality. There has been a general decrease in loyalty to national brands and a significant move to private labels (*i.e.,* retailer-controlled brands) because these brands often offer the same quality at lower prices.

▌ Consumer Complaint Behavior

If not satisfied, consumers can react in three ways.[118] The first and most common is simply not to buy again. A second reaction is to express dissatisfaction to others. As we saw in Chapter 16, such negative word of mouth is the most harmful effect of dissatisfaction because it has a multiplier effect that goes well beyond one consumer's reaction.

A third reaction is to seek redress. But few dissatisfied customers actively bring their complaints to the marketer's attention. One survey by the RAND Corporation, a nonprofit organization, found that even when they are injured by a product, only one in fifty consumers seek redress.[119] An earlier study by A. C. Nielsen of food products and health and beauty aids found that only 3 percent of all dissatisfied consumers brought their complaints to the attention of the manufacturer.[120] Both studies demonstrate that the manufacturer is almost totally cut off from direct consumer feedback regarding dissatisfaction with the product.

Why do so few consumers bother to take action in expressing their dissatisfaction? The reason is that they are not sufficiently involved with the product to go out of their way to complain. Many consumers in the studies cited earlier simply said it was not worth the time and effort. When financial risk and product involvement are higher, however, complaint behavior increases. When a wide array of higher-priced products was studied, one-third of all dissatisfied customers voiced complaints to manufacturers or retailers.[121]

Another possible explanation for the lack of consumer follow-up when dissatisfied is that there are no formal channels for redress. Letters of complaint are usually too much trouble to write and a minority of better-educated consumers is more likely to write them. Also, excessive red tape in retail stores frequently discourages product returns.

▌ Role of the Internet

The proliferation of Internet use, however, may be changing this pattern of consumer behavior when confronted with product dissatisfaction. The Internet enables people to find like-minded consumers more easily, making individuals feel less reticent to voice complaints. Several sites have emerged as consumer advocates. We noted several such sites in Chapter 16. For example, eComplaints forwards the customer complaint via email to the relevant company executives. Others, such as Epinions.com, proactively gather complaints, track and package them, and sell the data to the companies targeted.[122]

The Internet also affords companies an opportunity to learn about their customers and make decisions proactively to curb dissatisfaction. The Internet lowers the cost of information gathering and offers the possibility for two-way, real-time, or near-real-time communication between company and customer. For example, several Internet-based businesses, like Rhode Island–based Suretrade, are turning to live chats and cobrowsing to provide real-time, online customer service. Suretrade is an online brokerage firm that utilizes live chats to assist its customers so that customers can stay online while obtaining answers to questions in lieu of calling—a cumbersome procedure, since most still have only one telephone line for both Internet access and traditional telephone use.[123] This same concept can be applied by brick-and-mortar companies, which can use their web sites as an additional channel for customers to post complaints and receive assistance.

Many manufacturers supplement their web sites with toll-free telephone numbers. Whirlpool was among the first to do so and was followed by Procter & Gamble, General Electric, Clairol, Pillsbury, General Mills, and many others. General Electric has programmed over seven hundred fifty thousand possible answers to customer inquiries and complaints. Thus, when consumers call, representatives have a ready response.[124] A company's average cost to answer a complaint is about $3, often more than the cost of the product. However, the cost is generally worth it: One study found that quick and positive resolution of a complaint leads to repeat purchases 80 to 90 percent of the time.[125]

THE RIGHT TO BE A MINORITY CONSUMER WITHOUT DISADVANTAGE

The three additional consumer rights that have been discussed so far may have little relevance for low-income minority consumers. Minority consumers living in poverty

▌ are more exposed to unsafe products,

▌ have less access to information and fewer choices of alternative brands, and

▌ have less access to means of redress.

Compared with other consumers, low-income consumers do not always have the information necessary to make a satisfactory choice. They often lack the freedom to go outside their local community to engage in comparison shopping and lack the means for redress if the product fails.

Consumer activists also complain about marketing campaigns that they believe encourage unhealthy or unsafe product choices for minorities. They have been particularly forceful in their efforts to call attention to cigarette and alcohol advertising in minority neighborhoods, where incidents of lung cancer and liver damage are high. The Reverend Calvin Butts of Harlem, for one, has taken scores of his followers on marches through their neighborhood, where they paint over billboards selling cigarettes and alcohol. Some consumer organizations publish literature that attempts to educate minority consumers about how the major food, alcohol, and cigarette companies target them. The Center for Science in the Public Interest published two such books: *Marketing Disease to Hispanics* and *Marketing Booze to Blacks.*

Perhaps the most publicized protest (mentioned in Chapter 12) involved R. J. Reynolds's 1989 launch of Uptown, a cigarette that was targeted specifically to African Americans. The objective was to increase sagging sales by aiming at a segment that had a higher proportion of smokers. This was the first time that a new cigarette was designed especially for a minority group, instead of the usual practice of advertising existing brands across the racial spectrum. As a result, it drew a torrent of criticism, particularly since Uptown was very high in nicotine.[126] African-American leaders and consumer activists charged that the company was taking unfair advantage of inner-city minorities. In 1990, the secretary of health and human services said, "Uptown's message is more disease, more suffering, and more death for a group already bearing more than its share of smoking-related illness and mortality."[127]

R. J. Reynolds responded to the Uptown uproar by discontinuing the brand. Why the difference in its actions with Joe Camel and Uptown? Because the intended target saw the Uptown campaign as an affront, while the intended target for Joe Camel embraced the ads. By and large, cigarette and alcohol companies have not been overly responsive to complaints about their advertising tactics. The major beer companies, for example, continue to market their potent malt liquor brands almost exclusively to African Americans despite outrage by health officials. As a result, this area will continue to provide fertile ground for consumer advocates for some time to come.

At one time, the Internet presented another area of disadvantage for low-income and minority consumers. A 1997 study found that a "digital divide" existed between races and ethnicities. Internet users were more likely to be higher-income, better-educated white males. But as we saw in Chapter 12, the digital divide is disappearing. By 2000, over 40 percent of African Americans and Hispanic Americans were Web users, compared with 44 percent of the general population.[128] Even though the digital divide is disappearing on ethnic grounds, many disadvantaged groups still do not have web access and are unable to participate in the advantages of increased choice and greater price alternatives that web access offers. The proposed budget cutbacks in government programs to provide computers and Internet access to poor areas means that a socioeconomic divide may continue to exist with regard to the Web.

Social Responsibility

Based on the corporate actions cited in this chapter, the record of Corporate America is fairly mixed regarding the protection of consumer rights. The social responsibility of marketing organizations can be assessed in two areas: (1) their ability to restrain their own actions through a process of self-regulation and (2) their willingness to exert influence over social issues such as drug use and underage drinking and smoking, an application of influence that has come to be known as "social marketing." In short, companies have become increasingly aware of the new "triple bottom line"—financial, environmental, and social performance.[129]

SELF-REGULATION

Will marketing organizations accept their responsibilities to protect consumer rights through a process of self-regulation, or will they abdicate their responsibilities to government in the expectation of further legislation, more controls, and the establishment of more regulatory bodies?

The preference in a marketing society, on both pragmatic and ideological grounds, is for self-regulation rather than additional government regulation. For example, the advertising industry established the Children's Advertising Review Unit to try to regulate the nature and efficiency of advertising to children.[130] However, the record of corporate performance cited earlier is not encouraging. The failure of large companies to recall unsafe products, the inability of "smokestack" industries to establish adequate controls over air pollution, and the targeting of younger smokers by cigarette companies are all indications of the need for continued government controls. The corporate governance scandals in 2001–2002 demonstrated the willingness of companies like Enron and WorldCom to mislead their consumers, investors, and employees through fraudulent earnings reports and fueled the perception on the part of the public that many companies are not socially responsible and require greater government oversight.

However, marketing organizations have slowly been moving toward more responsible self-regulation. We have seen some companies take voluntary action to protect the environment. According to a study by *Fortune* magazine, companies such as Dow Chemical, IBM, and Xerox have effectively integrated environmental performance into their corporate goals.[131] Others such as Monsanto and DuPont have made major efforts to contain air and water pollution. Many companies have also accepted self-imposed industry standards for labeling, product safety, and children's advertising.

Of equal importance, many organizations have attempted to ensure consumer rights by providing better means to redress complaints through toll-free numbers and accessible web sites. Companies have also sought to improve communications with consumers through consumer affairs offices that formulate policies for handling consumer complaints. JCPenney, Eastman Kodak, and Giant Foods were among the first to establish such units. Companies have also used consumer affairs offices to educate consumers by disseminating information on nutrition, product content, and product safety. JCPenney was one of the first to establish a concerted effort in consumer education. It has published *Forum,* a publication for teachers of consumer education; *Insights into Consumerism,* a magazine providing teaching modules on consumer issues; and numerous buying guides containing factual product information.

Ultimately, companies must realize that it is in their self-interest to protect the consumer rights cited in this chapter. One indication of the importance of recognizing such corporate responsibility is a poll that found that 88 percent of consumers would be more likely to buy from a company that is socially responsible and a good corporate citizen.[132]

SOCIAL MARKETING

Marketing organizations can also demonstrate social responsibility by attempting to influence consumers to behave in a more socially responsible manner. Drinking and driving, smoking excessively, taking drugs, and refusing to recognize "safe sex" as a precaution against AIDS are four examples of consumer behavior that is not in the best interests of the consumer.

Social marketing is the use of marketing tools by organizations to try to influence such behavior, generally on a "pro bono" basis; that is, at no cost for their services. An example is the formation of a group of advertising agencies and media companies into the Partnership for a Drug-Free America to develop a communications campaign to reduce drug use. One recent television campaign shows a group of teenagers "hanging out" in a suburban garage. One teenager takes out a joint and starts passing it around the circle, but as the camera pans the circle of friends, it shows each person simply passing the joint on without taking a puff. The message is clear: Smoking marijuana is not "cool." Social marketing also involves sponsorship of events to assist causes. For example, the advertising firm of Kirshenbaum Gond & Partners developed ads to sponsor a race to benefit God's Love We Deliver, an organization that feeds homebound people with AIDS.

An offshoot of social marketing is **cause-related marketing,** which involves a firm sponsoring a charity or a cause that it then links to its name. For example, Revlon sponsors the annual Revlon Run/Walk for Women to benefit research into women's cancers. Similarly, Nabisco has sponsored the World Wildlife Fund and, in return, won the right to run a sweepstake for its brand of Animal Crackers that portray endangered species in cracker form. Similarly, British Petroleum (BP) forged an alliance with the Red Cross in 2001 to allow customers in BP stations across Europe to donate money to the organization. The link to the Red Cross was advertised, both online and in conventional media.[133]

It is estimated that American companies spent $600 million in 1996 on cause-related events and advertising.[134] One reason is that a 1994 study showed that 80 percent of consumers said they had a better image of a company that is involved in making the world a better place. And two-thirds said they would switch brands to support a cause-related marketing effort.[135]

SUMMARY

Our marketing economy does not always afford the consumer an environment for making an optimal or even an adequate choice. The necessity to promote consumer rights relative to the powers of big business is known as "the consumer movement," or "consumerism."

Consumerism is the set of activities of consumer organizations, government, and business to promote the rights of the consumer. The consumer movement in the United States is not new. Three distinct periods in the last century have been marked by increased activities to protect consumer rights: 1890–1915, 1933–1940, and 1962–1977. During each of these periods, increased prices and exposés of business practices led to legislation protecting consumer rights. The 1980s saw a marked decrease in government activities to protect consumer rights as a result of the Reagan administration's emphasis on self-regulation.

Consumerism is a global phenomenon, with strong consumer movements in Western Europe that originally began as protests carried out by Green parties in many countries against environmental pollution. Europeans' interest in consumer rights has expanded beyond the Green movement to include issues such as labeling for genetically modified foods, advertising to children, and the right to privacy. In contrast, the consumer movement has failed to capture the attention of the public in Asian countries, due in part to cultural differences, lack of enforcement mechanisms, and varying views on the role of government in consumer protection. Indications of change are emerging with new laws being passed in countries such as China and increased media attention to product defects and liability in places like Hong Kong.

The 1990s and early 2000s saw a rebirth of the consumer movement both in the United States and abroad. Under the Clinton administration, four issues emerged: (1) protection of the environment, (2) health and nutritional claims for food products, (3) the influence of advertising on children, and (4) the right to nondisclosure of private consumer information without consumers' consent. The fourth issue, in particular, has garnered much attention due to the growth of online commerce and the absence of laws and precedent to guide the governing of privacy in the online world. These issues have also been recognized abroad, particularly in Europe, where the emphasis is on EU legislation as the means to deal with the problems.

The chapter also reviewed four consumer rights that predate the rebirth of consumerism and were first spelled out by President Kennedy in the early 1960s, as follows:

1. The right to safety protects consumers against the marketing of hazardous goods.

2. The right to be informed means protection from misleading information and the need for a sufficient amount of accurate information to make an informed choice.

3. The right to be heard requires provision of the channels of communication to permit consumers to register complaints to business.

4. The right to be in the minority without disadvantage; that is, assurance that being a minority or low-income consumer does not mean deprivation of the foregoing rights.

These issues have also been addressed in Western Europe, where at times, more rigorous action has been taken in regard to pollution controls and product safety than in the United States.

Marketing organizations have a role in ensuring these rights. Some organizations have accepted their responsibilities by improving the means for registering complaints and by establishing consumer advisory boards and consumer affairs offices. However, there is still much to be done to encourage self-regulation aimed at ensuring consumer rights.

The advertising slogan of a discount retailer, "An educated consumer is our best customer," is a fitting conclusion to this chapter.

QUESTIONS FOR DISCUSSION

1. Do you agree with The Body Shop's policy of supporting social causes? Why or why not?

2. Why have consumer boycotts had mixed results in affecting social change?

3. The 1980s did not see the emergence of another period of consumer activity parallel to that of the 1970s. Why not?

4. What was the difference in the role of the FTC in regulating advertising under the Reagan and Clinton administrations?

5. How has the consumer movement in Europe differed from that in the United States regarding three forces cited in Figure 19.1?

6. What are the reasons for the increasing awareness of consumer rights and interest in the consumer movement in the 1990s and early 2000s?

7. How have governmental agencies reacted to the new environmentalism?

8. Why do most consumers express increasing concern about the environment, yet show greater reluctance to buy green products?

9. What are the pros and cons of eliminating all TV advertising to children under 8?

10. What are some of the differences in the ways Western Europe and the United States approached issues of the environment and health claims in the 1990s and early 2000s?

11. Why was there significant concern over Double Click's acquisition of Abacus? Were Double Click's actions sufficient to ensure privacy?

12. Cite an actual or hypothetical example of fraudulent, false, and misleading advertising. Clearly, the FTC should require advertisers to cease using fraudulent and false advertising. Should the agency require advertisers to cease misleading advertising? Why or why not?

13. Why did R. J. Reynolds withdraw Uptown, a cigarette positioned to African Americans, but continue to use Joe Camel ads in the face of criticism that the character appeals to children?

14. What role do socially responsible companies have in marketing social causes? What potential pitfalls should such companies be aware of in implementing cause-related marketing strategies?

RESEARCH ASSIGNMENTS

1 Visit the following web sites: *www.patagonia.com, www.benjerry.com,* and *www.thebodyshop.com.*

- Do these sites reflect support of social causes? In what ways?

- What are the differences in approach by each company on its web site?

2 Conduct a survey among forty to fifty consumers and identify those consumers who have taken some environmentally relevant action in the past month (*e.g.,* purchased recycled paper or brought materials to a recycling center). Identify the demographic and lifestyle characteristics of these consumers and their media habits.

- What are the differences in demographics, lifestyle, and media habits between the more environmentally conscious consumers and the rest of the sample?

- What are the implications for a campaign by the federal government to influence people to buy products that safeguard the environment?

3 Identify three companies that have consumer affairs departments. First determine the organization and objectives of the each department. Then determine the mechanisms for processing consumer complaints. What are the differences between these organizations regarding the purpose and operation of their consumer affairs departments?

NOTES

1. "Questioning Authority," *Across the Board* (January 2001), pp. 15–16.
2. "Body Shop's Founder Gives Up Control," *New York Times* (February 13, 2002), pp. W1,W7.
3. "Whales, Human Rights, Rain Forests—and the Heady Smell of Profits," *Business Week* (July 15, 1991), pp. 114–115.
4. "Ex-Global Body Shop Boss Opens Travel Ethics Site," *Marketing* (April 12, 2001), p. 4.
5. "Body Shop's Founder," pp. W1, W7; and www.bodyshop.com web site, Human Rights, as of November 30, 1999.
6. "The Body Shop: Truth & Consequences," *DCI* (February 1995), pp. 54–62.
7. "Questioning Authority," pp. 15–16.
8. See Robert O. Hermann, "Consumerism: Its Goals, Organizations and Future," *Journal of Marketing* 34 (October 1970), p. 56.
9. "Do Boycotts Work?" *Adweek's Marketing Week* (April 8, 1991), pp. 16–18; and "Facing a Boycott, Many Companies Bend," *Wall Street Journal* (November 8, 1990), p. B1.
10. "Cause for Concern," *Marketing Week* (February 11, 1999), pp. 28–31.
11. "Bottled Up: As Unicef Battles Baby-Formula Makers, African Infants Sicken," *Wall Street Journal* (December 5, 2000), p. A1.
12. Louisa Wah, "Treading the Sacred Ground," *Management Review* 87 (July/August 1998), pp. 18–22.
13. *New York Magazine* (February 11, 1991), p. 22.
14. Sanker Sen, Zeynep Gurhan-Canli and Vicki Morwitz, "Withholding Consumption: A Social Dilemma Perspective on Consumer Boycotts," *Journal of Consumer Research* 28 (December 2001), pp. 399–417.
15. "Cholesterol Claims at Issue," *Food Technology* (November 2001), p. 26.
16. "Cholesterol Crackdown," *Advertising Age* (May 20, 1991), pp. 1, 56; "P&G Gives In, Axes Its 'Fresh' Label," *Advertising Age* (April 29, 1991), p. 1; "U.S. Wants to Keep Menus Honest on Nutrition Claims," *New York Times* (June 10, 1993), pp. A1, A23.
17. "The Heart of the Matter," *Chemist and Druggist* (June 2, 2001), p. 1.
18. "Beware: Green Overkill," *Advertising Age* (January 29,1991), p. 26; "Green Products Sprouting Again," *Advertising Age* (May 10, 1993), p. 12; "It's Green, It's Friendly, It's Wal-Mart 'Eco-store,'" *Advertising Age* (June 7, 1993), pp. 1, 4.
19. "History of Consumer Protest," *New York Times* (September 16, 1985), p. 46.
20. George A. Steiner, "New Patterns in Government Regulation of Business," *MSU Business Topics* 26 (Autumn 1978), pp. 53–61.
21. John S. Healey and Harold H. Kassarjian, "Advertising Substantiation and Advertiser Response: A Content Analysis of Magazine Advertisements," *Journal of Marketing* 47 (Winter 1983), pp. 107–117.
22. William L. Wilkie, Dennis L. McNeill, and Michael B. Mazis, "Marketing's 'Scarlet Letter': The Theory and Practice of Corrective Advertising," *Journal of Marketing* 48 (Spring 1984), p. 11.
23. "The Consumer Movement: Whatever Happened?" *New York Times* (January 21, 1983), p. A16.
24. "Deregulation, Fast Start for the Reagan Strategy," *Business Week* (March 9, 1981), p. 62.
25. "It Sometimes Seems Like the Federal Tirade Commission," *New York Times* (June 3, 1984), p. C5. See also, "Consumers Are Getting Mad, Mad, Mad, Mad at Mad Ave," *Business Week* (April 30, 1990), pp. 70–71; and "F.D.A. Is Preparing New Rules to Curb Food Label Claims," *New York Times* (October 31, 1989), p. A1.
26. "U.S. Environmental Agency Making Deep Staffing Cuts," *New York Times* (January 3, 1982), p. 20.
27. "FTC Warns Agencies; Eyes Tobacco, Cable," *Advertising Age* (March 12, 1990), p. 6.
28. "Bush's Plan Would Slow, Not Halt, Rise in Emissions," *New York Times* (February 14, 2002), pp. A1 & A7.
29. "Bush Angers Europe by Eroding Pact on Warming," *New York Times* (April 1, 2001), section A.
30. Michael Jacobs, *Greening the Millennium?: The New Politics of the Environment* (Malden, Mass.: Blackwell, 1997).
31. Ecotopia web site http://www.ecotopia.be/ecotop/pubs/yearbook/epe2.html, as of January 2000.
32. Mikael Skou Anderson and Duncan Liefferink, *European Environmental Policy: The Pioneers* (New York: Manchester University Press, 1997).
33. Ernst U. Von Weizsacker, *Earth Politics* (London, N.J.: Zed Books, 1994).
34. European Union web site http://europa.eu.int/scadplus/leg/en/lvb/l32000.htm, as of January 2000.
35. "Environmental Product Standards, Trade, and European Consumer Goods Marketing," *Columbia Journal of World Business* (1995), p. 75.
36. Jonathan Golub, *New Instruments for Environmental Policy in the EU* (New York: Routledge, 1998); Charlotte Burns and Emma Harrison, "Setting Strategies for a New Europe," *Consumer Policy Review* (January/February 2000), pp. 25–29.
37. "Europe's Beef Ban Tests Precautionary Principle," *Chemical Week* (August 11, 1999), p. 42.
38. "Special—Genetically Modified Food: Food for Thought," *The Economist* (June 19, 1999), pp. 19–21.
39. Ibid.
40. European Union web site http://europa.eu.int/scadplus/leg/en/cha/c11509.htm, as of January 2000; and "World Health Meeting Approves Treaty to Discourage Smoking," *New York Times* (May 22, 2003), p. A11.
41. "The Changing Social and Political Environment and Japanese Business" from the web site http://www.japan-embassy.hu/English/jan98.html, as of January 2000.
42. "The Earth Has No Shortage of Fair-Weather Friends," *Adweek* (April 23, 2001), p. 20.
43. "Friend or Foe? Nature Groups Say Names Lie," *New York Times* (March 25, 1996), pp. A1, A12; and "Green Concerns Influence Buying," *Advertising Age* (July 30, 1990), p. 19.
44. "Green Attitude," *American Demographics* (April 1999), pp. 46–47.

45. "The Green Conundrum," *Across the Board* (May/June 2001), pp. 17–18.

46. "Environmental Defense," *Trusts & Estates* (June 2001), p. S26.

47. "Curbing Interstate Air Pollution," *Forum for Applied Research and Public Policy* (Fall 2001), pp. 21–27.

48. "Children's Health Is to Guide E.P.A.," *New York Times* (September 12, 1996), p. A14.

49. "Bush's Plan Would Slow, Not Halt, Rise in Emissions," pp. A1, A7.

50. "E.P.A. and Energy Department War Over Clean Air Rules," *New York Times* (February 19, 2002), p. A15.

51. "White House Calls for Cap, Trading Program for Carbon Dioxide Emissions," *McGraw-Hill's Power Markets Week* (November 20, 2000), p. 10.

52. "The Greening of McDonald's Environmental Houdini Act Transforms Chain from Rogue to Role Model," *Boston Globe* (January 24, 2000), p. C1.

53. "It's Not Trendy Being Green," *Advertising Age* (April 10, 2000), p. 16.

54. "FTC Green Guidelines May Spark Ad Efforts," *Advertising Age* (August 3, 1992), p. 1.

55. "Ad Claim Skeptics Still Bite," *Advertising Age* (May 7, 1990), p. S2.

56. "Alcohol Warnings Favored," *Advertising Age* (April 9, 1990), p. 1.

57. See "Groups Put Heat on FTC," *Wall Street Journal* (March 11, 1993), p. B8, for an example of consumer activism regarding health claims.

58. *Advertising Age* (January 22, 1990), p. 1.

59. "Marketers Nervous Over Labeling Rules," *Advertising Age* (May 7, 1990), p. S8.

60. "FDA Action Could Change Food Marketing on the Web," *New York Times* (February 14, 2001), p. C11.

61. "Food Claim Crackdown," *Washington Post* (June 19, 2001), p. WH6.

62. Nancy Stephens and Mary Ann Stutts, "Preschoolers' Ability to Distinguish Between Television Programming and Commercials," *Journal of Advertising* 11 (April/May 1982), pp. 16–25.

63. Deborah L. Roedder, Brian Sternthal, and Bobby J. Calder, "Attitude-Behavior Consistency in Children's Responses to Television Advertising," *Journal of Marketing Research* 20 (November 1983), pp. 337–349.

64. Elizabeth S. Moore and Richard J. Lutz, "Children, Advertising, and Product Experience: A Multimethod Inquiry," 27 *Journal of Consumer Research* (June 2000), pp. 31–48.

65. See Kenneth D. Bahn, "How and When Do Brand Perceptions and Preferences First Form? A Cognitive Developmental Investigation," *Journal of Consumer Research* 13 (December 1986), pp. 382–393; Alan R. Wiman and Larry M. Newman, "Television Advertising Exposure and Children's Nutritional Awareness," *Journal of the Academy of Marketing Science* 17 (1989), pp. 179–188; and Deborah Roedder John and John C. Whitney, Jr., "The Development of Consumer Knowledge in Children: A Cognitive Structure Approach," *Journal of Consumer Research* 12 (March 1986), pp. 406–417.

66. Joel B. Cohen, "Marketing and Public Policy at Odds Over Joe Camel," *Journal of Public Policy and Marketing* (Fall 2000), pp. 155–167.

67. "Teen Smokers, Read This," *New York Times* (August 23, 1996), p. A27.

68. "Poll Shows Camel Ads Are Effective with Kids," *Advertising Age* (April 27, 1992), p. 12.

69. Richard W. Pollay, S. Siddath, Michael Siegel, Anne Haddix, Robert K. Merritt, Gary A. Giovino, and Michael P. Eriksen, "The Last Straw? Cigarette Advertising and Realized Market Shares among Youths and Adults, 1979–1993," *Journal of Marketing* 60 (April 1996), pp. 1–16.

70. "Issue: Secret Documents Reveal Industry Focus on Children, Addiction," Action Alert, Smoking Control Advocacy Resource Center, October 26, 1995, p. 2.

71. "A Little Booze for the Kiddies?" *Business Week* (September 23, 1996), p. 158.

72. "Merchandising Means More to Kids Than TV Ads," *Marketing* (December 20, 2001), p. 18.

73. "FCC Adopts Limits on TV Ads Aimed at Children," *New York Times* (April 10, 1991), p. D7; and "White House Gets Bill Reducing Ads on Children's TV Programs," *New York Times* (October 2, 1990), p. A1.

74. "Top Health Official Demands Abolition of 'Joe Camel' Ads," *New York Times* (March 10, 1992), pp. A1, D1.

75. "Joe Camel Gets Reprieve, For Now," *Advertising Age* (June 6, 1994), p. 52.

76. Cohen, "Marketing and Public Policy," pp. 155–167.

77. "Business: Kid Gloves," *The Economist* (January 6, 2001), p. 60.

78. "Ad Groups Anxious Over Impending FTC Report," *Advertising Age* (September 4, 2000), p. 53.

79. "Tacky Toys With Crude Names," *Industry Week* (February 15, 1993), p. 26.

80. Catherine E. Vance, "Privacy: The Right, the Obligation, the Pending Battle," *Commercial Law Bulletin* (July/August, 2000), pp. 18–19.

81. *Doubleclick: Gathering Customer Intelligence* (Western Ontario: Richard Ivey School of Business, 2001), pp. 1–16.

82. Elizabeth de Grazia Blumenfeld, "Privacy Please: Will the Internet Industry Act to Protect Consumer Privacy Before Government Steps In?" *The Business Lawyer* (November, 1998), pp. 349–383.

83. *Firefly B* (Stanford, Calif.: Stanford University, Case OIT-22B, April 1998), pp. 1–3.

84. Wendy Melillo, "Privacy Matters," *Adweek* (June 19, 2000), pp. 14, 16.

85. Jacquelyn A. Ottman, "It's Not Just the Environment, Stupid," *In Business* (September/October 2000), p. 31.

86. "Japan Reports Progress in Pollution Reduction," *Chemical Week* (July 4–11, 2001), pp. 62–64.

87. "Asia Pacific: Japan's New Recycling Requirements Will Raise Costs," *World Trade* (February 2000), p. 24.

88. "Farmers Use Altered Seeds: Controversy over Genetically Modified Crops Heats Up Overseas," *Detroit News* (July 4, 2000), p. 12.

89. "World Business Briefing Asia: Japan Snack Recall," *New York Times* (March 26, 2001), p. 2.

90. "Filipinos Want Labels for Gene-Altered Food, Survey Says," *Businessworld* (April 23, 2001), p. 1.

91. "Business: Dysfunctional," pp. 71–72.

92. Ibid.

93. "Healthy PR Advice," *Marketing* (August 19, 1999), p. 33.

94. Allyson L. Stewart-Allen, "Rules for Reaching Euro Kids Are Changing," *American Marketing Association* (June 7, 1999), p. 10.

95. "Effort in WU to Ban TV Ads Aimed at Kids Gains Steam," *Los Angeles Times* (July 9, 2001), p. C3.

96. "Marketing to Children Sparks Criticism in Europe," *Wall Street Journal* (December 18, 2000), p. 1.

97. "EU Study Quashes Plan to Ban Ads for Children," *Campaign* (April 27, 2001), p. 2.

98. Stewart-Allen, "Rules for Reaching Euro Kids," p. 10.

99. Amy Zuckerman, "Culture Clash," *World Trade* (May 1999), p. 112.

100. James Heckman, "Marketers Waiting, Will See on EU Privacy," *American Marketing Association* (June 7, 1999), p. 4.

101. Executive Office of the President, Consumer Advisory Council, First Report (Washington, D.C.: U.S. Government Printing Office, 1963), pp. 5–8.

102. "BB Guns & Gun Control ABCs," *American Rifleman* (January 2002), pp. 40–41.

103. "Whirlpool to Recall 1.4 Million Dehumidifiers," *New York Times* (January 31, 2002), p. A23.

104. "CPSC, American Water Heater Recall Gas-Fired Units," *Reeves Journal* (December 2001), p. 12.

105. "Sunbeam to Face Lawsuit in Sprinkler Recall," *USA Today* (October 11, 2001), p. B3.

106. "Recent Consumer Product Safety Commission Product Recalls," *Home Textiles Today* (October 2001), p. 76.

107. "Environmental Due Diligence Is Now Routine," *European Venture Capital Journal* (October 1, 2001), pp. 32–39.

108. David M. Gardner, "Deception in Advertising: A Conceptual Approach," *Journal of Marketing* 39 (January 1975), pp. 40–46. See also J. Edward Russo, Barbara L. Metcalf, and Debra Stephens, "Identifying Misleading Advertising," *Journal of Consumer Research* 8 (September 1981), pp. 119–131.

109. "Car-Rental Firms Leave Drivers Dazed by Rip-Offs, Options, Misleading Ads," *Wall Street Journal* (June 1, 1990), p. B1.

110. "FDA Faults 'Misleading' Drug-Ad Images," *Wall Street Journal* (May 4, 2001), p. B8.

111. Michael B. Mazis, "FTC v. Novartis: The Return of Corrective Advertising?" *Journal of Public Policy & Marketing* (Spring 2001), pp. 114–122.

112. William L. Wilkie, Dennis L. McNeil, and Michael V. Mazis, "Marketing's 'Scarlet Letter': The Theory and Practice of Corrective Advertising," *Journal of Marketing* 48 (Spring 1984), pp. 11–31.

113. Ibid.

114. "Advertising Pitfalls in China," *Managing Intellectual Property* (September 1, 2001), p. 64.

115. "ASA Forces Maxtec to Amend Work," *Marketing Week* (January 31, 2002), p. 7.

116. "Critics Call Cuts in Package Size Deceptive Move," *Wall Street Journal* (February 5, 1991), p. B1.

117. "Court Tells Craftmatic to Halt Deceptive Ads," *New York Times* (February 12, 1992), p. D4.

118. See Jagdip Singh, "Consumer Complaint Intentions and Behavior: Definitional and Taxonomical Issues," *Journal of Marketing* 52 (January 1988), pp. 93–107, for a model of consumer complaint behavior.

119. "Product Liability: Who Sues?" *American Demographics* (June 1995), pp. 48–55.

120. George S. Day, "The Mystery of the Dissatisfied Consumer," *Wharton Magazine* (Fall 1977) p. 47.

121. Ibid.

122. Jo Ann S. Barefoot, "Trash—Talk—and Treasure—in Consumer Complaints," *ABA Banking Journal* (April 2000), pp. 25–30.

123. Charles Waltner, "Live Internet Service Set to Capture Customer Attention," *Information Week* (December 4, 2000), pp. 174–180.

124. "Customer Satisfaction Research Can Improve Decision Making," *Marketing News* 4 (February 5, 1990), p. 13.

125. *Wall Street Journal* (April 7, 1983), p. 31; see also Marsha L. Richins and Bronislaw J. Verhage, "Seeking Redress for Consumer Dissatisfaction: The Role of Attitudes and Situational Factors," *Journal of Consumer Policy* 8 (March 1985), pp. 29–44.

126. "After Uptown, Are Some Niches Out?" *Wall Street Journal* (January 22, 1990), p. B1.

127. Ibid.

128. "Online Rumba," http://abcnews.go.com, as of December 20, 2000.

129. Pamela Baxton, "Companies with a Social Conscience," *Marketing* (April 2000), p. 33.

130. "Give Self-Regulation a Hand," *Advertising Age* (October 15, 2001), p.16.

131. "Who Scores Best on the Environment," *Fortune* (July 26, 1993), p. 114.

132. Robert L. Gildea, "Consumer Survey Confirms Corporate Social Action Affects Buying Decisions," *Public Relations Quarterly* (Winter 1994–95), pp. 20–21.

133. "BP Set to Partner Red Cross Cause in European Deal," *Marketing* (September 20, 2000), p. 1.

134. "Cause and Effects Marketing," *Brandweek* (April 22, 1996), pp. 38–40.

135. "Promoting with a Cause," *Promo* (February 1995), pp. 67–70.

Glossary

absolute threshold Level below which the consumer cannot detect a stimulus; minimal stimulus values capable of being sensed. (6)

acceptable price range A price range the consumer views as realistic. If the product is priced below this range, quality is suspect. If the product is priced above, the consumer refuses to buy. (6)

acculturation The process of learning a culture different from the one in which a person was raised; learning the values of another culture (*e.g.,* a businessperson going abroad, immigrants moving to another country, foreign students). (11)

activation One of the three factors required for retrieval of information from long-term memory. The linkages between nodes must be activated before retrieval can take place. (7)

active adopter A consumer who has adopted a product and who actively gives positive information about the product to others. (16)

active rejector A consumer who has tried a product, found the product to be deficient, and actively gives unfavorable information about the product to others. (16)

actual self The concept individuals have of themselves based on who they think they are. (10)

adaptation level Point at which the consumer adjusts to a frequently repeated stimulus so that it is no longer noticed; the stimulus value (*e.g.,* brightness, loudness) to which the consumer is indifferent and with respect to which stimuli above or below it are relatively judged. (6)

advertising wearout Adaptation to a campaign over time that results in the consumer's boredom and fatigue; the consumer then "tunes out" the message. (6)

affective (feeling) component of attitudes The favorable or unfavorable disposition toward an object; consumers' evaluation of a brand on a positive to negative dimension represents the affective component of attitudes. (8)

age cohorts People of similar ages who have gone through similar experiences. (9)

AIO inventory A list of consumer activities, interests, and opinions constructed to measure lifestyle components empirically. (10)

anticipatory aspiration group Group that an individual aspires to belong to and anticipates joining at some future time. (14)

archetypes Commonly shared memories. (10)

aspiration group Group that a consumer aspires to be associated with, but of which he or she is not a member. (14)

assimilation/contrast theories Theories that combine the two views of assimilation and contrast and maintain that assimilation is more likely to occur if the disparity between experience and effect is likely. These theories state that when consumers are only slightly disappointed, attitudes are likely to change in the direction of expectations and remain positive. When consumers are very disappointed, a negative change in attitude is likely to occur after the purchase and may be exaggerated. (8)

assimilation effect Theory in social psychology that focuses on a desire to maintain balance between experiences and expectations by selectively accepting information consistent with expectations; the tendency in perception for the highly similar parts of a whole to look alike as much as possible; that is, to assimilate. Assimilation occurs when the stimulus differences among the parts are sufficiently small; if the differences are sufficiently large, the opposite phenomenon of contrast tends to occur. (2, 4)

attention The selective process of noticing a stimulus or certain portions of it; the momentary focusing of a consumer's cognitive capacity on a specific stimulus. (6)

attitude-specific strategy Requires comparison of each brand alternative on specific attributes. (7)

attitude toward the ad Consumers' predisposition to respond favorably or unfavorably to an ad. (17)

attitudes (*see* **brand attitudes**).

attribution theory A theory that states that people attribute a cause to their prior behavior. (5, 17)

baby boomers People born between 1946 and 1964, representing 76 million consumers. (9, 12)

baby busters The youths born between 1965 and 1976, representing 47 million consumers; also known as Generation Xers. (9, 12)

bait-and-switch pricing A form of deception in pricing practices that involves a low-price offer intended to lure customers into a store where a salesperson tries to influence them to buy higher-priced items. (19)

balance theory A theory that asserts that unbalanced cognitive systems tend to shift toward a state of balance.

Evaluation of an object is a function of consistently held beliefs about the object. When information about an object conflicts with consumers' beliefs, they achieve balance by either changing their opinion about the object, about their source of information, or a combination of both. The result is a balance in beliefs about the information and the object. (8)

behavioral component of attitudes The tendency to act based on favorable or unfavorable predispositions toward the object; generally measured by an intention to buy scale. (8)

behavioral segmentation An approach to segmentation that is based on the buying behavior of consumers after the product is in the marketplace. These segments are defined by brand usage, product category usage, and the level of product usage (*i.e.,* heavy to light). (18)

behaviorist school Concerned with observing changes in an individual's responses as a result of exposure to stimuli; developed two types of learning theories: classical conditioning and instrumental conditioning. (3)

benefit criteria The factors that consumers consider important in making a decision on one brand or another. (2)

benefit segmentation An approach to consumer segmentation that defines segments based on the common benefits consumers desire in a product. (18)

benefit segments Identification of a group of consumers based on similarity in needs. Often marketing opportunities are discovered by analysis of consumers' benefit preferences. Frequently, one or more segments are identified that are not being adequately served by existing alternatives. (2)

BOT A web site designed to help a consumer make a decision. A BOT can make a recommendation based on a consumer's needs, priorities, and price range. (7)

BOTS (shopping agents) A search-and-comparison tool on a web site that helps consumers locate a greater variety of items and make a decision among them. (1)

brand attitudes A consumer's learned tendencies to evaluate brands in a consistently favorable or unfavorable way. (8)

brand equity The value of a brand in the consumer's mind. (3)

brand leveraging A method in which a company uses a successful brand name on a product line extension, thus creating stimulus generalization. (6)

brand loyalty Repeat buying because of commitment to a brand. (3)

categorization Tendency of consumers to place marketing information into logical categories to process information quickly and efficiently and to classify new information. (6)

category-based strategy Involves evaluation of a brand as a totality rather than a specific attribute. (7)

cause-related marketing The sponsoring by a firm of a charity or other social cause, in which the firm links its name to the cause cited. (19)

chunking (grouping) information Organizing stimuli that summarize a wide range of information about a brand. A brand image is formed by information chunking, meaning the consumer is processing information by brand rather than by attribute. (6)

classical conditioning Conditioning in which an association is formed when a secondary stimulus is paired with a primary stimulus that already elicits a particular response. (3)

closure A principle of perceptual integration describing a perceiver's tendency to fill in the missing elements when a stimulus is incomplete. Experience tends to be organized into whole, continuous figures. If the stimulus pattern is incomplete, the perceiver fills in missing elements. (6)

cognitive (thinking) component of attitudes The tendency to act based on favorable or unfavorable predispositions toward the object; generally measured by an intention-to-buy scale. Beliefs link a brand to a set of characteristics and specify the extent to which the brand possesses each characteristic. (8)

cognitive consistency A basic behavioral principle to which balance theory conforms. This principle states that consumers value harmony between their beliefs and evaluations. If one is inconsistent with the other, consumers will change their attitudes to create harmony in their cognitive structure. (8)

cognitive economy The principle that consumers search for only as much information as they feel is necessary to adequately evaluate brands. (7)

cognitive learning theory A theory that views learning as a problem-solving process. Consumers go through a process of perceiving stimuli, associating the stimuli to their needs, evaluating alternative brands, and assessing whether products meet their expectations. (3)

cognitive response The thought a consumer develops that supports or counters claims made in marketing communication. (17)

cognitive school Views learning as problem solving and focuses on changes in the consumer's psychological set. (3)

cohort (*see* **age cohorts**).

Coleman-Rainwater Social Standing Hierarchy Often preferred to Warner's Index of Status Characteristics, this classification of social classes more directly reflects the power and prestige associated with each class and draws social class lines more sharply. The Social Standing Hierarchy also distinguishes between a middle class and a working class. (3)

collaborative filtering A micromarketing strategy that positions products to individuals based on knowledge of the individual's needs as reflected in past behavior and current preferences. This approach utilizes knowledge of the actions of consumers who have similar preferences to the target consumer, to personalize recommendations. (18)

communities of fantasy Communities that form on the Internet where users create new environments, personalities, or stories. (14)

communities of interest Communities that form on the Internet where users can interact extensively with others on a specific topic of common interest. (14)

communities of relationship Communities that form on the Internet based on certain shared life experiences. (14)

communities of transaction Communities that form on the Internet for the primary purpose of buying and selling products and services and delivering information related to these transactions. (14)

comparative influence The process of comparing oneself to other members of the group, providing a basis for comparing one's attitudes and behavior to those of the group. (14)

compensatory evaluation When using an attribute-specific evaluation method, consumers evaluate brands one at a time across a range of attributes. A good rating on one attribute can compensate, or make up for, a bad rating on another attribute of the brand. The evaluation of that brand is an overall evaluation, based on the sum of the ratings on all of the attributes. (7)

compensatory method (*see* **compensatory evaluation**).

complex decision making Making decisions through a process of active search for information. Based on this information, alternative brands are evaluated on specific criteria. The cognitive process of evaluation involves consumer perceptions of brand characteristics and development of favorable or unfavorable attitudes toward a brand. The assumption is that consumer perceptions and attitudes will precede and influence behavior. (2)

conditioned response A response that is the result of influence by primary and secondary stimuli. (3)

conjunctive strategy A strategy in which a consumer accepts a brand only if it is acceptable on key attributes. The consumer would eliminate a brand seen as negative on one or two of the most important attributes, even if it is positive on all other attributes. (7)

consumer equity Consumer loyalty that has been translated into a long-term commitment to the brand and the company based on interactive relationships. (3)

consumer information processing The nature of the consumer's search for and reactions to marketing communications; the process by which consumers perceive information in four steps—exposure to information, attention, comprehension, and retention of information. (7)

consumer movement The activities that are generally encompassed under the heading of *consumerism*; somewhat misleading term because there is no actual organ-

ization of consumers but, instead, a conglomeration of groups with separate concerns. (*See also* **consumerism**.) (19)

Consumer Product Safety Commission (CPSC) Agency established in the 1970s. It is empowered to set product safety standards to protect consumers from risk or injury. (19)

consumer socialization The process by which consumers acquire the knowledge and skills necessary to operate in the marketplace. The two most important types of consumer socialization are the socialization of children and the socialization of new residents in a community. (14)

consumer socialization of children The process by which young people acquire skills, knowledge, and attitudes relevant to their functioning in the marketplace. (15)

consumerism The set of activities of independent consumer organizations and consumer activists designed to protect the consumer. As a social movement seeking to augment the rights and power of buyers in relation to sellers, these organizations are concerned primarily with ensuring that the consumer's rights in the process of exchange are protected. (19)

context Setting. (5, 6)

continuity Principles of grouping that emerged from Gestalt psychology and that suggest that the basic flow of stimuli should be continuous and lead to a logical conclusion (*e.g.*, the flow of a sales message). (6)

contrast The opposite of adaptation; a change from the constant conditions a consumer is used to. Advertisers try to achieve contrast by using new, attention-getting stimuli. (6)

contrast effect States that a disparity between expectations and experiences may lead the consumer to magnify the disparity; implies that advertisers should moderate their claims so as not to increase consumer expectations to the point that dissatisfaction (*e.g.*, a disparity between expectation and experience) is likely to result. (2, 4)

co-optation Adapting the consumption values of another country (*i.e.*, America) to be consistent with local language, meaning, and beliefs. (13)

corrective advertising A means by which companies correct false claims publicly. (19)

counterargument Thoughts consumers develop that are designed to counter existing information (*e.g.*, a loyal RC Cola drinker develops thoughts to reject benefit claims made by Pepsi or Coca-Cola). (17)

cross-cultural influences Norms and values of consumers in foreign countries that influence strategies of multinational firms marketing abroad. (1, 11, 13)

cultivation theory According to this theory, children learn about a culture's norms and values from the media. The greater children's exposure to TV, the greater the likelihood that they will accept the images and associations seen. (15)

cultural context A concept that divides cultures into two groups: those that rely primarily on verbal and written communication to transmit meaning (low context cultures) and those that rely primarily on nonverbal communication (high context cultures). (16)

cultural homogeneity Identifies uniform cultures with little difference in norms, values, and socioeconomic status among groups (homophilous) versus more disparate cultures with wider difference among groups (heterophilous). (16)

cultural norms Those standards of behavior that govern proper social relations, means of ensuring safety, eating habits, and so forth. If behavior deviates from the cultural norm, society may place sanctions or restrictions on behavior. (11)

cultural values An especially important class of beliefs shared by the members of a society as to what is desirable or undesirable; beliefs that some general state of existence is personally and socially worth striving for. Cultural values in the United States include achievement, independence, and youthfulness. (11)

culture The implicit beliefs, norms, values, and customs learned from a society that underlie and govern conduct in the society. Culture leads to common patterns of behavior. (1, 11)

culture production system The individuals and organizations responsible for creating and producing products designed to meet cultural goals. (11)

database marketing Identifying individual consumers using databases of their characteristics and customizing product, service, or promotional offerings to meet their specific needs. (1, 9)

deceptive advertising Advertising that gives false information or that willfully misleads consumers about the brand's benefits. (17)

decoding The sequence of steps in consumer information processing from exposure to attention to comprehension of a message. Consumers translate the message so it is understood and possibly retained in memory. (17)

defense mechanism A strategy the ego uses to reduce tension. Conflicts that are not resolved in childhood influence later behavior in a manner of which the adult is unaware. (10)

demographic characteristics Objective descriptors of individuals and households; include age, income, family size, and employment status. (9)

demonstration principle Formulated by James Duesenberry, a Harvard economist, this principle states that due to increased mobility and purchasing power in America, consumers will come into increasing contact with new products and will be more likely to buy them; referred to as a social multiplier because ownership increases in multiples as a function of group influence and product visibility. (14)

depth interview An unstructured, personal interview in which the interviewer attempts to get subjects to talk freely and to express their true feelings. Can be conducted individually or in groups (*see also* **focus-group interview**). The latter have the advantage of eliciting more information because of group interaction. (10)

diffusion The process by which the adoption of an innovation is spread over time by communication to members of a target market. (16)

direct feedback Marketing communications that can be linked to sales results (*e.g.,* retail advertising announcing a sale can be related to the number of shoppers coming into the store). (17)

disclaimant group A group to which an individual belongs, although he or she rejects its values. (14)

disconfirmation of expectations Negative product evaluation resulting from consumption because expectations of product performance are not met. In such cases, consumers may develop more negative attitudes toward the product after the purchase. (8)

dissociative group A group to which an individual may regard membership as something to be avoided. (14)

downside price elasticity A measure of a consumer's sensitivity to decreases in price. If consumers are price elastic, they will change brands based on changes or differences in price. (18)

early adopter A category of adopters, who, while not the very first adopters, adopt early in the product's life cycle. They are moderately reliant on group norms and values, oriented to the local community, and very likely to be opinion leaders. (16)

early majority A category of adopters who deliberate carefully before adopting a new product. Their adoption process takes longer than an early adopter because they are likely to collect more information and evaluate more brands. (16)

ego Part of Freud's psychoanalytic theory—the individual's self-concept and the manifestation of objective reality as it develops in interaction with the external world. (10)

elaboration likelihood model (ELM) An information-processing model that postulates that the degree to which a consumer elaborates on a message depends on its relevance. The more relevant the message, the more elaborate the central processing that takes place. The less relevant the message, the more nonelaborate or peripheral the processing that takes place. (4)

encoding The translating, by advertisers or salespeople, of communications objectives into a message that conveys product benefits. (17)

enculturation The process of learning the values of one's own culture from early childhood. (11)

enduring involvement Continuous, more permanent involvement with a product; interest in product category on an ongoing basis. (4)

Environmental Protection Agency (EPA) A government agency that sets controls on industry emissions, toxic wastes, and automobile pollution. (19)

episodic memory Images in long-term memory that reflect our memory of past events. (7)

ethnocentric Assuming that foreign consumers have the same norms and values as domestic consumers. (13)

ethnographic research A type of research that involves in-depth observation, such as when a researcher observes or even lives with participants to observe their behavior. (1)

ethnography The study of culture by observation. Anthropologists determine cultural values through field studies in which they live with a group or family and observe its customs and behavior. (11)

Eurobrand A brand marketed in Europe with several languages on the same package under the same brand name. (13)

Euroconsumer A person who has many shared values with consumers in neighboring European countries. (13)

evaluative strategies Processing strategies for brand evaluation that require the organization of information about alternative brands; most likely to be used when involvement with a product is high. (7)

expected price range The range of prices the consumer expects to find in the marketplace, which tends to be a wider range than the consumer's acceptable price range. (6)

expert power Power based on the expertise of the individual or group derived from experience and knowledge (*e.g.*, a salesperson has expert power if the consumer regards him or her as knowledgeable). (14)

expert spokesperson Person who has a professional or technical relationship with a product or service. (17)

exposure Occurs when consumer's senses (sight, hearing, touch, smell) are activated by a stimulus. (6)

expressive roles Family purchase roles related to the need for social and emotional support (*e.g.*, decisions regarding style, color, or design). (15)

extended family A nuclear family with at least one grandparent living at home. (15)

extended self Extends our concept of self to what we own, wear, and use; incorporates some of our more important possessions into our self-concept. (10)

extinction Elimination of the link between stimulus and expected reward. If a consumer is no longer satisfied with a product, a process of extinction takes place. Extinction leads to a rapid decrease in the probability that the consumer will repurchase the same brand. (3, 7)

factor analysis A mathematical procedure for determining the intercorrelation between items and reducing the items into independent components or factors to eliminate redundancy; an analytical technique that reduces purchasing motives to a smaller number of independent need criteria. It is typically used to reduce a great amount of data into its more basic structure. (10)

false advertising A form of deceptive advertising that involves a claim–fact discrepancy. (19)

family Two or more people living together who are related by blood or marriage. (15)

family life cycle The progression of a family from formation to child rearing, middle age, and finally retirement; also reflects changes in income and family situation. (15)

Federal Communications Commission (FCC) A government agency that regulates communications media and practices. Among other things, it oversees advertising directed to children. (19)

Federal Trade Commission (FTC) A government agency established in 1914 to curb the monopoly powers of big business and unfair trade practices. It is also a watchdog over deceptive advertising. (19)

figure Stimuli that consumers distinguish as being more prominent and in the foreground. (5)

figure and ground Gestalt psychologists state that in organizing stimuli into wholes, individuals identify those stimuli that are prominent (the figure) and those stimuli that are less prominent (the ground or background). The figure appears well defined, at a definite location, solid, and in front of the ground. In contrast, the ground appears amorphous, indefinite, and continuous behind the figure. A principle of advertising is that the product should appear as the figure rather than as the ground. (6)

flexible globalization An attempt to standardize marketing strategies across countries but to be flexible enough to adapt components of the strategy to local conditions. (13)

focus-group interview An unstructured, personal interview in which the interviewer attempts to get groups to talk freely and to express their true feelings. This strategy has the advantage of eliciting more information than other types of interviews do, because of group interaction. (1, 10)

follower Individuals who are most likely to be influenced by word-of-mouth communications. (16)

Food and Drug Administration (FDA) A government agency created in 1906 to set product standards; it also requires disclosure of product contents. (19)

forgetting Forgetting occurs when information stored in memory is lost or when new information interferes with retrieval of stored information. Occurs when the stimulus is no longer repeated or perceived. Lack of use of a product or elimination of an advertising campaign can cause forgetting. (3, 7)

framing Situation in which the usage puts the product in a relevant context for consumers. (5)

fraudulent advertising A straightforward lie; a form of deceptive advertising. (19)

frequency The number of times an individual consumer or household is exposed to a message marketers send. (17)

functions of attitudes There are four functions served by attitudes: a utilitarian function, a knowledge function, a value-expressive function, and an ego-defensive function. Marketing strategies can attempt to influence attitudes serving each of these functions. (8)

gatekeeper Information gatherer who controls the level and type of stimuli flowing from the mass media to the group; the person who has the greatest expertise in acquiring and evaluating information from various sources and is most aware of alternative sources of information but does not necessarily disseminate them. (16)

Generation X (*see* **baby busters**).

Generation Y Consumers born between 1977 and 1994, representing 67 million people. (9, 12)

Generation Z People born after 1994, representing 35 million children as of 2003. (9)

geodemographic analysis Demographic data analyzed by geographic area, generally based on census data. (1, 9)

Gestalt psychology A German school of psychology that focuses on total configurations or whole patterns. Stimuli, such as advertising messages, are seen as an integrated whole. In short, the whole is greater than the sum of the parts. (6)

global influences Common needs and values across countries. (13)

grassroots innovator An innovator in a lower socioeconomic group (generally from a rural area) who disseminates tastes and influence to higher socioeconomic groups. (16)

ground Stimuli that consumers distinguish as being less prominent and in the background. (5)

habit Repetitive behavior resulting in a limitation or absence of information seeking and evaluation of alternative choices. (3)

hedonic need The need to achieve pleasure from a product; most likely associated with emotions or fantasies derived from consuming a product. (2)

heterophilous groups Groups outside of an individual's primary social network or personal network; secondary groups. (16)

hierarchy of effects Stipulates the sequence of cognitive states the consumer goes through in reaching a tendency to act. Needs are formulated, beliefs are formed about the brand, attitudes develop toward the brand, and the consumer then forms an action predisposition. (2, 4, 8)

high-involvement purchase Purchase that is important to the consumer. It is closely tied to his or her ego and self-image and involves some financial, social, or personal risk. (4)

homophilous groups Groups that are part of an individual's personal network; primary groups. (16)

household Any individual living singly or together with others in a residential unit. (15)

household life cycle A more modern version of the family life cycle that includes categories such as divorced couples, married couples without children, and remarried people with children and stepchildren. (15)

id (libido) Part of Freud's psychoanalytic theory; the component of personality that controls the individual's most basic needs such as hunger, sex, and self preservation. (10)

ideal self The concept that individuals have of themselves based on who they think they would like to be. (10)

image A total perception of an object formed by processing information from various sources over time. (6)

impulse buying A tendency to buy on whim with little preplanning. (4)

inconsistency Information delivered to consumers that communicates varying and conflicting messages or ideas about a brand. Inconsistency in information can inhibit activation or retrieval of a brand. (7)

Index of Status Characteristics (ISC) A multi-item index combining several socioeconomic variables into one index of social class. The ISC measures four variables: occupation, source of income, house type, and dwelling area. (9)

indirect feedback Measures used to evaluate the effectiveness of communications when marketing communications cannot be directly related to sales results. Indirect criteria include exposure to and awareness, comprehension, and retention of the marketing communication. (17)

inertia A passive process of information processing, brand evaluation, and brand choice. The consumer frequently purchases the same brand by inertia to save time and energy. (3, 4)

inference Involves the development of an association between two stimuli; for instance, consumers may associate high price with quality. (6)

infomediary A web site designed to provide product information by bringing together information from various other sources.(2, 7, 17)

information overload A concept that refers to the situation where consumers' ability to process information is surpassed because of excessive information; as a result, decision making becomes less effective. (7)

informational influence The influence of experts or experienced friends or relatives on consumer brand evaluations. (14)

innovativeness The early adoption of a new product. Innovativeness is distinct from opinion leadership in that it is a behavioral variable (*e.g.*, adoption). In contrast, opinion leadership is measured by the consumers' perception regarding their interpersonal influence on others. (16)

innovator A category of adopters who are the first of all those who will adopt. Innovators are eager to try new ideas and products, usually have higher incomes, more education, are more cosmopolitan, and are more active outside of their communities. Innovators are less reliant on group norms, more self-confident, and more likely to obtain their information from scientific sources and experts. (16)

inoculation theory A theory proposing that consumers can be "inoculated" against negative thoughts about a product when processing a marketing message with messages that anticipate these negative thoughts and refute them. (17)

instrumental actions Actions necessary to complete the purchase of a brand (*e.g.,* obtaining financing for a car). (2)

instrumental conditioning Conditioning that requires the development of a link between a stimulus and a response. (3)

instrumental roles Family purchasing roles related to task-oriented functions meant to provide direction to the group. Decisions on budgets, timing, and product specifications are task-oriented. (15)

instrumental values As defined by Rokeach, instrumental values are the means to attain cultural goals. As applied to consumers, instrumental values are consumption-specific guidelines. (11)

integration The tendency to perceive stimuli as an integrated whole; for example, a brand image. (6)

interference Occurs when a related information node blocks the recall of the relevant information. Competitive advertising often causes consumers to be unable to recall advertising for a related brand; or consumers may sometimes confuse one brand with another. (7)

involvement A state when the consumer feels a product is important to him/her and is motivated to process information about the product. (2)

irresponsible advertising Advertising that depicts or encourages irresponsible behavior or portrays groups in an irresponsible manner. (17)

just-noticeable difference (JND) The minimal difference that can be detected between stimuli. The consumer is not able to detect any difference between stimuli below his or her differential threshold. The JND varies not only with (a) the sensitivity of the receptor and (b) the type of stimuli, but also with (c) the absolute intensity of the stimuli being compared. (6)

laddering As applied to the means-end chain, laddering involves a series of consumer interviews to determine the links among product attributes, consumption goals, and cultural values. (11)

laggard A category of adopters who are last to adopt. They are independent from group norms because they are tradition bound, and they make decisions in terms of the past. Laggards usually have the lowest socioeconomic status and are suspicious of new products. (16)

late majority A category of adopters who adopt a product because most of their friends have already done so. The late majority is skeptical and relies heavily on group norms. They are usually older and below average in income and education. (16)

learning A change in behavior occurring as a result of past experience.(3)

lexicographic strategy A procedure that requires consumers to rank product attributes from most important to least important. Consumers will choose the brand that dominates on the most important criterion; if two or more brands tie, then consumers will examine brands on the second attribute and so on until the tie is broken. A lexicographic rule follows a sequential approach. (7)

lifestyle An individual's mode of living as identified by his or her activities, interests, and opinions. Lifestyle variables have been measured by identifying a consumer's day-to-day activities and interests. (10)

limen The threshold level at which perceptions occur. Perceptions below the conscious level are subliminal. (*See also* **subliminal perception**.) (7)

long-term memory The place where the consumer stores and retains information on a long-term basis. (7)

low-involvement purchases Purchases that are less important to the consumer. Identity with the product is low. Because it may not be worth the consumer's time and effort to search for information about brands and to consider a wide range of alternatives, low-involvement purchases are associated with a more limited process of decision making. (4)

mainstreaming The theory proposing that individuals tend to see the world around them largely based on information from the mass media. Therefore, heavy viewers of TV will develop similar perceptions of reality because they are exposed to similar stimuli. (13)

market maven A consumer with information on many kinds of products, places to shop, and other facets of markets who can initiate discussions with consumers and respond to requests from consumers for market information. (16)

market segmentation A strategy of identifying consumers with similar needs or characteristics, grouping them, and targeting them with product offerings. (18)

marketing concept The philosophy that marketing strategies rely on a better knowledge of the consumer. (1)

marketing stimuli Any component of a product's marketing plan (*e.g.,* price, package, advertising, the store that sells the brand, and the brand itself). Most marketing stimuli are symbolic in nature; that is, representations of the product, not the product itself. (6)

mass customization A strategy of offering consumers products or services designed to meet their individual needs and offering this facility to a broad group of consumers. (1, 18)

materialism A traditional American value that reflects the desire for affluence as a means of enhancing one's social status through conspicuous consumption, or visible displays of wealth and privilege. (11)

mature market Consumers born before 1946, representing 68 million consumers. (9, 12)

means–end chain As described by Gutman, the interface between culture and consumer behavior. That is, the means (product attributes) are the vehicle for attaining personal values (the ends) with the consumption goals as an intermediary between them. (11)

membership group A group to which an individual belongs and in which he or she has face-to-face communication with other members; groups to which a person is recognized by others as belonging. (14)

memory Represents information that the consumer retains and stores and that the consumer can recall for future use. (2)

micromarketing Reaching individual consumers based on their demographic characteristics. It is an extension of market segmentation in that it breaks the market down into more finite components. (1, 9, 18)

misleading advertising A form of deceptive advertising that involves a claim-belief interaction. The advertisement interacts with a consumer's beliefs and results in a misleading claim. (19)

moods Passing feelings that occur at a point in time (*e.g.,* feeling happy, sad, silly, anxious, sexy, and so forth). (17)

motivational research Research into consumer motives, particularly unconscious motives. These are determined through indirect assessment methods that include projective techniques and depth interviews. On this basis, hypotheses are developed regarding the motivations for consumer behavior. (10)

motives General drives that direct a consumer's behavior toward attaining his or her needs. (2)

multiattribute models Models that measure attitudes on a multidimensional basis by determining how consumers evaluate brands across product attributes. The sum of these ratings weighted by the value placed on each attribute represents consumers' attitude toward the brand. (8)

myths Stories or character representations in fantasy form that attempt to portray cultural values. (11)

new reality The realization that there are limitations to growth in the American economy and that these limits translate into restricted future purchasing potential. (11)

node Each word or image in long-term memory. Each node is linked to other words or images (*e.g.,* good food and fast service are nodes that a consumer may link to the McDonald's node). (7)

noncompensatory evaluation A model of attitude structure in which brands are evaluated on a few of the most important attributes. Weakness of a product or brand on one attribute cannot be compensated for by its strength on another. As a result, the brand can be eliminated from consideration based on one or two attributes. This method requires consumers to process information by attribute across brands. (7)

nonevaluative strategies Techniques for brand evaluation that involve the use of a simple decision rule to avoid the necessity to evaluate brands (*e.g.,* some consumers simply buy the cheapest brand). (7)

normative influence The influence exerted on an individual to conform to group norms and expectations. (14)

norms Rules of behavior in particular circumstances that specify actions that are proper and those that are improper; beliefs held by a consensus of a group concerning the rules of behavior to which group members are expected to conform. These are rules and standards of conduct (generally undefined) that the group establishes. (14)

nuclear family Married couple with one or more children. (15)

one-to-one marketing A type of micromarketing that focuses on the needs of individual consumers, rather than larger groups or segments. (18)

opinion leader An individual who is most likely to influence others through word-of-mouth communications. (16)

passive consumer A consumer who has adopted a product but does not give information to others or exert influence over others. (4)

passive learning Learning that occurs when consumers learn about brands with little involvement and purchase with little evaluation of alternative brands. Consumers are more likely to form attitudes after, rather than before, a purchase. (4)

penetration strategy A strategic option establishing a competitive price for a new product entry. A mass marketing approach would be used. It is most relevant for continuous innovation. (16)

perceived risk Degree of risk consumers perceive in a purchase; composed of two elements: (1) uncertainty about the decision and (2) potential consequences of the decision. (6)

perception The process by which people select, organize, and interpret sensory stimuli into a meaningful and coherent picture; the way consumers view an object (*e.g.,* their mental picture of a brand or the traits they attribute to a brand). (2)

perceptions A consumer's selection, organization, and interpretation of marketing and environmental stimuli to form a coherent picture. (6)

perceptual defense Consumers' distortion of information so that it conforms to their beliefs and attitudes. This function operates to protect the individual from threatening or contradictory stimuli. (6)

perceptual equilibrium/disequilibrium Consumers seek to maintain equilibrium in their psychological set by screening out information that does not conform to their predispositions. When consumers choose information consistent with prior beliefs or interpret information to conform to these beliefs, they are processing information to ensure perceptual equilibrium. Acceptance of contradictory information means consumers are in a state of perceptual disequilibrium. (6)

perceptual mapping A group of quantitative techniques that seeks to position various brands on a "map" based on the way consumers perceive them. The closer one brand is to another on the map, the more similar it is to the other brand. The basic assumption is that if consumers see two brands as being similar, they will behave similarly toward the two brands. (8)

perceptual organization The organization of disparate information so that it can be comprehended and retained. (6)

perceptual vigilance A form of selective perception whereby the consumers' needs determine the information perceived; the tendency of consumers to select the information that helps them in evaluating brands to meet their needs (*e.g.,* words that connote important values are often perceived more readily. As a result, consumers will recognize preferred brand names more quickly than they will nonpreferred brand names). (6)

performance roles Roles prescribed to individuals, which, along with ritual artifacts and a script, are one of the three common elements of a consumption ritual. (11)

permission marketing A concept of marketing on the Web that states that since consumers are able to choose which web sites to visit and what messages to receive, marketers on the Web must now ask consumers directly for permission to market to them. (1)

personality A person's consistent and enduring patterns of behavior. Represents a set of consumer characteristics used to describe target segments. (10)

placement The second of three factors required for retrieval of information from long-term memory. Placement determines to which other nodes consumers will connect the activated node. (7)

preattentive processing When a consumer has been exposed to an ad but has not been motivated to actively process the information. (6)

primary data Data collected for the specific purpose of answering research questions. (1)

primary formal groups Groups the consumer frequently comes in contact with that have some formal structure (*e.g.,* school or business groups). (14)

primary informal groups Groups the consumer frequently comes in contact with that have no formal structure (*e.g.,* the family and peer groups). These groups have the greatest influence on the consumer. (14)

primary (intrinsic) stimuli Unconditioned stimulus; that is, the initial stimulus (*e.g.,* cowboy) that another stimulus is linked to (*e.g.,* Marlboro cigarettes) to produce a conditioned response. In marketing, the product and its components (package, contents, physical properties) are primary stimuli. (6)

primary (unconditioned) stimulus An object, character, or person that elicits a particular response. (3)

product concept A bundle of product benefits that can be directed to the needs of a defined group of consumers through symbolism and imagery. The product concept represents the organization of marketing stimuli into a coordinated product position that can be more easily directed to consumers. (6)

product positioning Communication of the set of benefits the product is designed to meet. Such benefits are communicated through advertising and other marketing strategies. (6)

projective techniques Techniques used for detecting and measuring wants and attitudes not readily discernible through more direct methods. They consist of the presentation of ambiguous materials (*e.g.,* ink blots, untitled pictures, etc.). In interpreting this material, the viewer "projects" tendencies of which he or she may be unaware or may wish to conceal. Thus, these techniques are diagnostic devices in which interpretation of ambiguous stimuli is taken to reveal something about the observer, based on previous experience and motivations, needs, and interests in play at the time. (1, 10)

proximity Closeness. The tendency to group stimuli by proximity means that one object will be associated with another based on its closeness to that object. (6)

psychoanalytic theory Theory developed by Sigmund Freud that emphasizes the conflict among id, ego, and superego in childhood and the resolution of these conflicts in adult behavior. The dynamic interaction of these elements results in unconscious motivations that are manifested in observed human behavior. (10)

psychographic characteristics Consumer psychological characteristics that can be quantified; represented by two classes of variables: lifestyle and personality. (10)

psychological set The consumer's state of mind toward an object; that is, his or her needs, attitudes, and perceptions relative to various brands. The psychological set is represented at a given point in time prior to the decision process. It will change during the decision process when the consumer processes new information, resulting in changes in needs, attitudes, and perceptions. (2)

qualitative research Designed to provide more information about consumers' underlying motives by asking them questions in an unstructured manner. (1)

reach The number of people exposed to the message that the marketer sends. (17)

reactance A situation where consumers may reject the group norms and display independence when group pressures become too intense. (14)

reference group Any group with which an individual identifies such that he or she tends to use the group as a standard for self-evaluation and as a source of personal values and goals; a group that serves as a reference point for the individual in the formation of beliefs, attitudes, and behavior. Such groups provide consumers with a means to compare and evaluate their own brand attitudes and purchasing behavior. (1, 14)

reference (standard) price The price consumers expect to pay for a certain item that serves as a frame of reference by which consumers compare prices of alternative brands. (6)

referent power Power based on the identification of the individual with members of the group. The greater the similarity of the individual's beliefs and attitudes with those of group members, the greater the referent power of the group. A salesperson has referent power if the consumer sees the salesperson as similar to him- or herself. (14)

referent spokesperson A person to whom consumers can easily relate. (17)

reinforcement Repeated satisfaction. (3)

relationship marketing An area of marketing in which marketers must maintain a relationship with their customers after the purchase. Service marketers attempt to establish a one-to-one relationship with consumers over time. (1, 3, 9, 18)

reservation price In the context of comparing prices of alternative brands, the higher end of the acceptable price range or the upper limit above which consumers would judge an article too expensive. (6)

response elasticity A measure of consumers' sensitivity to changes in marketing strategies. Types of response elasticity include price, deal, coupon, advertising, and package size elasticity. (18)

reward power Power based on the ability of the group to reward the individual. (14)

risk barrier A type of barrier to adopting an innovation; represents the consumers' physical, economic, performance, or social risk of adopting the innovation. (16)

risky shift phenomenon The hypothesis that joint decision making encourages the group to make riskier decisions because, in this way, all members of the group can share the failure of a wrong decision. (15)

ritual A series of symbolic behaviors that occurs in sequence and is repeated frequently—for example, those that occur in grooming and gift-giving and during holidays. (11)

ritual artifacts In rituals, these are often in the form of consumer products. For example, colored lights, mistletoe, wreaths, and Santa Claus are artifacts of Christmas rituals. (11)

roles Functions assumed by or assigned to individuals by the group in the attainment of group objectives. (14)

rules-based systems A micromarketing strategy that positions products to consumers on the Web by developing a statistical relationship between a consumer's characteristics and behavior, and his or her likelihood to purchase. (18)

sacred consumption Consumption of goods that promote beauty, the preservation of nature, and cooperation. (11)

scanner data Data collected from scanners that link consumers' exposure to advertising and subsequent behavior. (17)

schema A cluster of concepts or beliefs that represent an individual's perception of an object or situation. (6, 7)

script A prescription of how, when, and by whom products will be used, which, along with ritual artifacts and performance roles, are the three common elements of a consumption ritual. (11)

search engine Web sites designed to identify other relevant web sites based on key words. (7)

secondary (conditioned) stimulus A stimulus that is linked to a primary stimulus and evokes the same response. (3)

secondary data Existing data from published sources or from company records. (1)

secondary (extrinsic) stimulus A stimulus that is repeatedly linked to a primary stimulus to produce a conditioned response. Communications designed to influence consumer behavior are secondary stimuli that represent the product or stimuli associated with the product (price, store in which purchased, effect of salesperson). (6)

secondary formal groups Groups with some formal structure with which the consumer meets infrequently (*e.g.*, alumni groups, business clubs, and tenant organizations). These groups are likely to have the least amount of influence on the consumer. (14)

secondary informal groups Groups with no formal structure with which the consumer meets infrequently (*e.g.*, shopping or sports groups). (14)

secular consumption Consumption of goods that promote technology, the conquest of nature, and competition. (11)

selection The first component of perception. Consumers pick and choose marketing stimuli based on their needs and attitudes (*e.g.*, a car buyer will be more attentive to car ads). (6)

selective perception Consumers perceive marketing stimuli selectively to reinforce their needs, attitudes, past experiences, and personal characteristics. Selective perception means that two consumers can perceive the identical ad, package, or product very differently. (6)

selective retention A phenomenon that occurs when a consumer retains information in long-term memory that is most important to his or her needs. Information is thus retained selectively. (7)

self-concept (self-image) theory A theory that maintains that a person's self-concept causes the individual to see herself or himself through the eyes of other persons. In doing so, an individual takes into account the other person's behavior, feelings, and attitudes. This evaluation is closely related to the perceptions of whether other persons in the reference group will approve or disapprove of the "self" presented to the reference group. (10)

semantic memory Words and sentences stored in long-term memory that reflect facts and concepts that we remember. (7)

semiotics A field of study established to study the interrelationship among three components: object (brand), the signs and symbols associated with the object, and the consumer who does the associating. To understand how people derive meaning from symbols, researchers must understand the shared meaning of various signs in a culture. (6)

short-term memory The place where a consumer briefly evaluates perceived information to determine whether it is to be stored in long-term memory. (7)

similarity A principle of grouping that suggests stimuli will be grouped together by similarity in their characteristics. (6)

situational influences Temporary conditions or settings that occur in the environment at a specific time and place. (5)

situational involvement Temporary involvement with a product only in specific situations, such as when a purchase decision is required. (4)

skimming strategy A strategic option establishing a high price for a new product entry and "skimming the cream of the market" by aiming at the most price inelastic consumer. Advertising and sales promotion are limited to specific targets, and distribution is selective. It is the most relevant strategy for discontinuous innovations. (16)

social class A division of society made up of persons possessing certain common social and economic characteristics that are taken to qualify them for equal-status relations with one another and that restrict their interaction with members of other social classes. (9)

social judgment theory Sherif's theory that describes an individual's position on an issue based on his or her involvement with the issue. Sherif identified a latitude of acceptance, a latitude of rejection, and a latitude of noncommitment to operationalize this concept of involvement. The greater the involvement, the narrower the latitude of acceptance and the wider the latitude of rejection on various positions. (4)

social marketing The use of marketing tools by organizations, generally on a pro bono basis, to try to influence consumers to take more socially responsible behavior. (19)

social mobility Movement of an individual or household from one social class to another. (9)

social multiplier effect As a result of the demonstration principle, ownership increases in multiples as consumers come into contact with and acquire new products. The social multiplier effect illustrates the volatility of group influence in the American economy. (*See also* **demonstration principle**.) (14)

social stratification The ranking of people in society by other members into higher or lower positions such as upper, middle, and lower class, to create a hierarchy of respect or prestige. (9)

social-cultural theories Theories of personality development that are based on Freud's theories but differ in that they believe that a person's social and cultural variables are more important than biological drives in personality development. (10)

socialization The process by which an individual learns the norms and values of the group and of society. (14)

source bolstering When viewing ads in low-involvement situations, the tendency for consumers to react positively to the source of the message as opposed to the message itself. (17)

source credibility The level of expertise and trustworthiness consumers attribute to the source of the marketing message. (17)

source derogation When viewing ads in low-involvement situations, the tendency of consumers to react negatively to the source and, therefore, to tend not to believe the message. (17)

spurious loyalty When a brand achieves a minimum level of satisfaction, the consumer repurchases it on a routinized basis; the consumer appears to be brand loyal but is not. (4)

standard price Also known as the consumer's reference price, this is the price that consumers expect to pay for a certain item. The standard price serves as a standard frame of reference by which consumers compare prices for alternative brands. (6)

status The rank of an individual in the prestige hierarchy of a group or community; the position the individual occupies within the group. High status implies greater power and influence within the group. (14)

status symbol A possession that indicates a person's status in society—for example, a uniform or membership in an exclusive club. (9)

stimuli Any physical, visual, or verbal communications that can influence an individual's response. (6)

stimulus generalization Consumers' ability to perceive differences in stimuli. It allows consumers to judge brands selectively and to make evaluative judgments about preferences of one brand or another. (6)

subcultural influences Differences in norms and values among subcultures within a society. (12)

subcultures Parts of the total culture of a society that are distinct from society in certain respects (*e.g.*, an ethnic group, a social class group, a regional group); the ways of behaving that distinguish a particular group from a larger one. (1, 11, 12)

subculture of consumption A part of the total culture of a society that is distinct from society due to the central role of product interests or activities. The product can serve as a total lifestyle focus, define a common value system, establish a social hierarchy related to expertise with the product, and/or generate intense interest and enduring involvement with the product among members of the subculture of consumption. (12)

subliminal embeds Tiny figures inserted into magazine ads by high-speed photography or by airbrushing. (6)

subliminal perception Perception of a stimulus below the conscious level. If the stimulus is beneath the threshold of conscious awareness but above the absolute threshold of perception, it is known as subliminal perception. (The conscious level is referred to as the limen; thus, perception below the conscious level is subliminal or below the absolute threshold.) (6)

subtyping Developing a subcategory of a broader category (*e.g.*, Federal Express established the subcategory overnight delivery within the general category of package delivery). (6)

superego Part of Freud's psychoanalytic theory; the component of personality that is the leash on the id and works against its impulses. (10)

support arguments Thoughts evoked in response to advertising when viewed by consumers who support what is read or said. (17)

surrogate consumer An agent retained by a consumer to guide, direct, and/or transact marketplace activities. They have essentially assumed the decision role for the consumer. (16)

symbolic aspiration group A group in which an individual does not expect to receive membership, despite the acceptance of the group's norms and beliefs. (14)

technographics An approach to segmenting consumers based on consumers' motivations, desires, and ability to invest in technology products. (16)

terminal values As defined by Rokeach, cultural goals to be attained. Applied to consumers, terminal values are their ultimate purchasing goals. (11)

theory of reasoned action A modification of Fishbein's multiattribute model; proposes that, to predict behavior accurately, it is more important to determine the person's attitude to that behavior than to the object of behavior. (8)

threshold level Level of sensory discrimination; ability to discriminate stimuli. (6)

trait theory A quantitative approach to the study of personality postulating that an individual's personality is composed of definite predispositional attributes called traits. The most empirical basis for measuring personality, it states that personality is composed of a set of traits that describe a general response predisposition. (10)

transfer The third of three factors required for retrieval of information from long-term memory. Transfer determines the information consumers will retrieve from long-term to short-term memory. Generally, consumers will transfer information that is most important in making a decision. (7)

transformational effect The effect that occurs when the attitude consumers have toward an ad carries over to the brand. Explains why consumers who cannot tell the difference between soft drinks in blind taste tests have strong brand preferences when they can choose labeled brands. (7)

trickle-across effect The process of diffusion occurring across groups regardless of socioeconomic status; a horizontal pattern of diffusion. (16)

trickle-down effect The process of information and influence traveling from higher to lower socioeconomic groups; a vertical pattern of diffusion. (16)

trickle-up effect The phenomenon that occurs when lower-class groups influence the purchases of those farther up the ladder (*e.g.*, jeans were originally designed for blue-collar workers and made their way up to designer jean status). (16)

unconditioned response The response to primary (unconditioned) stimuli. (3)

unplanned purchases A buying action undertaken without buying intention prior to entering the store. Four types of unplanned purchases are (1) pure impulse, (2) reminder effect, (3) suggestion effect, and (4) planned impulse purchases. (4)

upside price elasticity A measure of a consumer's sensitivity to increases in price. If consumers are price elastic, they will change brands based on changes or differences in price. (18)

usage barrier A type of barrier to adopting an innovation; occurs when an item is not compatible with the existing practices or habits of consumers. (16)

utilitarian needs Need to achieve some practical benefit from a product. These needs are associated with product attributes that define performance. (2)

value barrier A type of barrier to adopting an innovation; represents a lack of performance relative to price compared with substitute products. (16)

value system The relative importance cultures place on cultural values. (11)

values Shared beliefs among group members as to what behaviors are desirable and undesirable. (14)

vicarious (observational) learning When people imitate the behavior of others as a result of observing them. (3)

viral marketing A marketing strategy that encourages the spread of information about a product or service from one person to the next, to the next, much like the spread of a virus. (16)

vocabulary of product attributes and benefits A set of adjectives to describe a product's characteristics and benefits generally obtained from consumer depth interviews (*e.g.,* a vocabulary for soft drink brands might include terms like mild, sweet, carbonated, thirst-quenching). (8)

Weber's law A law of psychological relativity. Subject discriminations are not bound to absolute characteristics of stimuli but to relations between them. The size of the least detectable change or increment in intensity is a function of the initial intensity; the stronger the initial stimulus, the greater the difference needs to be (*e.g.,* the higher the price of a product, the greater the price difference between two brands of that product must be for consumers to detect it). (6)

word of mouth Interpersonal communication between two or more individuals, such as members of a reference group or a customer and a salesperson. People exert purchase influence through such communication. (16)

Name Index

Subject Index

Supplements

INSTRUCTOR'S RESOURCE MANUAL

Written by the text author, each chapter in the manual includes chapter objectives, teaching suggestions, answers and guides to end-of-chapter questions, and guidelines for research assignments.

TEST BANK AND COMPUTERIZED TEST BANK

The test bank contains multiple-choice and true/false questions as well as short-essay questions. In addition, *HM Testing*, an electronic, Windows version of the test bank, allows instructors to generate and change tests easily on the computer. The program also prints an answer key for each version of the text. A call-in test service (800-733-1717), which allows instructors to select items from the test bank and order printed tests, is also available.

VIDEOS

The video package spotlights a variety of examples that correspond with the concepts and topics highlighted in the text. The video guide provides complete teaching notes to help instructors prepare for each video presentation as well as in-class discussion.

POWERPOINT

This classroom presentation package (downloadable from the Web) provides clear, concise text and art to create a total presentation package. Instructors who have access to PowerPoint can edit slides to customize them for their presentations. Slides can also be printed as lecture notes for class distribution.

INSTRUCTOR WEB SITE

This password-protected site provides lecture notes and PowerPoint slides for downloading, as well as additional classroom resources.